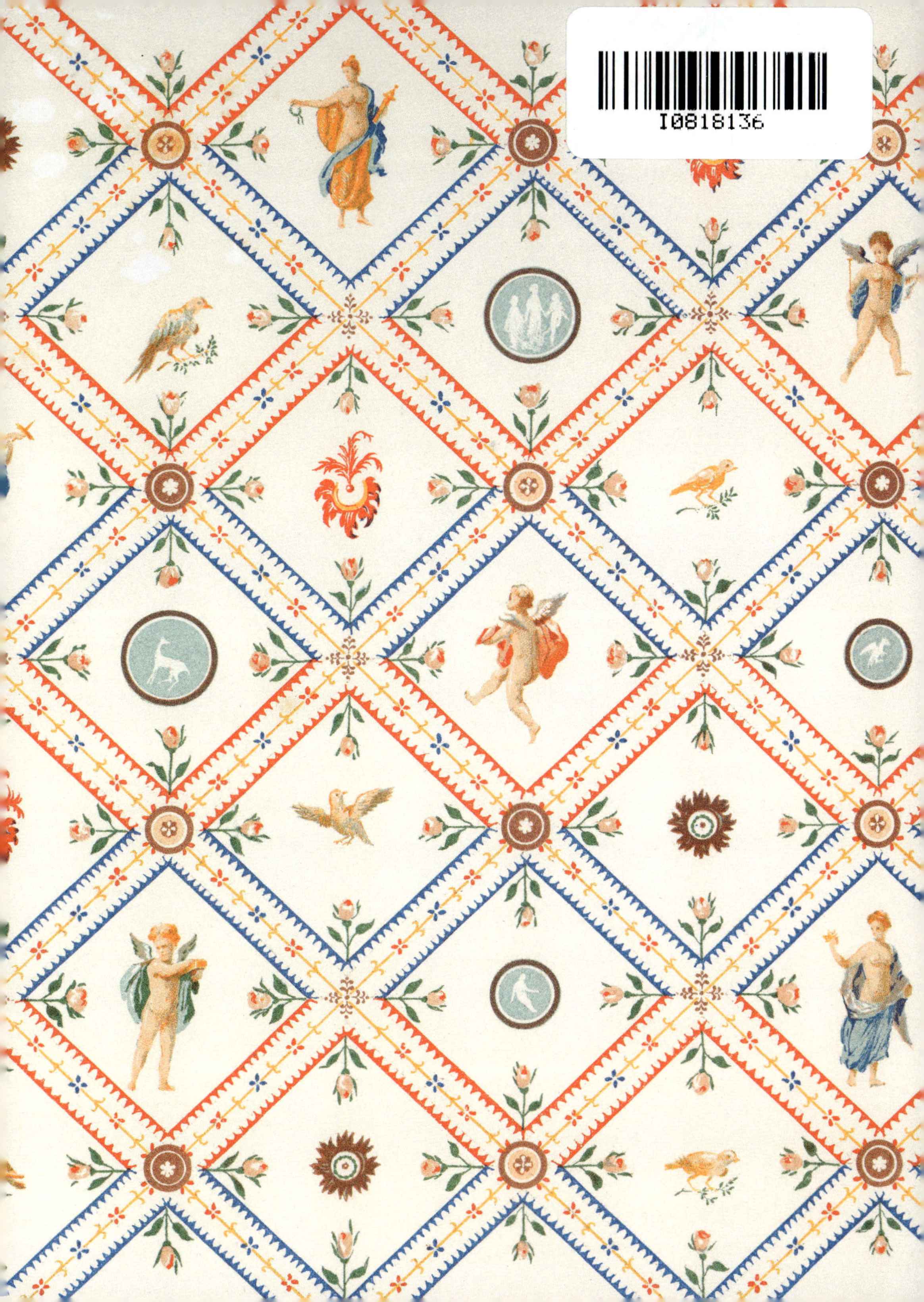
I0818136

LE CASE
ED
I MONUMENTI
DI
POMPEI

NAPOLI

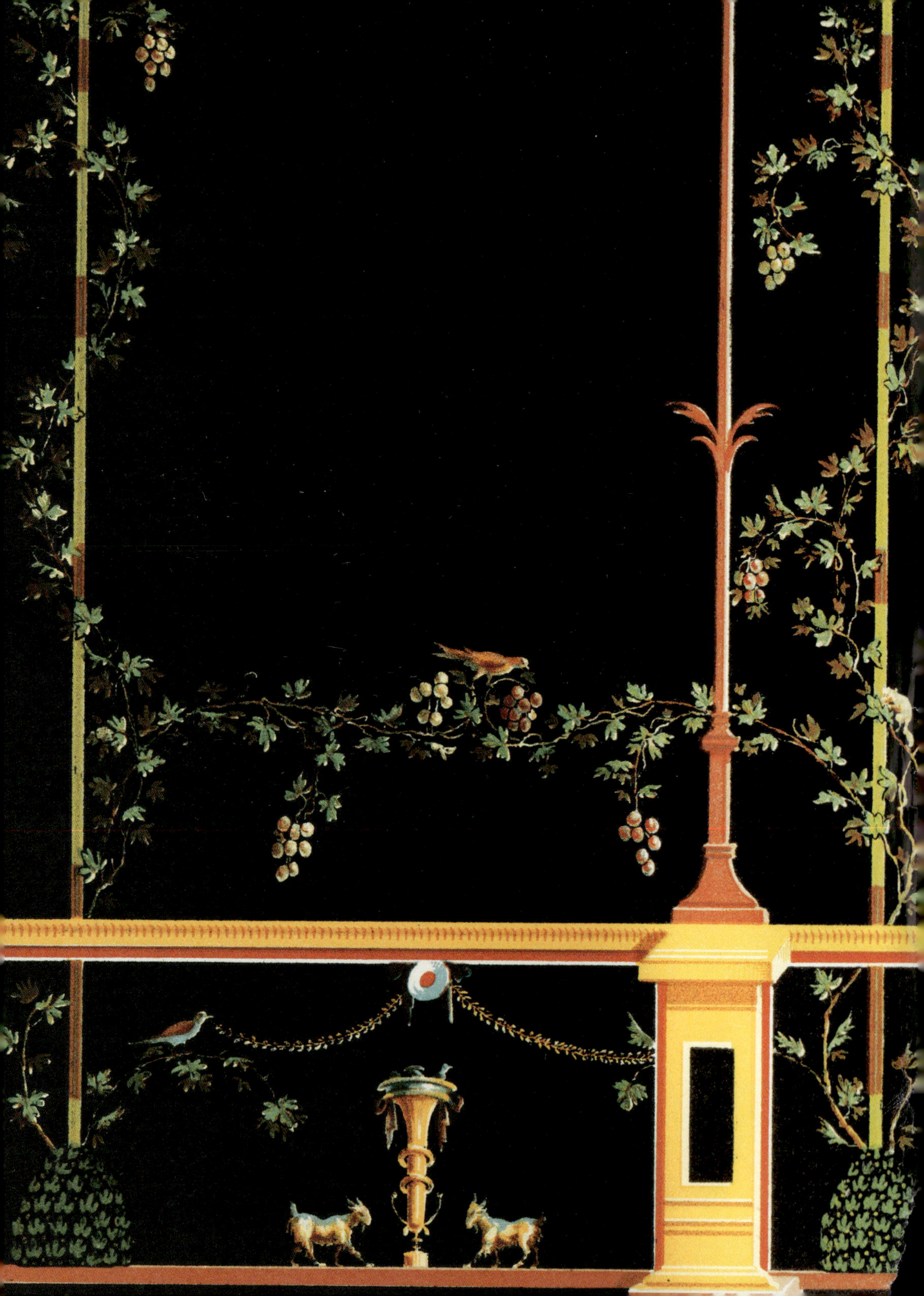

FAUSTO & FELICE NICCOLINI

HOUSES AND MONUMENTS OF POMPEII

Essays by
VALENTIN KOCKEL & SEBASTIAN SCHÜTZE

Designed by
ANDY DISL

Directed and produced by
BENEDIKT TASCHEN

TASCHEN

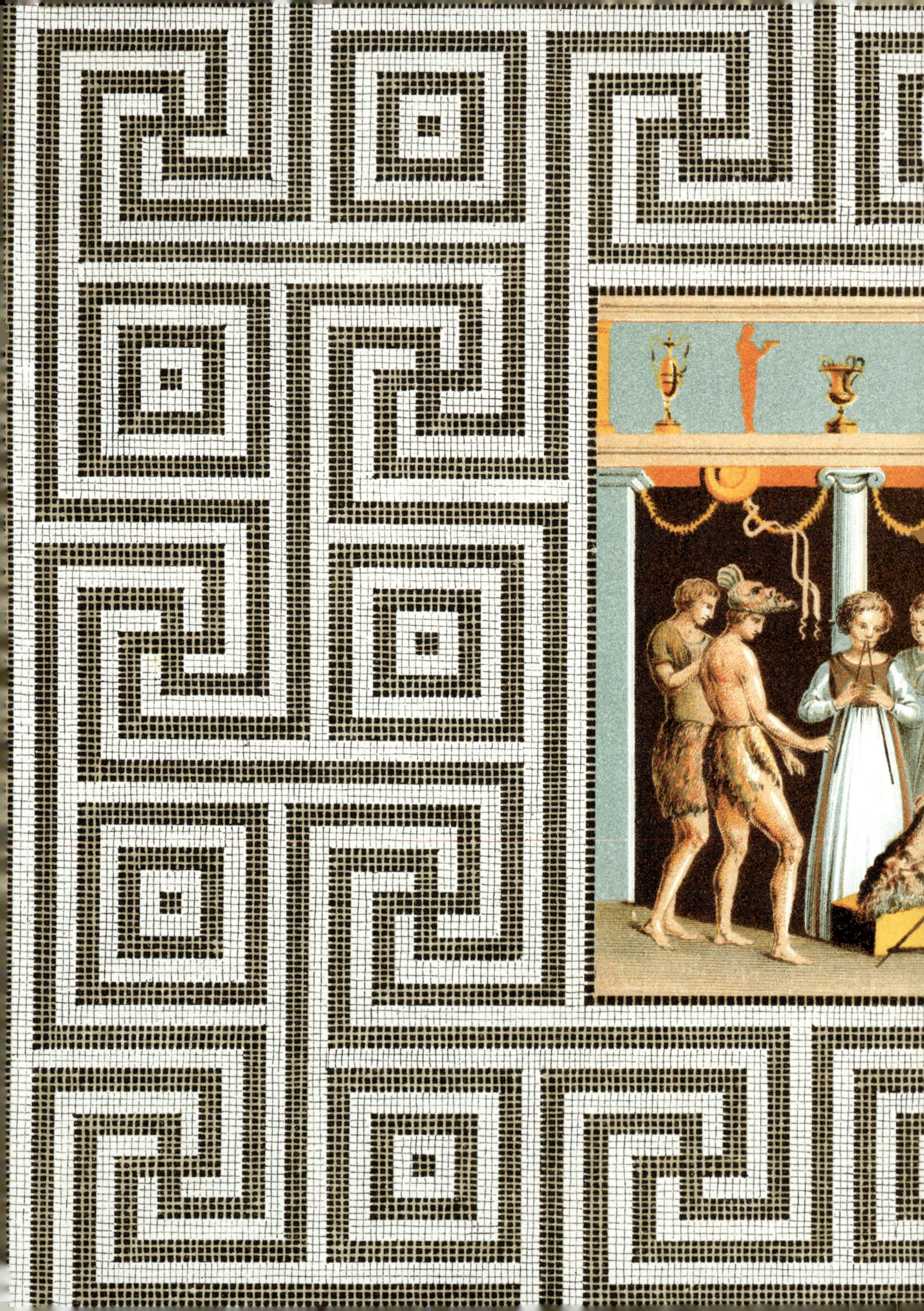

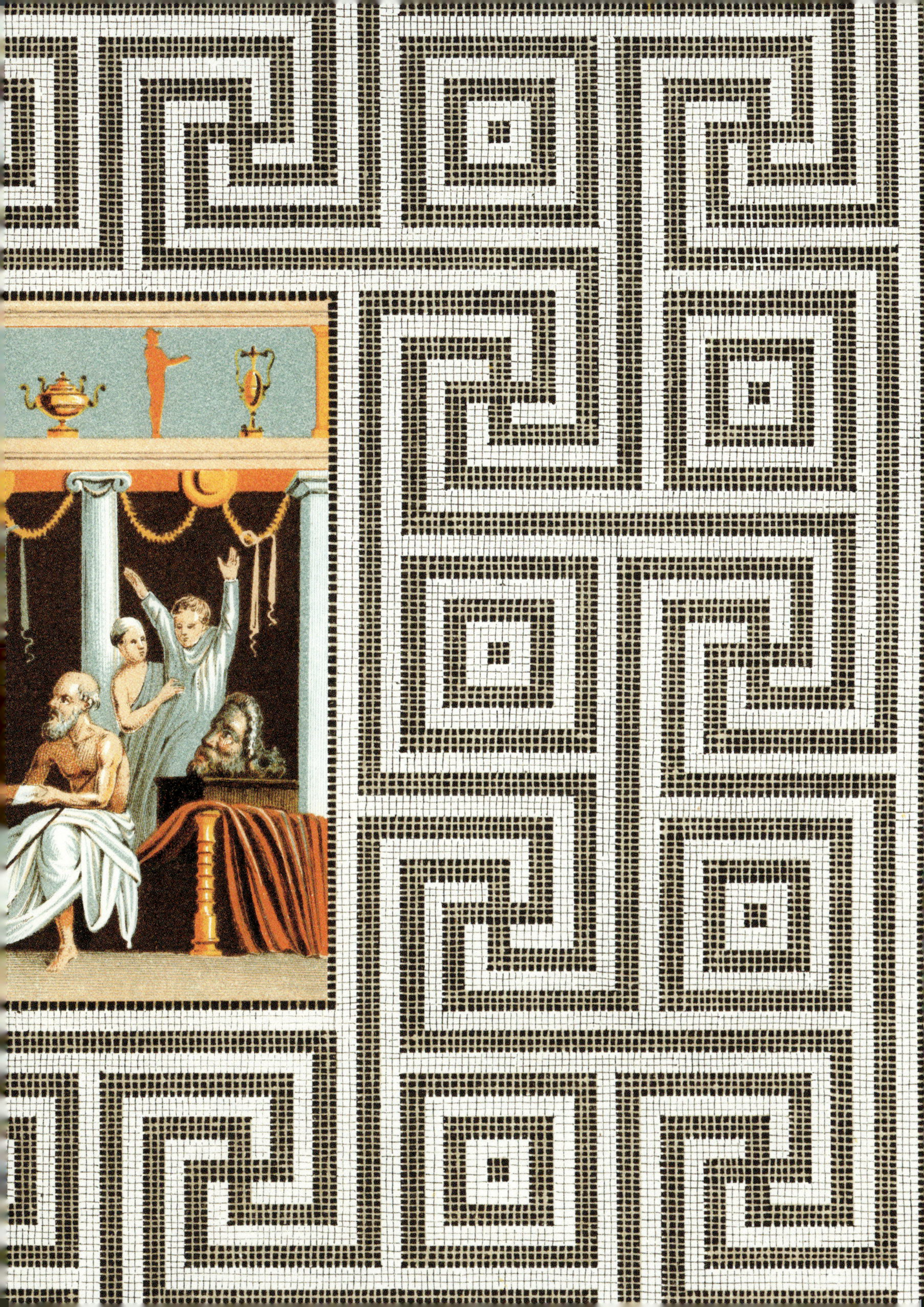

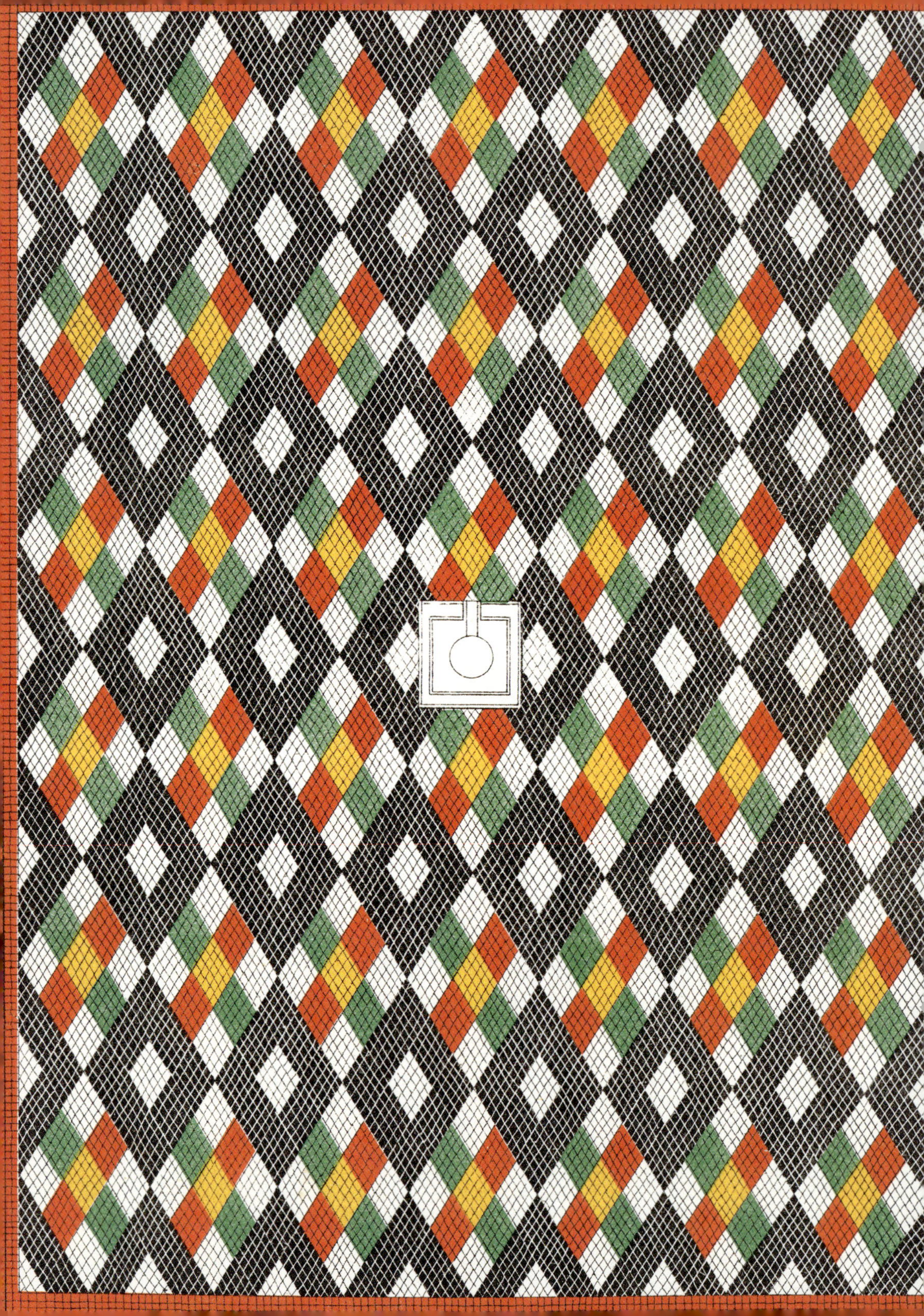

Contents

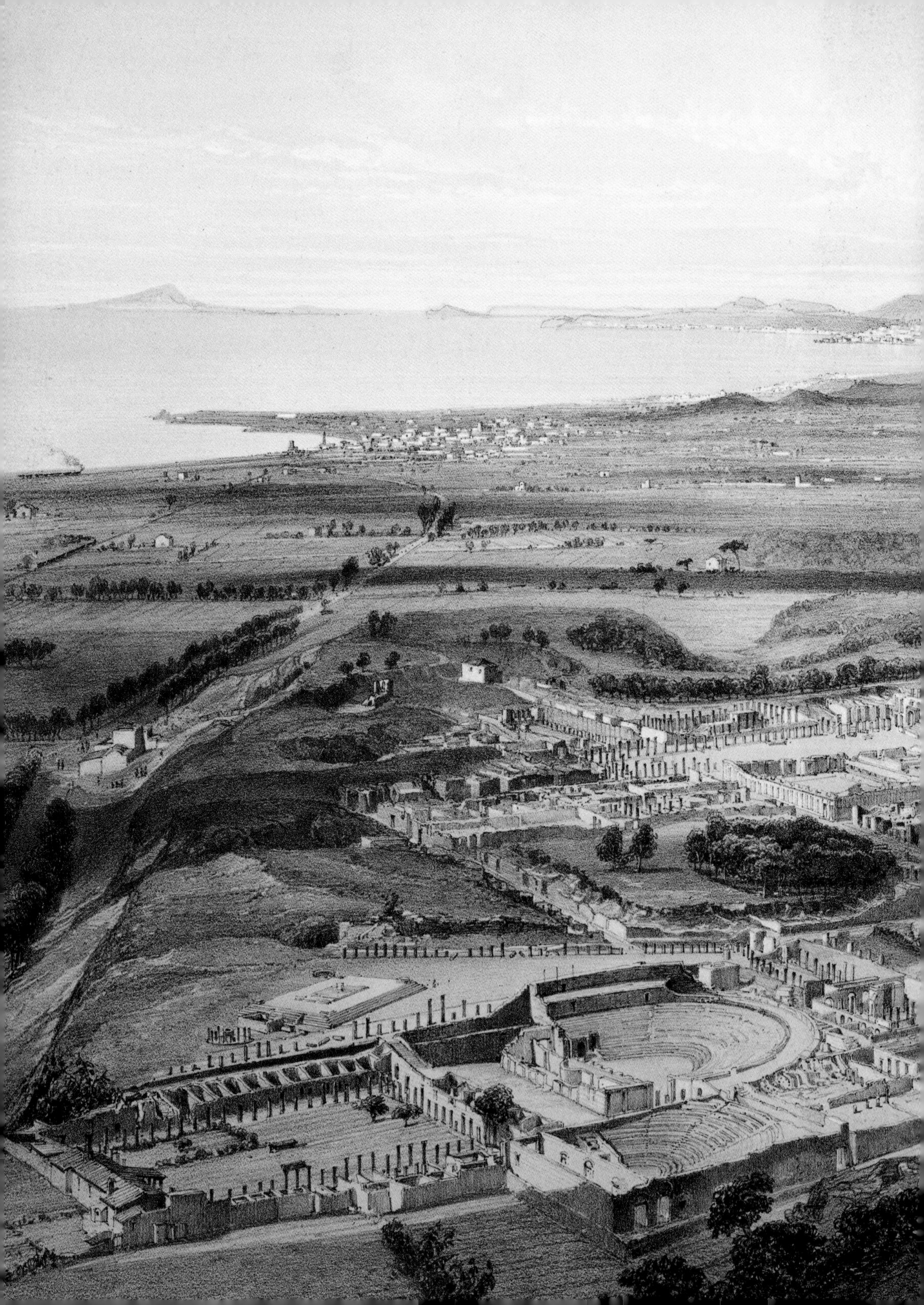

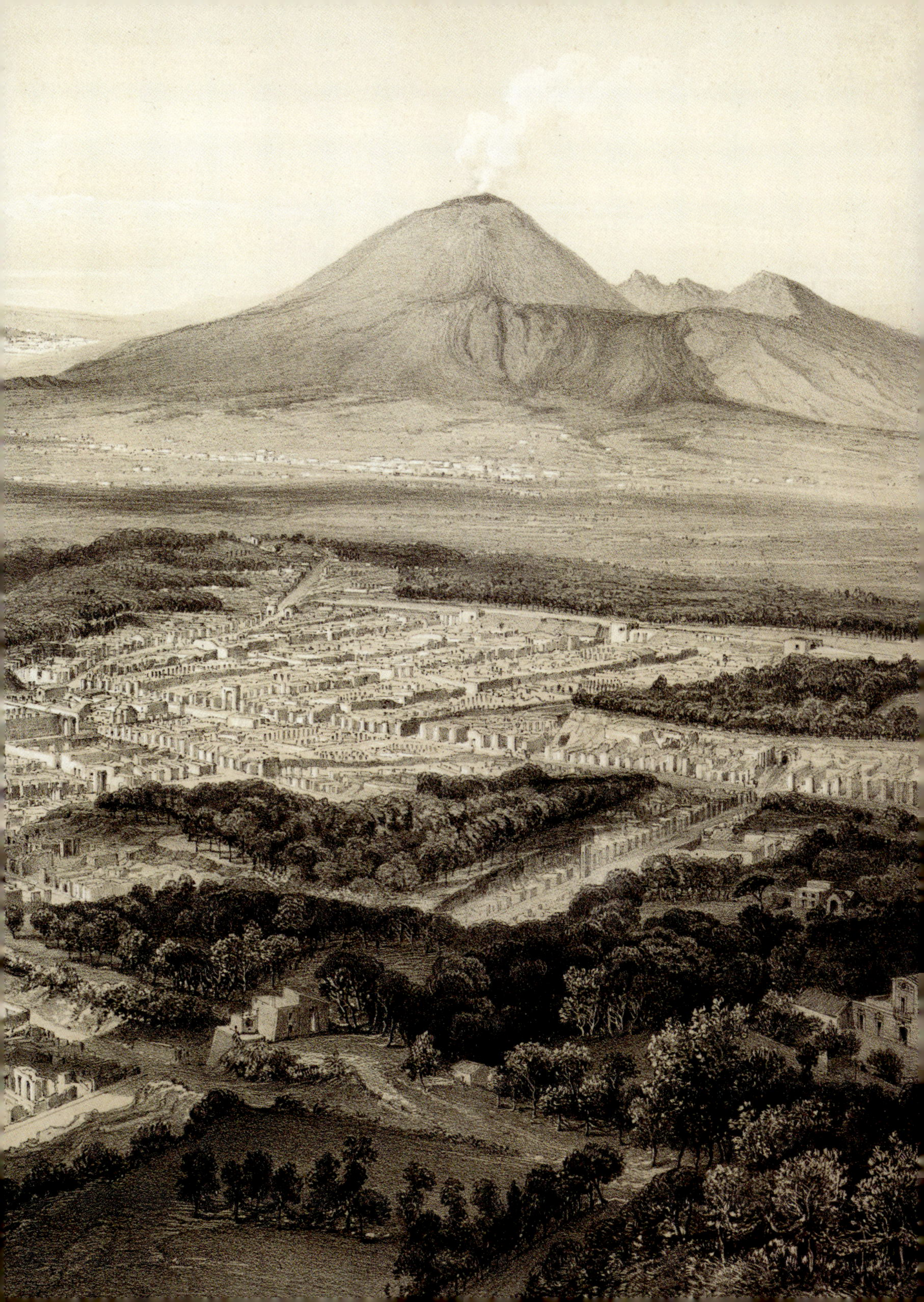

THE REDISCOVERY AND VISUALISATION OF POMPEII

The work by the Niccolini brothers and its context

The Preface (Proemio)

This work ... is the first in our land that makes Pompeii known in its entirety, and this has been achieved with the aid of all the means the arts of our country, as well as technical inventions from abroad, can offer us. – Fausto and Felice Niccolini

With these solemnly pronounced words, the brothers Fausto and Felice Niccolini began the preface in which they presented their great publishing project, *Le Case ed i monumenti di Pompei.* Started in 1854, it would not be completed until more than 40 years later, long after both the brothers had died, by their nephew Antonio. Ultimately it would come to comprise four volumes, almost 500 plates and several hundred pages of text – a monumental work both in scope and format. The fact that it could actually be completed was by no means a matter of course, for it was produced during a period of great political and social upheavals in Naples. The project was inaugurated during the time of the Kingdom of the Two Sicilies, but this latter soon collapsed in the wake of Garibaldi's invasion and in 1861 was assimilated into the new Kingdom of Italy. Naples was now merely a province, and many members of the old elite were replaced or else withdrew from public office. The phrase "the first in our land" nevertheless remained significant: with the *Case e monumenti*, the Niccolinis had succeeded in matching the magnificent publications from countries north of the Alps, producing a work that was second to none in its size and illustrations and which combined the forces of Italian artists and academics. They also made use of the very latest printing technology, colour lithography, which had only just been introduced into Naples and which gave the illustrations an entirely new luminosity. In their sheer quantity, too, the illustrations far surpassed all other archaeological works on Pompeii.

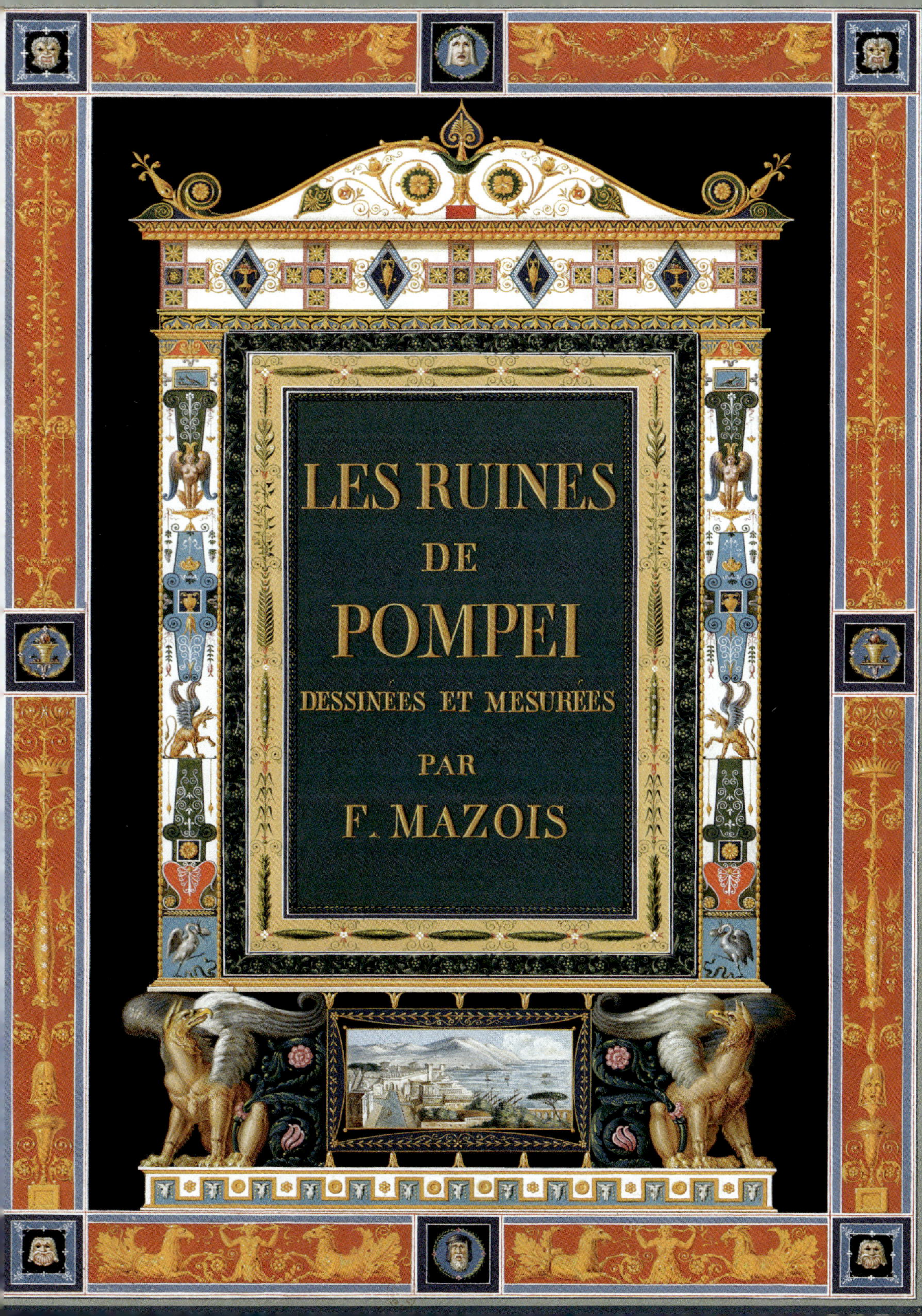
LES RUINES
DE
POMPEI
DESSINÉES ET MESURÉES
PAR
F. MAZOIS

But what was the background to this publishing project? Who were its editors, with what other works did it have to compete, how was it conceived, and what were its aims?

Excavation and documentation – discovery and excavations in the 18th century

The rediscovery of the cities of Herculaneum, Stabiae and Pompeii, destroyed in AD 79 by the eruption of Vesuvius, is closely bound up with political events in the Kingdom of Naples in the first half of the 18th century. In 1734 the Spanish Infante Carlos was crowned Charles VII. After a first successful war to secure his new realm, the young king planned the building of a royal palace, the Reggia, in Portici beneath Mount Vesuvius. A well shaft was discovered in the course of the building work, which had already been used in 1711 by the Austrian lieutenant general Prince d'Elboeuf to recover a number of ancient statues. In 1738 these subterranean excavations were successfully reopened under the direction of officers from the Royal Engineers and large parts of the ancient city – which lies barely 100 feet (30 metres) below today's ground level – could be accessed via galleries and further shafts. The rich finds of bronze and marble statues initially found their way into the rooms and courtyards of the large Reggia complex under construction in the immediate vicinity. Later a dedicated museum was created in the neighbouring Palazzo Caramanica under the name of the Herculanense Museum.

After the remains of Roman villas had earlier been uncovered – and filled in again – in ancient Stabiae, above modern-day Castellammare, in 1749 excavations were begun north of the River Sarno (pp. 72–73), at a site with the field name *cività* (city), always in the hope of rich finds for the royal collections. Here, as in Stabiae, it was possible to reach the ruins from the surface, without digging tunnels, which greatly facilitated operations. The first digs were undertaken with no particular system and were filled in again afterwards, with the landowner receiving a compensation payment. The so-called Villa des Cicero was among the buildings temporarily uncovered during this phase (1754), together with the property *(praedium)* of one Julia Felix (1754–1757). It was not until 1763, however, when the discovery of an inscription in front of a city gate (later designated the Herculaneum Gate) clearly identified the location as ancient Pompeii, that the decision was made not to fill in the excavations again after they had been opened up. All the finds continued to be sent to Portici, along with the finest of the wall paintings, which were cut out, backed with slate and provided with wooden frames so that they could be hung like panel paintings in their own gallery. At the same time, excavators abandoned their practice – criticised by visitors – of destroying paintings that had not been cut out in order to prevent thefts. The area of excavation around the city gate now remained visible and was slowly extended towards the city centre, while the large Theatre (1764 onwards) and its accompanying portico, and above all the Temple of Isis and, outside the city to the north, the so-called Villa of Diomedes (1771–1775), were also uncovered. Since it

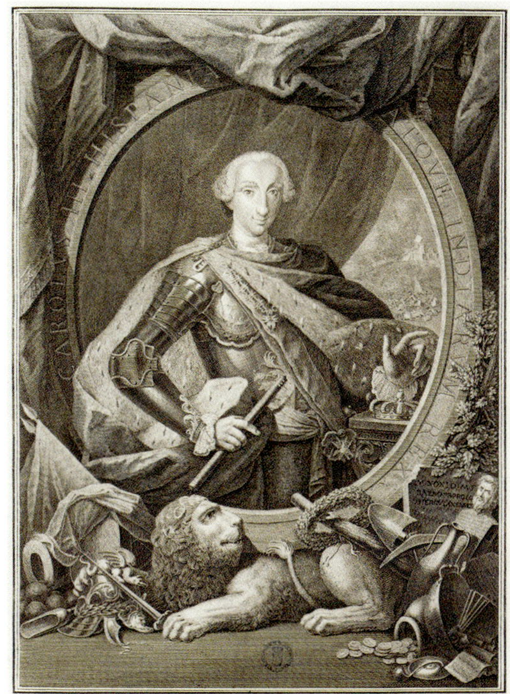

was almost impossible to visit the tunnels in Herculaneum, in the 18th century the three still separate areas of excavation in Pompeii attracted increasing numbers of visitors from all over Europe, who spent several weeks in Naples, mainly in winter, as part of their Grand Tour. Both the museum and the excavations in Pompeii itself could only be visited with a permit. These were evidently given out in such numbers that towards the end of the 18th century, at the suggestion of the excavation management, a Taverna del Rapillo (Pumice Inn) was opened, where tourists could obtain refreshments. Visitors were always strictly supervised and were not allowed to make either drawings or take notes – a regulation bemoaned in all the accounts of the day.

News of the discovery of Herculaneum and Pompeii spread rapidly amongst European academics and *dilettanti*, and people waited impatiently to learn more. To begin with, Charles VII and his most important advisor, the Marchese Tanucci, treated the results of the excavations as classified information. In 1755, however, the Accademia Ercolanese was founded as a scholarly society with the task of publishing the finds in books with engraved plates accompanied by commentaries. A new paper factory had to be established in order to produce the large-format volumes, and young artists were specially trained as draughtsmen and engravers. Of the originally 40 planned volumes of *Le antichità di Ercolano esposte* (The Antiquities of Herculaneum Displayed; hereafter *Antichità d'Ercolano*), however, just eight were actually published: five on painted works, two on bronzes and one on lamps and candelabra. Issued successively between 1757 and 1792, the volumes were at first reserved for presentation as gifts by the king, as a token of his particular favour, and were consequently somewhat

Camillo Paderni, ***Portrait of King Charles III of Spain with Military and Archaeological Trophies***, 1757
Copper engraving. From: *Le Antichità di Ercolano esposte*, vol. 1, Naples 1757, frontispiece

Page 11
François Mazois, ***Title-Page*** for ***Les ruines de Pompéi***
Watercolour drawing. Paris, Bibliothèque nationale de France, Gd 12d rés. ft.4, frontispiece

rare and difficult to examine despite their large editions of 1,500 copies. Only from the 1770s onwards did it become possible to purchase them as well from the book trade. This restrictive access both to the antiquities and to information about them led to the appearance of illegal publications. The first such book appeared in 1754 and featured paintings made on the basis of drawings executed from memory after visits to the museum. One of its two authors, the painter Nicolas Cochin, felt that the ancient murals were "mal dessinées ... [avec] peu de connaissance des formes et des détails de la nature" ("badly drawn ... [with] little knowledge of the forms and details of nature"), a verdict delivered from the standpoint of the 18th century and which would remain stuck to these works for a very long time. The accounts published in German and French by Johann Joachim Winckelmann following his visits in 1758 and 1762, which contained no illustrations, expressed strongly negative views regarding the competence of the excavators – views that were later shared and reiterated by many visitors. A first more substantial and cohesive report, with numerous illustrations, can be found in the second volume of the *Voyage pittoresque* (1782) by the Abbé de Saint-Non. The sole plan of the city, by Francesco Piranesi, also appeared in Rome in 1782. Images of the Vesuvian cities, their architecture and artworks only reached a wider public from the 1770s onwards, with the appearance across Europe of cheaper reprints of the *Antichità d'Ercolano*.

For the young kingdom, the excavations meant a great boost for legitimacy and prestige. The finds, which at least in Herculaneum were brought up from below ground like mineral resources extracted from a mine, resulted in the creation of a museum that was comparable in its significance with the papal collections in Rome. The importance attributed to these finds is demonstrated by the frontispiece of the first volume of the *Antichità d'Ercolano* (ill. p. 13): beneath the portrait of the king in military dress lies a lion, while on the left, a helmet, cannonballs and a powder scoop symbolise the ruler's military successes. To the right of the lion, however, the club of Hercules and his victor's crown stand for Herculaneum, and are accompanied by digging tools and archaeological finds such as inscriptions, coins and bronze utensils. The finds were instrumentalised as means of consolidating the power and integration of the young dynasty, and their value was further increased by their limited accessibility, despite the very high level of interest by the European general public.

The "French decade"

Amidst the storms of revolution and the rule of the French Empire, the Kingdom of Naples also temporarily collapsed, but the symbolic importance of the ruins and finds remained as great as before. This is illustrated by a bizarre episode that occurred during the short-lived Parthenopean Republic, which was set up after the conquest of Naples by French troops in

François Mazois, ***Casa di Championnet***, ca. 1810
Watercolour drawing. Paris, Bibliothèque nationale de France, Gd 12e rés. ft. 4, pl. XX, no. 48

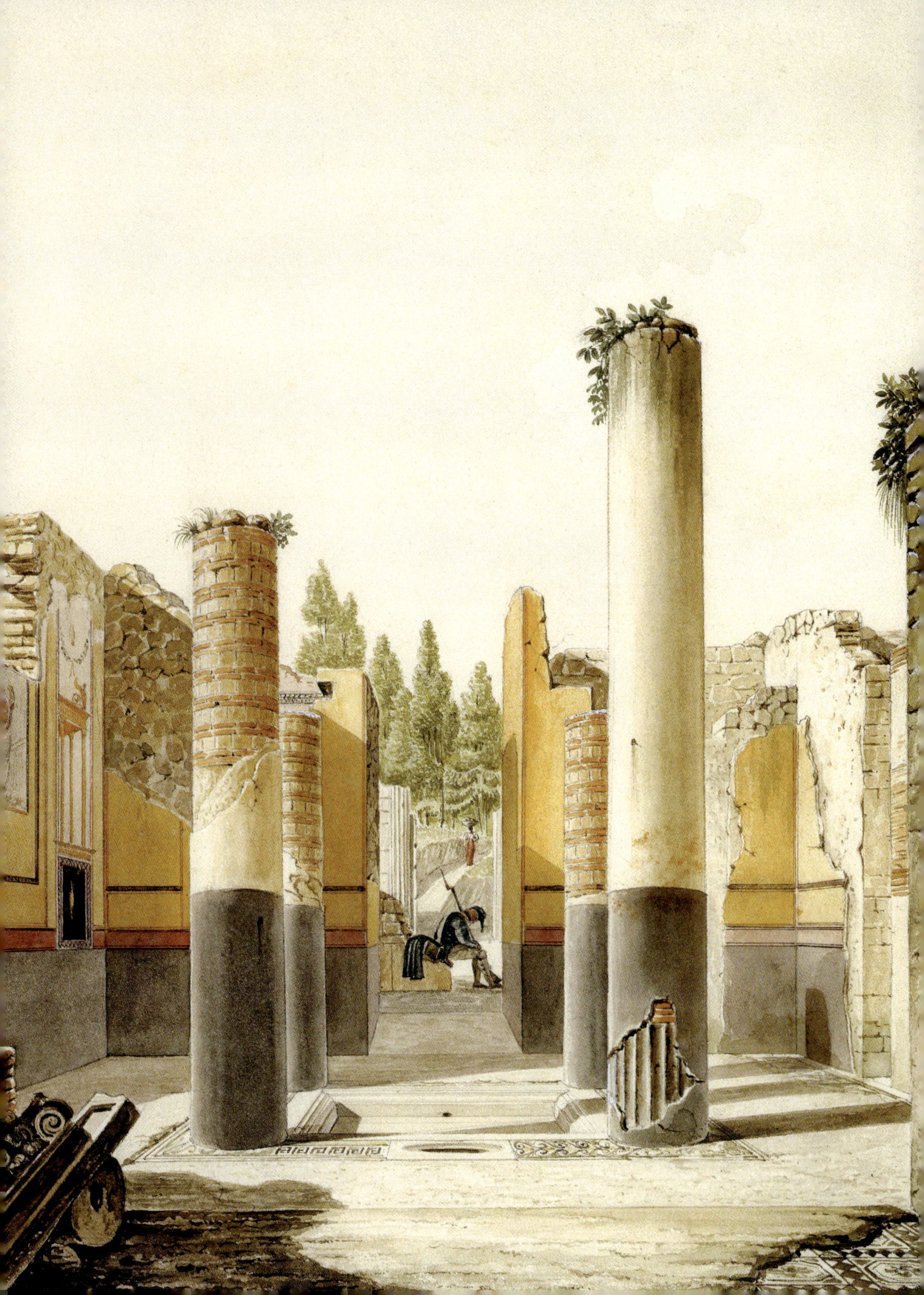

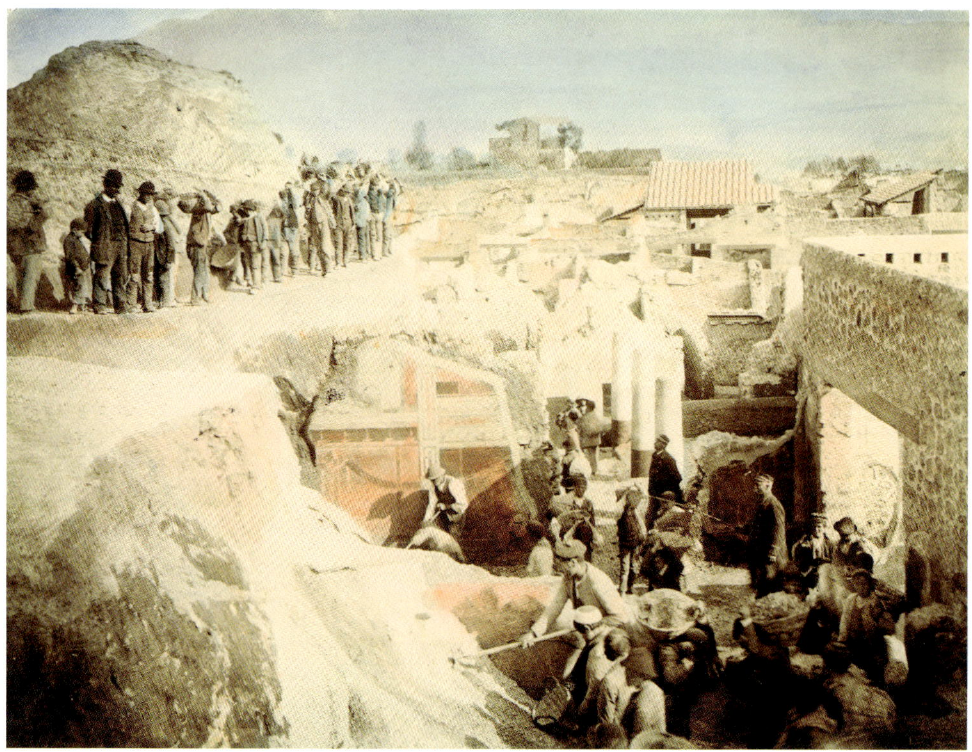

Achille and Pasquale Esposito, ***Excavations in Pompeii (Casa delle Nozze d'Argento)***, 1894
Albumen silver print, 19.2 x 24.3 cm / 7½ x 9⅝ in. Private collection

1799 and lasted only a few months. King Ferdinand IV, a son of Charles VII, had fled into exile to Palermo and taken important parts of the collection with him, thereby underlining the fact that they belonged to the sovereign. Meanwhile, the French not only sought to ship back to France the remaining artefacts which had been recovered from the Vesuvian cities, but immediately began their own excavations in Pompeii with a workforce of 1,000 (!) soldiers. Their efforts were largely unsuccessful though and the antiquities themselves got no further than Rome, but in 1802, after the Treaty of Florence, Ferdinand IV was forced to present a substantial quantity of ancient finds from Pompeii as personal compensation to First Consul Bonaparte, which immediately passed into the private possession of Empress Josephine.

Properly speaking, the French decade only began in 1806, however. For the first time now, a long-term plan of excavations was drawn up with the aim of systematically investigating Pompeii as a city. It was decided both to link up the still separate areas of excavation and to follow the line of the city wall in order to establish the shape of the city and locate the whereabouts of its gates. On the main street, the Casa di Sallustio and Casa di Pansa were uncovered, among others, as well as the south side of the Forum. Queen Caroline Murat, one of Napoleon's sisters, partially financed the excavations herself. As a result she considered the finds her personal property and had them taken to her private museum, the so-called Museo Palatino, in the royal palace. In 1816 she took many objects with her into exile and later sold some of them to Ludwig I of Bavaria.

The Bourbon Restoration

The restoration of Bourbon rule spelled little change for the excavation programme and its aims. The ever diminishing amount of money available for the excavations, however, meant that everything advanced more slowly. Several major discoveries were nevertheless made in the years between 1817 and 1860, including not only the complete uncovering of the Forum and its surrounding area, but also the two very well-preserved complexes of thermal baths and the gradual exposure of the ancient network of streets, linking the old excavation sites into a single area. Of particular importance are the numerous houses, some of them with their painted décor still in very good condition, that were uncovered above all in regions VI and VII. The Casa del Poeta tragico (1824/25) was followed by the Casa dei Dioscuri (1828/29), the Casa del Fauno (1830–1832) and a whole series of houses, some of them magnificently decorated and furnished, whose most important paintings and mosaics (such as the Alexander mosaic) were cut out and taken to the museum, now transferred to Naples and called the Real Museo Borbonico (Royal Bourbon Museum). Although several important houses had already been excavated in the north of the city from the 18th century onwards, it was only now that the full spectrum of Roman domestic architecture became apparent. Surpassing all expectations, in particular, were the mythological pictures that were brought to light in large numbers.

Improved means of transport in the 19th century resulted in a sharp increase in visitors to Pompeii. Following the Napoleonic Wars and the Continental Blockade, these visitors had chiefly been English travellers who were resuming the Grand Tour. Now, however, the building of Italy's first railway line from Naples to Portici in 1839, and its extension to Castellammare in 1844 with a station at Pompeii, made it much easier to reach the excavations. When Pope Pius IX visited the ancient city in October 1849, he too arrived by train, pulled by an engine named the "Pompei". To meet demands, several guidebooks were published in a handy octavo format in both Italian and French, along with plans of the city, some of them hand-coloured, which were regularly updated to show the latest excavations (ill. pp. 72–73). The archaeological sites thus also became a significant aspect of the kingdom's growing tourist industry.

Within the excavation administration and behind the doors of the Accademia Ercolanese, reorganised in 1817 as part of the Società Reale Borbonica, the situation was by no means idyllic: there were problems over money intended for the excavations instead going into private pockets, not to mention the power wielded by individual members and committees

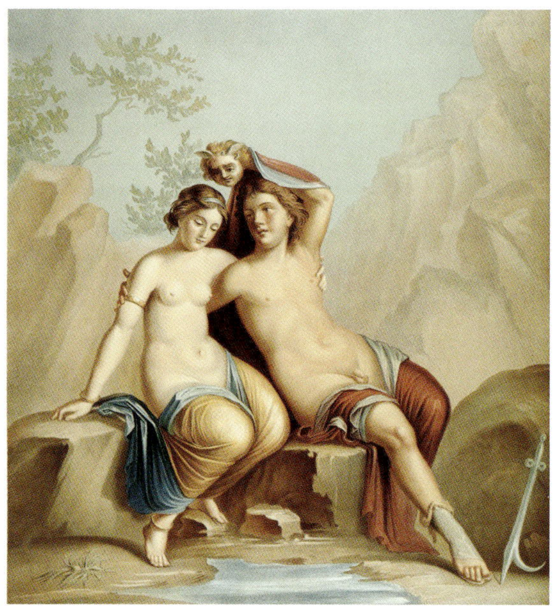

and disagreements over publication rights. New finds could only be illustrated after a fixed period of three years, and even then only with direct permission. Authorisations more generous than the normal rule were nevertheless granted – over the heads of those who were technically responsible for them – to foreigners with friends in high places. Visits from the European aristocracy also became occasions for the "excavation" of certain finds deliberately placed there in advance. One of the most prominent victims of such intrigues would be Giuseppe Fiorelli (1823–1896), who as a young man in 1846 was appointed Ispettore of Pompeii. Together with Raffaele D'Ambra (1814–1892), he was a member of a committee that in 1848 was asked to put forward proposals for a reorganisation of the museum administration. They drew up a lengthy text which bluntly pointed to many failures in the existing system, including thefts from the museum, absenteeism among the staff, nepotism and corruption. Fiorelli, who was a vocal supporter of the constitution and the king, was subsequently imprisoned during the final phase of the Restoration. His draft of 1848 later became the starting point, however, for the comprehensive reforms Fiorelli would implement in the new Kingdom of Italy.

The unification of Italy and Giuseppe Fiorelli

In 1860, the last year of the Kingdom of the Two Sicilies, the excavations came to a complete standstill. However, the very first proclamations issued by Garibaldi after seizing power on September 7 that year also related to the museum and Pompeii. On October 22 Garibaldi visited the excavations accompanied by a large retinue, and on October 24 with King Vittorio

Wilhelm Zahn
Casa dei Capitelli colorati: Perseus Shows Andromeda the Head of the Medusa Reflected in the Water
Casa dei Dioscuri: Jupiter Crowned by a Victory
Colour lithographs. From: Wilhelm Zahn, *Die schönsten Ornamente und merkwürdigsten Gemälde aus Pompeji, Herculanum und Stabiae*, vol. 3, Berlin 1849–1859, plate 24 (above), plate 14 (opposite)

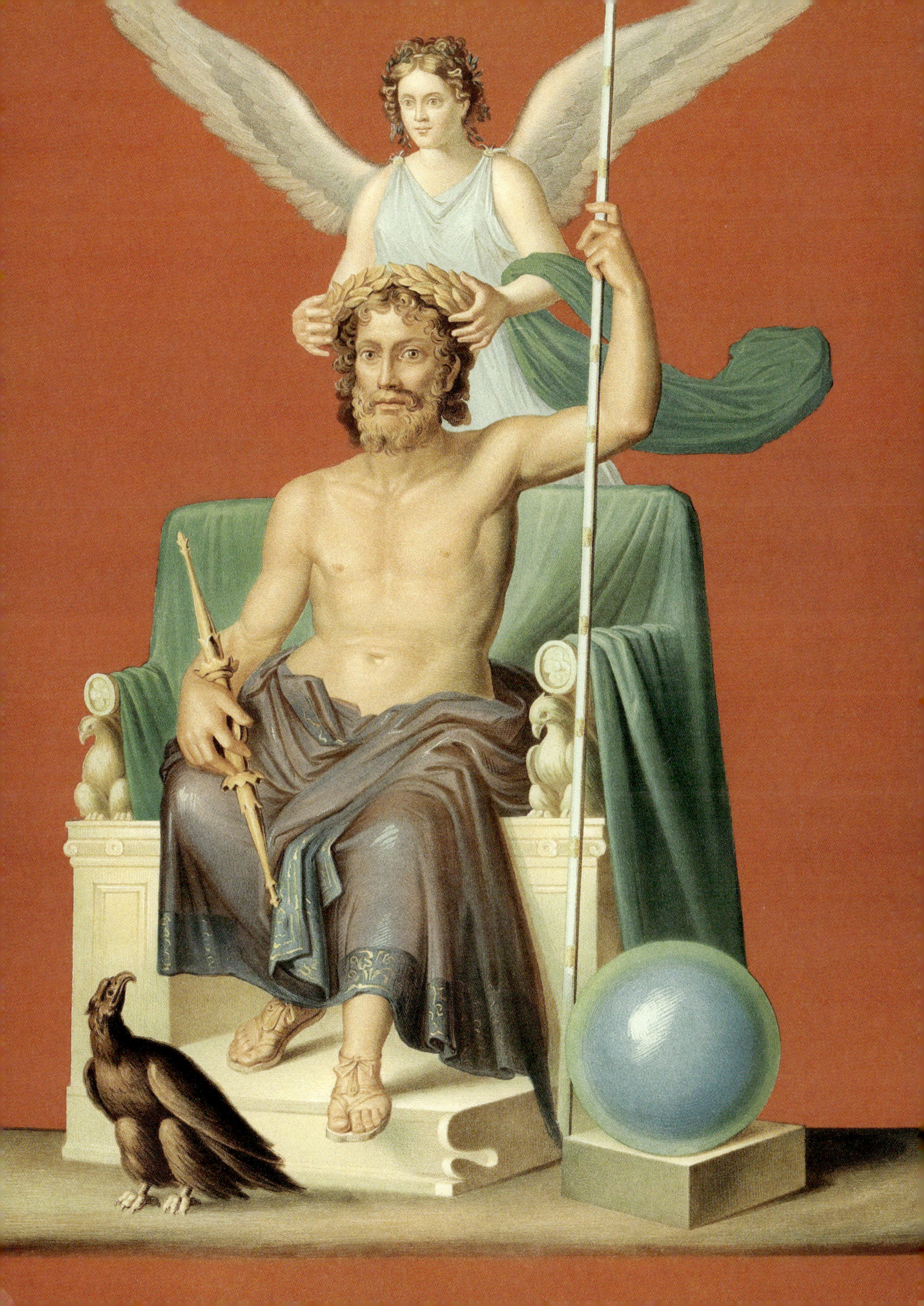

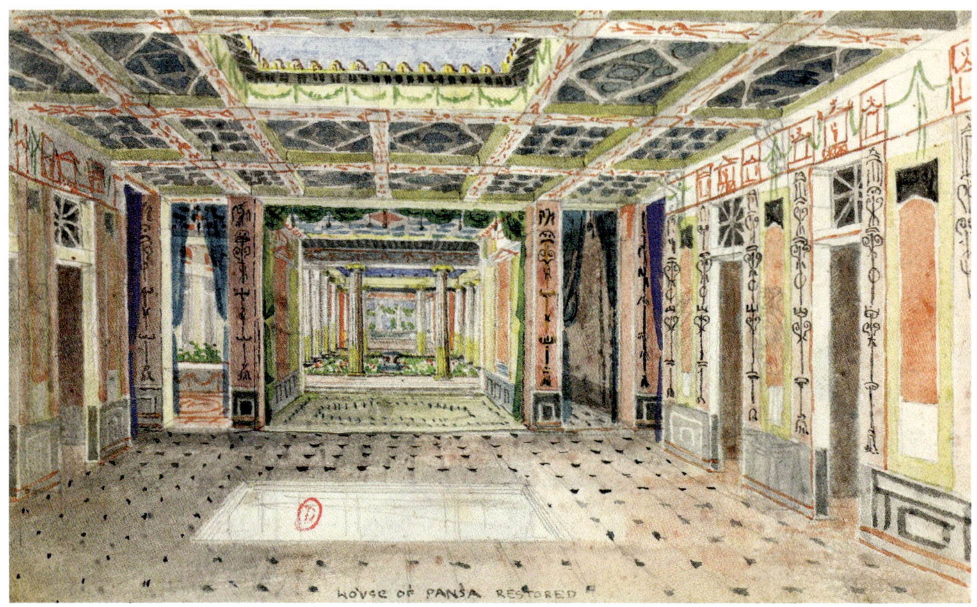

William Gell, ***Casa di Pansa: Reconstruction of the Atrium***
Watercolour drawing, ca. 1818. Paris, Bibliothèque INHA, MS. 180, 1, plate 41

Emmanuele. In December Giuseppe Fiorelli returned to the stage, initially as Ispettore of excavations at Pompeii, and this time the post served him as a springboard for a rapid ascent. As early as 1863 Fiorelli took over from the previous Soprintendente after the latter's death, and as director of the museum and Soprintendente of excavations he held the fate of Pompeii in his hands from this time on. In this capacity he founded in 1866, the Scuola Archeologica di Pompei, in which young men trained to become archaeologists – at that time a new profession.

In Pompeii itself Fiorelli now had the opportunity, as well as the funding thanks to a budget increase from the coffers of the new state, to implement the reforms he had proposed back in 1848. Some of the changes were administrative, such as increasing the price of admission, so that visitors would contribute to the costs of the excavations in return for right of entry. Fiorelli's division of Pompeii into regions and blocks of houses and his introduction of a house-numbering system are still in use today; based on his own historical research, this served to simplify discussion and communication about the various buildings and finds in Pompeii. Other improvements included longer-term systematic planning of the excavations. In particular, the countless mounds of earth still lying between the dig areas (ill. p. 16) were removed, with a modern light railway being employed for this purpose. From now on, blocks of houses were excavated completely and not left half buried in the incessant search for interesting objects. Some of the innovations popularly attributed to Fiorelli, on the other hand, had in fact already been introduced in the last decade of the Bourbon Restoration. One example is the decision to stop excavating houses from the original street level, since the resulting earth pressure destroyed the ancient walls. Instead, the teams of diggers began removing the debris of the Vesuvian eruption evenly from above, so that for the first time the remains of roofs and upper storeys could be studied. Fiorelli's most spectacular idea was also based on earlier experiments: in 1863, under his direction, plaster casts were made for the first time from the body-shaped cavities left in the volcanic ash where victims of the eruption had perished. The resulting figures conveyed the suffering of the Pompeians with an immediacy that touched all of Europe, thanks not least to the new medium of photography, which ensured that the images spread rapidly. The same can be said of the 1:100 scale model of the city, greatly admired then as now, and the regularly updated mapping (ills. pp. 25, 26–27). Meanwhile, Fiorelli's openness with regard to sharing the results of the excavations proved particularly beneficial. Already in 1850 he had sought to publish old excavation reports but was prevented from doing so by a court ruling. From 1860 to 1864 he was now able to print these reports in several volumes and so for the first time facilitated public access to a wealth of information on the course of the excavations and the origins of the objects in the museum. In the summer of 1861 he also founded the *Giornale degli scavi di Pompei*, a monthly journal that reported on current excavations. The international world of scholarship had never before been kept up to date on such an intensive, almost day-to-day basis. Fiorelli furthermore supported the production of a whole series of academic works, mainly by German scholars, who were generously permitted to work in the

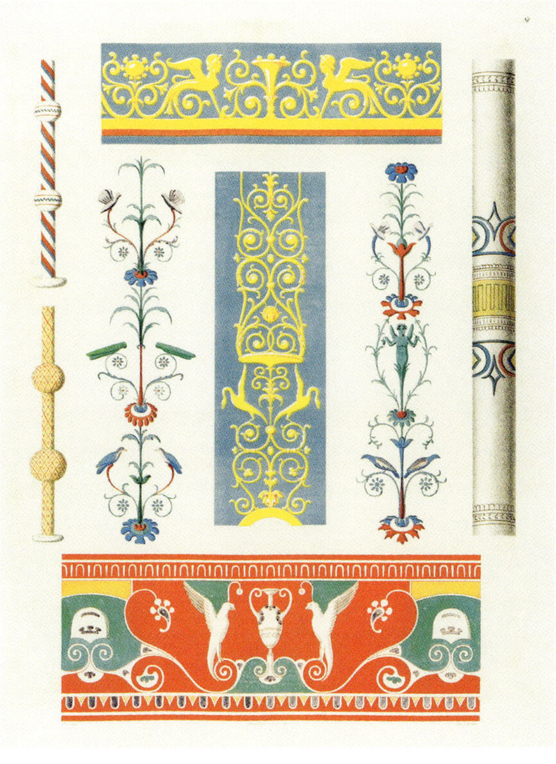

Wilhelm Zahn, ***Ornamental Details from the Casa delle Vestali and Other Houses in the Vesuvian Cities***
Colour lithograph. From: Wilhelm Zahn, *Die schönsten Ornamente und merkwürdigsten Gemälde aus Pompeji, Herculanum und Stabiae*, vol 1, Berlin 1828–1829, plate 81

Museo Nazionale and in Pompeii. The at times positively eulogistic accounts of Fiorelli and his achievements must also be seen against this backdrop.

But there were also shortcomings in excavation practice under Fiorelli. Although curbs were placed, for example, on the previously standard procedure of cutting out wall paintings and taking them to the museum, no adequate protective measures were introduced to preserve the paintings in situ. Meanwhile, the documentation of Pompeian wall decorations in drawings and watercolours, so extensively undertaken in the 1820s and up until the 1840s, was tailing off and likewise only inadequately replaced by photography. Houses uncovered in the 1860s are consequently often both particularly badly preserved and poorly documented. Fiorelli's appearance on this stage nevertheless signified a fundamental shift in the way Pompeii was understood. The ancient city and its finds were no longer considered the private property of the king, but instead it became a sort of world heritage site which on principle was accessible to everyone. The young German archaeologist Wolfgang Helbig went so far as to proclaim: "Pompeii and its treasures do not belong to Italy alone but to all civilised nations. Nevertheless, it is Italy that administers it and thus bears a great responsibility to the public."

Fiorelli had assumed national stature as early as 1865 with his appointment as Senator of the Kingdom, and in 1875 he moved to Rome to take charge of Italy's newly founded Directorate General of Antiquities and Fine Arts. His students Giulio De Petra (1841–1925) and Antonio Sogliano (1854–1942) continued the excavations in Pompeii along his lines, and at the end of the century houses were for the first time extensively reconstructed even as work progressed while larger finds were conserved in situ. The old dream of recreating the contexts of daily life in antiquity was thus fulfilled as far as was possible. The most famous example of this, the Casa dei Vettii (ill. p. 511), is illustrated in the final plates of the *Case e monumenti*.

Documentation and conservation

Since the first excavations at Pompeii, the directors of the work (architects or engineers) made plans of the uncovered buildings and also drew up constantly updated maps of the city. The wall paintings, in particular, were carefully documented. Whole walls had to be drawn before the sections earmarked for the museum were cut out, in order to preserve their context, while selected pictures were copied in a more manageable size. The *regolamenti* (regulations) set out the working procedure for the artists, with the director of excavations first of all bringing together the pictures that were to be copied. Draughtsmen then traced the newly uncovered motifs using transparent paper and took colour samples or made watercolours in front of the newly exposed wall. In reduced format, the pictures could then serve as the basis for the engravings in the *Real Museo Borbonico*. The accuracy of the drawing also had to be confirmed, and then finally the watercolours were sent to the Academy of Fine Arts and the tracings to the Accademia Ercolanese, so that their respective members could write accompanying texts for the *Real Museo Borbonico*. But the sluggishness of officialdom, squabbles over jurisdiction, the ever dwindling budget and probably also the unreliability of certain of the artists made a speedy execution of these procedures next to impossible, such that towards the end of the Bourbon era there was a large discrepancy between commissions and finished drawings. The quality of the sheets can also be seen to vary. Alongside artists such as Francesco Morelli (active until 1829), Giuseppe Marsigli (active 1824–1837), Giuseppe Abbate (documented from 1835, d. 1877) and later Vincenzo Loria (1849, documented until 1911) and Geremia Discanno (1839–1907), there are also more modest talents, whose qualification evidently consisted in their connection to one of the artists already employed. Nevertheless, the modern viewer is regularly astonished to see how meticulously copied ancient forms were transformed, in the course of their reduction to a smaller scale, into classicist figures that – for all their iconographical accuracy – undeniably reflect the style of their day. An initiative in 1854 to replace the slow and expensive process of documentation by drawings with photography failed to get off the ground.

Many sheets remain missing even today; others could only be reacquired after the artist's death by purchasing them from his widow, while others again (or copies of them) were sold directly by the artists to tourists and perhaps also to the Niccolinis. This situation too was greatly lamented in the above-mentioned report compiled by the committee in 1848. Concerning the pictures, the authors stated: "We only know that there must be many [drawings], some in the royal printing works, others in the Ministry, others with Cavaliere Antonio Niccolini or in the secretariat of the Accademia Ercolanese, and finally others in dusty boxes in the museum offices ..."

Similarly considered regulations governed the maintenance and restoration of Pompeii's uncovered buildings. The thoroughly modern stipulation that, in the case of stabilisation works, the old must always remain distinguishable from the new, had to be checked by a separate committee, which made on-site inspections for this purpose.

Since about 1820 staff at the museum had also been working on a three-dimensional form of documentation: a large wood and cork model of the city on a scale of 1:48. Individual group of buildings were painstakingly and comprehensively reproduced right down to every wall and plaster fragment. The model-builder Domenico Padiglione (1756–1832) and his sons copied the state of the ruins on site in the course of extended stays in Pompeii. The *regolamenti*, moreover, stipulated that the draughtsmen making copies of wall decorations should also produce miniature versions for the model. Ultimately, however, the scale proved too large to be able to represent the whole city in a fully coherent manner. Fiorelli therefore commissioned Felice Padiglione (ca. 1810–1864) to make a new model at a scale of 1:100, which was begun in 1860 and continued until nearly the end of the century (ills. pp. 25, 26–27). It contains a great deal of information about rooms and walls that are today completely destroyed.

Finally, Pompeii's public buildings and individual houses were documented in an almost systematic undertaking by the French winners of the Prix de Rome, although the vast majority of these works remained unseen up until the end of the 20th century in departments of prints and drawings and in academies of art. By contrast, some of the other techniques employed to bring the ancient city to life were positively spectacular and targeted at large audiences. It was only natural, for example, that the big 360-degree panoramas that were shown in specially built rotundas in London and Paris – the first mass medium – should include Pompeii among their subjects. During the winter of 1823/24, two views of Pompeii (seen from vantage points on the Forum and inside the Theatre) were even on show in London at the same time in the Strand and Leicester Square. A smaller variant was the so-called room panorama, a speciality of the painter Carl Georg Enslen (1792–1866). His surviving studies from 1826 clearly testify to his striving for documentary accuracy, but thanks to their low horizon they also capture the landscape around Pompeii, which the artist rendered in loving detail (the watercolours belong to the St. Annen-Museum in Lübeck). Lastly, the bird's-eye view also offered an entirely new view of the city as a whole, comparable with looking down upon the model in the museum. A sheet on Pompeii can also be found in the series *L'Italie à vol d'oiseau* (1849) by Alfred Guesdon (1808–1876), offering an accurate picture of the state of excavations at the time (ill. pp. 8–9).

The spread of knowledge through publications

While the number of publications remained very small up until the end of the "French decade", apart from the *Antichità d'Ercolano*, this situation altered considerably with the Bourbon Restoration. The most impressive and for many decades the standard work of reference on Pompeian architecture and town planning was *Les ruines de Pompéi* by François Mazois (1783–1826), the publication of which was financed by Queen Caroline Murat (see ills. pp. 11, 15). The French architect had attended the excavations continuously from 1809 to 1811 and subsequently visited them several times. The first two volumes of his work appeared in large folio before his death in 1826, while Franz Christian [François] Gau (1790–1853) edited volumes III and IV between 1829 and 1836. Mazois prefaced each architectural style with a substantial introduction, before describing the monuments in Pompeii individually and illustrating them with ground plans, orthogonal views, cross-sections and many details in numerous plates. In particular with his study on the Roman house, in which he combined an in-depth knowledge of Classical authors with an equally thorough familiarity with the houses of Pompeii, he laid the foundations of research into ancient domestic architecture. His drawings were regularly copied right up to the end of the 19th century.

The English-language *Pompeiana*, published in London between 1817 and 1819 by the antiquarian William Gell (1777–1836) and architect John P. Gandy (1787–1850; see ill. p. 20), was aimed at a different, less academically oriented and above all British public. The two quarto volumes include many drawings of Pompeian architecture and fragments of wall paintings, as well as numerous vedute. These views of the city, made with the aid of a camera lucida (at the

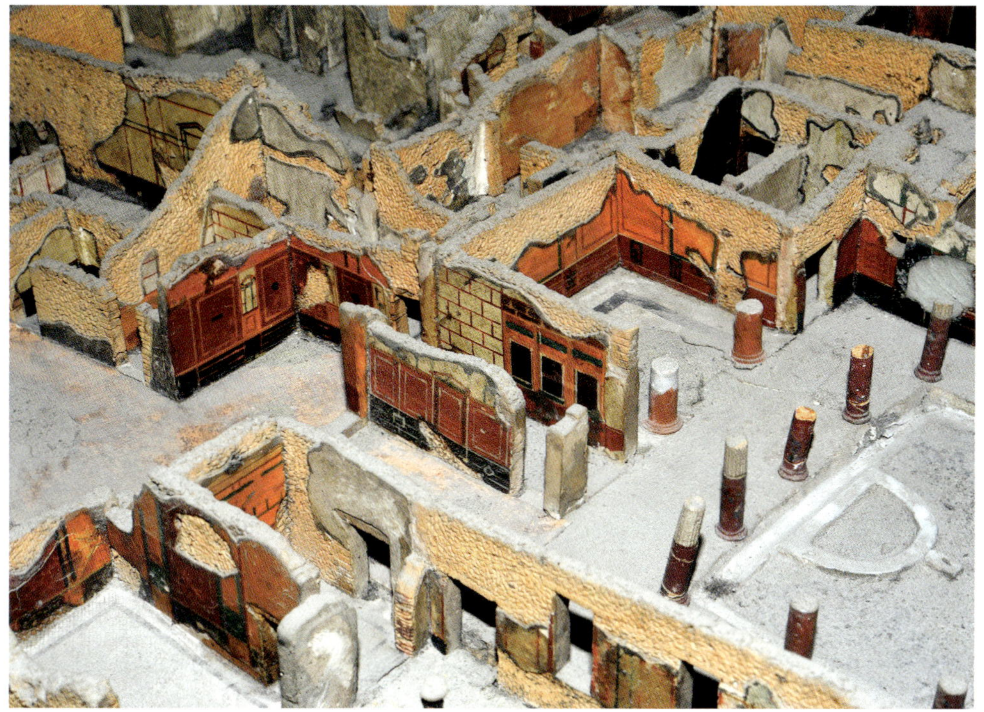

Above and pages 26–27
Felice Padiglione, ***Cork Model of Pompeii at a Scale of 1:100***
Detail: Casa del Citarista (I 4, 5 and 25), View Looking West, 1861 ff.
Overview of the Forum and Regio VII, View Looking East, 1861 ff.
Naples, Museo Archeologico Nazionale

time still a new invention), were considered particularly accurate. Compared with Mazois's *Les ruines de Pompéi*, the text is written in a lighter style but is none the less very thorough in its discussion of even the most recent finds, which Gell was in some cases permitted to draw. The *Pompeiana* passed through several editions up to the 1860s and was also translated into French. In 1832 Gell published a sequel in the same format.

Despite the major differences in their size, price and target readership, the publications by Mazois and Gell have one thing in common: they chiefly concentrate on the ruins in Pompeii itself and only occasionally make reference to finds removed to the museum. The most extensive publication of the time, however, had a different objective: the *Real Museo Borbonico* was devoted overwhelmingly to the artworks housed in Naples and only featured a short annual report on the results of the excavations in Pompeii. Altogether 16 volumes appeared between 1822 and 1857, containing more than 900 plates. The project was initiated by the Società

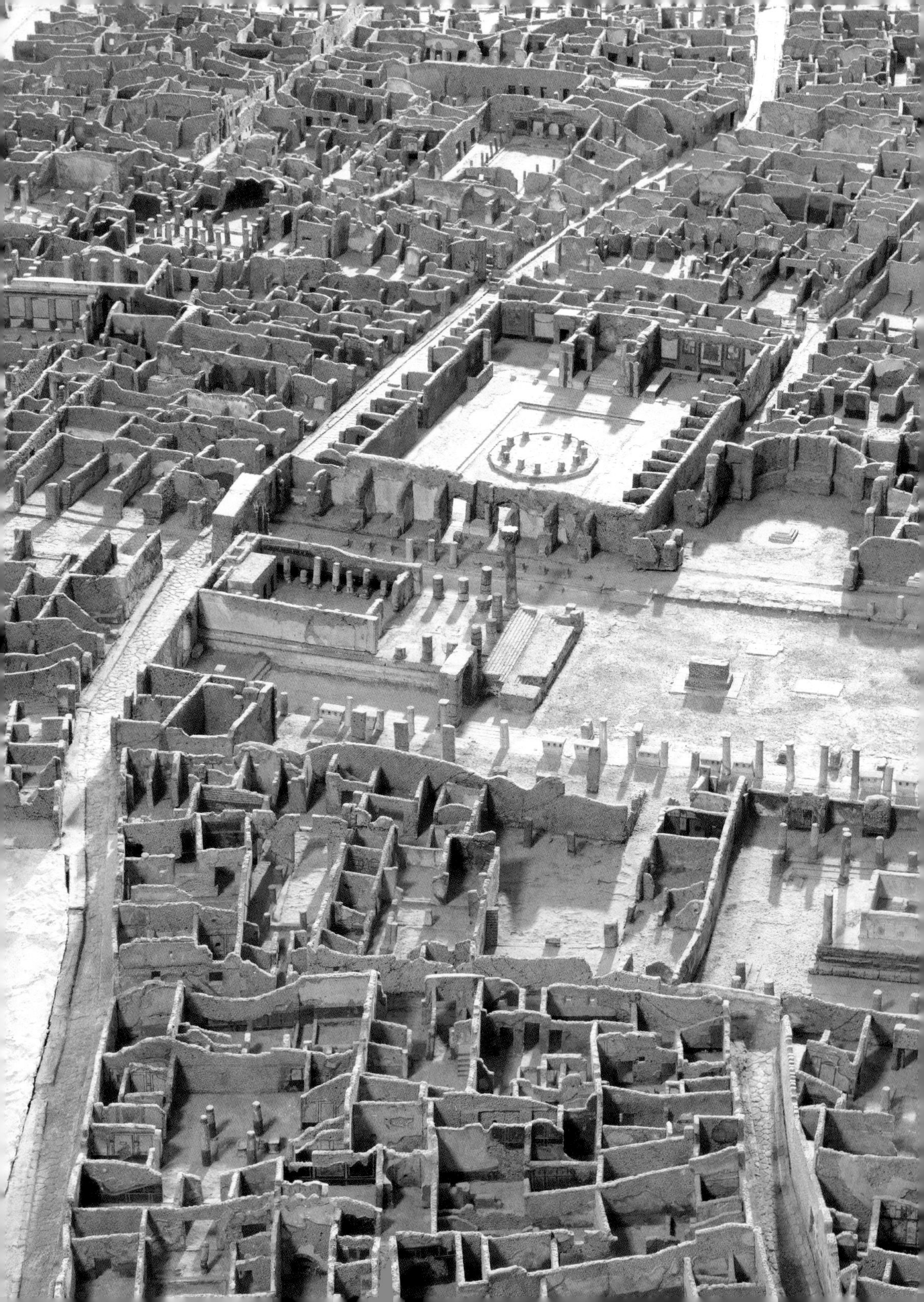

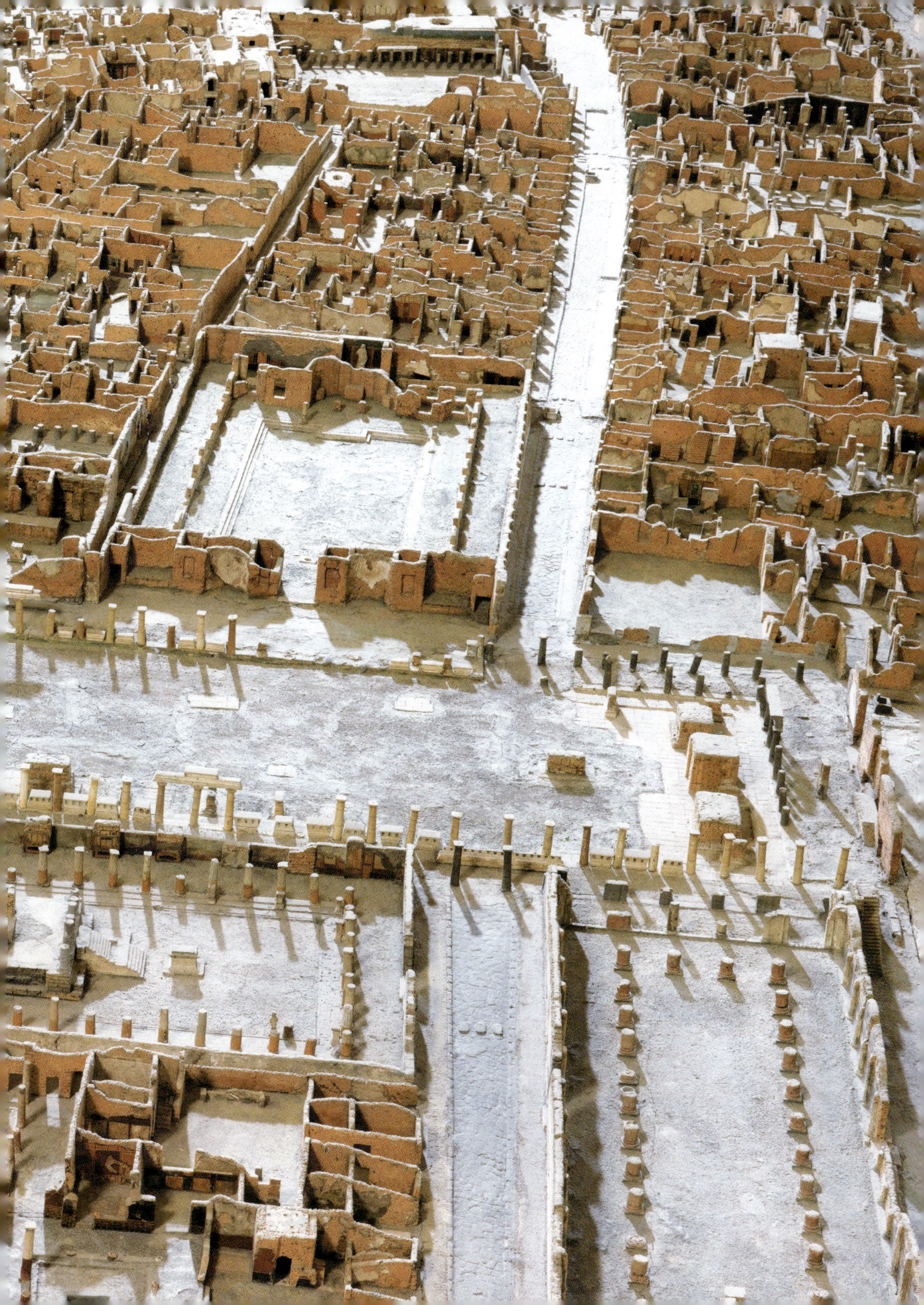

FUSSBODEN DES SÜDLICHEN KUPPELSAALES.

I.

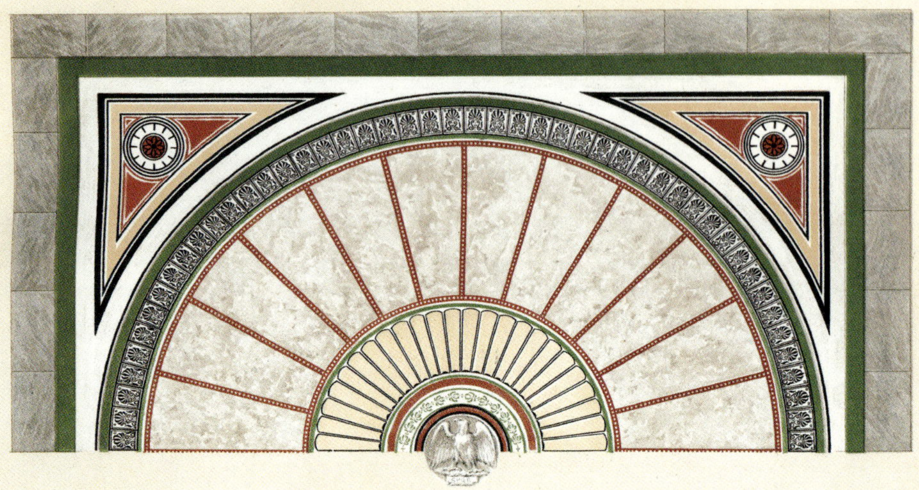

FUSSBÖDEN IN DEN SÄLEN FÜR GYPSABGÜSSE NACH DER ANTIKE.

III.

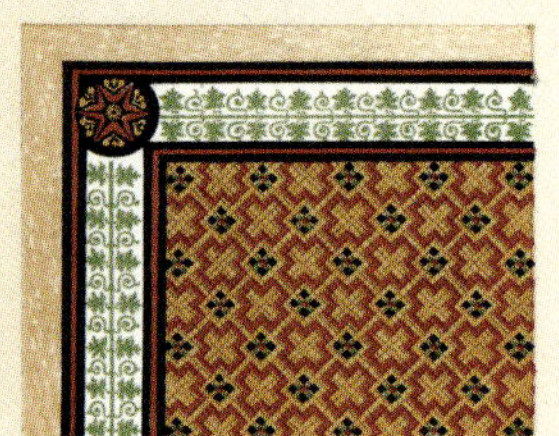

IV.

V.

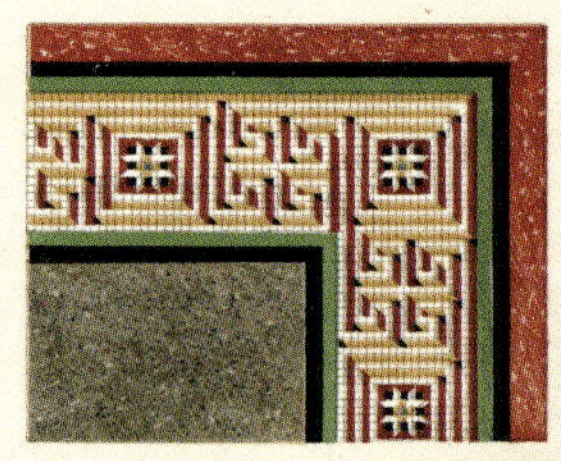

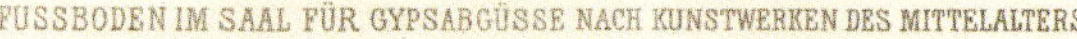

FUSSBODEN IM SAAL FÜR GYPSABGÜSSE NACH KUNSTWERKEN DES MITTELALTERS.

VI.

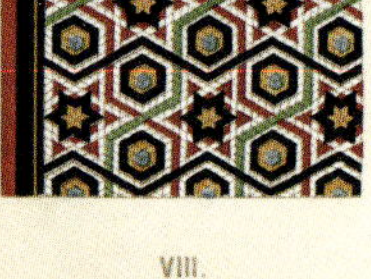

VIII.

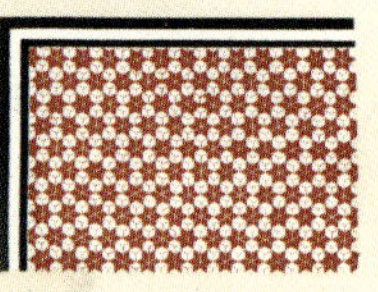

X.

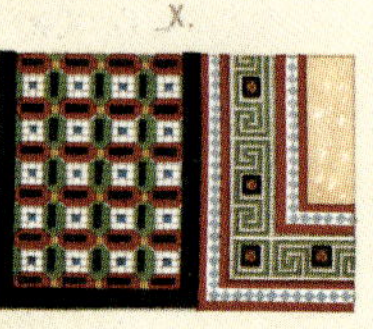

II.

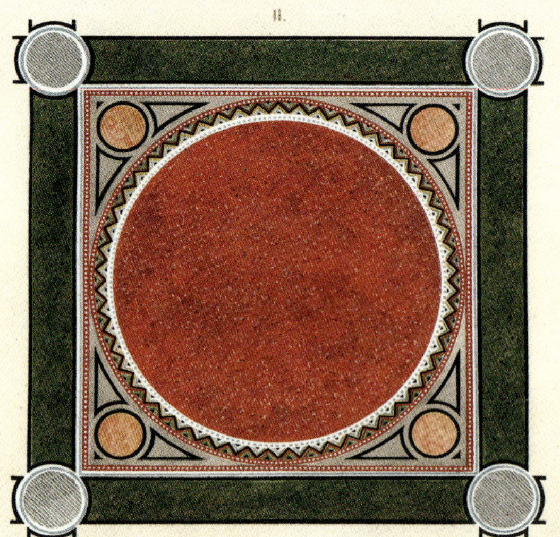

VII.

IX.

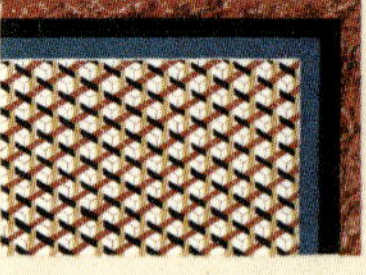

XI.

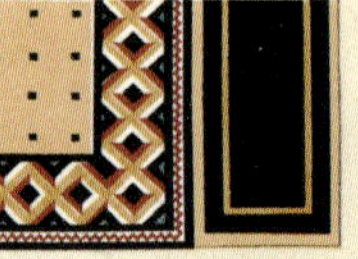

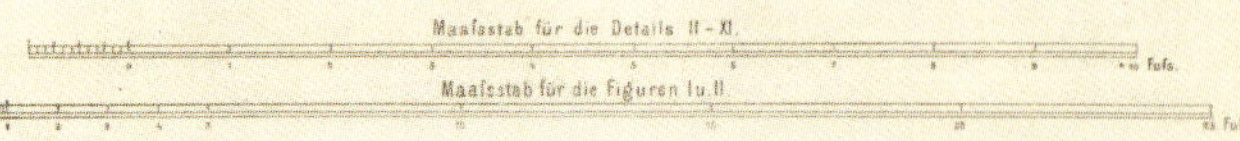

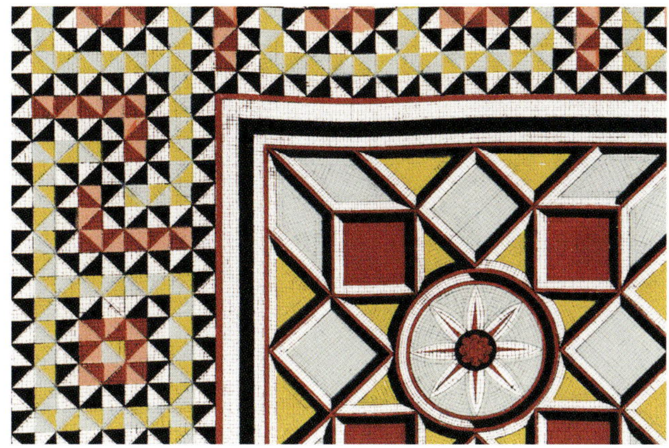

Reale Borbonica, of which the Accademia Ercolanese was a part, and thus stood under the patronage of the king, who also provided the funding. Consequently it was oriented towards comparable publications originating from other major European museums. The Società commissioned Antonio Niccolini, in his capacity as director of the Accademia delle Belle Arti, to act as editor and manager of the project. Niccolini evidently chose the draughtsmen and engravers himself, while the explanatory texts were written by members of the Società Reale. The work was intended to be completed within four to five years (one fascicle per month, one volume every four months), but the last three volumes only appeared after Niccolini's death, under the direction of his sons Fausto and Felice. Details of the publication and its proposed schedule were set out in a call for subscriptions. Each volume was published in an edition of 1,400 copies, but even though the price was set deliberately lower than that of the *Antichità d'Ercolano*, sales left a great deal to be desired, at least at the start.

A comprehensive analysis of the concept of the *Real Museo Borbonico* lies outside the scope of the present essay. One essential innovation the work presented in relation to the *Antichità d'Ercolano*, however, was the flexibility of its combination of the most different areas of interest and its inclusion of objects of daily life, the so-called *instrumentum domesticum*. Pompeii itself is apostrophised as the museum's "most important monument", and as its inexhaustible source: only in Pompeii is it possible to familiarise oneself with all aspects of public and private life. The large number of illustrations in the volumes of the *Real Museo Borbonico* devoted to practical utensils testifies to the editors' interest in this sphere.

On aesthetic grounds and also for reasons of cost and time, simple line engravings were chosen for the illustrations (with the exception of the hand-coloured). For the vedute in particular, however, it was also decided to use lithography – newly introduced in

Friedrich August Stüler, ***Mosaic Floors in the Neues Museum in Berlin***
Colour lithograph. From: Friedrich August Stüler, *Das Neue Museum in Berlin*, Berlin 1862, plate 16

Wilhelm Zahn, ***Mosaic Floor from Pompeii,*** Naples, Real Museo Borbonico
Colour lithograph. From: Wilhelm Zahn, *Die schönsten Ornamente und merkwürdigsten Gemälde aus Pompeji, Herculanum und Stabiae*, vol. 1, Berlin 1828–1829, plate 81 (detail)

Naples – on account of its tonal quality, even though it was considerably more expensive. In the two final volumes, a total of six colour lithographs make their appearance, printed by the Lithographische Druckerei Richter & Cie., the same printers Fausto and Felice were at that stage already working with for the *Case e monumenti*. The first fascicle was very poorly received by archaeologists: fundamental doubts were expressed about Antonio Niccolini's level of expertise and there was criticism both regarding the selection of objects, most of which were already known, and the quality of the illustrations, which were seen as being too small and in many cases inaccurate. The texts too were harshly judged: several were said to be no more than banal descriptions, while others expounded theoretical information that had little to do with the objects themselves. References to the dimensions of objects and where they had been found were evidently considered unimportant and omitted, and the pieces were thus stripped of any context.

Despite these criticisms, the *Real Museo Borbonico* was of crucial significance for the production of the *Case e monumenti*. The work begun by Antonio Niccolini was taken over and completed by his sons Fausto and Felice, who quite evidently had access, therefore, to their father's library of images. They made extensive use of these earlier drawings for their own plates, making only minor alterations in the process. The colour lithographs of the *Case e monumenti* also reveal the same particular interest in the objects of daily life exhibited by the *Real Museo Borbonico*, although the two publications were nevertheless very different in their fundamental conception.

Competition and yardstick: Wilhelm Zahn and the others

In many respects the most important publication on Pompeii in the first half of the 19th century was the three-volume work by Wilhelm Zahn (1800–1871), *Die schönsten Ornamente und merkwürdigsten Gemälde aus Pompeji, Herculanum und Stabiae* (1828–1859; ills. pp. 18, 19, 21, 29). Zahn spent the years 1824–1827 in Naples and over the summer months had the privilege of living in Pompeii itself, in a farmhouse situated within the bounds of the ancient city. Further lengthy stays followed during the 1830s. Thanks to his high-level patronage, Zahn was able to make direct tracings of many freshly uncovered wall paintings. On his way home from Italy in 1827 he stopped in Weimar to visit Goethe, who greeted Zahn's works with enthusiasm and supported his project to publish them. In 1828 Zahn had his *Neu entdeckte Wandgemälde in Pompeji* printed by Cotta, comprising 40 plates of black-and-white line engravings of Pompeian motifs. At almost exactly the same time he issued a call for subscriptions to *Die schönsten Ornamente*, the first series of which with its 100 plates appeared in 1829 to glowing reviews from Goethe. This new work surpassed the *Neu entdeckte Wandgemälde* in every respect. Its physical dimensions were almost doubled, on the grounds that this would allow many items to be reproduced full scale. Most significantly, however, the very first fascicle included not only line engravings but also two colour lithographs. Recent studies have shown that Zahn was right in claiming to have invented colour lithography. The gradual evolution of this sophisticated technique, which demands extreme precision in the positioning of the heavy stone plates, can be traced through the three volumes of *Die schönsten Ornamente*. In the early plates the individual, wholly opaque colours are printed next to each other and only in a few places have they been "improved" by a little hand-colouring, whereas the later illustrations are very much more differentiated, thanks also to the development of new colours. Figural images consequently make their first appearance only in volume II and mythological scenes in the third and final volume (ills. pp. 18, 19). The plates are accompanied by very short texts in German and French which nevertheless always give the precise source of each motif and, in the case of the line engravings, information about the colours of the original and the scale of the reproduction. They often include remarks that reveal a very practical interest, for example, observing that this ornamental design or that mosaic, which has been drawn stone by stone, could be recreated in modern interiors on the basis of the reproduction. As he wrote in his short introduction, Zahn hoped that a detailed knowledge of ancient styles of ornament would exert a positive influence on contemporary taste. He thereby placed himself firmly in line with 18th-century tradition, which saw in ancient art a schoolmistress for the present. In this way many plates also resemble pattern books with examples of bands of ornament or decorative systems executed in mosaic (ill. p. 21). In 1843 Zahn went on to produce a separate publication devoted to ornamental designs, *Ornamente aller klassischen Kunst-Epochen*, a work that was influential in Germany and a precursor to the more wide-ranging *Grammar of Ornament* by Owen Jones (1806–1874) published in 1856.

Die schönsten Ornamente made a great impact, not least as a sourcebook for "interior decorations by house painters and craftsmen", as Eduard Gerhard wrote. In particular its many illustrations of mosaics found an echo in the floors of public as well as private buildings, even if their origin was not always known (ill. p. 29). The quality of its lithographs became the yardstick for rival publications throughout Europe.

Another important work documenting the finds in Pompeii from this period was that by Wilhelm Ternite (1789–1871). Ternite won the support of the Prussian royal family while still a young man and in 1824/25 was able to travel to Italy as the companion of the art-collecting Count Ingenheim (1789–1855, illegitimate son of Frederick William II of Prussia). Probably under the latter's influential patronage, he made drawings and watercolours of the wall paintings in Naples and Pompeii, and in 1827 showed them to Goethe in Weimar – just a few months before Wilhelm Zahn's visit, in fact. Despite Goethe's enthusiastic response, for financial reasons Ternite was for a long time unable to issue his works as lithograph prints. The first fascicle of *Wandgemälde aus Pompeji und Herculanum nach den Zeichnungen und Nachbildungen in Farbe von W. Ternite* did not appear until 1839, to be followed in the years up until 1858 by only eleven of the announced instalments, and evidently in very small editions. The illustrations were accompanied by texts in three languages by the archaeologists Karl Otfried Müller

(1797–1840) and Friedrich Gottlieb Welcker (1784–1868). At 27½ x 21½ inches (70 x 55 cm), Ternite's *Wandgemälde* is one of the largest publications. Each part is dedicated to a different European sovereign and the work is clearly aimed at the interests of a small elite. The concept of the *Wandgemälde* may be considered the most unusual out of the three anthologies of reproductions all published at more or less the same time. Of the 88 plates in each part, only one is reproduced as a colour lithograph. The remainder show details life-size, in which the heads of the figures are rendered in great detail and in differentiated tones, while the bodies appear only in outline. Ternite had no interest in mythological subjects and none at all in the contexts of his pictures; what mattered to him was the style in which the paintings were made and the personal signature of their artists.

Désiré Raoul-Rochette (1789–1854), one of the leading French archaeologists in the first half of the 19th century, likewise visited Italy in 1826/27 and made an extended stay in Pompeii. Two publications appeared after this trip. The first, co-authored with the architect Jules-Frédéric Bouchet (1799–1860), was a monograph on the Casa del Poeta tragico, which had been uncovered in 1824/25. This work, which contains 28 plates with hand-coloured engravings, presents the architecture of the house in the systematic manner of the "envois de Rome" sent back to Paris by Prix de Rome scholars. It enriches this format, however, with numerous illustrations of entire walls and the most important of the mythological paintings, as well as a comprehensive text by Raoul-Rochette. Only many years later did he publish his *Choix de peintures de Pompéi* (1844–1856), a far more influential selection of mythological paintings in folio format (24 x 17 ⅜ in. / 61 x 44 cm). The 28 plates (32 had been planned) are systematically ordered by subject and are accompanied by detailed commentaries. Although all the pictures are from Pompeii, Raoul-Rochette treats them not in the context of their original rooms but as iconographical sources for ancient mythology. On occasion he specifically refers to the sources on which his illustrations are based, in order to emphasise their quality. Thus his first plate, which also reproduces cracks and other areas of damage to the design, is based on a tracing (in other words, 1:1) by the late Giuseppe Marsigli (1795– ca. 1835), another was based on a work by a "competent Neapolitan artist", a third on a sheet that was made available to him by the king. It is only by using such firsthand sources that the "vrai caractère" of the painting can be recognised, unlike in the corresponding illustrations in the *Real Museo Borbonico*.

Another compendium on the finds from the Vesuvian cities issued during these same years follows an entirely different concept. Henri Roux (active 1820–1855), who had earlier worked for Raoul-Rochette, and Louis Barré (1799–1857) together published – the first as draughtsman and engraver, the second as author – almost 800 illustrations of antiquities and

Anonymous, ***Pasticcio of Pompeian Motifs***
Oleograph. From: Johannes Overbeck, *Pompeji in seinen Gebäuden, Alterthümern und Kunstwerken*, Leipzig 1856, front cover

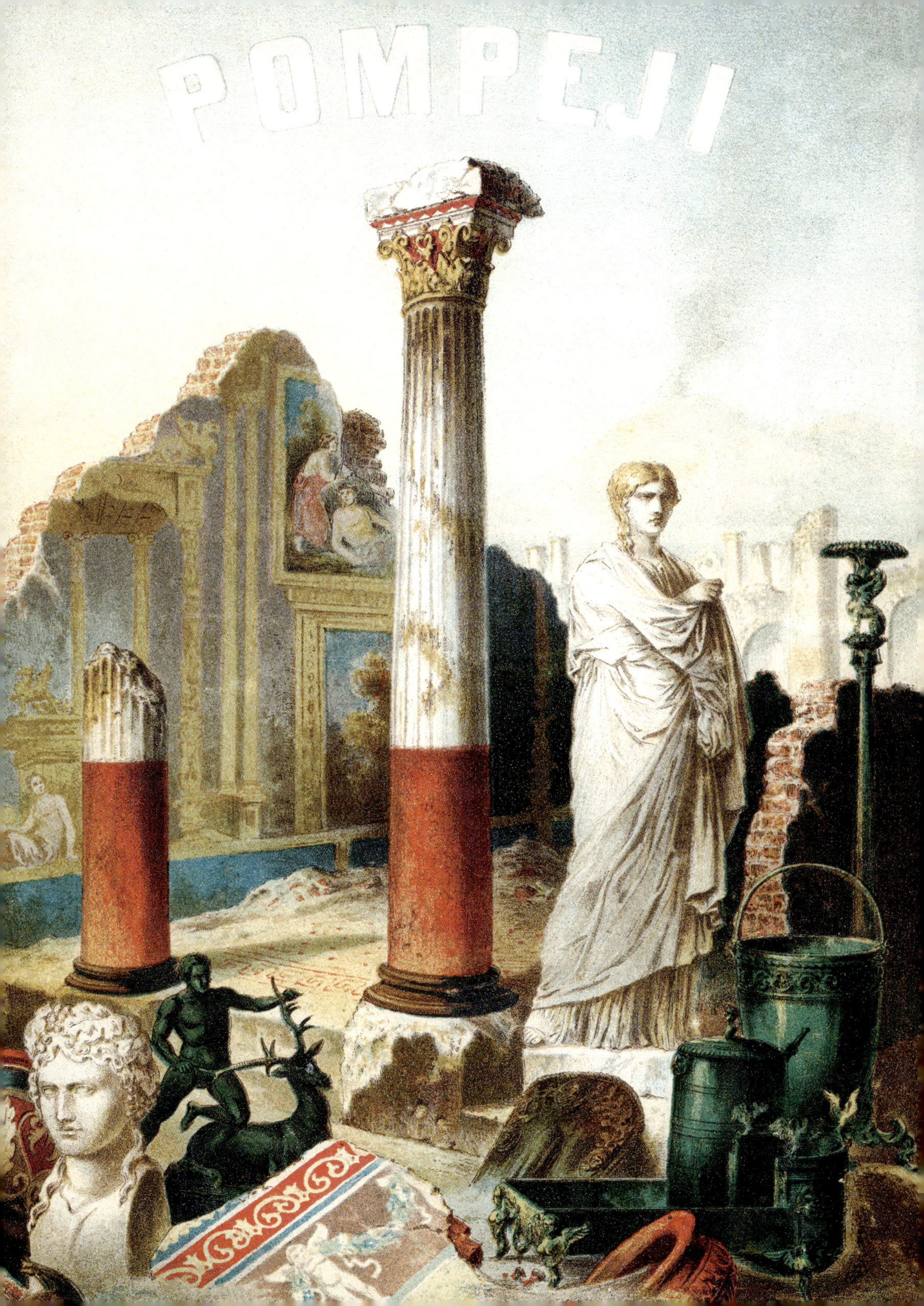
POMPEJI

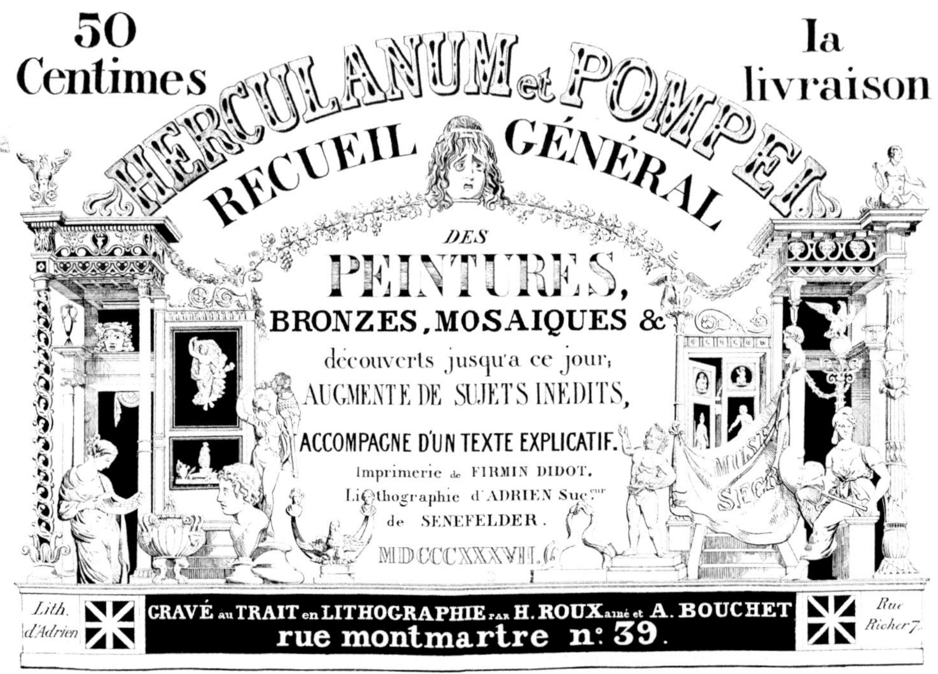

Henri Roux, *Call for Subscriptions for the Work*
Herculanum et Pompéi. Recueil Général des Peintures, Bronzes et Mosaïques, 1837
Paris, Bibliothèque nationale de France, Département des Estampes et de la Photographie

wall paintings from the Vesuvian cities, in simple line engravings. Between 1837 and 1841, eight volumes appeared in an affordably priced and above all quickly issued and complete edition (see above). The visual sources are clearly identified in the title to each illustration and are drawn chiefly from the *Antichità d'Ercolano* and the *Real Museo Borbonico*, as well as from more recent publications. The "Roux-Barré", as it is called in archaeological circles, was a great success and was translated into German as well as Italian.

The contemporaries

The years in which the Niccolini fascicles appeared were marked by changes not only in the political sphere (with the associated consequences for Pompeii's administration), but also changes in academic approaches and the way in which the latest discoveries were communicated to a wider public. In 1855 and 1856 respectively there appeared two handy-sized publications – the French *Pompeia* by Ernest Breton (1812–1875) and the German *Pompeji* by Johannes

Overbeck (1826–1895) – which for many years, in their numerous new editions, would offer readers a first point of access to Pompeii. Both authors organised their material in a new, systematic fashion, devoting separate sections to public and private spheres of life in the city and the art associated with each, and thereby clearly differed from the Niccolinis' concept. The quarto volumes were also no longer addressed primarily to visitors walking round the actual ruins, who wanted quick information about what they were looking at, but to readers who "wished to learn more about the subject at home". To his subsequent fury, the first edition of Overbeck's work was nevertheless given a three-colour printed cover that was probably intended to encourage sales but whose design seemed more appropriate for a younger readership than for a serious work. These books were intended to be affordable and tailored to a middle-class public (ill. p. 33). During this same period, meanwhile, Pompeii also acquired a new historical profile, thanks chiefly to the efforts of German archaeologists. The studies by Richard Schöne (1840–1922), Heinrich Nissen (1839–1912) and August Mau (1840–1909) demonstrated for the first time that the state of the city at the moment of the Vesuvian eruption should be understood as the result of a process that had begun several hundred years earlier, whose traces repeatedly overlaid each other but were still distinguishable. This perspective is encountered in the Niccolinis' texts only on isolated occasions.

Appearing in direct competition with the *Case e monumenti* towards the end of the century were the various compilations by Emil Presuhn (1844–1881) and Pasquale D'Amelio (dates unknown; ill. p. 39). In plates of a similar size, both authors offered a selection of Pompeii's finest wall paintings as colour lithographs, with the text playing only a subordinate role. Both also used draughtsmen and printers who had already worked for the Niccolinis and who had no compunction about speaking ill of their rivals: "the scrupulous fidelity in their plates does leave something to be desired". Antonio Niccolini responded to this rivalry by compiling selected plates from his own volumes into new booklets and selling these at a much lower price than the series as a whole.

Genesis, structure and conception of the *Case e monumenti*

The Niccolinis – a well-connected family

Antonio Niccolini the Elder (1772–1850) arrived in the French-ruled kingdom in 1807. He had already worked as a successful set designer and theatre architect in his native Tuscany and now made a name for himself in the same line of work in Naples too.60 His greatest success as a set designer would be his work for L'ultimo giorno di Pompei, the opera by Giovanni Pacini (1796–1867), which in 1825 was greatly praised for its archaeological accuracy. As an architect in the service of the king, Niccolini was also commissioned to build the new Teatro di San Carlo (1816) and soon afterwards the complex of the Villa Floridiana and its gardens. Significant in our context is his work for the Reale Accademia delle Belle Arti, where in 1822 he was appointed director. In this capacity he took over the editorship of the Real Museo

Borbonico, and wrote for it a long article on the so-called Alexander mosaic from the Casa del Fauno. As head of the Academy and numerous committees, Antonio enjoyed great influence and evidently used this to promote the careers of his two sons Fausto (1812–1886) and Felice (1816–1886). After architectural training in Florence, Fausto followed his father into the profession of royal theatre architect, designing and building new theatres in the kingdom. At the start of the 1850s Fausto Niccolini led the private excavations by Leopold, Count of Syracuse, in Cuma and introduced the young archaeologist Giuseppe Fiorelli to the Count. After Fiorelli's dismissal from government service he was employed as the Count's personal secretary. Later, as Soprintendente, Fiorelli thanked his friend Fausto for this support by appointing him in 1866 "Architect 1st class for the interior decoration of the museum". In this role Niccolini designed a decorative scheme for a number of museum galleries based on the Stabian Baths in Pompeii, and thus established a concrete connection between the excavations and the presentation of the finds.

Less is known about his younger brother Felice. At the latest from 1861 he held the post of secretary at the Soprintendenza and proceeded to rise to director of the museum in 1882, again thanks to Fiorelli's support. Until 1867 he was occupied with the publication of the final volumes of the *Real Museo Borbonico* and wrote several texts himself for the last volume. From 1854 onwards he also worked on the *Case e monumenti*, for which he likewise wrote an increasing number of texts.

The publication remained in family hands even after the death of the two brothers, when the project was taken over by Fausto's son Antonio. The change makes itself visible in the plates of volumes III and IV, where altogether 149 plates – a third of the entire work – carry Antonio's name. The only formal modifications are seen in the stamp and the signature below the pictures, in which *Fratelli Niccolini* becomes *(A.) Niccolini*. Antonio the Younger parted company with the printers Richter & Cie. and worked first of all with Litografia Artistica Zucchi & De Luca (later Autoriello & De Luca) and finally with Officina Litografica Casa Editrice Fausto Niccolini.

The three generations of the Niccolini family were able to assert themselves under three political systems in Naples over a period of almost a century. Antonio the Elder clearly made the transition from French rule to the Bourbons without problems and acquired a very influential position in all areas of artistic life in Naples as well as at the excavations in Pompeii. His sons received their start in professional life thanks to their father's connections. But they subsequently attached themselves to circles that welcomed the emerging Kingdom of Italy under Savoy rule and were thus able to establish a foothold in the new state with no difficulty. Their friendship with Giuseppe Fiorelli was thus of the greatest significance: the young nation's most important archaeologist not only supported their vast publication on Pompeii but also exerted a crucial influence upon its conception.

An editorial adventure

The specifications of the *Case e monumenti* are extraordinarily high. The format alone – roughly 23½ x 17 in. (60 x 43 cm) – places the volumes alongside the most lavish editions of the time. Each plate (with a pictorial field of ca. 20½ x 14¼ in. / 52 x 36 cm) was printed on a very much larger cartoon, which bears an oval stamp at the bottom in which the word *POMPEI* in the centre is framed by the names *FAUSTO E FELICE NICCOLINI*. After the brothers' death, the stamp was changed to *A. NICCOLINI EDITORE*. Each instalment appeared in a half-title wrapper that carried the title of the work in white on a red ground and sometimes also the fascicle number. The hand-painted letters vary slightly from one half-title to the next and were therefore evidently redone each time. The fascicles also included transparent interleaves carrying the title of the chapter and the number of the plate, likewise in large hand-painted letters, lithographically printed in red. The large sheets were sometimes trimmed by libraries after binding and the stamp damaged as a result. The information on the actual title-pages of the four volumes also appears in hand-drawn red letters (ill. p. 1). These give the title of the work, the number of the volume and the place and year of publication, the latter being largely fictive since production extended over many years. The name of the publisher appears nowhere.

With this design concept the Niccolinis positioned themselves very consciously in line with the works of Mazois, Zahn, Raoul-Rochette and Ternite. But in the scope of their text (548 pages) and the number of reproductions (451 plates) they far surpassed all other works on Pompeii. The printing and commercial distribution of the fascicles seem to have been protracted and at times almost chaotic affairs. Although roughly four instalments of eight pages with three plates were issued every year, they by no means appeared in the sequence as planned. From a chance report we learn that three fascicles belonging to three different chapters in two separate volumes all came out at once. Since no call for subscriptions has yet been discovered, and since the Niccolinis' own *Proemio* says nothing specific on the subject, it is unclear how large the work was initially intended to be. In bibliographic notes dating from the end of the 1870s the total is understood to be about 60 fascicles, but by around 1890 this figure had risen to 124 according to the information of booksellers. In fact, the final part carries the number 137.

How the enterprise was organised financially, we do not know. However, a recently discovered document from 1859 shows for the first time that the palace supported the editors by purchasing a large number of fascicles outright for a considerable sum. The high production costs were reflected in correspondingly elevated prices: in 1891 the bookseller Friedrich Furchheim gave the price of one fascicle as 15.30 lire, which corresponded to about 12 goldmarks. According to the same source, the most recent edition (1884) of the *Pompeii* book by Johannes Overbeck cost 20 marks; two Niccolini fascicles were thus substantially more expensive than a whole book. This unusually high price, sustained continuously over 40 years, also answers to a certain extent the question of the size of the edition: only large libraries were in a position to purchase the complete series and the work consequently remained confined to a small circle of academics and art lovers.

The concept behind the contents of the *Case e monumenti*

From the rather stilted preface by the Niccolini brothers it is not easy to understand their overall concept for the work and its contents. The short introduction, under the scholarly heading of *Proemio* (proem) as befitting an academic publication, is a mixture of topical observations on the significance of Pompeii as a source for Classical antiquity – "the most eloquent book on the history of antiquity that we possess" – and reflections on the nature of a publication of this diversity which anticipate many of the criticisms that might be levelled against it. The authors were conscious of the impossibility of presenting a systematic portrait of Pompeii in a work that was to be issued in instalments, and therefore alluded to a new plan of the city and an index (never published) at the end of the work, which would identify all the different subjects covered. The project was to start with a *Descrizione generale*, a general description of the city dealing with all aspects of civic life. Only then were its monuments – houses, temples etc. – to be examined individually. As far as the plates were concerned, it was intended to use colour illustrations and simple or hatched line drawings, as required. Objects in the museum were also to be included. The texts were to remain short and would be written for an academic public and for lovers of art. Lastly, the Niccolinis wanted to counter the old reproach that the treasures of Pompeii had been studied in the first place by foreigners rather than in Naples itself.

This preface was complemented by a second, written on the occasion of the appearance of the first fascicle. It issued from the pen of Giulio Minervini (1819–1891), a leading member of the Accademia Ercolanese and a highly regarded figure in the world of Neapolitan archaeology, and at that time the most likely candidate for the position of director of the Soprintendenza. He summarised the programme of contents sketched out in the *Proemio* in laudatory terms and likewise heaped praise on the lavish design and production of the work: thanks to the drawings by Abbate and the German lithographers Richter and Frauenfelder, it could already be placed on a par with foreign publications; only a few lithographs by Zahn were perhaps still superior. He even found praise for the elegant Gaetano Nobile typeface, a Bodoni font that in reality was commonplace at the time. Minervini, who himself wrote the text of the first fascicle, also tells us that the king, who had placed the Niccolinis' enterprise under his royal patronage, desired the texts to be written by members of the Accademia – a wish that was implemented in the first fascicles. Lastly, Minervini makes mention of a sumptuous frontispiece, although none such is found in any of the surviving copies: did it perhaps pay tribute to the royal house but then fall victim to the political upheaval of 1860?

The arrangement of the chapters in the Niccolini volumes, as indicated to the binders by the contents page, does not correspond to the order as originally announced. Thus the *Descrizione generale*, which was supposed to appear before the other descriptions, instead appears at the end of volume II and is later resumed and continued in an *Appendice*, *Supplemento* and the *Nuovi Scavi* in volumes III and IV. It provides a detailed description of Pompeii's topography in place of the historical and cultural-historical introduction first announced. This latter only appears – unexpectedly, given the heading – in the text on the *Topografia di Pompei* at the start of the third volume. Volume I instead contains a total of 17 chapters, each concerned with a single house, public building or tomb. In the best cases, the text is accompanied by a ground plan, details of the architecture and a series of illustrations of the wall paintings and a number of the finds, and in conclusion a vedutà. The criteria according to which individual buildings were selected seem to vary: in some cases the aim is to include the latest excavations (Casa di Marcus Lucretius, Casa di Sirico, Stabian Baths) and in others to present the most famous monuments (Casa del Poeta tragico, Casa del Fauno, Temple of Isis, Theatre, Amphitheatre, Street of Tombs). The texts, each separately paginated, are in most instances very thorough and reflect the current state of scholarship. They describe the objects and conclude with a fresh round-up of all the finds known from excavation publications. This is a very modern concept and one that had never before been applied so consistently to a large number of houses. When compared especially with the somewhat indiscriminate compilation of plates in the *Real Museo Borbonico*, and also with the illustrated works by Zahn, Ternite and Raoul-Rochette with their focus solely on details, the significance of this context-oriented approach

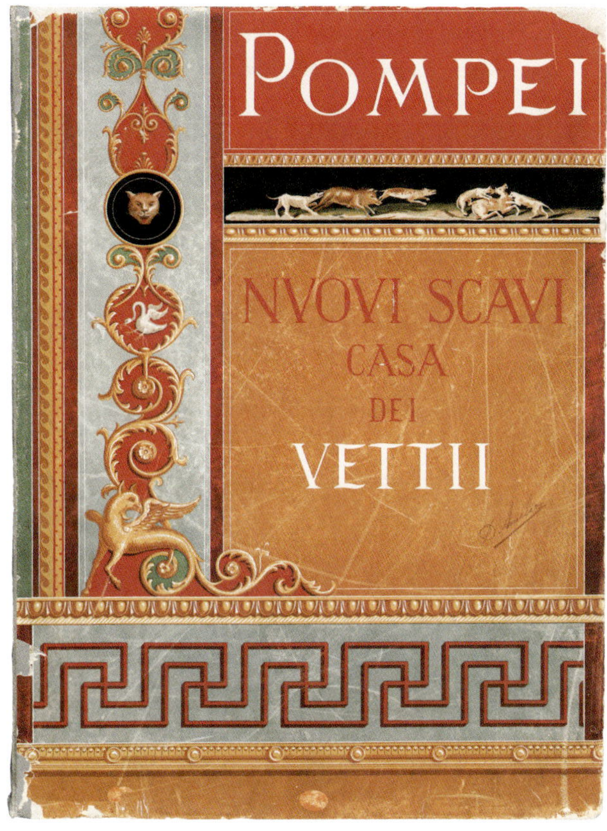

Pasquale D'Amelio
Cover for *Pompei. Nuovi Scavi. Casa dei Vettii*, Naples 1899

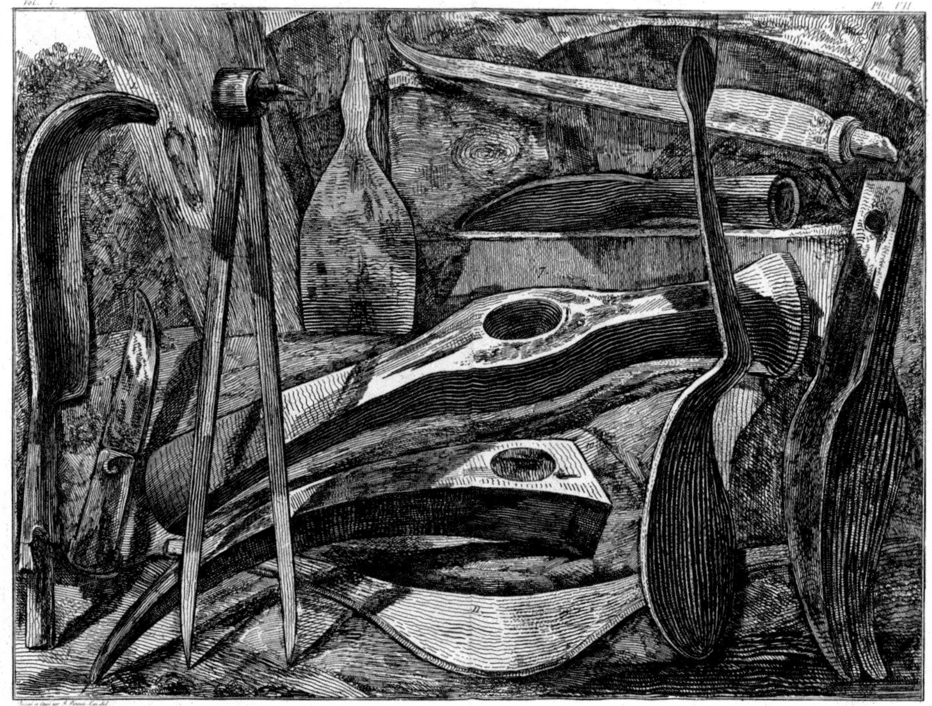

Francesco Piranesi, ***Agricultural Implements***
Copper engraving. From: Francesco Piranesi, *Les Antiquités de la Grande Grèce aujourd'hui Royaume de Naples, vol. 1*, Paris 1807, plate 7

becomes clear: what had previously been divided between excavation site and museum gallery was to some extent once again rendered visible as a whole.

The second large section, planned from the start and differently conceived in terms of its content, was titled *Descrizione generale* and takes up the entire second half of volume II. It consists of a detailed description of all the buildings in Pompeii excavated to date in topographical order, starting with the Street of Tombs and Regio VI beyond the Herculaneum Gate. The text is complemented by a series of plans at the start of volume 3, which provide the insulae and house numbers that are vital for the reader's orientation. Both concepts – that of the individual building as a contextual whole, and the systematic topographic description of a rationally organised city – clearly reflect the ideas of the young Fiorelli. One can sense the discussions taking place between the friends and see how the publication became Fiorelli's manifesto, so to speak.

The plate sections, not just in the Descrizione generale but also in the later Appendice and Supplemento, defy any such clear logic, however. Their links to the text become ever vaguer and their mostly brief captions allow us at best to identify what is shown. The plates themselves seem to have been compiled with variety in mind, with new finds occasionally slipped in. A new concept appeared later on, probably only introduced under Antonio Niccolini the Younger: with the chapters Mestieri e Industrie (The Trades and Industries of the Pompeians), Forme in Gesso (The Victims of the Vesuvian Eruption) and L'Arte in Pompei (The Arts in Pompeii), volume III took up categories also found in the latest books on Pompeii by Johannes Overbeck and Ernest Breton (see above). Substantial texts give these sections a certain weight. Last of all, the series of reconstructions in volume IV has regularly been criticised, and rightly so. The illustrations have either been taken directly from the drawings of William Gell or François Mazois or are composite images that demonstrate little knowledge of their subject and are often not even very appealing to the eye. Here we sense the publisher Antonio Niccolini, who may have been hoping for a large market for such pictures.

The Niccolini illustrations are strictly regimented. With the exception of the vedute, objects are presented in orderly rows and walls shown in orthogonal projection. Many of the plates group together a selection of small bronzes and other finds from various sources and thereby echo the academic style of other museum publications of the time. Small wall sections, for example showing floating figures, are commonly combined into panels, as can be seen even today in the Museo Nazionale. Only a few of the plates, devoted to items of glassware, break out of this spectrum and monumentalise their objects. In this way they follow the style of a number of sheets by Francesco Piranesi that were very well known to archaeologists (ill. p. 40). Also favoured were the plates featuring examples of ornamental patterns, decorative borders and sections of mosaic whose internal symmetry meant they could be easily repeated. Even if this is rarely stated in the captions, these compilation plates were inspired by the same thinking that lay behind Wilhelm Zahn's *Die schönsten Ornamente* and Owen Jones' *Grammar of Ornament* (ill. p. 43): they were intended to serve as design sources for tasteful contemporary décors.

The sources, artists and colours

The Niccolini brothers were able to draw upon an extremely rich corpus of pictorial sources. They had at their disposal the plates of the *Real Museo Borbonico* or the corresponding originals, as well as the *Ornati* and numerous drawings in the museum archives, often the only testaments to walls long ago destroyed.

Each plate carries not only the name of the editor (F[rate]lli Niccolini or A. Niccolini) but also that of the printer and the artist. In the case of these two latter, it is frequently impossible to know which is which. The task is easiest where a name is accompanied by the abbreviation Lit., Lith. or lit., which refer to the lithographic printers. The names associated with the Richter & Cie. lithographic firm sound chiefly German: G. Frauenfelder, K. Grob, C. Weidenmüller and J. Müsli. This changes in volumes III and IV with the switch to a new printer, after which the majority of the plates are produced by the lithographer D. Capri. Many of the artists signing themselves as draughtsmen (dis[egnavit]; dip[inxit]) are not found in artists' dictionaries. Often all they had to do was transfer the various originals on to the stone, but there are exceptions. The best known are the members of the so-called Scuola di Posillipo, which in the 19th century supplied a large, tourist-oriented market with vedute of Naples and its surroundings. The Niccolinis used no fewer than ten sheets by the most prominent of them, Giacinto Gigante (1806–1876), who as a young man had already worked for the volumes of the *Real Museo Borbonico*. Teodoro Duclère (1814–1869), Gigante's most important pupil, is represented with three views, while other sheets, although not signed, can perhaps also be attributed to him. Of the remaining names, most are associated with the documentation of the excavations in Pompeii. Thus the first two volumes contain no fewer than 62 plates drawn by Giuseppe Abbate. Abbate had first worked as an assistant to Wilhelm Zahn, before in 1835 being appointed a junior draughtsman and from 1838 "First Draughtsman" at the Soprintendenza. He rose to international prominence in 1853 when he was engaged to work on the decoration of the Pompeian Court in the Crystal Palace in Sydenham. After the end of the Great Exhibition of 1851, Matthew Digby Wyatt and Owen Jones rebuilt Sir Joseph Paxton's Crystal Palace in south London and turned it into a museum of world cultures. The Pompeian Court was one of a series of exhibition features devoted to different historical periods which also presented a full-scale reconstruction of a Roman atrium house inspired by similar residences uncovered in Pompeii. For his contributions to the *Case e monumenti*, Abbate was very often able to make use of his own drawings, some of them already reproduced in the *Real Museo Borbonico*, as well as a volume of plates published under his name and containing 150 engravings of objects from the museum. Among the other artists, mention should also be made here of the genre and landscape painter Vincenzo Loria, who supplied numerous contributions from volume II onwards, and towards the end of the century also worked for Pasquale D'Amelio in competition with the Niccolinis. Another name that surfaces regularly in volumes III and IV is that of Geremia Discanno. Having started out as a landscape and genre painter, by 1870 he was working freelance for Fiorelli and from 1876 this employment was made official. He used his outstanding knowledge of Pompeian wall painting to decorate several interiors in the Pompeian style, not only in Naples and the surrounding area but also in the Achilleion built for Empress Elisabeth of Austria on Corfu. Discanno also contributed

Owen Jones, ***Compilation of Ornamental Mosaics from Pompeii***
Colour lithograph. From: Owen Jones, *The Grammar of Ornament*
London 1856, plate XXV (Pompeian No. 3)

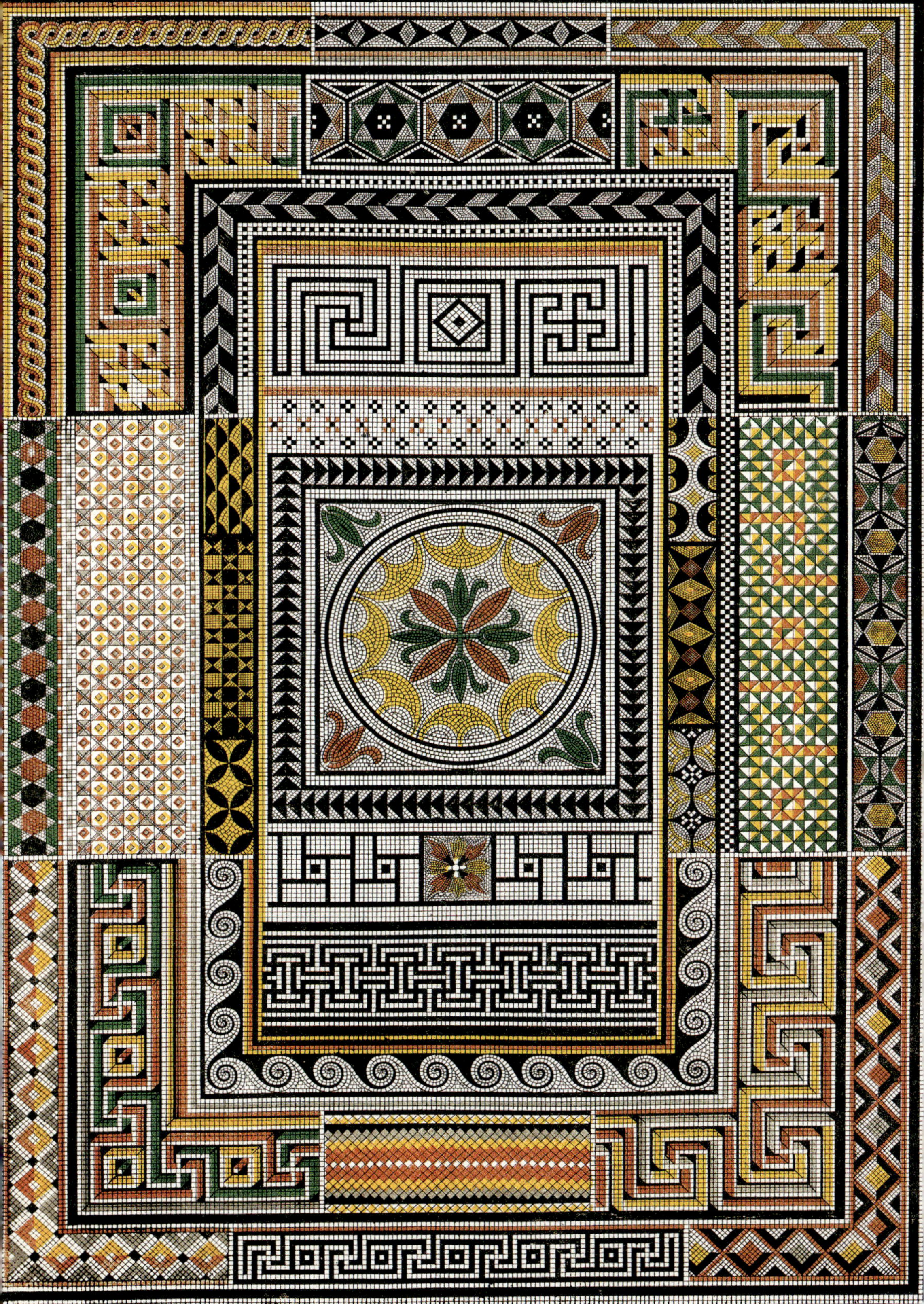

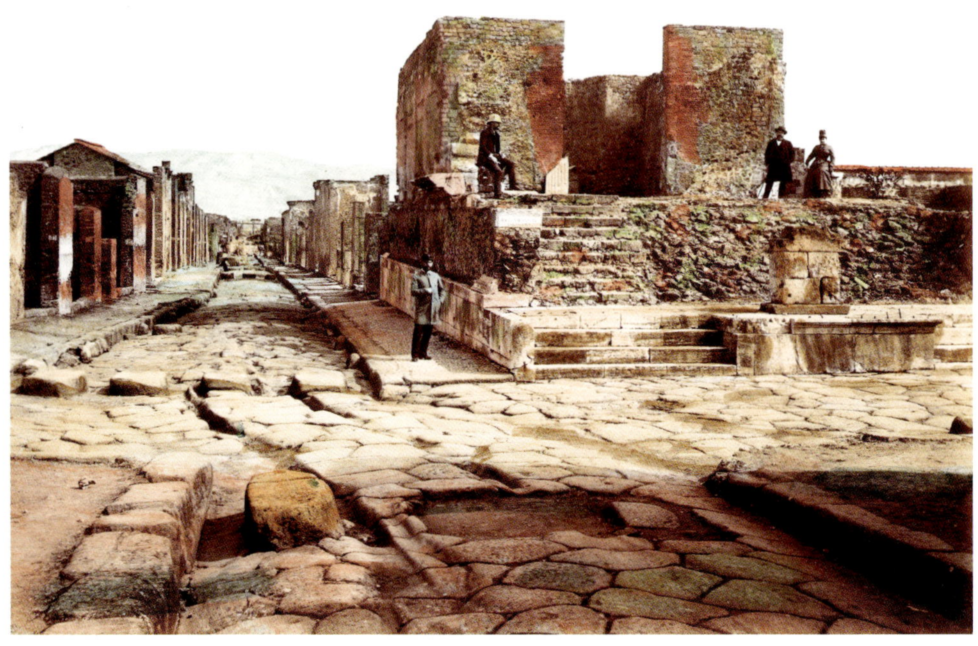

Giorgio Sommer, ***Temple of Fortuna Augusta,*** 1870s
Coloured albumen silver print, 20.2 x 26 cm / 8 x 10¼ in.
Los Angeles, Getty Research Institute, Los Angeles (2003.R.14.1)

to the publications by Fiorelli and August Mau, who greatly appreciated the accuracy of his drawings. The differing levels of skill wielded by the artists contributing to the Niccolinis' vast project are reflected in the resulting plates. In the later stages, the colours of the lithographs became less subtle and the precision of the prints declined. A simplified process using just one or two printing plates was also increasingly employed.

The Niccolinis and the new medium of photography

In 1854 colour lithographs were still a brand-new visual medium in Naples. Over the 40-year course of the *Case e monumenti*'s publication, however, they not only lost their novelty value but gave way with the arrival of another medium, photography, which because of its objective accuracy would ultimately supplant all graphic methods of documentation. Several members of the Soprintendenza were quick to recognise the value of this invention as a means of recording the excavations. A camera made available on loan was employed from 1847 and in 1854 excavation Inspector Gaetano Genovese (1795–1875) arranged for the purchase of a French camera. In this way, Genovese argued, it would be possible to photograph, during the course of excavations, important finds and objects that would otherwise be lost for ever. It was also later suggested that photo albums might be sold to tourists, who were prohibited from taking pictures themselves. But this commercial argument proved to be counterproductive since the palace had no interest in encouraging competition for the Niccolinis' work. Unfortunately, nothing today survives of these first attempts to document the finds using modern means. On the other hand, some early series of pictures are still known that were taken in the 1850s by Neapolitan photographers, who required a special permit for their work. From the 1860s onwards the excavators worked regularly with such photographers, who were required to supply reference copies of all their pictures. A special position was held here by Giorgio Sommer (1834–1914), who worked closely with Fiorelli. Under the Bourbon dynasty Sommer had been granted a longer-term photography permit and also worked with stereo cameras. His stereograph of Garibaldi's visit to the Pantheon (today the Macellum) on October 22, 1860 became a historic image. In 1863 Sommer also photographed the first plaster casts by Fiorelli, whilst in a sales brochure of 1886 he was able to offer no fewer than 77 motifs from Pompeii (ills. pp. 44, 47). Fiorelli collected these photos and sent them to the Ministry in Florence as evidence of his work. Sommer was followed by the Esposito brothers (biographical dates unknown) and Giacomo Brogi (1822–1881), and later the Alinari brothers. Their pictures could be purchased on site in Naples or ordered from a printed catalogue. The majority of these photographs show views of buildings; pictures of individual walls were, at this stage, still rare. The photos from Pompeii were complemented by numerous pictures of objects in the Museo Nazionale. Painters such as Sir Lawrence Alma-Tadema (1836–1912) owned large collections of such photos and used them as sources for their works.

It is interesting in this context to consider how the Niccolini brothers viewed this new medium. The note "dalla Fotografia" (sic!) below the colour lithograph of the dancing faun in the chapter on the Casa del Fauno (volume I, pl. 5), the three fascicles of which appeared in 1855, indicates the brothers' early use of a photograph as a visual source and is probably intended to stress the authenticity of the reproduction. It seems that photographs were consulted in particular for the many illustrations of sculptural works. This applies very much as well to the pictures of the eruption victims in volumes II and III, where it is possible to identify the specific Sommer photographs on which they were based. Some of the lithographed views – in particular in volume IV – certainly derive from photos. Like many artists and publishers of their day, in other words, the Niccolinis also used cost-effective photographs and translated them into a print medium that was very much easier to reproduce.

Epilogue

Through his [Fausto Niccolini's] work, our Pompeii has acquired such lustre and dignity that we can take much pride in his splendid publication, which knows no comparison in all of Europe ...

Fiorelli's effusive characterisation was part of a personal reference written for Fausto Niccolini in order to help him secure a new position. But like every good exaggeration, it contains a nugget of truth. With the *Case e monumenti* the Niccolinis succeeded in producing a work that surpassed in magnificence all other publications on Pompeii and portrayed the city in a clearer light. For the first time Pompeii could be seen as a whole, from its architecture and its decoration to the smallest finds. As influenced by the ideas of Giuseppe Fiorelli, this approach to the archaeological object – seeing it not as an individual piece but as part of a larger context – was emphatically modern. Even in its own day, the great wealth and variety of the work's illustrations will have distracted many a reader from the text and tempted them to leaf slowly through the plates. While archaeologists have underlined the flaws in the work, such as the inaccurate drawings, inaccurate data and texts considered too sparse, today, we see this differently. The *Case e monumenti* lies before us as the independent monument of an era in which it was possible, for the first time, to reproduce the colours and hence the most important quality of Pompeian walls in the grand style. With this historicisation of the four volumes, we gain the distance we need in order to accept their idiosyncrasies as such. This is true of the porous structures of the lithographs as much as for the sometimes overly strong, sometimes milky-matt colours of this reproduction technique. They filter reality in a distinctive way that allows us to experience it anew. Moreover, with its new view of the contexts of the finds and its full exploitation of colour lithography, the *Case e monumenti* is an impressive testament to an age of profound academic and artistic change in approaches to the ruins of Pompeii.

Giorgio Sommer, ***Casa del Balcone pensile***, 1870s
Coloured albumen silver print, 25.3 x 20.3 cm / 10 x 8 in.
Los Angeles, Getty Research Institute, Los Angeles (2003.R.14.5)

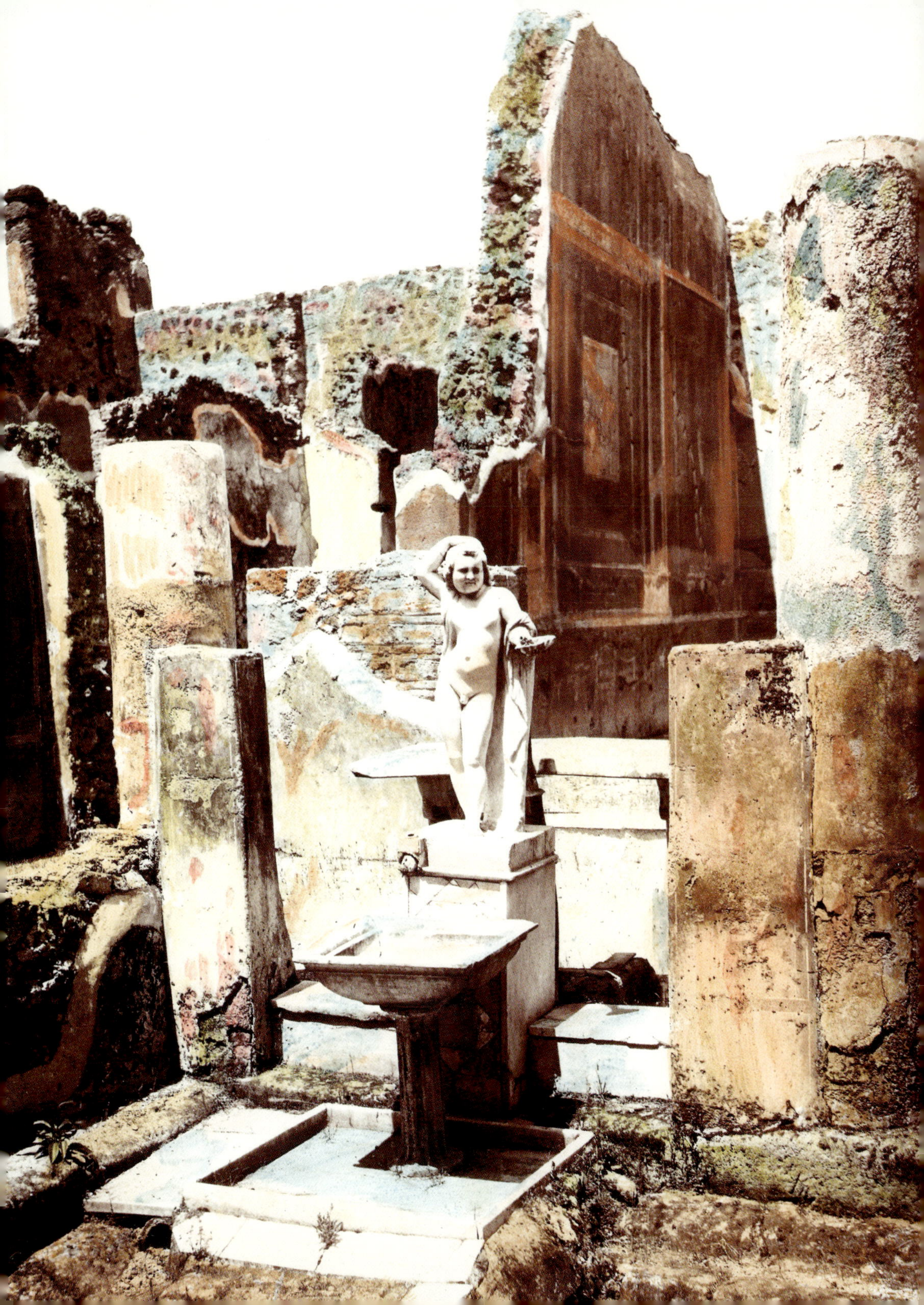

"ROME IS SIMPLY A VAST MUSEUM; POMPEII IS A LIVING ANTIQUITY"

The art of the Vesuvian cities between appropriation and reinterpretation

In his famous letter to his friend, the Roman historian Tacitus, Pliny the Younger described the devastating Vesuvian eruption of AD 79 in antithetically heightened terms as "a catastrophe which destroyed the loveliest regions of the Earth". At the same time, he expressed his belief that this "remarkable natural occurrence" would ensure the immortal fame not just of his uncle, Pliny the Elder, who had died during the eruption, but also of the cities which had been affected and the people who lived there (ill. p. 49). In fact, it was only with the rediscovery of Herculaneum and Pompeii and the beginning of the excavations – in 1738 and 1748 respectively – instigated by Charles VII, King of Naples and Sicily (from 1759 Charles III, King of Spain), that the Vesuvian cities would emerge from the shadows of literary accounts and arise, as it were, out of the ashes and lava into the spotlight of Western culture. Their reception history belongs to the "densest" discourses in the history of ideas and culture. It has made an unparalleled mark upon architecture and the fine arts as well as literature, poetry, music and film right up to our own day, and has profoundly shaped and reshaped our notions of Antiquity.

From the middle of the 18th century onwards it was not only the ever new sections of these ancient cities that were uncovered, but at the same time the scope of their significance and how they came to be interpreted was also being constantly expanded. The Bourbon excavations were primarily aimed, for all their early Enlightenment spirit, at the discovery of new artefacts that would enrich the holdings of the royal museum, at that time located in Portici but later transferred to Naples. In keeping with their nature as the preserve of a courtly elite, both the museum collections and the special publication of the excavation finds in *Le Antichità di Ercolano esposte* ("The Antiquities of Herculaneum Displayed"; Naples 1757–1792) were only accessible to a limited few. Numerous

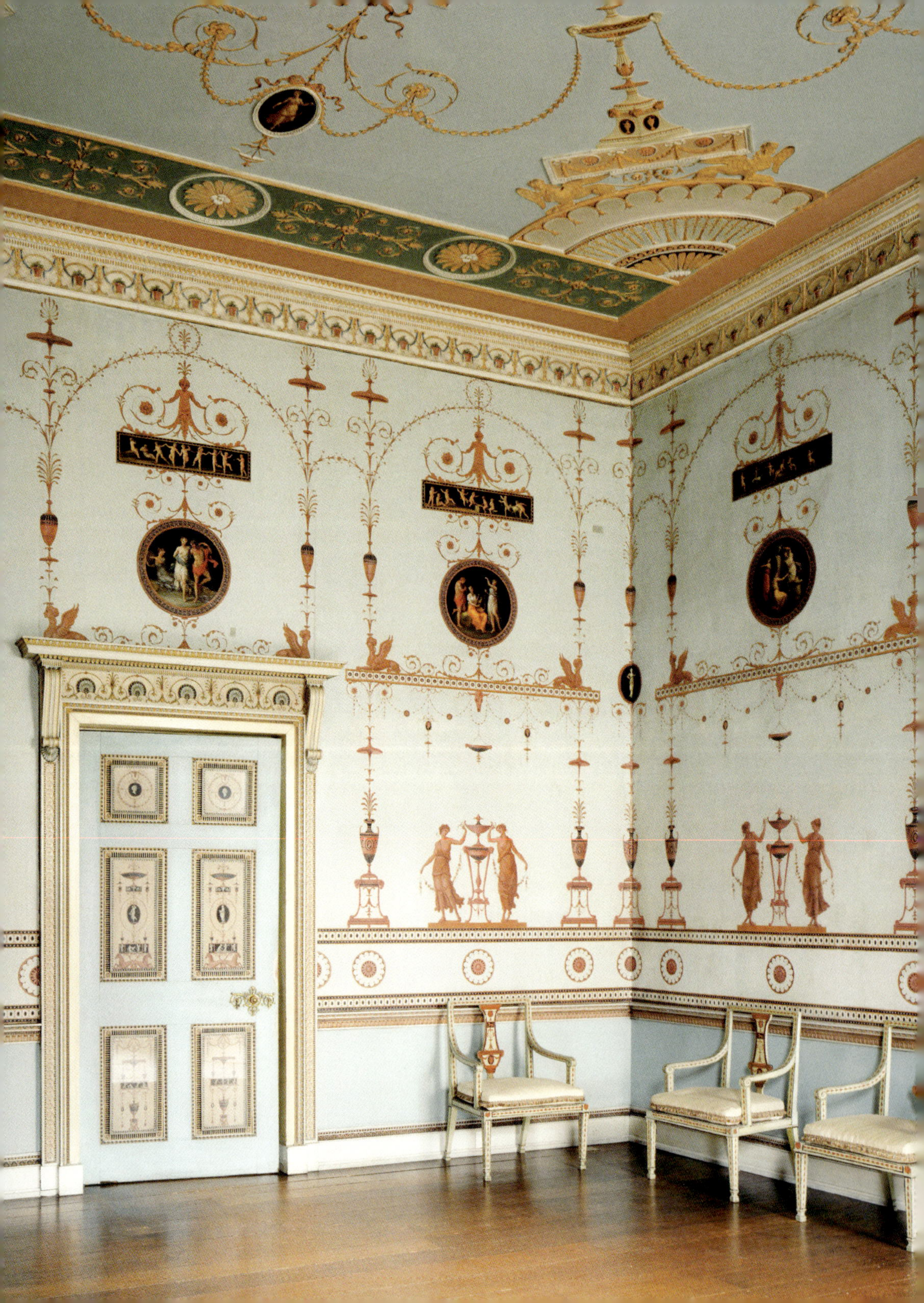

contemporary travel journals give a lively impression of the difficulties that faced even such famous visitors as Scipione Maffei (1675–1755), Charles de Brosses (1709–1777), Johann Joachim Winckelmann (1717–1768), Vivant Denon (1747–1825) and Johann Wolfgang von Goethe (1749–1832) when it came to obtaining access to the excavations and finds.

It was not until the 19th century, as the age of the bourgeoisie began to dawn, that the Vesuvian cities and their treasures were gradually opened up to a wider public. This continuous but by no means linear process corresponded, from a cultural historical perspective, to the decline of the Grand Tour and the beginnings of modern mass tourism, and was accompanied as well as fuelled by radical political upheavals and spectacular technological innovations. Thus the years of Napoleonic rule in Naples under Joachim Murat, from 1808 to 1815, and the unification of Italy in 1861, also represent important milestones for the progress of excavations in the Vesuvian cities. From the middle of the century, the new medium of photography revolutionised the documentation of excavation sites and successively replaced both drawings and engravings. In 1839 Italy's first section of railway line opened between Naples and Portici and was soon extended to the Pompeii excavations, where the "Pompei/Scavi" railway station opened in 1844. In October 1849 Pope Pius IX himself visited the ancient cities using this new means of transport, followed a few years later, in October 1860, by Giuseppe Garibaldi. By now, at the latest, the modern age had reached Pompeii. On September 16, 1860, shortly before his visit, Garibaldi issued a decree in which he declared Pompeii to be a subject of both national political and cultural-political importance: "Seeing that the Pompeii excavations have been most regrettably abandoned for several months, to the distress of the academic world and to the detriment of the local population, and considering that our revolution must be truly Italian, that is to say worthy of the motherland of the arts and the sciences, I hereby decree that the excavations of Pompeii, as national property, shall be granted 5,000 *scudi* per annum and that works shall be resumed immediately."

This radical, if here only hinted at, "structural change in the public sphere" is also reflected in the major publications on the excavations. Thus the eight volumes of *Le Antichità di Ercolano esposte*, published by the Accademia Ercolanense from 1757 to 1792, were highly scholarly works but were circulated only in small editions and as royal gifts to selected recipients. Not even the appearance of pirated editions and copies of individual plates succeeded in altering this situation to any significant degree. It was only with François Mazois' *Les Ruines de Pompéi* (Paris 1812–1838; p. 24, ills. pp. 11, 15), William Gell's *Pompeiana. The Topography,*

Page 49
Pierre-Henri de Valenciennes, ***The Eruption of Vesuvius in AD 79*** (detail), 1813
Oil on canvas, 147.5 x 195.5 cm / 58 x 77 in. Toulouse, Musée des Augustins

Robert Adam, ***Etruscan Room***, 1761–1780
London, Osterley Park

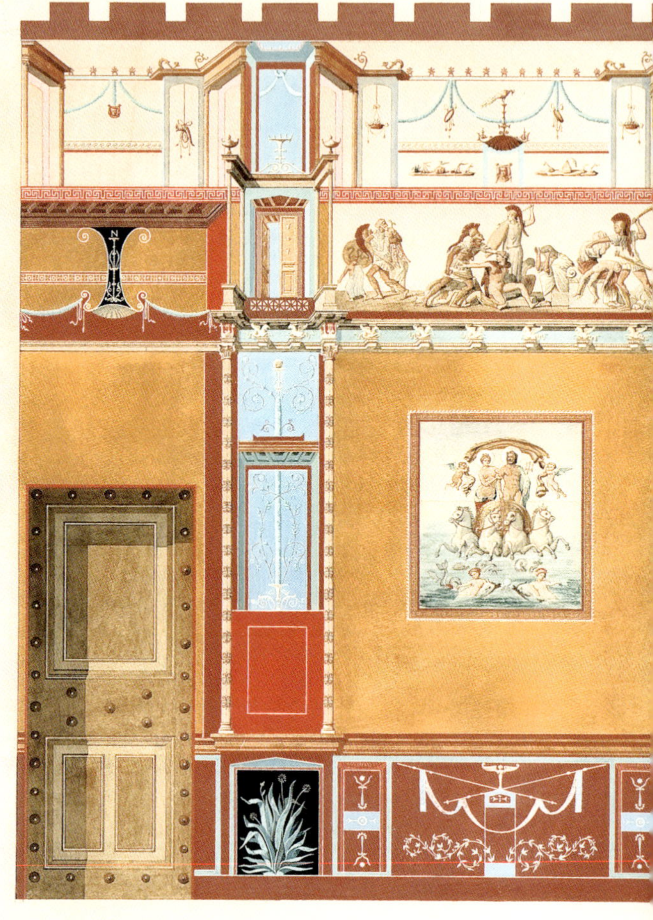

Edifices and Ornaments of Pompeii (London 1832; p. 25, ill. p. 20), Antonio Niccolini's *Real Museo Borbonico* (1824–1857; ill. pp. 29–30) and Wilhelm Zahn's *Die schönsten Ornamente und merkwürdigsten Gemälde aus Pompeji, Herculanum und Stabiae* (Berlin 1828–1858; pp. 30–31, ills. pp. 18, 19, 21, 29) that scholarly publications began to reach a wide international public. The magnificent volumes of the *Case ed i monumenti di Pompei* ("Houses and Monuments of Pompeii"; Naples 1854–1896) published by Fausto and Felice Niccolini can be understood as the sum and provisional end point of this development. Detailed descriptions and over 400 colour lithographs convey a comprehensive impression of Pompeii to the reader: not only by way of the vedute and maps of the city, the views and ground plans of its public buildings and private houses along with detailed plates compiling the artworks and practical utensils found there, but also through "animated" reconstructions of everyday life in Antiquity in shops, bars and workshops, public squares, temples, theatres and baths. In their foreword, the editors proudly mention the large number of celebrated contributors to their work and described the *Case ed i monumenti di Pompei* as the first comprehensive attempt to document "civic life in this ancient town". Pompeii has "not been resurrected for a privileged few, but for the admiration of the whole world and the study of all those who devote their efforts to such noble disciplines".

Even if the art and architecture of Pompeii were of a somewhat provincial character in comparison with the monuments of Classical Athens or Imperial Rome, they nevertheless promised something quite unique: an "authentic" impression, a snapshot of everyday

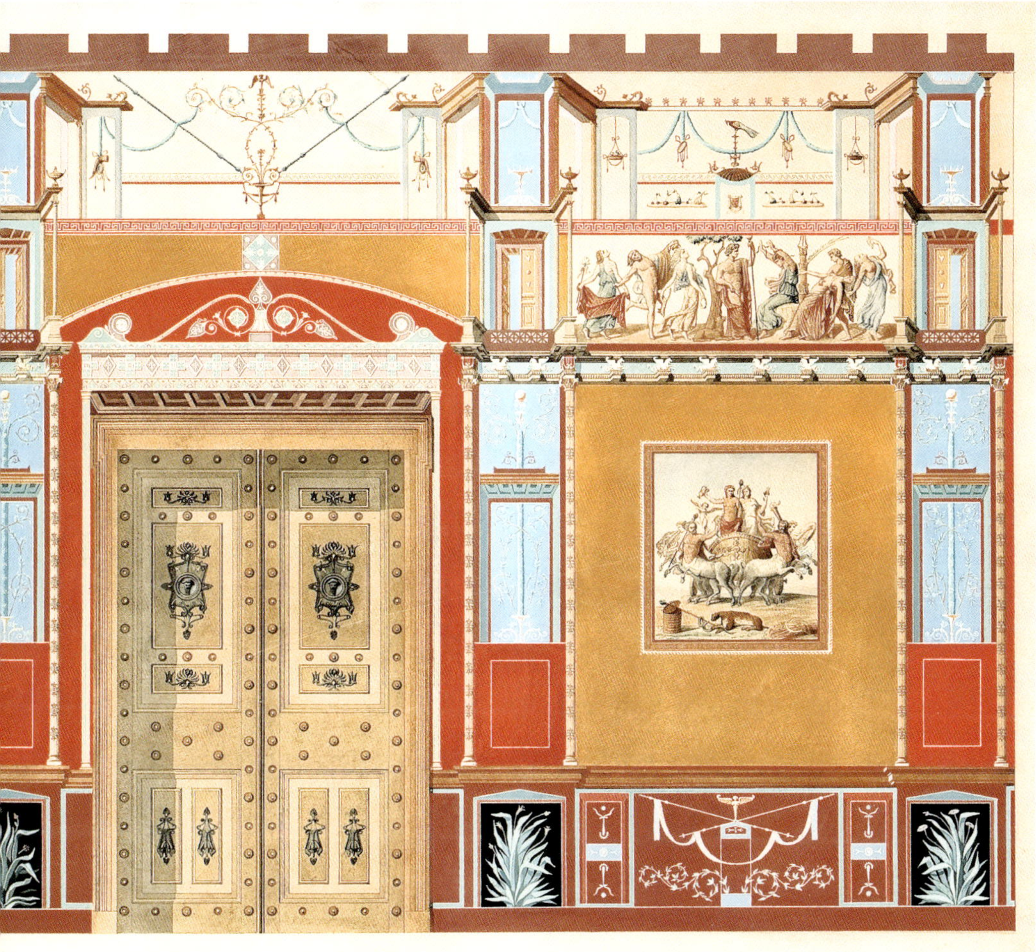

Alfred-Nicolas Normand, ***Design for a Wall Decoration for the Atrium of the Maison Pompéienne***, 1860
Graphite, watercolour, pen and brown ink and tempera, 47 x 89 cm / 18½ x 35 in.
Paris, Musée des Arts décoratifs, Cabinet d'Arts graphiques

life in Antiquity preserved by pyroclastic rocks. This is emphatically expressed in the *Lettre de M. Taylor à M. Ch. Nodier sur les villes de Pompéi et d'Herculanum* with which François-René de Chateaubriand (1768–1848) concluded his published account of his trip to Naples: "Herculaneum and Pompeii are so important for the history of Antiquity that to study them properly one must live there, reside there ... Rome is simply a vast museum; Pompeii is a living Antiquity." Its qualities as a living Antiquity were also, for the Niccolini brothers, what made the "modest Pompeii" a serious rival to Athens and Rome. Against this backdrop, the topography and urban planning of the ancient city and its preservation assumed ever greater importance: priority now lay not with the discovery of individual pieces for the royal collections, but with the comprehensive excavation and conservation of the city complex as a whole – as a social space and a unique testament to ancient civilisation. At the same time, this paradigm shift meant that Pompeii increasingly took over from Herculaneum as the focus of excavations, since here the ancient buildings lay buried under a much thinner, less solidly encrusted layer of ash and stone. The idea that the entire city was an "incomparable museum" was first voiced as early as 1748 by the famous antiquarian Scipione Maffei. However, this modern, holistic approach would only be implemented systematically under Giuseppe Fiorelli (1823–1896), for many years the head of excavations at Pompeii, as Ispettore degli Scavi di Pompei from 1860 and from 1863 to 1875 as Soprintendente degli Scavi and director of the museum in Naples.

Pompeian, Etruscan or *à la grecque*

With the discovery of the Vesuvian cities, ancient room decorations of a previously unseen wealth and variety were revealed, in an excellent state of preservation and with colours still vivid and bright. The restrictive access to these finds, and the appearance only gradually of publications in which they were presented, merely stimulated the public's curiosity yet further and made the "unseen and long-awaited reports" of Winckelmann's *Sendschreiben von den Herculanischen Entdeckungen* ("Letter on the Discoveries at Herculaneum") a Europe-wide antiquarian bestseller when it was published in 1762. Alongside Rome, the Vesuvian cities became the most important stop on every educational tour and the style variously described as Pompeian, Etruscan or *à la grecque* conquered the whole of Europe. Royal palaces, the residences of the nobility and soon, too, bourgeois homes were now fitted with a Pompeian Cabinet or a Pompeian Room complete with furnishings, utensils and porcelain in the Pompeian style. These were modelled on ancient originals, although increasingly too upon their neoclassical interpretations and reinterpretations. Trend-setting examples of such decorative schemes included the interiors by Robert Adam (1728–1792) at Osterley Park (ill. p. 50), James "Athenian" Stuart (1713–1788) at Spencer House, Friedrich Wilhelm von Erdmannsdorff (1736–1800) in Wörlitz and Dessau, Charles Cameron (1745–1812) in Tsarskoye Selo, and Karl Friedrich Schinkel (1781–1841) in the Berlin Stadtschloss. In Italy, significant interiors in the Pompeian style were created in the Palazzo Altieri in Rome, the Palazzo Milzetti in Faenza, the Palazzo Baciocchi in Bologna and the Villa Doria d'Angri and Palazzo di Capodimonte in Naples.

Anton Raphael Mengs, ***Jupiter and Ganymede***, 1758/59
Fresco on canvas, 178.7 x 137.5 cm / 70⅜ x 54⅛ in.
Rome, Galleria Nazionale d'Arte Antica, Palazzo Barberini

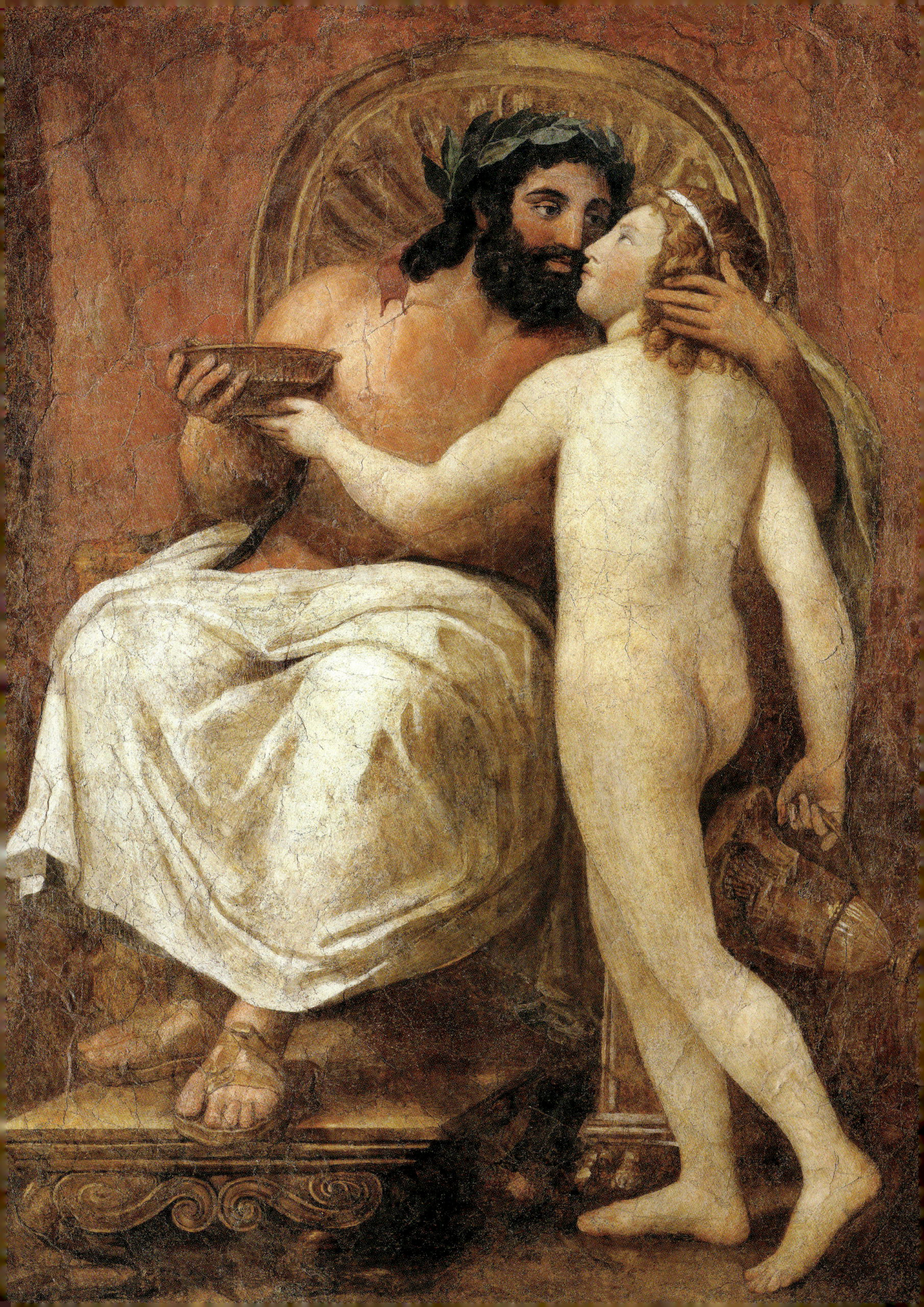

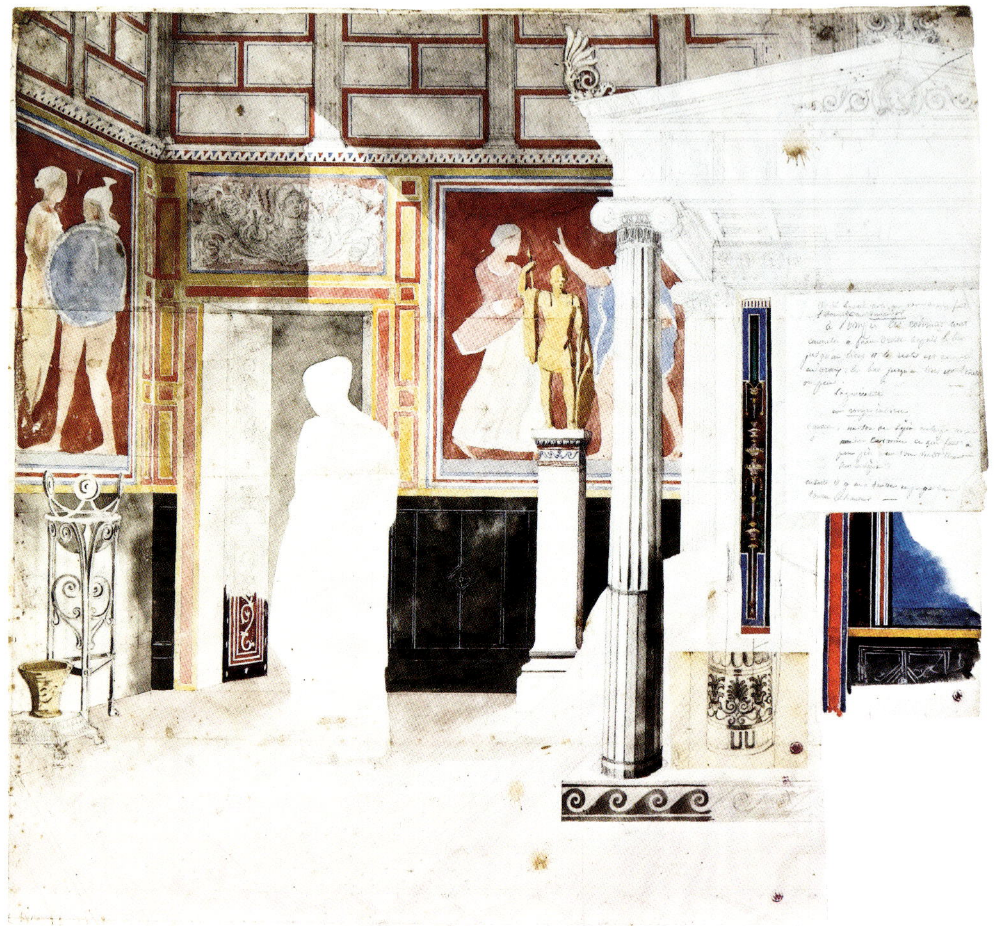

Jean-Auguste-Dominique Ingres, ***Antiochus and Stratonice***, 1840
Pen and watercolour, 50 x 65 cm / 19¾ x 25⅝ in. Montauban, Musée Ingres

Two of the most ambitious projects of all were the Pompejanum in Aschaffenburg and the Maison Pompéienne in Paris. In 1839 Ludwig I of Bavaria (1786–1868) commissioned his court architect Friedrich von Gärtner (1791–1847) to build an idealised reconstruction of the Casa dei Dioscuri, which had been excavated just a few years earlier in 1828–1829. Gärtner had already visited Pompeii in 1816 during his student days and made various drawings of wall decorations. He now travelled a second time to Pompeii on behalf of the king and according to his own account spent ten days in the Casa dei Dioscuri. As soon as 1842 the designs were finalised and construction work began on the Pompejanum, on a terrace above the River Main and surrounded by vineyards and Mediterranean gardens. The interior décor was likewise intended to satisfy the most exacting antiquarian demands: Johann Martin von Wagner (1777–1858), the king's most important artistic advisor, selected suitable originals in Naples, which were then copied – in some cases inside the Real Museo Borbonico itself – by the painters Christoph Friedrich Nilson (1811–1879), Joseph Schlotthauer (1789–1869) and Joseph Schwarzmann (1806–1890). Open to the public right from the start, the Pompejanum was conceived as a synthesis of the arts that would convey an authentic impression of the way in which people lived in Antiquity. Its aim was "to give the image of a Roman building complete with all its furnishings on German soil", as the king wrote to Wagner in a letter of March 22, 1843. Almost completely destroyed in the Second World War, the Pompejanum was subsequently rebuilt but today we must look first and foremost to Gärtner's design drawings to appreciate the extraordinary quality of the original interiors.

Similarly ambitious was the Maison Pompéienne, built between 1854 and 1857 for Prince Jérôme Napoléon (1822–1891) according to plans by Jakob Ignaz Hittorff (1792–1867) and Alfred-Nicolas Normand (1822–1909). Normand had visited Pompeii in 1849 and 1851 and made early use of photography to document some of what he saw. The residence on Avenue Montaigne was modelled on the Villa di Diomede, the Casa di Pansa and the Casa del Poeta tragico. In 1866, however, the house was sold and in 1891 demolished altogether. Normand's drawings and an album of photographs he compiled nevertheless convey a vivid impression of this homage to Antiquity in the heart of Paris (ill. pp. 52–53). Here too, the architecture, wall decorations, furniture and furnishings were modelled on Pompeian originals. For all its formal similarities to Ludwig I's Pompejanum, however, the Maison Pompéienne was founded on a different set of ideas, as can be seen most plainly in a painting from 1861 by Gustave Boulanger (1824–1888), in Versailles at the Musée national des châteaux de Versailles et de Trianon. The picture shows rehearsals for *Le Joueur de flûte*, a play by Émile Augier (1820–1889), and its accompanying prologue, *La Femme de Diomède*, by Théophile Gautier (1811–1872), which were performed at the inauguration of the Maison Pompéienne on February 14, 1860. All the characters are dressed in ancient costume, as are the writers Augier and Gautier, who are coaching the actresses Maria Favart and Madeleine Brohan. The scene is set in the atrium of the Maison Pompéienne, where a marble statue of Emperor Napoleon I (1769–1821) is naturally also part of the décor. Whereas Ludwig I was motivated above all by his antiquarian interests and enthusiasm for Antiquity, the Maison Pompéienne carried stronger political connotations: it was conceived as a utopian alternative to modern times and as a programmatic statement of the restoration under Napoleon III (1808–1873).

Pages 58–59
Lawrence Alma-Tadema, ***The Vintage Festival*** (detail), 1871
Oil on canvas, 77 x 177 cm / 30¼ x 69¾ in. Hamburg, Hamburger Kunsthalle

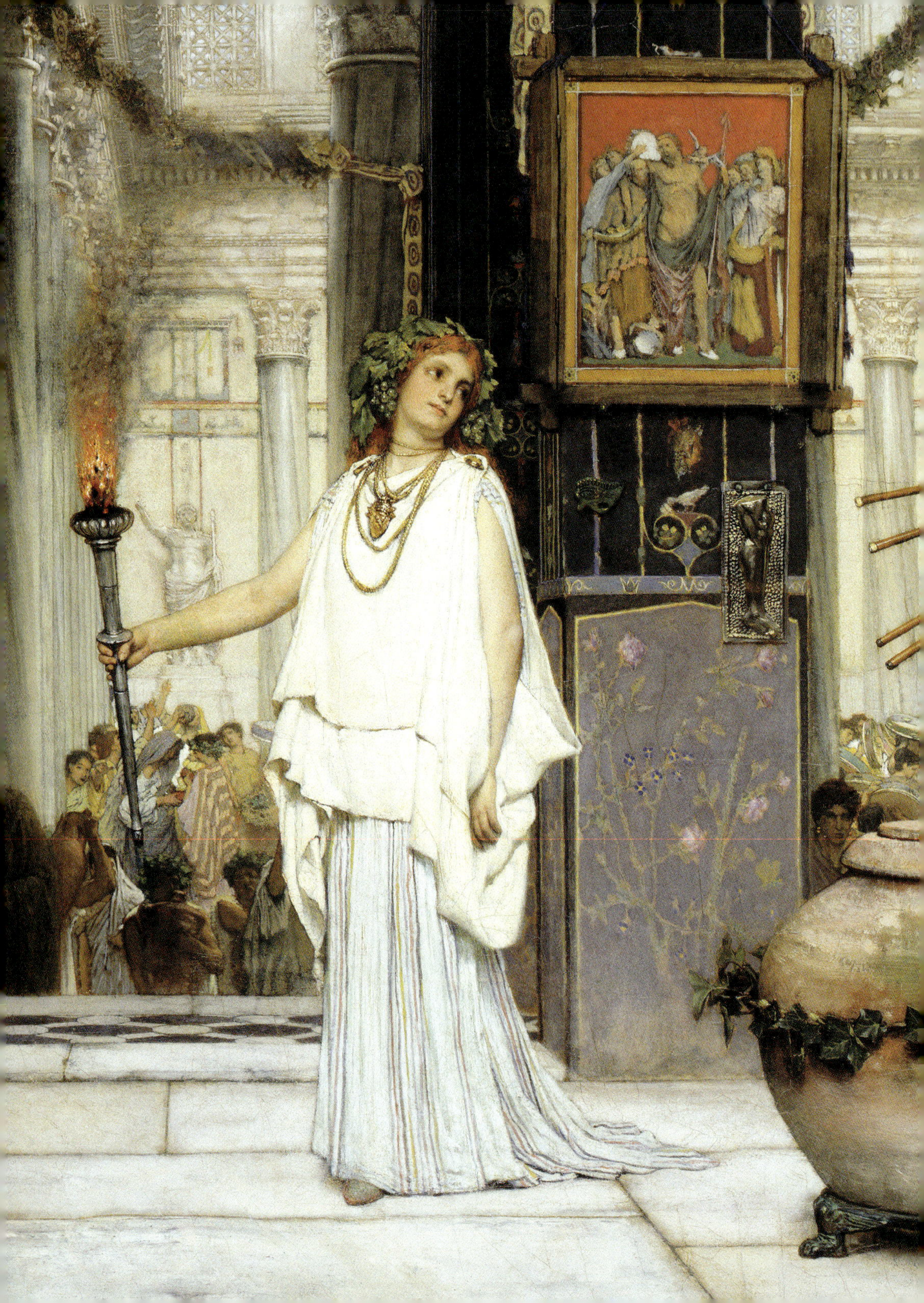

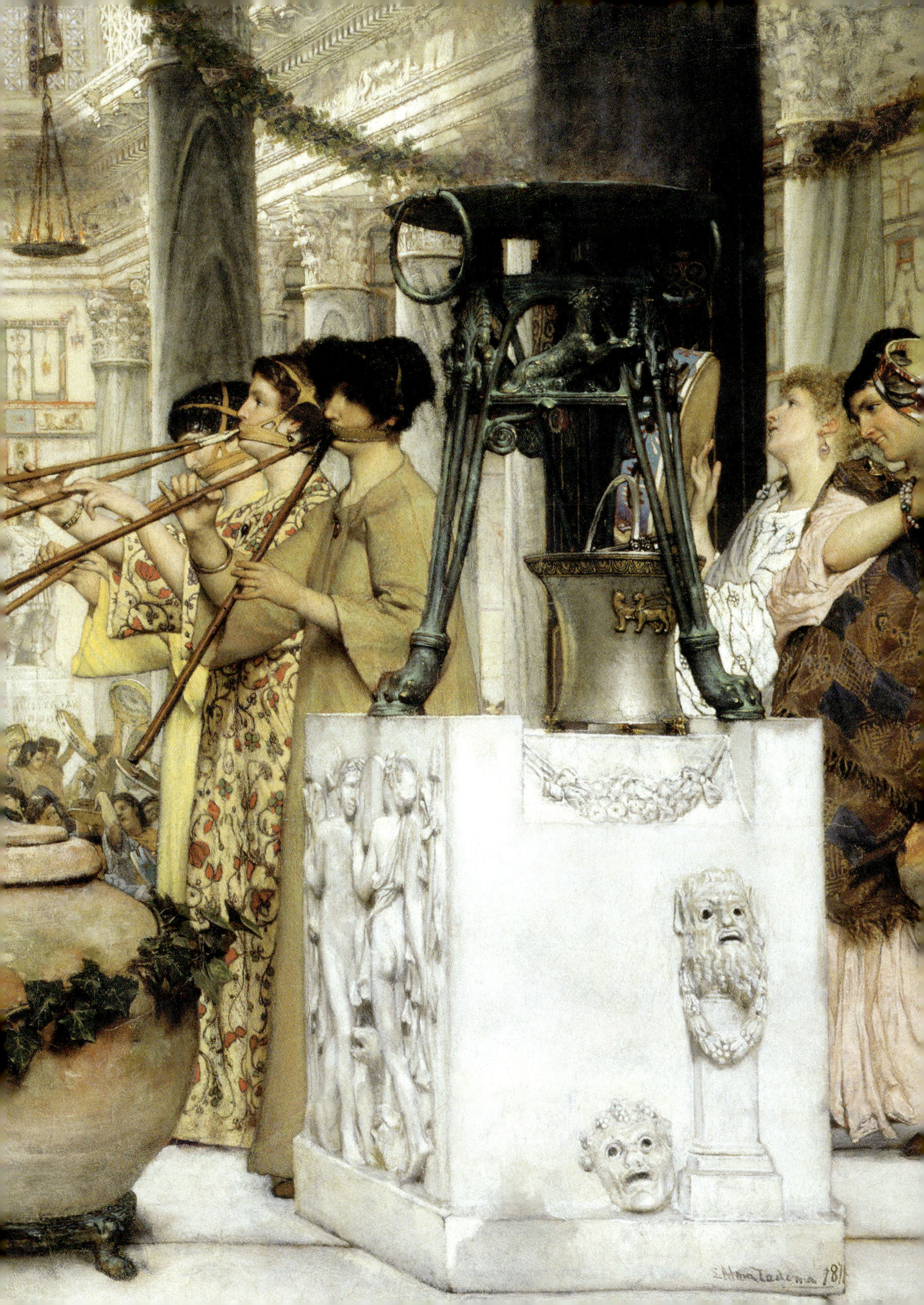

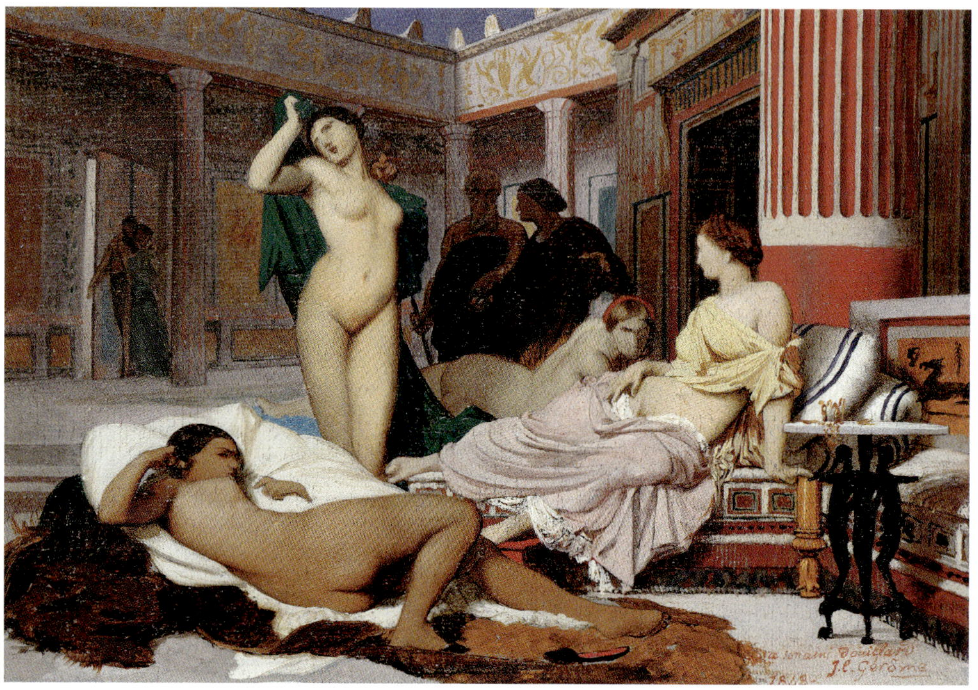

Jean-Léon Gérôme, ***Greek Interior,*** 1848
Oil on canvas, 15.5 x 21 cm / 6 x 8¼ in. Paris, Musée d'Orsay

Pompeian architecture and interiors remained in vogue even into the opening decades of the 20th century, as witnessed by the Salone Pompeiano in the Villa Rendel in Naples (1886–1895) and the atrium of the Palazzo Feltrinelli in Gargnano on Lake Garda (1904–1907). In the wake of the Greek Revival, Pompeian interiors were also created in North America. Among the earliest examples were the Pompeian-style murals (1856–1858) by Constantino Brumidi (1805–1880) for the meeting-room of the Committee on Naval Affairs in the Capitol in Washington. A final synthesis of the arts in the spirit of the Vesuvian cities can be seen in the Getty Villa, completed in 1974 for J. Paul Getty (1892–1976) in Los Angeles. It was designed by Stephen Garret on the model of the Villa dei Papiri in Herculaneum and today houses the Getty Museum's collection of antiquities.

History painting from classicism to modernism

Even more spectacular than the rich decoration schemes found in Herculaneum, Pompeii and Stabiae were the large-scale mythological wall paintings uncovered in both public and private buildings. Famous examples include *Chiron and Achilles* from the Basilica in

Herculaneum, and from Pompeii, the *Sacrifice of Iphigenia* from the House of the Tragic Poet, Narcissus from the House of Marco Lucrezio Fronto, *Isis Receiving Io in Canopus in Egypt* from the Temple of Isis, and *Perseus and Andromeda* from the Casa dei Dioscuri. Such testaments to ancient monumental painting were barely known in the Renaissance and Baroque eras. When the *Aldobrandini Wedding* (Vatican Museums) was discovered in 1606 within the Gardens of Maecenas on the Esquiline Hill, it caused a veritable sensation. In the caption to an engraving made by Pietro Santi Bartoli (1635–1700) around 1674, the ancient fresco is described as "artis exemplar, et miraculum" ("model and miracle of art"). Giovanni Paolo Pannini (1691–1765), in his programmatic 1755 representation of *Roma Antica*, combined vedute of Roman monuments with masterpieces of ancient sculpture (ill. pp. 70–71). A copy of the *Aldobrandini Wedding* is visible in the centre, where, as the sole example of ancient fresco-painting it is being admired by a group of art connoisseurs. Prior to the discovery of Herculaneum and Pompeii, knowledge of the masterpieces of ancient painting was essentially confined to the literary descriptions contained in the writings of Pausanias, Lucian or Philostratus. Many artists sought to reconstruct these in paint, as in *The Calumny of Apelles* by Sandro Botticelli (1445–1510; Florence, Galleria degli Uffizi) and *The Sacrifice of Iphigenia of Timanthes* by Pietro Testa (1611–1650; Rome, Galleria Nazionale di Palazzo Spada).

With the Vesuvian murals, works of "great" history painting now appeared for the first time in substantial numbers alongside ancient sculpture. In this context it was significant for their reception that they were removed from the walls where they had been painted and then hung in the manner of framed gallery pictures in the Real Museo Borbonico. Their style presented a marked contrast to the naturalism and dynamism of Baroque painting and its expression of the affects, and could be compellingly assigned to Winckelmann's categories of noble simplicity and quiet grandeur. The monumental figures in most cases face forward or are seen parallel to the pictorial plane and avoid complex foreshortening. Their expression is classically calm. Local colours dominate, laid down in large areas and exhibiting the light tones associated with the fresco technique, while interior modelling is very restrained. Compositions are restricted to a few figures and seem almost deliberately devoid of dramatic content. They are images of a "decommissioned history" of sublime "naïveté" and served the great neoclassical painters – Anton Raphael Mengs, Angelika Kauffmann, Johann Heinrich Wilhelm Tischbein, Asmus Jakob Carstens, Joseph-Marie Vien, Jacques-Louis David, Jean-Auguste-Dominique Ingres, Vincenzo Camuccini and Felice Giani – as justification for a radical reorientation in keeping with the spirit of Antiquity. The Vesuvian cities supplied an inexhaustible repertoire of pictorial inventions to which artists could allude through their choice of subject or with an obvious visual quotation, as in the case of Vien, who in his *Cupid Seller* of 1763 (Fontainebleau, Palace) cites the famous mural from the Villa Arianna in Stabiae. The ultimate aim, however, was to reinvent a "Homeric" style. Characteristic of the intensity with which this goal was pursued is the fresco of *Jupiter and Ganymede* (ill. p. 55), executed by

Mengs in 1757–1758 during a stay in Naples, which even Winckelmann took to be authentic and in 1764 celebrated as a masterpiece of ancient painting in the first edition of his *Geschichte der Kunst des Alterthums* (*History of the Art of Antiquity*). Whether the fresco by Mengs was indeed conceived as a fake, or instead represents a particularly ambitious attempt to imitate the style and technique of Antiquity, remains a matter of dispute among scholars even today.

The pictures from the Vesuvian cities are omnipresent in neoclassical painting and appear as *exempla* alongside ancient sculpture and vase decorations as well as alongside the masterpieces of Raphael (1483–1520), Annibale Carracci (1560–1609) and Nicolas Poussin (1594–1665) and the line drawings of John Flaxman (1755–1826). From the middle of the 18th century onwards, they exerted a profound influence upon the development of history painting and the scholarly discourse concerning this highest-ranking genre in the western canon. Works such as Mengs' *Perseus and Andromeda* of 1777–1778 (Saint Petersburg, The State Hermitage Museum), Tischbein's *Iphigenia and Orestes* of 1788 (Bad Arolsen, Stiftung des fürstlichen Hauses Waldeck und Pyrmont) and the series of three paintings Kauffmann executed in 1785 in Naples for George Bowles – *Cornelia, Mother of the Gracchi* (Richmond, Virgina Museum of Fine Arts), *Virgil Writing his own Epitaph in Brundisium* (Portland, private collection) and *Pliny the Younger and his Mother in Misenum, AD 79* (Princeton, Art Museum) – testify to the programmatic imitation of ancient style and subject matter. A prime example of just how strongly the art of the Vesuvian cities influenced conceptions of ancient wall-painting as a whole can be seen in the pictorial reconstructions of the murals by Polygnotus at Delphi that were attempted by the Riepenhausen brothers based on the descriptions by Pausanias – as is particularly clear in the colour engravings of the late edition of their work from 1829.

Alongside the mounting volume of archaeological evidence, the idea that Herculaneum and Pompeii provided an "authentic" insight into daily life in Antiquity was a key determining factor in their reception. Equally major roles were played by "living" reconstructions of the past and the superimposition and interaction of ancient and modern. Thus the view of the ruins of the Temple of Isis in Pompeii, complete with Grand Tourists, reproduced by the Abbé de Saint-Non in his *Voyage pittoresque* (Paris, 1781–1786), is accompanied even at this early date by an idealised reconstruction in which the temple becomes the nocturnal setting for a sacrificial rite attended by numerous figures. In the Palazzo Sessa, the Neapolitan residence of Sir William Hamilton (1731–1803), Emma Hart (1765–1815), the later Lady Hamilton, captivated a cosmopolitan public with her famous "Attitudes", in which she dressed and posed as ancient statues and figures from Pompeian murals. Views of Pompeii were increasingly peopled not only with sketching artists, excavators and tourists, but with imaginary ancient protagonists. This emphatic trend towards bringing Antiquity back to life and cementing it

Mario Sironi, ***Justice Between Law and Order*** (detail), ca. 1936
Mosaic. Milan, Palazzo di Giustizia

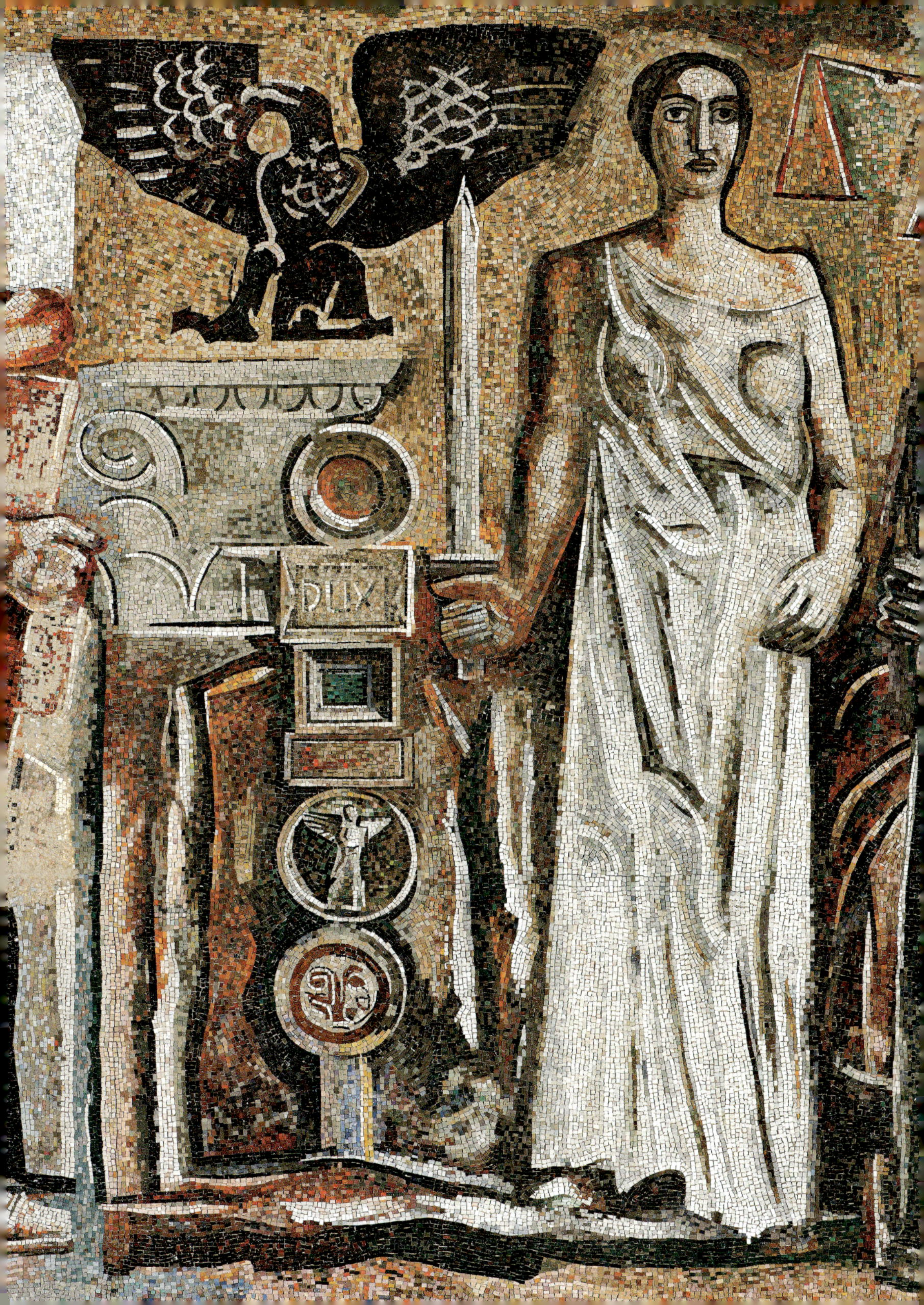
DUX

within a contemporary context developed in the second half of the 19th century into a distinct representational tradition. In 1813–1814, Ingres had visited Naples and the Vesuvian cities during his student years. The Pompeian murals remained inscribed almost genetically within his art, even as late as his 1856 *Portrait of Madame Moitessier* (London, National Gallery), whose pose is derived from the allegorical figure of Arcadia found in the mural of *Hercules and Telephus* in the Basilica in Herculaneum. In his *Antiochus and Stratonice* of 1838 (Chantilly, Musée Condé), Ingres staged the drama within a Pompeian interior and modelled the figure of the Macedonian princess on that of Penelope in a mural discovered in 1818–1822 in the Macellum in Pompeii. A detailed preliminary drawing for the composition (ill. p. 56) highlights the meticulous accuracy with which the artist created his ancient setting.

If these references still served, in the case of Ingres, to lend authenticity to his history painting, a few years later Pompeii instead provided Jean-Léon Gérôme (1824–1904) and Théodore Chassériau (1819–1856) with a framework for the erotic fantasies of the 19th century. Gérôme's *Greek Interior* (ill. p. 60) was exhibited at the Salon of 1850–1851 and immediately purchased by Jérôme Napoléon, the future builder of the Maison Pompéienne. The atrium of a Pompeian house, furnished with the archeologically accurate representation of a bronze tripod with satyrs from the Villa of Julia Felix, here served as the legitimation for a brothel scene with voluptuous female nudes. Chassériau's *Tepidarium at the Baths in Pompeii* of 1853 (Paris, Musée d'Orsay) reproduces a view of the tepidarium at the Forum Baths in Pompeii with almost philological precision. The artist had visited the excavations in 1840 and made drawings while he was there, but his painting appears directly based on an accurate perspective view in William Gell's *Pompeiana*. Although Gell clearly identified the tepidarium as part of the men's wing of the complex, in Chassériau it is full of women relaxing and drying themselves after the bath. Chassériau's tepidarium thus has something of the erotic ambience of an orientalised harem – another popular vehicle for 19th-century projections. In the central figure of the young woman with her arms raised and breasts bared we can probably see a direct reference to the imprint of a woman's bust, discovered in 1771 but today lost, which would inspire the erotic fantasies of not just the young Octavien in Théophile Gautier's 1852 novella *Arria Marcella: Souvenir de Pompéi*. Gautier was an enthusiastic admirer of Chassériau and praised his *Tepidarium* as "an antique fresco stolen from a wall in Pompeii".

The works by Gérôme and Chassériau appealed to 19th-century public taste and ushered in a whole wave of neo-Pompeian painting in which an archeologically faithful representation of ancient architecture, wall decorations and furnishings was combined with a spirit of sensuality and figural motifs related to the contemporary interest in eroticism. The contrast between the authenticity of the settings and the "modern" protagonists inhabiting them generated a rich tension that also characterised the numerous works by the Neapolitan School, such as *The Pompeian Bath* of 1861 by Domenico Morelli (1826–1901; Milan, Fondazione internazionale Eugenio Balzan) and *The Pompeian Bedroom* of 1871 by Federico Maldarelli (1826–1893;

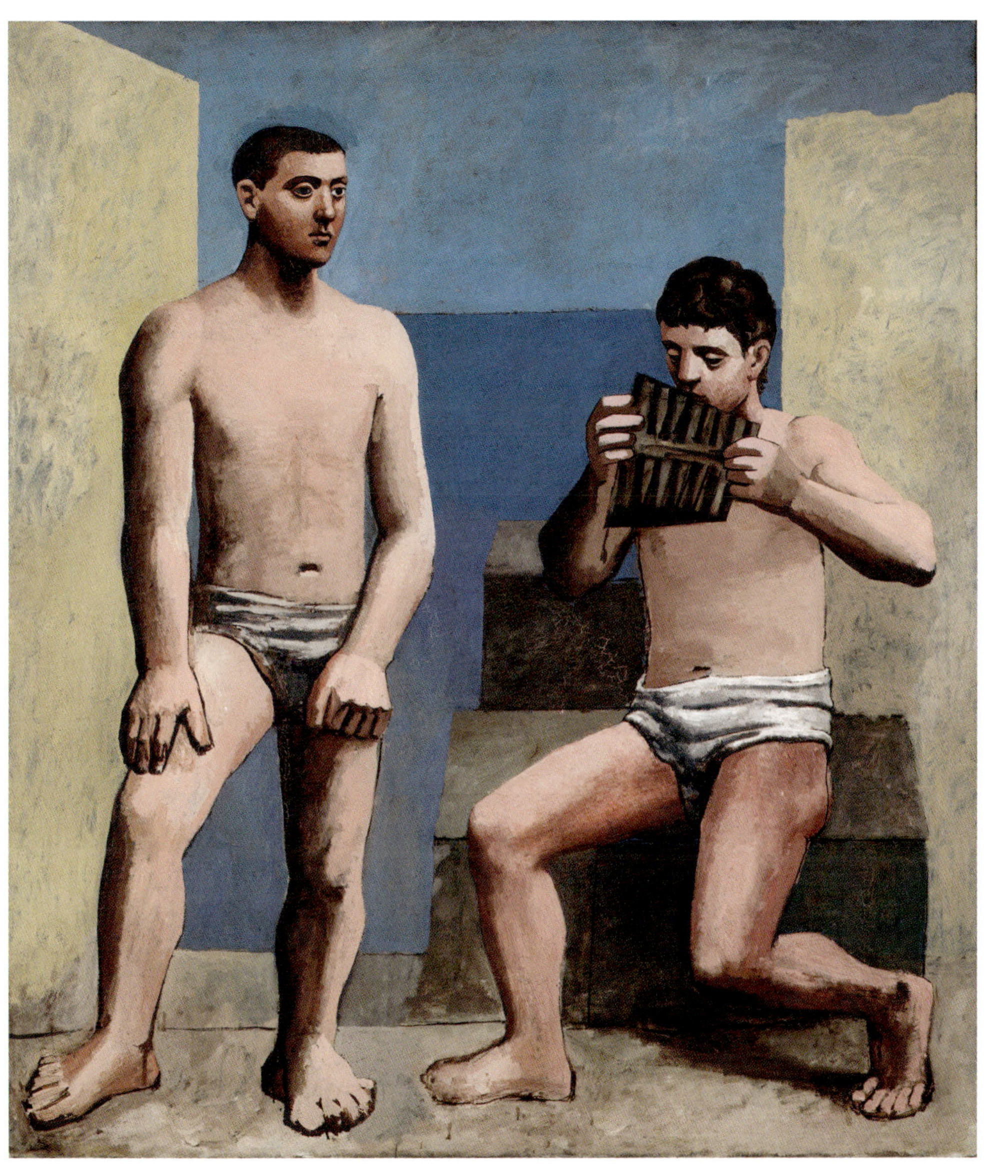

Pablo Picasso, *The Pan Pipes*, 1923
Oil on canvas, 205 x 174 cm / 80¾ x 68½ in. Paris, Musée Picasso

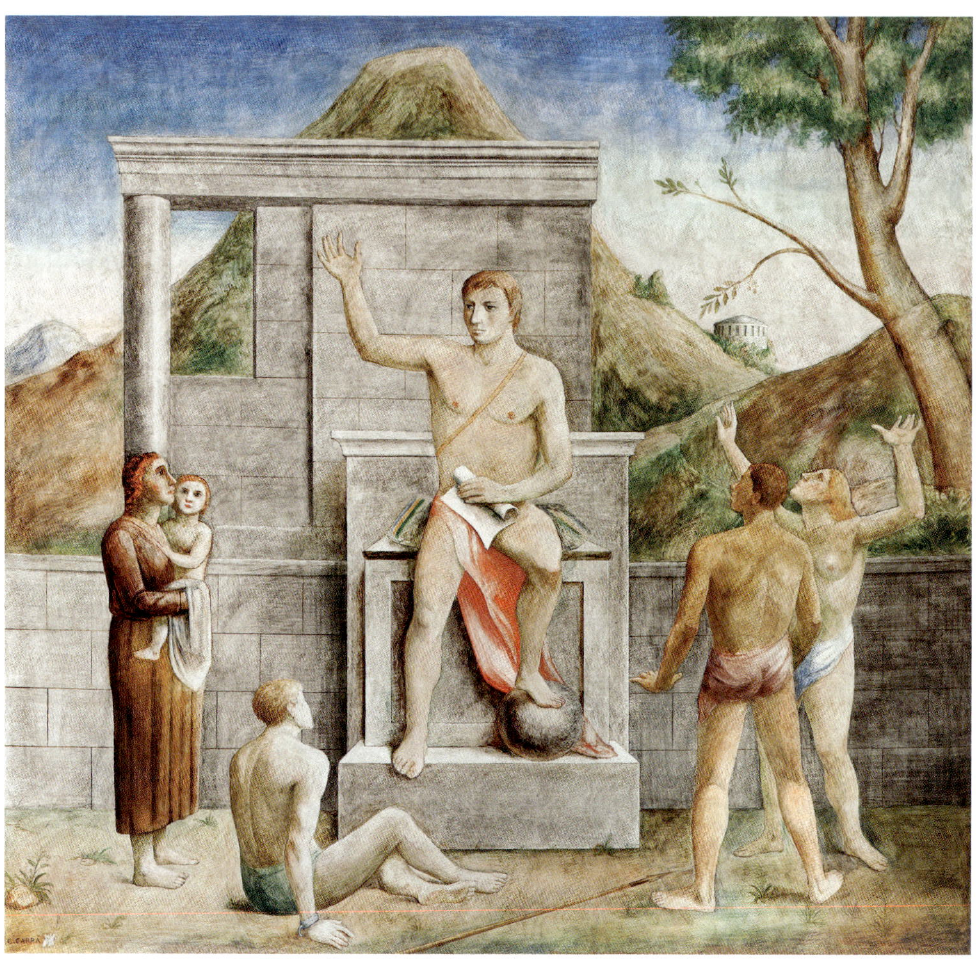

Carlo Carrà, ***Justinian Gives a Slave his Freedom***, 1938
Fresco. Milan, Palazzo di Giustizia

Rome, Galleria Nazionale d'Arte Moderna). The most successful of these neo-Pompeian painters was Lawrence Alma-Tadema (1836–1912). He first visited Naples on his honeymoon in 1863 and subsequently visualised the ancient Vesuvian cities in the spirit of the Victorian age in paintings made primarily in London. Among his early works is *The Vintage Festival* of 1870 (Hamburger Kunsthalle), which shows a procession of men and women, crowned with wreaths and making music in homage to Dionysus, in the hall of a Pompeian house. Not only the statues, vases, reliefs and pictures, but also the vessels, practical utensils and musical instruments were copied with the greatest accuracy from ancient originals. Two paintings in vibrant

Pompeian red are shown hanging in gilt frames like gallery pictures on the hall's black pillars. While individual pictures painted on marble or wood were indeed found in the Vesuvian cities, they were nevertheless integrated within the wall decoration. In Alma-Tadema's later works, such antiquarian detail receded more and more, and the main focus now fell upon the relationships – in most cases erotically charged – between the protagonists. Antiquity, more strongly than ever, became the screen on to which Victorian yearnings could be projected.

Within a few years of Alma-Tadema's death, Pompeian wall painting would find itself back under scrutiny from an entirely different perspective as it came under the gaze of modernism. In the 1920s and 1930s, after the systematic deconstruction of all traditions and the move into abstraction, after an increasingly rapid succession of isms replacing one another and with the traumatic experiences of the First World War, modernism in many places entered a phase of classicist self-reflection. A return to order, the "ritorno all'ordine", was the new catchphrase, one that simultaneously implied a return to tradition. The search for new mythologies and "grand" form led artists to turn their attention once more to Antiquity. In its choice of subject and stylistic means, *The Pan Pipes*, painted in 1923 by Pablo Picasso (1881–1973), programmatically embodies this Arcadian current within modernism (ill. p. 65). At more or less the same time, Giorgio de Chirico (1888–1978) was painting his metaphysical worlds, inspired by the perspectivism of Friedrich Nietzsche (1844–1900) as much as by wall paintings from the Vesuvian cities. The example of Pompeii was also a key influence in the modernist renewal of wall painting, as pursued by Oskar Schlemmer (1888–1943) and the great painters of the Novecento in Italy. In the *Manifesto della pittura murale* written by Mario Sironi (1885–1961) in 1933 and jointly signed with Achille Funi (1890–1972), Carlo Carrà (1881–1966) and Massimo Campigli (1895–1971), the great tradition of Italic wall painting is underscored as the reference point and powerful catalyst of a new Fascist painting (ills. pp. 63, 66), which is to be "ancient and entirely modern" at the same time. Funi translated this in programmatic fashion into his cartoons for the decoration of the Palazzo dei Ricevimenti e Congressi in Rome, for example, in *Aeneas' Flight from Troy* (Rome, Archivio Centrale dello Stato).

"Death, like a sculptor, has taken a cast of his victim"

Visitors to the Vesuvian cities throughout the centuries have been particularly moved by the idea that the inhabitants, overtaken by the eruption, met their death in the very middle of their daily lives. The regular recurrence of fresh eruptions in the years 1631, 1774, 1794, 1826, 1858, 1872, 1906 and most recently 1944 provided a vivid reminder of the threat continuously posed by the volcano. The dramatic eye-witness account by Pliny the Younger was visualised in paintings such as *The Eruption of Vesuvius, AD 79*, executed in 1813 by Pierre-Henri de Valenciennes (1750–1819; ill. p. 49). The collective imagination was probably shaped most enduringly, however, by *The Last Day of Pompeii* (Saint Petersburg, The State Hermitage Museum) by Karl Pavlovič Briullov (1799–1852), completed in 1833. This monumental canvas, measuring some 15 x 21 feet (456 x 651 cm), was frequently reproduced and also inspired the famous novel by Edward Bulwer-Lytton (1803–1873), *The Last Days of Pompeii*, published in 1834.

It was only natural that, during the course of the digging, skeletons should have regularly come to light. In 1863 the director of excavations, Fiorelli, made the first plaster casts from the negative moulds left by the bodies of the victims in the layers of ash and lava. Some of the resulting figures look as if they have died in their sleep; others seem to be huddling together, while others again betray the desperate struggle of their final moments. We see men, women and children, squatting on the ground, lying down, or writhing in agony – silent witnesses of the devastating natural catastrophe who lend the historical event a personal, individual countenance. The powerful impact of these casts is reflected in the reactions of several contemporaries. For Chateaubriand, "Death, like a sculptor, has taken a cast of his victim". The writer Luigi Settembrini (1813–1877), a friend of Fiorelli, was also deeply moved when he saw the first casts: "They have been dead for 18 centuries, but they are human creatures whom we see in the throes of death. This is not art, not imitation, but their bones, the relics of their bodies and their clothes mixed with plaster; it is the agony of death that here assumes shape and form."

The plaster figures convey the impression of an authentic snapshot and were exhibited along with the other finds in the Museo Archeologico in Naples. In the form of photographs and print reproductions, they quickly reached a wide audience and thus added a crucial dimension to the Pompeii experience. The popular Pompeii albums by the photographer Giorgio Sommer (1834–1914), or Michele Amodio (active 1850–1890), almost always included pictures of the victims (ill. p. 69). In modern times, these expressive images of death captured in plaster surpass even the celebrity of such famous Vesuvian bronzes as the *Seated Hermes* from the Villa dei Papiri in Herculaneum and the *Dancing Faun* from the Casa del Fauno in Pompeii. The pathos of authenticity and their media presence have made the Pompeian casts into archetypes upon which artists such as Auguste Rodin (1840–1917), Arturo Martini (1889–1947) and Henry Moore (1898–1986) no less than Duane Hanson (1925–1996) and George Segal (1924–2000) have all drawn. Among the most impressive activations of these formulae of pathos are the large memorials created by Hanson to the Vietnam War and by Segal to the Holocaust. In Hanson's 1967 installation *War (Vietnam Piece*; Duisburg, Lehmbruck Museum), dead and wounded soldiers lie spattered in blood on the scorched ground. The hyperrealistic figures in polyester resin and fibreglass are painted in colour. The stiffened bodies and prevailing ash-grey colour directly evoke the Pompeian casts, while the combat trousers, steel helmets and cartridge casings, together with the clearly visible traces of blood, localise and at the same time intensify the scene. In Segal's 1984 *Holocaust Memorial* (San Francisco, Legion of Honor Park), the naked corpses lie rigid on the ground, as if unceremoniously flung down. The figures, originally made in plaster, were cast in bronze and painted white for the open-air installation. Men, women and children can be made out, some with arms flung wide, others lying quietly. Through the uniform white and the absence of any attributes, they appear robbed of all individuality.

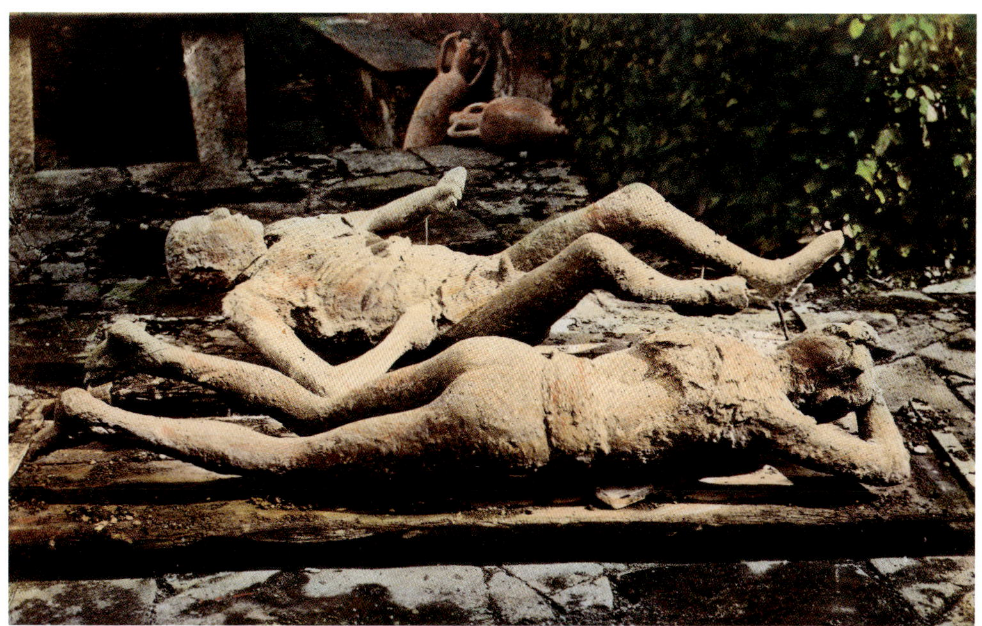

Michele Amodio (?), ***Plaster Casts of Two Victims of the Vesuvian Eruption***, spring 1875
Coloured photograph. Private collection

The reference to Nazi concentration camps and the Holocaust is made explicit only through the man standing at the barbed-wire fence, gazing into the distance. Like their Pompeian archetypes, Hanson's and Segal's figures are based on casts made from human models.

The major and minor avenues of Pompeii's reception history could easily be explored much further. It is the sense of continuity, the artistic pre-eminence and the multiplicity of perspectives which have ensured the unbroken topicality of Pompeii and its fellow Vesuvian cities in European art for over 250 years. Texts and images have been of crucial significance for the way Pompeii has been perceived and the continuously changing horizons of experience and expectation of its visitors. The *Case ed i Monumenti di Pompei* marks, as was noted at the start of this essay, a milestone in the structural change affecting the public sphere and the paradigm shift that goes with it, and must be counted amongst their powerful multipliers. For as so aptly summarised by Stefano De Caro, the long-serving Soprintendente of Naples and Caserta, the work of the Niccolini brothers represents the "first virtual reconstruction of Pompeii".

Pages 70–71
Giovanni Paolo Pannini, ***Roma Antica***, ca. 1755
Oil on canvas, 169.5 x 227 cm / 66¾ x 89⅜ in. Stuttgart, Staatsgalerie

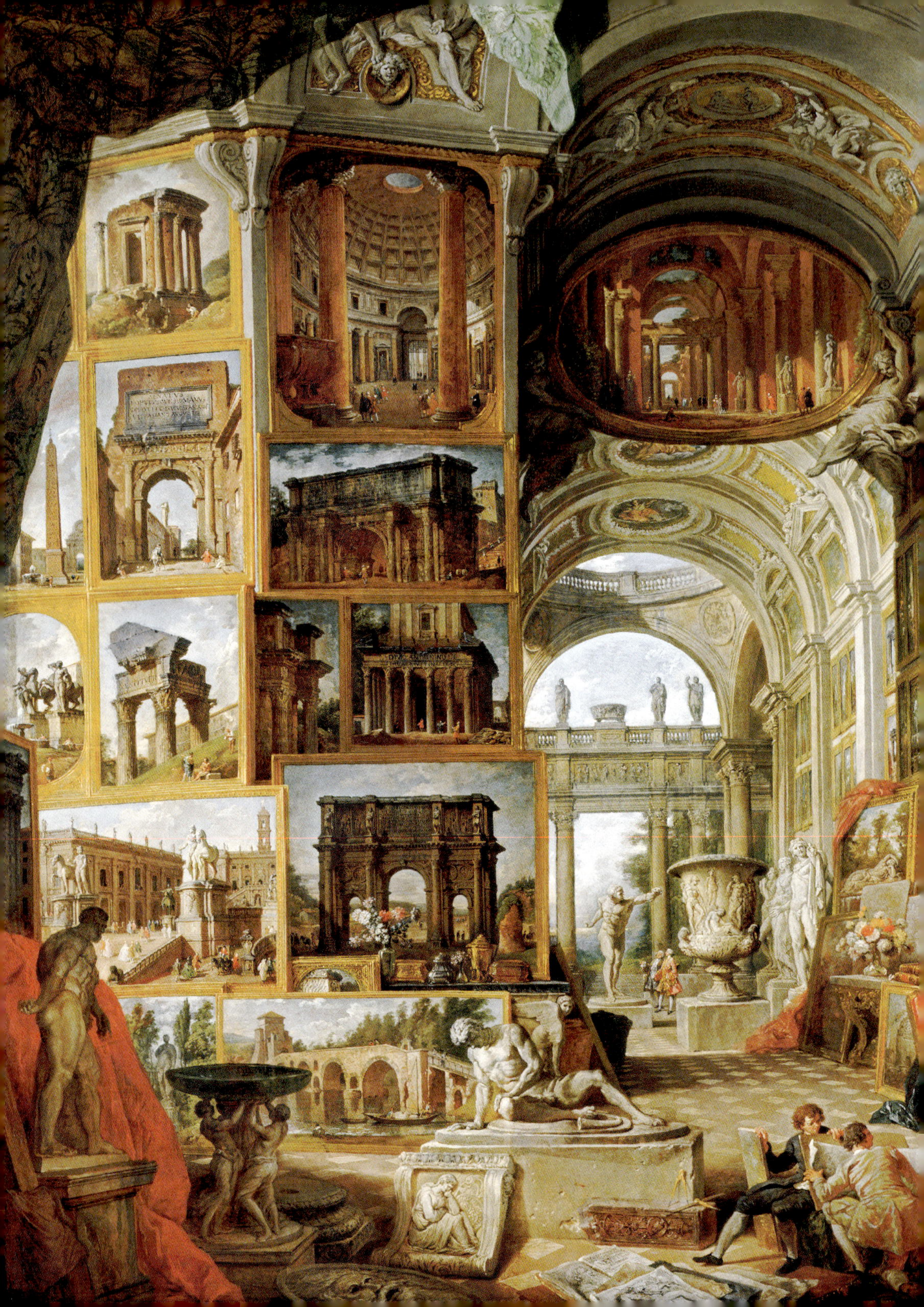

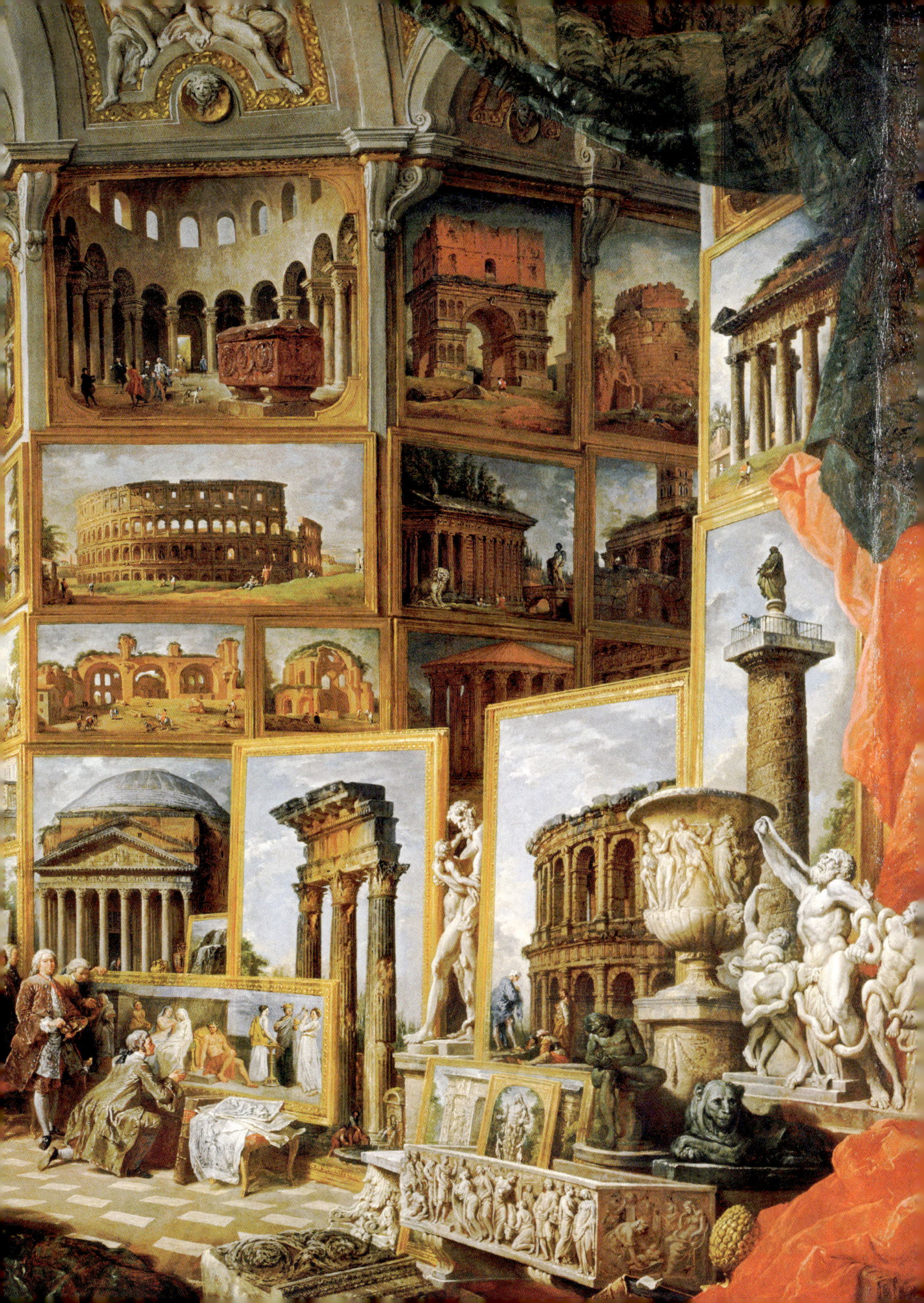

POMPEII: EXCAVATIONS 1748–1900

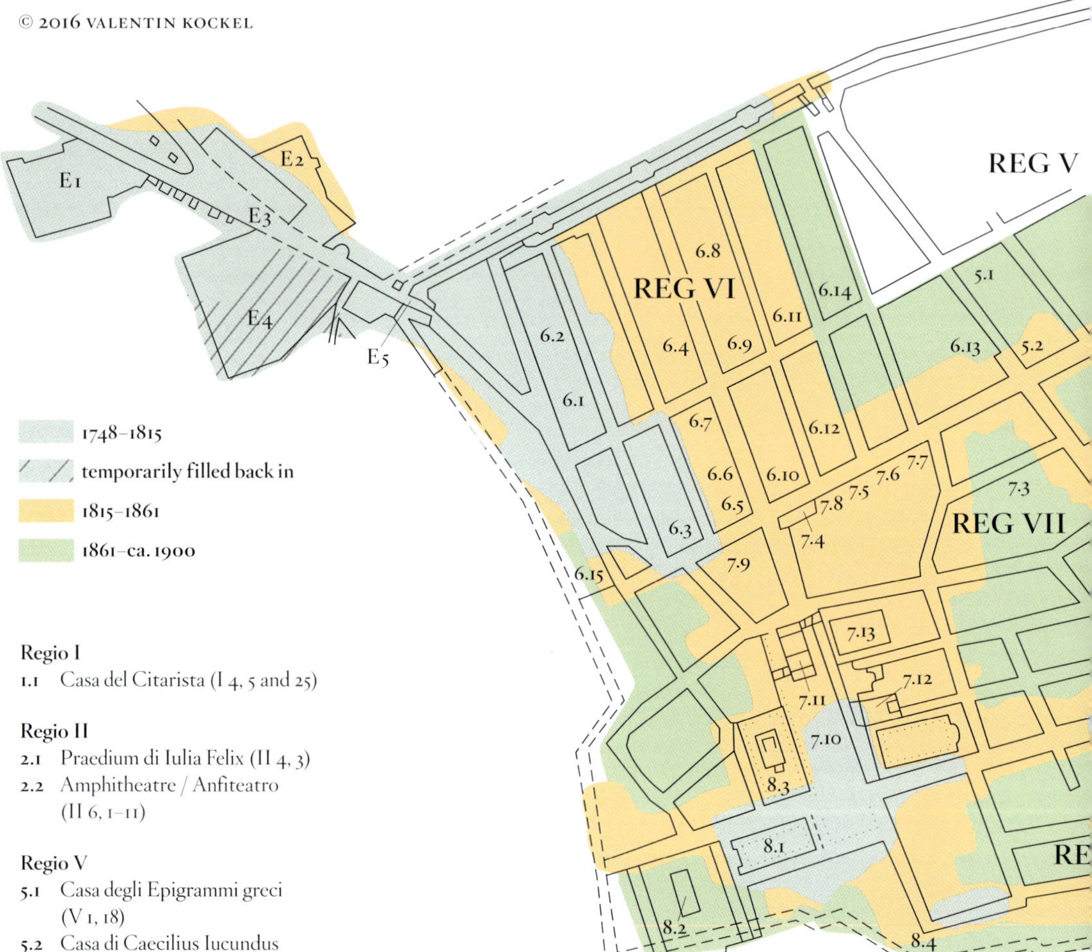

Regio I

1.1 Casa del Citarista (I 4, 5 and 25)

Regio II

2.1 Praedium di Iulia Felix (II 4, 3)
2.2 Amphitheatre / Anfiteatro (II 6, 1–11)

Regio V

5.1 Casa degli Epigrammi greci (V 1, 18)
5.2 Casa di Caecilius Iucundus (V 1, 26)
5.3 Casa delle Nozze d'Argento (V 2, i)

Regio VI

6.1 Casa di Sallustio (VI 2, 4)
6.2 Casa delle Amazzoni (VI 2, 14)
6.3 Casa di Pansa (VI 6, 1)
6.4 Casa di Inaco e Io (VI 7, 19)
6.5 House of the Tragic Poet / Casa del Poeta tragico (VI 8, 3 and 5)
6.6 Fullonica (VI 8, 20)
6.7 House of the Small Fountain / Casa della Fontana piccola (VI 8, 23 and 24)
6.8 Casa di Meleagro (VI 9, 2)
6.9 House of the Dioscuri / Casa dei Dioscuri (VI 9, 6–9)
6.10 Casa del Naviglio (VI 10, 11)
6.11 Casa del Labirinto (VI 11, 9–10)
6.12 House of the Faun / Casa del Fauno (VI 12, 2)
6.13 Casa di Orfeo (VI 14, 20)
6.14 Casa dei Vettii (VI 15, 1)
6.15 Casa del Bracciale d'Oro (VI 17, Insula occidentalis 42)

Regio VII

7.1 Stabian Baths / Terme Stabiane (VII 1, 8)
7.2 House of Siricus / Casa di Sirico (VII 1, 25)
7.3 Casa di Popidius Priscus (VII 2, 20)
7.4 Temple of Fortuna Augusta / Tempio della Fortuna Augusta (VII 4, 1)
7.5 House of the Figured Capitals / Casa dei Capitelli figurati (VII 4, 29 and 57)
7.6 House of the Coloured Capitals / Casa dei Capitelli colorati (VII 4, 31 and 51)
7.7 Casa della Caccia antica (VII 4, 43 and 48)
7.8 Casa della Parete nera (VII 4, 59)

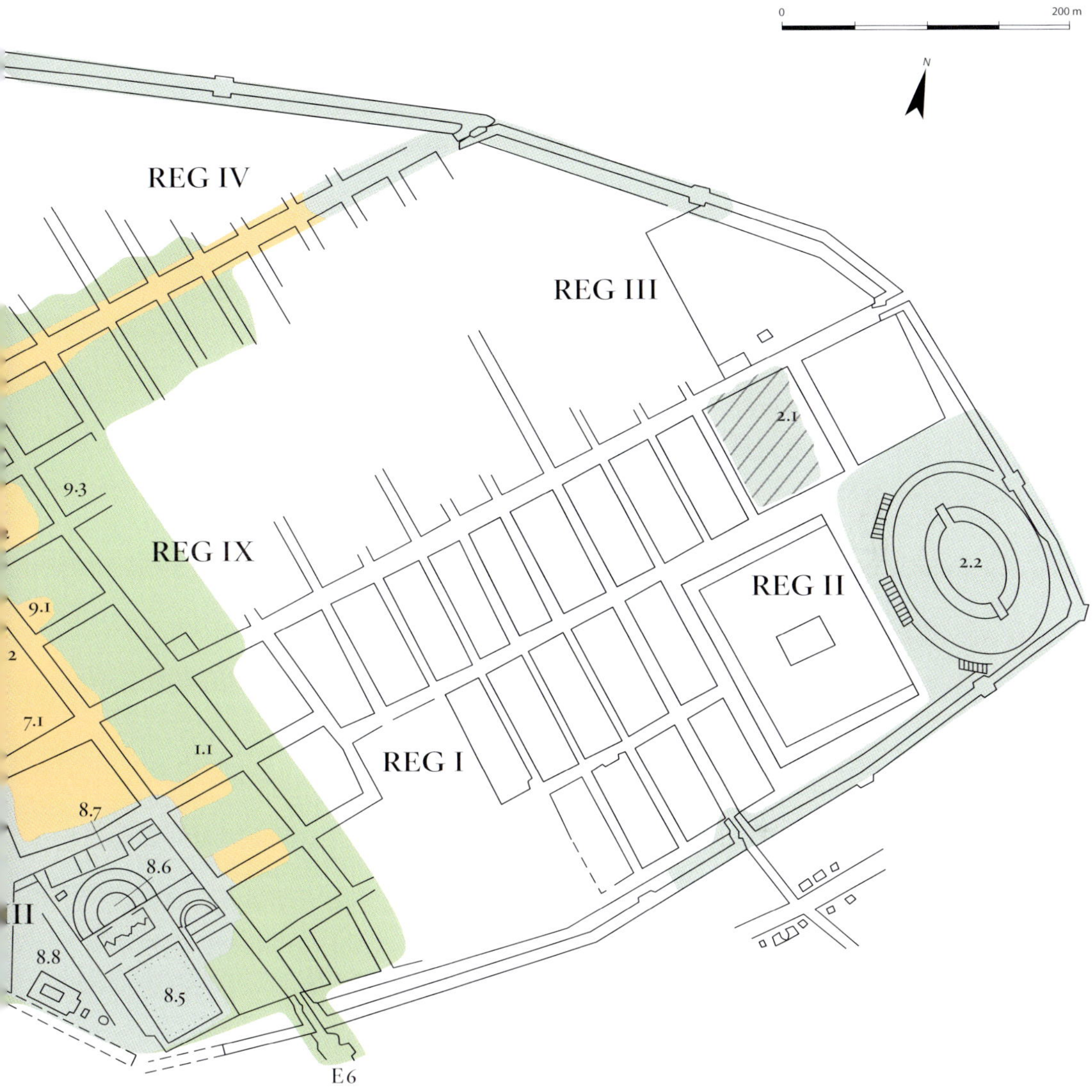

7.9 Forum Baths / Terme del Foro (VII 5, 7 and 24)
7.10 Forum (VII 8)
7.11 Capitolium (VII 8, 1)
7.12 Temple of Vespasian / Tempio di Vespasiano (VII 9, 2)
7.13 Macellum (VII 9, 8 and 19)

Regio VIII

8.1 Basilica (VIII 1, 1)
8.2 Temple of Venus Pompeiana / Tempio di Venere (VIII 1, 3)
8.3 Temple of Apollo / Tempio di Apollo (VIII 1, 32)
8.4 Terme del Sarno (VIII 2, 17–21)
8.5 Gladiators' Barracks / Caserma dei Gladiatori (VIII 7, 16)
8.6 Theatres / Teatri (VIII 7, 20)
8.7 Temple of Isis / Tempio di Iside (VIII 7, 28)
8.8 Triangular Forum / Foro triangolare (VIII 7, 30)

Regio IX

9.1 Casa del Gallo II (IX 2, 10)
9.2 House of Marcus Lucretius / Casa di Marcus Lucretius (IX 3, 5 and 24)
9.3 House of Fortuna / Casa della Fortuna (IX 7, 20)

Outside the walls

E 1 Villa of Diomedes / Villa di Diomede
E 2 Villa delle Colonne a Mosaico
E 3 Street of Tombs / Via dei Sepolcri
E 4 Villa di Cicerone
E 5 Porta Ercolano
E 6 Porta Stabiana

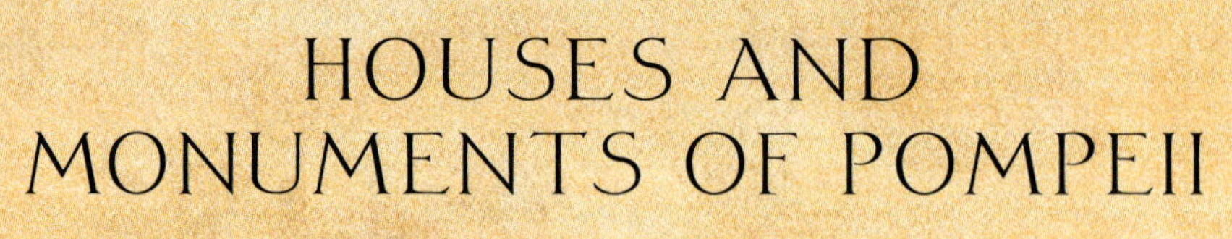

HOUSES AND MONUMENTS OF POMPEII

Le case ed i monumenti di Pompei (1854–1896)

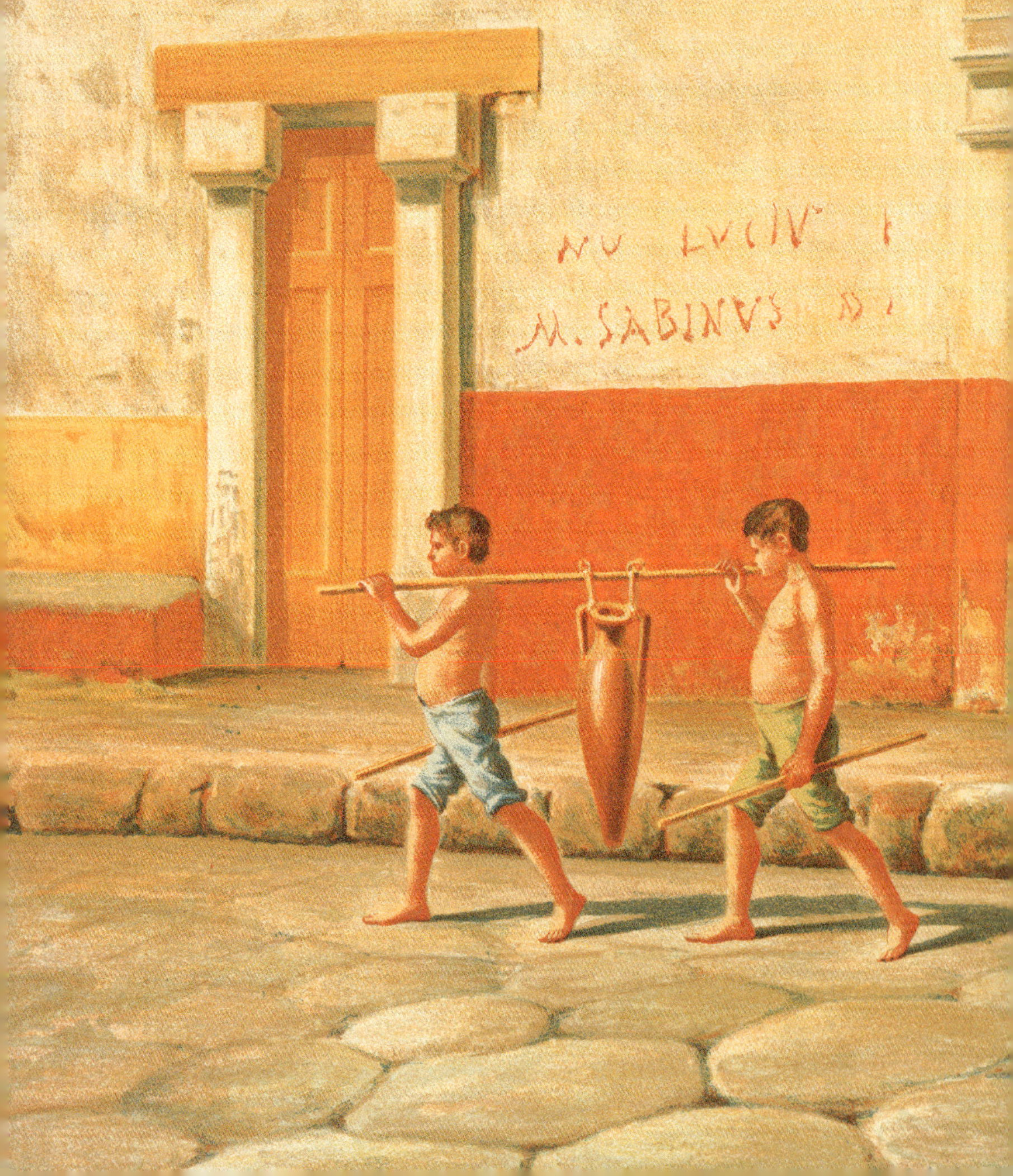

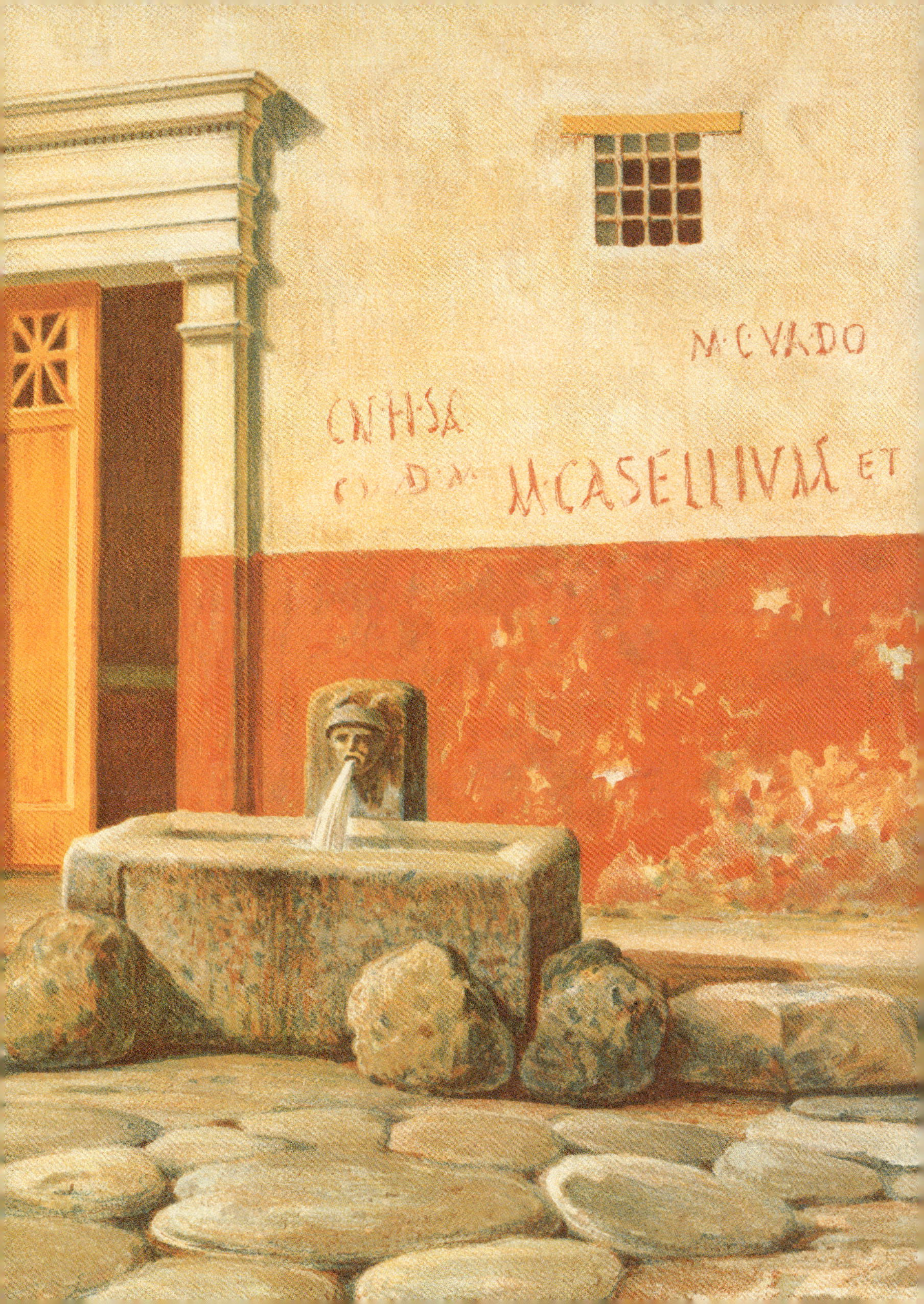
M·C·VADO
CN·H·SA
M·CASELLIVM ET

CASA DEL POETA TRAGICO

House of the Tragic Poet

(also Casa Omerica)

The first instalments of the Niccolini brothers' great work appeared in 1854/55. These included the descriptions of the Casa di Marco Lucrezio, the Casa del Fauno and other more recent excavations. The printed table of contents later specified a different order for the bookbinders: the Casa del Poeta tragico (VI 8, 3 and 5), which had been unearthed in 1824/25 and whose description was published in 1858, was now placed at the start. As this rearrangement makes clear, the Casa del Poeta tragico was the epitome of the Pompeian house and only it could form the opening to this work.

For many years the excavators had been working in and around Pompeii's Forum and as a result had only uncovered public buildings. Not until they set about linking the previously separate areas of excavation around the city gate and the Forum, by working along the Via delle Terme, did they start to encounter the well-preserved houses that make Pompeii such a unique source of information about life in antiquity. The discovery of a cache of jewellery (pl. 3) in November 1824 announced the house that greeted the archaeologists with its now famous "CAVE CANEM" (Beware of the dog) mosaic. The ground plan (pl. 1) was quickly uncovered: laid out around the atrium and peristyle, it was smaller in overall size but otherwise of a mostly standard shape, with only the largest room – a triclinium adjoining the peristyle (15) – extending beyond the otherwise rectangular outline of the complex. What was unusual, however, was the exceptionally rich decoration of the house, with wall-paintings of very high quality. In the atrium alone, visitors were surrounded by six large pictorial fields with mythological themes. They are commonly thought to show scenes from Homer's *Iliad*, although their interpretations remain speculative: the marriage of Zeus and Hera (pl. 2); Briseis being led from the tent of Achilles; the release of Chryseis; Venus and (?); Poseidon and

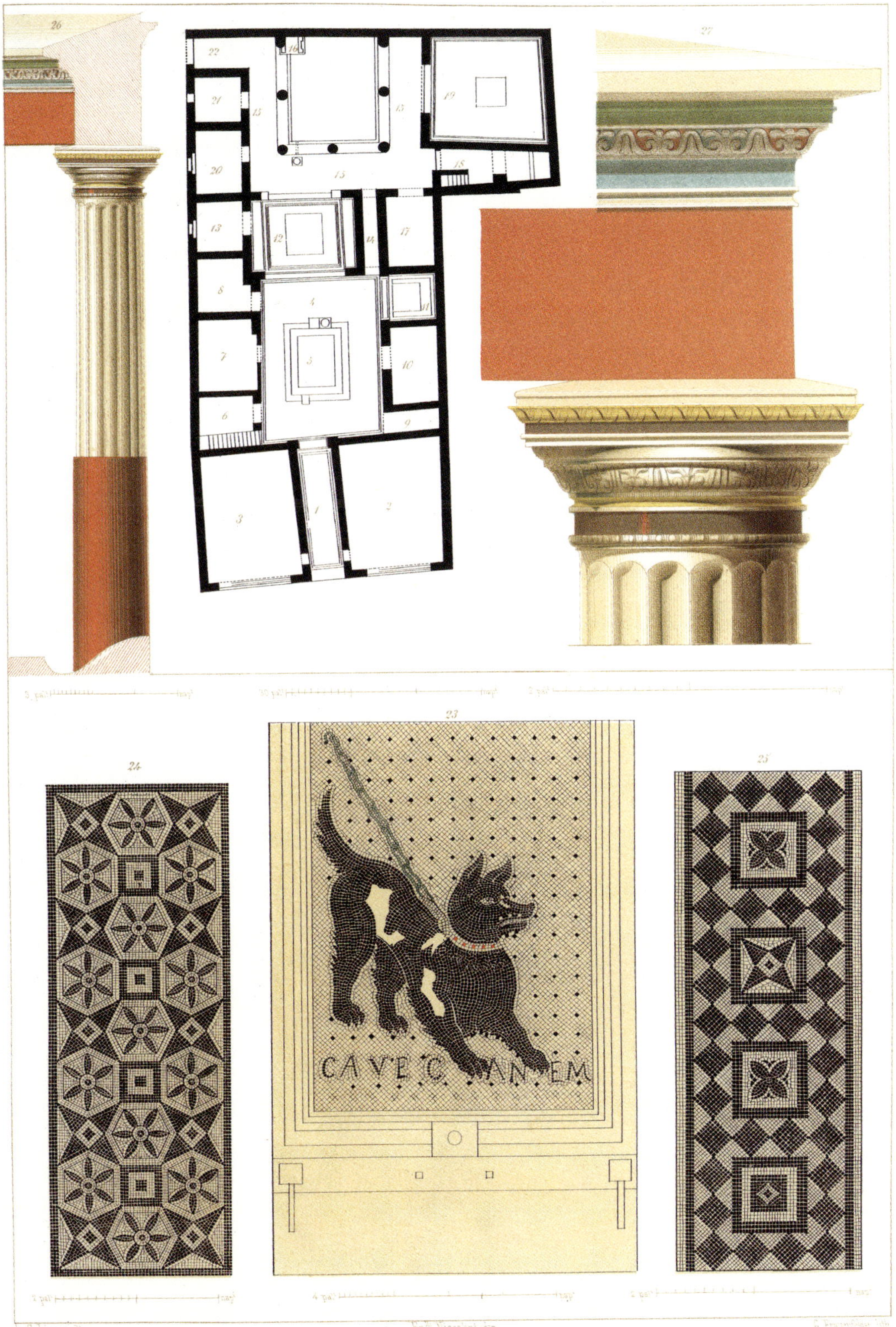

26

27

5 pal. — nap.

30 pal. — nap.

2 pal. — nap.

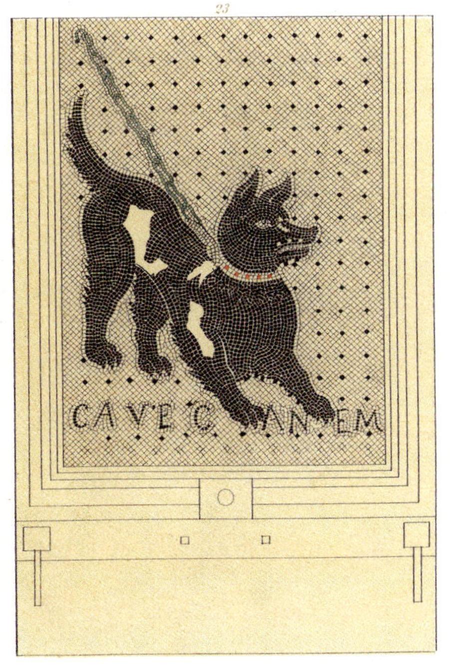

23

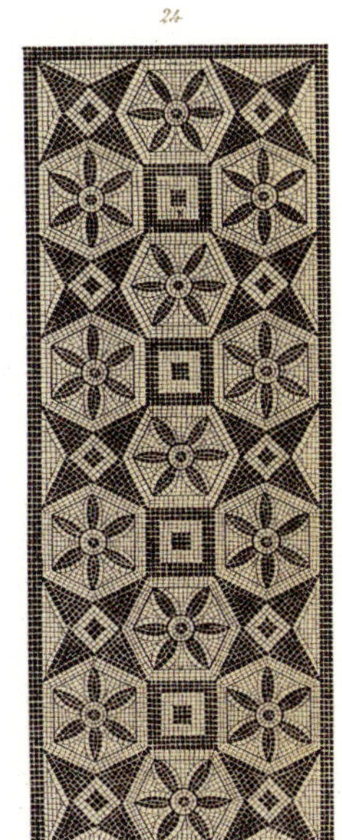

24

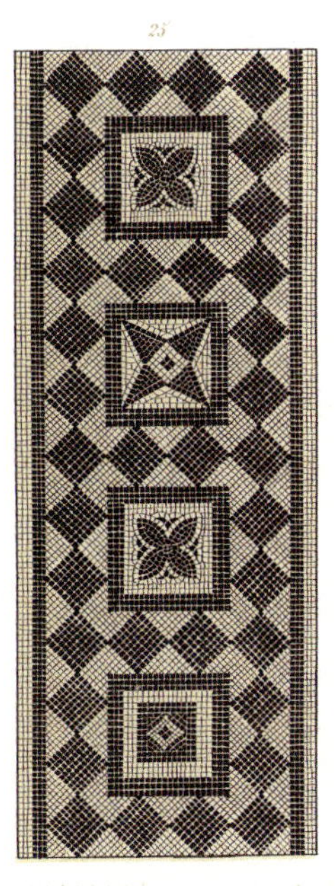

25

2 pal. — nap.

4 pal. — nap.

2 pal. — nap.

V. Schioppa dis. Fr.co Niccolini dir. G. Frauenfelder lith.

Lit. Richter e C. in Napoli

Amphitrite (?); a battle scene. The Sacrifice of Iphigenia at Aulis in the peristyle complements this Homeric theme. By way of contrast, however, the triclinium was decorated with scenes of happy and unhappy love, presented within the larger architectural framework: Theseus abandoning Ariadne; Artemis and Calisto; the buying of erotes (pl. 6). An older floor mosaic in the tablinum (12) of good quality shows a group of actors rehearsing (pl. 3) and thus underlines the level of culture and education the house's decoration was presumably intended to convey.

Soon after these wall-paintings had been uncovered, it was decided – contrary to the usual practice at the time – to leave them in situ and to reconstruct the house. For technical, methodological and conservation reasons, however, these plans came to nothing and most of the pictures were taken to Naples. In 1828 a hand-coloured monograph on the Casa del Poeta tragico was produced by French scholar Désiré Raoul-Rochette and architect Jules Bouchet. The house was discussed in detail by William Gell in the 1832 edition of his *Pompeiana* and was accompanied by a reconstruction drawing of the atrium. But it was Edward George Bulwer-Lytton's novel *The Last Days of Pompeii*, published in 1834, that carried the fame of the House of the Tragic Poet beyond the smaller circle of scholars and artists. The book's fictional hero, the Greek – and later Christian – Glaukos, lives in this house, described in detail by the author and whose sophisticated and superior-quality decoration seemed appropriate in view of Glaukos' Greek background. Today, visitors to Pompeii barely notice the house, which is mostly closed. Only the dog mosaic may easily be seen. For archaeology, however, the house's decoration remains an important touchstone when it comes to the methodology of interpreting pictorial subjects and in particular the question of whether a common concept underlies their selection. An attempt in the 1990s to reconstruct the house in England as a full-scale walk-through replica failed due to costs.

Pages 74–75
Scene in the Via di Mercurio (detail) – With a fountain and the Casa della Fontana piccola (Vol. IV, pl. 2). With regard to the actual situation, a number of details have been modified.

Page 77
Plate 1 — *[I. Schioppa]*
1–22 Ground plan of the house. *23* Black and white mosaic with a representation of a guard dog inside the entrance door (CAVE CANEM). *24–25* Details of the black and white floor mosaics at the threshold of the atrium (1) and in the right-hand ala (11). *26–27* Details of the architecture in the small peristyle garden.

Plate 2 — *[G. Abbate]*
Atrium, south wall – Marriage of Zeus and Hera (?).

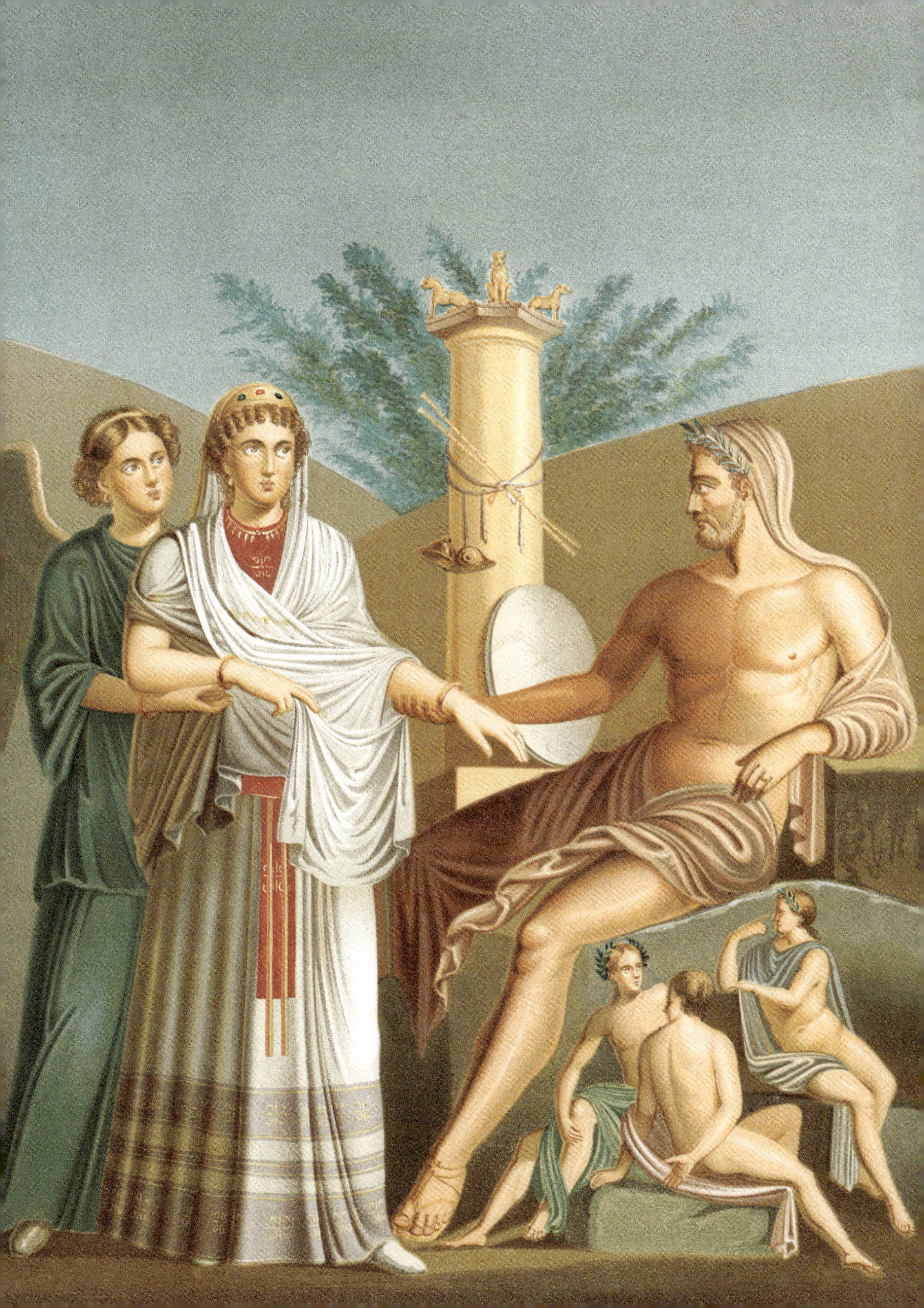

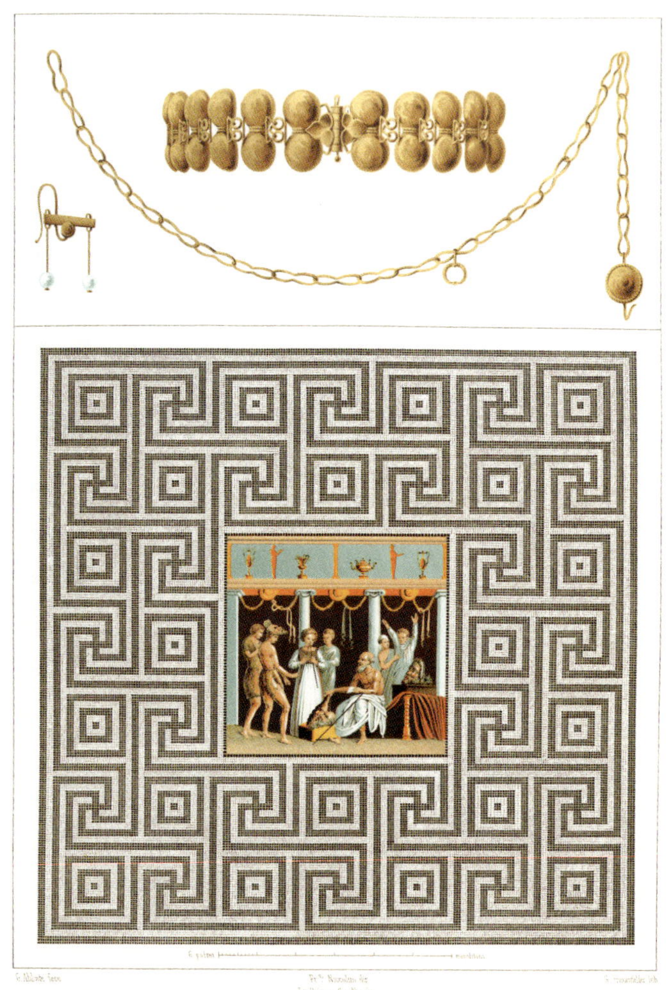

Plate 3 — *[G. Abbate]*
Gold jewellery – Bracelet, necklace, earring. ***Mosaic floor from the tablinum (12)*** – A double meander border (still in situ) surrounds the representation of a troupe of actors rehearsing a play about satyrs. The house is named after this mosaic.

❖

Plate 6 — *[G. Abbate]*
Back (north) wall of the triclinium (19) – In the central scene, two lovers are considering the purchase of some small erotes.

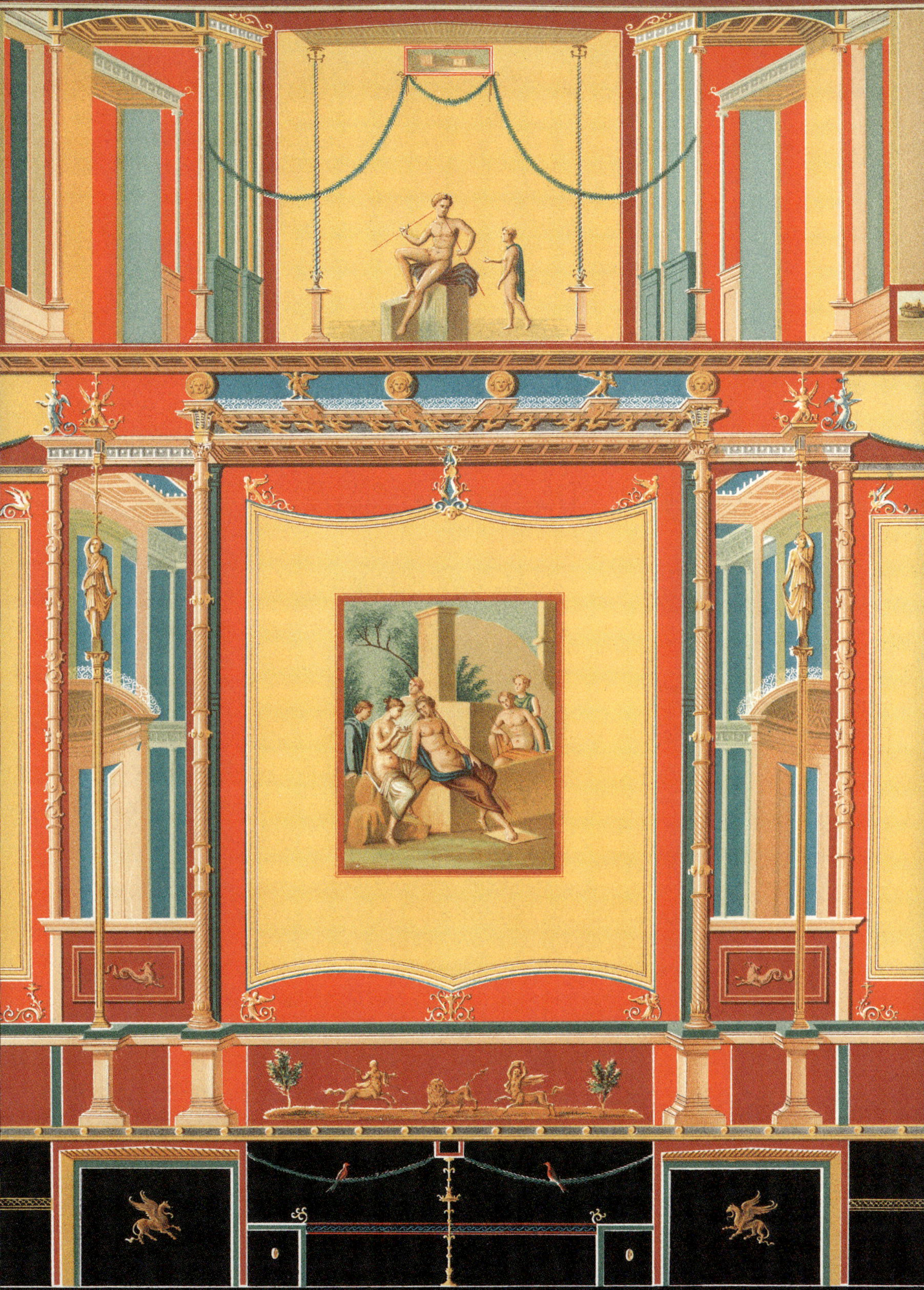

CASA DEI DIOSCURI

House of the Dioscuri

(also Casa di Castore e Polluce)

The property initially referred to as the Casa del Questore, but which soon became known as the Casa dei Dioscuri or Casa di Castore e Polluce (VI 9, 6–7), lay at one end of the Via della Fortuna and was excavated at great speed in 1828/29. Consisting of three substantial atrium houses that were made into one in the 1st century BC, it is one of late Pompeii's most splendid residences. It is unusual because of its wide variety of rooms, different atria and peristyles as well as very large dining rooms. The relatively small number of finds – worth mentioning are two gold chests *(arcae)* in the vicinity of the Corinthian atrium, which still contained gold coins – and the absence of the marble cladding which had originally been a feature of the grandest room in the house (48) indicated to the excavators that valuable materials had been salvaged from the house soon after it had been buried. By contrast, the painted decoration, which had been completely redone shortly after the earthquake of AD 62, was still in excellent condition. Many important pictures were cut out and taken to the museum, whilst roofs were set up over the murals left in situ to protect them from the weather and from visitors.

The House of the Dioscuri owes its name (never much liked by the Niccolini brothers) to two wall-paintings in the entrance area, which show the divine twins Castor and Pollux with their horses. Several of today's most famous mythological paintings from this house were concentrated – like in a picture gallery – in and around the Corinthian atrium (7) and the peristyle to the south (44). There were two scenes from the life of Achilles facing each other on either side of the tablinum (26): the discovery of Achilles amongst the daughters of Lycomedes after Odysseus had exposed him by trickery (pl. 4 and pl. 6) and Achilles' anger at Agamemnon (largely destroyed; not illustrated). Plate 3 shows the death of Niobe's children in a most unusual composition.

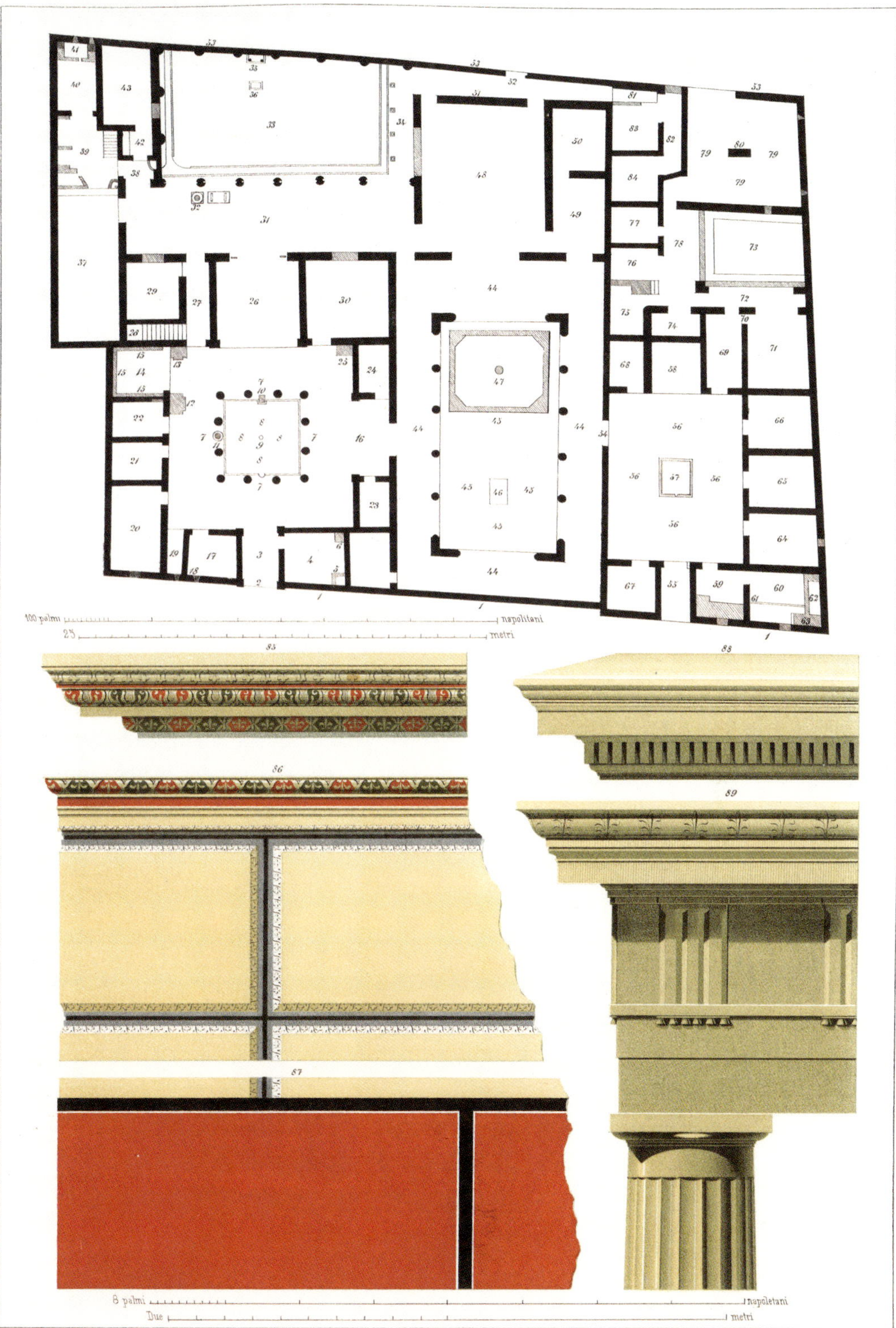

G. Abbate fece. Fr.lli Niccolini dir. Lit. Richter e C. in Napoli. G. Frauenfelder lit.

It was long ago recognised that both the style of the mythological paintings and the design and details of the wall decorations so closely resembled those of the Casa dei Vettii (see vol. IV) and the Macellum (vol. I) that we may assume the same team of artists worked in all three buildings. The owner of the House of the Dioscuri, and hence their employer, may have been one Cn. Alleius Nigidius Maius, one of the most influential men in Pompeii during the reigns of Nero and Vespasian. The decoration of the Macellum was commissioned by his daughter Maia, which would explain why the same workshop was active in both locations. To what extent the pictures in the House of the Dioscuri make reference by way of their subject matter to the person of the owner remains, however, a matter of debate.

The discovery of the Casa dei Dioscuri had far-reaching consequences. King Ludwig I of Bavaria chose it as the model for his idealised Pompeian villa, the Pompeianum, in Aschaffenburg. At the king's command, in April 1839 architect Friedrich von Gärtner developed his ideas for the project based on a plan of the northern group of rooms. The ground plan was made more regular and the upper storey – known to have existed formerly but now entirely destroyed – was replaced by his own design. In 1846 Carlo Ruspi also made copies for Ludwig of individual pictures in the museum at Naples, some of which were used in Aschaffenburg, most notably the Dioscuri and the large paintings from the tablinum, but also many smaller decorative details. Completed in 1850, the Pompeianum was the first replica of a Pompeian house constructed north of the Alps and the only one still surviving today. After comprehensive restoration to repair the heavy damage it suffered in the Second World War, the building is once again open to the public.

Page 83

Plate 1 — *[G. Abbate]*

1–84 Ground plan of the two combined houses. *85–86* Coloured stucco decorating the façade. *88* Entablature of the Corinthian order in the peristyle (7). *89* Doric order in the garden peristyle (33).

❖

Plate 4 — *[G. Abbate]*

Tablinum, central picture on the south side – Discovery of Achilles amongst the daughters of Lycomedes. Part of an outstanding decoration in the 4th style.

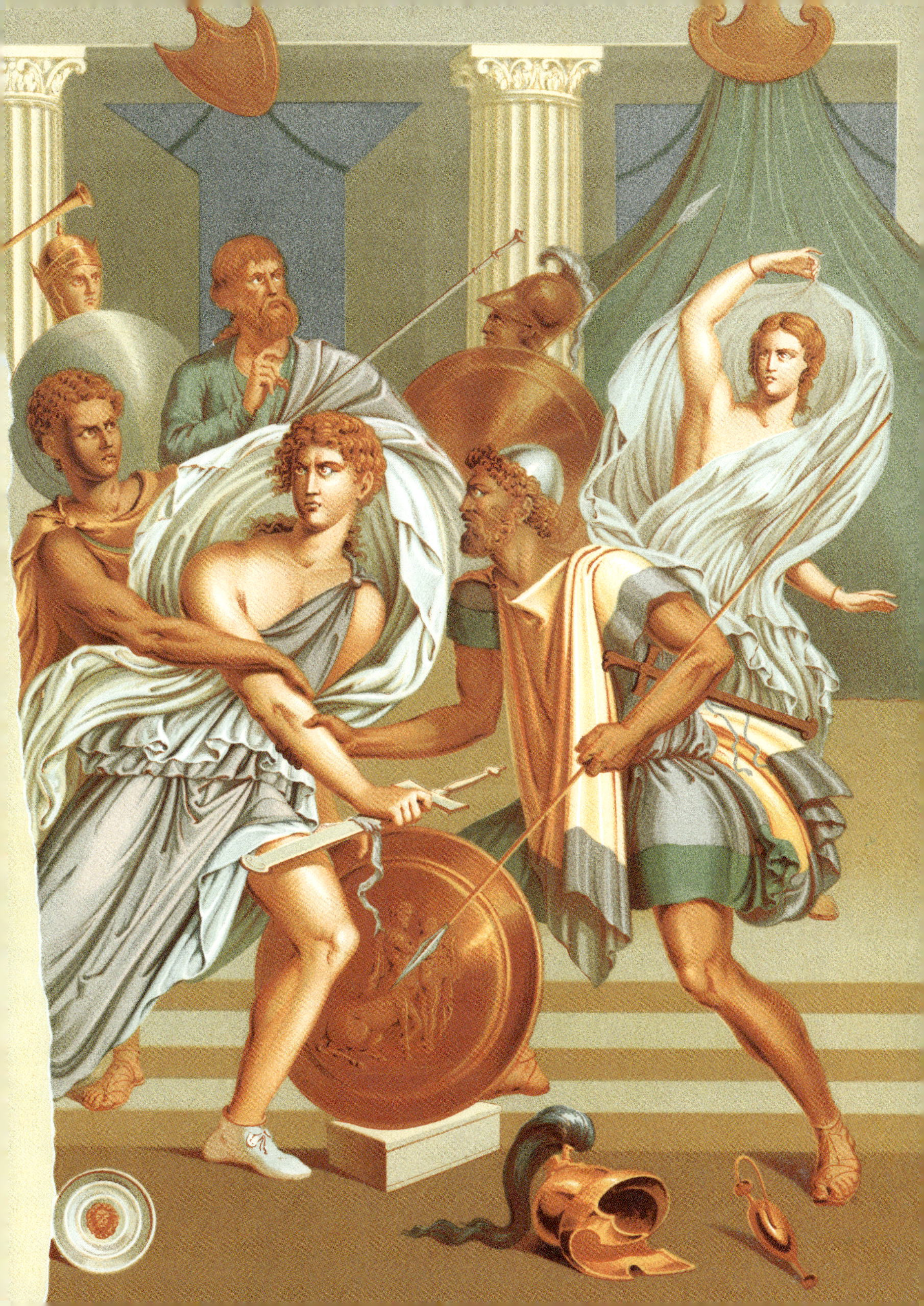

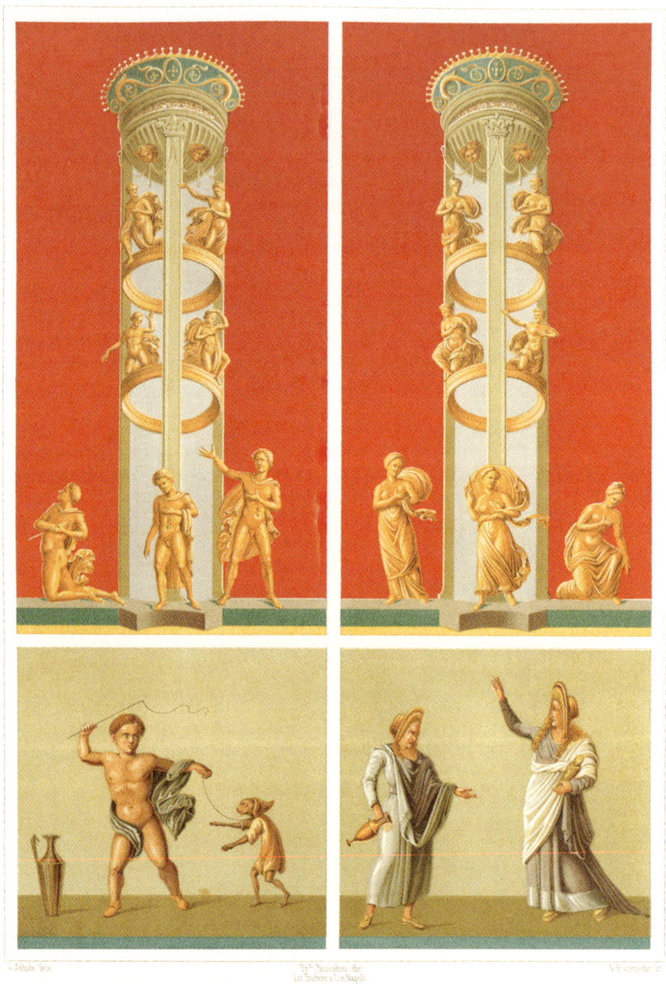

Plate 3 — *[G. Abbate]*
West pilasters of the peristyle (45) – Two tall tripod structures, with Niobe's children enclosed by their feet; Apollo and Artemis kill them with arrows. *Peristyle (45)* – Dwarf playing with monkey. *Viridarium (45)* – Two actors with tragic masks.

Plate 10 — *[G. Abbate]*
Cubiculum (17) – Wall decoration.

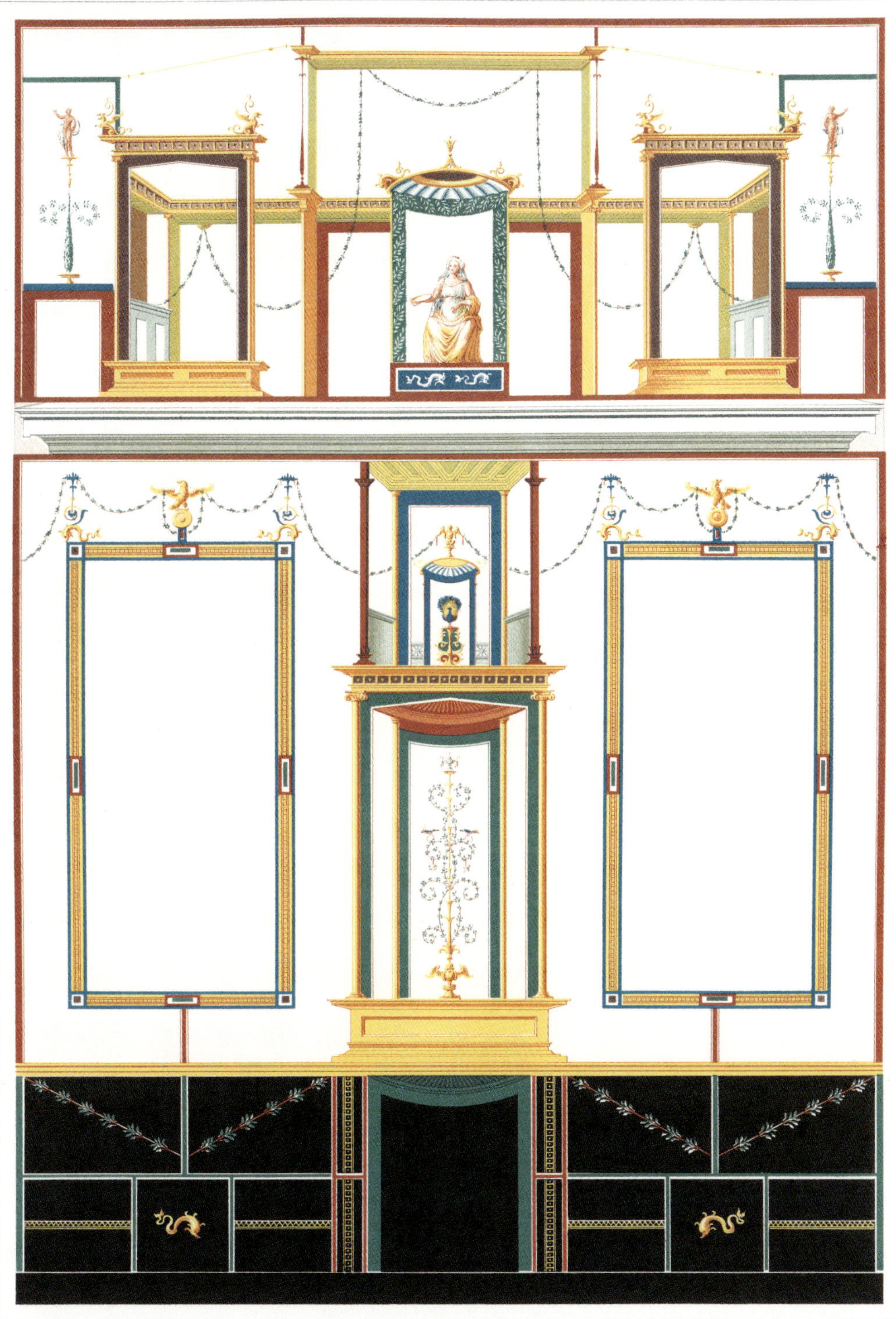

G. Abbate fec. Frat[lli] Niccolini dir. G. Frauenfelder lit.

Lit. Richter e C. in Napoli.

6 palmi 1 2 3 4 5 6 Napoletani

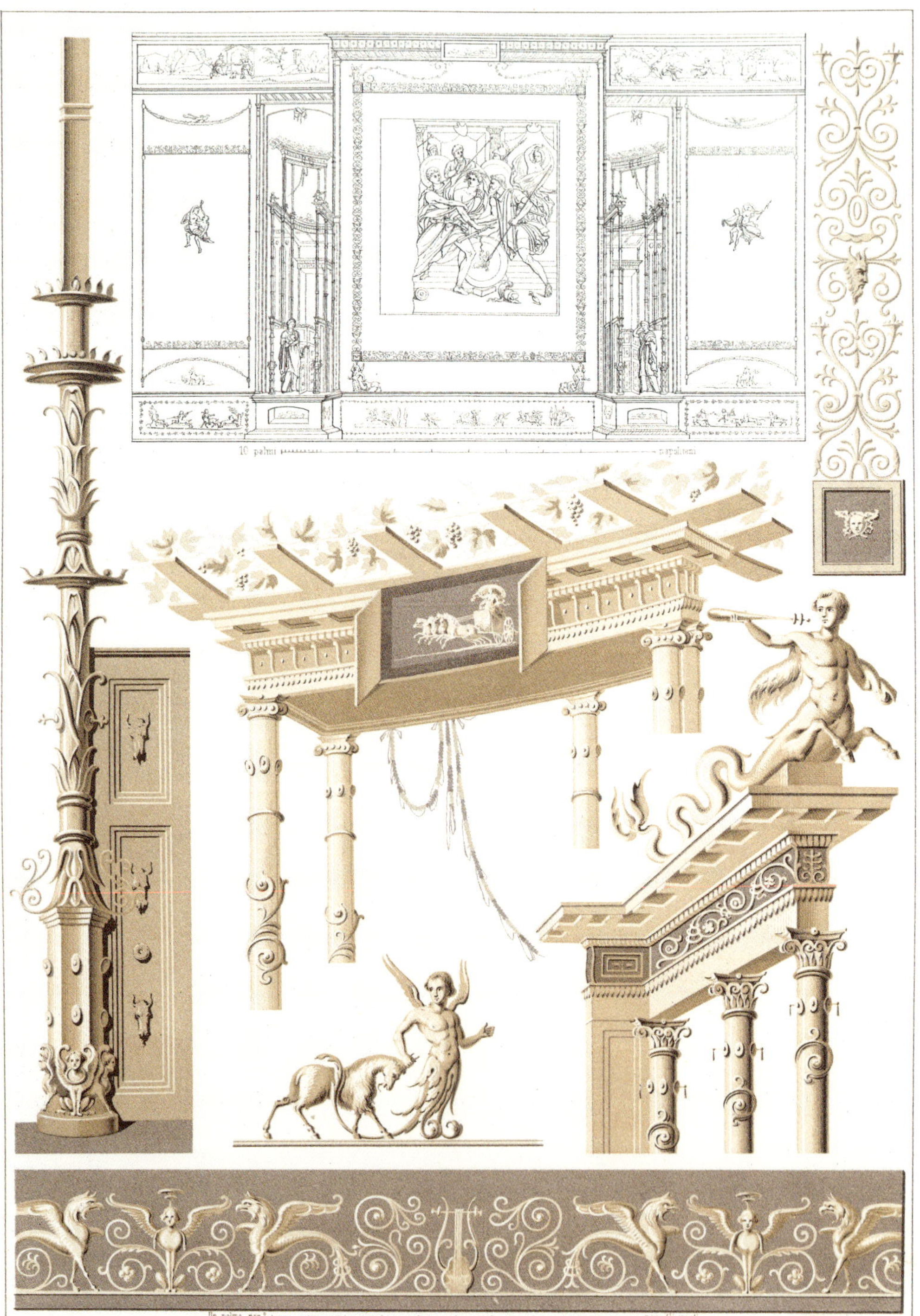

G. Abbate fece — Fr.^co Niccolini dir. Lit. Richter e C. in Napoli — G. Frauenfelder lit.

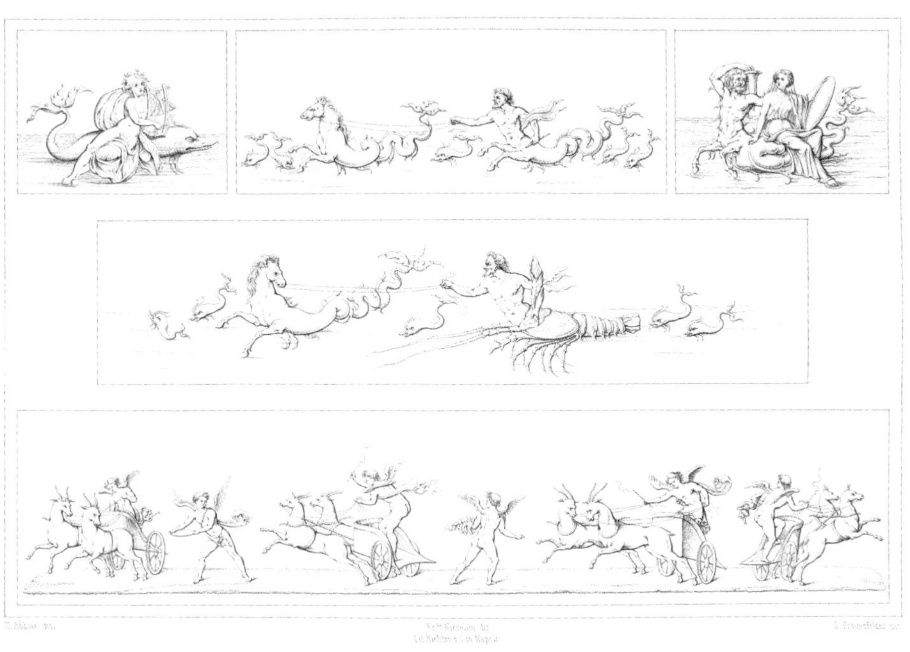

Plate 6 — *[G. Abbate]*
Tablinum (26) – South wall in full, and details. Today largely destroyed.

Plate 7 — *[G. Abbate]*
Oecus (30), north wall – Arion, playing the cithara, is borne across the sea by a dolphin. ***Oecus (30), predella*** of the ***south wall*** – Sea centaur reining back a sea horse, accompanied by dolphins. ***Oecus (30), predella of the south wall*** – Sea centaur bearing Thetis with Achilles' armour across the sea; lobster with the upper body of a man reining back a sea horse, accompanied by dolphins. ***Tablinum (26), predella of the south wall*** – Erotes on chariots *(bigae)* drawn by goats.

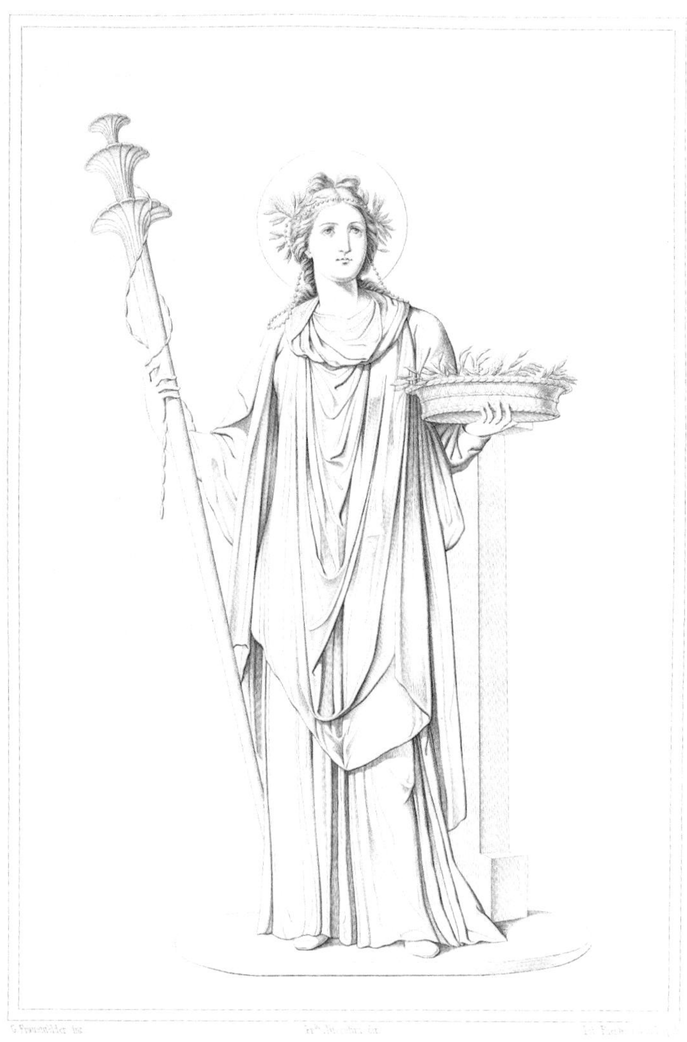

Plate 5 — *[Anonymous]*
Atrium (9) – Ceres with torch and fruit basket.

✤

Plate 11 — *[G. Gigante]*
View from the ala (16) of the atrium into the large peristyle (45) looking south-east (1857) – The female visitor seems to be more interested in the young man standing in the doorway than in her companion's commentary.

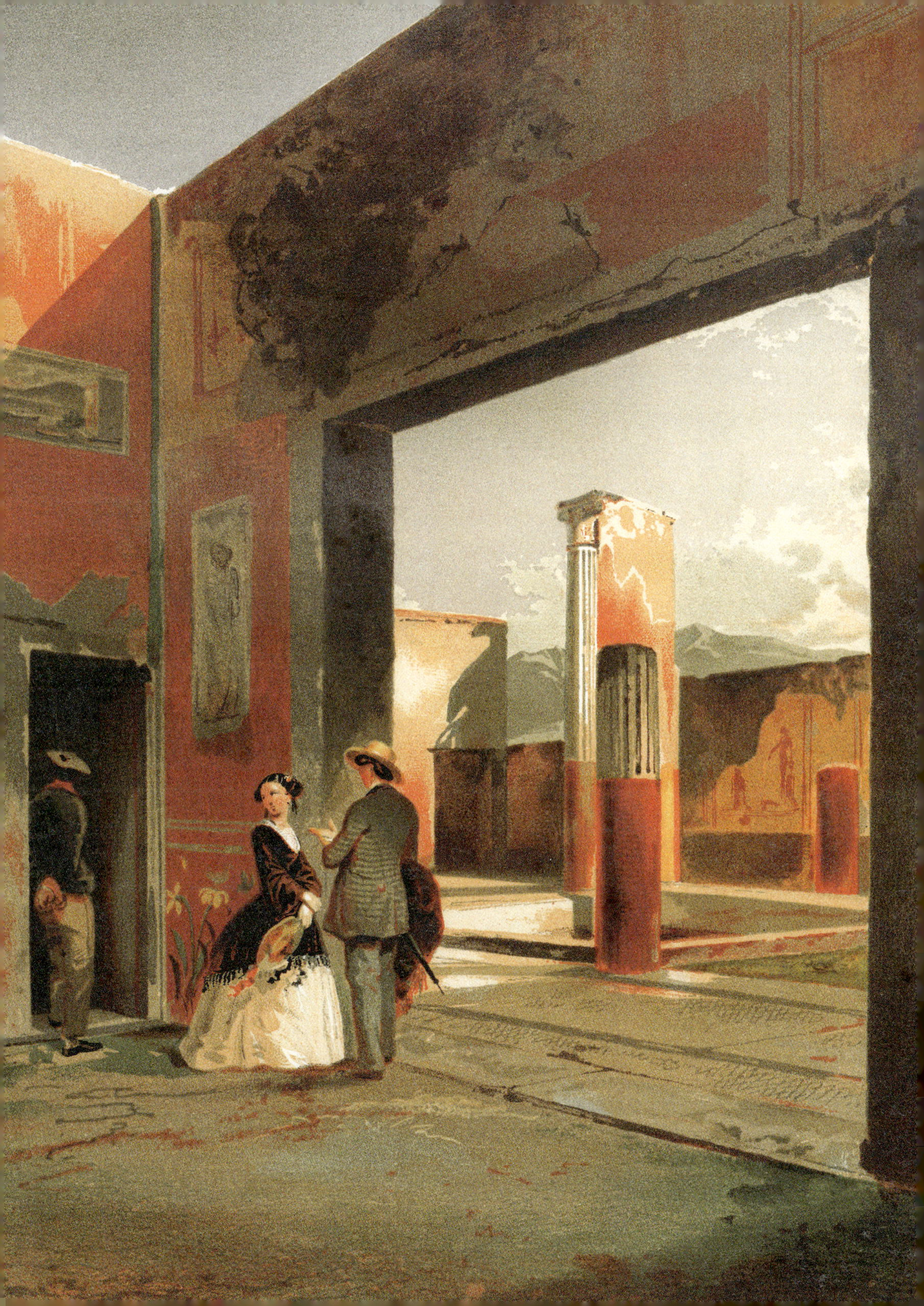

CASA DELLA FONTANA PICCOLA

House of the Small Fountain

(also Casa della seconda Fontana)

In the 1820s, excavations followed the Via di Mercurio to the north. Arriving at the first intersection at the start of 1827, workers came across this relatively modest house. The house takes its name from the fountain that was uncovered in June, in the presence of Francis I, the king of Naples, and the royal family. Since the house adjoining to the south was known as the Casa della Fontana (grande), this one became known as the Casa della seconda Fontana, later Fontana piccola (VI 8, 23–24). The House of the Small Fountain consists of two older houses which had been converted into a single property in the Augustan period and enlarged with the creation of rooms in an upper storey. The mosaic in plate 1 (no. 36) is a remnant of this earlier phase of decoration, as perhaps too are the bronze lamp-stands (pl. 6) from the same era. After the earthquake of AD 62 the house was redecorated. The mosaic fountain in the peristyle may also date from the period before the earthquake. Its asymmetrical siting was calculated so that it could be seen all the way from the entrance, lending it additional prominence as an impressive feature. The rear wall of the peristyle is decorated with large landscape scenes between painted half-columns (pl. 4). The statuettes in front of the fountain in plate 3 are older than the fountain itself, and their different materials and varying quality suggest that they have been randomly arranged. It is also conceivable that they were brought together by the excavators in order to impress the royal visitors (see also vol. III, I Mestieri, pl. 3). Since the walls here featured no spectacular examples of individual pictures nothing was cut out, and instead the house was largely roofed over, so that the condition of the walls today is still astonishingly good.

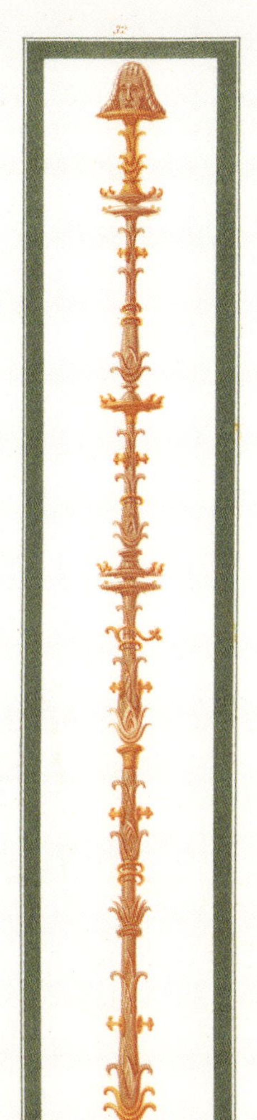

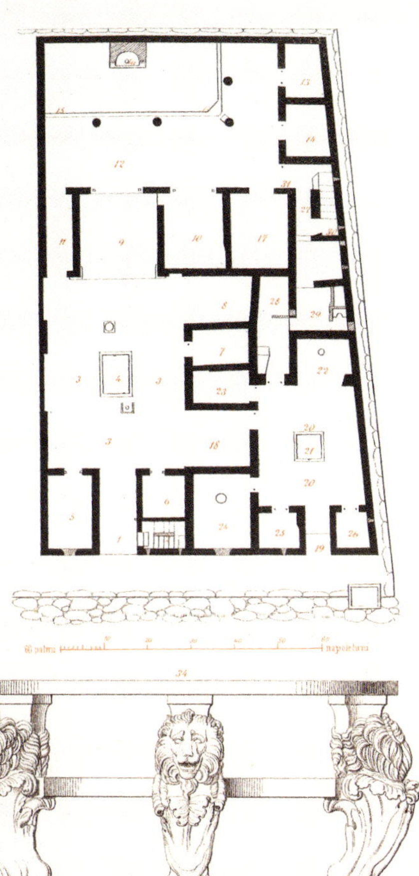

35

M HOLCONIVM
PRISCVM·II VIR·I·D· POMARI·VNIVERSI
CVM·H·FLVIO·VESTALE·ROG

36

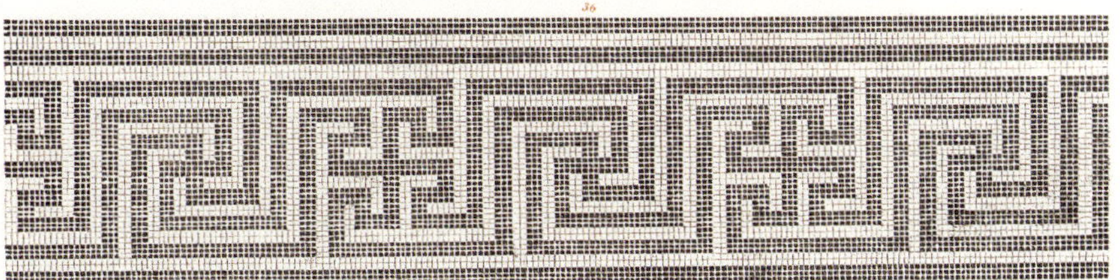

G. Abbate fec. — Fr.co Niccolini dir — Lit. Richter in Napoli — G. Frauenfelder es

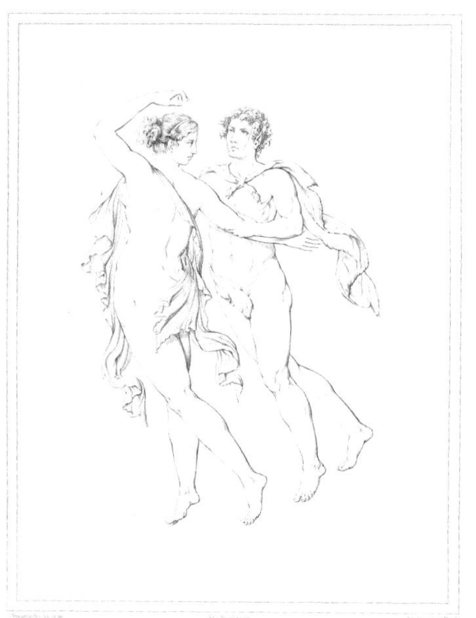

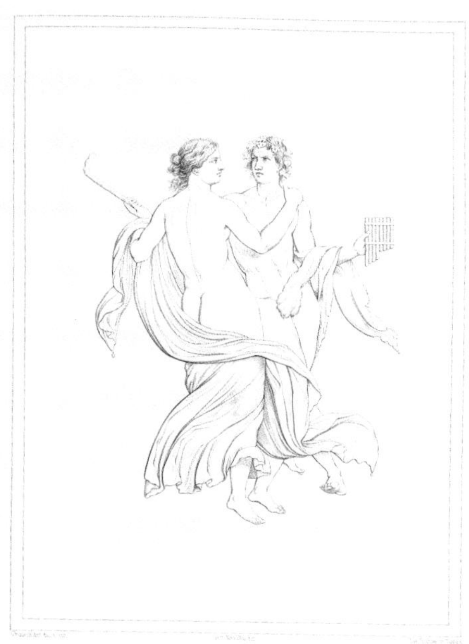

Page 93

Plate 1 — *[G. Abbate]*

1–31 Ground plan of the house. *1* Entrance. *3* Main atrium. *16* Mosaic fountain in the garden. *20* Lesser atrium. *32–33* Painted candelabra from the wall divisions in the lesser atrium (20) and room (25). *34* Table with three legs in the form of lions supposedly from room (13) or (14). *35* Election address for M. Holconius Priscus from the front façade. *36* Tablinum (9): section of the meander border from the floor mosaic.

Plate 2, 5 — *[G. Trauenfelder]*

Atrium (3), south wall – Floating satyr and maenad couple.

Plate 3 — *[G. Trauenfelder]*

Fountain in the garden (16) – Mosaic façade and water-spouting bronze and marble figures.

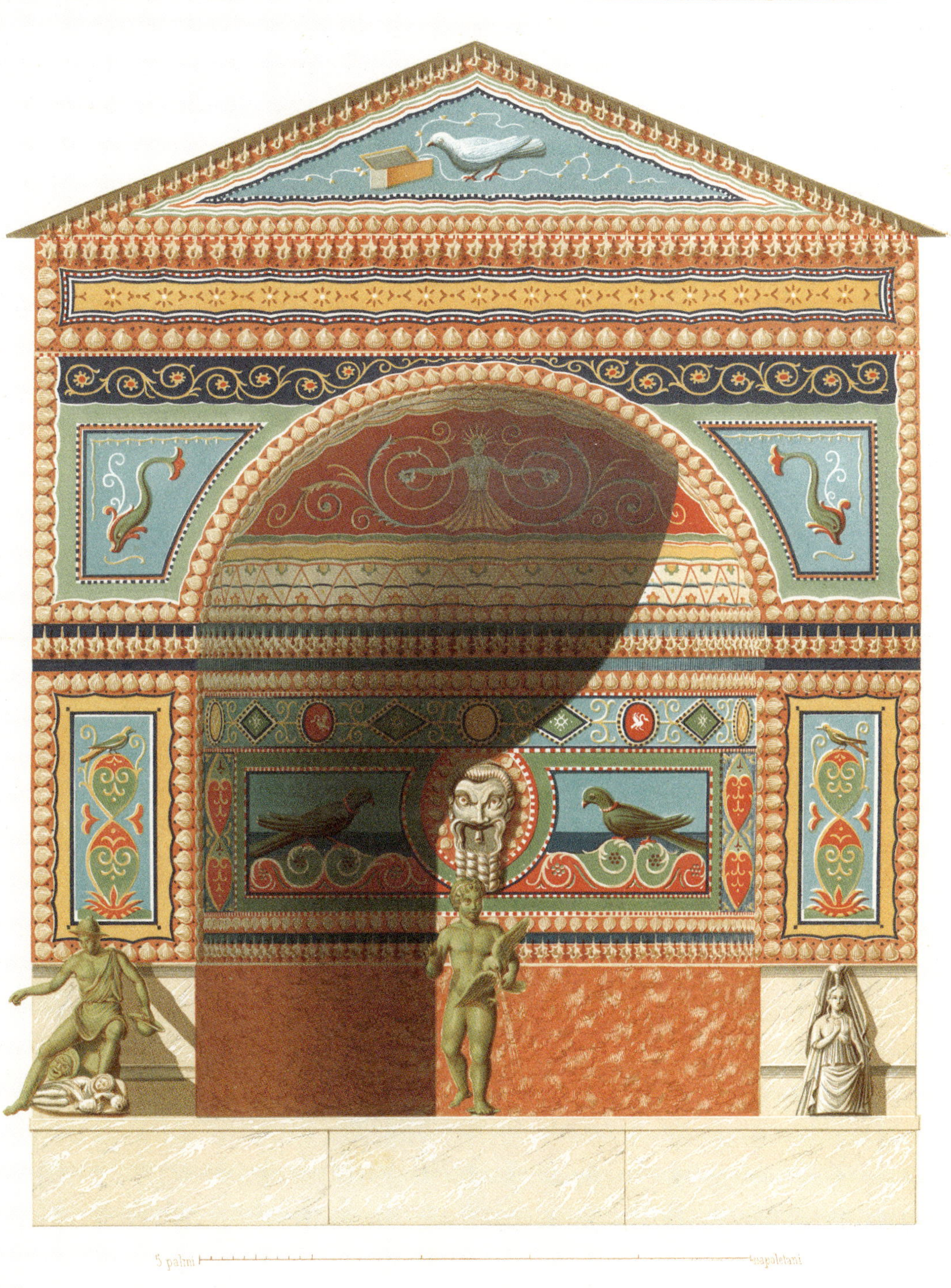

C. Abbate fec. Fr.lli Niccolini dir. G. Frauenfelder es.

Lit. Richter in Napoli

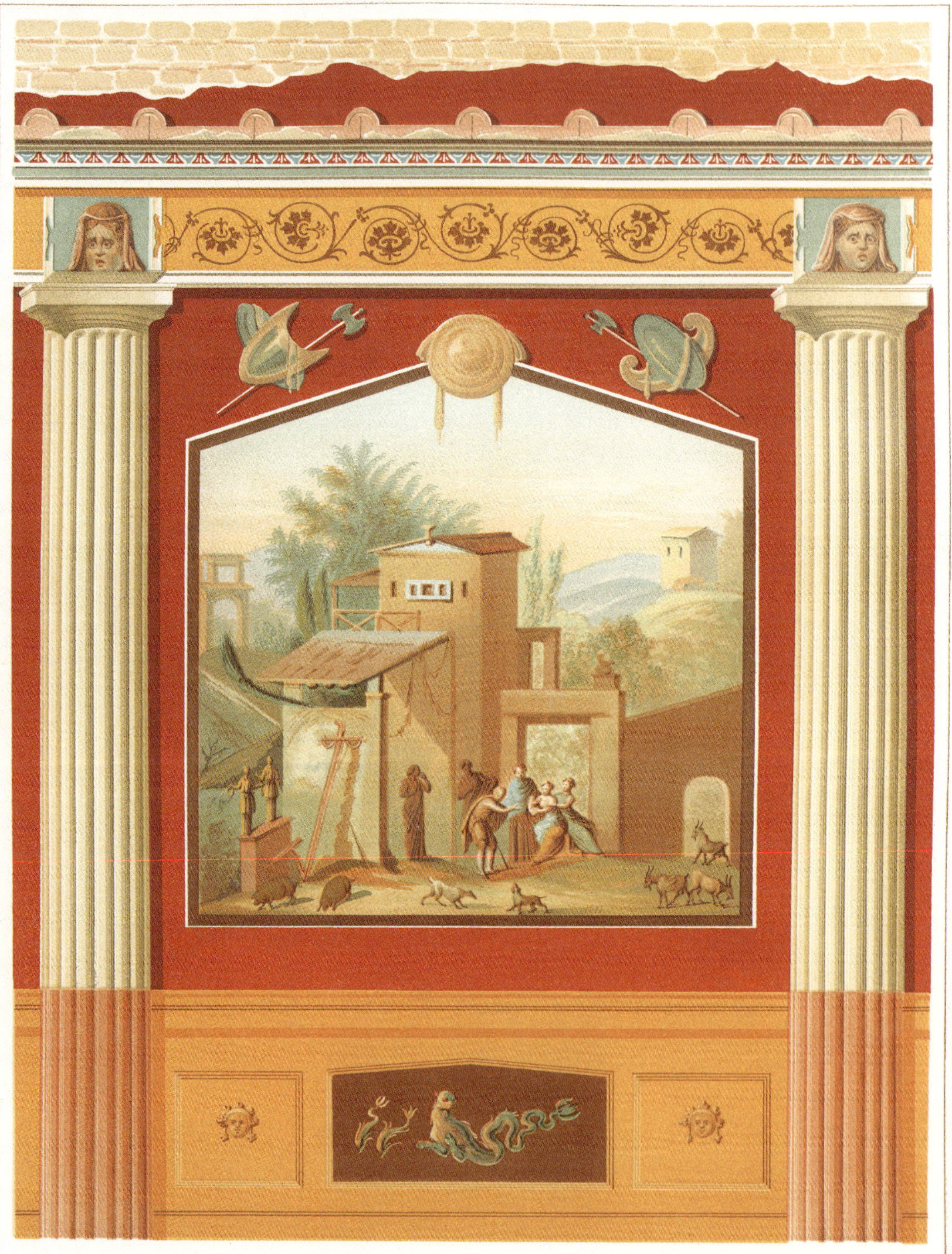

G. Abbate fece · Fr.sco Niccolini dir · Lit. Richter in Napoli · E. Frauenfelder ec.

8 palmi napoletani

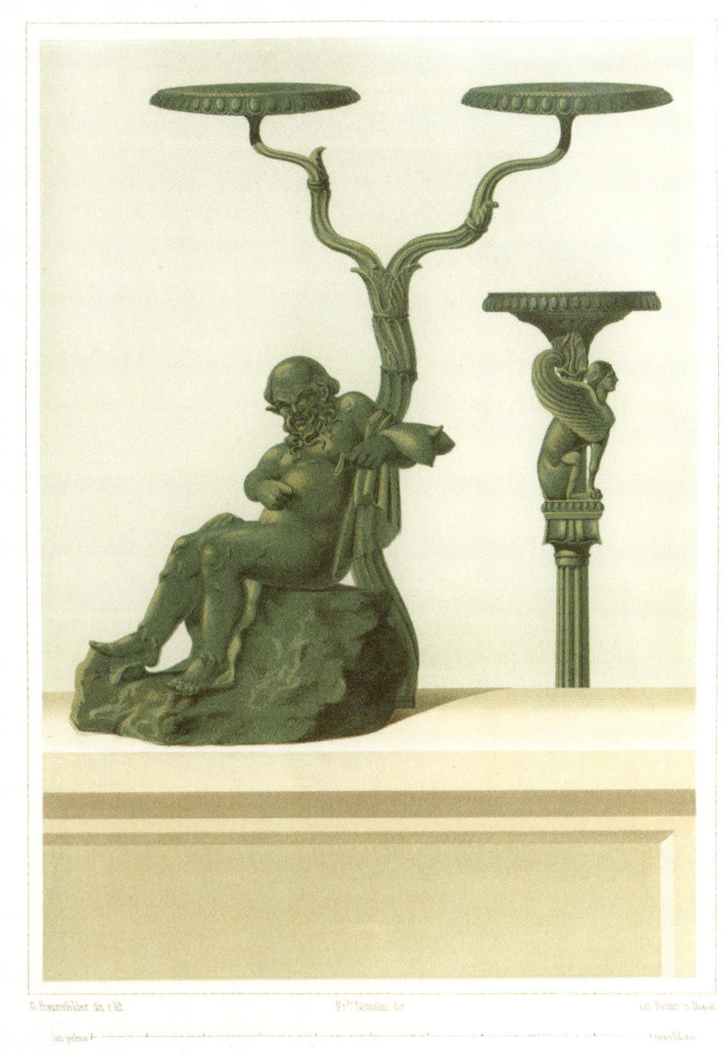

Plate 4 — *[G. Abbate]*
Garden – Right-hand section of the west wall with landscape scene.

Plate 6 — *[G. Frauenfelder]*
Two bronze lamp-stands from the upper storey of the atrium (3) – A seated silenus leaning against a vegetal lamp-stand and pouring wine from a skin into a vessel (now missing). ***From the ala (3)*** – Sphinx seated on the capital of a column.

TEMPIO DELLA FORTUNA

Temple of Fortuna Augusta

In the winter of 1823/24 workers uncovered a small temple (VII 4, 1) on a major intersection north of the Forum. The temple interior *(cella)* of the west-facing building was entered from the street via steps leading up to a central platform, where the altar stood – a solution similar to the arrangement employed in the Capitolium on the Forum. On this platform, iron railings with two gates separated the area used for worship from the general public area. The temple itself consisted of a long rectangular *cella* and a deep portico fronted by four columns. Inside there were two niches for statues on either side, and, in a small apse, a plinth with columns at each corner for the statue of the goddess Fortuna (pl. 1). A series of inscriptions informs us that the temple was erected to Fortuna Augusta, the personification of the Emperor Augustus' good fortune, by one M. Tullius on his own land and at his own expense. Tullius was one of the most prominent figures in Augustan Pompeii, and with this temple he probably laid the foundation stone for the first imperial cult in the city. The rooms adjoining the temple on the south side accommodated the people responsible for maintaining the cult. In its architecture, the building corresponds to temples in Rome from the same time, and with its exceptionally lavish décor it must have created a striking impression: not only were the columns and their very high-quality Corinthian capitals made of marble, still rare in Pompeii at this date, but the whole building was entirely faced in marble – even using coloured variants inside. Columns, sections of cladding and the statue of Fortuna had already been looted when the excavators arrived, but digging none the less uncovered two well-preserved statues, as well as the fragments of at least one more. The two figures, one female and one male, are illustrated in plate 2 with the colour decoration at that time still visible, but today lost.

Plate 1 — *[I. Schioppa]*
1–14 Ground plan of the temple. *15–24* Capitals and other architectural details.
25 Inscription by the donor, M. Tullius Marci Filius.

Pages 100–101
Plate 2 — *[G. Abbate]*
Two marble statues of local dignitaries found in the temple – When they were uncovered, they still carried clear traces of painted decoration.

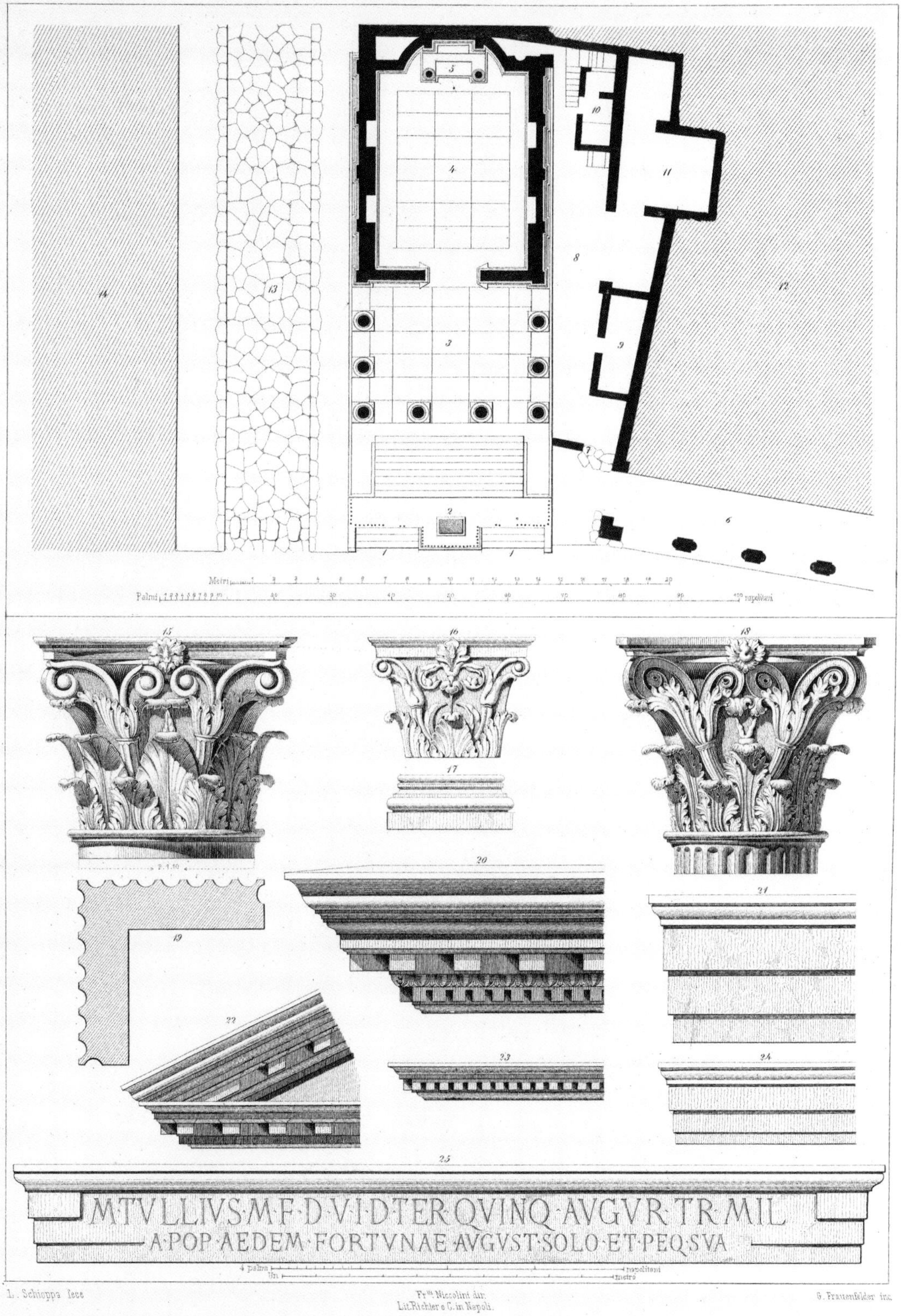

Metri 1 2 3 4 5 6 7 8 9 10 11 12 13 14 15 16 17 18 19 20

Palmi 1 2 3 4 5 6 7 8 9 10 20 30 40 50 60 70 80 90 100 napolitani

M·TVLLIVS·M·F·D·V·I·D·TER·QVINQ·AVGVR·TR·MIL
A·POP·AEDEM·FORTVNAE·AVGVST·SOLO·ET·PEQ·SVA

4 palmi napolitani
Un metro

L. Schioppa fece

Fr.lli Niccolini dir.
Lit. Richter e C. in Napoli.

G. Frauenfelder inc.

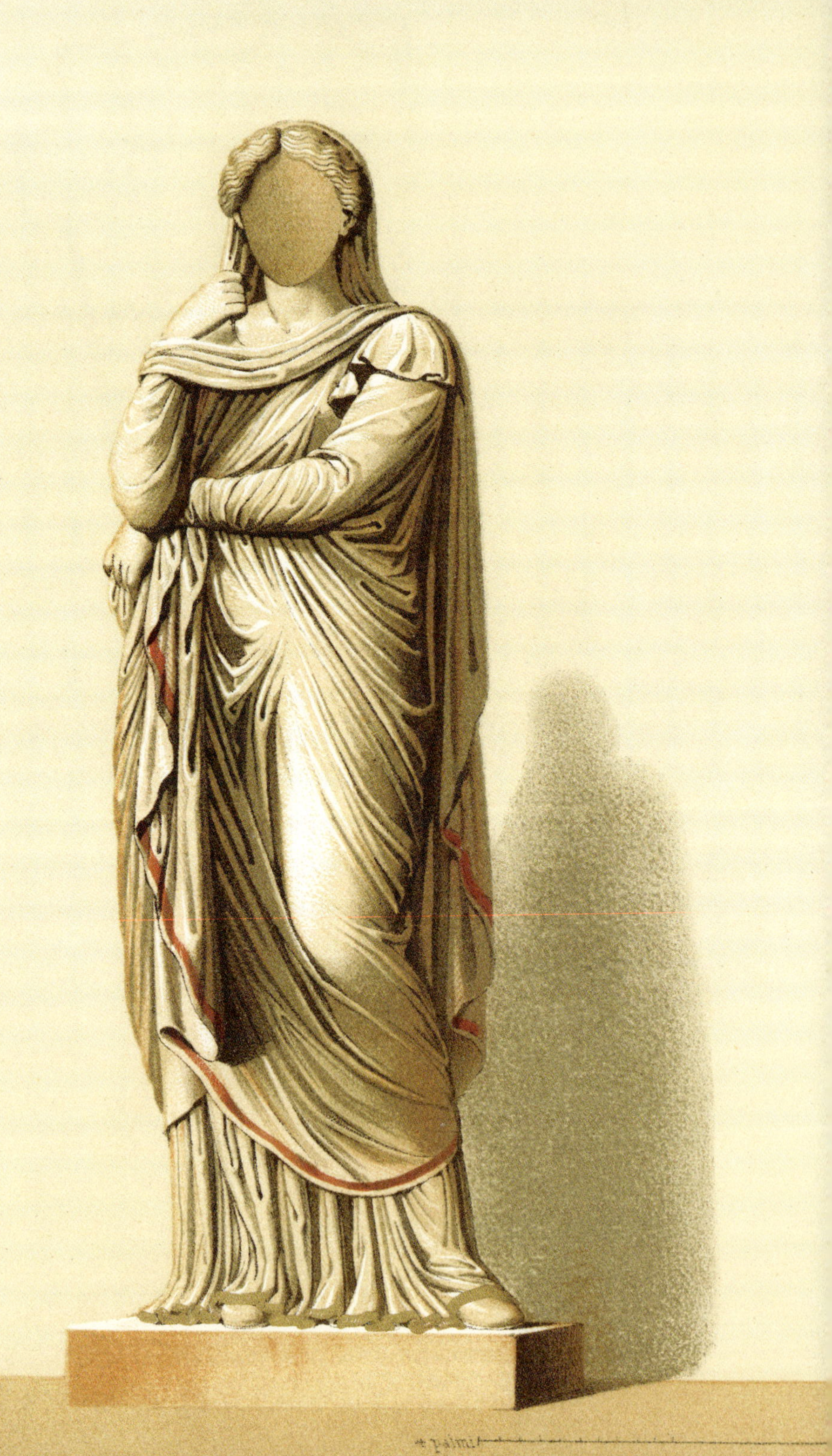

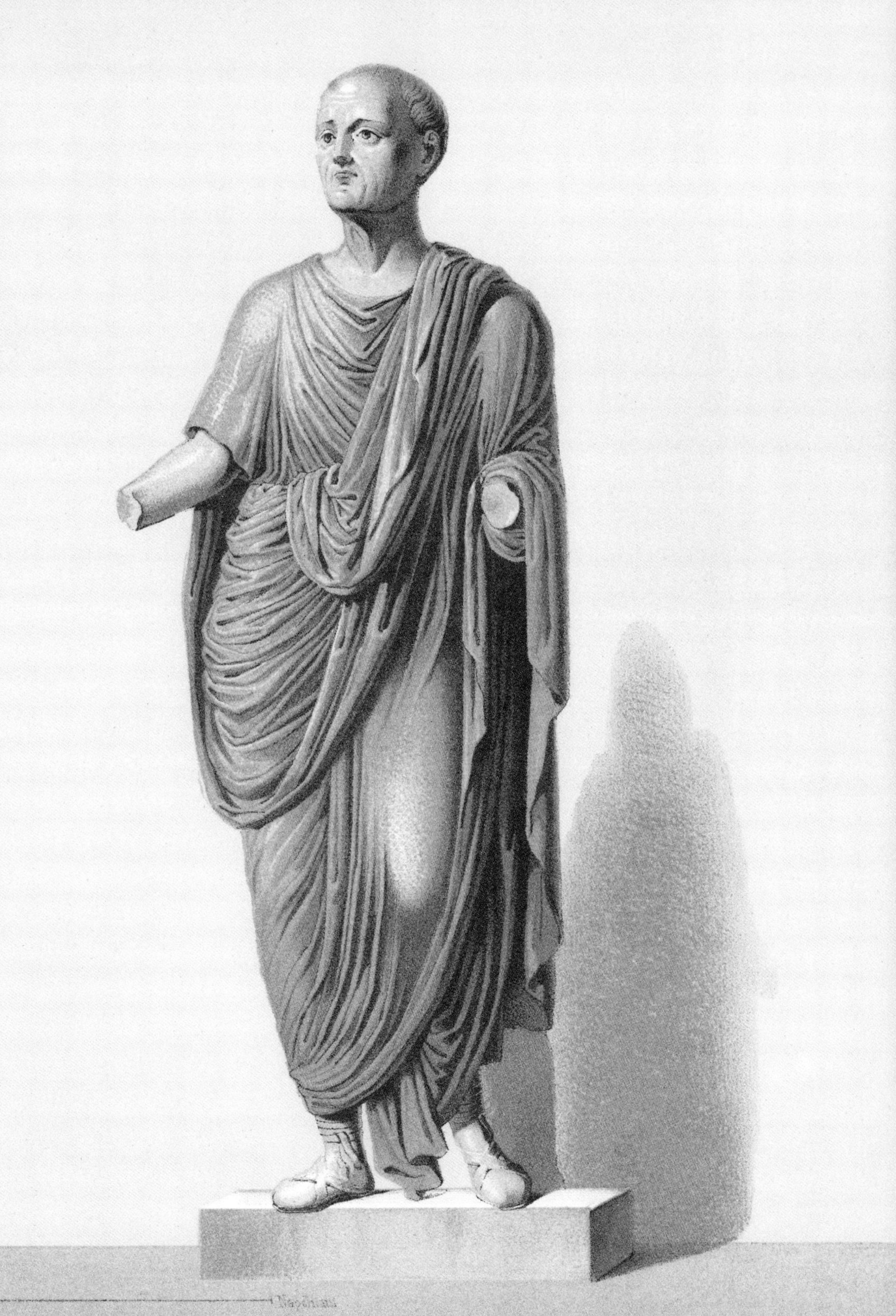

CASA DEL FAUNO

House of the Faun

When workers excavating on October 7, 1830, turned their attention to a promising house entrance on the Via della Fortuna, they had no idea that the largest and most magnificent house in Pompeii lay before them. It occupies an entire block of the city and with its surface area of almost 3000 m² not only does it exceed in size virtually every other house in Pompeii, but is comparable in scale – as we know today – with the palaces of the Hellenistic rulers in Pergamon and at Pella (Macedonia). The Casa del Fauno (VI 12, 2), as it became known shortly after the discovery of the bronze statuette of a dancing faun in its atrium (pl. 5), was a startling discovery, however, not simply on account of its size. It consisted of two parallel atria – one Tuscan without columns, and one Corinthian with four columns – alongside two large peristyle halls with a series of reception rooms, abundantly decorated with figural mosaic floors. All of this was clearly visible from the main entrance, unfolding along a straight line of sight in front of the visitor. The most important find, however, came to light on October 27, 1831. In a rectangular exedra of a particularly elaborate architectural design, workers uncovered a mosaic depicting a battle between Alexander the Great and Darius, King of Persia. It is probably the most significant work of art Pompeii has yielded to date. The remaining decoration of the rooms, by contrast, proved to be less interesting. Throughout the house the owners had kept with the 1st-style stucco ornamentation dating from the 2nd century BC, in which figural representations make almost no appearance. Individual finds were also not as plentiful as the excavators might have hoped. In plate 8 the most important pieces are set out in an imaginary room, while plate 4 shows the jewellery of a woman who died in the Corinthian atrium.

⁂

Plate 1 — *[Anonymous]*

1–54 Ground plan of the house. *7–9* *Fauces* with mosaic floor. *11–12* Tuscan atrium with faun statuette. *25* Exedra with Alexander mosaic. *11, 13, 14, 15, 20, 21, 27* Rooms with mosaic floors. *22* First peristyle. *30* Second peristyle. *39* Tetrastyle atrium. *34–36* Kitchen area. *55–56* Oscan inscriptions. *57* Limestone wellhead. *58* Capital from the entrance. *59* Cornice (depicted upside down). *60* Doric capital from the second peristyle. *61–62* Ionic column from the first peristyle. *63* Corinthian capital from the exedra (25).

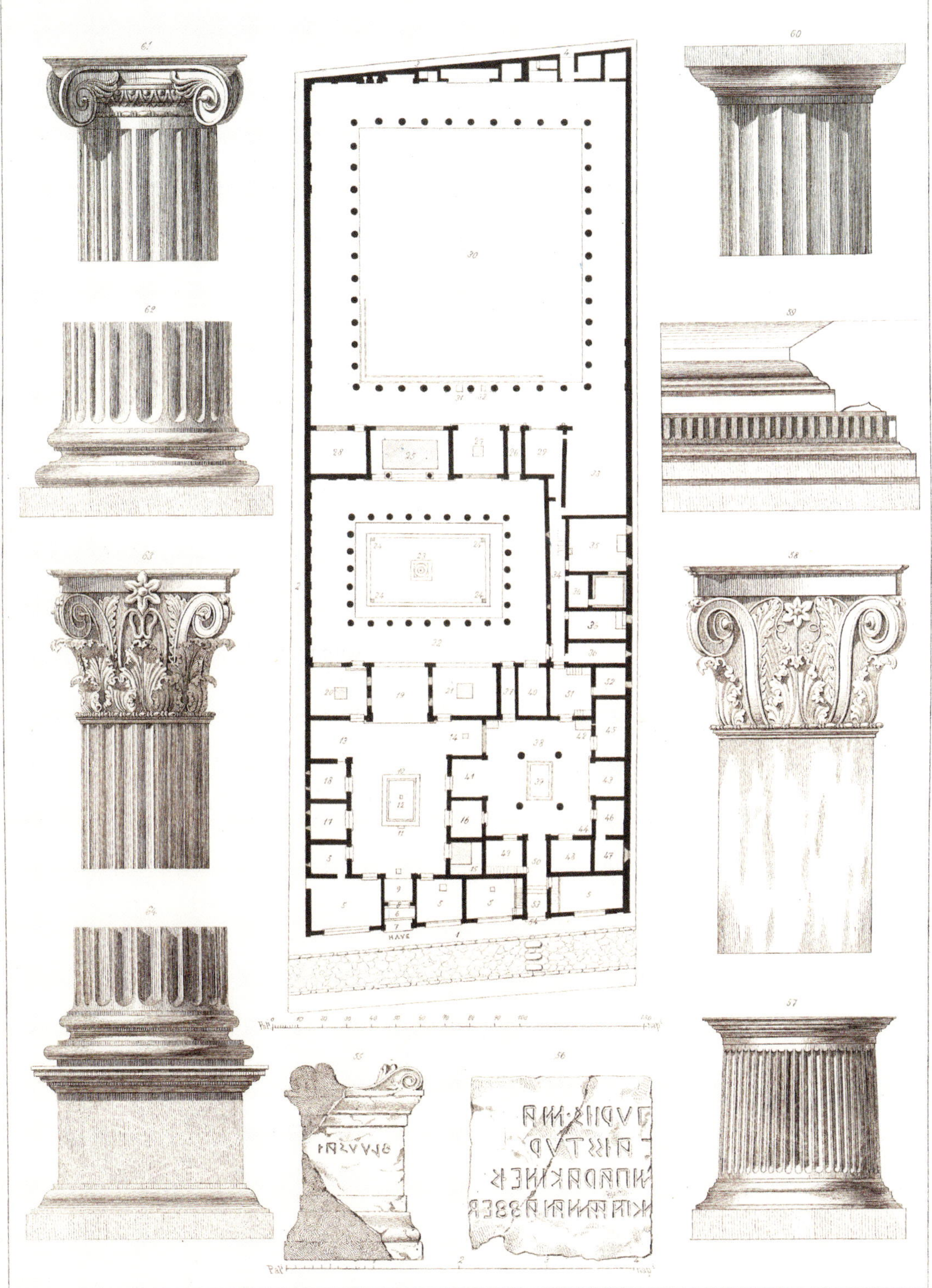

Fr.co Niccolini dir
Lit. Richter in Napoli

A first large version of the house was built on top of earlier remains in the first half of the 2nd century BC. Towards the end of the century this complex was altered and improved, amongst other things with the creation of a peristyle to the north in place of a simple garden. The outstanding interior decoration with its mosaics and stucco work was executed between 120 and 90 BC, during which period several new rooms were also added. It is today generally assumed that the mosaic artists, in particular, were foreign and had perhaps come direct from Greece's eastern empires. Many elements suggest that the owner of the house had links with Egypt (e.g. Alexandria; see the Nile landscape in plate 6 below). Someone working as a merchant *(mercator)* in Pompeii at this time could have had such connections. On the other hand, the Latin greeting "HAVE" (pl. 9), inlaid for all to see in the pavement in front of the entrance, is tantamount to a statement of Roman allegiance in a city that was still completely Oscan, and thus suggests the owner simultaneously enjoyed good relations with Rome. With its almost 200-year-old décor still fully preserved, the house must have seemed like a museum that demonstrated the venerability of the owner's family.

It was originally proposed that the Casa del Fauno, like the Casa del Poeta tragico (vol. I), should be rebuilt. In the end, however, this plan was dropped and the Alexander mosaic was transported to Naples – in a single piece and under hazardous conditions. The illustrations of the Casa del Fauno in *Case e monumenti* probably come closest to the Niccolini brothers' overall vision for their work. They start with a page dedicated strictly to the house's architecture and end with a painterly vedutà. In between are seven plates showing the key finds, including seven mosaics, in which the significance of the Alexander mosaic is emphasised with a separate detail view showing the Persian king. The 12-page text guides the reader through the house and discusses the individual finds and where they were discovered. Together they provide a complete picture of this house.

Plate 3 — *[G. Abbate]*
Room (21) – The winged infant Dionysus riding on a lion-headed tiger. He is wearing a wreath and holding a large drinking vessel (kantharos). The double frame around the central motif features garlands and masks with a meander border. The surface around the central picture consists of irregularly laid coloured stones.

Page 106
Plate 2 — *[G. Abbate]*
Mosaic emblemata – *1* Casa del Labirinto: dove (of Aphrodite?) pulling a mirror out of a small basket. *2–7* ***Casa del Fauno:*** *2* Oecus (27): lion. *3* Ala (13): doves pulling a pearl necklace out of a jewellery box. *4* Mosaic from the threshold of the atrium: garlands of fruit with theatre masks, triangles. *5* Room (20): sea scene with fish. *6* Ala (14): mosaic with two registers. Above: a cat catching a bird. Below: ducks, fish and sea creatures. *7* Meander border at the entrance to the tablinum (19).

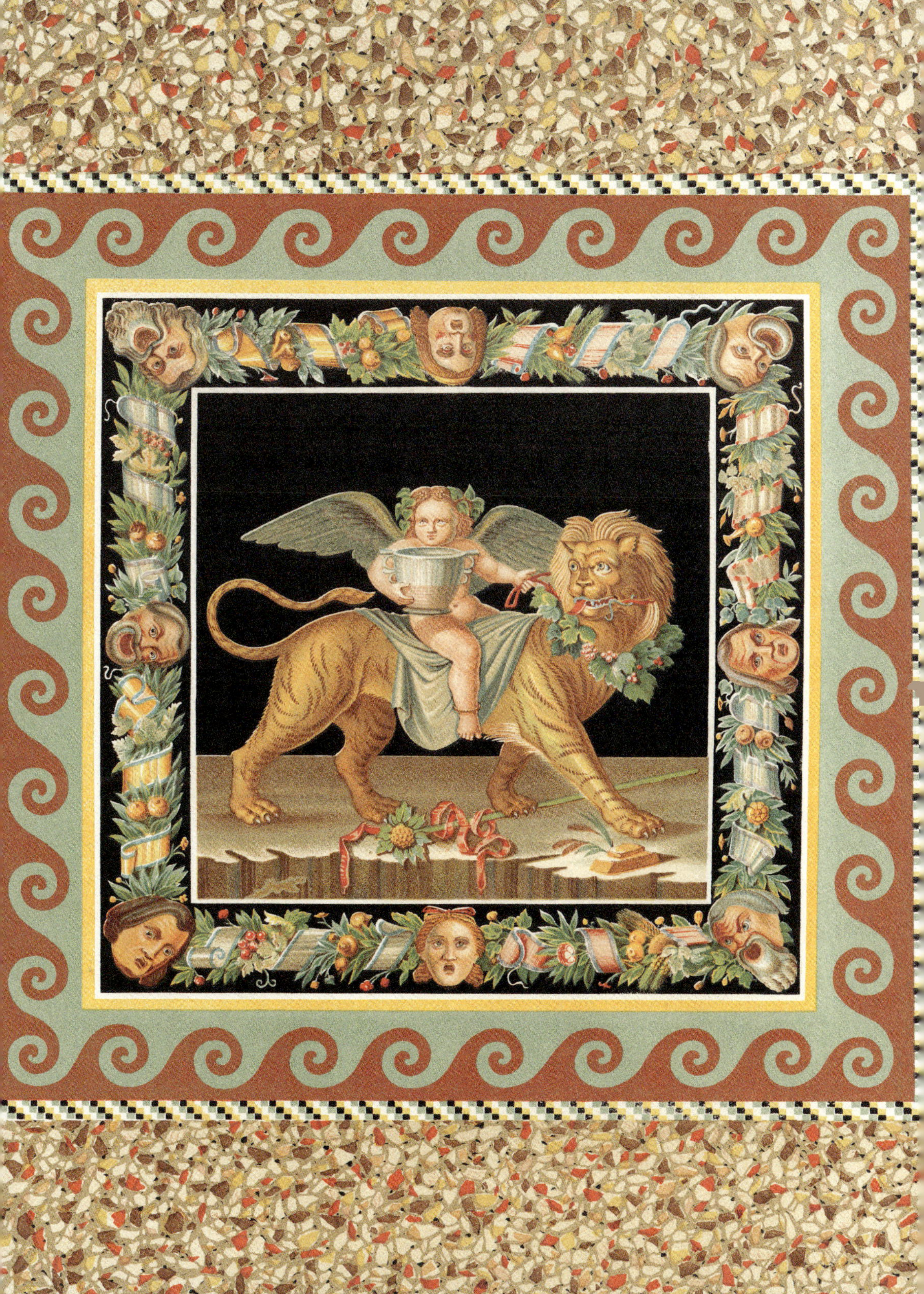

1

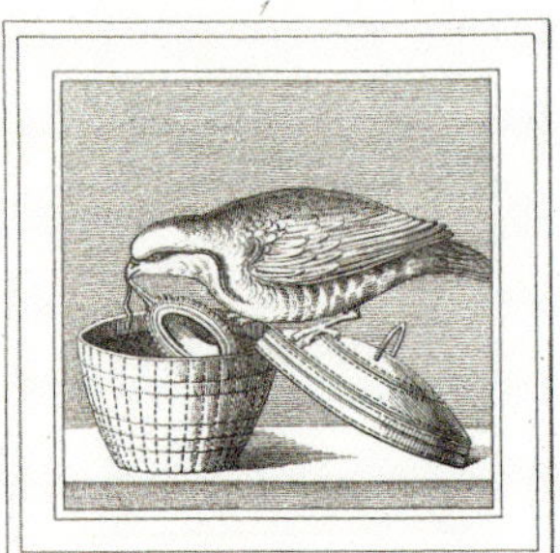

2

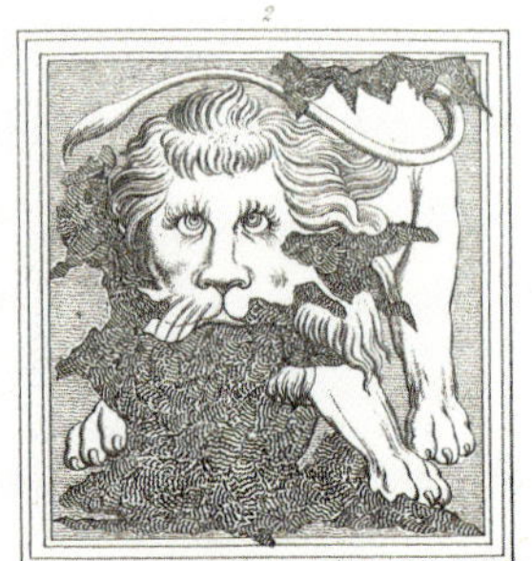

3

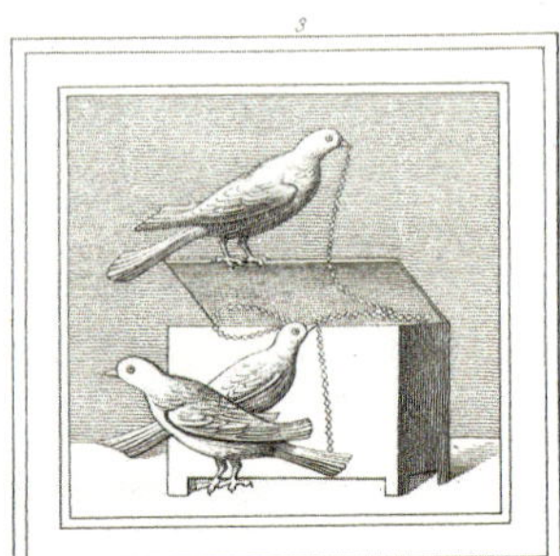

4

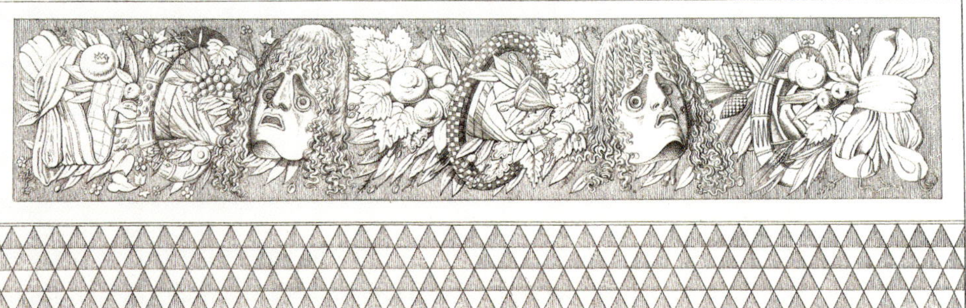

5

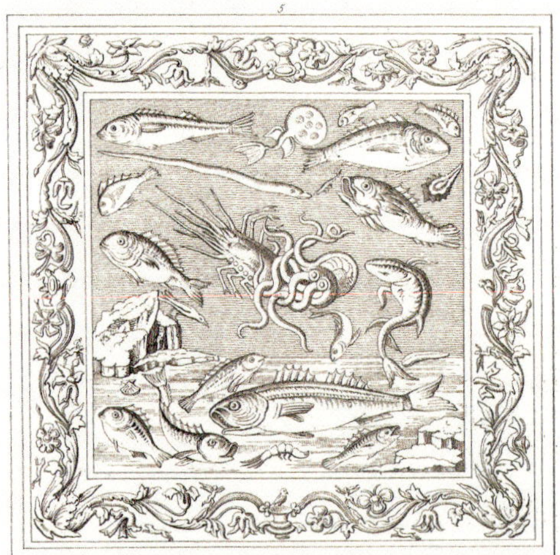

6

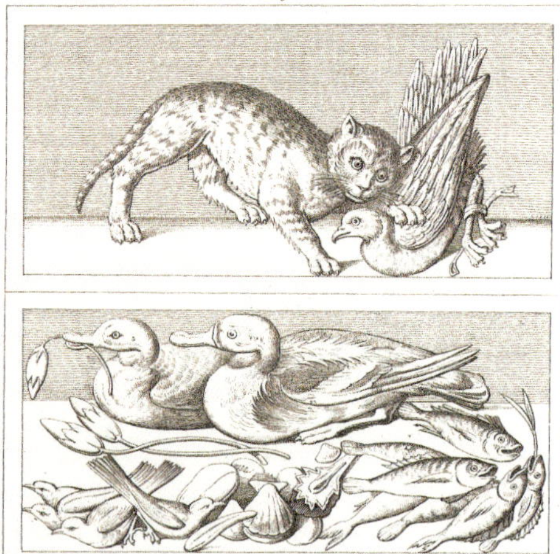

7

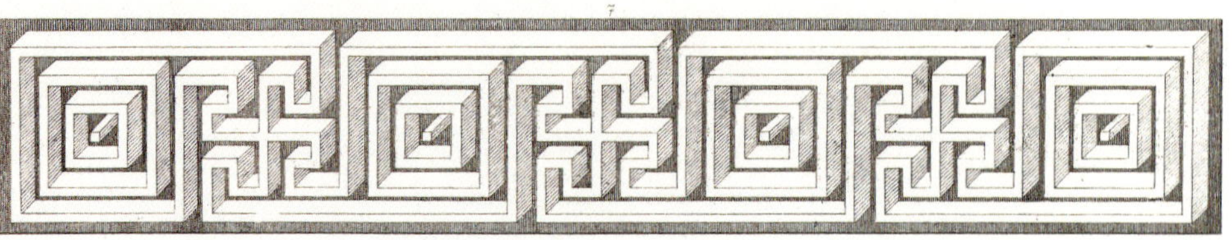

G. Abbate fec. | Fr.lli Niccolini dir. | G. Frauenfelder dis.

Lit. Richter in Napoli

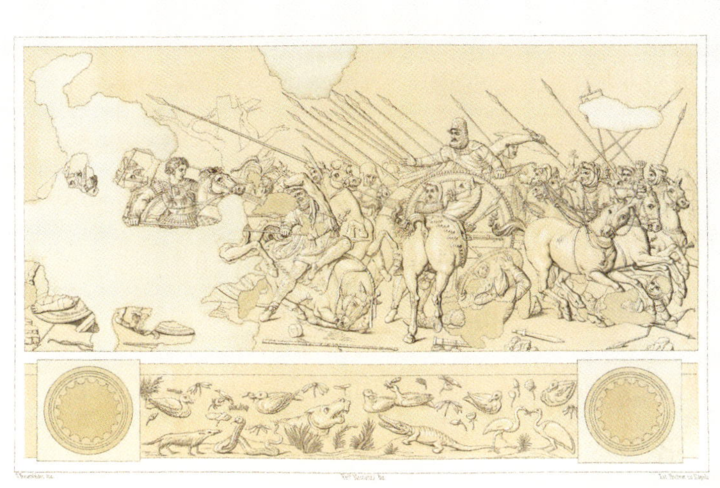

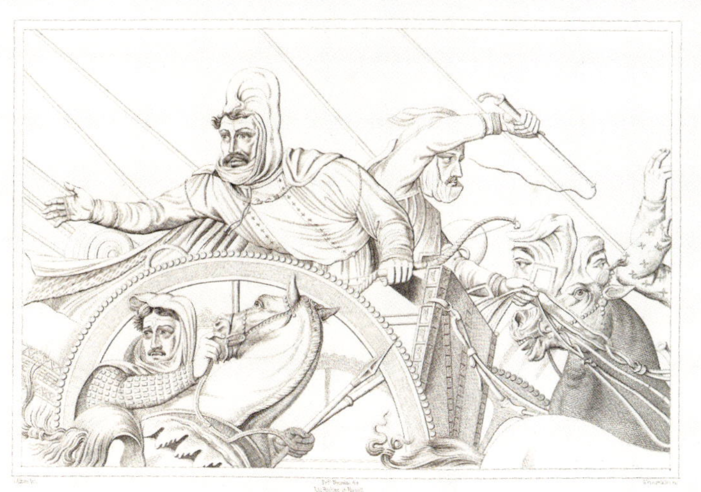

Plate 6 — *[Anonymous]*
Exedra (25) – Mosaic floor with representation of a battle between Alexander the Great and Darius, King of Persia. Below: Nile landscape with aquatic and land animals. Mosaic between the columns at the entrance to the exedra.

✠

Plate 7 — *[G. Abbate]*
Exedra (25) – Detail of the Alexander mosaic:
Darius in his battle chariot fleeing before Alexander.

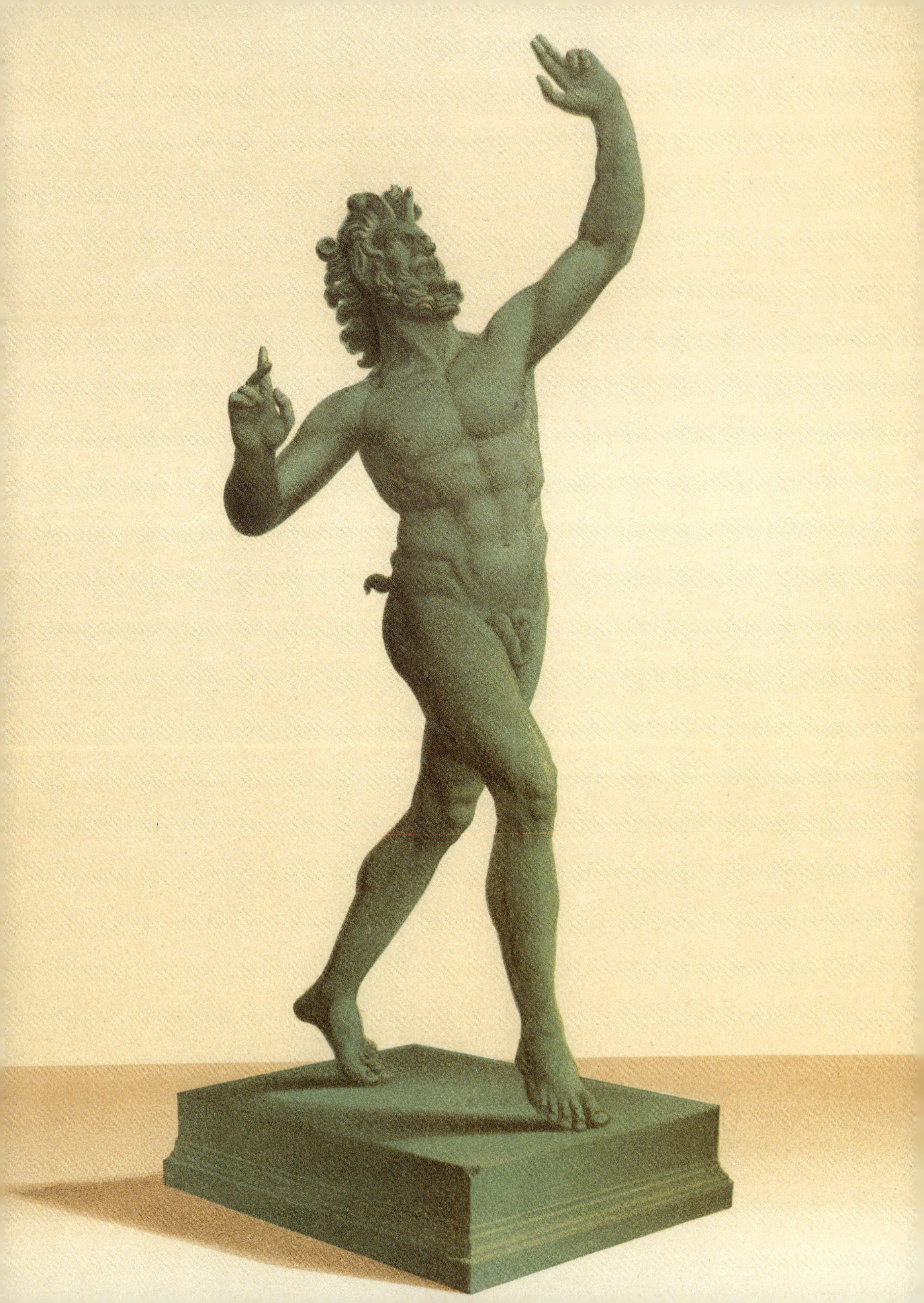

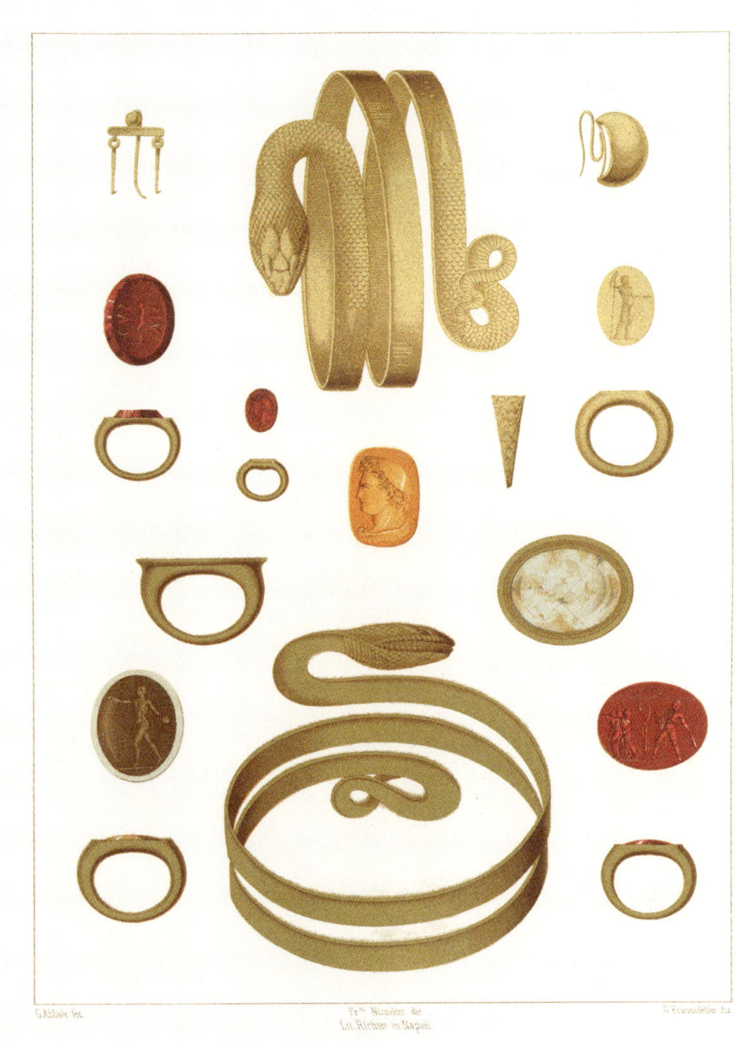

Plate 5 — *[Anonymous]*
Atrium (11) – The bronze statuette of a dancing faun from which the house was given its name. Probably 2nd century BC.

❖

Plate 4 — *[G. Abbate]*
Corner of the tetrastyle atrium (44) – Gold jewellery and rings belonging to a woman who died on this spot.

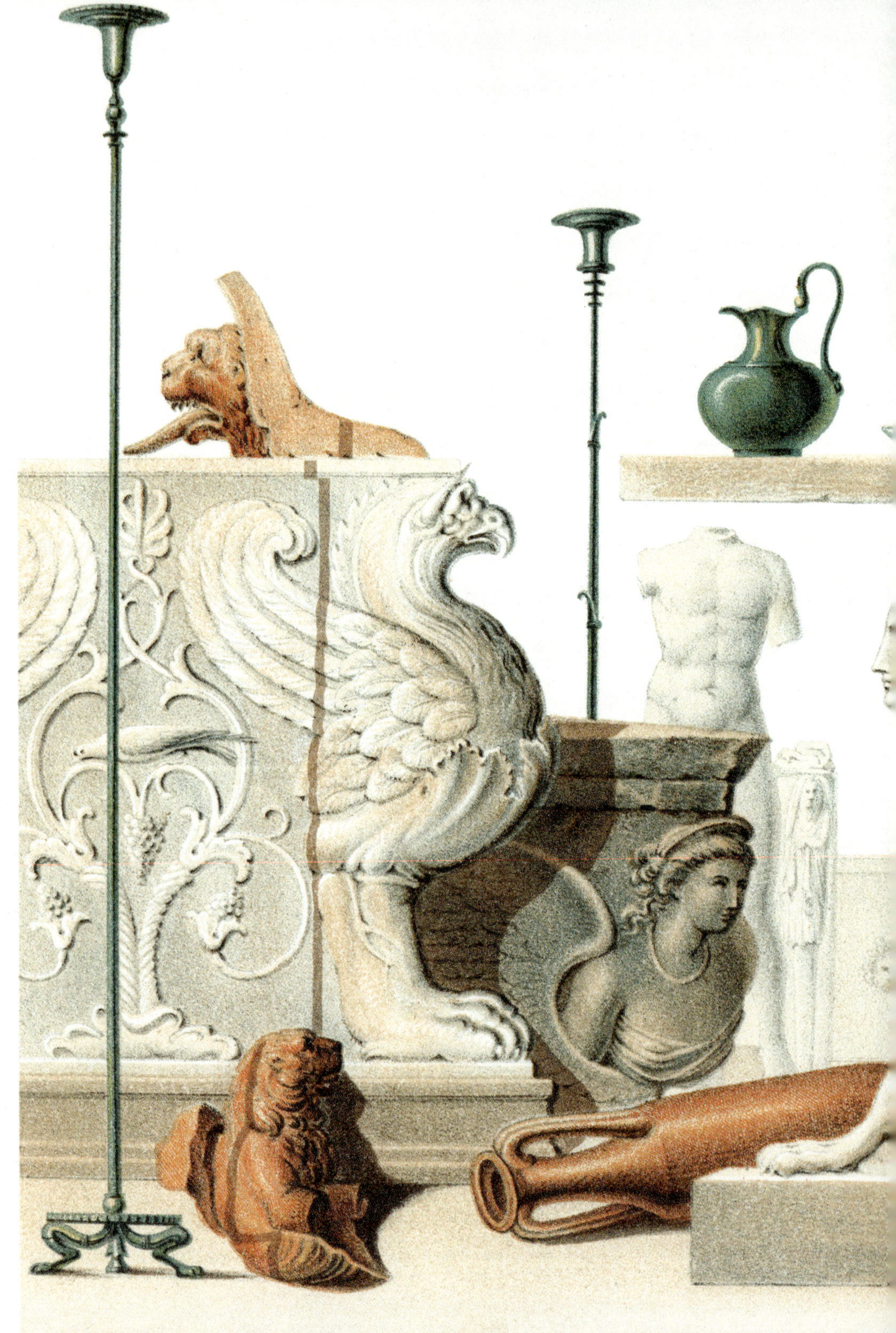

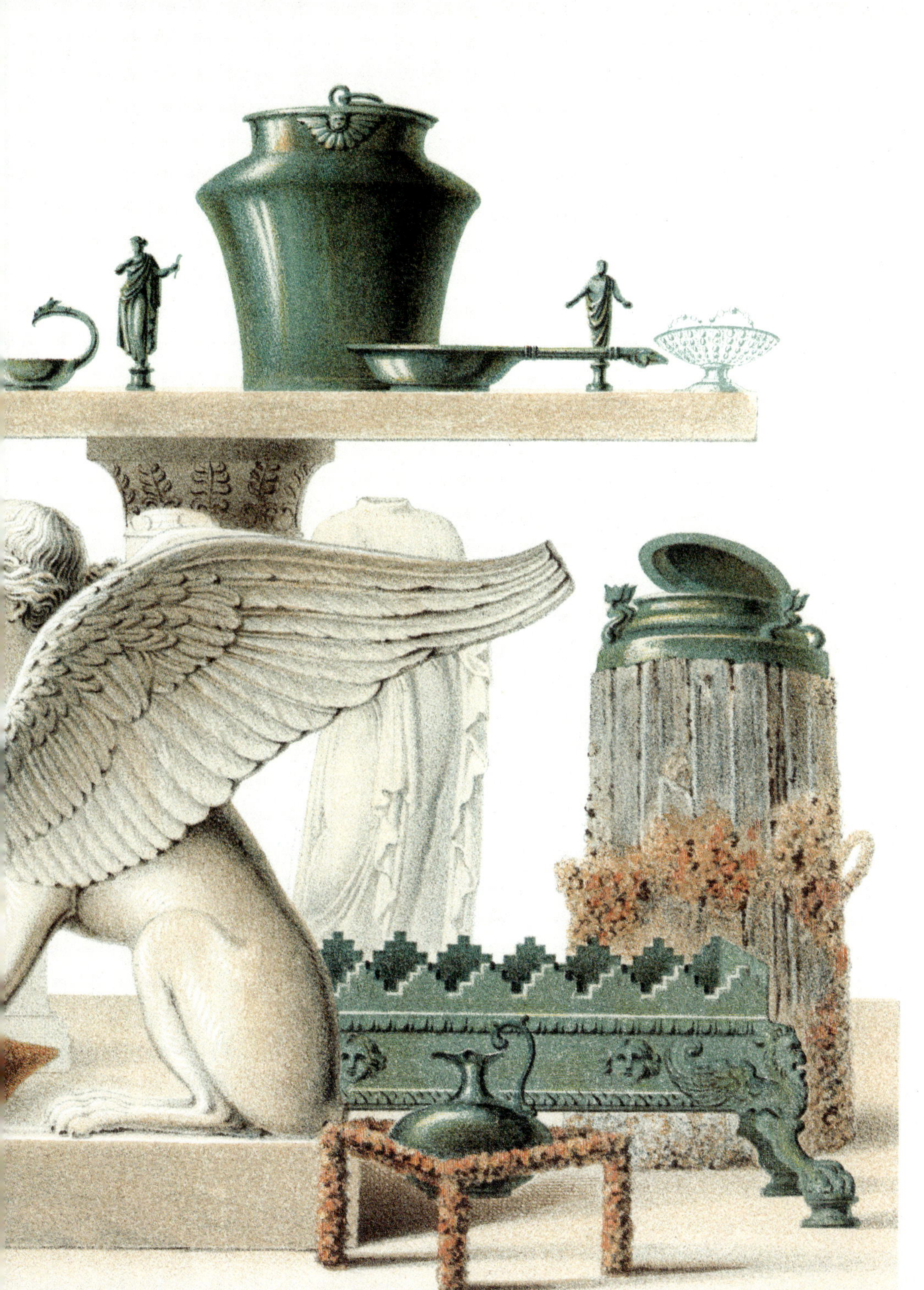

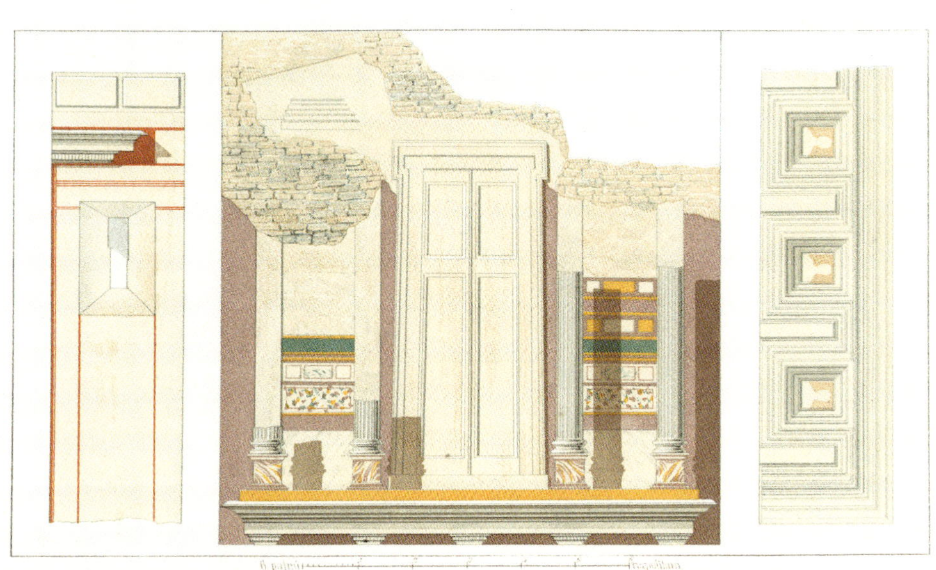

Pages 110–111 and above

Plate 8 — *[G. Abbate]*

Above: 1st-style wall decoration. A small "temple façade" from the *fauces* (9) and wall of a room with a window. Below (pp. 110–111): collection of decorative and utility items variously made of marble, bronze and terracotta.

Plate 9 — *[T. Duclère]*

View of the Casa del Fauno – Looking through the *fauces* towards the atrium and the first peristyle, with Vesuvius smoking in the background. On the ground in front of the entrance, the word "HAVE" (Welcome).

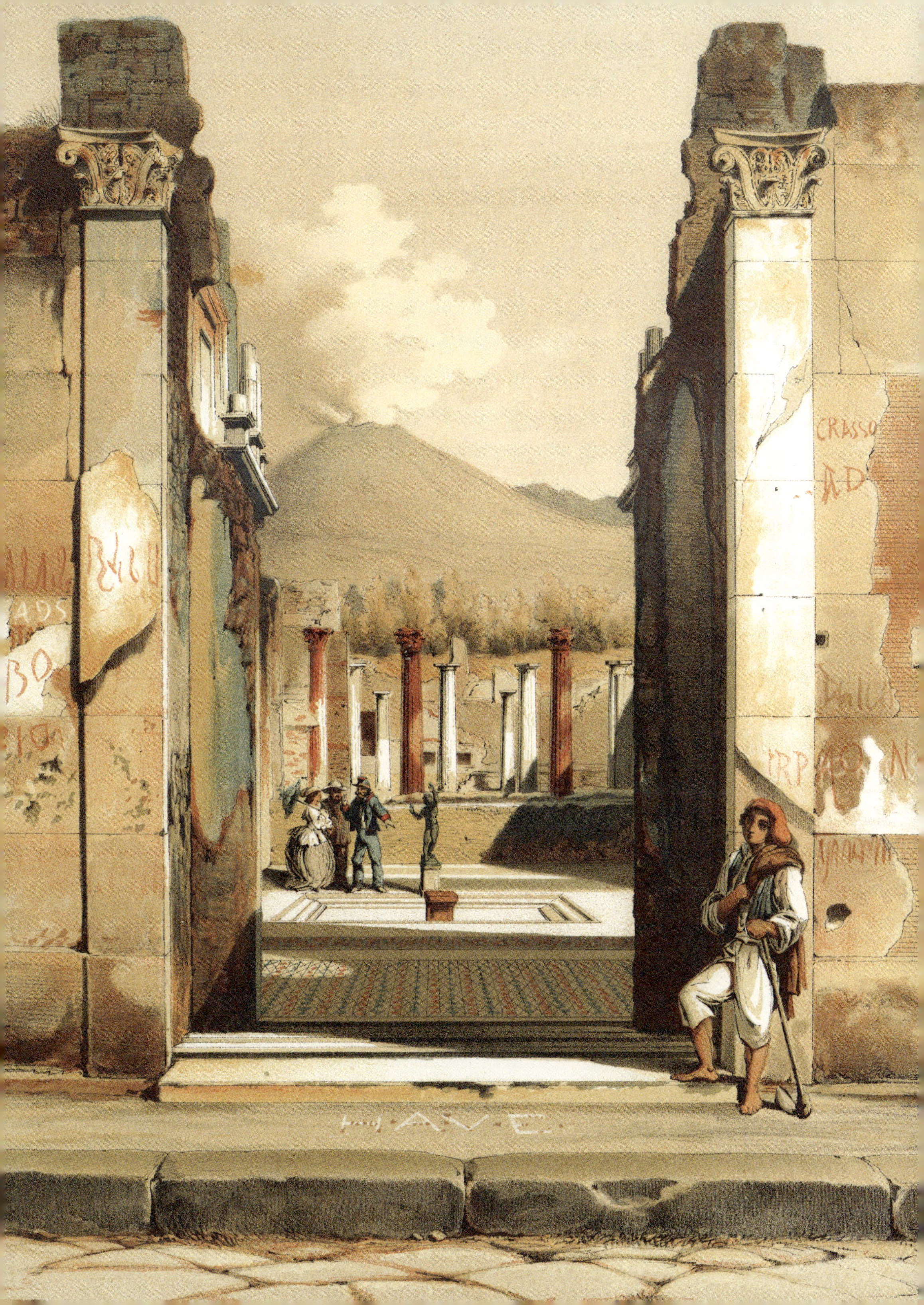
CRASSO
A·V·E

CASA DI SIRICO

House of Siricus

(Via Stabiana, Casa no. 57 / Casa di Sirico)

Beginning in March 1852, a house on the Via Stabiana was quickly uncovered working back from its entrance (at that time no. 57). It soon became clear, however, that this first house was connected via a narrow corridor to a second one, whose entrance lay on the Vicolo del Lupanare and which was subsequently excavated in 1857. This proved to be the main entrance of the unusual complex (VII 1, 25 and 47), which comprised two atrium houses and a bakery that had probably been amalgamated in the late 1st century BC. Following the discovery of a signet ring bearing the name [Vedius] Siricus, the property became known as the Casa di Sirico."Hail wealth", the welcome greeting at the entrance (47), has been interpreted as a reference to the business affairs of the house's owners (Casa di Sirico, pl. 1). After the earthquake of AD 62, a programme of complete redecoration was begun, but this work could not be finished. The house's importance rests on the magnificent wall-paintings completed in just a few of the rooms, together with its marble furnishings, some of them older in date. The Niccolini plates themselves document a very fresh excavation, but reproduce only a small selection of the wealth of decorations uncovered. The excavations were conducted by Gaetano Genovese, the architect responsible for Pompeii from 1852 to 1861, and here brought into use a new method. For the first time the earth was removed stratigraphically, i. e. in layers starting from the top, making it possible to observe the remaining traces of upper storeys and roof constructions. One of the results of this "modern" excavation technique finds its way into plate 1 for Casa no. 57, which includes the first systematic representation of roof tiling. With only a few exceptions (the picture of the wounded Aeneas), the murals were left in situ and – apart from the exedra (7) – are as a result today largely destroyed (see also vol. III, Arte, pl. 17).

Plate 1 — *[G. Abbate]*

1–16 Ground plan of house no. 57 on the Via Stabiana. *1* Entrance from the Via Stabiana. *3* Atrium. *10* Peristyle. *14* Garden. *17–23* Elements of a tiled roof. *24* Atrium (5), cross-section through the impluvium. On the left, a table leg with griffin décor, in front of it a pedestal with the remains of a bronze statuette, to the right a small marble pedestal table (10). *25* Frieze of a battle between Greeksand Amazons (today lost).

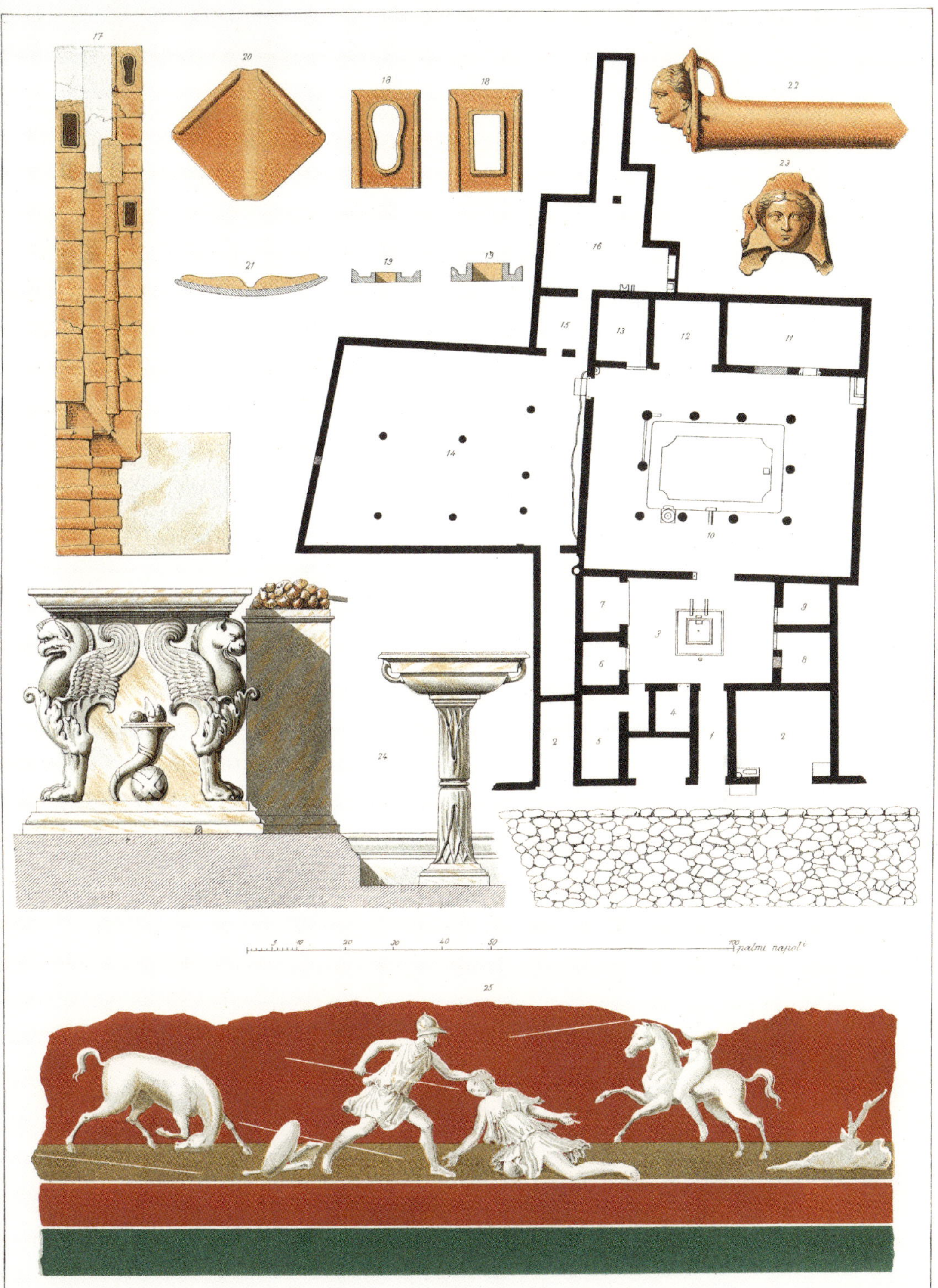

G. Abbate fec. Fr.co Niccolini dir G. Frauenfelder lith.

Lit. Richter in Napoli

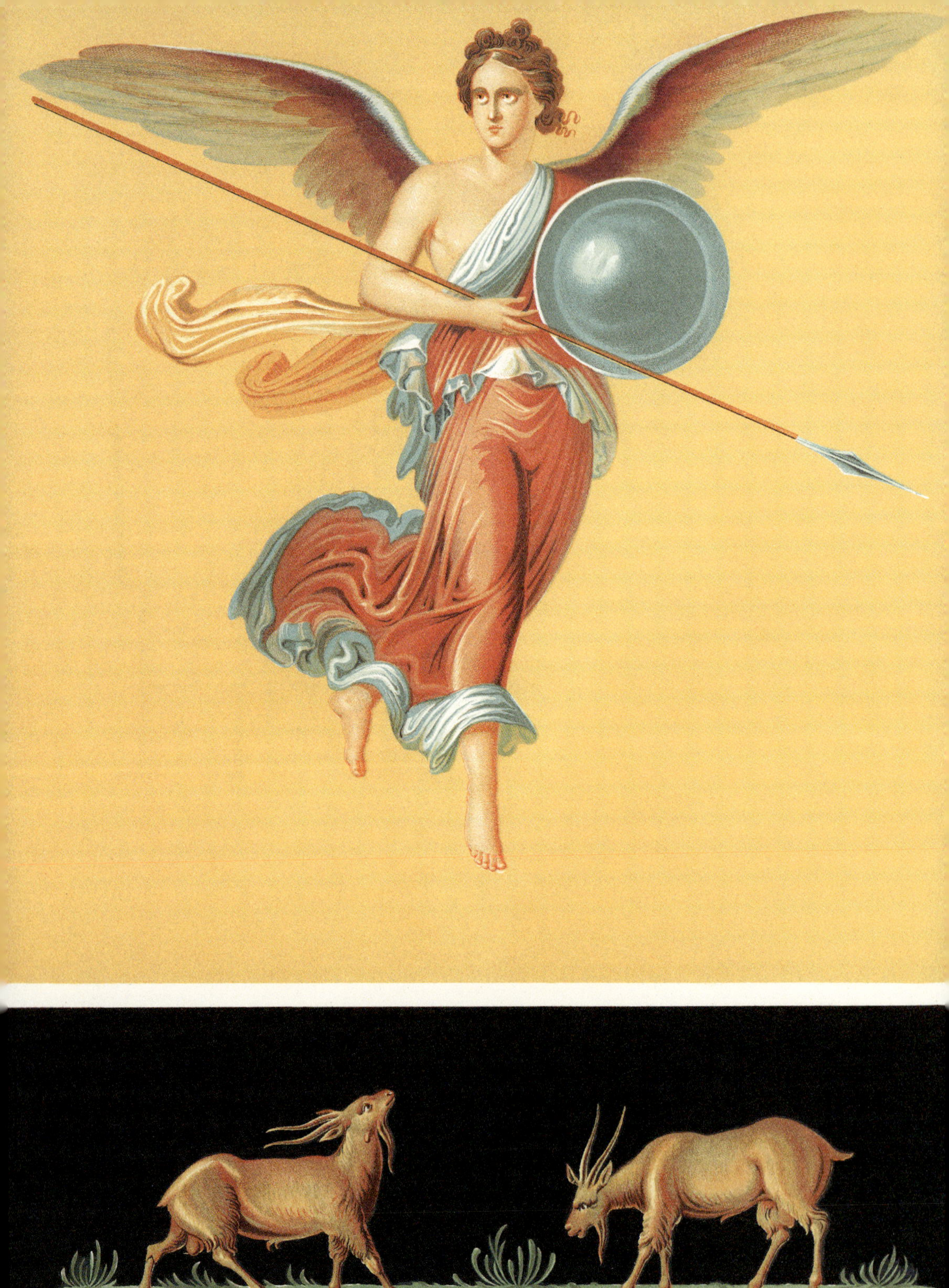

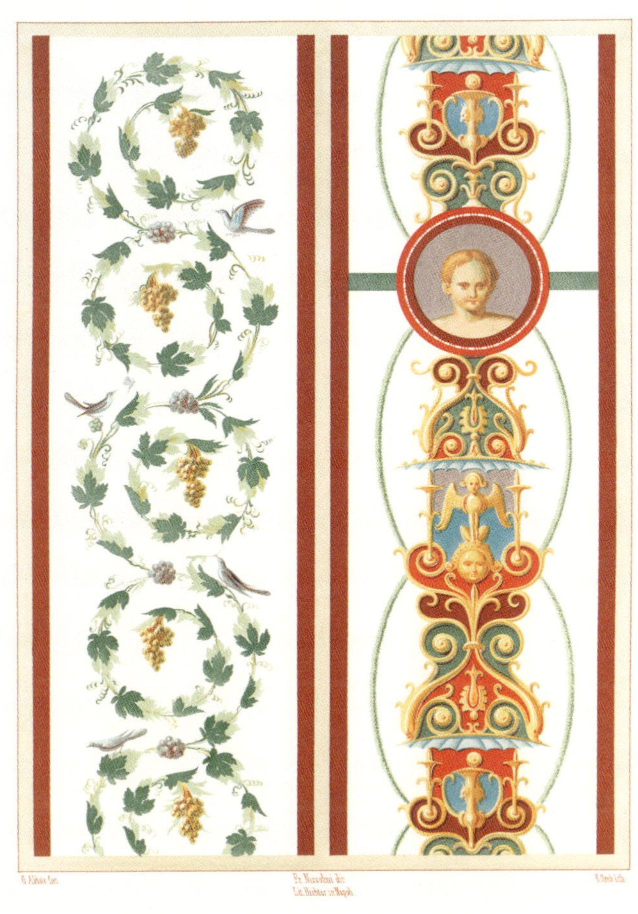

Plate 2 — *[G. Abbate]*
Peristyle, east wall (10) – Floating winged Victory with shield and lance (today destroyed). Two grazing goats.

✻

Plate 3 — *[G. Abbate]*
Exedra (12) – Decoration of the pilasters with a frieze of vines and a candelabrum with portrait medallion.

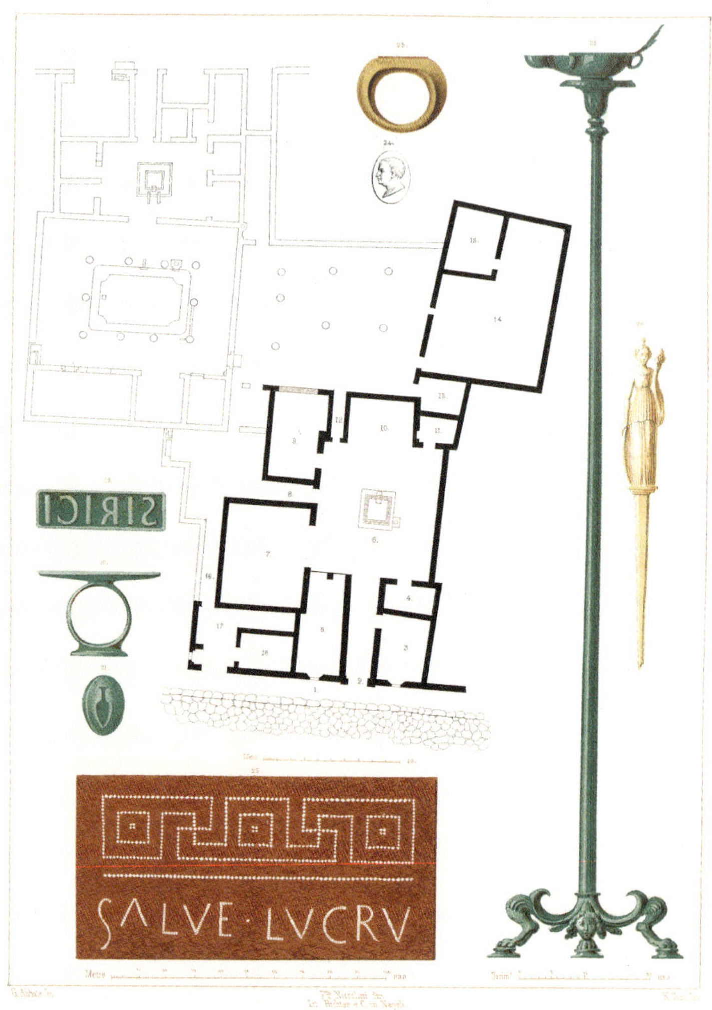

Plate 1 — *[G. Abbate]*

1–18 Ground plan of the house at entrance no. 47, along with the ground plan of Casa no. 57. *2* Entrance. *6* Atrium. *7* Exedra. *8* Corridor to the rest of the house. *9* Triclinium. *19–21* Signet ring of the house-owner ("Property of Siricus"). *22* Floor mosaic at the entrance (2): "SALVE LUCRU" (Hail wealth).

❖

Plate 2 — *[G. Abbate]*

Triclinium (9), front part – Wall decoration, late 3rd/early 4th style: central scene with the wounded Aeneas being attended by a doctor in the company of his son Ascanius and his mother Venus.

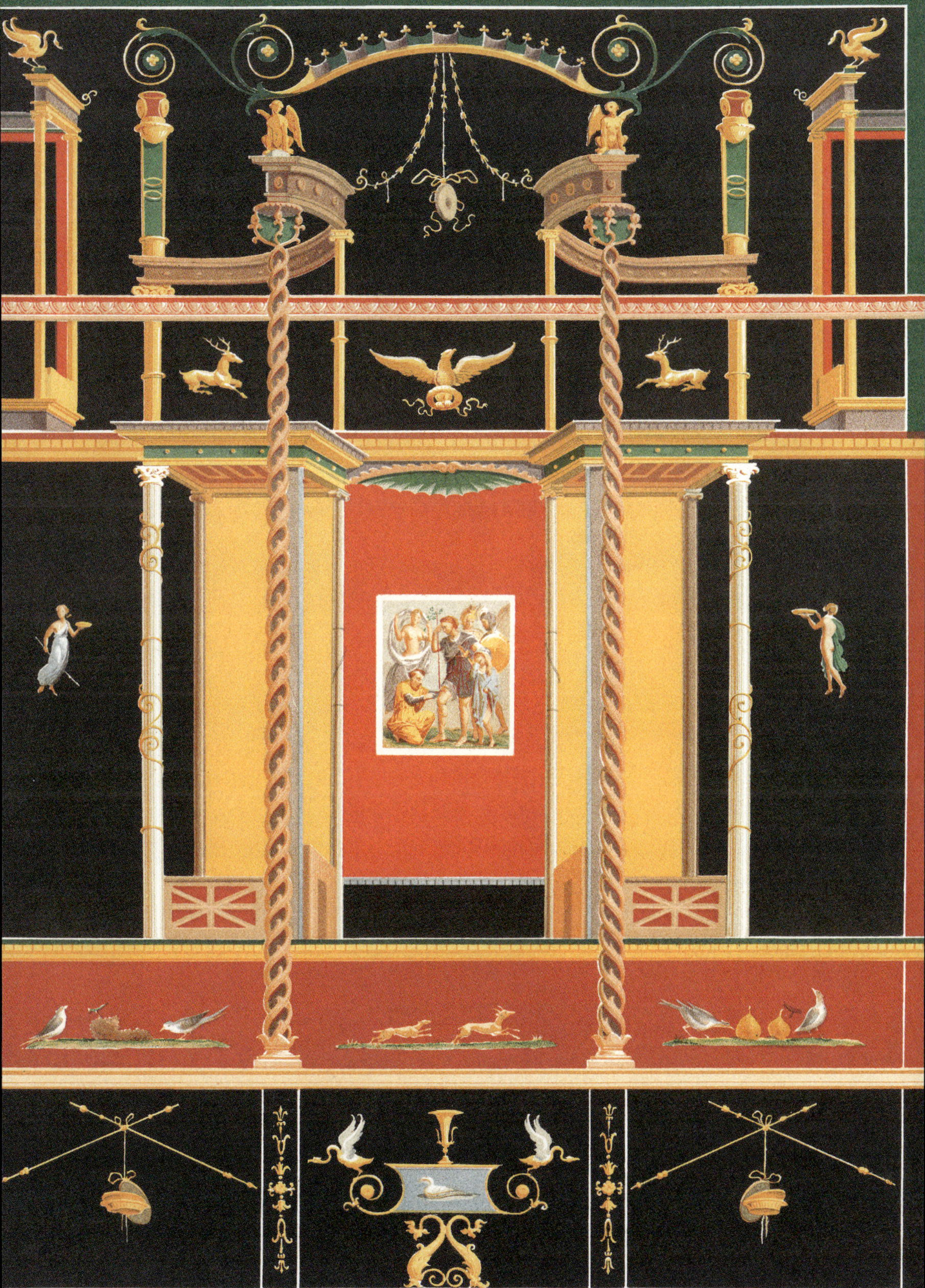

MACELLUM

Macellum

The Macellum (VII 9, 7; formerly known as Pantheon) in the north-east corner of the Forum was built as part of efforts by the civic authorities to impose some structure on the multiple functions served by Pompeii's main square. As a covered market, it allowed for the hygienic separation and storage of foodstuffs (pl. 1). Within the colonnade there were only north-facing, shaded shops, while a light, twelve-cornered structure in the middle of the courtyard served as a fish market. In view of its central position, this construction was initially thought by the excavators to be a Pantheon. In the time of the Caesars, the east side of the courtyard was occupied by a small building for the imperial cult, an assembly room for cult members and a counter selling fresh meat (?). The mural decoration, which today only survives on the sheltered west wall, was of astonishing quality. Large black areas, containing small mythological scenes and floating figures (pl. 5), alternate with architectural prospects of a sophisticated design, in which we appear to look through an opening in which a number of figures are calmly standing (pl. 2). The typically conventional upper zones are here replaced by large, simply painted still lifes that make reference to the Macellum's function, in so far as they show storage containers and foods (vol. II, Descrizione generale, pl. 87). This haphazard combination of completely different subjects is hard for us to understand today. Two well-preserved, life-size statues and a large hand holding a globe, undoubtedly belonging to the statue of an emperor, were found in the small temple dedicated to the imperial cult. The intact statues do not include any members of the imperial family, however, only local high-ranking individuals with hairstyles typical of the day, comparable with the statues from the Temple of Fortuna Augusta (vol. I, pl. 2).

❧

Plate 1 — *[Anonymous]*

The ground plan, which is oriented to face the east, shows the courtyard complex with its surroundings, and must have been drawn after 1860 since its scale is in metres. *A* Interior courtyard with wooden pavilion. *B* Four-sided colonnade. *C* Entrance from the Forum. *D* Sacellum for the imperial cult. *E* Market room with masonry counter. *F* Assembly room for cult members.

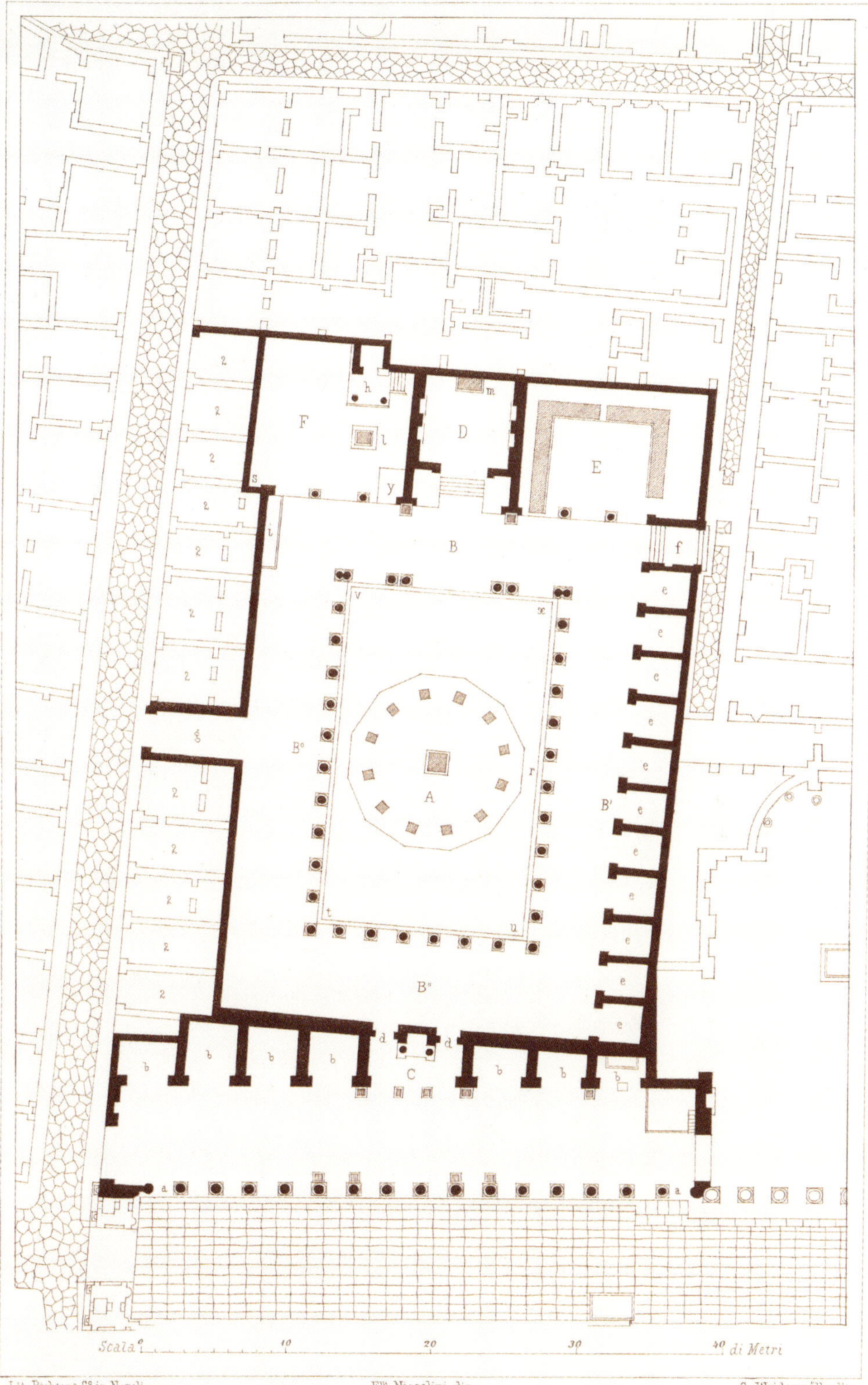

Lit. Richter & Cᵉ in Napoli. Fˡˡⁱ Niccolini dir. C. Weidenmüller lit.

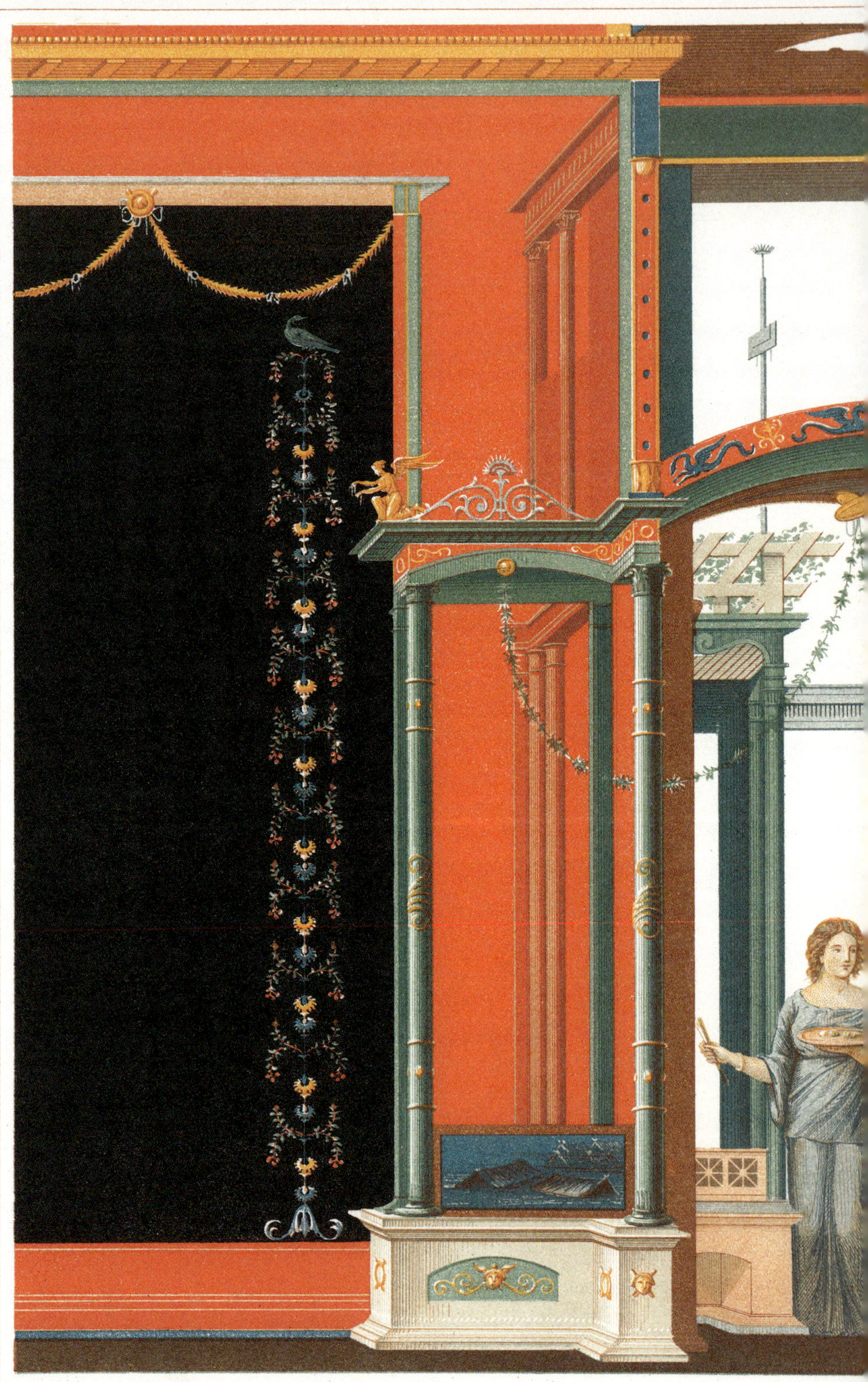

Lit. Richter & C° in Napoli. F.lli

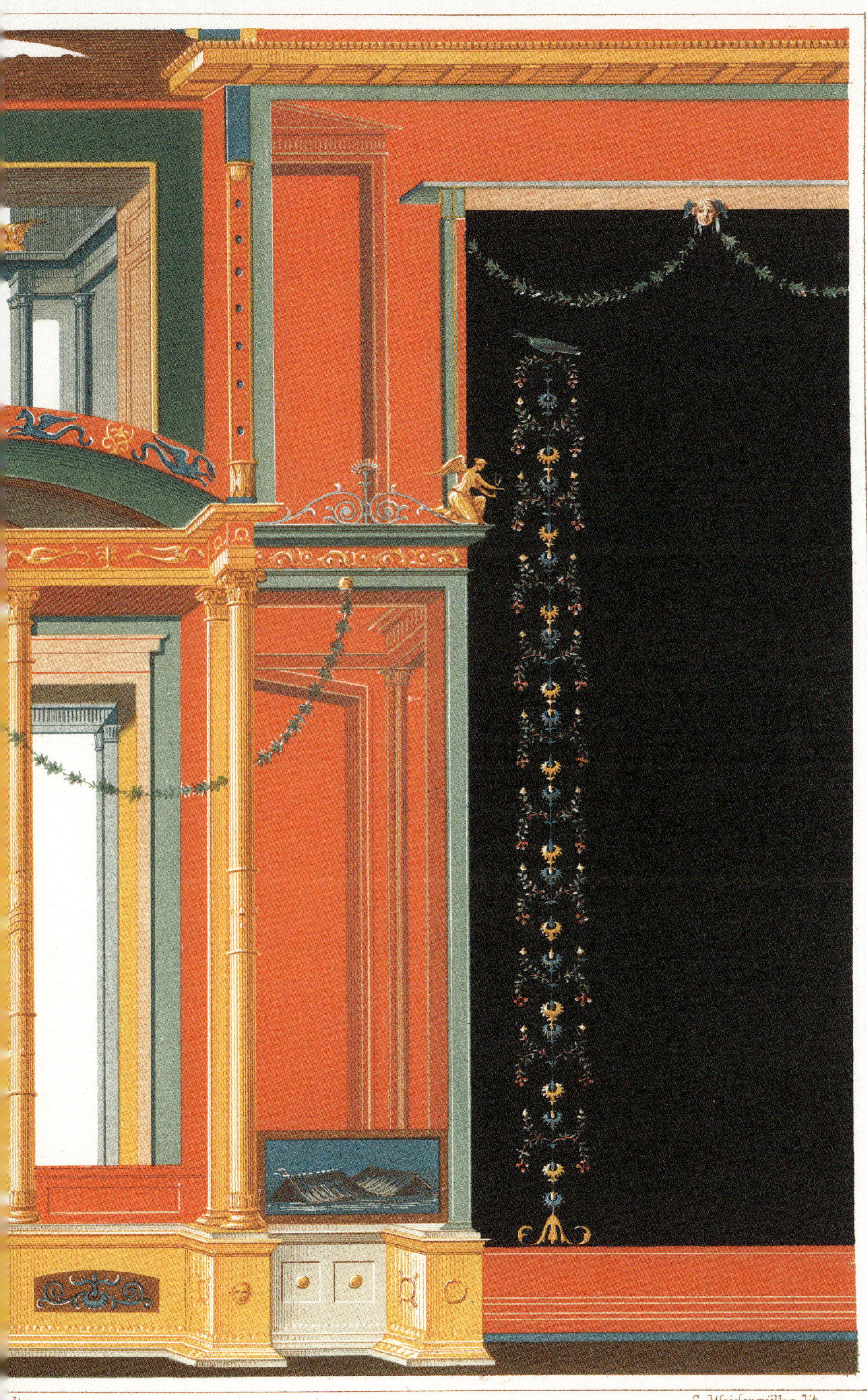

dir. G. Weidenmüller lit.

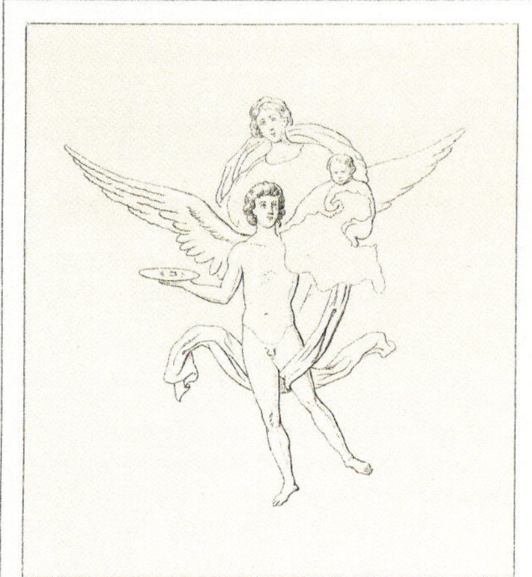

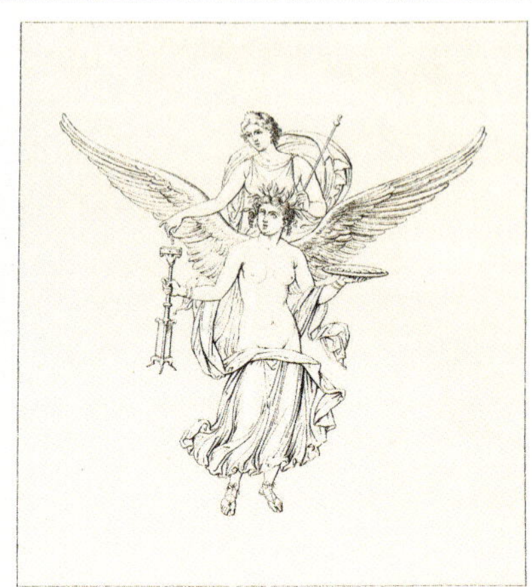

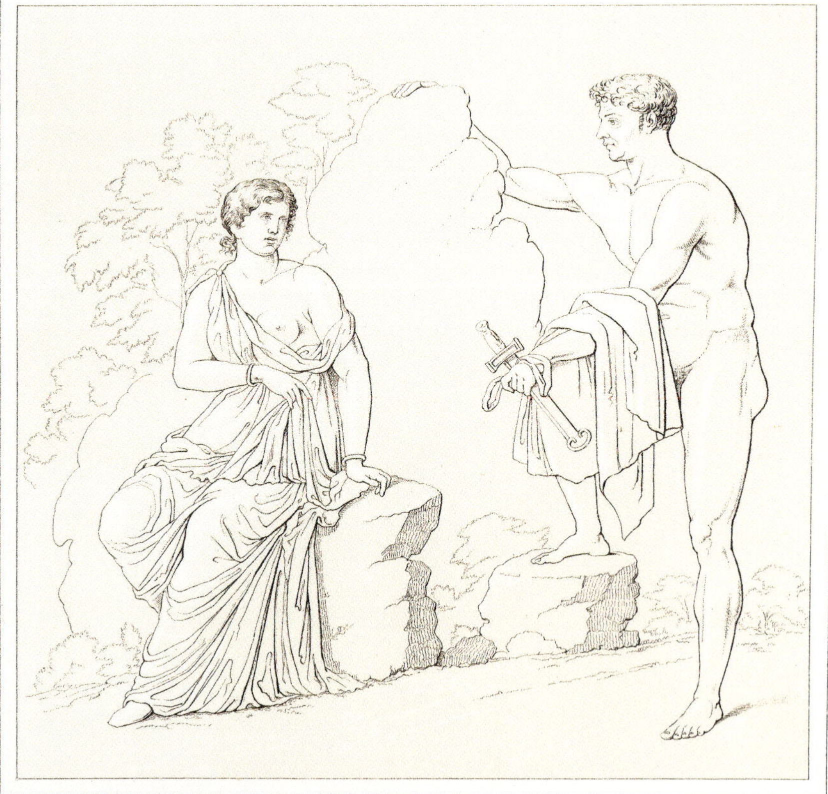

Lit. Richter & C.° Napoli — F.lli Niccolini dir. — Vin.zo Mollame inc.

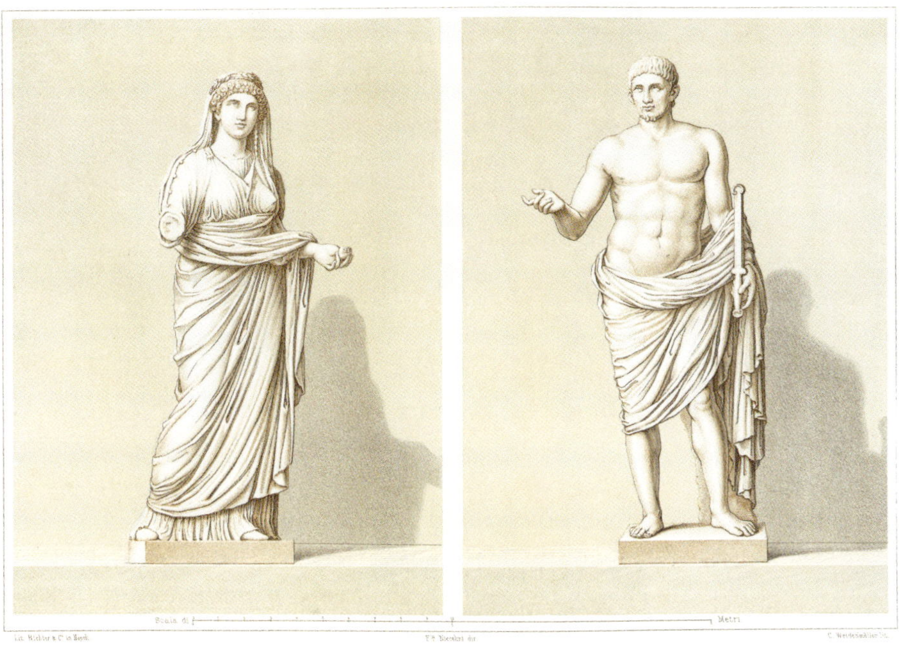

Pages 122–123

Plate 2 — *[Anonymous]*

West wall of the peristyle, southern section – Detail of the middle zone of the architectural prospect in the 4th style. A serving girl with a dish stands in what is skilfully painted to resemble an open doorway with space beyond. Pictures of warships appear on top of the plinths on either side.

Plate 5 — *[Anonymous]*

West wall of the peristyle – Above, two floating groups: a naked youth with a dish (left) and a winged Fortuna (right). Below, central picture on a pale ground: Argus guarding Io.

Plate 6 — *[Anonymous]*

Sacellum in the middle of the east side – Two life-size statues of local dignitaries from the niches of the small building used for the imperial cult. The male figure wears a "military" costume with a sword and his cloak fastened around his hips. The female figure is dressed in the style of a married woman and holds a pomegranate.

SEPOLCRI DI UMBRICIUS SCAURUS E DI NAEVOLEIA TYCHE

Tombs of Umbricius Scaurus and Naevoleia Tyche

During the years of French rule (1806–1815), a section of the road from Pompeii to Naples in front of the Herculaneum Gate was excavated, and was found to be lined with tombs, bars and villas. The layout of the two tombs presented here is typical of a design in general use: a courtyard surrounds the tomb structure itself, and the crypt in the substructure has space for an entire *familia*, with urns for both the natural members as well as slaves. The chamber is surmounted by a monumental altar with an inscription facing the road. Niccolini's text on the tomb of Umbricius Scaurus chiefly discusses the stucco reliefs found on the plinth, which succumbed to a winter frost shortly after their discovery in 1812. The reliefs illustrate scenes from the most important day of the gladiatorial games which were financed by a certain Numerius Festius Ampliatus for the Pompeians on the occasion of an honour or official appointment. They depict the baiting of wild beasts and combat between gladiators armed with different weapons, and thereby correspond closely with descriptions of such games in ancient literature.

The altar on top of the tomb of Naevoleia Tyche is faced with marble on three sides (pl. 1). As its inscription reveals, Tyche built the tomb in her lifetime for her deceased husband, the wealthy freedman Munatius Faustus, and their dependants (pl. 1, no. 4). Faustus had been granted the right to sit on a seat for two people *(bisellium)* at the theatre in recognition of a public donation he had made. In the pictorial field below the inscription we see Munatius Faustus standing on the right, with two slaves in front of him distributing free grain from sacks to the Pompeian populace. The right and left sides of the altar illustrate respectively a sailing ship (pl. 1, no. 5) – Faustus' wealth evidently came from maritime trade – and the *bisellium* seat (no. 6) with which he was honoured. The popular interpretation of the ship as a metaphor for the voyage of life, as also proposed by Niccolini, is erroneous in this context. The inscriptions and pictorial themes on Pompeian tombs refer exclusively to the life and achievements of the deceased (cf. vol. II, Cenotafio di Calvenzio Quieto).

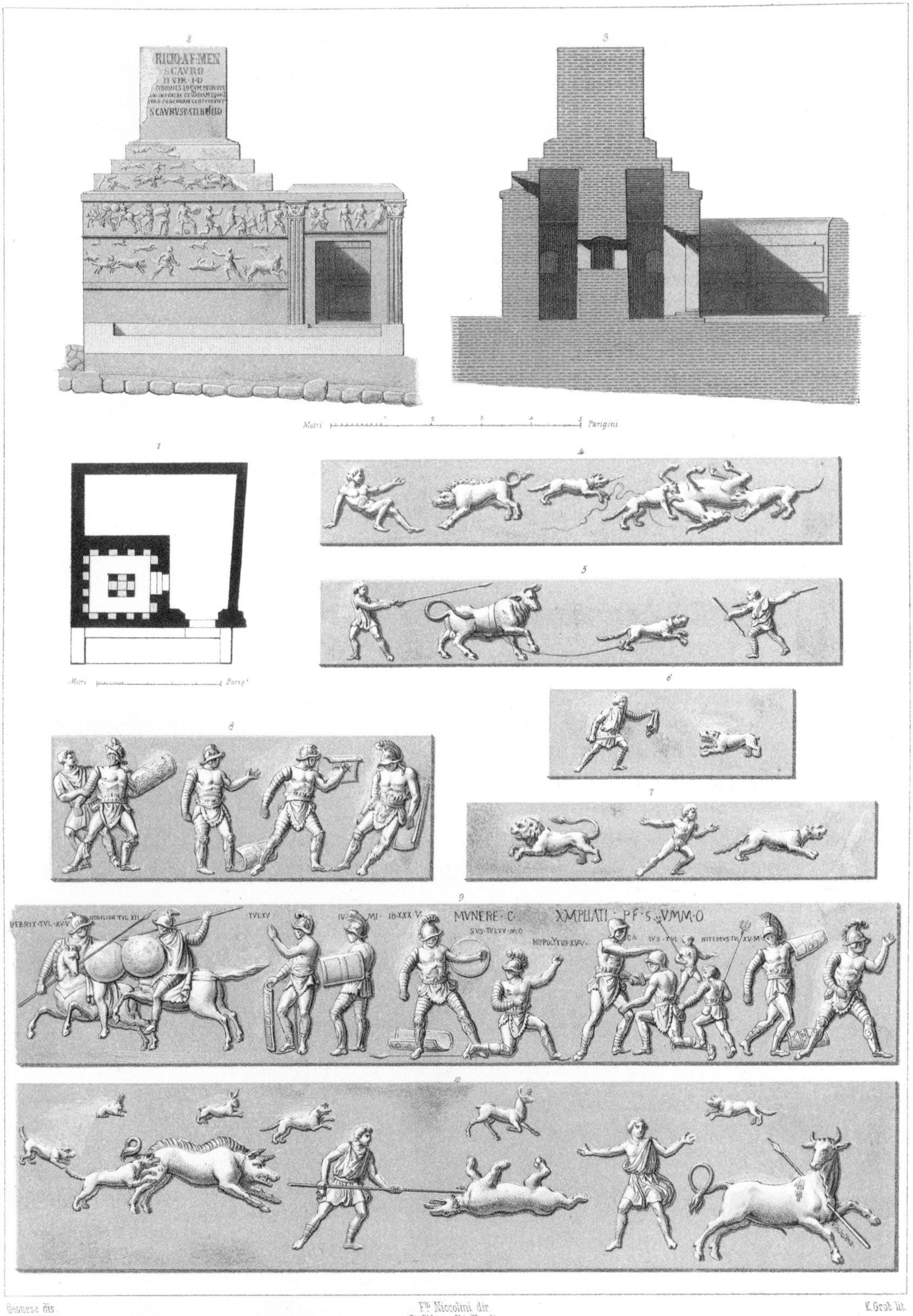

2

3

Metri 1 2 3 4 5 Parigini

1

Metri Parig.

4

5

6

8

7

9

MVNERE·C· XMPLIATI·PF·S·VMM·O

10

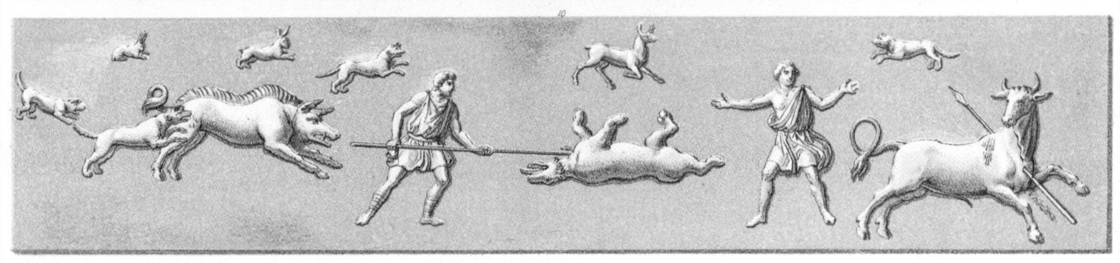

Gennese dis. F.lli Niccolini dir. Lit. Richter e C. in Napoli. K. Grob lit.

Page 127

Plate 1 — *[Genuese]*

1–3 Ground plan, view and cross section of the tomb. *4–10* Stucco reliefs (today destroyed) from the façade. *4–7, 10* Baiting of wild beasts *(venatio)*. *8–9* Scenes from the most important day of the games, featuring gladiatorial combats.

⁂

Plate 1 — *[G. Frauenfelder]*

1–3 Ground plan, view and cross section of the tomb. *4* Front of the tomb altar: inscription with portrait of Naevoleia and representation of Munatius Faustus' public donation of grain. *5* Right side: merchant ship. *6* Left side: seat of honour *(bisellium)* of Munatius. *7* Cross section of a lead container with a glass urn standing inside it.

2 3

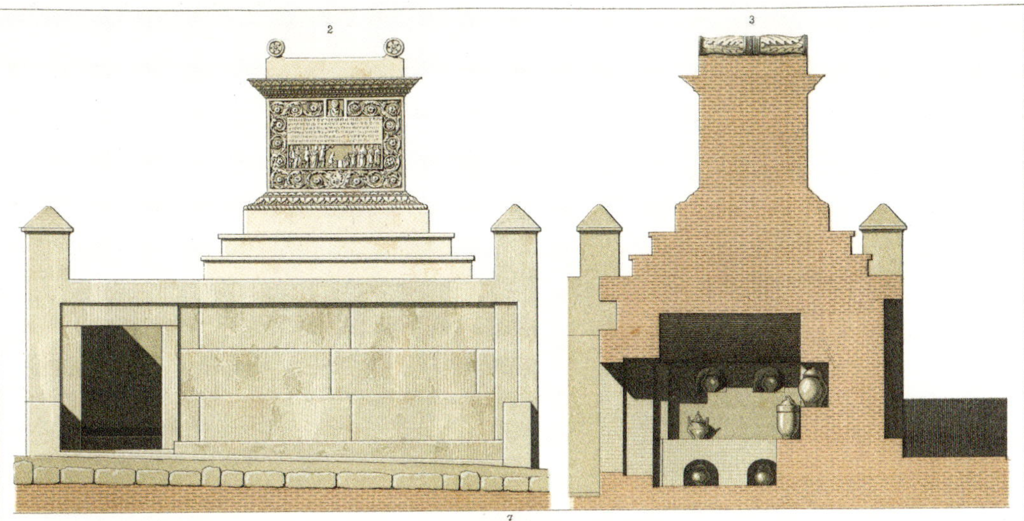

10 palmi napolitani

3 metri

7

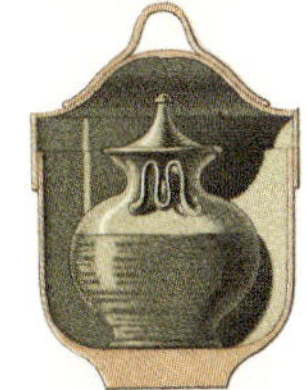

5

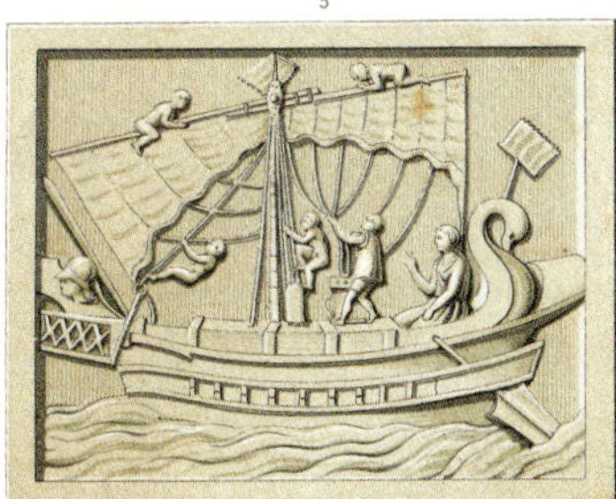

6

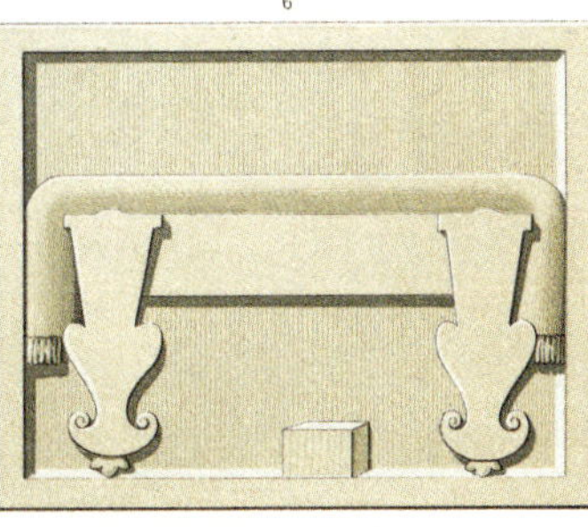

1

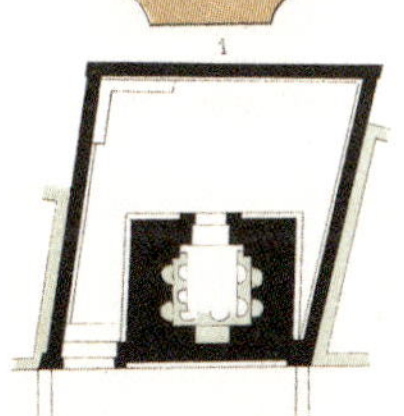

40 palmi napolitani

4

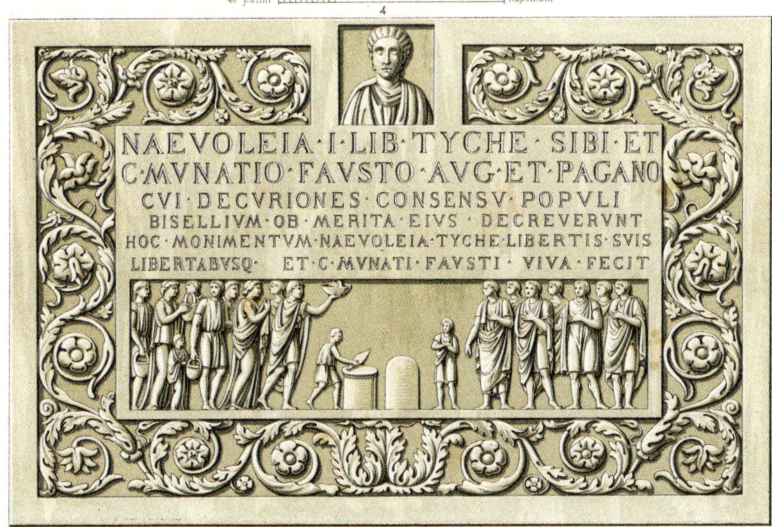

4 palmi napolitani

Un metro

G. Frauenfelder dis. e lit. Fr^lli Niccolini dir Lit. Richter e C. in Napoli

TEMPIO DI VESPASIANO

Temple of Vespasian

(also Tempio di Mercurio, Temple of Mercury)

During the excavation of the Forum and adjacent buildings in 1817, a number of complexes were discovered that were closely associated with the imperial cult. These included the small temple at the rear of a courtyard halfway along the east side of the Forum. A narrow vestibule led into the courtyard, which was built only with very shallow niches and pilaster strips rather than with a colonnade. Against the rear wall – and directly attached to it – was a small podium temple with a platform before it, which could only be entered via steps on either side. As the excavators observed, the marble panels that once extensively clad the podium and steps had been looted along with other architectural elements following the burial of the city. A small marble-clad altar in the centre of the courtyard is the best-preserved feature of the complex. The scene on the front shows the preparations for an animal sacrifice, on the sides are objects associated with ritual practice, and on the rear is a shield of honour crowned by a wreath and flanked by two small laurel trees. These last symbols, in particular, clearly allude to the veneration of an emperor, and hence the complex is no longer known as the Temple of Quirinus or Mercury, but the Temple of Vespasian (VII 9, 2). Recent investigations have shown that the complex, or at least the altar, dates back in modified form to the early 1st century and was perhaps originally dedicated to Emperor Tiberius. Niccolini based his view of the temple on a watercolour by Giacinto Gigante, and evidently borrowed from the drawings by François Mazois for the ground plan and details of the architecture and altar. The temple area was for a long time fenced off and used for storing stone fragments. Consequently, some of the details illustrated do not belong to the original decoration.

✻

Plate 1 — ***[Anonymous]***

1–2 Ground plan and view of the temple precinct and of the temple with the altar in front. *3–6* Marble altar showing its decoration: on the front, sacrificial scene; on the sides, sacrificial paraphernalia beneath garlands; on the back, the Augustan wreath of oak leaves *(corona civica)* and two laurel trees. *7–8* These architectural fragments were kept in the courtyard, which was used as a storage area, and do not belong to the temple.

2

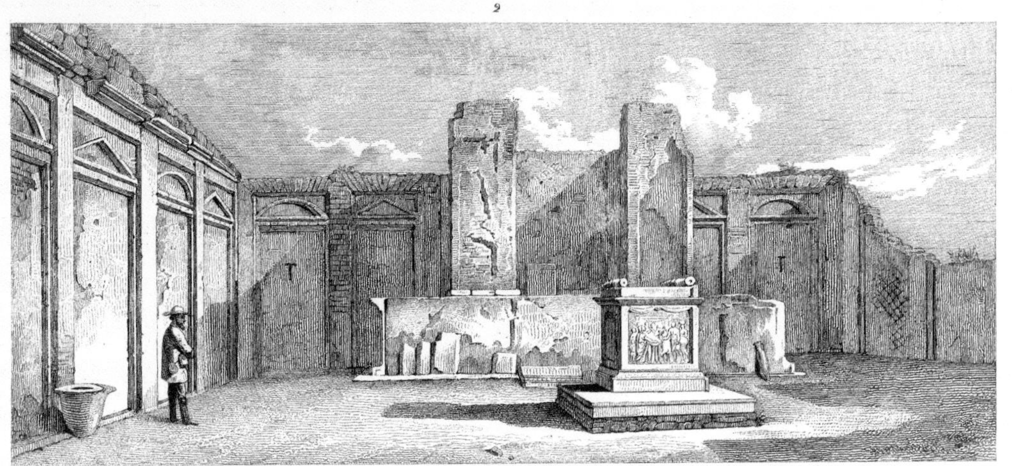

7

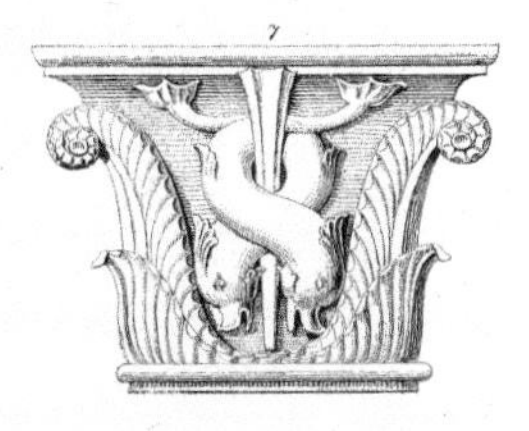

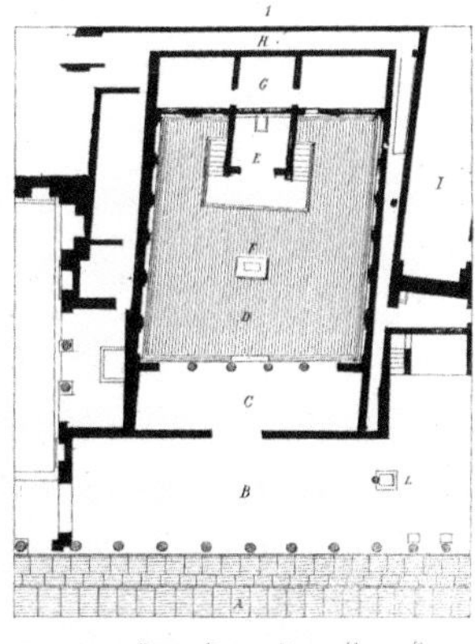

6

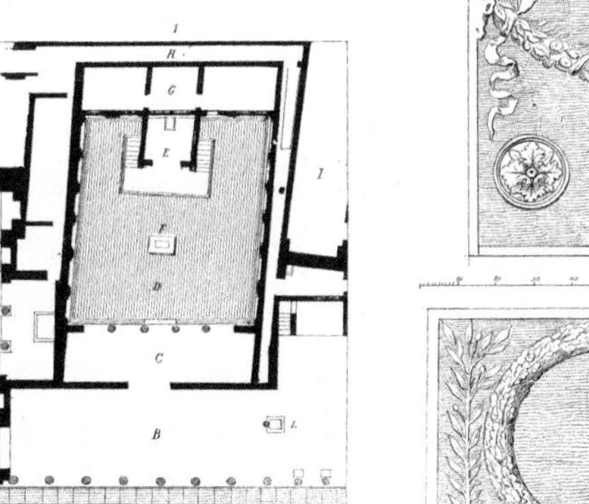

8

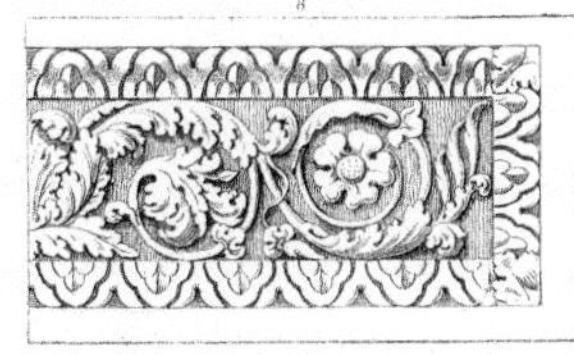

5

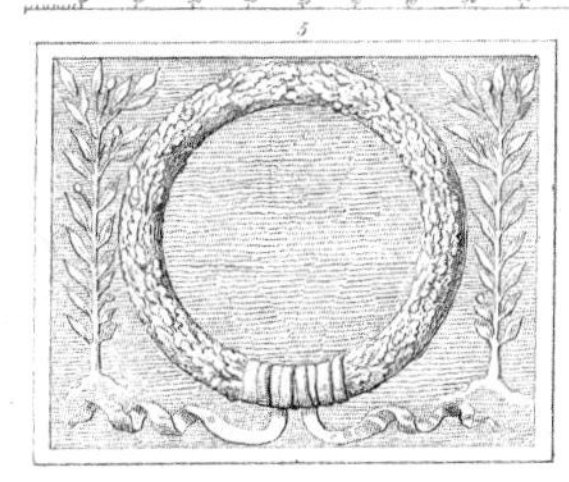

3

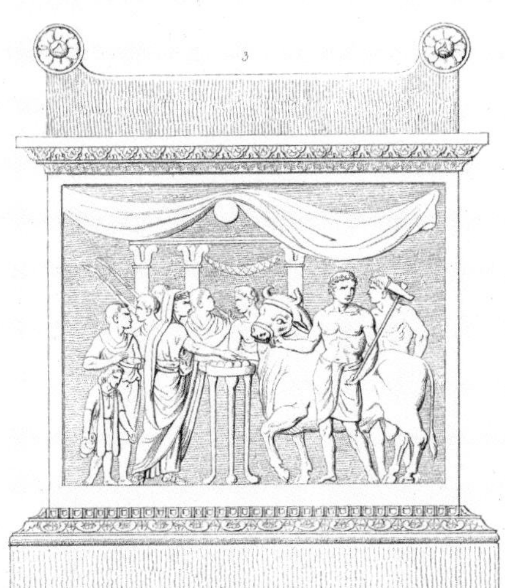

4

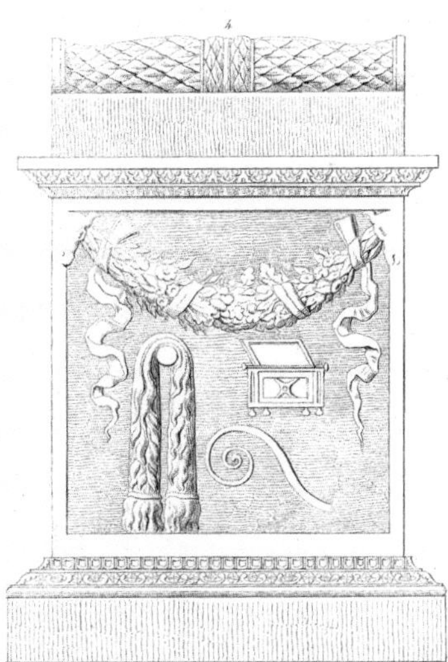

Grob inc. — F.lli Niccolini dir. — Lit. Richter e C.

CASA DEI CAPITELLI COLORATI

House of the Coloured Capitals

The Casa dei Capitelli colorati (VII 4, 31–33. 50 and 51), so called because of the colourfully painted Ionic capitals in its southern peristyle (18/19), is one of the large houses dating from the 2nd century BC and therefore from Pompeii's Oscan period. It extends right across an entire insula, from the Via della Fortuna to the Via degli Augustali, where its main entrance originally lay. The house covers almost 2000 m2 and contains a great many rooms, to which fresh alterations and extensions were made shortly before the eruption of Vesuvius. Little survives of the building which previously stood on the site apart from its walls and columns. The painted decoration dates from the years after the earthquake of AD 62, when the residential part of the house was probably reduced to just the southern end and the northern peristyle was given over to agricultural activity (an oil press). The excavators, who uncovered most of the house in 1833, were disappointed with the finds it yielded. The marble cladding had already been removed from the walls and pool (perhaps even in antiquity?) and other decoration they had expected to find was also missing. The majority of the often small mythological paintings which remained were cut out and sent to Naples. Only rooms 13, 17, 24 and 25 were given a protective roof and as a result are in relatively good condition today. The house was thoroughly documented in illustrations by various members of the excavation team and many of its mythological pictures were reproduced and discussed in volumes of the *Real Museo Borbonico*. We can follow this working process particularly clearly in the surviving sheets by Antonio Ala, which range from actual-size tracings to scale drawings of whole walls. With just four plates, the house is, however, only modestly represented here, but further illustrations are included later on in *Case e monumenti* (see also vol. III, Arte, pl. 54).

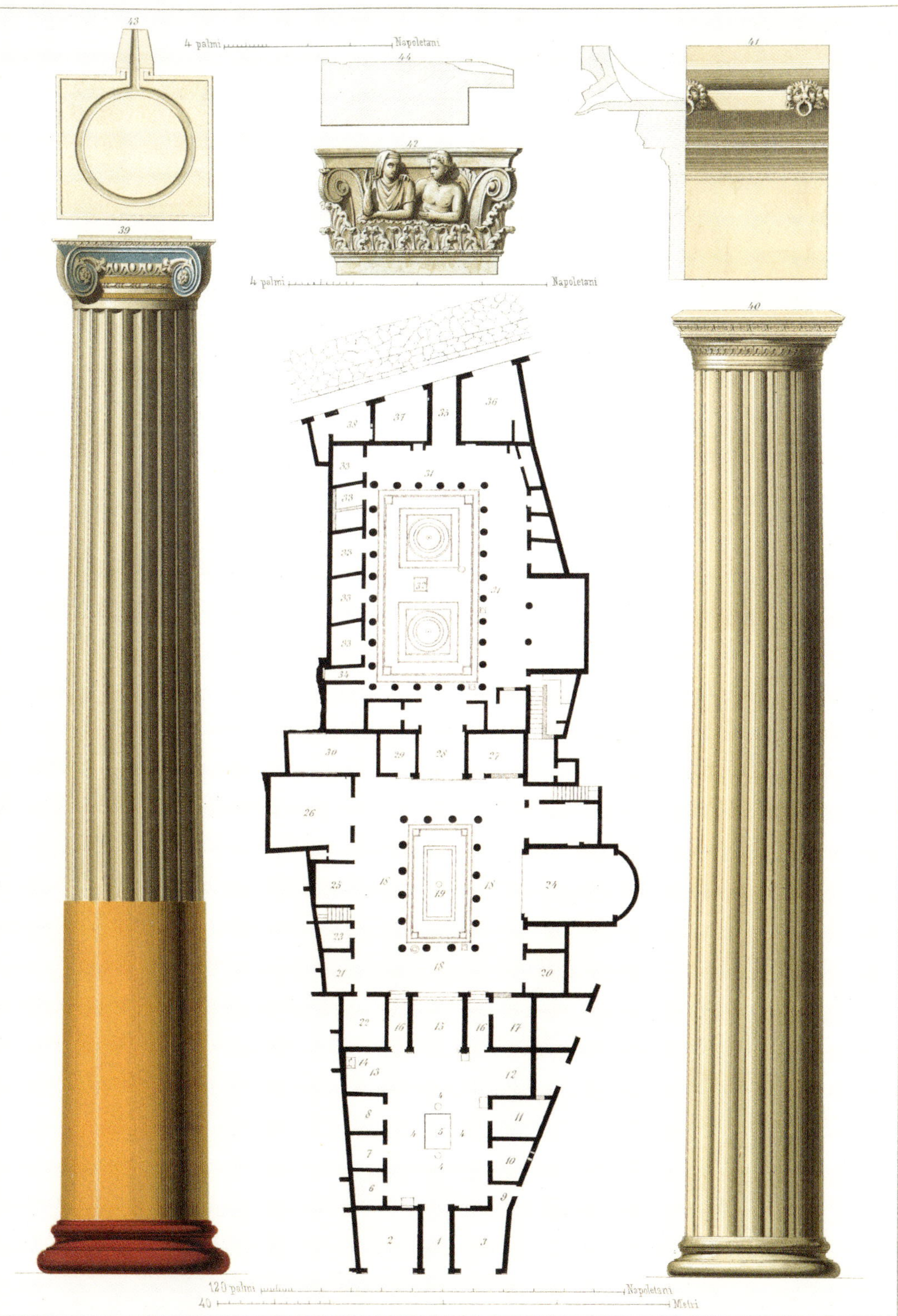

G. Frauenfelder dis. e lit

Fr.lli Niccolini dir

Lit. Richter e C. in Napoli

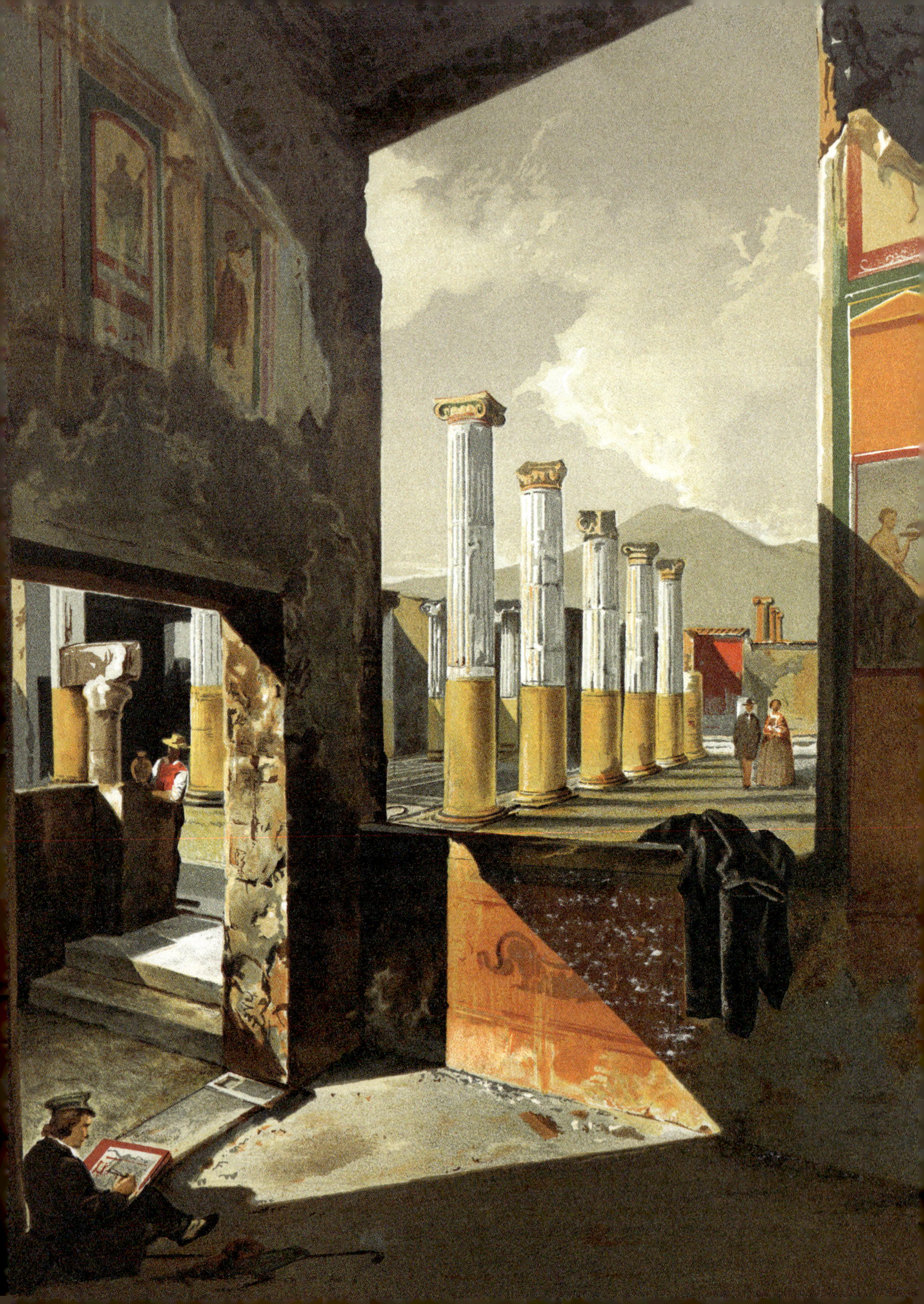

Page 133

Plate 2 — *[G. Frauenfelder]*

1–38 Ground plan of the house. *39* Ionic column in the south peristyle. *40* Originally Doric, then stuccoed column from the north peristyle. *41* Entablature from the north peristyle. *42* Figural capital from the entrance to the Casa dei Capitelli figurati (cf. vol. II, Casa dei Capitelli figurati, pl. 1). *43–44* Stone block from an oil press, found in the north-east corner of the peristyle (31).

❖

Plate 1 — *[G. Gigante]*

View from room (17) into the first peristyle (18) – The picture of Ganymede and the eagle of Zeus next to the window was later cut out.

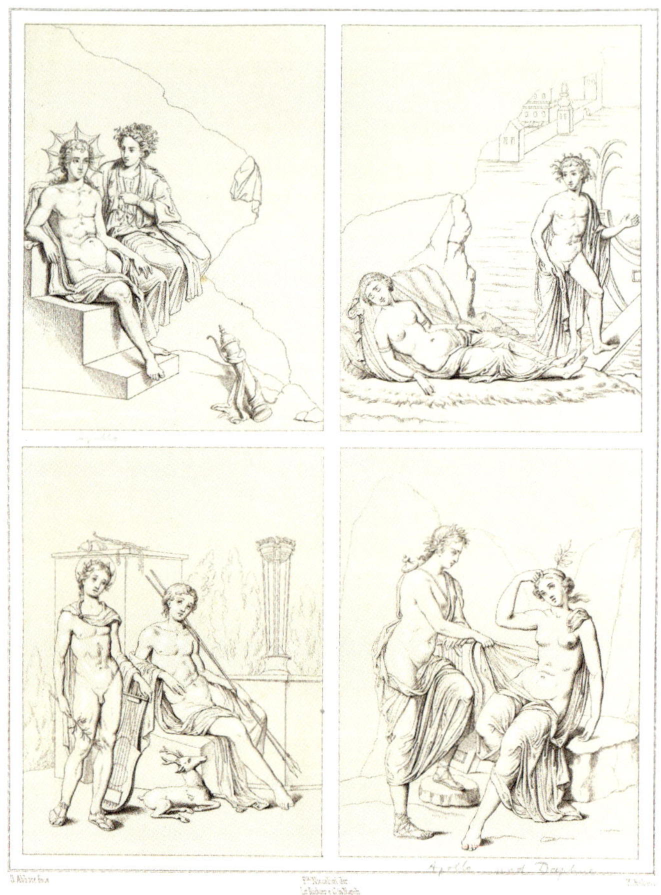

Plate 3 — *[G. Abbate]*

Oecus (26) – Central picture on the south wall whose subject is disputed (Apollo-Helios and his consort Rhodos?). ***Oecus (20)*** – Central picture on the north wall: Theseus abandons the sleeping Ariadne on Naxos. ***Oecus (17)*** – Central picture on the east wall: Apollo and Kyparissus with a cypress branch (?) in his right hand. ***Ala (7)*** – Central picture on the west wall: Apollo standing before the seated Daphne, who recognises him with surprise. A laurel branch is sprouting from her head.

Plate 4 — *[G. Abbate]*

Oecus (17) – Central picture on the south wall: Venus riding a sea centaur across the sea, accompanied by erotes.

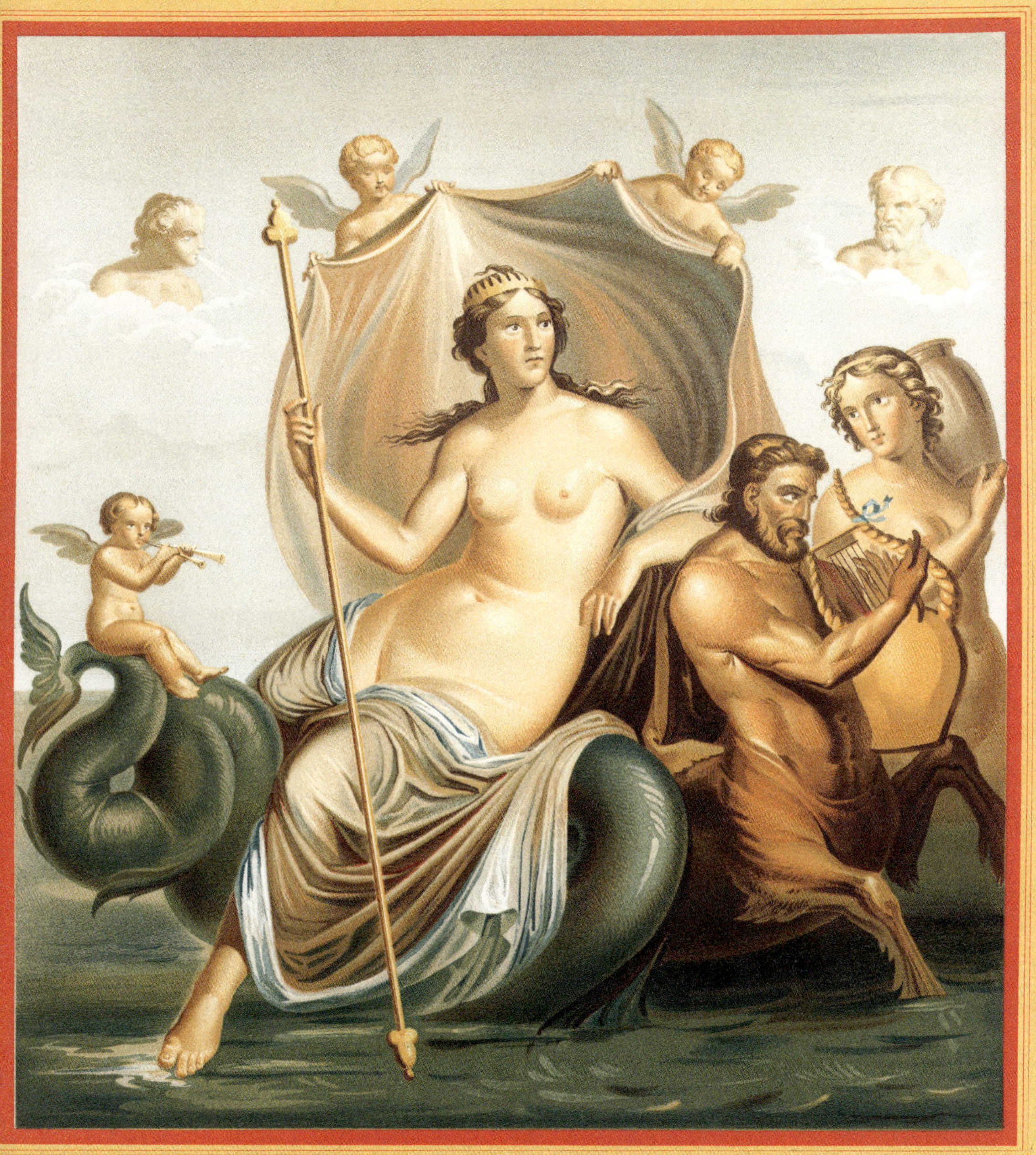

CASA DI MARCO LUCREZIO

House of Marcus Lucretius

A private residence that was uncovered east of the Via Stabiana in the first half of 1847 soon became known as the House of Marcus Lucretius (IX 3, 5 and 24) after the city councillor who was thought to have lived there. Its irregular and unusual ground plan shows that it consisted of two smaller units that were only amalgamated in the Imperial age (pl. 1). The surviving interior décor dates from the period shortly before the volcanic eruption. In particular the rooms around the large peristyle are distinguished by the very high quality of their decorations, whose central pictures take as their theme either the theatre or the legendary strength of Dionysus (pl. 2–3 and 5–9). What lends the house special significance, however, is a garden that was laid out in place of the usual peristyle and furnished with a great number of small marble statues of different subjects and of varying quality (pl. 1 and pl. 4). Since the site slopes upwards towards the east, the garden could easily have been seen not only from the surrounding rooms but all the way from the entrance itself. A small alcove in which the figure of a satyr is standing also contains a basin from which water runs down over some steps into a circular pool with a small fountain in the middle. Creatures from the world of Dionysus – satyrs and sileni, erotes and dolphins – frolic round about, along with ducks, ibises and other animal species. In the 19th century the garden was replanted in the antique fashion and the statuettes were left in place. For over a hundred years this ensemble remained as an example, visible from the street outside, of what a Pompeian garden looked like – until some of the statues were stolen and the rest were removed and placed in storage. But this mythologically themed landscape also attracted criticism from certain quarters: the garden was variously described as "thoroughly tasteless", "bizarre" and "of very uneven quality".

⁂

Plate 1 — *[G. Abbate]*

1 Ground plan of the house. *2–3* Right-hand ala: attributes of Dionysus in the predella zone. *4* Connecting room: small picture of writing utensils, on the sealed white letter the address which gives the house its name: *M(arco) Lucretio Flam(ini) Martis Decurioni Pompei(s)* (For Marcus Lucretius, Priest of Mars, Councillor of Pompeii). *5* Ala: head of an elephant. *6* Garden: graffito of a stylised labyrinth and the inscription: *Hic habitat Minotaurus* (The Minotaur lives here). *7–9, 12–14* Small marble sculptures associated with Dionysus from the pool area. *10–11* Marble sculptural groups: dolphins saving erotes from giant squid.

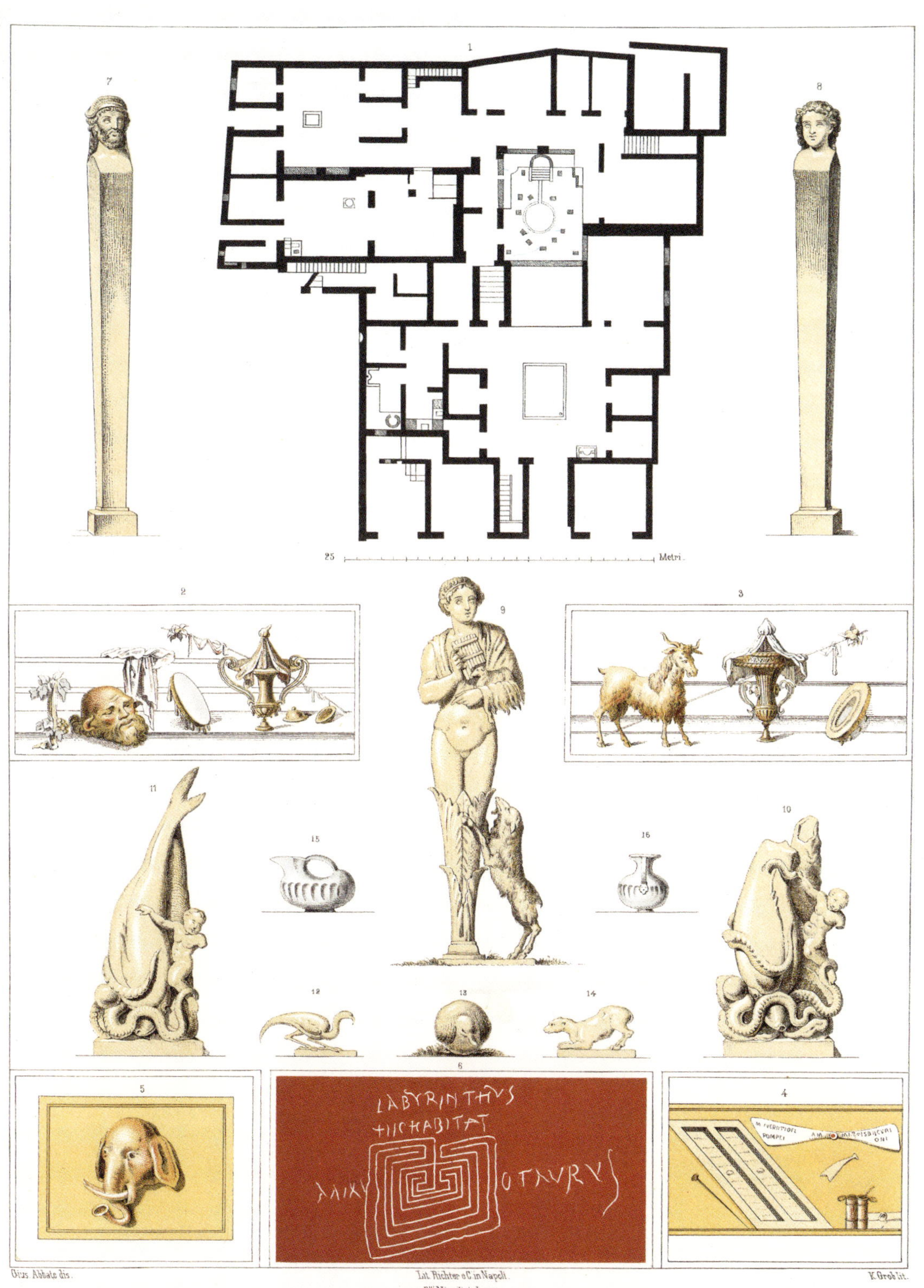

Gius. Abbate dis. Lit. Richter e C. in Napoli. K. Grob lit.

F.lli Niccolini direx.

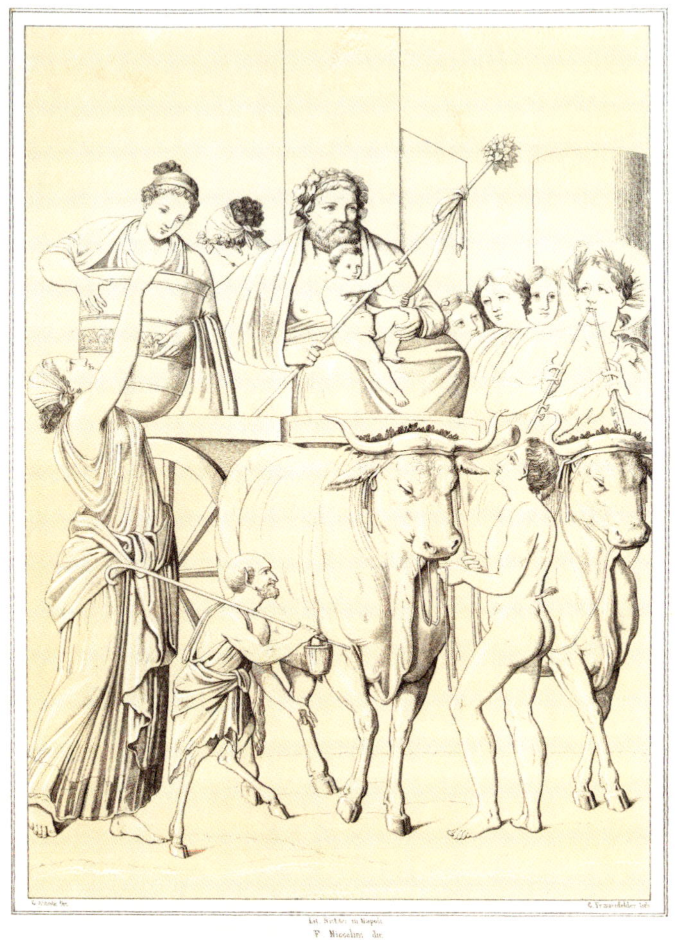

Plate 2 — *[G. Abbate]*
South wall of the triclinium – As befitting the banqueting room, the entire pictorial decoration is devoted to episodes from the life of Dionysus: the infant Dionysus sitting on Silenus' lap in an ox-drawn cart (see also pl. 5, 8 and 9).

✱

Plate 3 — *[G. Abbate]*
Cubiculum beside the atrium, north wall – 4th-style wall decoration: in the central picture, a seated Venus, fishing.

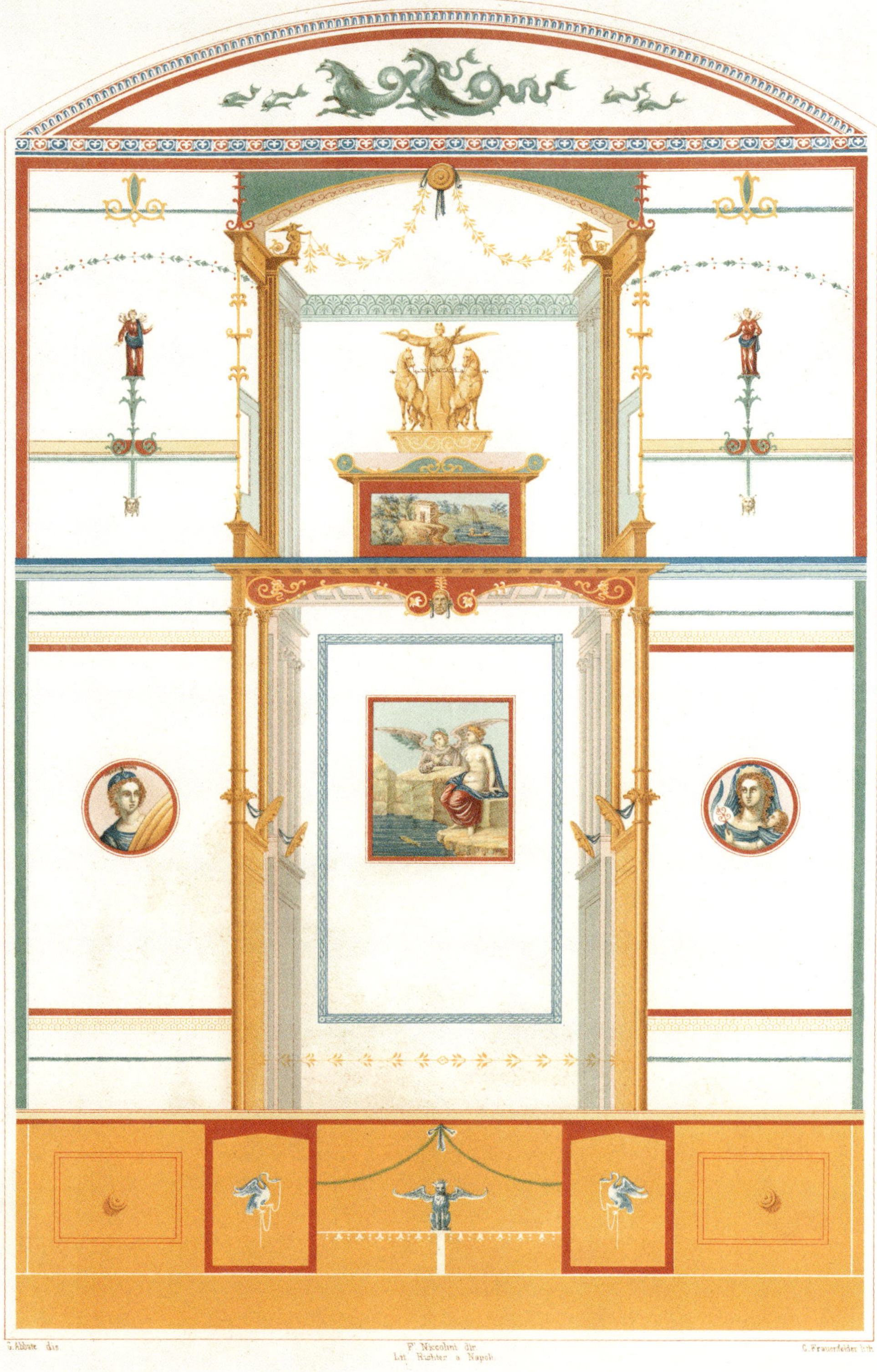

G. Abbate dis. F. Niccolini dir. C. Frauenfelder lith.
Lit. Richter a Napoli

Palmi 1 2 3 4 5 6 7 8 napolitani

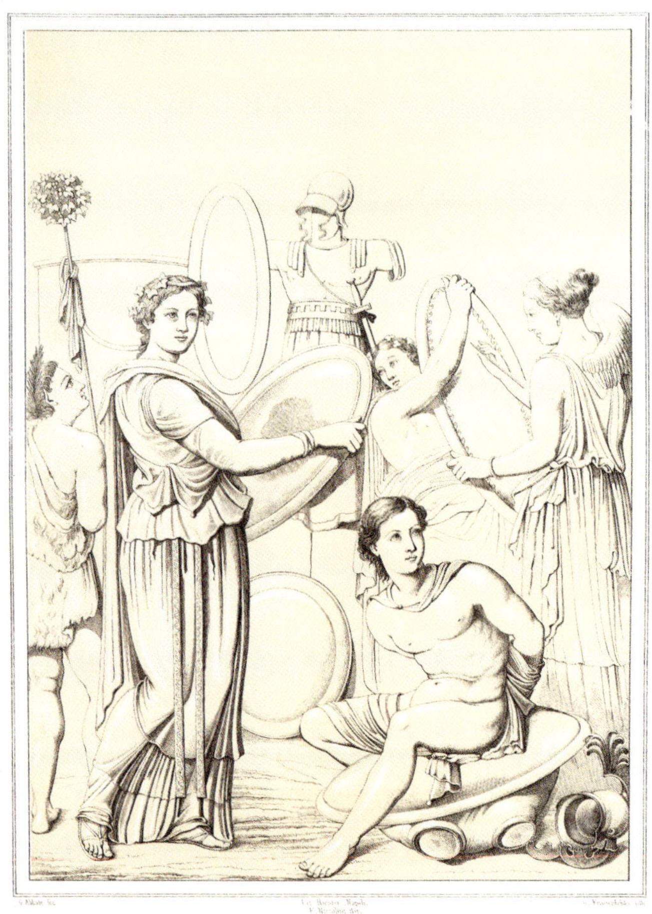

Plate 5 — *[G. Abbate]*
North wall of the triclinium – Triumph of Dionysus. The god is standing in the foreground with a prisoner seated on a pile of weapons in front of him. In the background, a tropaion – a victory monument made of weapons – is being erected, with Victory writing the triumphal announcement on a shield.

Plate 4 — *[G. Abbate]*
1 View of the fountain area and the objects and sculptures uncovered there. *5* Marble statuette of a satyr. *6* Statuette of a silenus leaning against a support. *7* Sculptural group: Pan extracting a thorn from a satyr's hoof. *8* Floor mosaic in the tablinum. *10* Lantern.

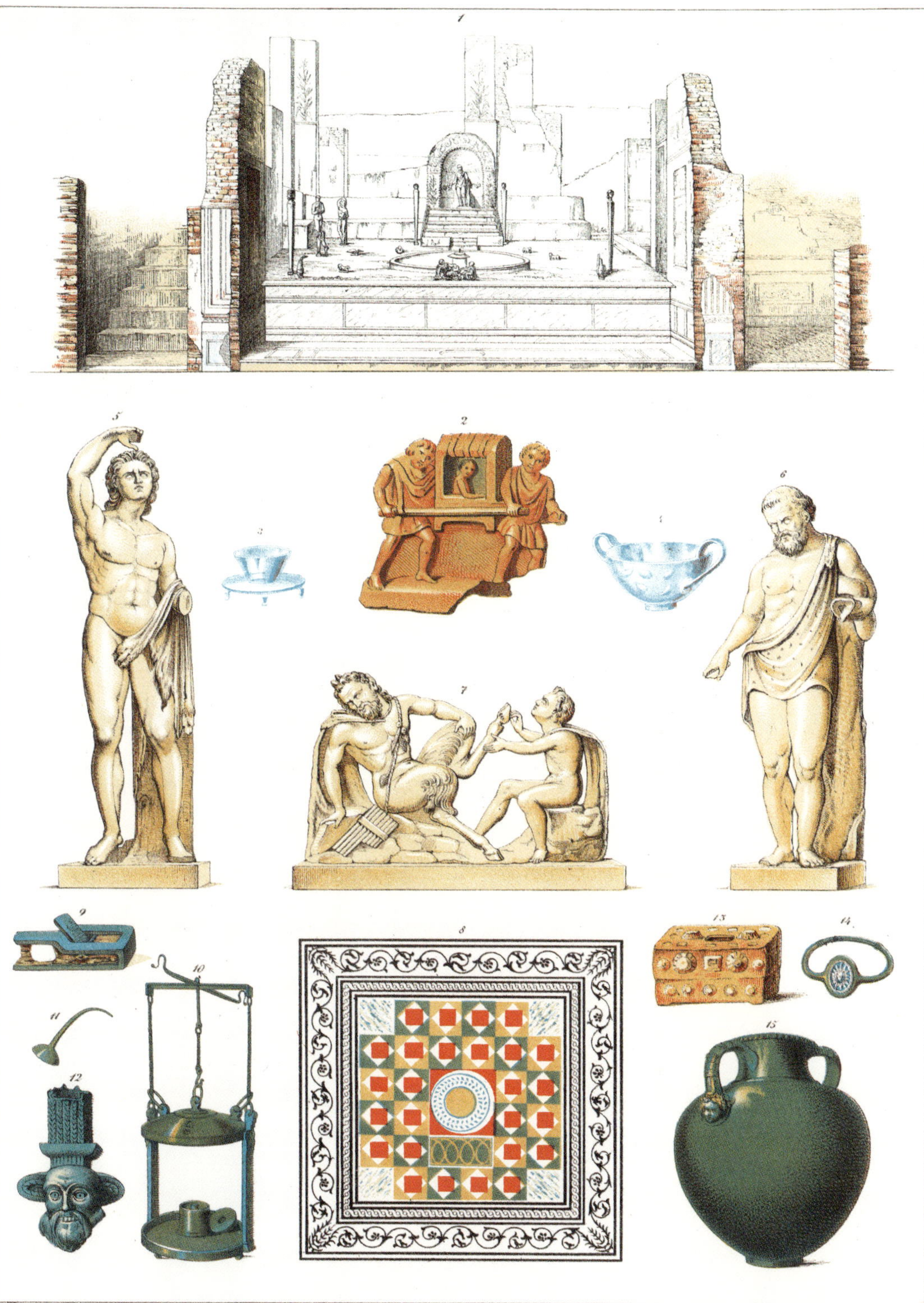

C. Abbate fec. F.lli Niccolini dir. G. Frauenfelder lith.
Lit. Richter, Napoli

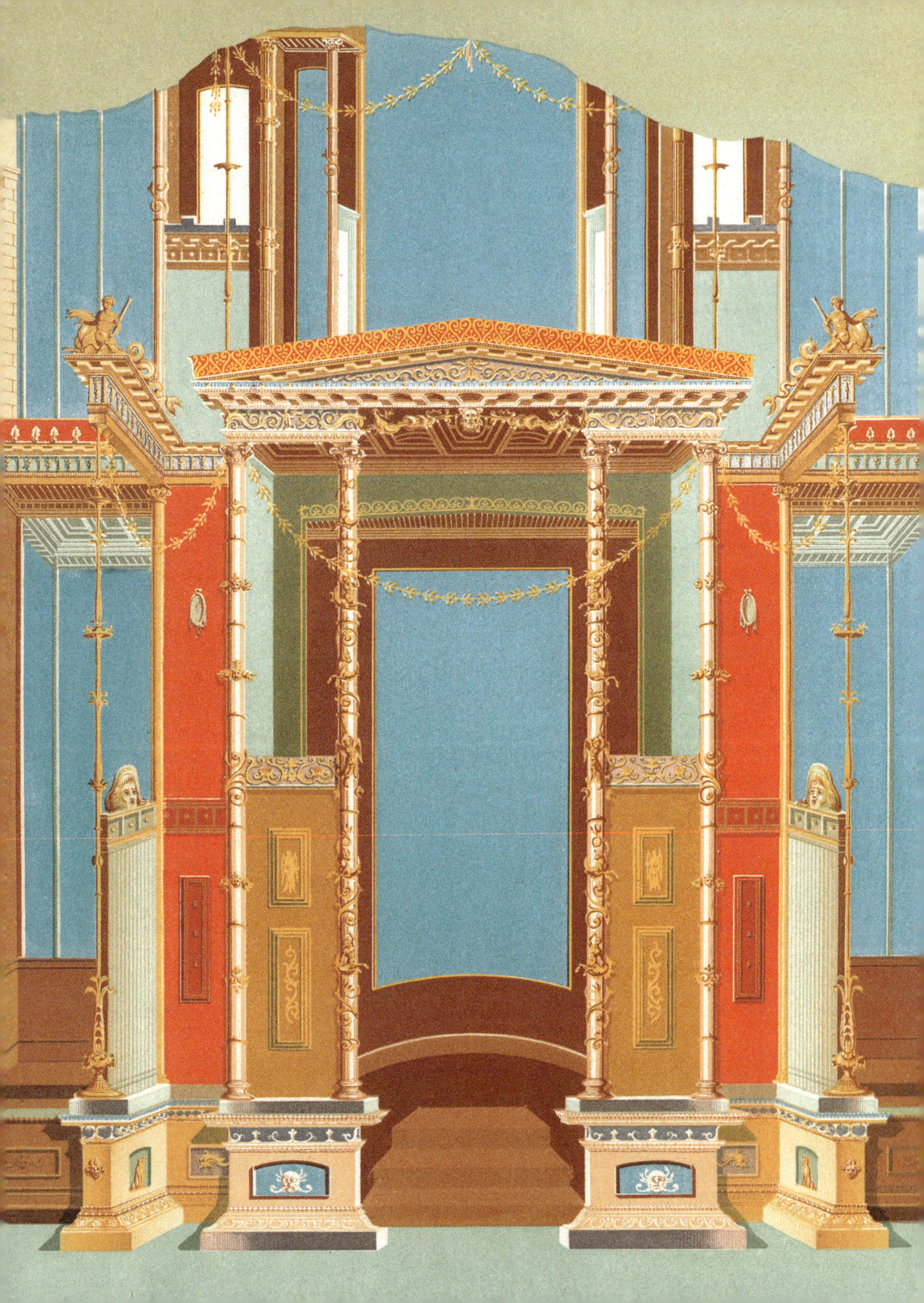

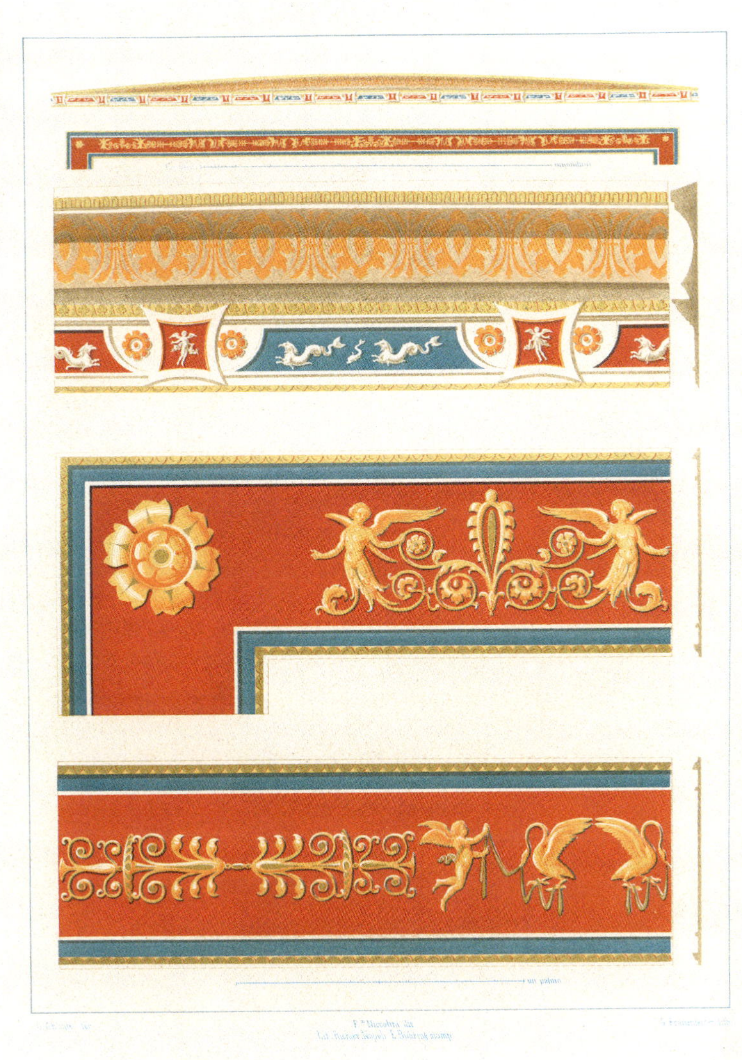

Plate 6 — *[G. Abbate]*
Atrium – 4th-style wall decoration.

✻

Plate 7 — *[G. Abbate]*
Upper zone of the tablinum – Painted decorative and stucco borders that Giuseppe Abbate found in the debris and pieced together.

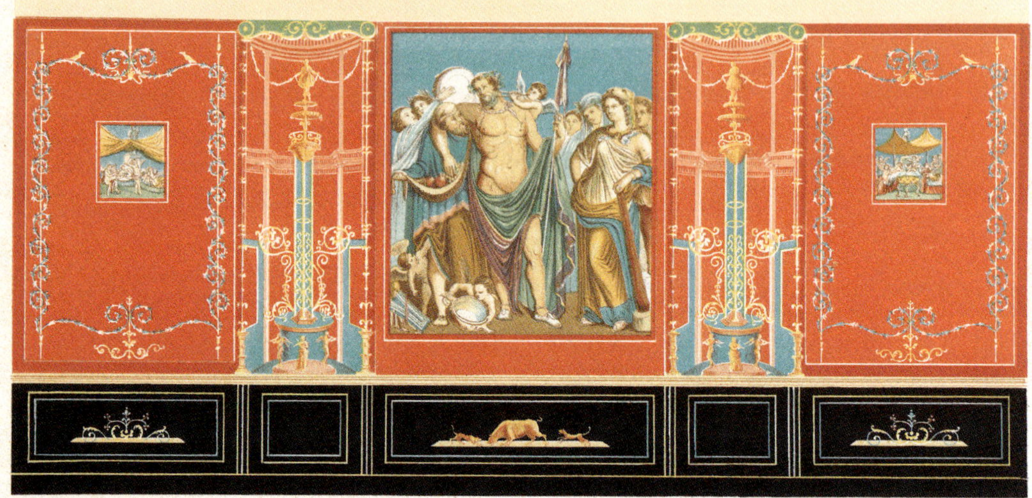

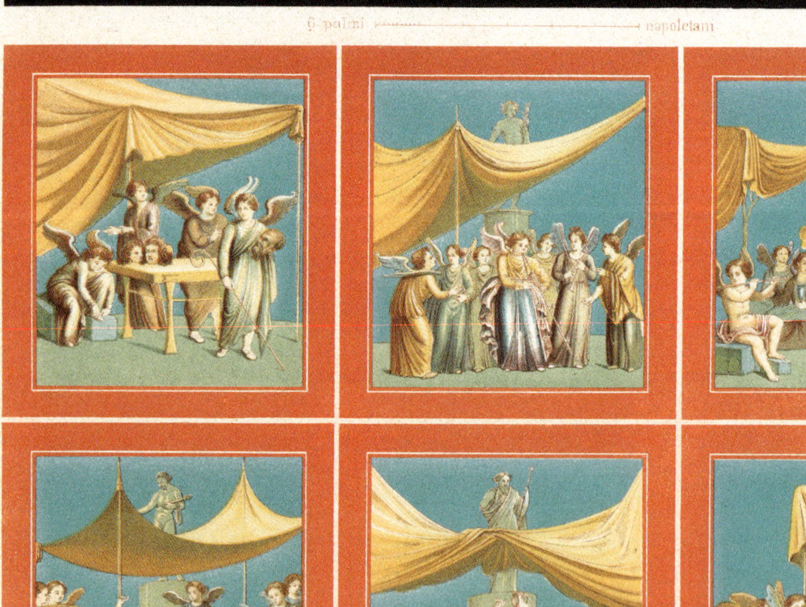

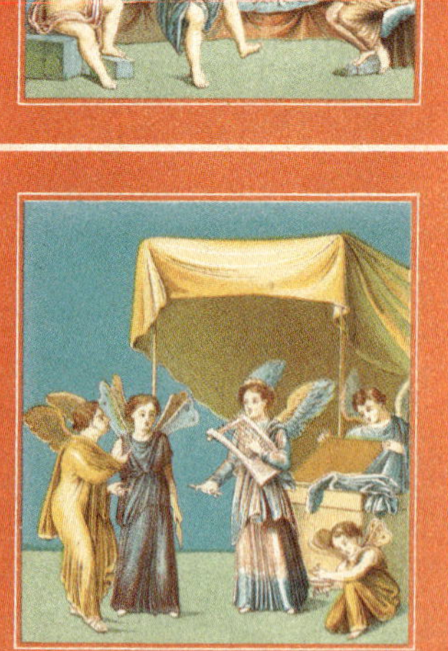

G. Abbate fec. F.[co] Niccolini dir. G. Frauenfelder lith.
Lit. Richter Napoli

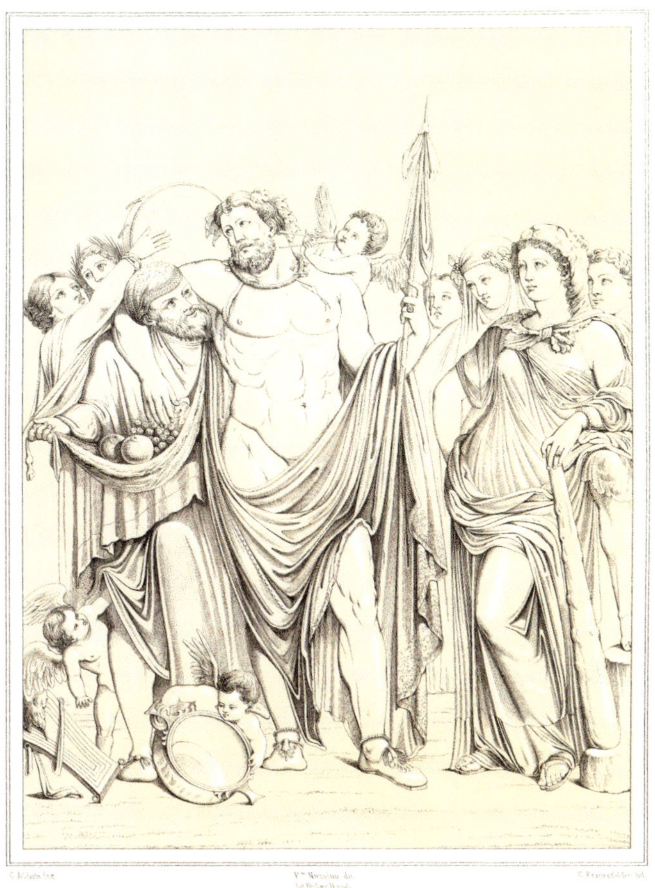

Plate 9 — *[G. Abbate]*
East wall of the triclinium – Above: view of the entire wall decoration with the drunken Hercules as the central picture (see pl. 8). Below: six scenes of celebrating cupids and psyches, which appeared in the right- and left-hand fields on the room's walls.

Plate 8 — *[G. Abbate]*
East wall of the triclinium – The Strength of Dionysus: the drunken Hercules has to be supported; the giant kantharos lies empty before him. Omphale stands beside Hercules, with his club and lion skin.

TERME STABIANE

Stabian Baths

(also Terme presso la Porta Stabiana)

Following the excavation of the first public baths at Pompeii near the Forum in 1825 (see vol. III), in 1853 a second complex – today known as the Stabian Baths (VII 1, 8) – was discovered on the Via Stabiana, near the Stabian Gate (presso la Porta Stabiana). The actual bath complex is lined with shops along its south and west faces, with the income from their lease going towards operating costs. The baths themselves consist of a peristyle courtyard with an open-air pool and separate facilities for men and women, laid out in mirror image on either side of the boiler room. They follow the standard sequence of apodyterium, frigidarium, tepidarium and caldarium. Thanks to their solid barrel-vault construction a number of ceilings and their stucco decoration have survived in good condition and these are shown in plates 2–4. The interior decoration of the baths had not yet been completed by AD 79 and the wall-paintings, like the stucco decorations in the courtyard, thus appear remarkably fresh and colourful. Today the Stabian Baths hold great significance for archaeological research on account of the many alterations carried out to the complex since the 3rd or 2nd century BC. These make it possible to trace the development of Roman bath culture in detail, both with regard to the engineering involved and the ways in which the baths were used.

With eight plates devoted to the Stabian Baths, the Niccolini brothers were the first to publish anything concerning this particularly magnificent complex, and very soon after its excavation. Moreover, they also took inspiration from the decorations of the Baths for their own architectural designs. Between 1864 and 1870, Fausto Niccolini, as the architect responsible for what had meanwhile become the "National" Museum in Naples, designed the interior décor for four of its large galleries. The stucco cladding on the ceilings, in particular, was very closely informed by the vaults of the apodyterium, its vestibule and the tepidarium.

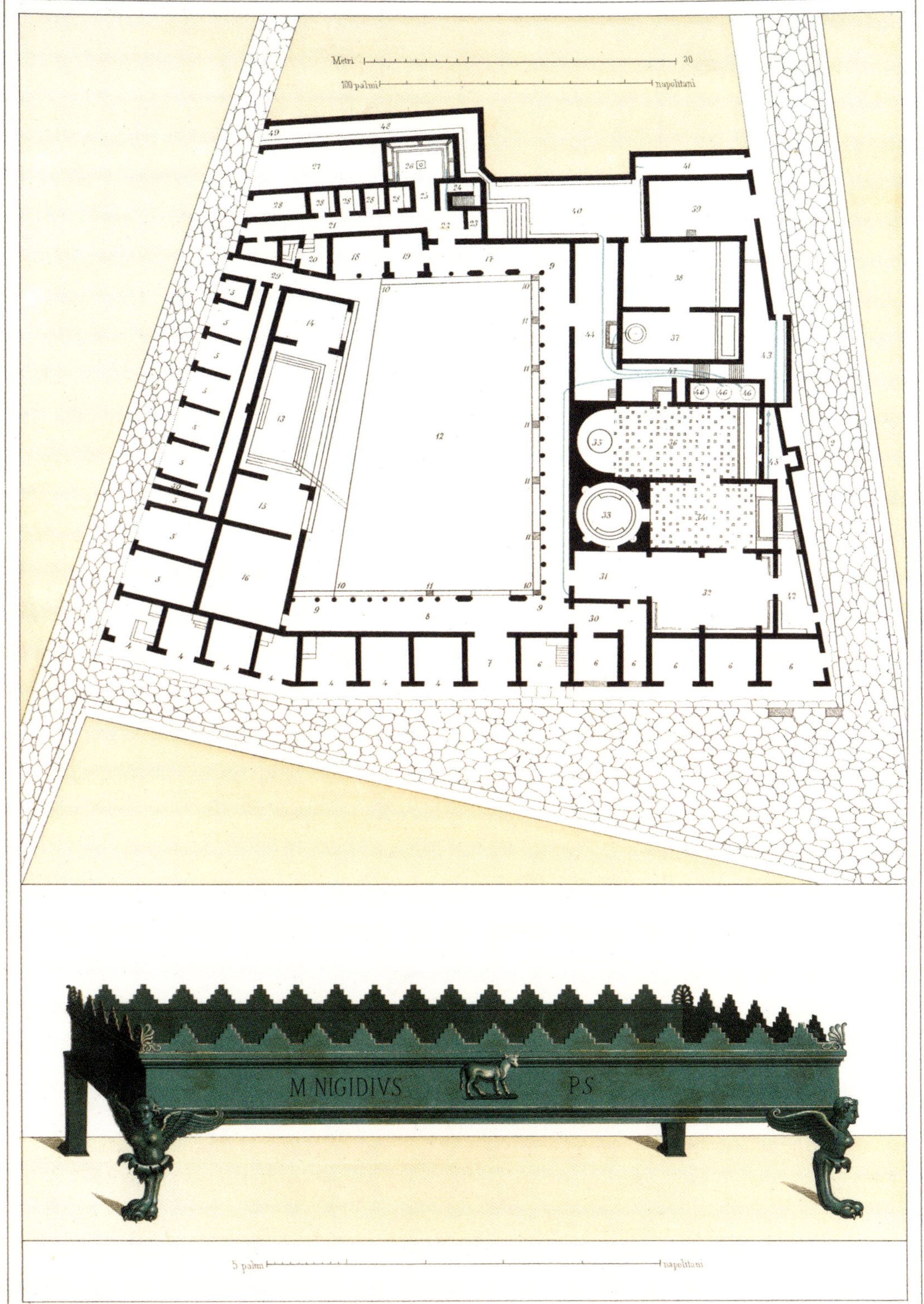

G. Abbate fece
Fr.llo Niccolini dir
Lit. Richter e C. in Napoli
G. Frauenfelder lith

Page 149

Plate 1 — ***[G. Abbate]***

Above: ***Ground plan of the Stabian Baths*** – ***7, 21, 39*** and ***42*** Different entrances. ***12*** Palaestra. ***13*** Swimming pool *(natatio)*. ***26*** Latrine. ***31–36*** Men's baths. ***37–40*** Women's baths. ***46*** Three water boilers. Below: ***Brazier*** – From room (19), donated by one M. Nigidius Vaccula (his cognomen, meaning "heifer", is represented by a young cow). The letters "PS" stand for "Pecunia Sua" (paid for with his own money).

✠

Plate 4 — ***[G. Abbate]***

Vestibule of the apodyterium (31) – Detail of the stucco decoration of the barrel vault: in the fields against blue backgrounds, Hora with a tambourine together with floating animals and erotes.

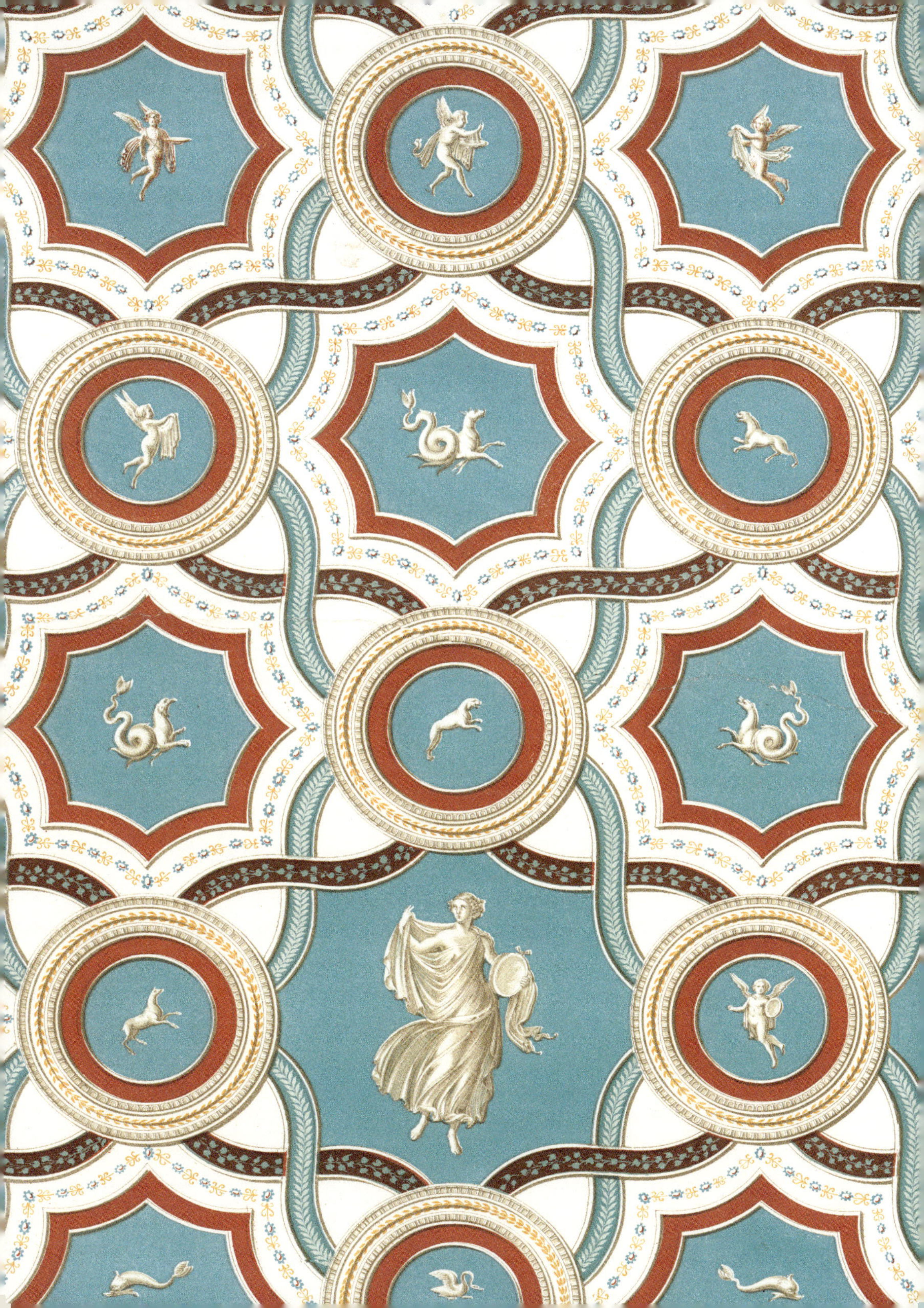

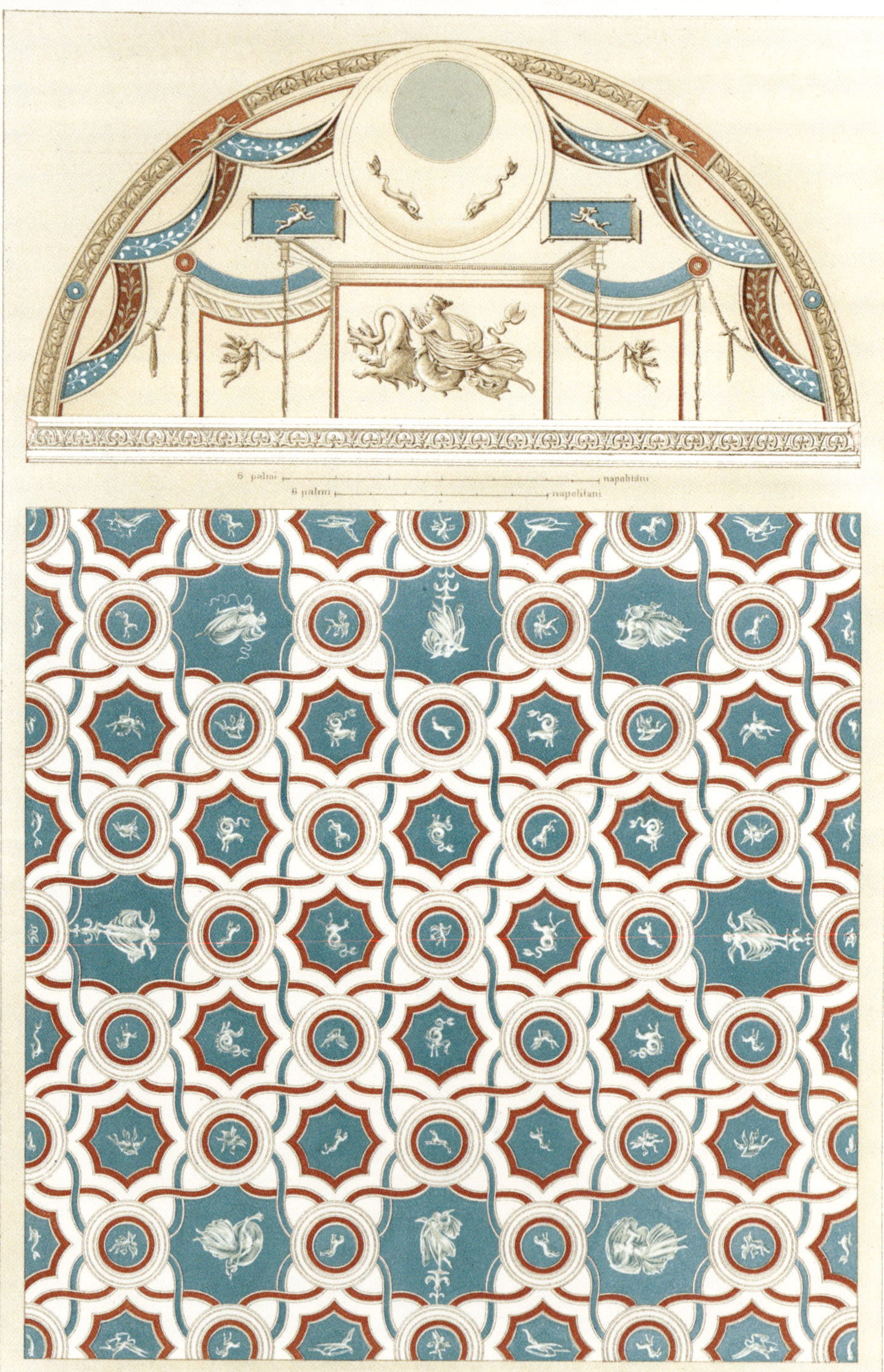

G. Abbate fec. F.lli Niccolini dir G. Frauenfelder lith.
Lit. Richter, Napoli

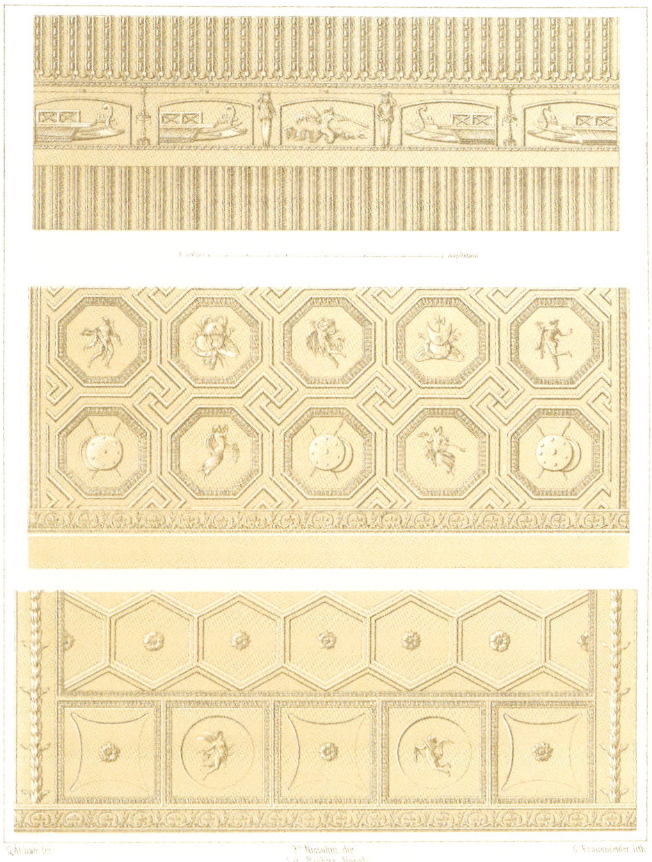

Plate 3 — *[G. Abbate]*
Vestibule of the apodyterium (31) – Stucco decoration of the barrel vault and the lunette on the west wall: interlacing bands form differently shaped fields with a blue ground, containing various flying or floating figures.

Plate 2 — *[G. Abbate]*
Elements of the stucco decoration – *A* Frieze along the top of the wall in the tepidarium (34), showing warships, sea creatures and supporting figures (cf. pl. 6.2).
B–C Details from the apodyterium (32): floating figures and trophies.

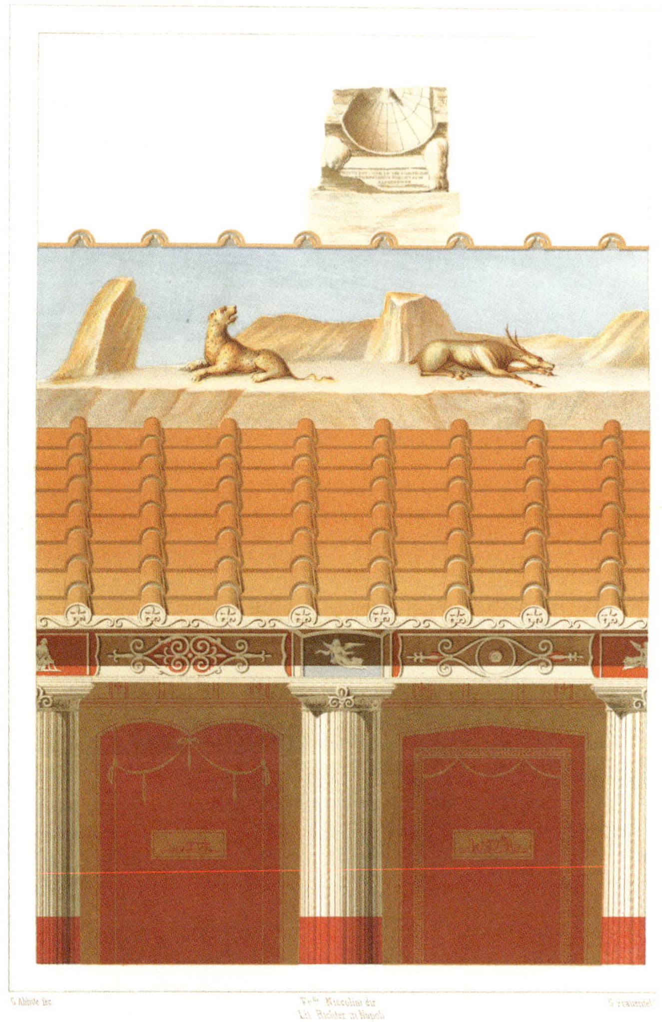

Plate 5 — *[G. Abbate]*
View of the eastern wing of the palaestra – With a sundial dating from the 2nd century BC, found in situ.

Plate 7 — *[G. Abbate]*
Frigidarium (33) – Wall decoration on the east side: Silenus reclining in a garden, propped against a wineskin.

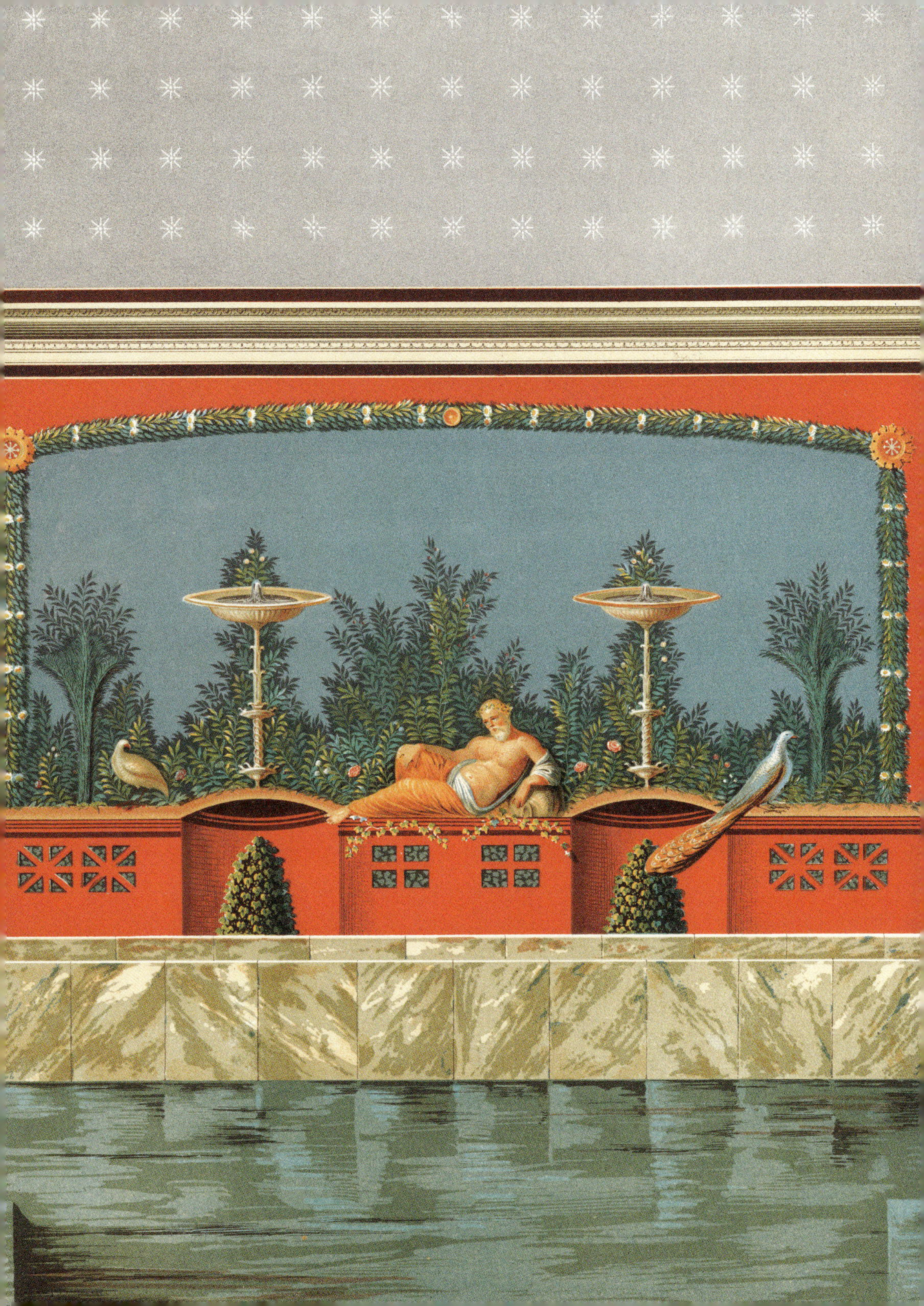

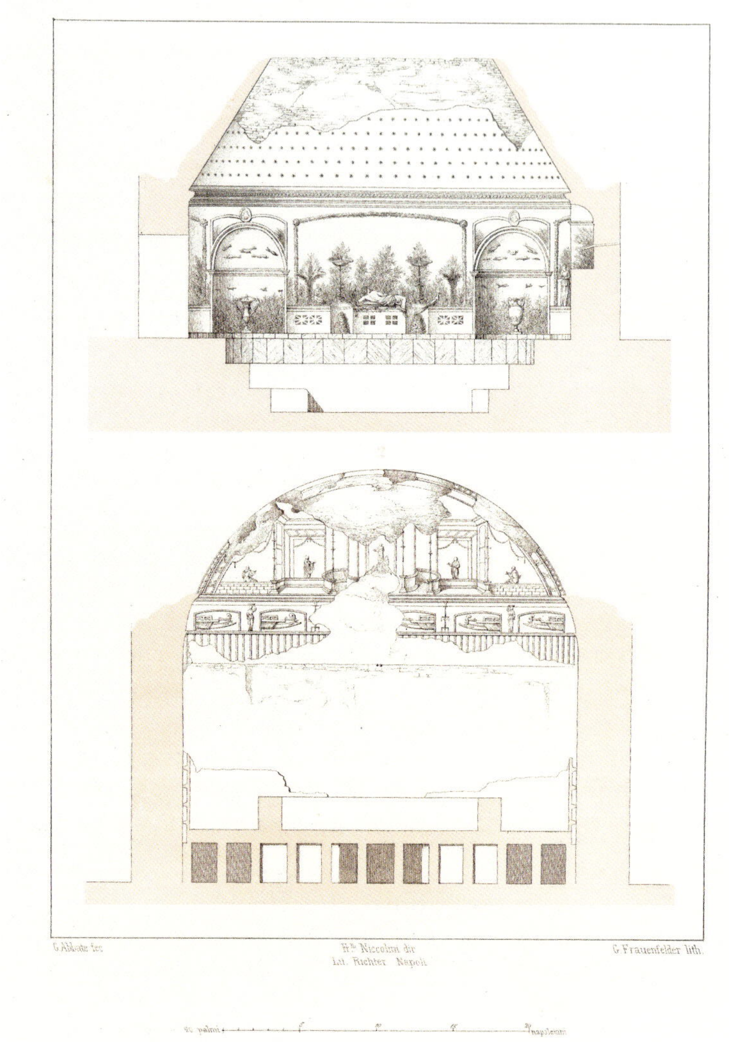

Plate 6 — *[G. Abbate]*

1 North-south cross section through the circular frigidarium (33) with rear view of a reclining figure. *2* North-south cross section through the tepidarium (34) with the stucco frieze and lunette decoration on the east wall.

Plate 8 — *[G. Abbate]*

Palaestra façade of room (16) – Detail of the stucco decoration: lavish architectural prospect from Pompeii's final years. In the centre, drunken Hercules with young Eros.

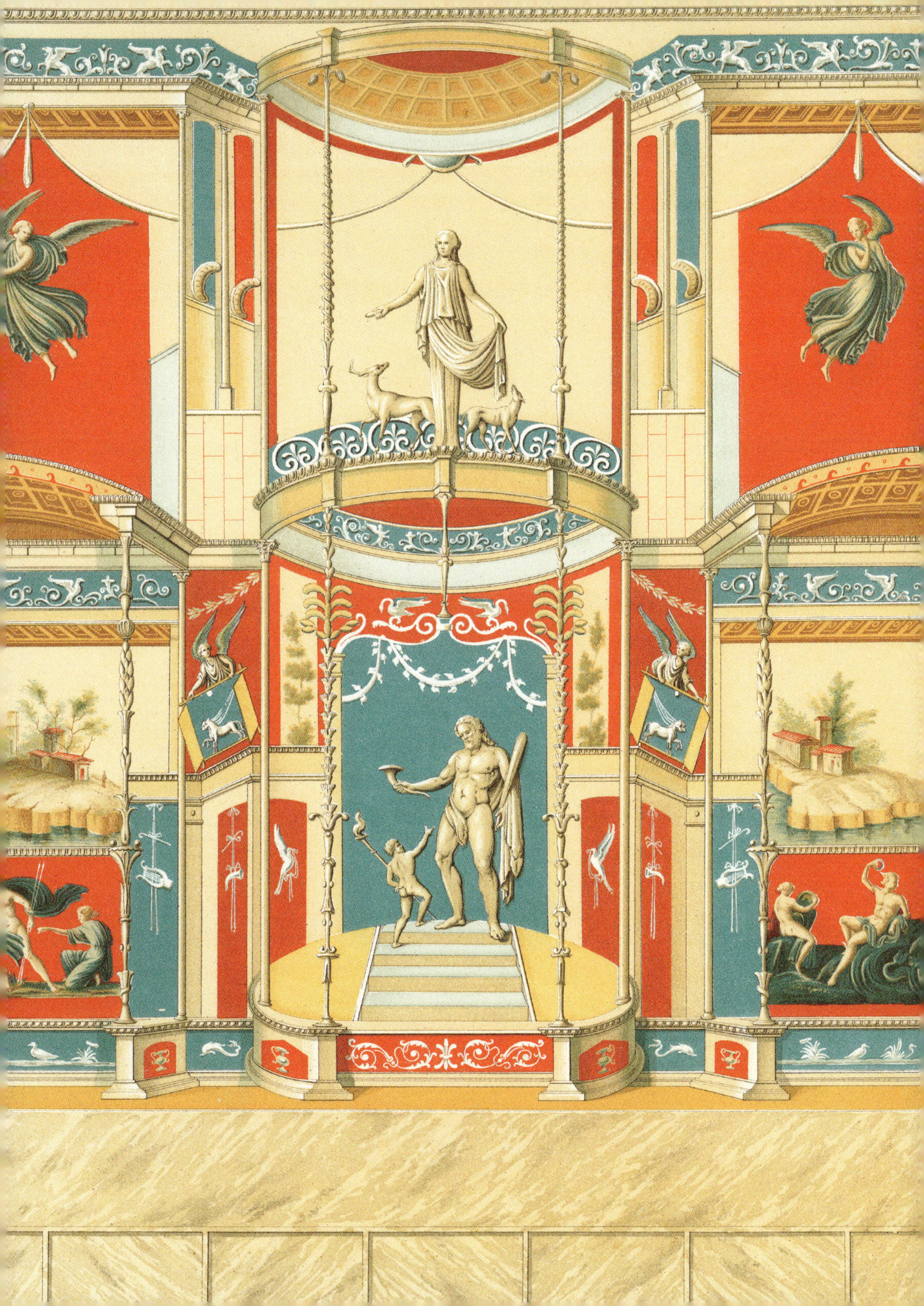

CASERMA DEI GLADIATORI

Gladiators' Barracks

(also Portico of the Theatre)

Attached to Pompeii's large Hellenistic theatre was a colonnaded square that was used by the public during intervals in performances or else – according to a more recent interpretation – served as gymnasium. At the latest after the earthquake of AD 62, however, this area was assigned a different use. Behind the porticos, on two storeys, were several small rooms in which a large number of helmets and leg guards were found in 1766/67. These were identified in the 19th century as items of gladiators' armour, suggesting that this was a *ludus gladiatorius* – a combined residential and training complex for gladiators. Along with a wealth of graffiti concerned with gladiators, the decoration of one of the larger rooms (pl. 1, B and C) confirms this interpretation – hence the name Caserma dei Gladiatori (VIII 7, 16 and 17) used by the Niccolini brothers. The fights themselves took place in the amphitheatre and occasionally in the Forum.

In the 18th century the Gladiators' Barracks was the entrance point for visitors to the excavations and where the guides promptly related one of the (false) myths about Pompeii: the discovery of the skeleton of a woman wearing lavish jewellery led to the claim that the eruption of Vesuvius had surprised a high-society lady during a tryst with a gladiator. In reality, she was one of a group of women here overtaken by death as they attempted to flee.

The richly ornamented ceremonial helmets were probably only worn by the gladiators during parades, but not in actual combat. Alongside motifs from the mythological worlds of Hercules and Dionysus, the decoration on the helmets also employed imperial ideology with subjects such as the conquest of Troy or Rome enthroned. The weapons continue to serve today as models for history paintings and "swords-and-sandals" movies.

⁂

Plate 1 — *[G. Abbate]*

A Ground plan, oriented facing the west. *1–3* Main east entrance from the Via Stabiana. *43* Steps up to the "*lanista*'s quarters". *45* Prison. *B–C* Wall-painting with representation of gladiators' armour and weapons from room (37). *D–E* Details of column orders. *F* Leg irons for prisoners, found in room (45).

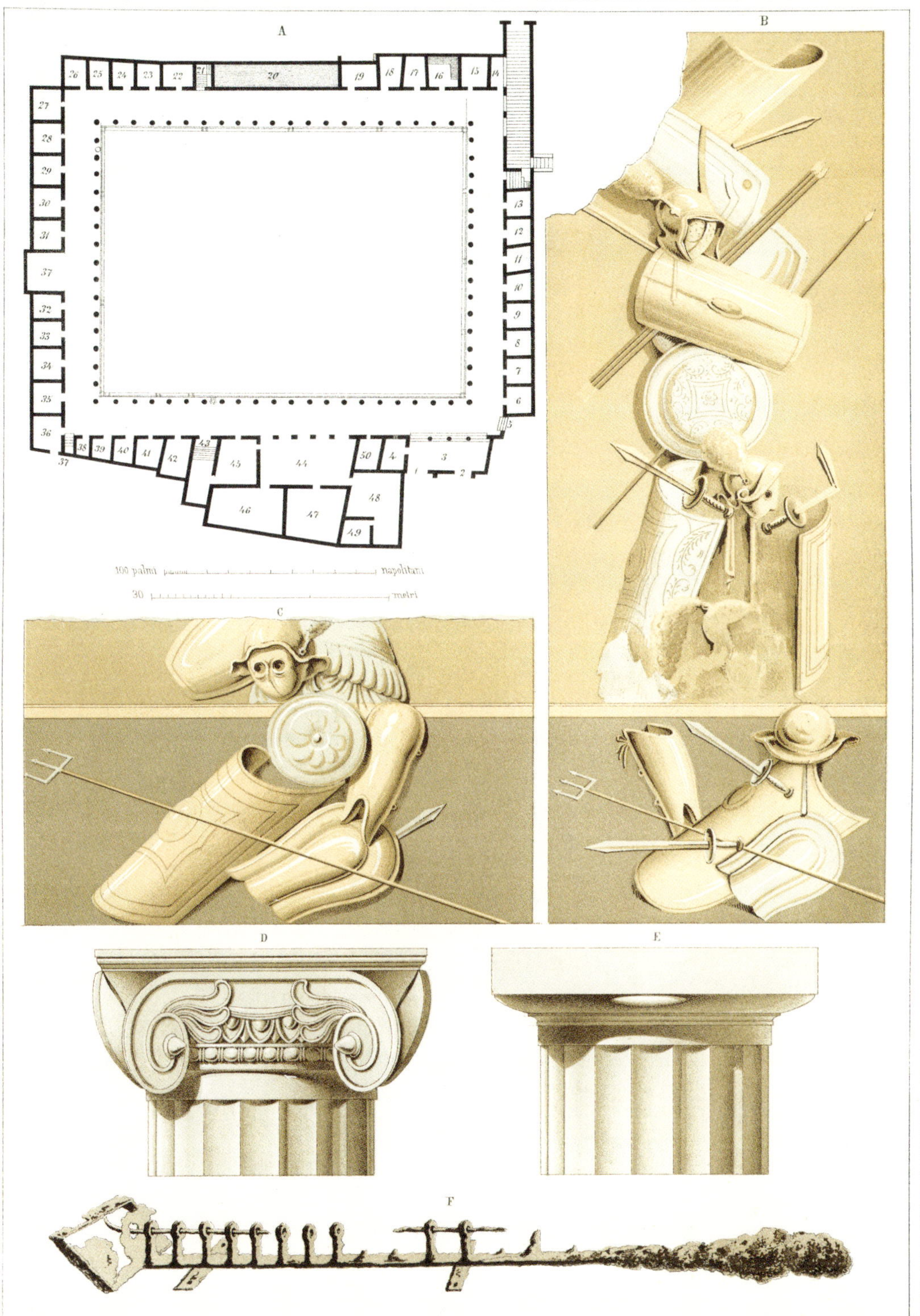

G. Abbate dis.

Fr.co Niccolini dir.
Lit. Richter e C. in Napoli

G. Frauenfelder lit.

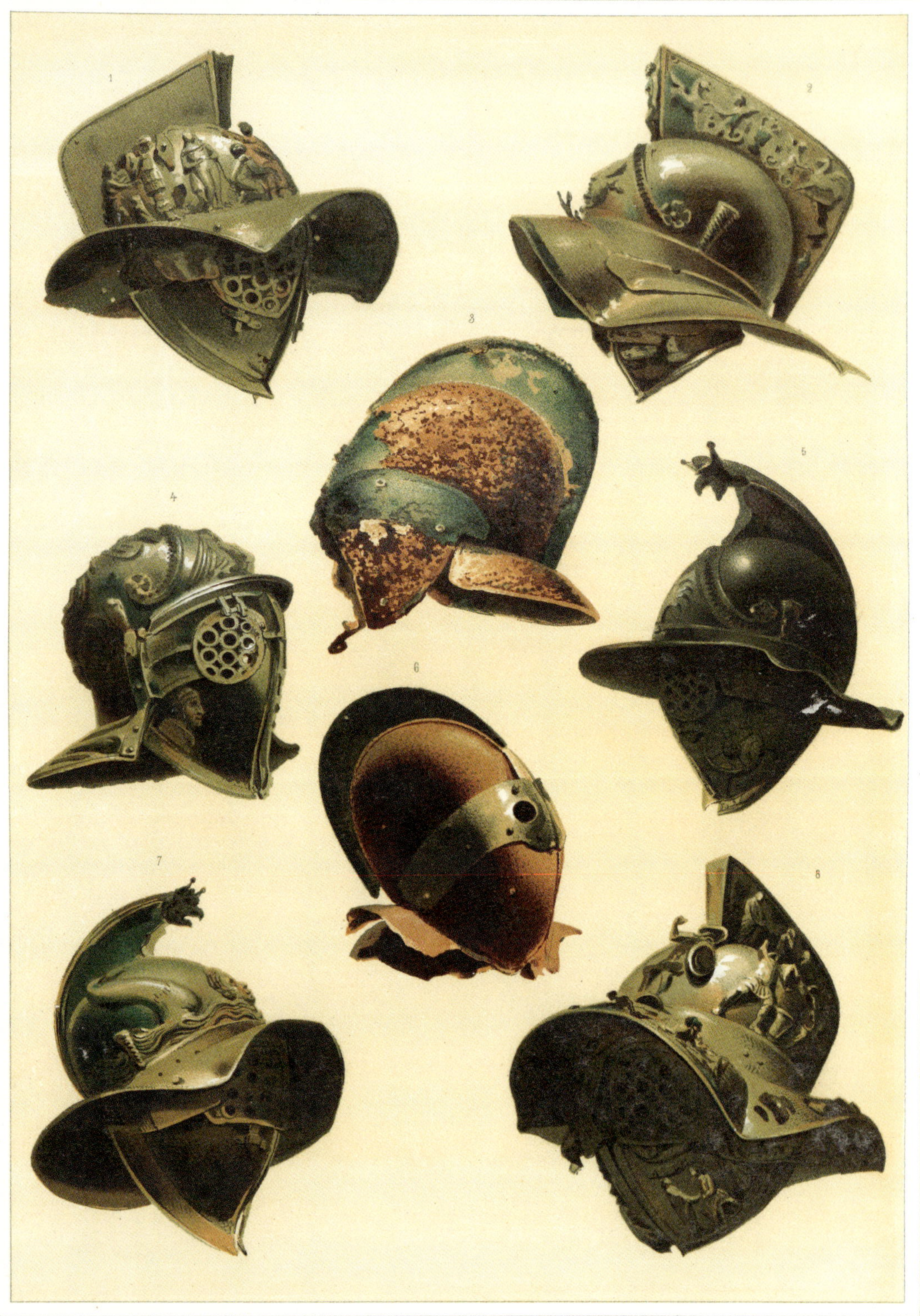

F. Mattej dis. Flli Niccolini dir. Lit. Richter e C. in Napoli. K. Grob lith.

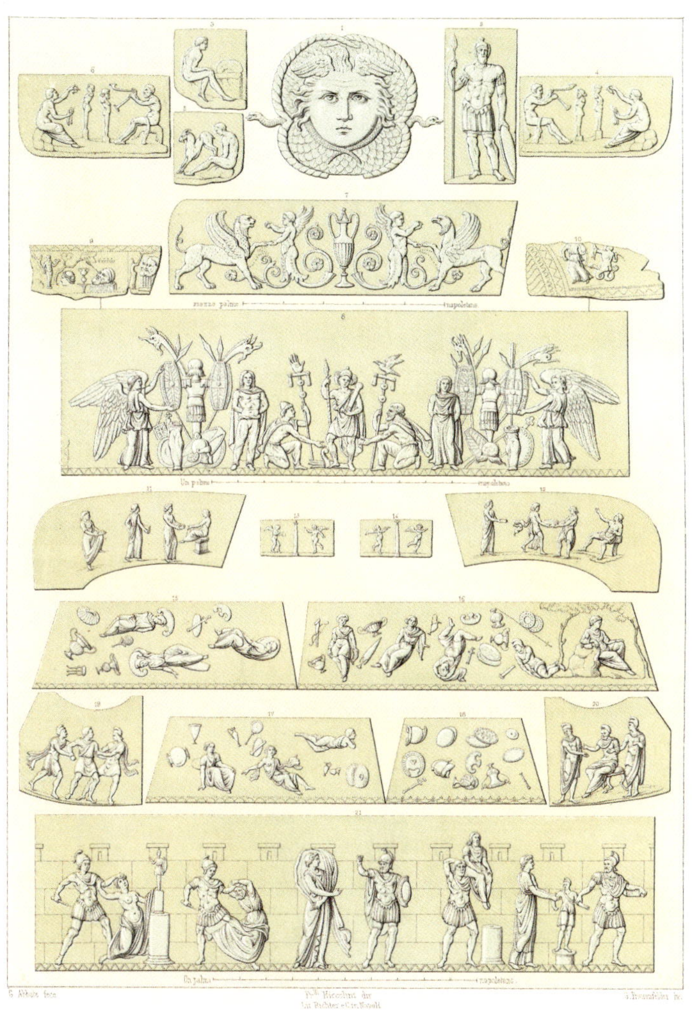

Plate 2 — *[P. Mattej]*
Gladiators' helmets in Naples.

✠

Plate 3 — *[G. Abbate]*
Decorative details of the helmets in plate 2.

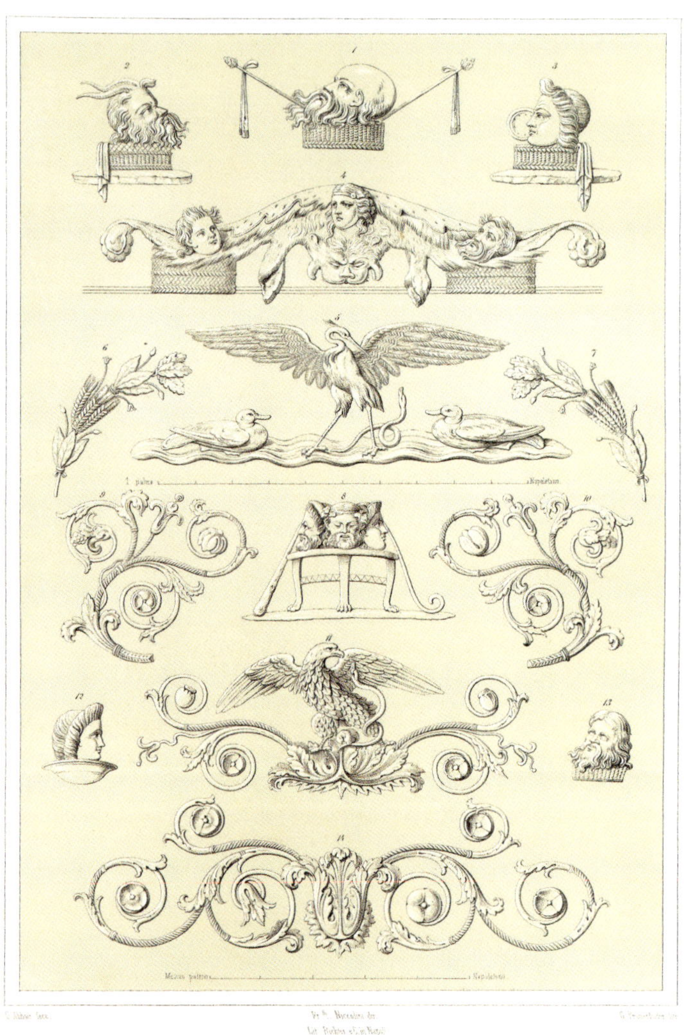

Plate 5 — *[G. Abbate]*
Ornamental details of the armour in plate 4.

Plate 4 — *[P. Mattej]*
1–8 Pieces of gladiators' armour: shoulder guards, shield, leg guards and a fragment of scale armour.
9 Part of a belt. *10* Sword from Stabiae.

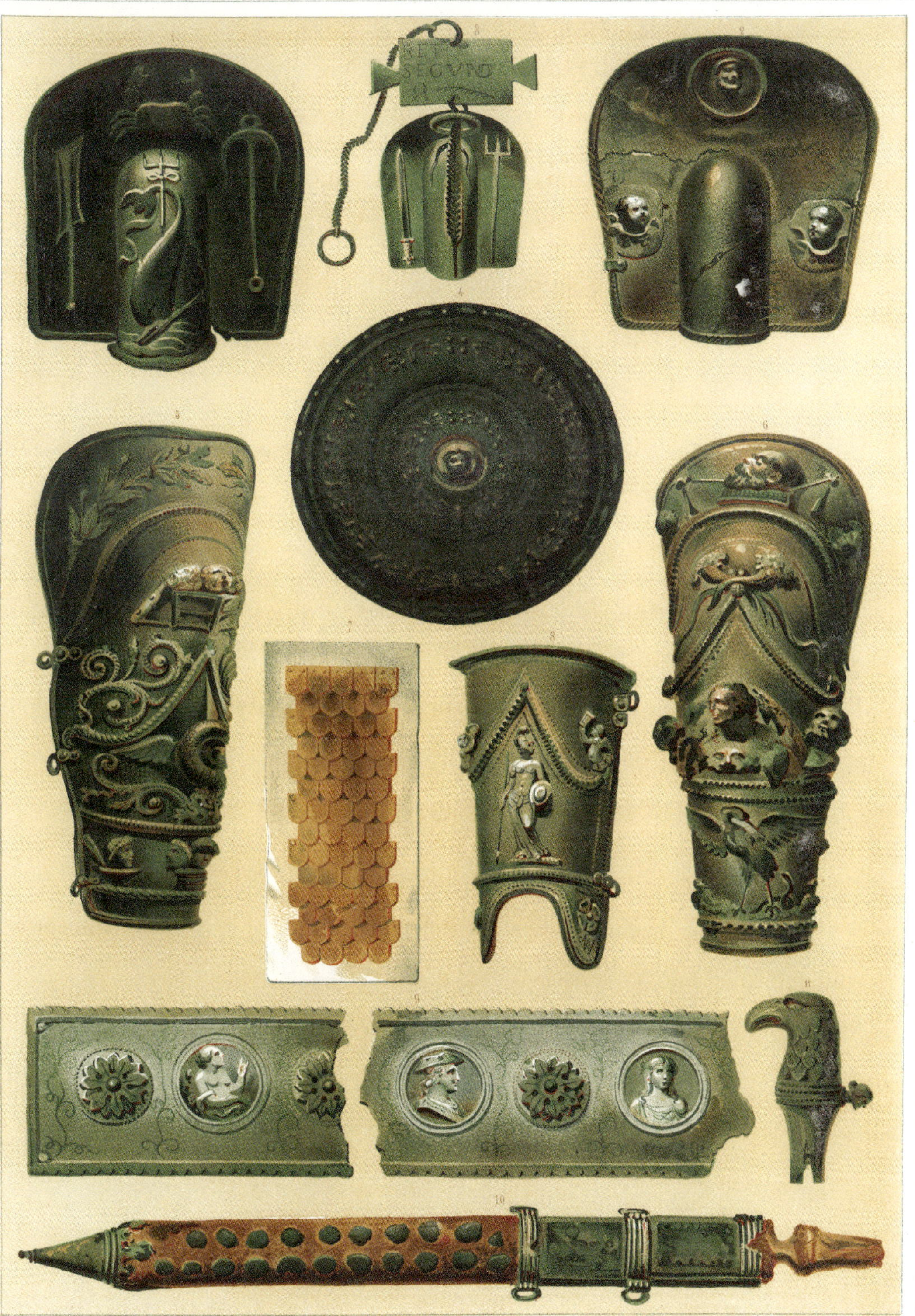

E. Mattej dis. Fco Nicoolini dir. K. Grob lith.

Lit. Richter e C. in Napoli.

TEATRI

Theatres

Pompeii had two theatres, which were located right next to each other on the steep southern slope of the city's hill and exploited this topography for their auditoriums. The considerably larger (VIII 7, 20–21. 27 and 30) of the two was built in the 2nd century BC and adapted in the Augustan era to meet Roman requirements. Although most of the marble is now missing, remains of some of the seats of honour, which belonged to particularly important citizens, can still be seen (pl. 1, no. 28). Evidence of the places where tall posts once stood suggests that the theatre was equipped with large sun awnings *(vela)*, which could be unfurled above the spectators – something freely mentioned as a particular luxury in announcements for the games (pl. 2, no. 3). The second theatre (VIII 7, 17–20) is expressly described in an inscription as a *theatrum tectum* and was therefore fully roofed. It was built soon after Pompeii became a Roman *colonia* in 80 BC, and was commissioned by the same two magistrates who were responsible for the construction of the amphitheatre. The antiquated supporting figures in the *cavea* also date from this period (pl. 2, no. 5). The juxtaposition of an open-air theatre and a smaller, roofed assembly house is not uncommon in Southern Italy. This duplication may be connected with the influx of colonists, who brought with them new administrative structures and hence the need for more public buildings. The two theatres were easy to identify among the ruins and were excavated, with certain interruptions, between 1764 and the end of the 18th century. For a long time they ranked among Pompeii's most important sights and hence were frequently reproduced in vedute and panoramas. Giovanni Battista Piranesi produced the first detailed drawings of their architecture in the 1770s (for the theatre complex see also vol. I, Caserma dei Gladiatori).

Plate 1 — *[Anonymous]*
1–27 Ground plans of the two theatres and cross sections through their cavea and stage house respectively. *9* Orchestra. *12* Front of the pulpitum (stage). *10* Location and *29* detail of the seat of honour reserved for M. Holconius Rufus.

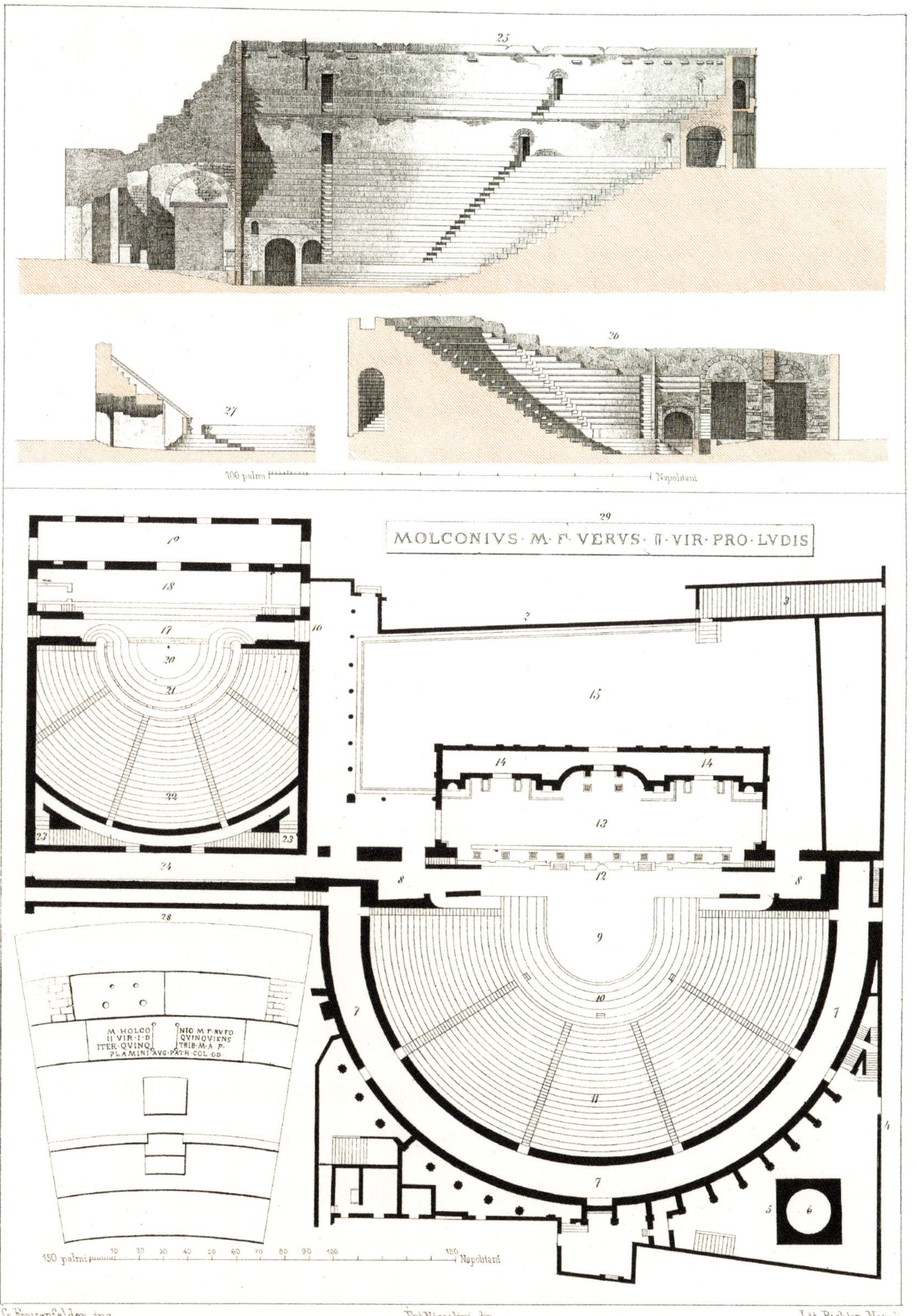

G. Frauenfelder inc. Frᵗ Niccolini dir. Lit. Richter, Napoli

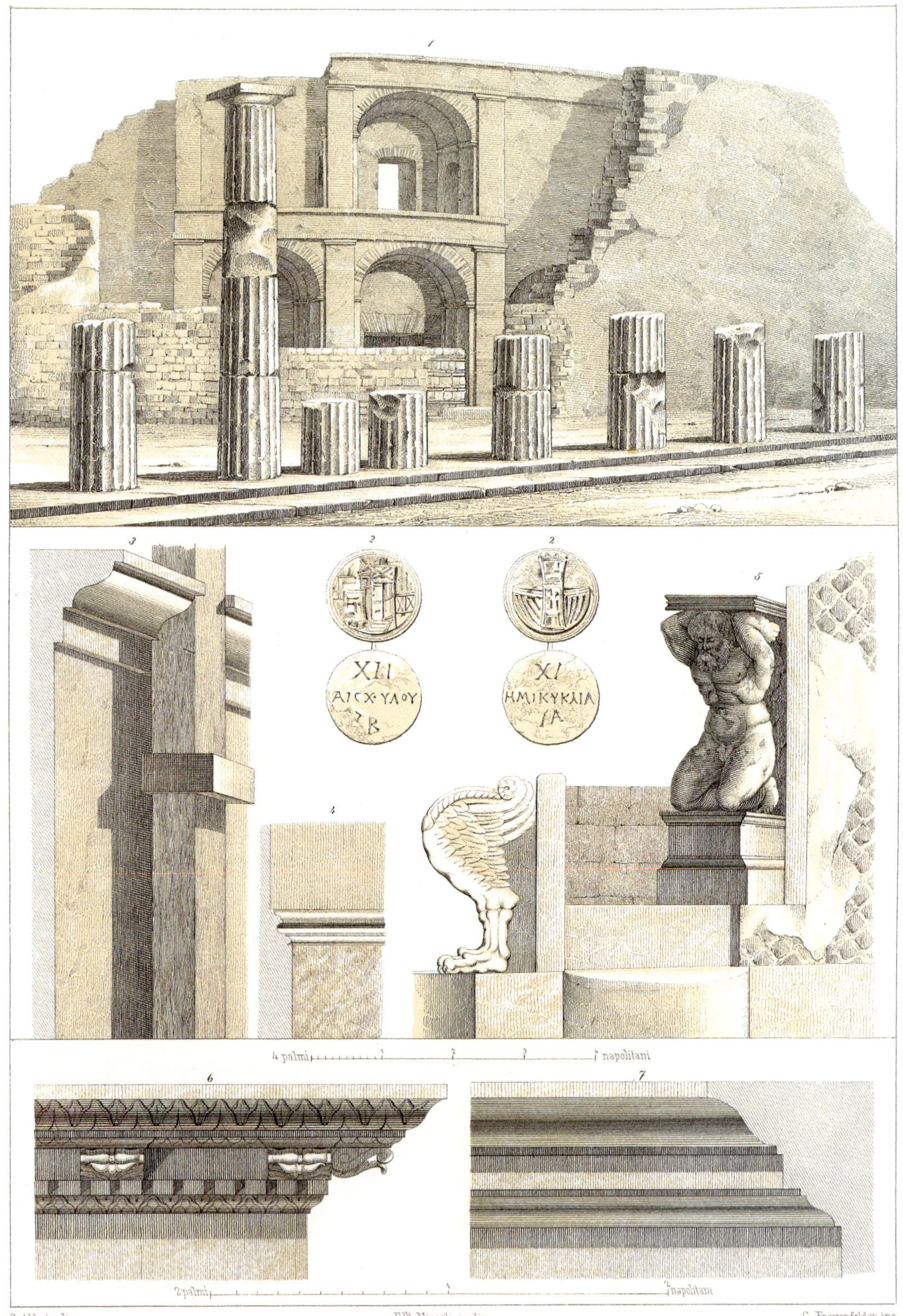

G. Abbate dis.

F.lli Niccolini dir.
Lit. Richter e C.i, Napoli

G. Frauenfelder inc.

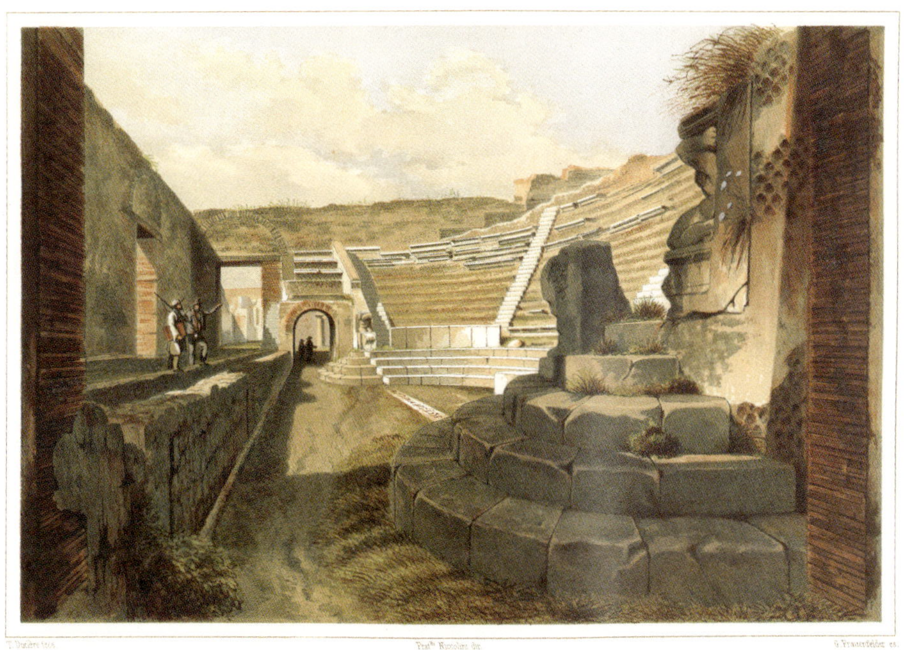

Plate 2 — *[G. Abbate]*
View and various details of the theatre – *1* View from the Triangular Forum.
2 Entry tokens *(tesserae)* made of bone. *3* Projecting slab supporting the posts for the *vela* (awnings).
5 Tuff figures in the *theatrum tectum.*

✠

Plate 3 — *[T. Duclère]*
View into the *theatrum tectum* from the entrance on the Via Stabiana.

TEMPIO D'ISIDE

Temple of Isis

The Ancient Egyptian cult of Isis reached Italy towards the end of the 2nd century BC in the Hellenised form it had assumed in the 3rd century in Alexandria. Even before Rome, the first centres of worship were established in Campania at Puteoli (today Pozzuoli), at the time Italy's most important port. The cult of Isis had to contend with political resistance until the Imperial age, when – despite certain secret practices – it finally became widely accepted. The Temple of Isis in Pompeii was founded at some point in the 2nd century BC. What the excavators discovered in December 1764, however, and what they went on to reveal during the next two years, had only just been completed when Vesuvius erupted and was thus extraordinarily fresh. An explanation is provided by the large inscription over the entrance (pl. 2 and pl. 5): the six-year-old Numerius Popidius Celsinus had completely rebuilt the Temple of Isis (VIII 7, 28) from the ground up after the earthquake of AD 62. He was consequently made a member of the Pompeii city council – an office his father, as a freed slave, could never have occupied.

The small temple precinct, bounded by a high wall (ca. 20 x 22 m / 65,6 x 72,2 feet), lay somewhat outside the old city centre in an area above the theatre that was home to several cults. From the outside the only entrance was by a door, and the exterior walls were plastered and plainly decorated. Inside was a somewhat irregular peristyle with the transverse temple standing on a podium in the courtyard, together with a number of altars and other small buildings necessary for the Isis cult (pl. 1). The rear walls of the colonnade are painted red above an ochre plinth and show a rhythmic sequence of architectural vistas (pl. 11). A continuous frieze of leafy scrolls divides the middle from the upper zone (pl. 7), and the decoration corresponds to the usual repertoire of Pompeian mural painting, with only the small figures of priests of Isis and initiates holding cult objects alluding to the building's function (pl. 12 below). The rectangular temple itself incorporated small side niches for further cult figures

A

N·POPIDIVS·N·F·CELSINVS
AEDEM·ISIDIS·TERRAE·MOTV·CONLAPSAM
A FVNDAMENTO·P·S·RESTITVIT·HVNC·DECVRIONES·OB LIBERALITATEM
CVM ESSET ANNORVM·SEXS·ORDINI·SVO·GRATIS·ADLEGERVNT

B

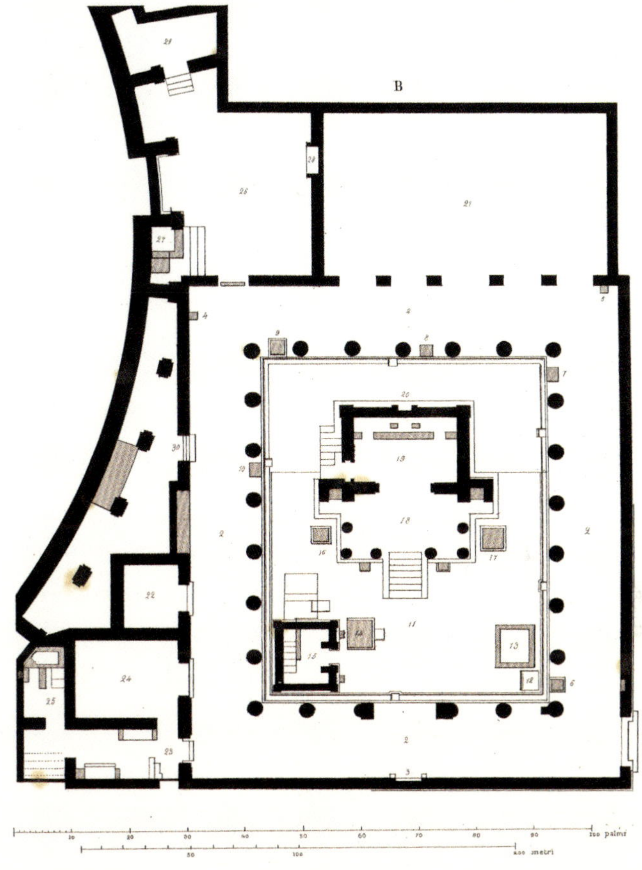

C

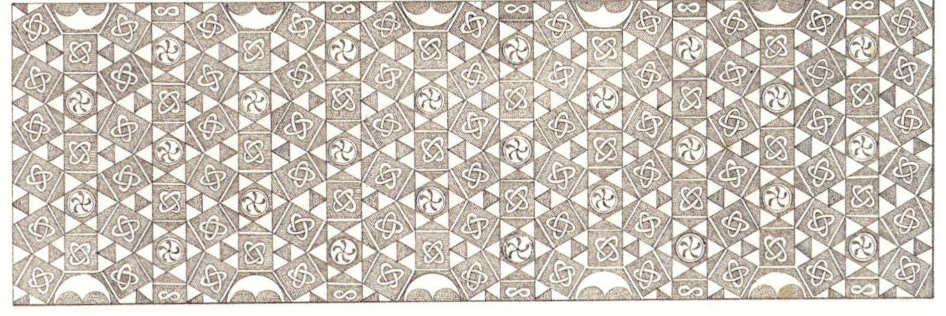

K. Grob inc. Fco Niccolini dir. Lit. Richter e C. in Napoli

(Anubis, Harpocrates?). In front of the temple stands an open-roofed, house-shaped masonry structure which enclosed the steps leading down to a pool of water used for ritual purposes. Like the temple, it is faced with magnificent stucco-work, whose pictorial themes relate to the cult only on the façade (pl. 9). Small statues of Isis (pl. 6), a Venus (pl. 8) and the bust of one Norbanus Sorex (pl. 10) stand inside the colonnade. The room behind the temple was used by the priests of the mysteries and was decorated with large paintings, one of which shows Io, after her flight to Egypt, being received by Isis in Canopus (Alexandria; pl. 12). Although only a few Egyptian and cult objects were excavated in the temple itself, *sistra* (rattles) and other items uncovered elsewhere in Pompeii clearly point to a domestic cult of Isis, often in conjunction with Fortuna.

The Temple of Isis was among the first excavations in Pompeii that were not filled in again and which consequently remained visible for visitors. After the customary removal of all the valuable pictures, a protective roof was built to cover – temporarily, at least – what remained in situ. To what extent the temple in Pompeii fuelled the Egyptomania already prevalent in the 18th century, or the subsequent Egyptian Revival in architecture, is difficult to judge. Like Pompeii as a whole, the precinct came to light at a moment in time when the cultural climate was ready for its reception. Then as now, the image of priests conducting cult ceremonies already known from a wall-painting in Herculaneum, and easily transferable to the temple at Pompeii, undoubtedly captivated the popular imagination, at least indirectly. In this way, Isis-themed porcelain table decorations made in Naples were greeted with rapture. But the notion that the 14-year-old Mozart during his visit to Pompeii in 1770 found inspiration for aspects of his *Magic Flute* is probably no more than wishful thinking.

Page 169
Plate 2 — ***[Anonymous]***
A Inscription by the donor N. Popidius Celsinus. *B* Ground plan of the temple precinct, oriented towards the west, with the theatre on the left. *C* Detail of the floor mosaic inside the temple.

⁂

Plate 5 — ***[Anonymous]***
Reconstruction of the entry door to the temple precinct in front view and cross section. Plan drawing of the doorstep.

⁂

Pages 172–173
Plate 1 — ***[G. Gigante]***
View of the Temple of Isis from the east.

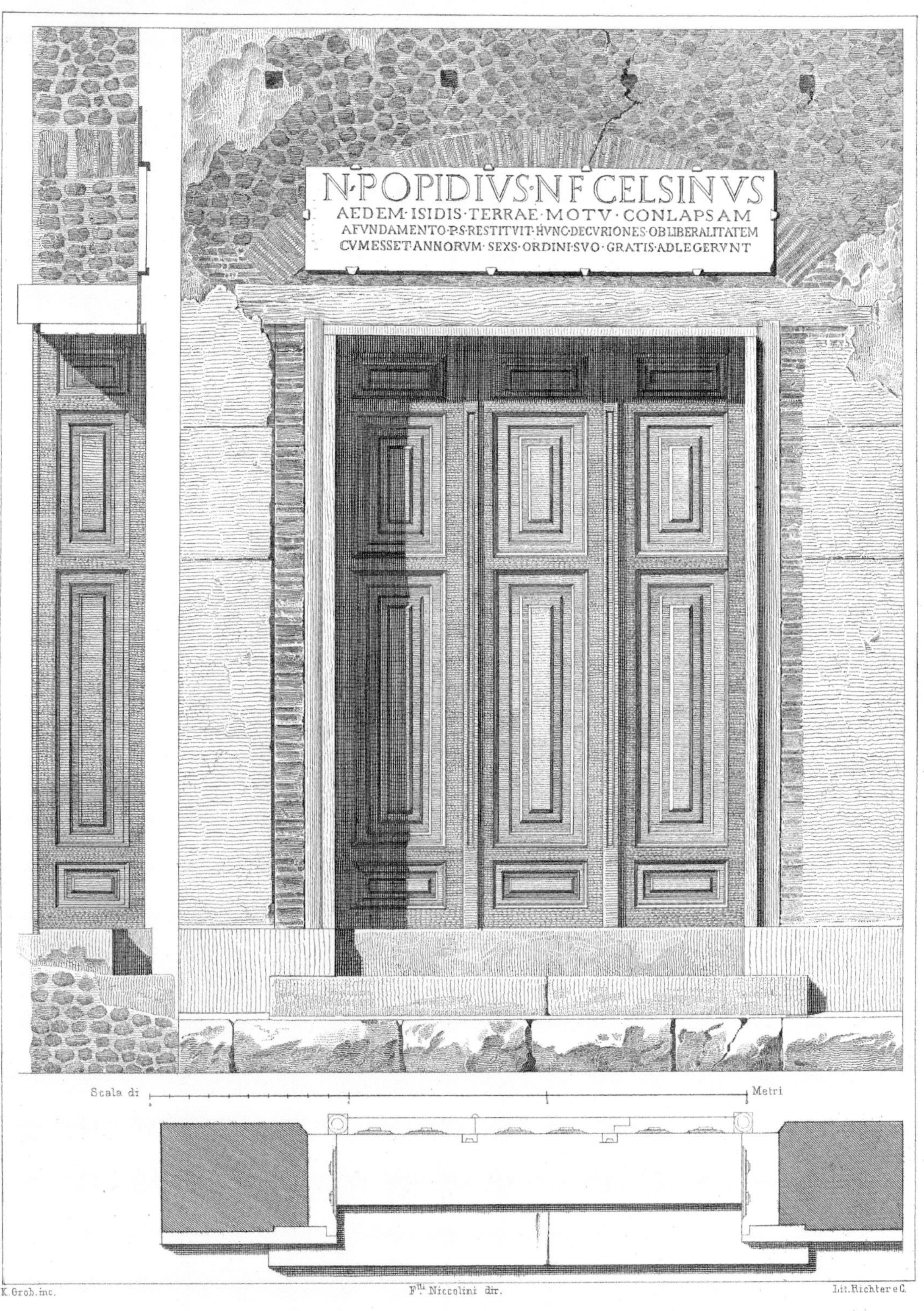
N·POPIDIVS·N·F·CELSINVS
AEDEM·ISIDIS·TERRAE·MOTV·CONLAPSAM
A FVNDAMENTO·P·S·RESTITVIT·HVNC·DECVRIONES·OB LIBERALITATEM
CVM ESSET·ANNORVM·SEXS·ORDINI·SVO·GRATIS·ADLEGERVNT
Scala di
Metri
K. Grob. inc.
F.lli Niccolini dir.
Lit. Richter e C.

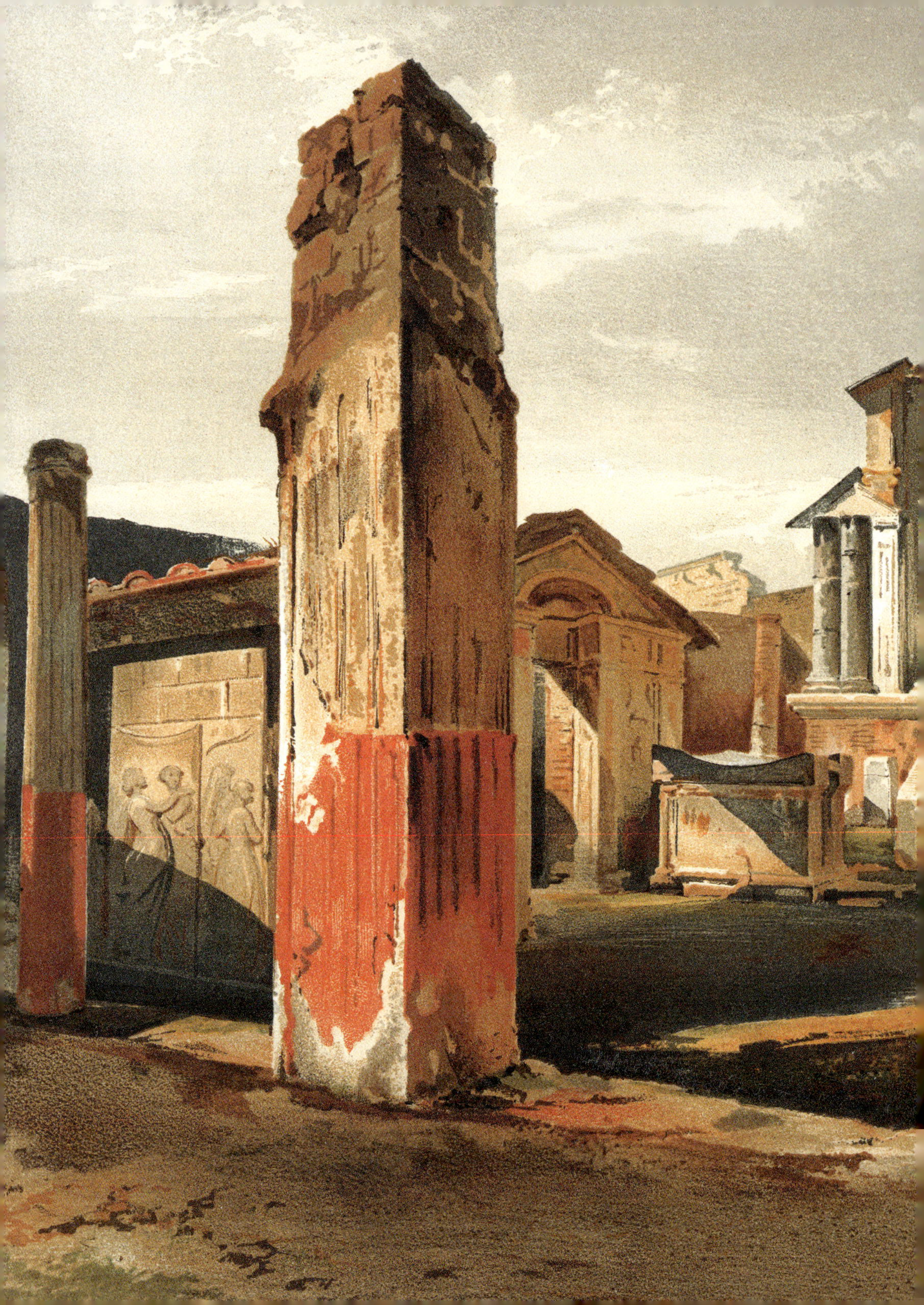

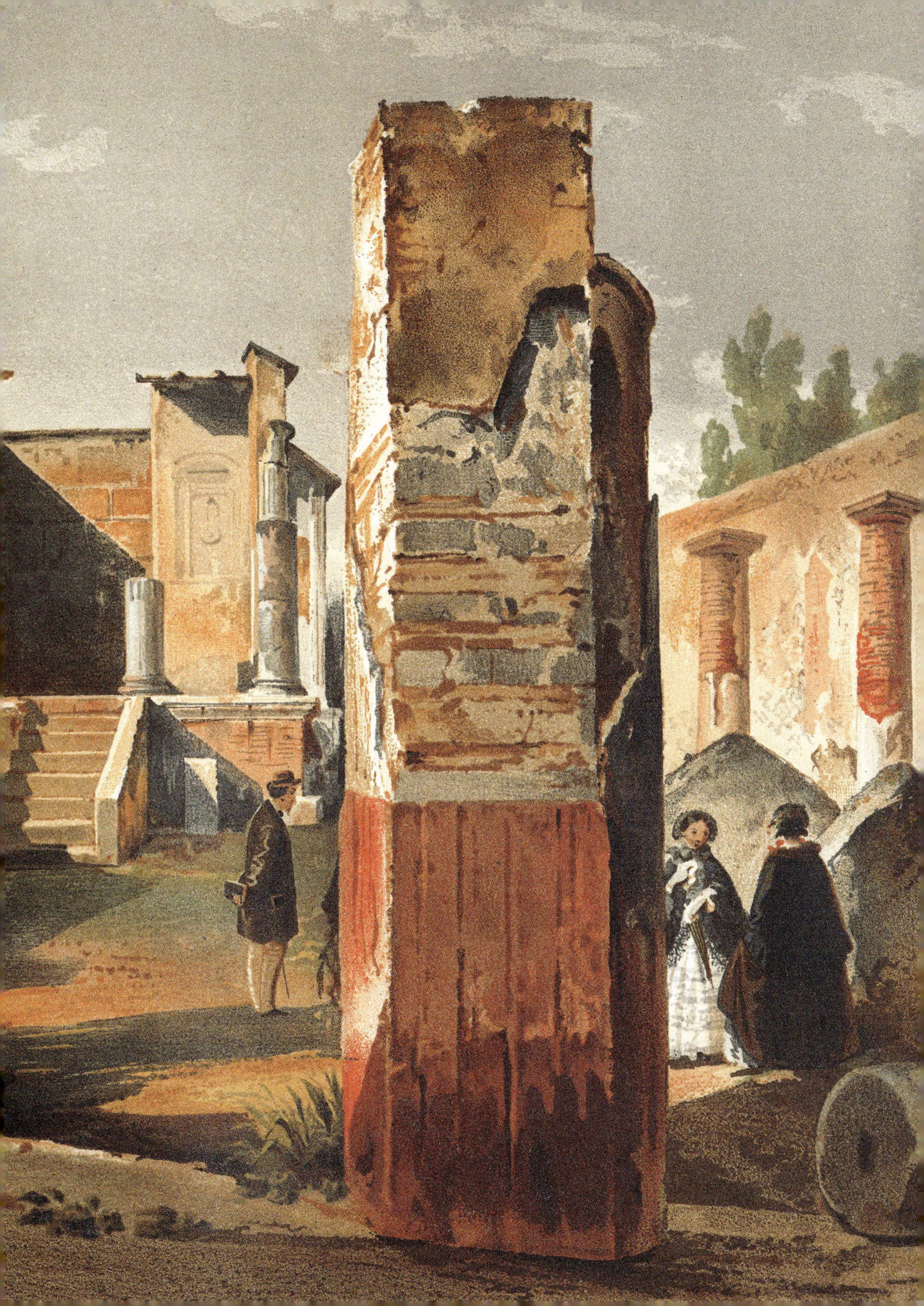

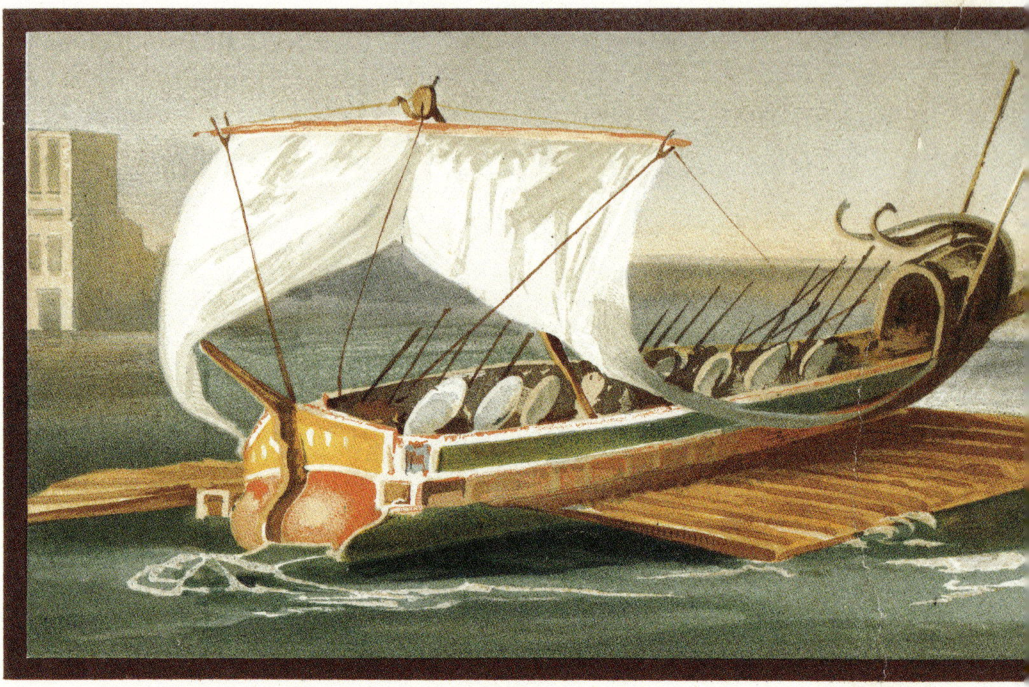

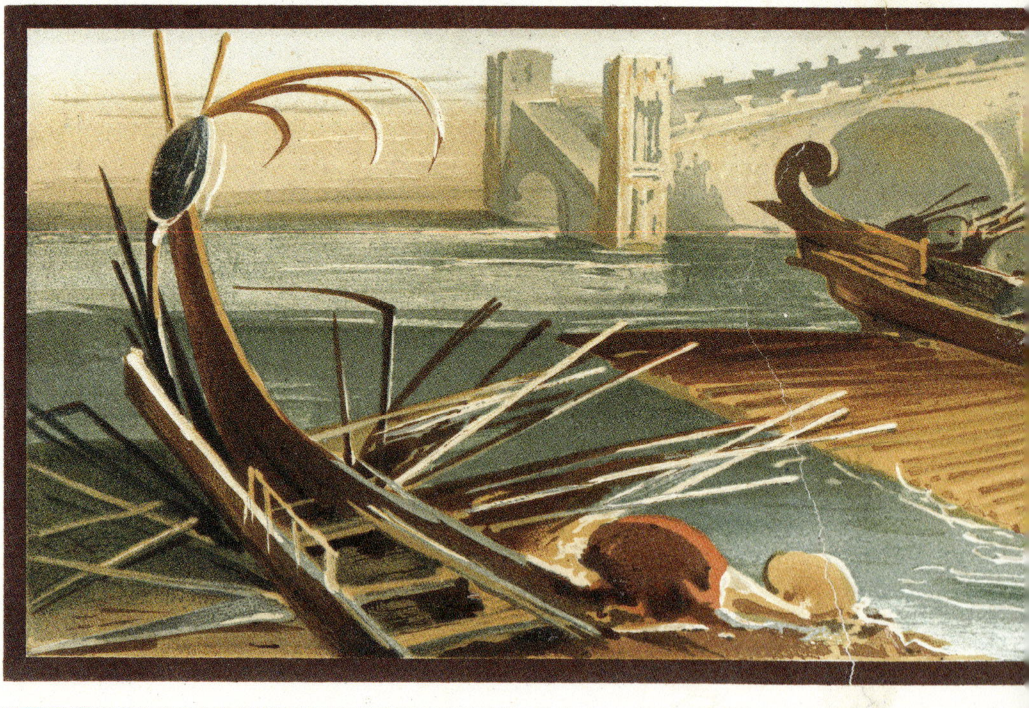

G. Gigante fec.

F^{lli} N

Lit. Rich

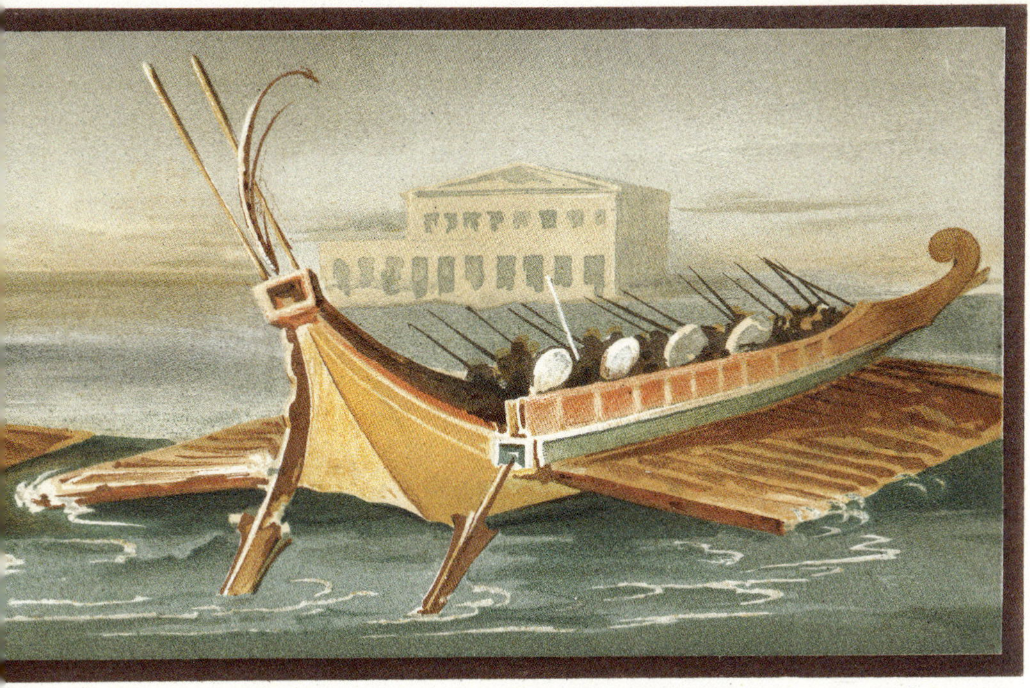

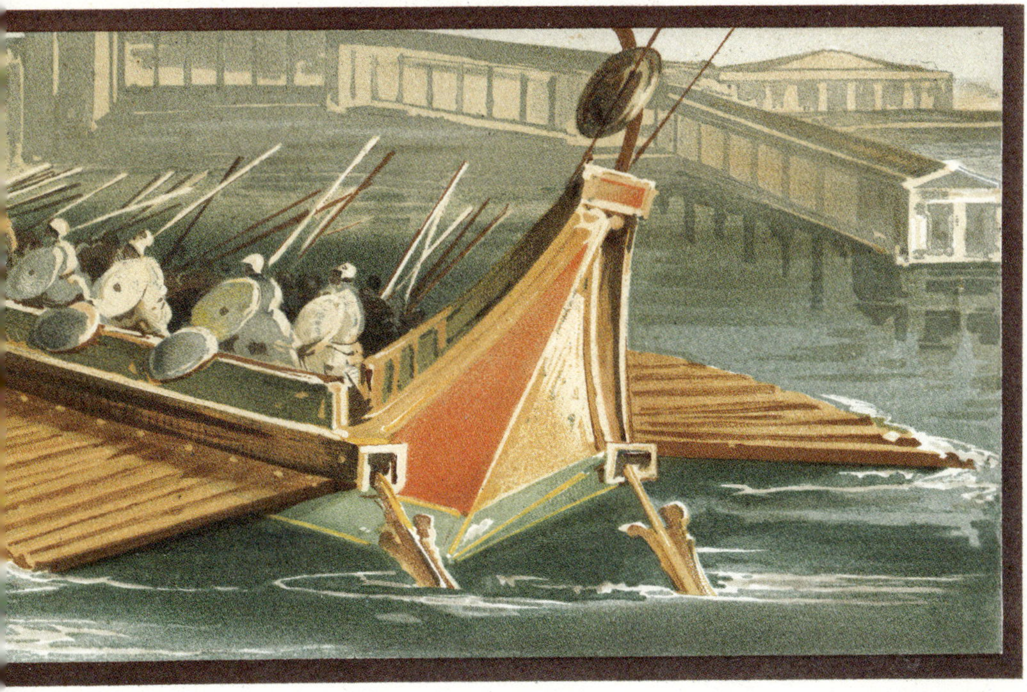

r.
apoli.

K. Grob lit.

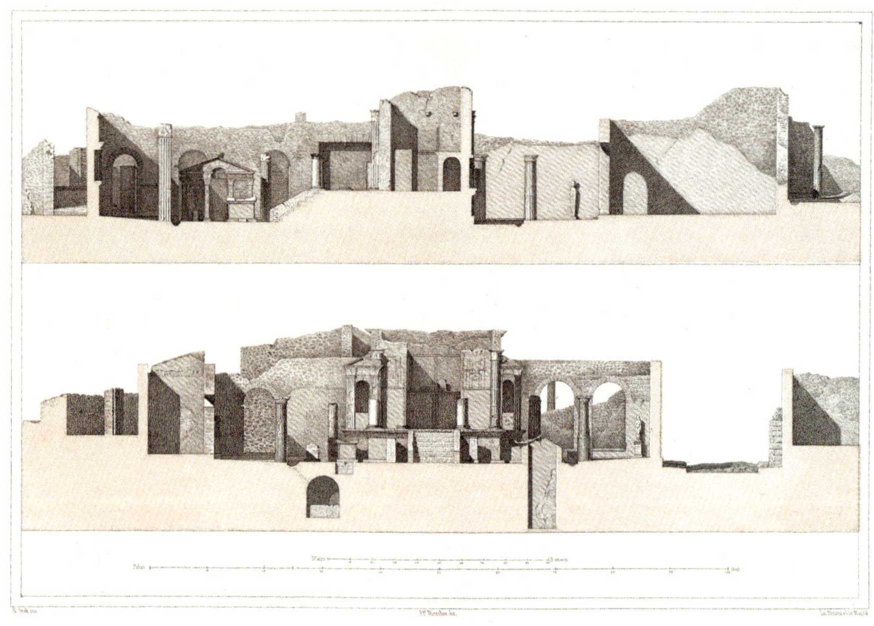

Pages 174–175

Plate 4 — *[G. Gigante]*

Pictures of naval battles from the south and north sides of the perimeter wall.

✻

Plate 3 — *[Anonymous]*

East-west and north-south cross sections through the temple precinct.

✻

Plate 6 — *[K. Grob]*

North-east corner of the courtyard – Statue of Isis on its pedestal with an inscription naming Caecilius Phoebus as the donor.

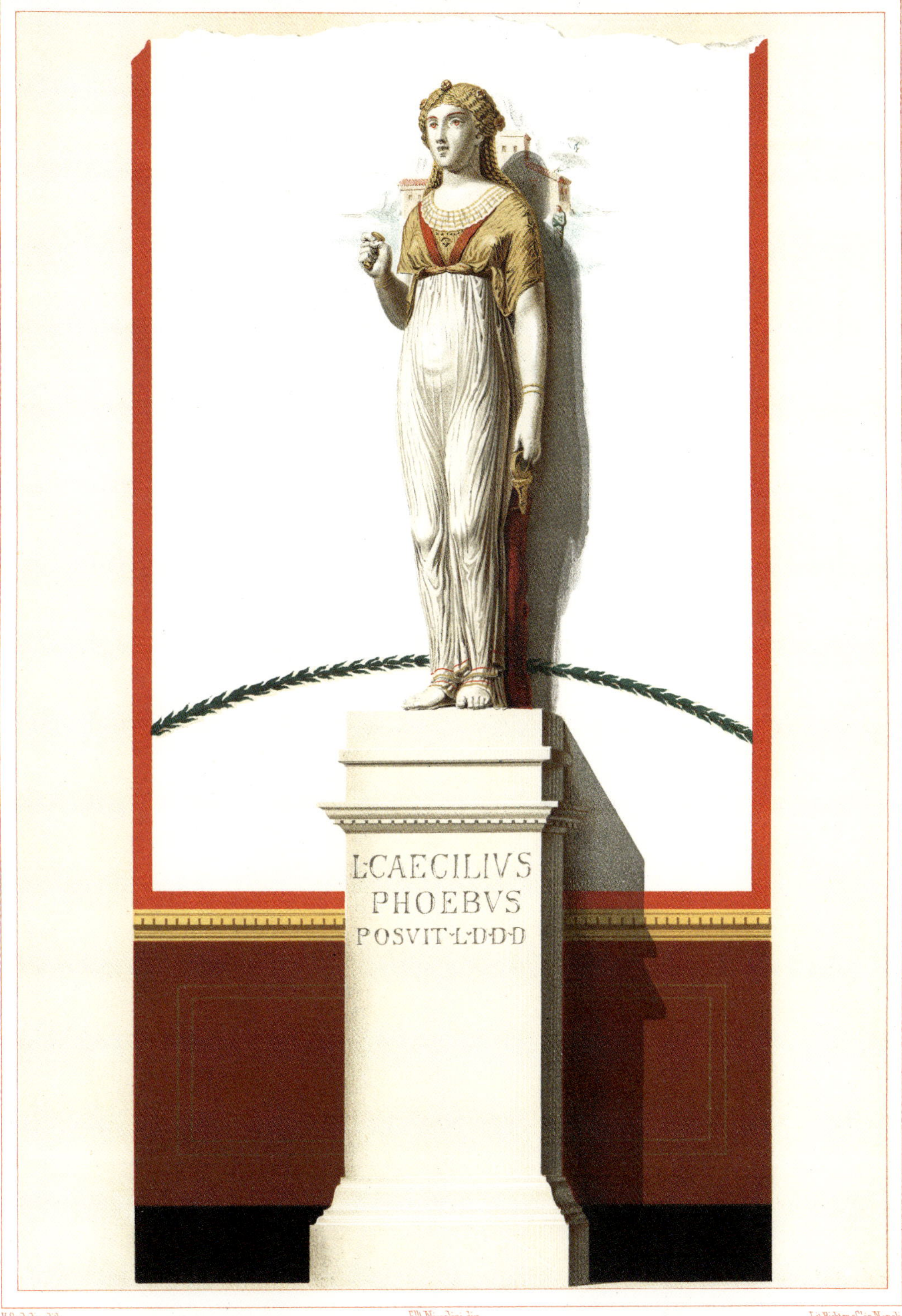

K Grob dis e lith. F^lli Niccolini dir. Lit. Richter e C. in Napoli

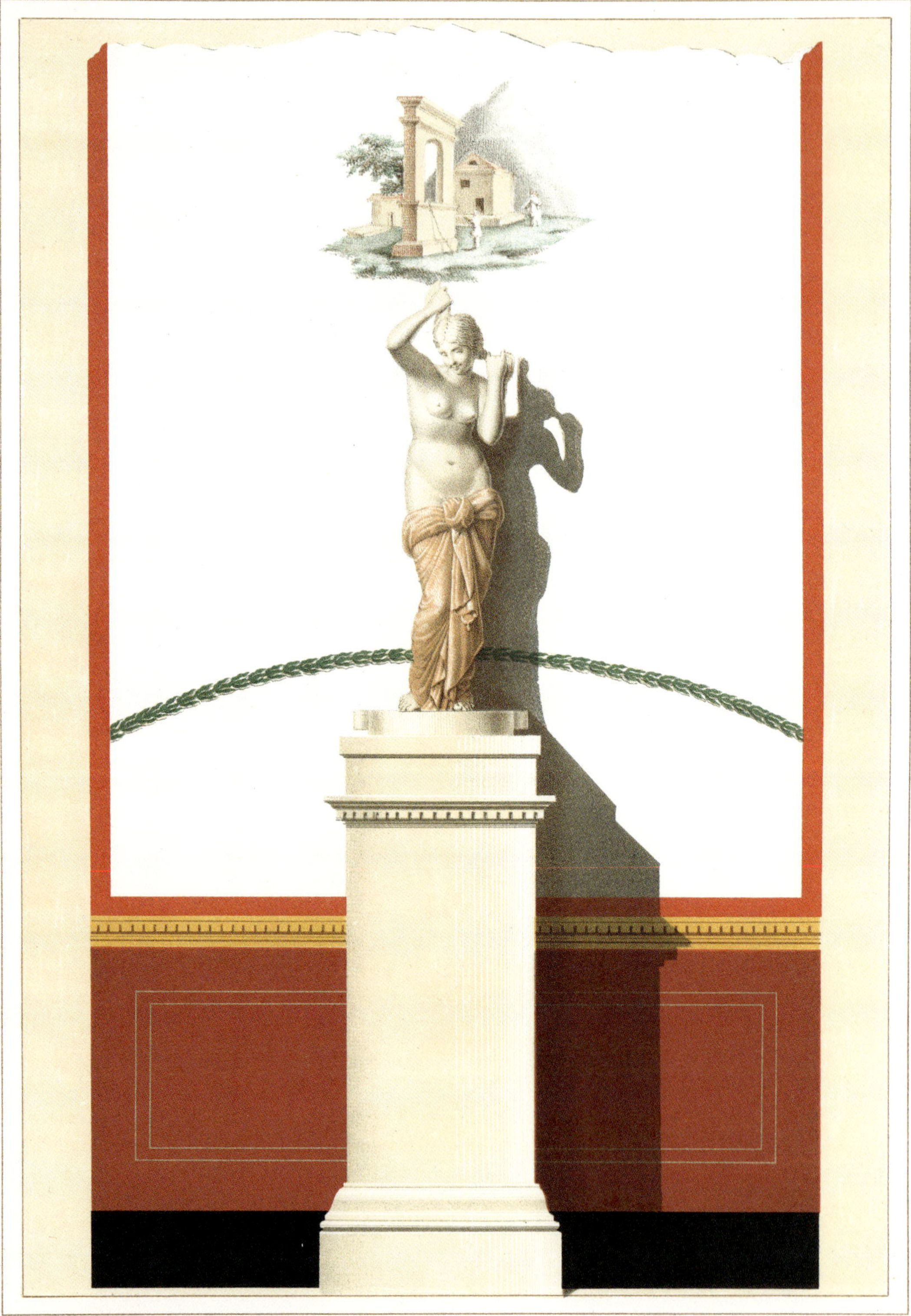

Lit: Richter e C.º in Napoli. F.lli Niccolini dir. V. Mollame lit.

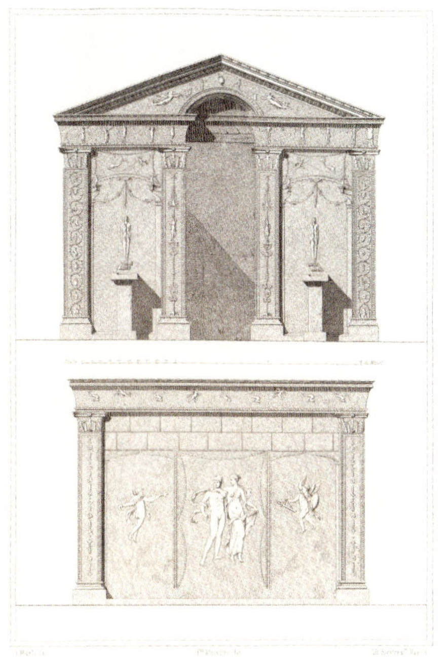

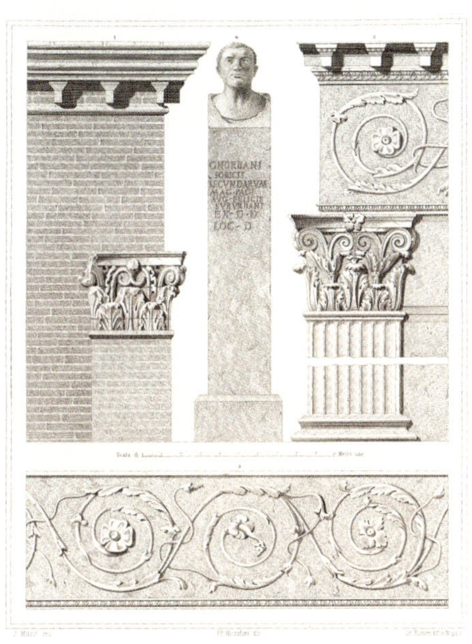

Plate 8 — *[Anonymous]*
Western part of the south perimeter wall – Statuette of Venus Anadyomene on a plinth. Venus is rising out of the sea, or her bath, and drying her hair.

✻

Plate 9 — *[Anonymous]*
So-called *purgatorium,* in which holy water from the Nile was kept, seen from the north and east.

✻

Plate 10 — *[Anonymous]*
1–3 Architectural details, made of stucco, from the Temple of Isis: ***1 and 3*** Outer order. ***2*** Inner order.

✻

Pages 180–181
Plate 11 — *[Anonymous]*
Western part of the south perimeter wall – Detail with a central motif showing a priest of Isis with a *situla* in his right hand.

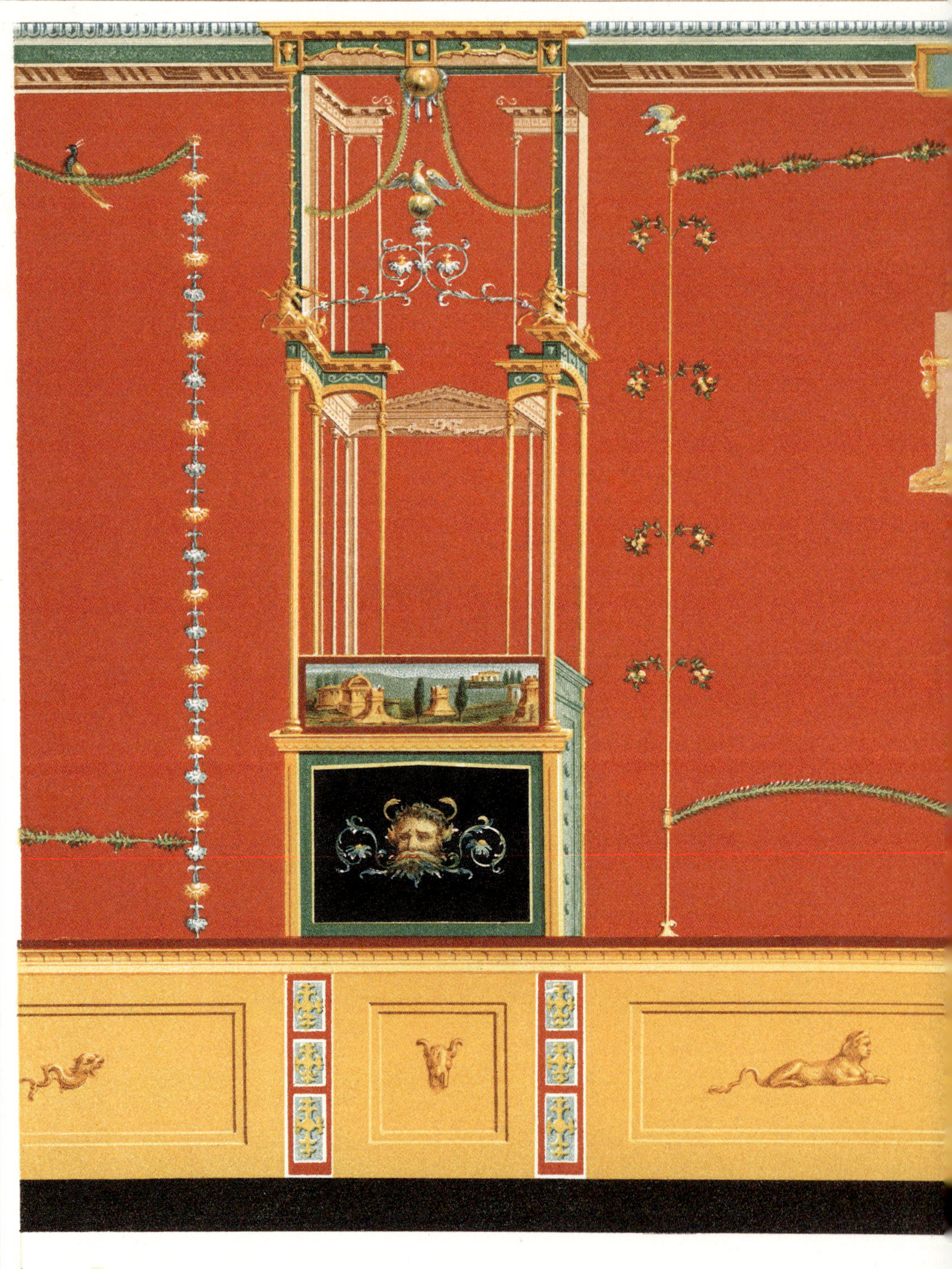

Lit. Richter & C° Napoli.

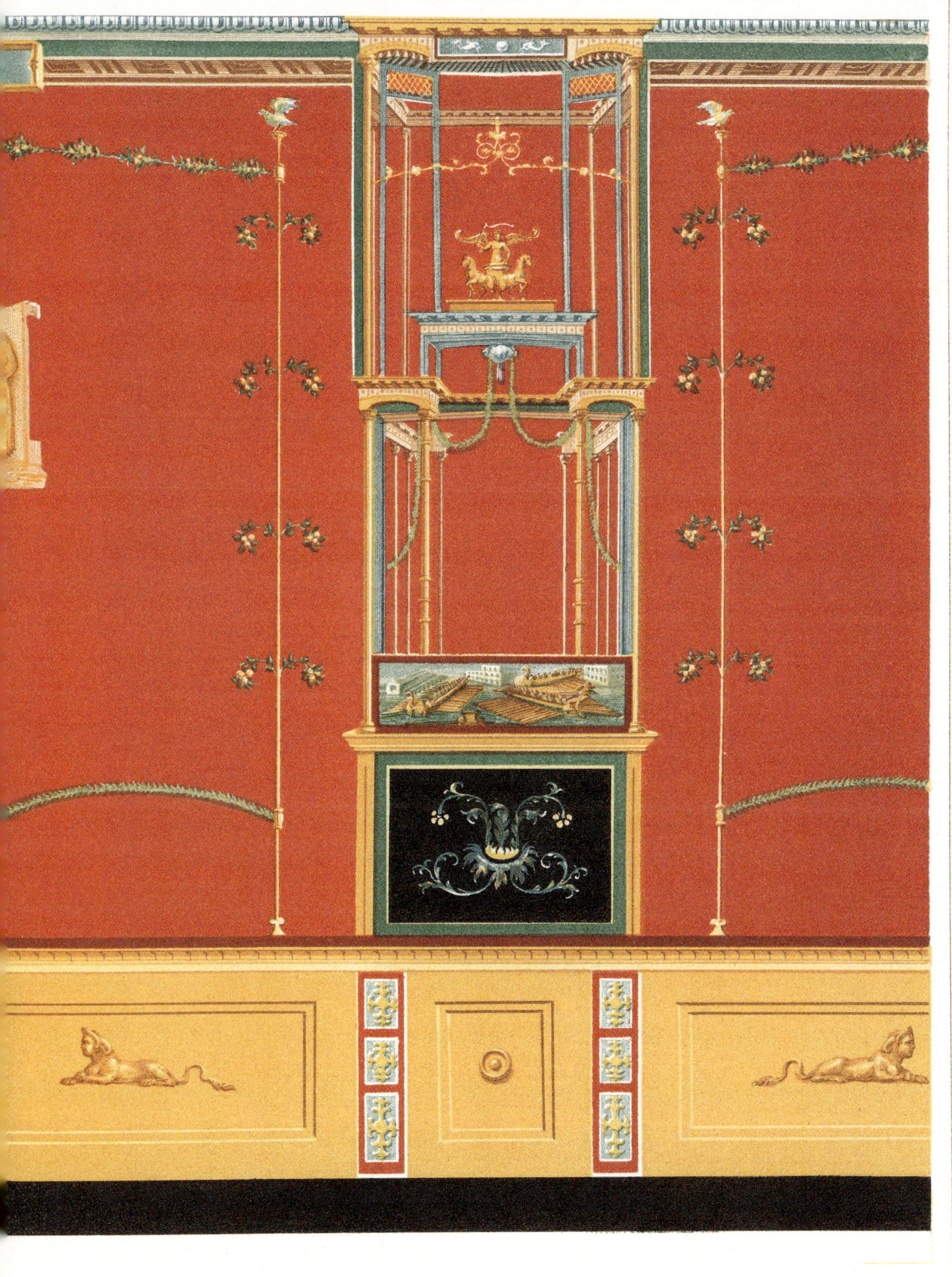

ḋir.

C. Weidenmüller lit.

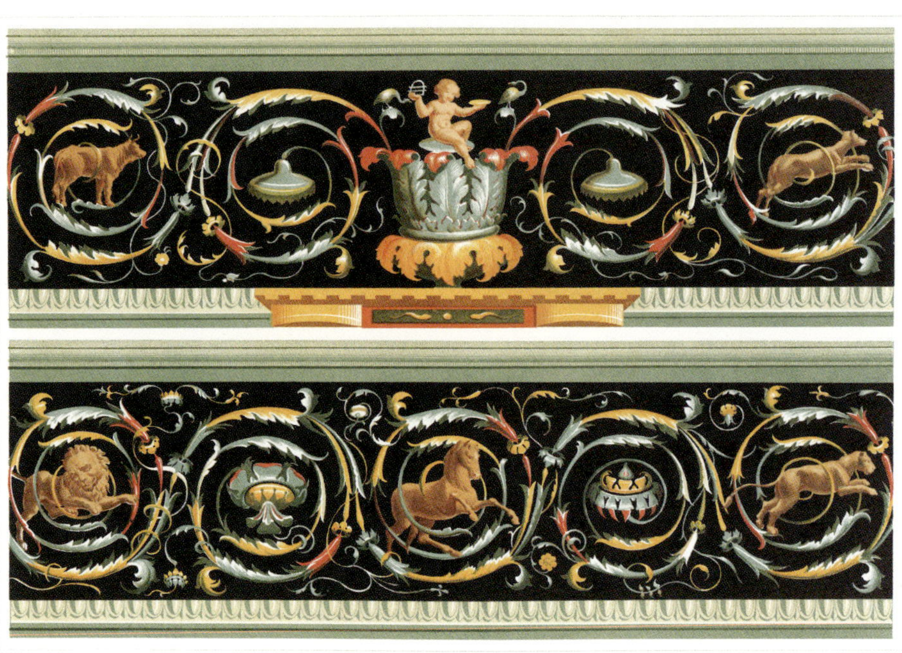

Plate 7 — *[G. Abbate]*
East perimeter wall – Frieze of scrolls with a pygmy sitting in a calyx, holding a *sistrum* in his right hand. The second section shows a lion, horse and tiger leaping through the scrolling tendrils.

✠

Plate 12 — *[Anonymous]*
A Ekklesiasterion (assembly room) – central picture from the south wall: Io flees to Egypt, where she is carried by the personification of Nile from Canopus to a temple of Isis and there welcomed by the goddess. In the background, priestesses with cult objects. *B* Five vignettes with central motifs from the mural decoration of the courtyard. Priests of Isis with cult objects, one figure wearing an Anubis mask.

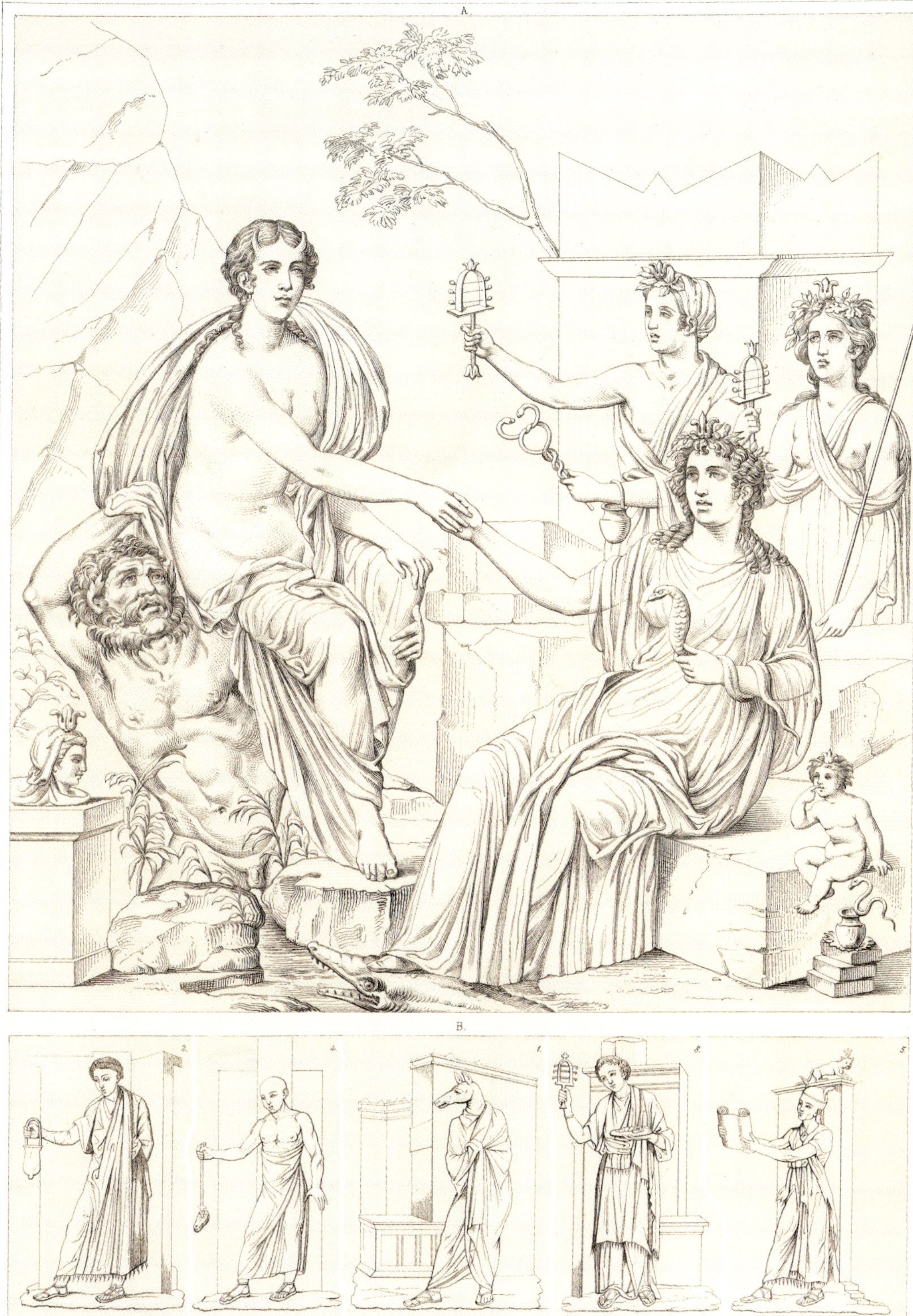

Lit. Richter & C.º Napoli. F.lli Niccolini dir. G. Weidenmüller lit.

VILLA DI DIOMEDE

Villa of Diomedes

Between 1771 and 1774 the excavators uncovered a large suburban villa outside the Herculaneum Gate. This was one of the first buildings not to be filled in again but to remain accessible to visitors. Its name is erroneously derived from the tomb inscription of one Arrius Diomedes, found in the vicinity. The villa, formerly with three floors, was oriented towards the Gulf of Naples, so that its owners had a spectacular view of the bay. The street entrance opened directly on to a small peristyle courtyard, which gave access in turn to the main reception rooms and to a well-appointed suite of baths. The garden was situated on a lower level with a pillared portico around its border, beyond which were a number of vaulted rooms. On one side was a substantial wing for the household's management. Although the objects found in the house were not especially rich, the discovery of a group of 18 dead bodies caused a particular stir. Their bodies, long since decayed, had left cavities in the hardened ash, and these negative impressions were cut out and taken to the museum. The imprint of the torso of a (young?) woman was on show in the museum for many years and inspired Théophile Gautier to write his successful novella *Arria Marcella*, published in 1852.

In the 18th century, only the Villa of Diomedes corresponded to contemporary ideas of what a residence fit for the Romans should look like. Since its well-preserved wall paintings contained almost no mythological scenes, little was cut out. The overall structure as it stood was still extensively documented in the 18th century, allowing it to be accurately reconstructed today. While individual views of the villa had already appeared as engravings, the Niccolini publication now also included colour reproductions of entire walls. Since these latter offered no interesting central motifs, the chapter was supplemented with additional plates showing floating figures that had been discovered and cut out decades earlier from the so-called Villa di Cicerone, and which belonged to the most popular subjects of Pompeian wall painting (pl. 5).

❖

Plate 1 — *[R. Sifo]*

1–44 Ground plan of the villa (oriented towards the SW): the upper storey is drawn in black, the lower storey in grey.

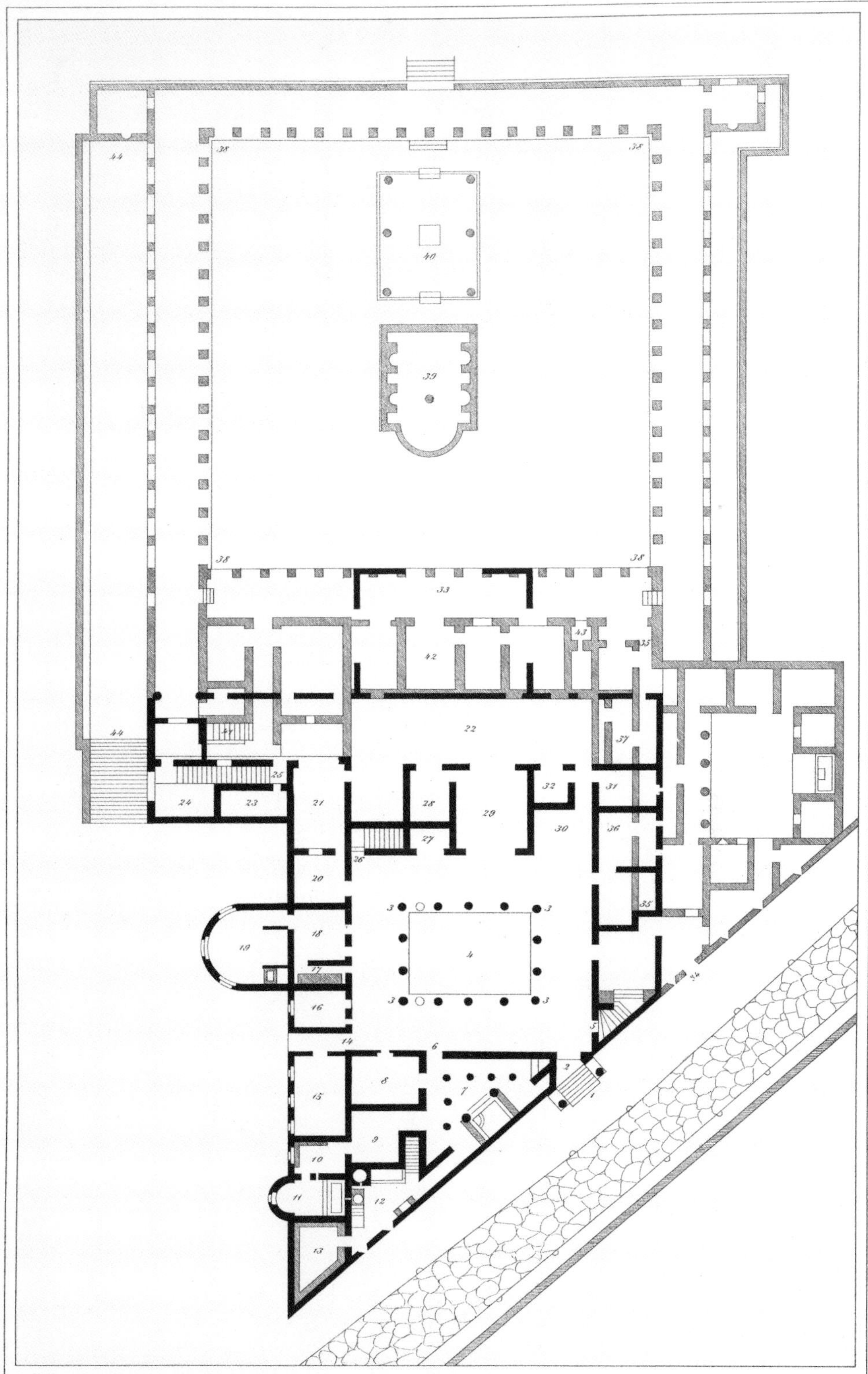

Lit Richter & C Napoli　　F.lli Niccolini dir.　　R. Sifo inc.

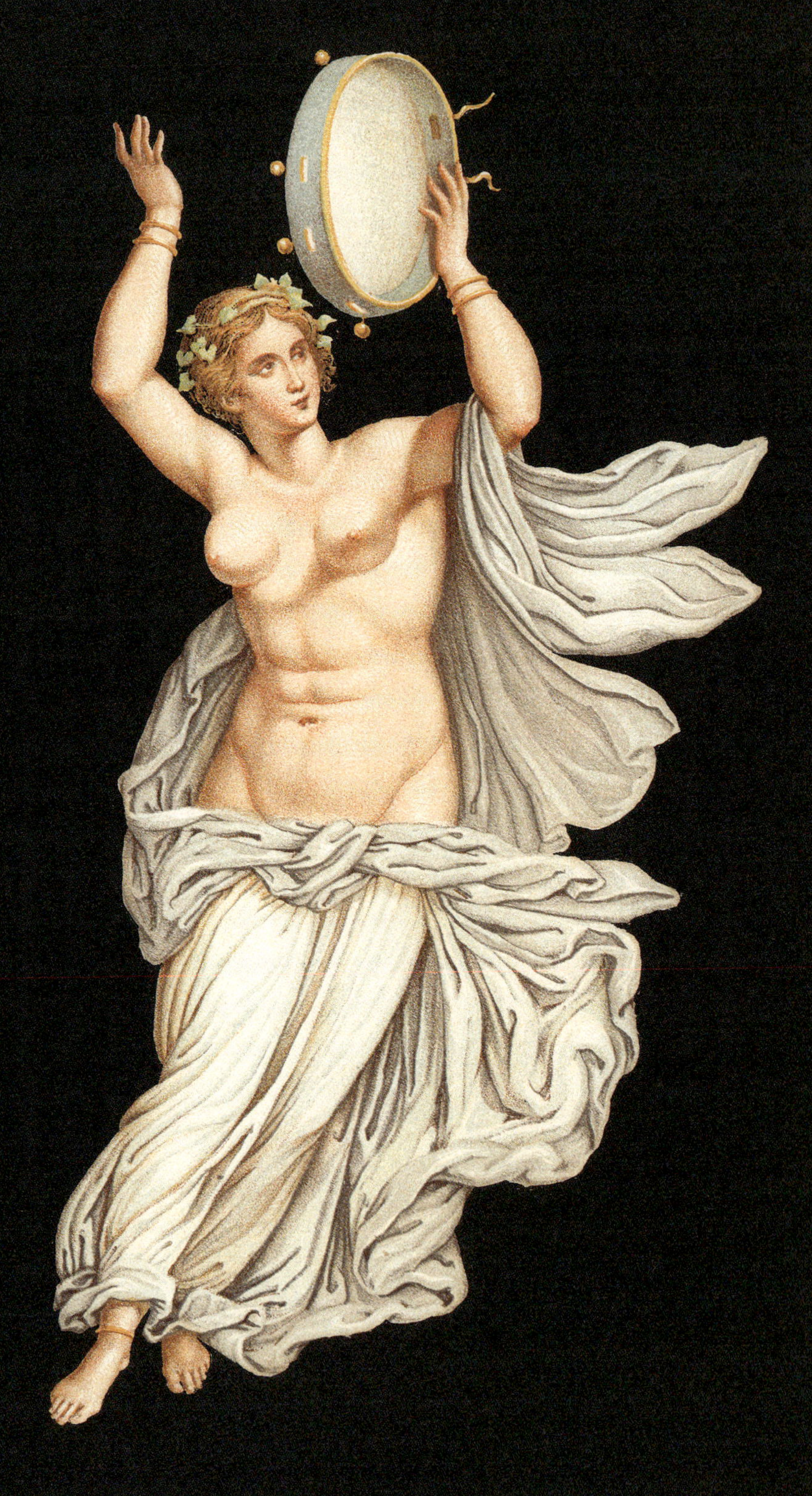

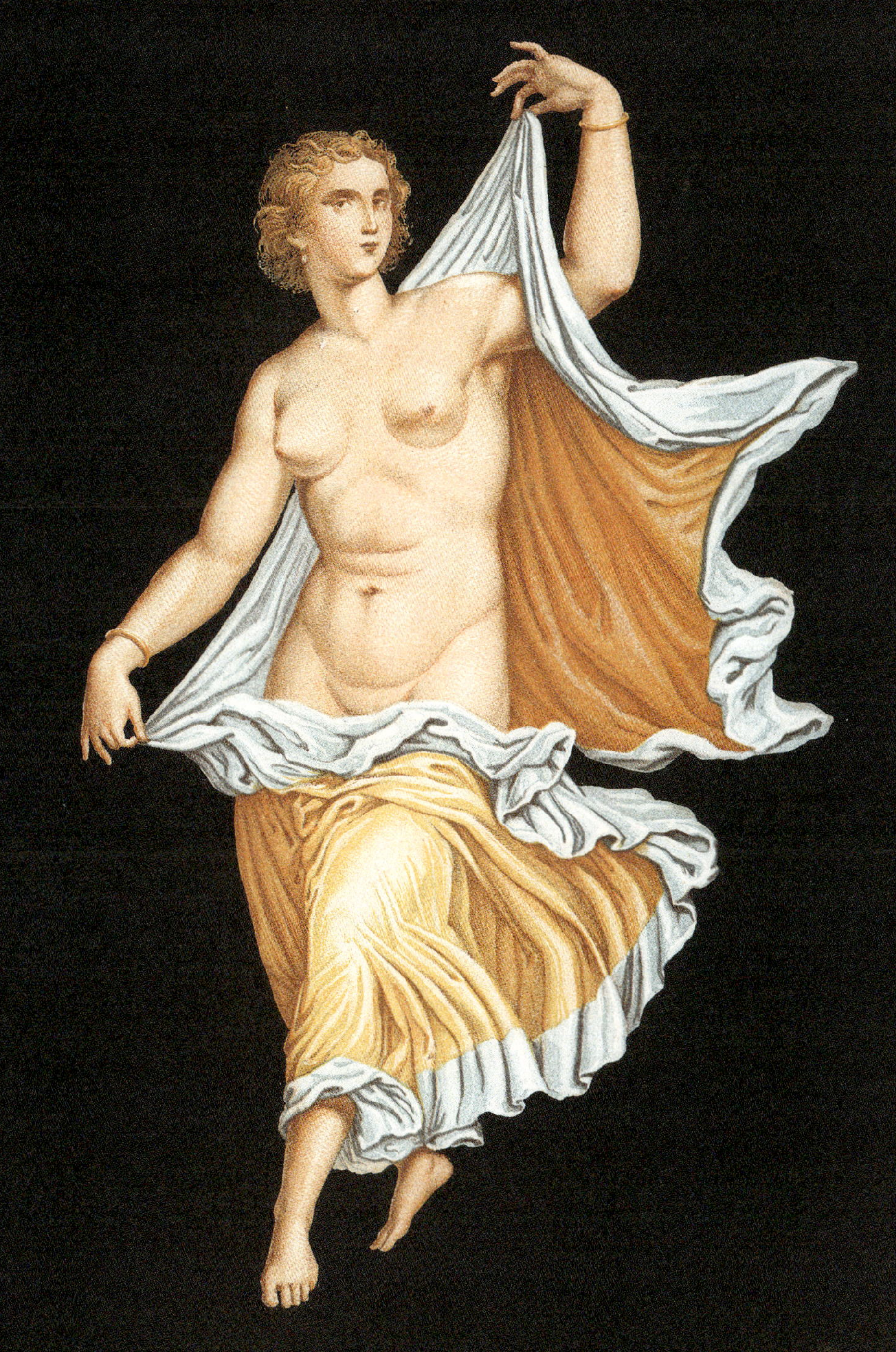

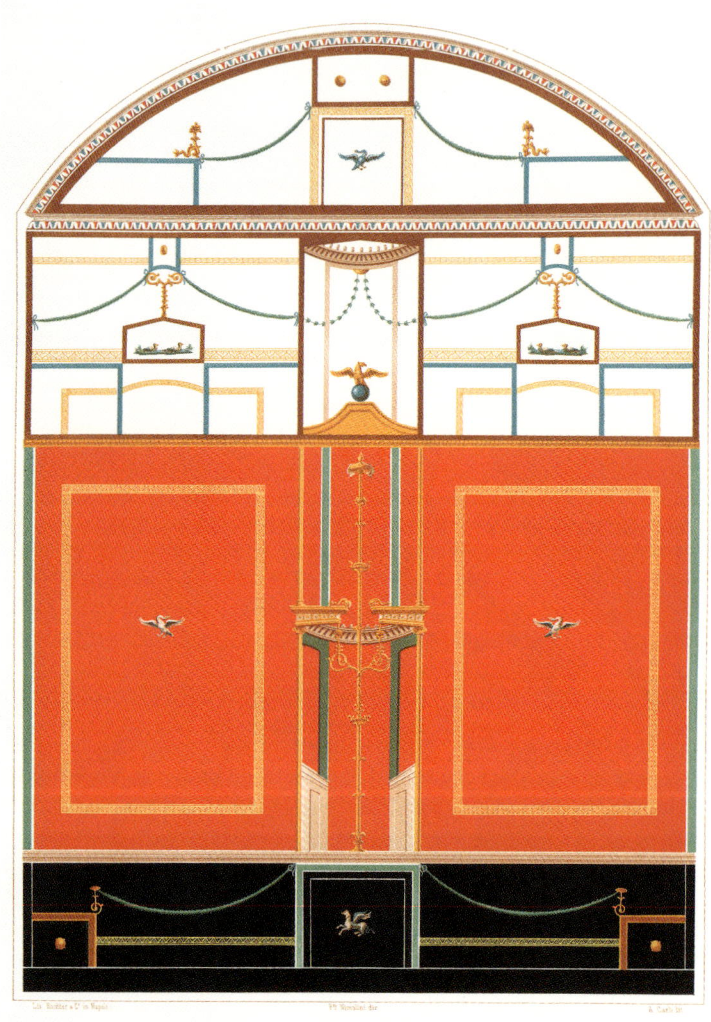

Pages 186–187
Plate 5 — *[V. Mollame, C. Weidenmüller]*
So-called Villa di Cicerone – Floating maenads.

❖

Plate 4 — *[A. Carli]*
Villa di Diomede – Wall decoration from room (42) on the east side of the lower peristyle.

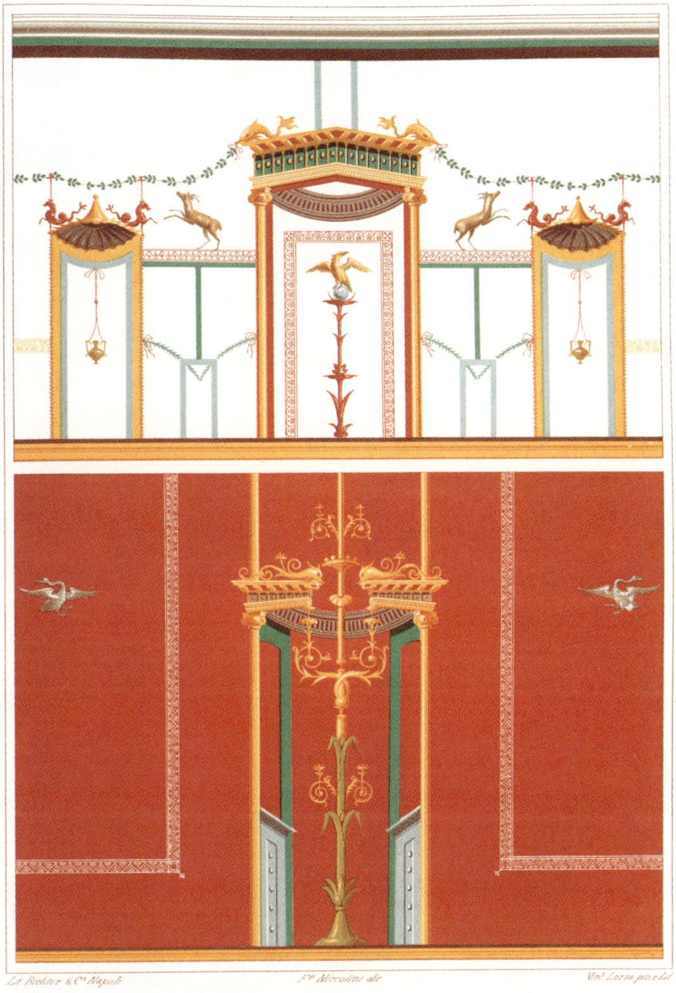

Plate 6 — *[V. Loria]*
Two sections of mural décor from an unknown room – The decoration closely resembles that in plate 4 and could therefore show a wall from room between (42) and (43), which had largely been laid out as a pendant to (42).

Pages 190–191
Plate 7 — *[C. Weidenmüller]*
View over the garden towards the main villa buildings – In the background, parts of the Villa delle Colonne a Mosaico on the Street of Tombs.

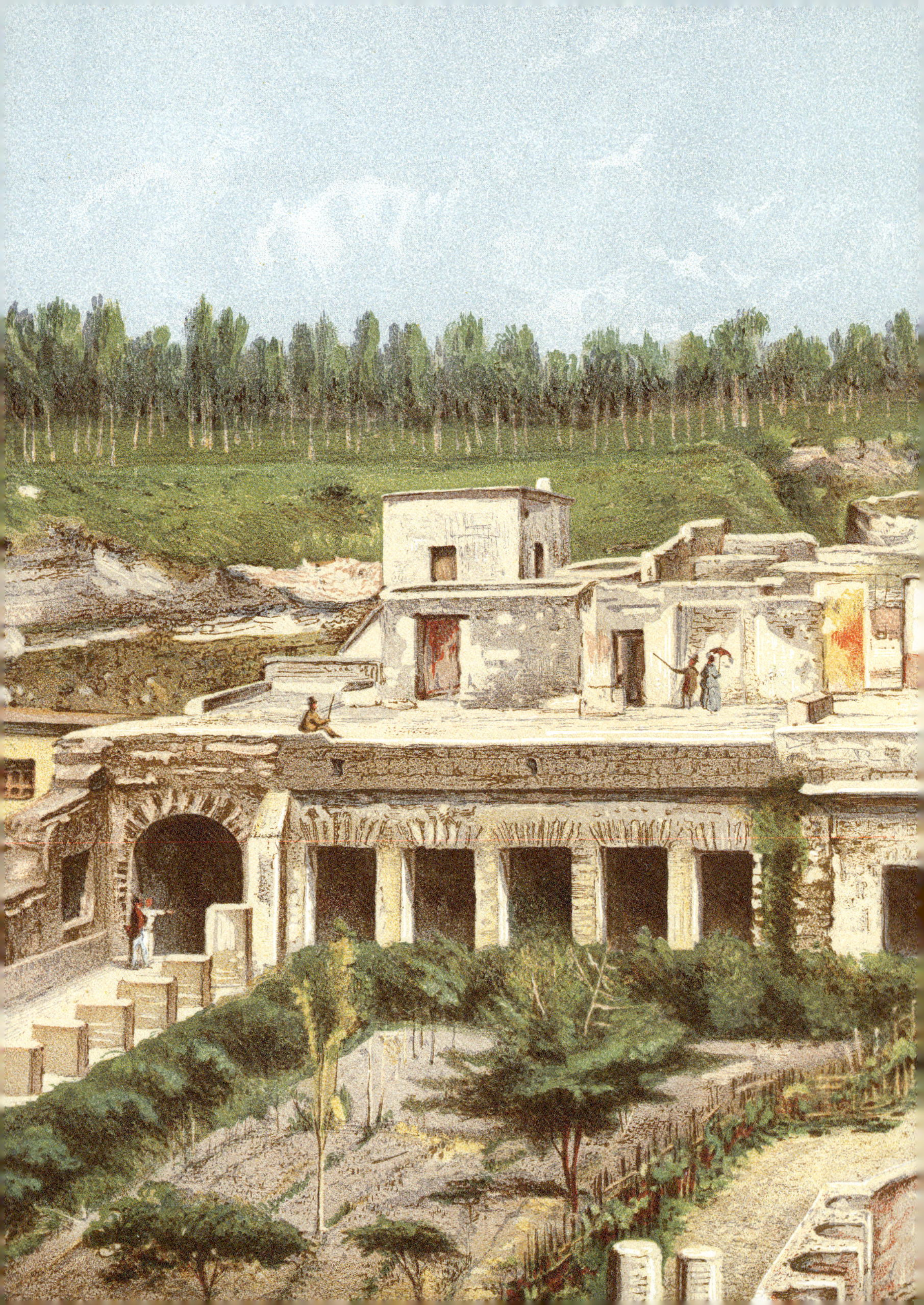

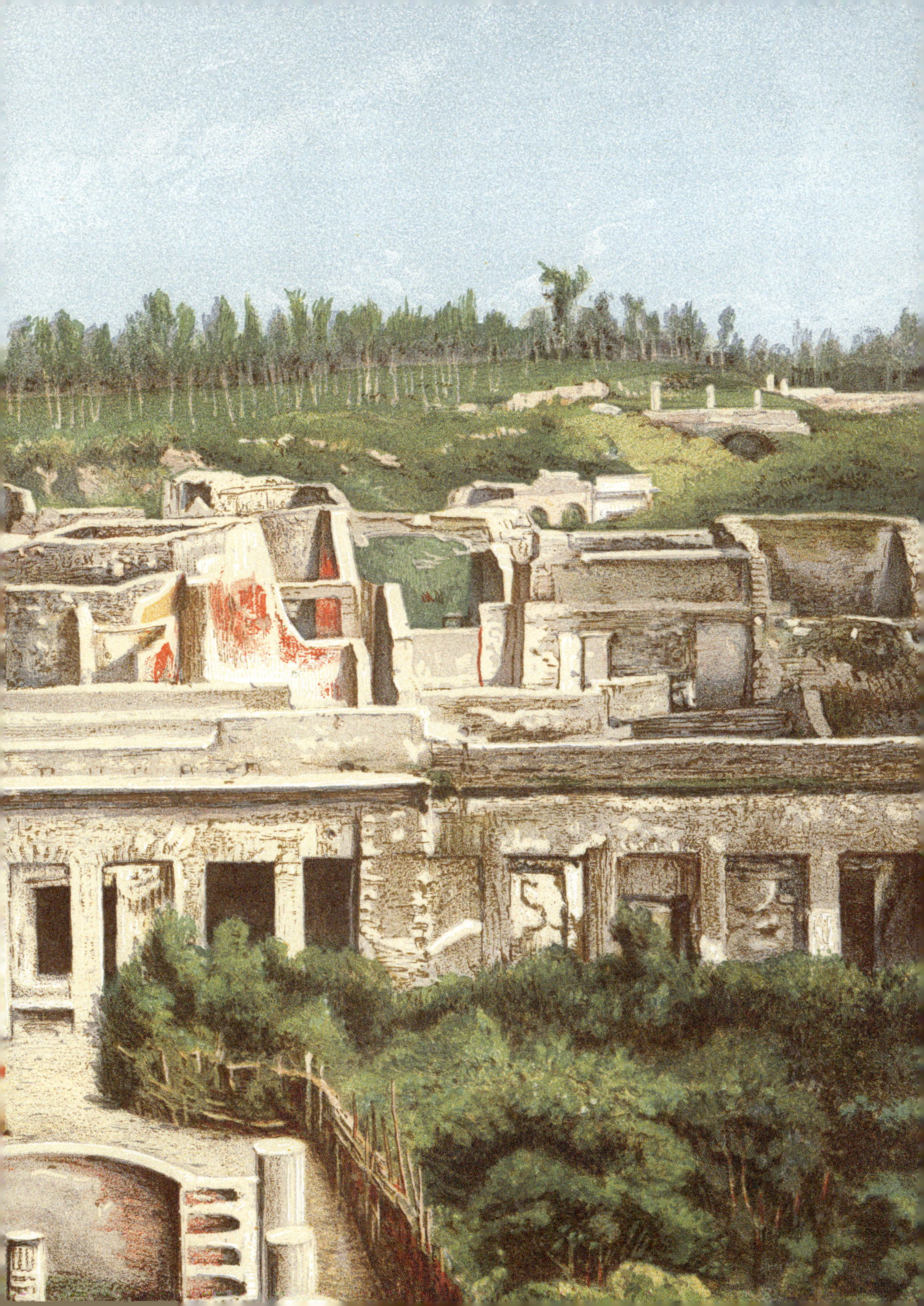

CASA DEI CAPITELLI FIGURATI

House of the Figured Capitals

The initially nameless house (VII 4, 57), "opposite the Casa del Fauno" on the Via di Nola, was uncovered in 1832/33. Within its elongated ground plan it contained all the elements of a typical Late Hellenistic house: an atrium with side rooms and a handsome peristyle court with two reception rooms opening on to it. Unlike the Casa del Fauno and other previously discovered houses with fine interior decorations, such as the Casa del Poeta tragico, it aroused little interest. Its only spectacular features were the two pilaster capitals with their figural carvings situated to the right and left of the entrance (pl. 1, 3–5). These represent new interpretations of Corinthian capital forms and show a Dionysian couple (a satyr/silenus with a maenad) facing the street and a human couple facing into the entrance passage. Some of the figures are resting on cushions, and the corner volutes of the capitals seem to form the back of a sofa. The capitals date from the end of the 2nd century BC and belong to the house's original construction phase. The meaning of their imagery remains disputed, with interpretations ranging from Dionysian mysteries and hopes for the afterlife to equating the masters of the house with the retinue of Dionysus, as found, for example, in traditions of the rulers of Egypt. Almost nothing survives of the house's later mural decoration from the early and middle Augustan period or from the years shortly before the earthquake, nor indeed its mosaics. It is thus unsurprising that modern-day visitors to Pompeii give the house little attention and turn instead to the Casa del Fauno opposite.

✻

Plate 1 — *[F. Tessitore]*

1 Ground plan of the house. *2, 4* Capital on the west of the entrance, seen from the street and the *fauces* respectively. *3, 5* Capital on the east of the entrance, seen from the street and the *fauces* respectively. *6* Central mosaic in the tablinum. *7* Peristyle, sundial. *8* Mosaic strip in a cubiculum. *9* Decorative silver disk from a bridle. *10* Threshold mosaic at the entrance to the tablinum.

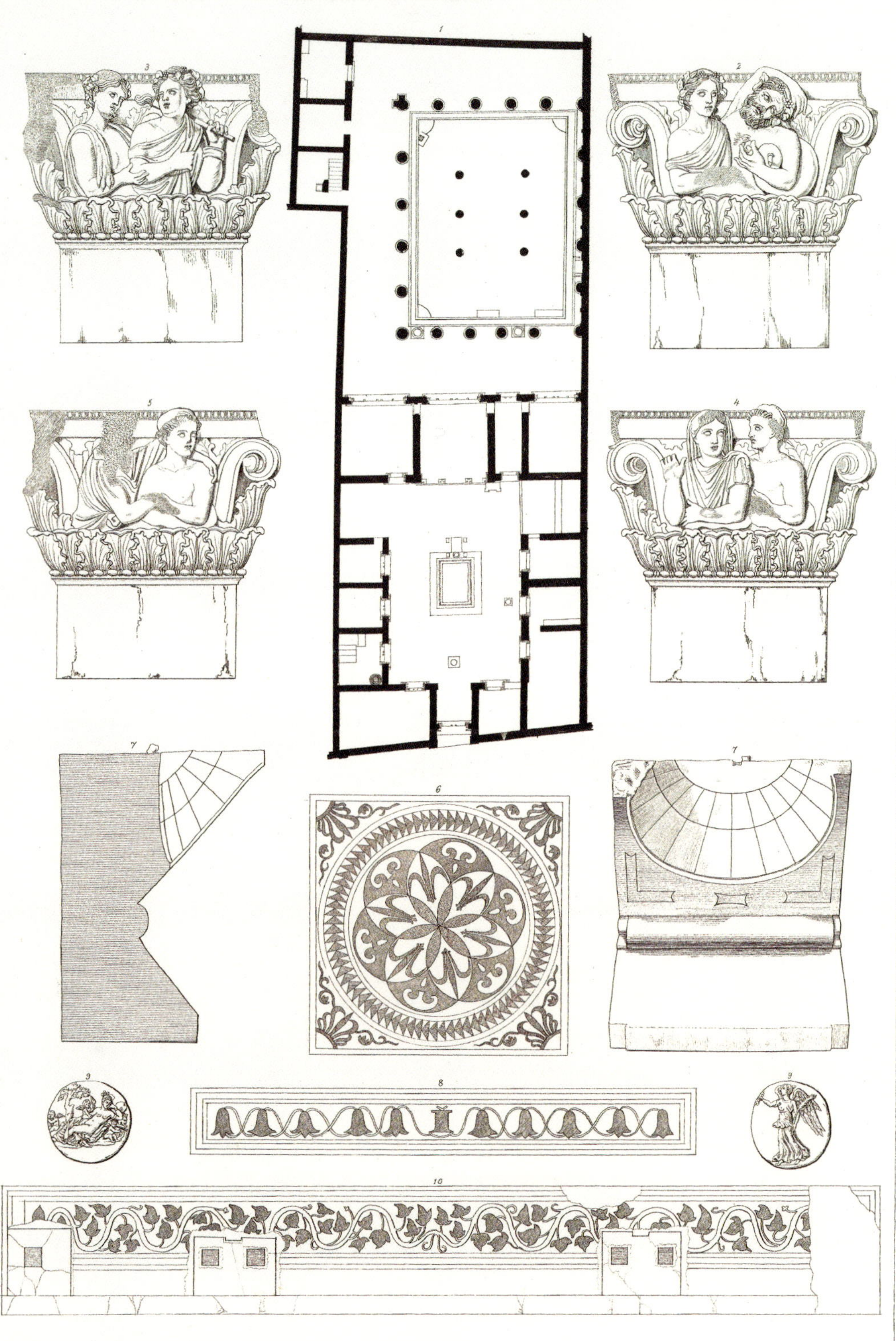

Fco. Tessitore inc. Flli Niccolini dir. Lit. Richter & Co.

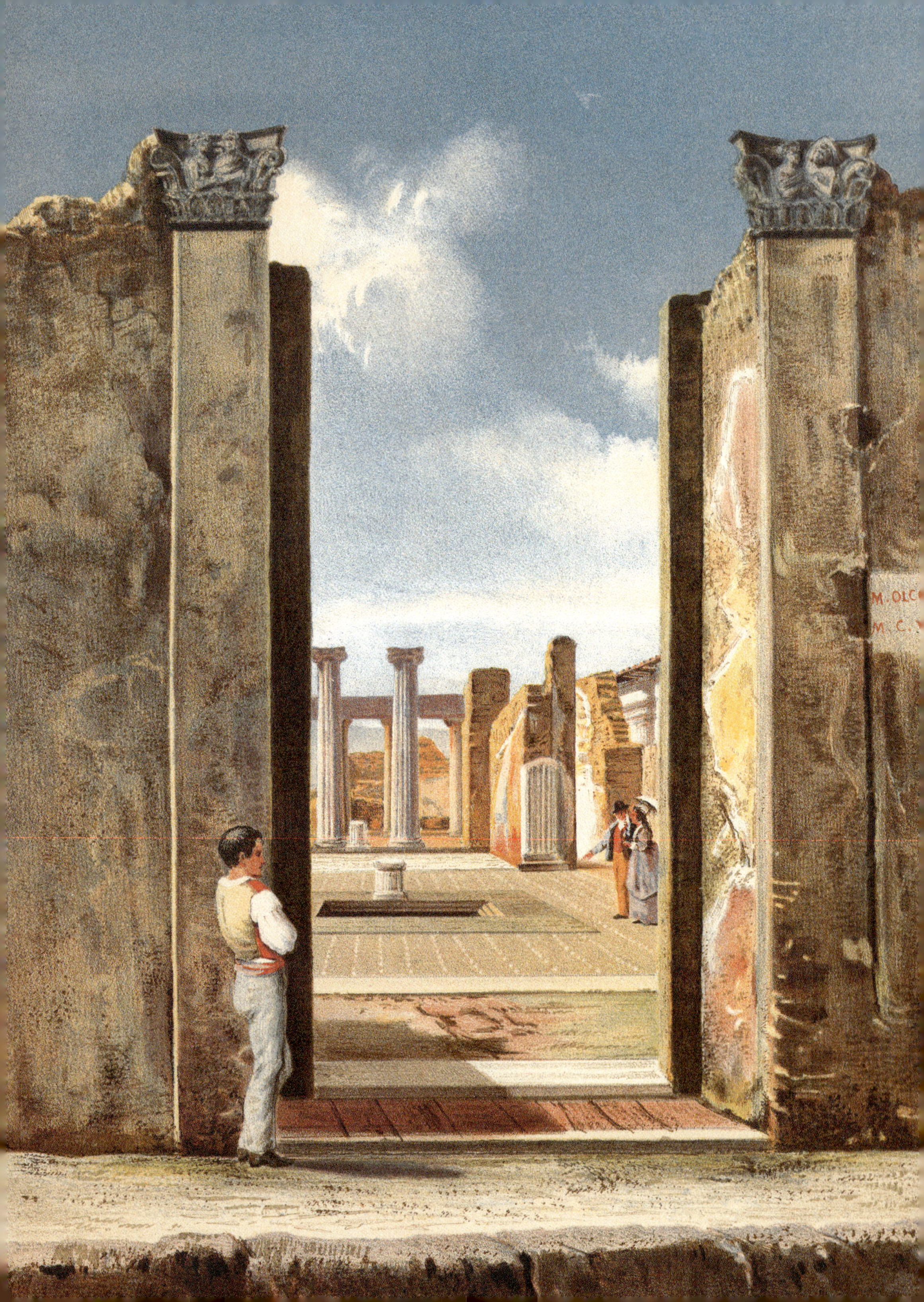

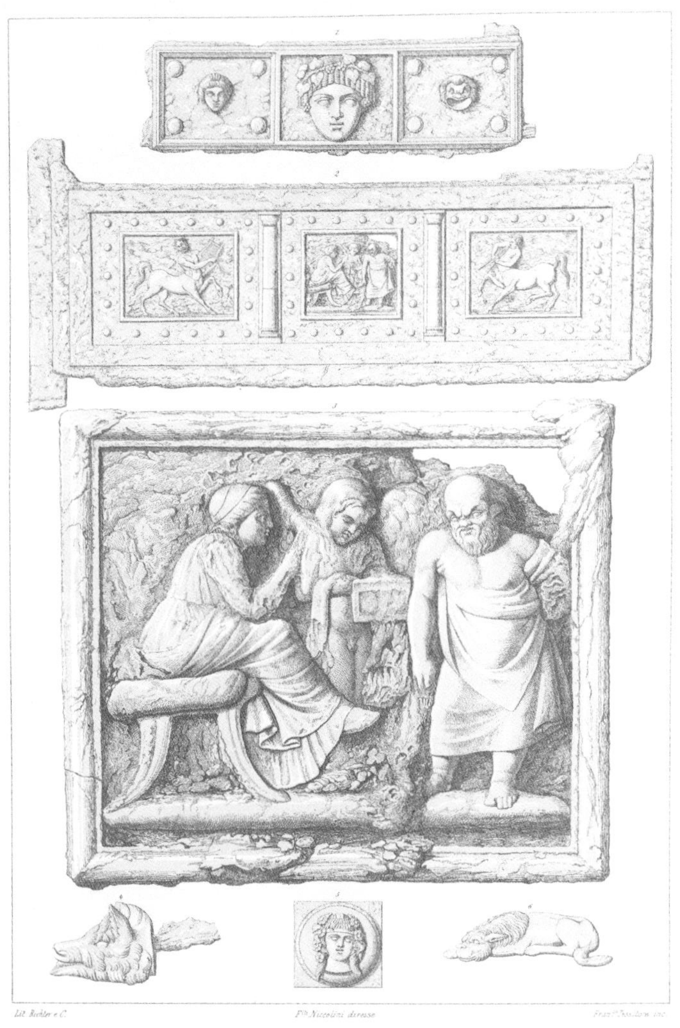

Plate 2 — *[V. Mollame]*
View of the house from the Via di Nola – The figural capitals are today housed in the Pompeii depository.

❖

Plate 3 — *[F. Tessitore]*
Atrium – Metal fittings from a money chest *(arca)*: centaurs and the education of Eros.

DESCRIZIONE GENERALE

General Description

After several chapters devoted to individual excavation sites in the first volume of *Case e monumenti*, volume II contains the single largest chapter in the work as a whole: Descrizione generale, a general description of the city of Pompeii in 80 pages of text with 96 plates. The Niccolini brothers had already announced the inclusion of this chapter in their foreword to the complete work, written before 1860. The city was to be described in topographical order and the text accompanied by numerous plates, which would present the full scope of those finds from Pompeii that could not positively be classified according to a strict system or assigned to a specific excavation site. Only in this way was it possible to do justice to the work's claim, as formulated in its title, to represent the houses and monuments of Pompeii. The chapter opens with a short history of the city based on the (few) literary sources, followed by a brief summary of excavations conducted up to the start of the 1860s. The description itself was written over many years, from approximately 1862 to 1876 (with the last plate only appearing in 1880), and proceeds building by building and area by area. It thereby follows the system proposed in 1858 by Giuseppe Fiorelli, who divided the city into districts (regiones) and blocks of houses (insulae). This system, still in use today, is employed here for the first time – even before Fiorelli used it himself in a larger work, in his own *Descrizione di Pompei* of 1875. But in an idiosyncratic mix of tradition and innovation, as so often with the Niccolini brothers, they then adapted this abstract order to fit the usual circuit, which starts at the Street of Tombs outside the Herculaneum Gate and ends at the theatres. After looking first at the tombs and the nearby suburban Villas of Diomedes and Cicero, the reader is led through the city gate into Regio VI, then into Regiones VII, VIII and IX and lastly into parts of Regio I. The buildings in each insula are all treated in varying degrees of detail, including references to the chapters on individual houses in volume I. The Niccolini brothers

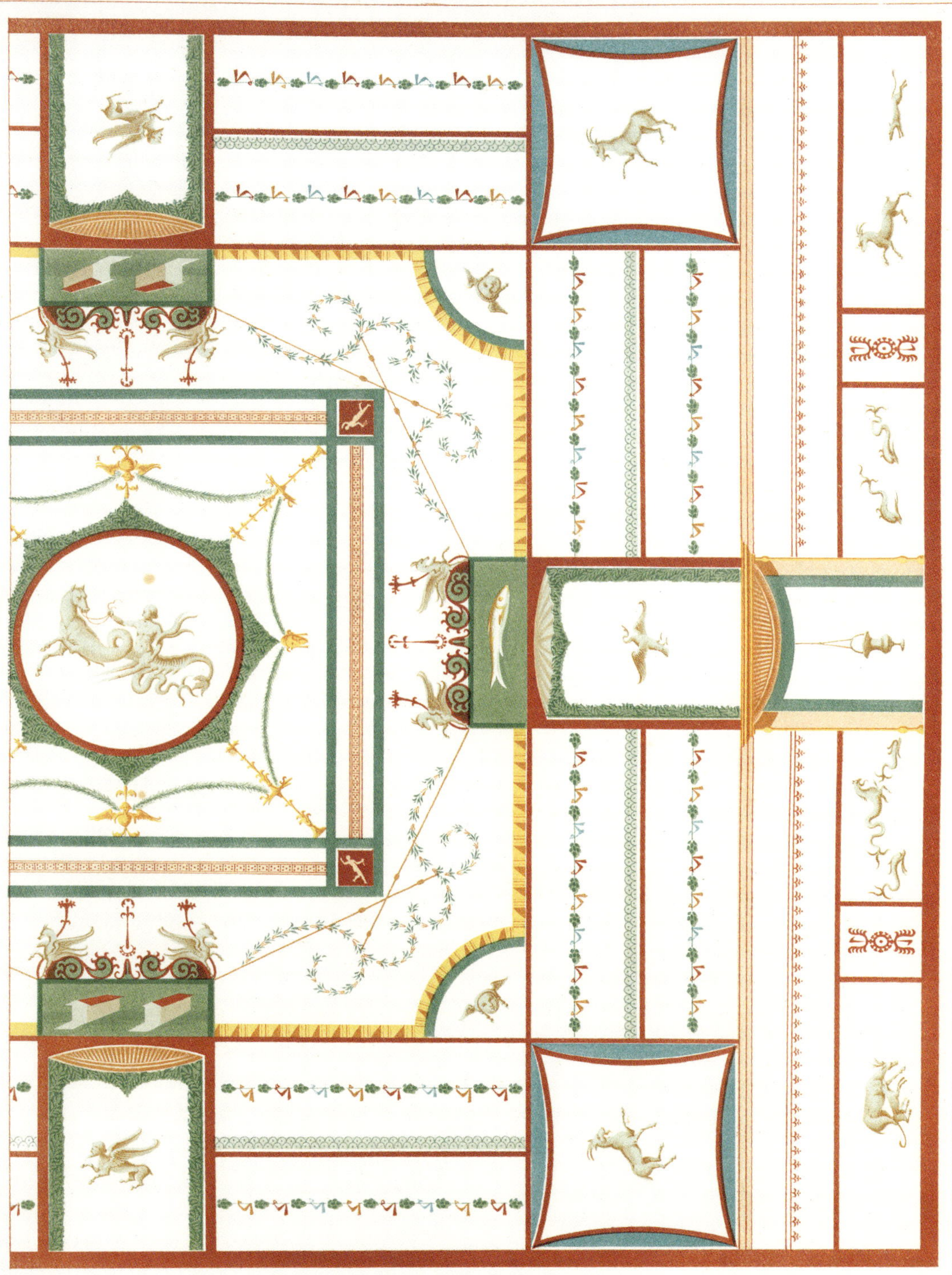

G. Abbate fece | Fr.lli Niccolini dir. Lit. Richter in Napoli | G. Frauenfelder es.

¼ palmi ——— 1 Napolitani

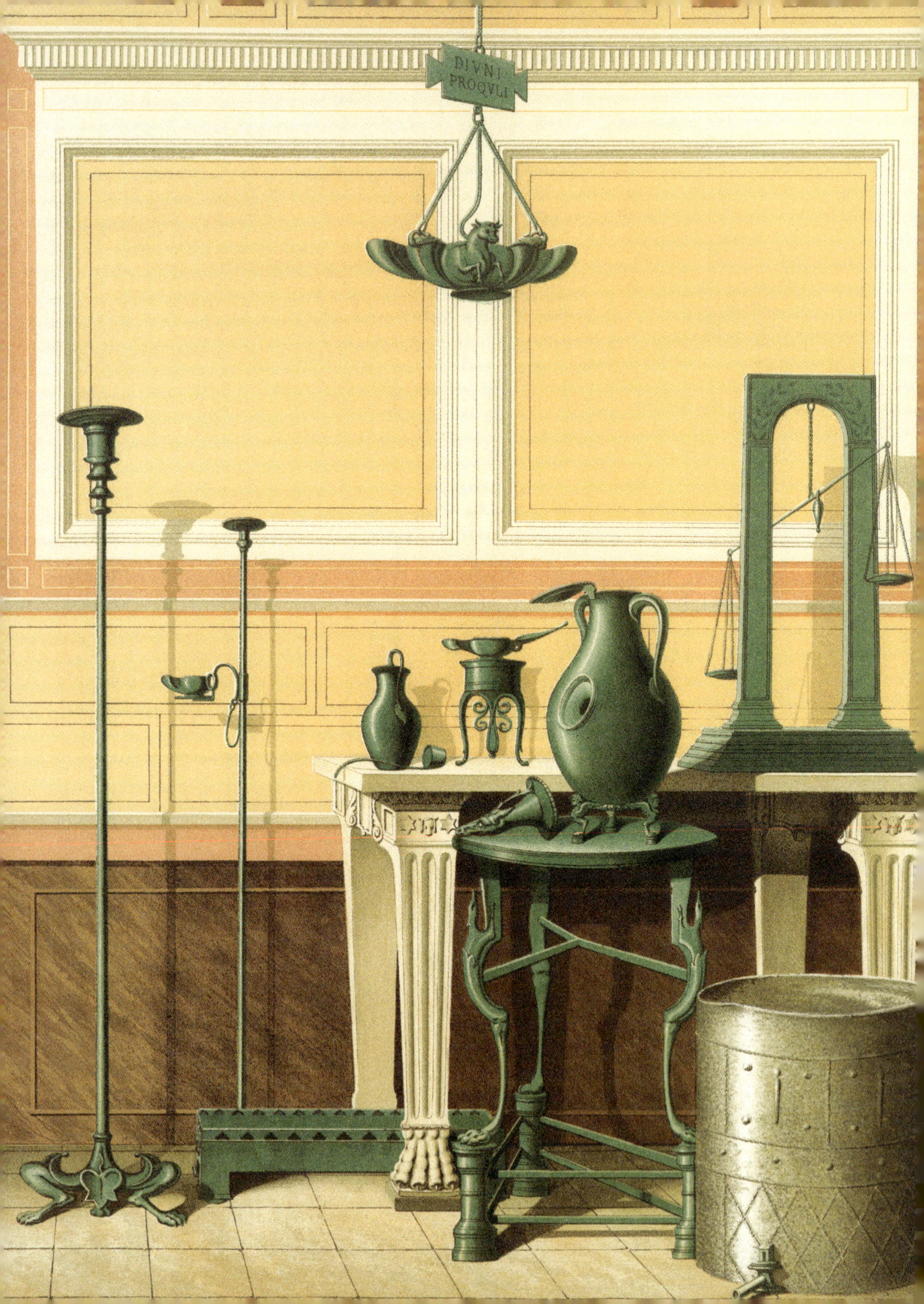
DIVNI
PROQVLI

show themselves to be very well informed. They draw upon the excavation reports from the Bourbon period (*Pompeianarum Antiquitatum Historia*, recently published by Giuseppe Fiorelli between 1860 and 1864) as well as the latest literature: Wolfgang Helbig's complete description of the wall paintings (*Wandgemälde der vom Vesuv verschütteten Städte Kampaniens*, 1868); the volume edited by Karl Zangemeister devoted to Pompeii's wall inscriptions (1871), in the *Corpus Inscriptionum Latinarum* series; and Giuseppe Fiorelli's previously mentioned *Descrizione* (1875), to name only the works they mention most frequently. References to the plates occur frequently in the early pages, especially to those in the chapter Topografia di Pompei in volume III, which must therefore have been compiled at the same time even if it was only published in the third volume. The text ends abruptly: the editors needed to bring the second volume to a close, as they explained, but would continue the description of the most recent excavations in a supplement in volume III; in the end, it appeared in volume IV.

There is only a loose connection between the 96 plates and the text, and even the six pages of plate descriptions confine themselves largely to essentials. Only among the first ten plates, which were delivered before 1860 and hence in advance of the first pages of text, are there a few which follow the progress of the description, in so far as they relate to the Street of Tombs and the villas and tombs lying along it (pl. 4, 6, 7, 10; see also in this volume the chapters on the Villa di Diomede and the Cenotafio di Calvenzio Quieto). In the case of various other plates, their inclusion may have been prompted by the relative recentness of the finds they illustrate – even if we do not know the precise order in which the instalments were published. This is true of the bronzes in plates 14, 15 and 19 and even more so for the sensational casts of bodies made in 1863 (pl. 18), a topic that would be taken up again in volume III. The gold lamp (pl. 42) found in the same year in the Temple of Venus Pompeiana and perhaps donated by Emperor Nero also falls into this category, as do the wax tablets from the archives of Caecilius Iucundus (pl. 60), only discovered in 1875. With the statuette of the satyr pouring wine from the Casa del Centenario (pl. 94), a new find from 1880 was even added right at the very end.

For the rest, the plates present that quality of Pompeii which the Niccolini brothers outlined in their Proemio, with the city itself being "the most eloquent book on the history of Antiquity that we possess". Thus subjects of all different kinds follow one another in richly

Page 197

Plate 1 — *[G. Abbate]*

Casa VII 3, 21 – Ceiling painting of the triclinium, excavated in 1843.

⁂

Plate 2 — *[G. Abbate]*

Collection of household utensils made of bronze and lead – Pendant lamp, lamp candelabra, charcoal brazier, table, jug, drinking vessel *(rhyton)* and a set of scales. Below right, a lead water tank. The precise origin of the individual objects is unknown.

varied succession. A series of vedute shows, among other things, two views of the *Street of Tombs* (pl. 7 and 29) and three of the otherwise largely neglected Forum (pl. 11, 16 and 20). The plates devoted to wall paintings present not only whole walls but also ornamental details and several monochrome reproductions of mythological themes, regardless of whether they were housed in the museum or were still in situ (and are therefore today mostly destroyed). A major area of focus is small bronzes, both in the shape of fountain statuary and as holders for lamps or receptacles in dining rooms (pl. 15, 16, 19, 21, 41, 52, 80, 94 and 95). The large money chest (*arca*, pl. 33) from an atrium and a number of bronze locks and keys (pl. 56) recall the morning reception at which the *patronus* appeared in front of his freedmen and clients. The above-mentioned wax tablets from a banker's archive include lease and rental contracts between private individuals, but also with the municipality of Pompeii (pl. 60). Lastly, a series of plates presents jewellery and domestic utensils *(instrumentum domesticum)* from daily life. These include rings, silver spoons and gold vessels from a temple treasury (?; pl. 34, 42). There are astonishingly modern-looking items of medical equipment (pl. 93), along with lamps and bronze candelabra from which lamps could hang or else be placed standing upright. One plate is devoted entirely to the culture of bathing (pl. 62). The majority of the pictures are based on earlier illustrations in the *Real Museo Borbonico*, either as direct copies or assembled into composite images. By way of exception, however, the plates devoted to glassware were created especially for the Niccolini book. While it is true that representations of the same objects had already been engraved for the *Museo Borbonico* and, earlier still, for the never-published volumes of the *Antichità di Ercolano*, artist Vincenzo Mollame here succeeds in lending the shimmering vessels a presence that leaves the otherwise mostly sober representations far behind (pl. 43, 83 and vol. IV, Supplemento, pl. 25).

Any attempt to find a system in the organisation of the plates is unlikely to succeed. The Niccolini brothers themselves, after listing various categories, acknowledged in their foreword that such rigorous classifications could never be implemented satisfactorily in practice. It is also probable, however, that the composition of the Descrizione generale was greatly influenced by considerations of which we are ignorant: factors ranging from the recentness of the finds to the availability of images, and the wish to compile attractive instalments on different topics, will all have played a role.

Plate 4 — *[G. Abbate]*
Four details from the walls of different houses – Flying erotes, a candelabrum and a section of the upper zone of a wall painting.

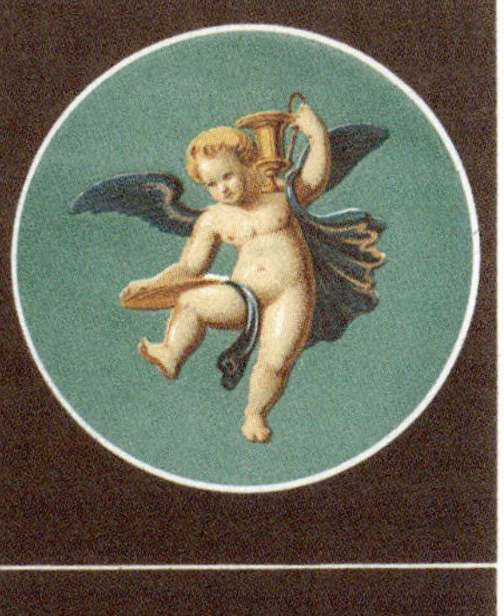

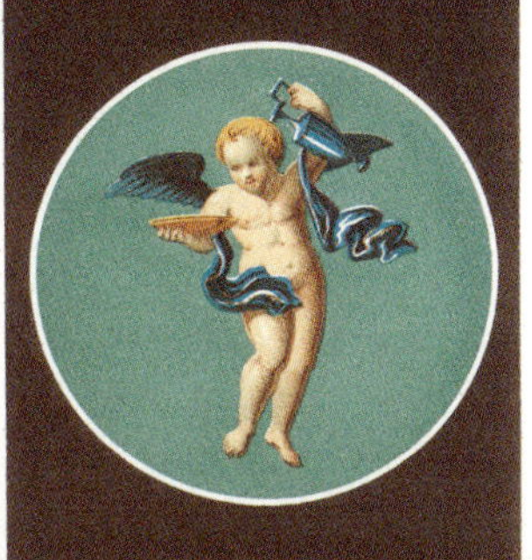

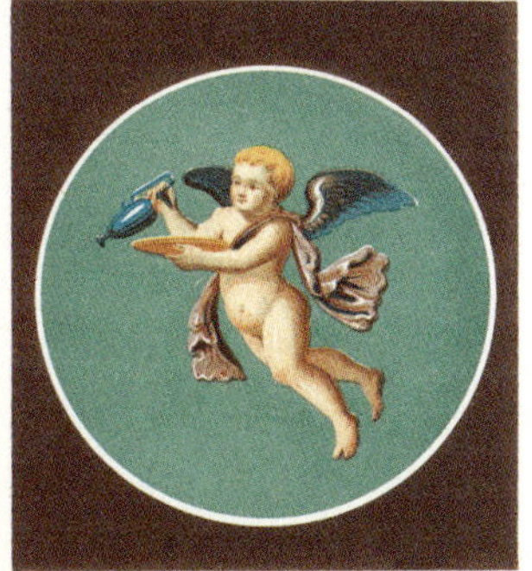

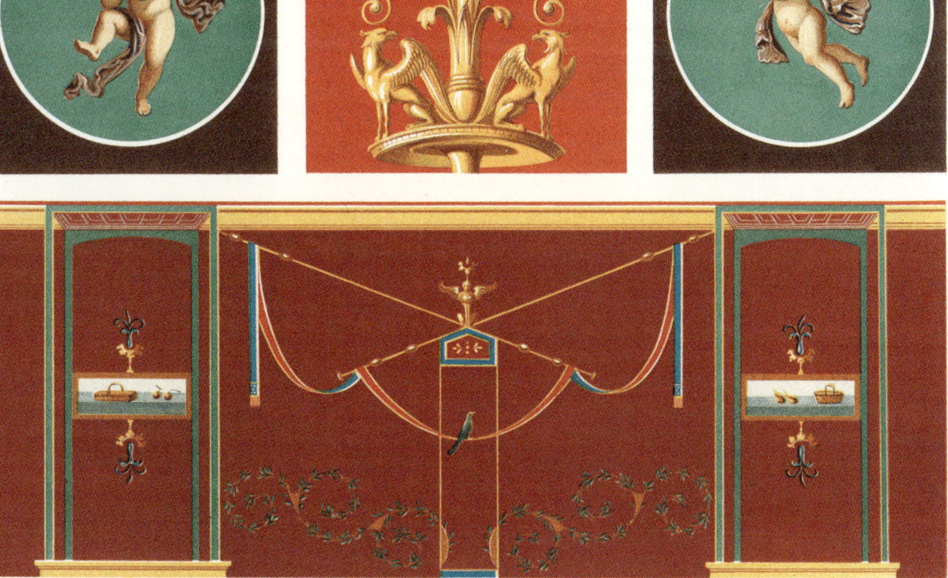

G. Abbate fece

Fr.[lli] Niccolini dir.
Lit. Richter e C. in Napoli

G. Frauenfelder lith.

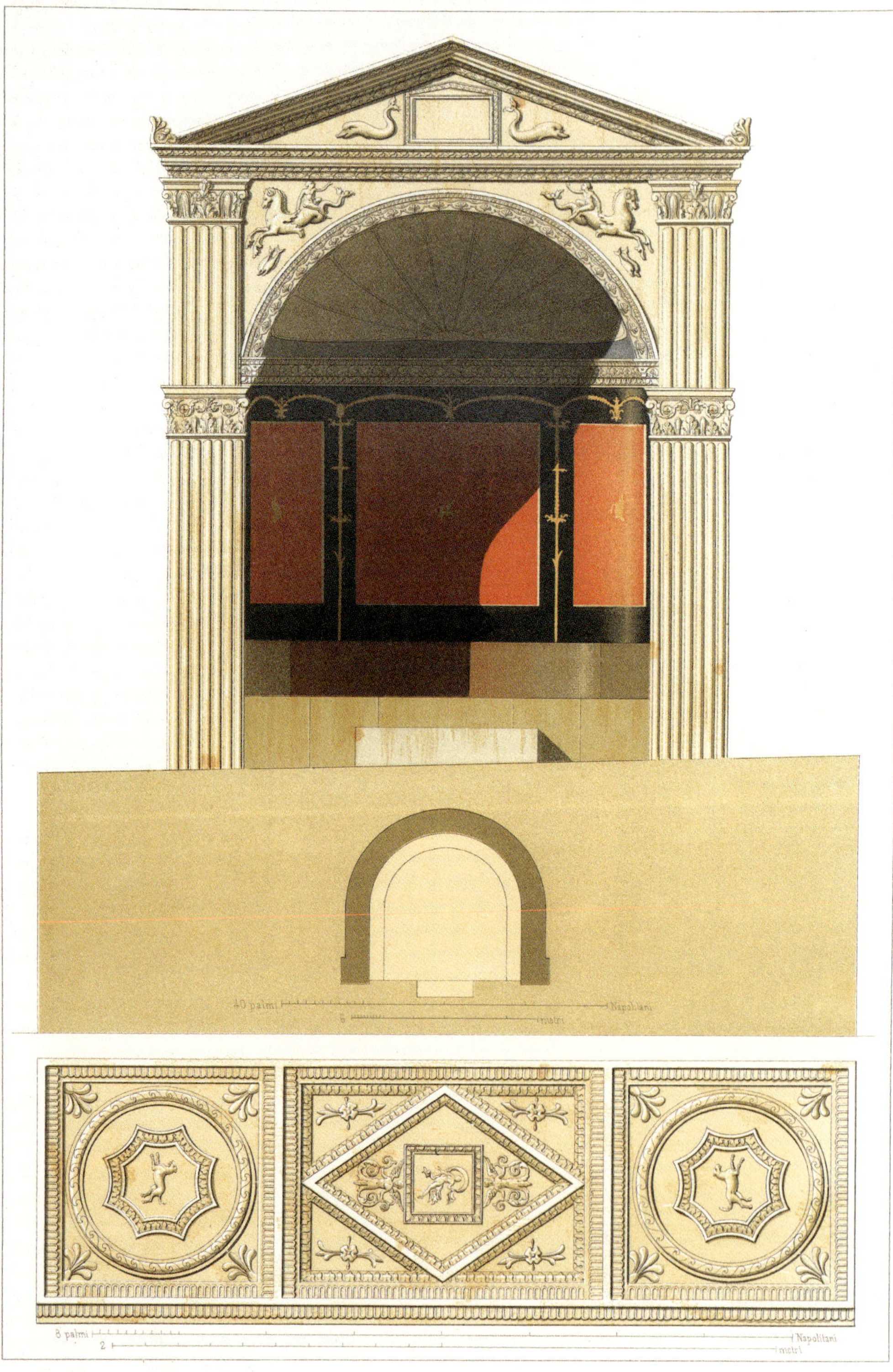

G. Abbate fece

Fr.lli Niccolini dir.
Lit. Richter e C. in Napoli

G. Frauenfelder lit

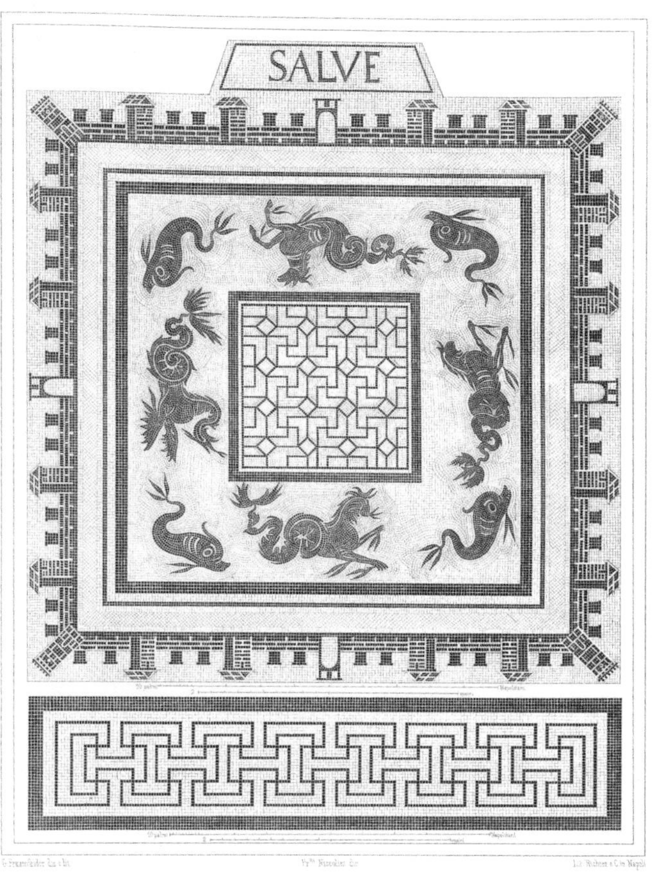

Plate 6 — *[G. Abbate]*
Street of Tombs in front of the Herculaneum Gate – Lavishly stuccoed exedra with frescoed interior. View, ground plan and detail of the stucco work on the inside of the arch.

Plate 5 — *[G. Trauenfelder]*
Black-and-white floor mosaic with a procession of fabulous sea creatures – The central motif is surrounded by a stylised city wall with towers and city gates. The sheet combines various fragments from Pompeii and Stabiae into a new mosaic.

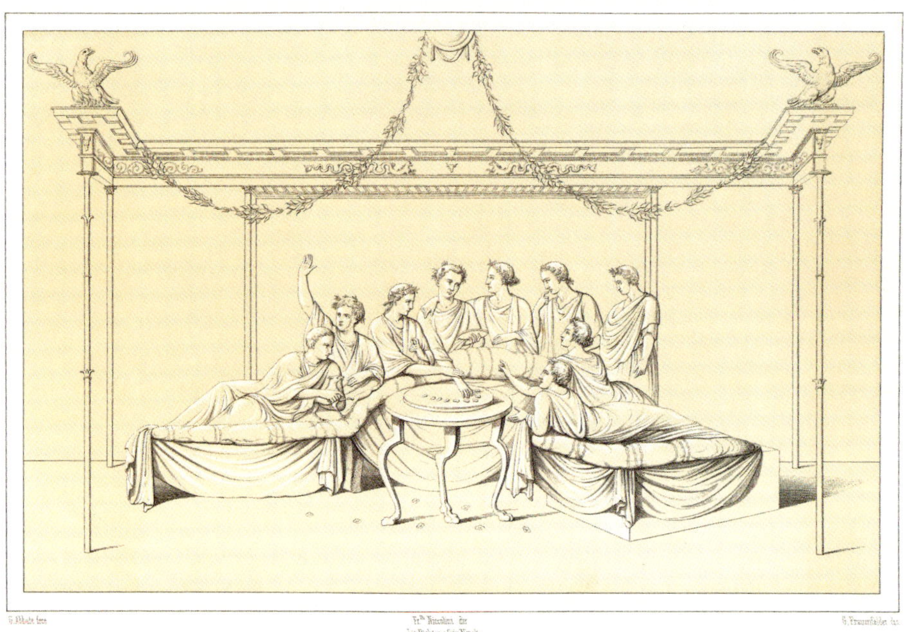

Plate 3 — *[G. Abbate]*
Wall painting of a dining scene with guests, set inside a pavilion – The mural was found in 1844 in a tavern on the south side of the Via di Nola but was afterwards destroyed.

Plate 8 — *[G. Abbate]*
Marble memorial statue of Marcus Holconius Rufus – In its reconstructed position in front of the Stabian Baths.

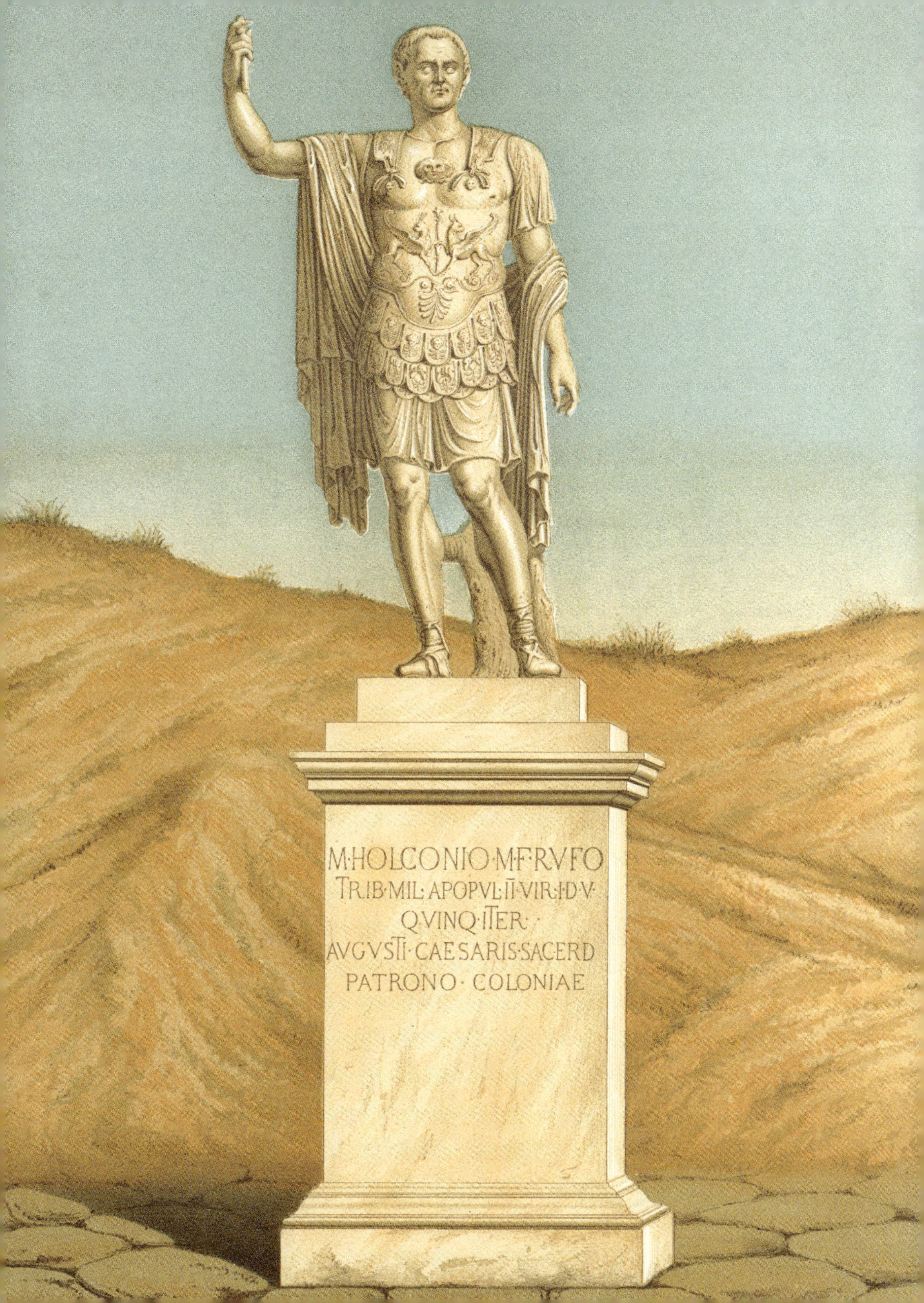
M·HOLCONIO·M·F·RVFO
TRIB·MIL·A·POPVL·II·VIR·I·D·V·
QVINQ·ITER·
AVGVSTI·CAESARIS·SACERD
PATRONO·COLONIAE

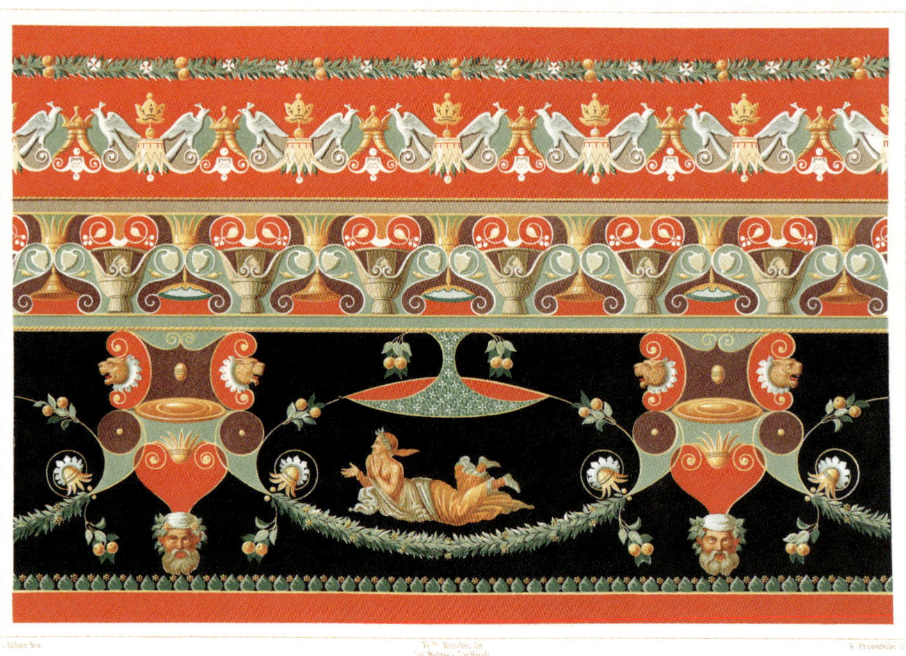

Plate 9 — *[G. Abbate]*
Insula occidentalis – Ornamental band in the 3rd style (1st half of the 1st century AD), reconstructed from numerous fragments.

⁂

Plate 10 — *[G. Abbate]*
Street of Tombs in front of the Herculaneum Gate, Tomb North 8 (?) – Vessel of so-called cameo glass: idyllic scenes showing erotes at the vintage are carved out of an outer layer of opaque white glass.

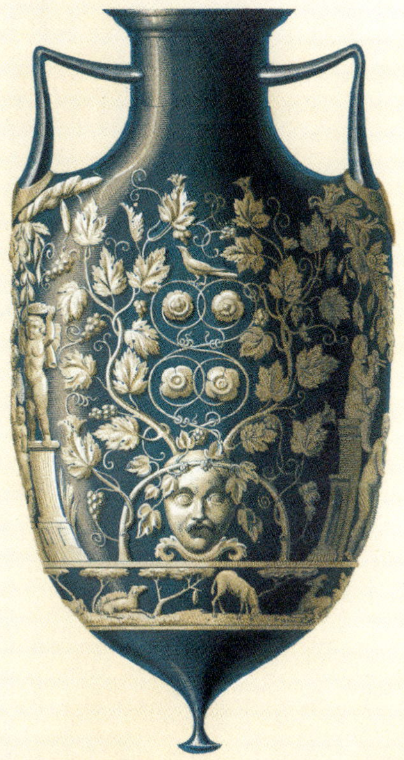

Un palmo Napolitano

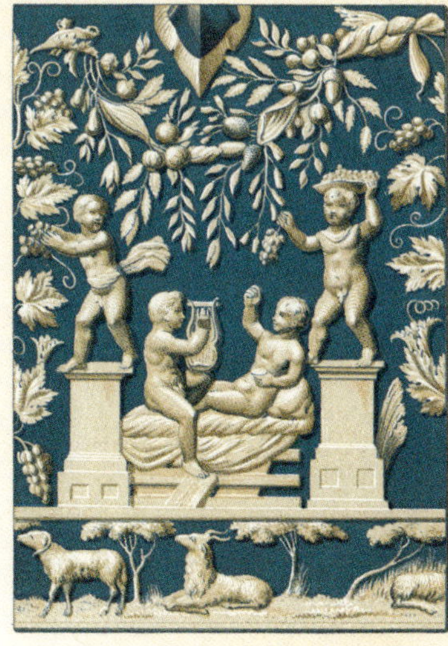

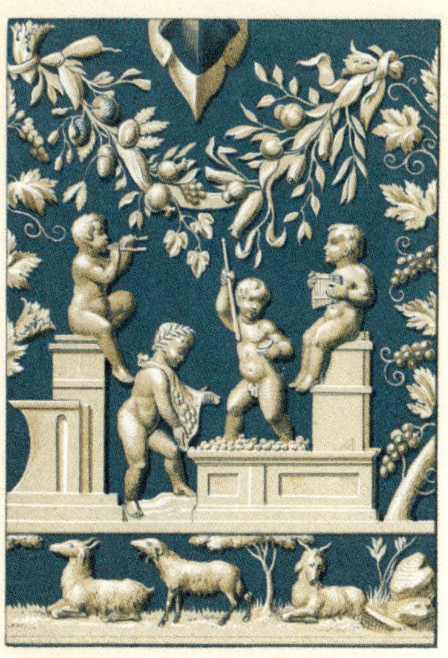

G. Abbate fece. Fco Niccolini dir. Lit. Richter e C. in Napoli

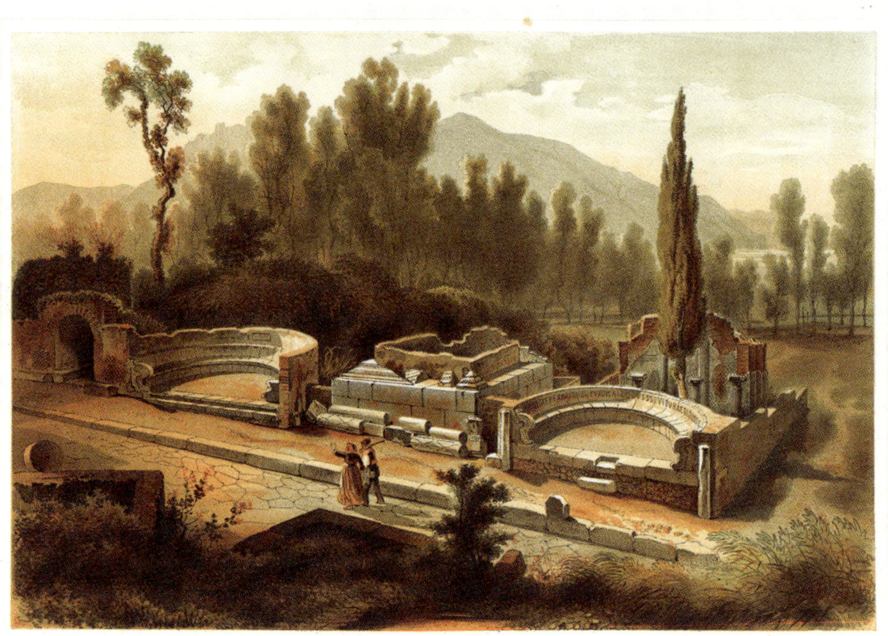

Plate 7 — *[T. Duclère]*
Street of Tombs in front of the Herculaneum Gate – Bird's-eye view with several tombs; another part of the necropolis can be seen in plate 29.

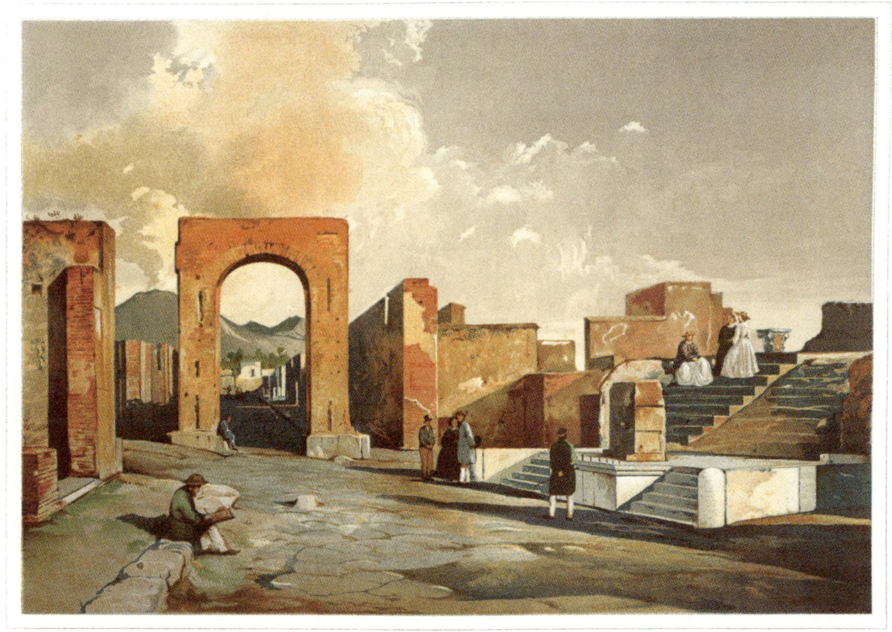

Plate 11 — *[G. Gigante]*
Via del Foro – Looking north, with a triumphal arch, stripped of its marble cladding, at the start of the Via di Mercurio and Vesuvius behind. On the right, the ruins of the Temple of Fortuna Augusta (vol. I), on the left the artist drawing.

Pages 210–211
Plate 16 — *[G. Gigante]*
View of the Forum from the north – Right: Capitolium, with the Monti Lattari range behind.

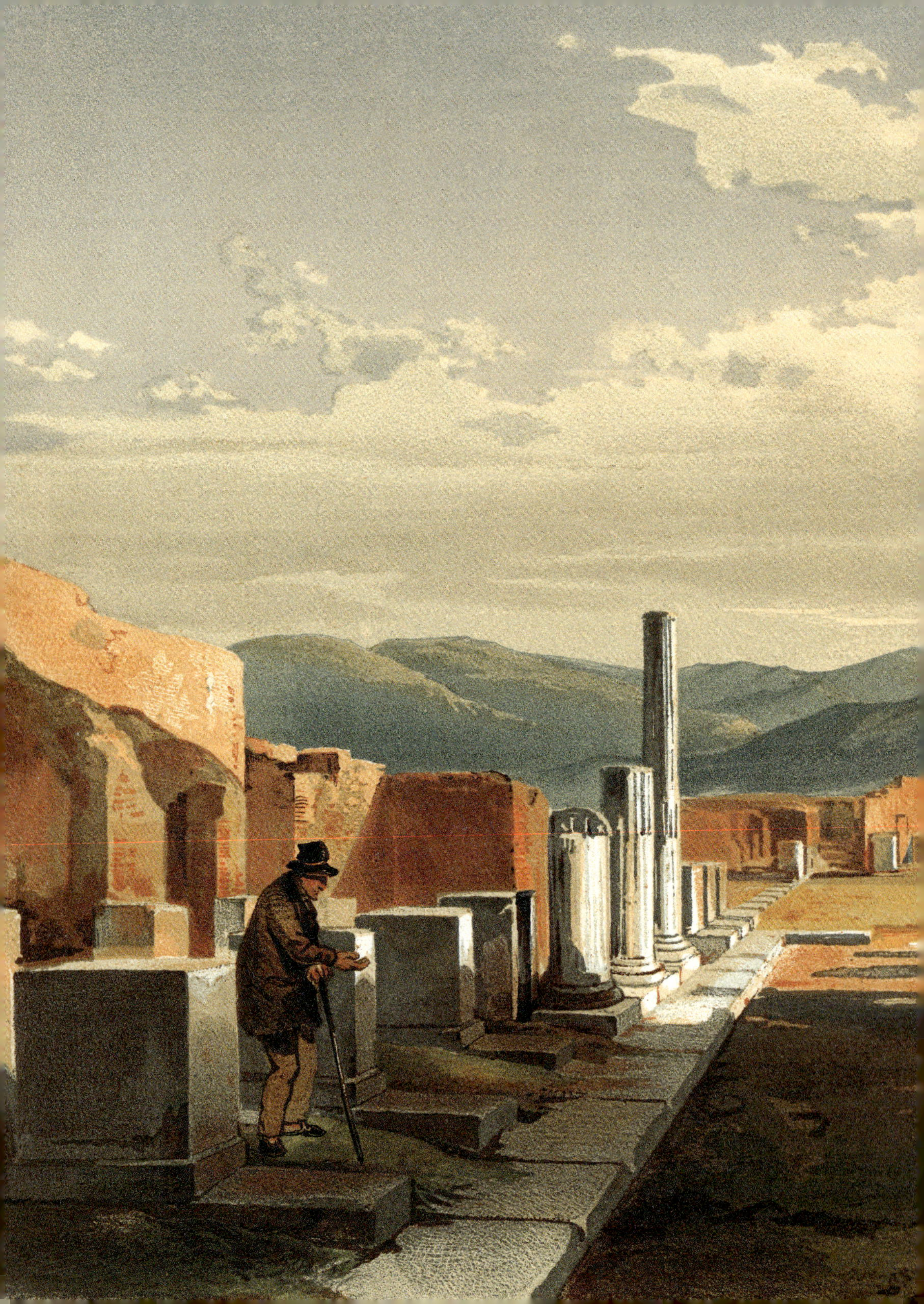

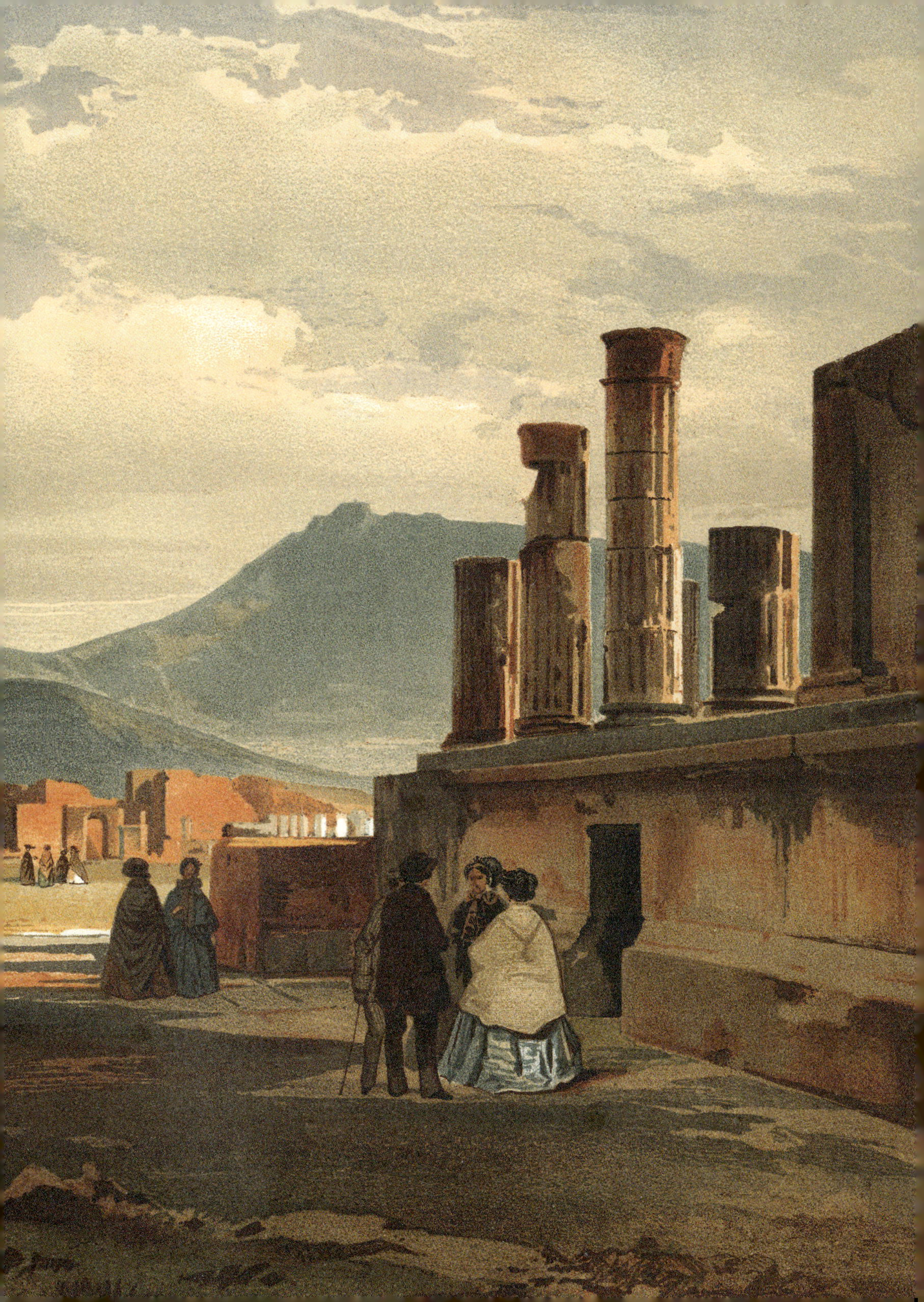

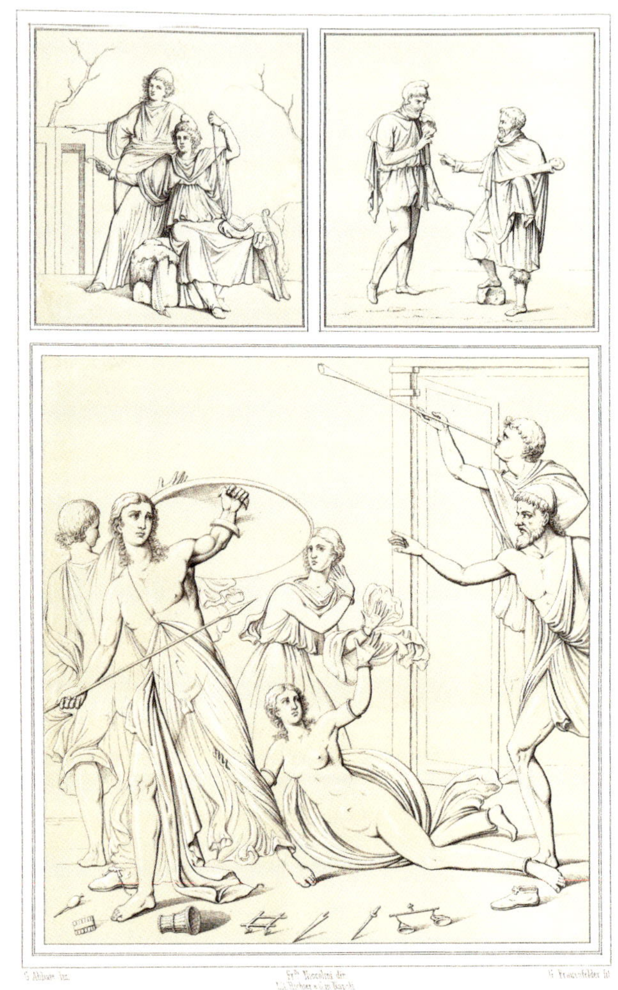

Plate 13 — *[G. Abbate]*
Above: ***Casa di Cornelius Rufus (VIII 4, 15 and 30), oecus (m) overlooking the peristyle*** (ca. 65 x 57 cm / 25 ½ x 22 ½ in.) – The significance of the figures in Oriental dress is unclear. Below: ***Casa di Holconius Rufus (Casa dei Postumii, VIII 4, 4 and 49), triclinium (33)*** – Odysseus discovers Achilles with the daughters of Lycomedes on Skyros. All the pictures are today destroyed.

Plate 12 — *[G. Abbate]*
Candelabra and other details from a wall painting and a painted cornice in the 4th style. Unknown origin.

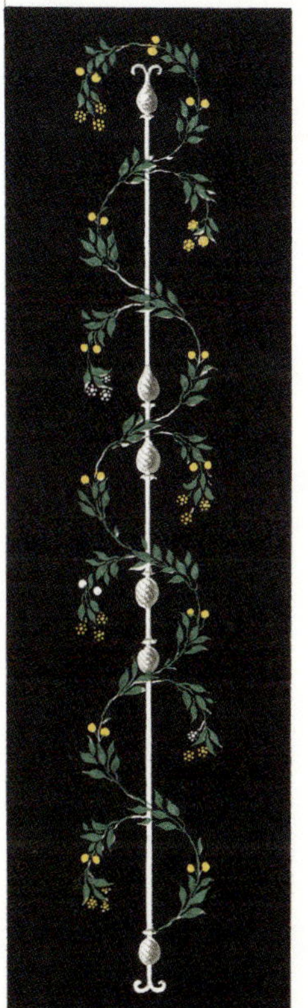

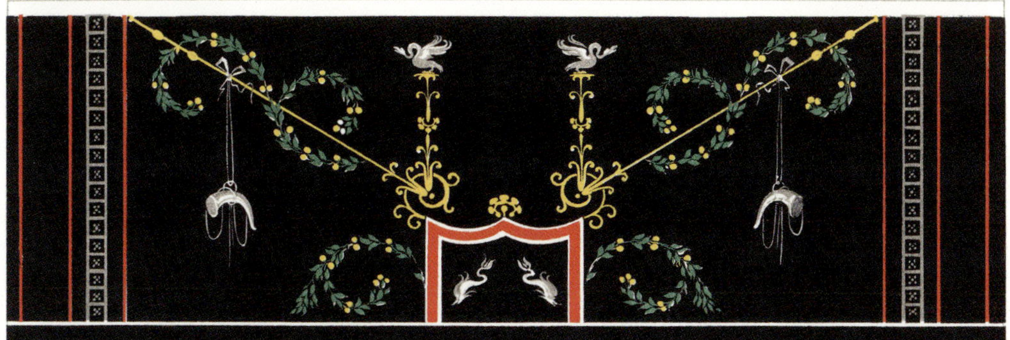

G. Abbate fec. — F.lli Niccolini dir. Lit. Richter e C.ie in Napoli — K. Grob lith.

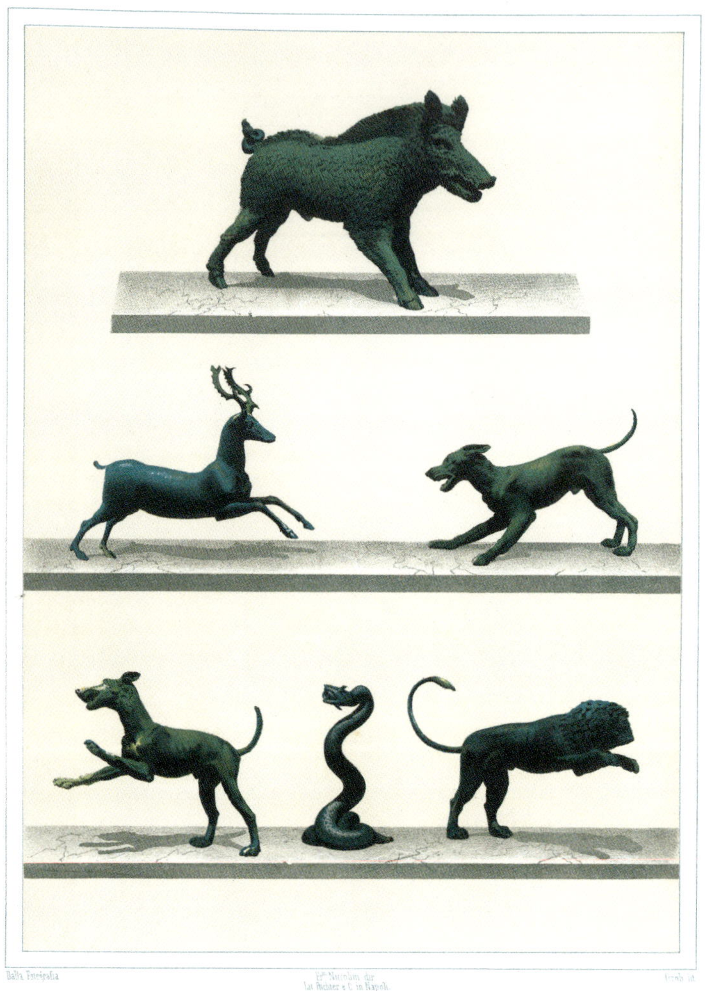

Plate 14 — *[K. Grob]*
Casa del Citarista (I 4, 5) – Six bronze animal figures from a fountain in the garden peristyle.

✱

Plate 15 — *[K. Grob]*
Casa VII 12, 17 and 21, side room (b) – Bronze statuette of a Dionysus.

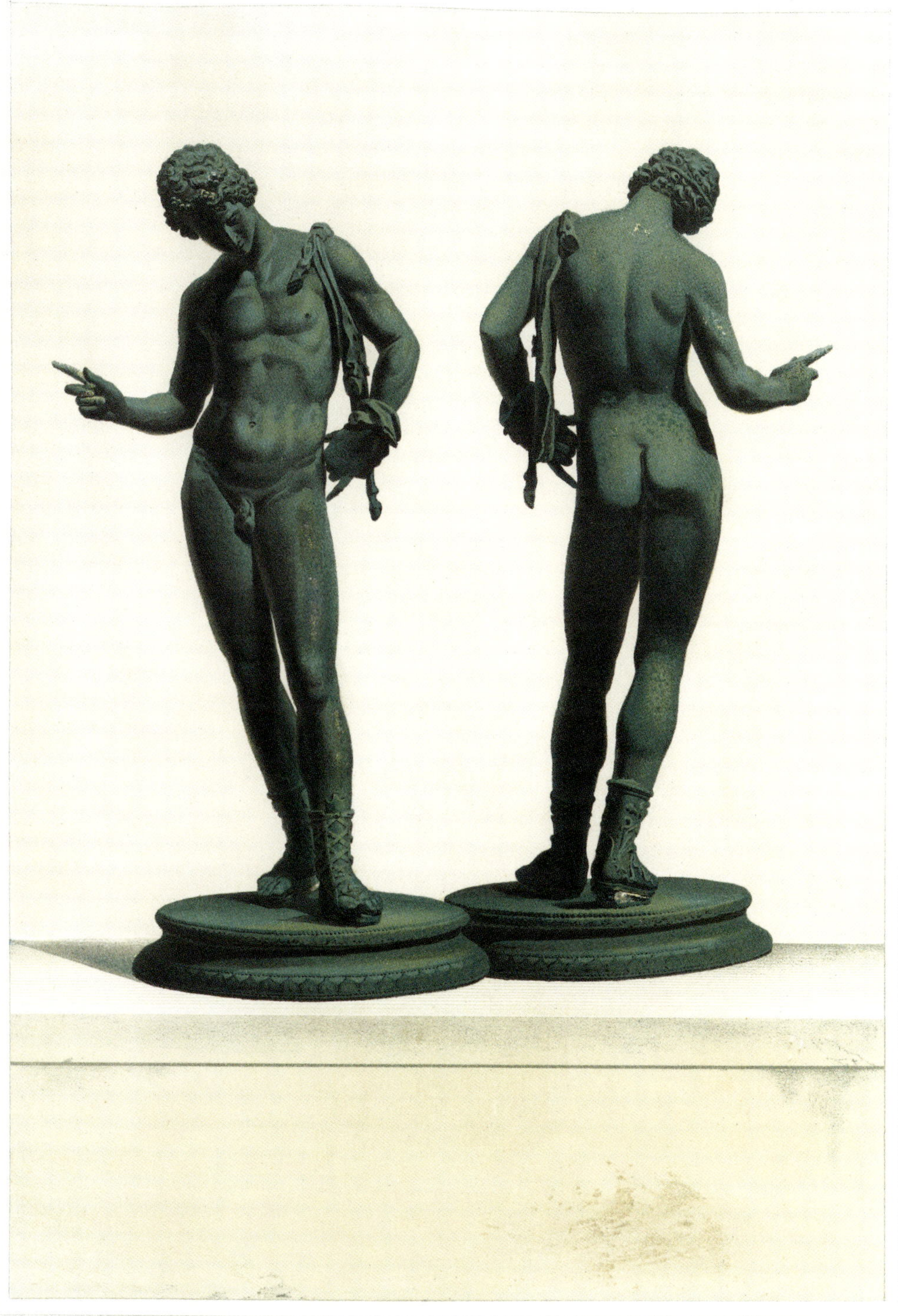

Della Pace, dis. e lit. da K. Grob. F.lli Niccolini dir. Lit. Richter e C.° Napoli

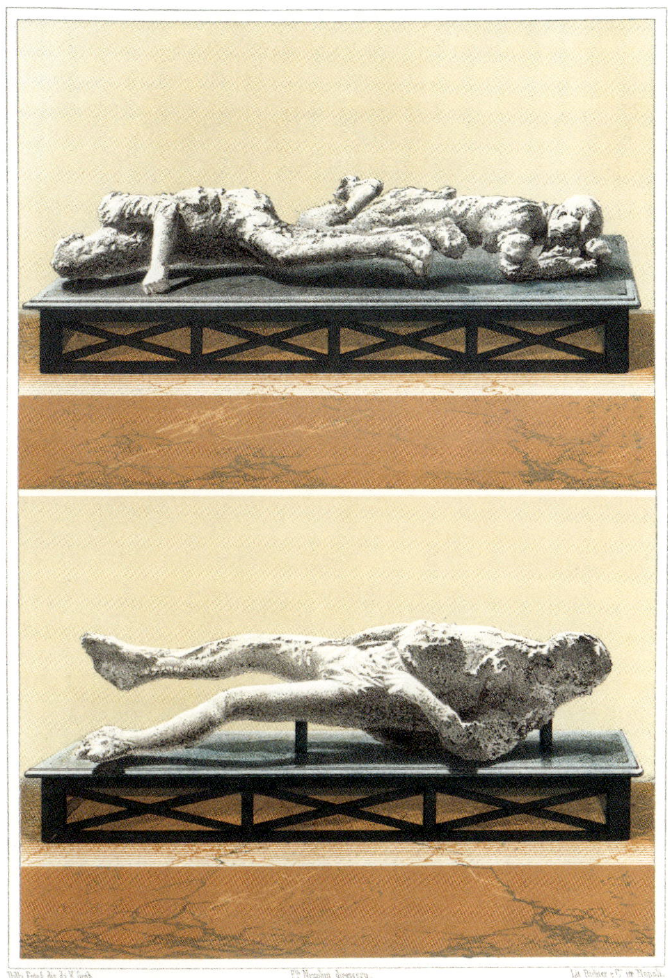

Plate 17 — *[G. Abbate]*
Casa dei Capitelli colorati (VII 4, 31–35), exedra 31 – Pasticcio of ornamental details: in the middle, a motif from a 4th-style wall painting that was destroyed in the 19th century.

❖

Plate 18 — *[K. Grob]*
Plaster casts of the bodies of three victims of the Vesuvian eruption of AD 79 – The casts were made in February 1863 from the cavities left by the bodies, which were found in the Vicolo degli Scheletri along with a small treasure trove (see also pl. 34).

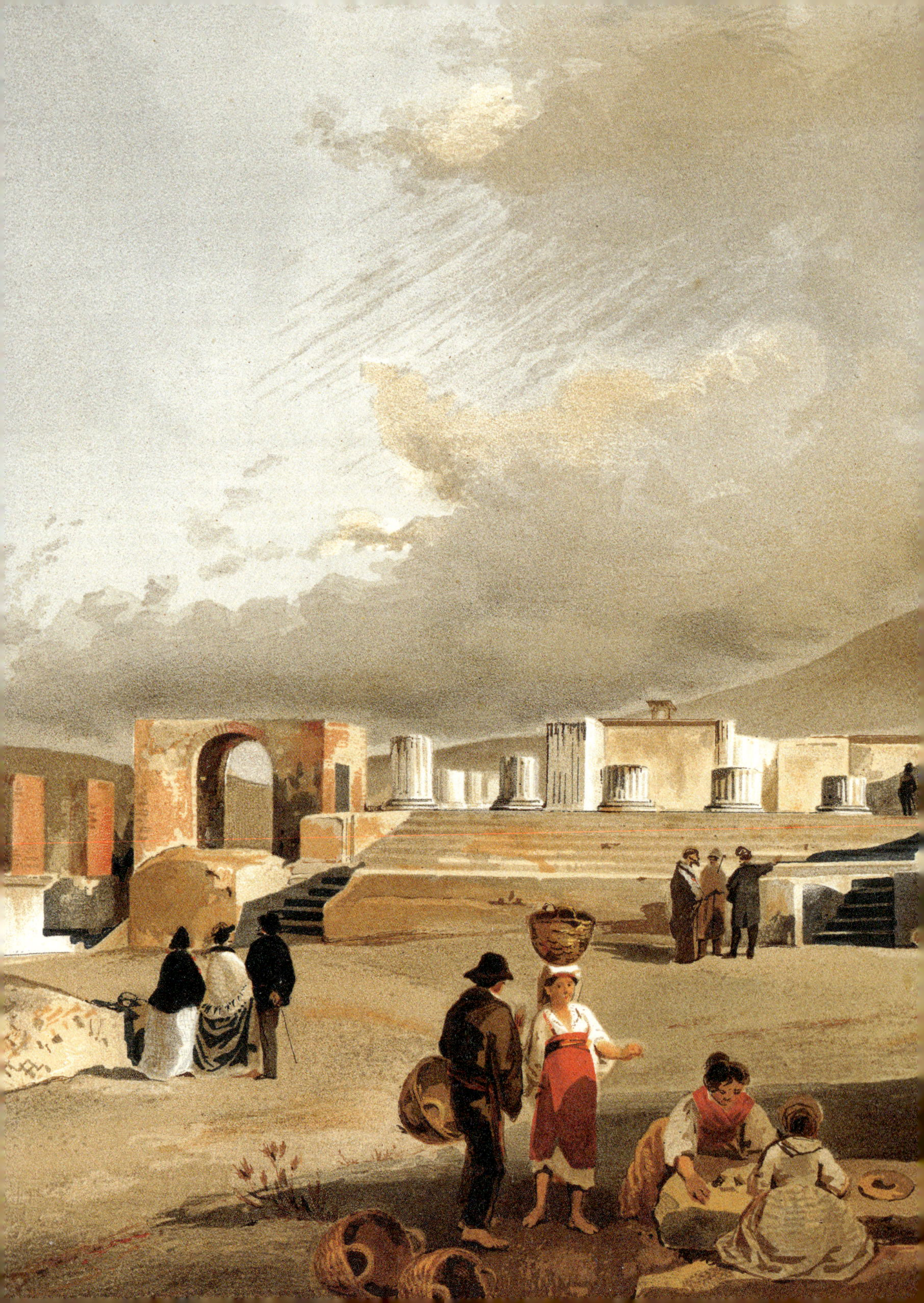

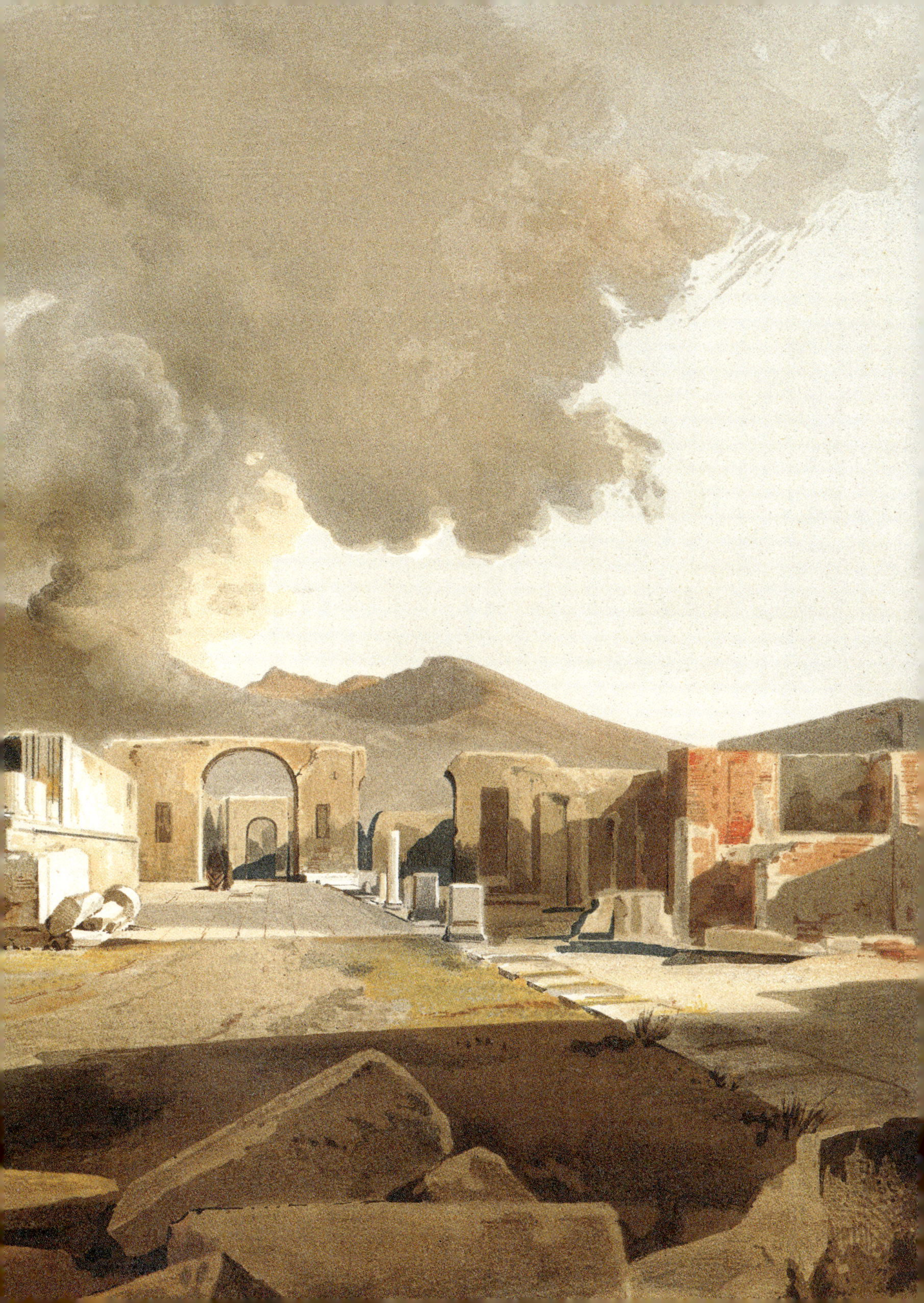

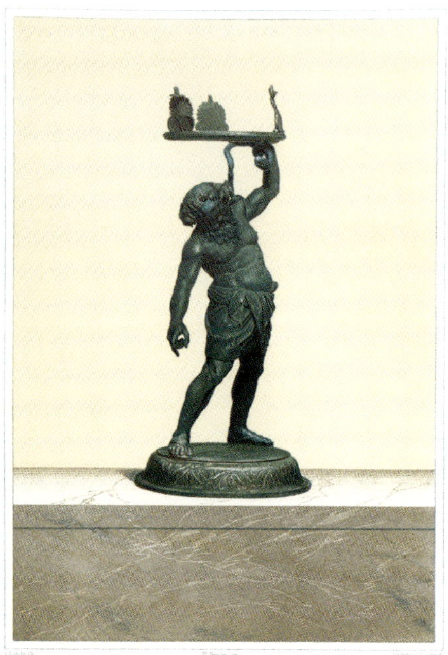

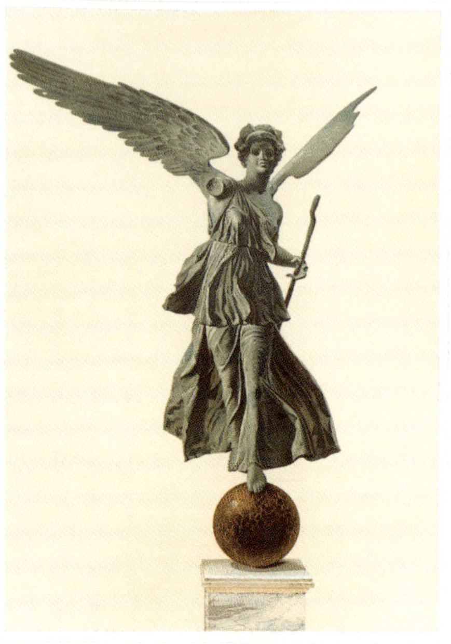

Pages 218–219

Plate 20 — *[G. Gigante]*

Forum – View from the south with a smoking Vesuvius in the background.

⁂

Plate 19 — *[K. Grob]*

Casa di Popidius Priscus or Casa dei Marmi (VII 2, 20) – Bronze statuette of a satyr, holding up a (missing) wine vessel with his left hand. The statuette, found in May 1864, evidently appealed to the tastes of the day. It was greatly admired and frequently reproduced, with copies cast in bronze.

⁂

Plate 21 — *[K. Grob]*

Bronze statuette of a winged Victory – Found in 1823 in Pompeii according to the Niccolini brothers. The statuette has an eyelet on the back and so was capable of being suspended "in flight". Like the satyr in plate 19, casts of the figure were made by the Chiurazzi art foundry.

⁂

Plate 23 — *[G. Abbate]*

Two sections of a candelabrum and another decorative motif from the period of the 4th style. Origin unknown.

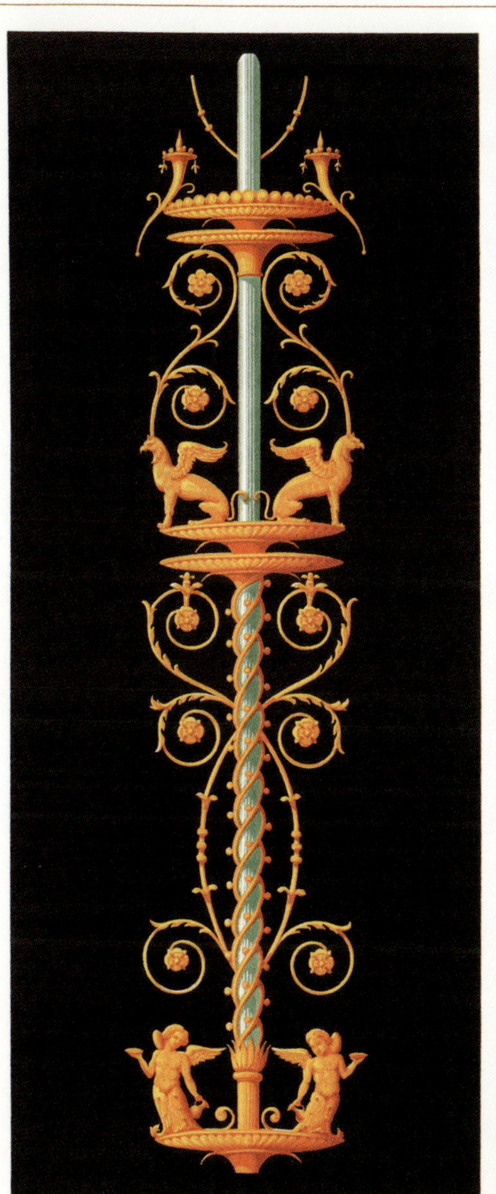

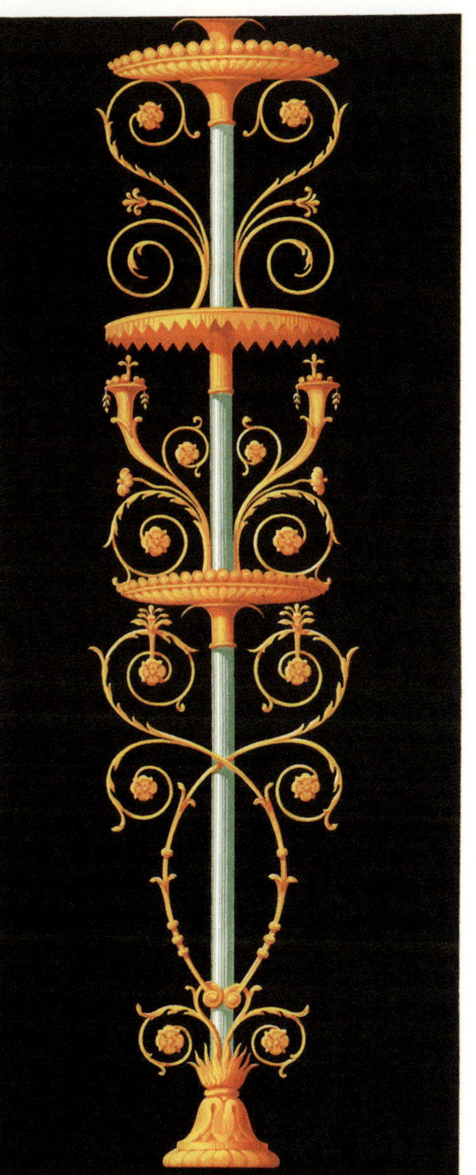

G. Abbate fece. | F.lli Niccolini dir. | A. Carli lit.

Lit. Richter e C.o in Napoli.

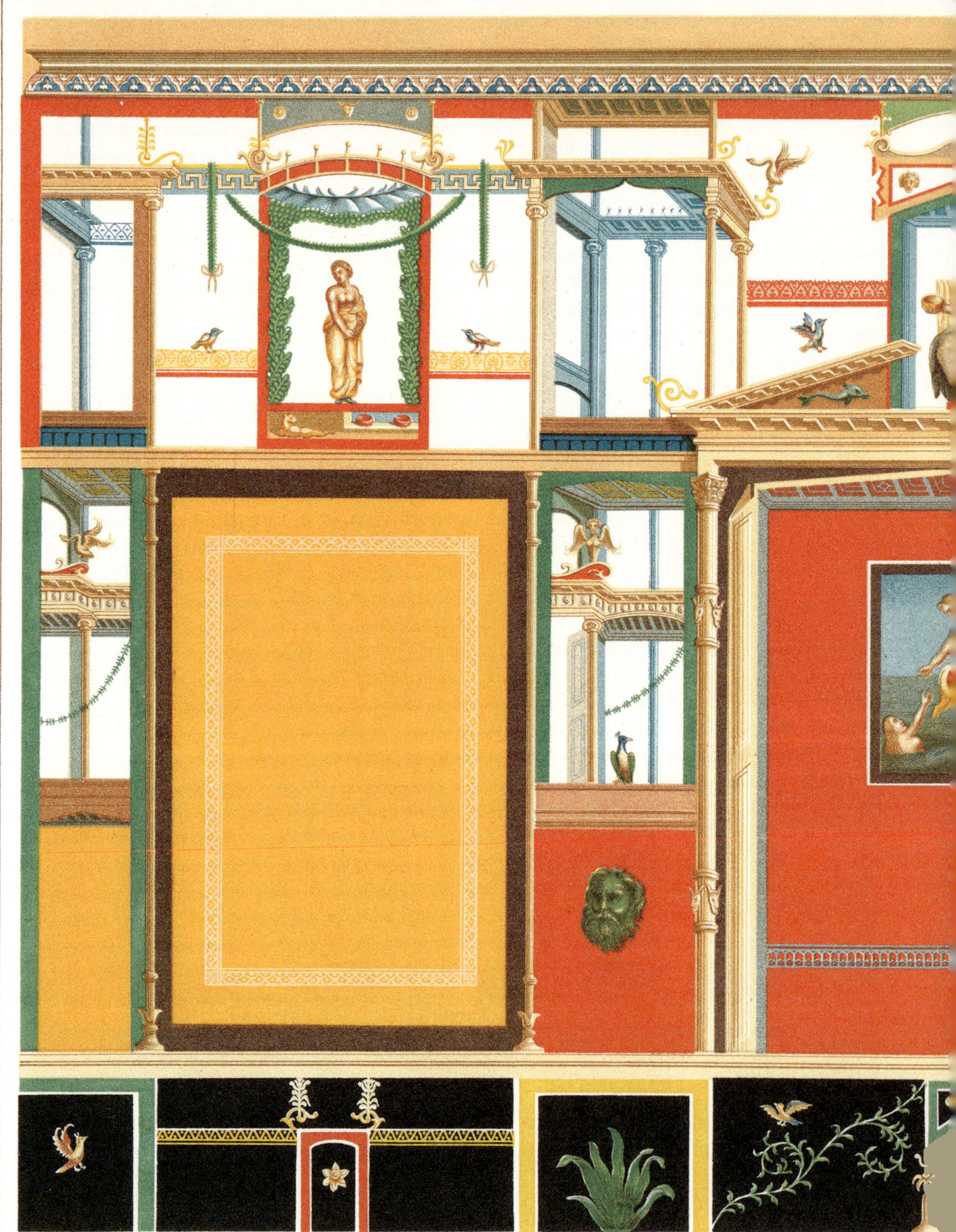

Lit. Richter e C.o Napoli.

F.III

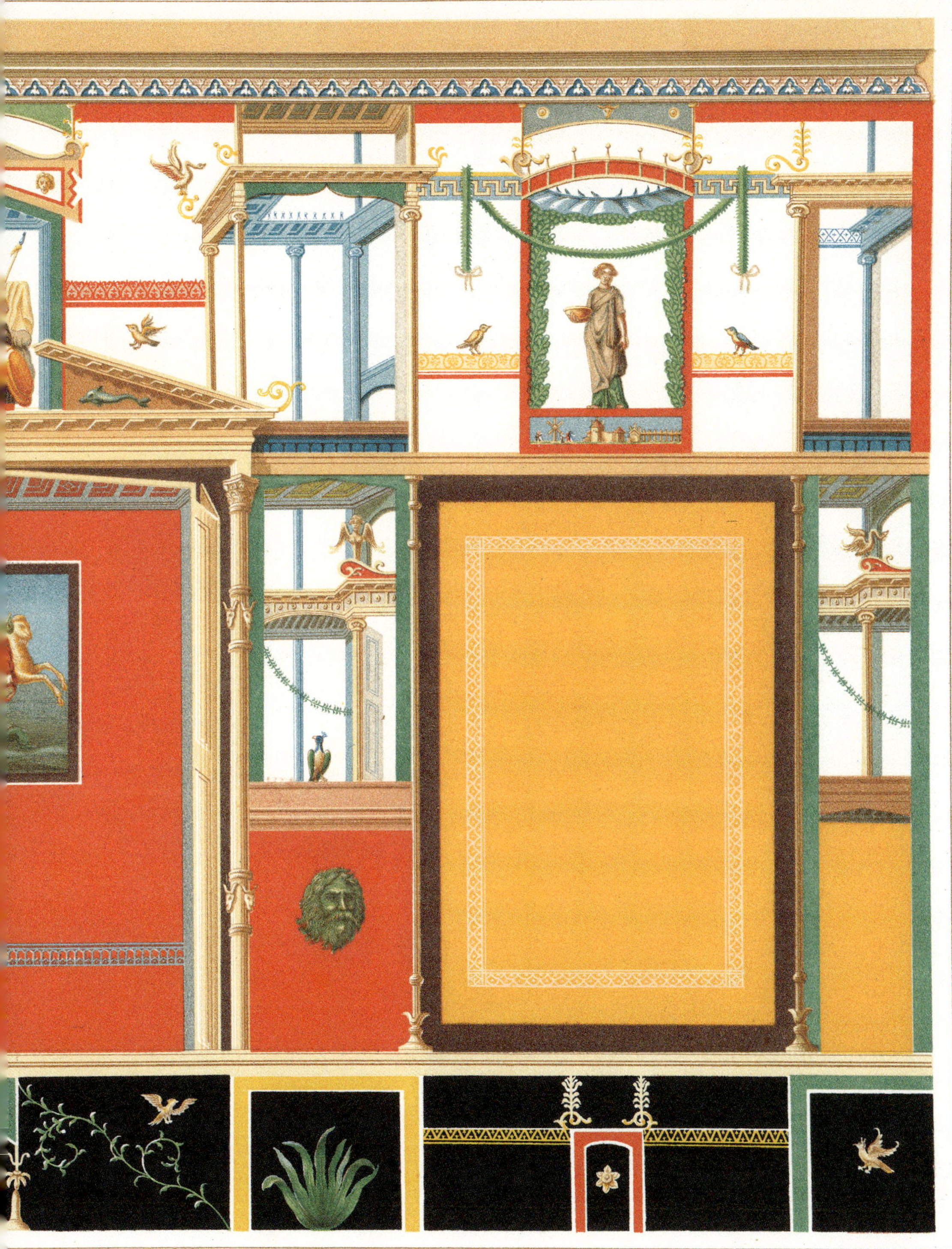

dir. A. Carli lit.

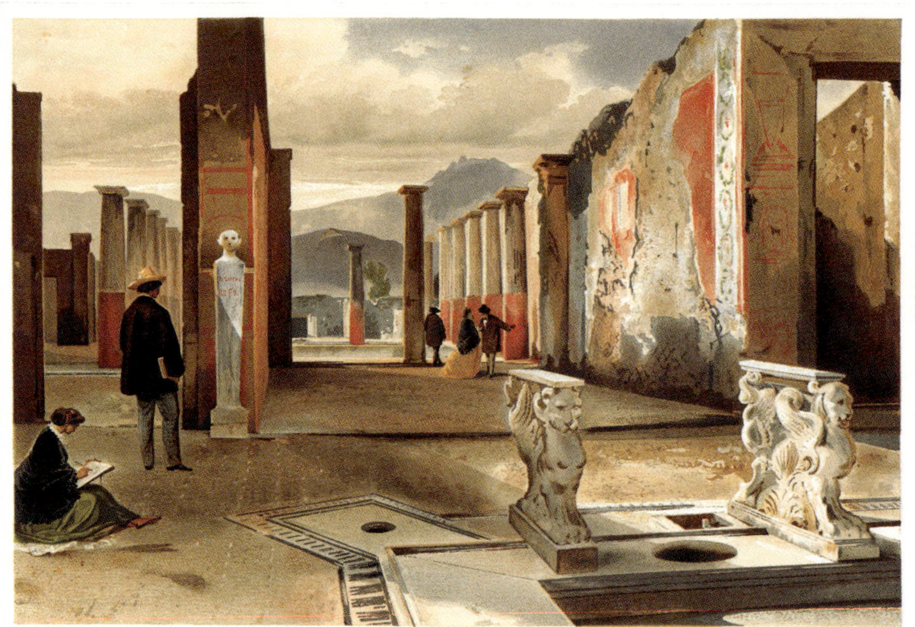

✻

Pages 222–223

Plate 22 — *[A. Carli]*

Casa di Modesto (VI 5, 13), tablinum, or Regio VI, Insula occidentalis – Heavily reconstructed wall with a central picture that shows the myth of Phryxus and Helle. The wall was destroyed in the 19th century.

✻

Plate 25 — *[G. Gigante]*

Casa di Cornelius Rufus (VIII 4, 15) – View of the atrium with the marble legs of an ornate table.

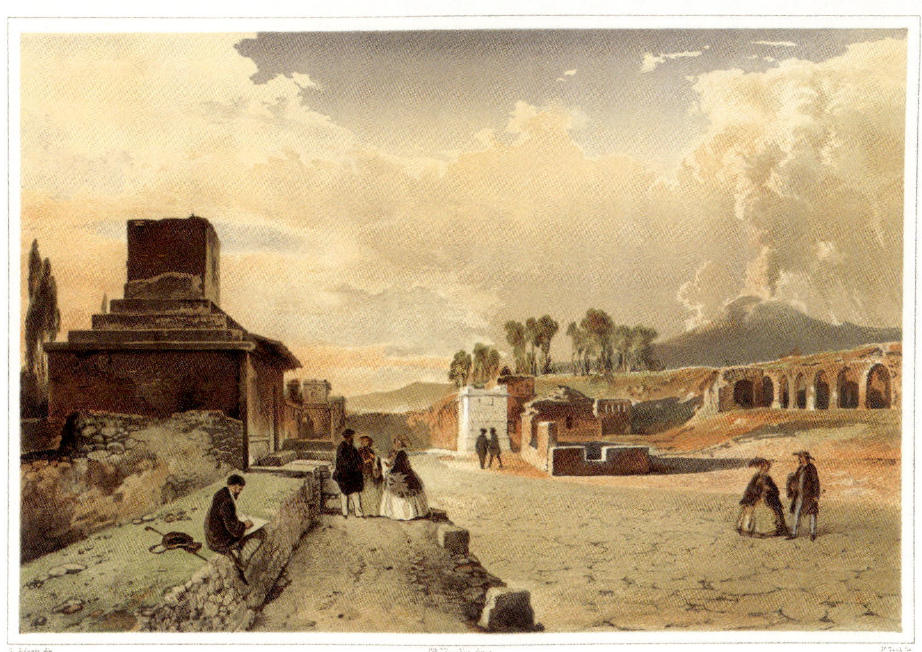

Plate 29 — *[G. Gigante]*
Street of Tombs – View towards the north, with Vesuvius in the background and the artist drawing on the left. Another part of the necropolis can be seen in plate 7.

Pages 226–227
Plate 27 — *[A. Carli]*
Casa della Parete nera (Casa dei Bronzi, VII 4, 59), south wall of the exedra – Upper zone of a wall painting in the 3rd style with seated Zeus, *ca.* AD 20–30. Today destroyed (see also pl. 31, from the same wall).

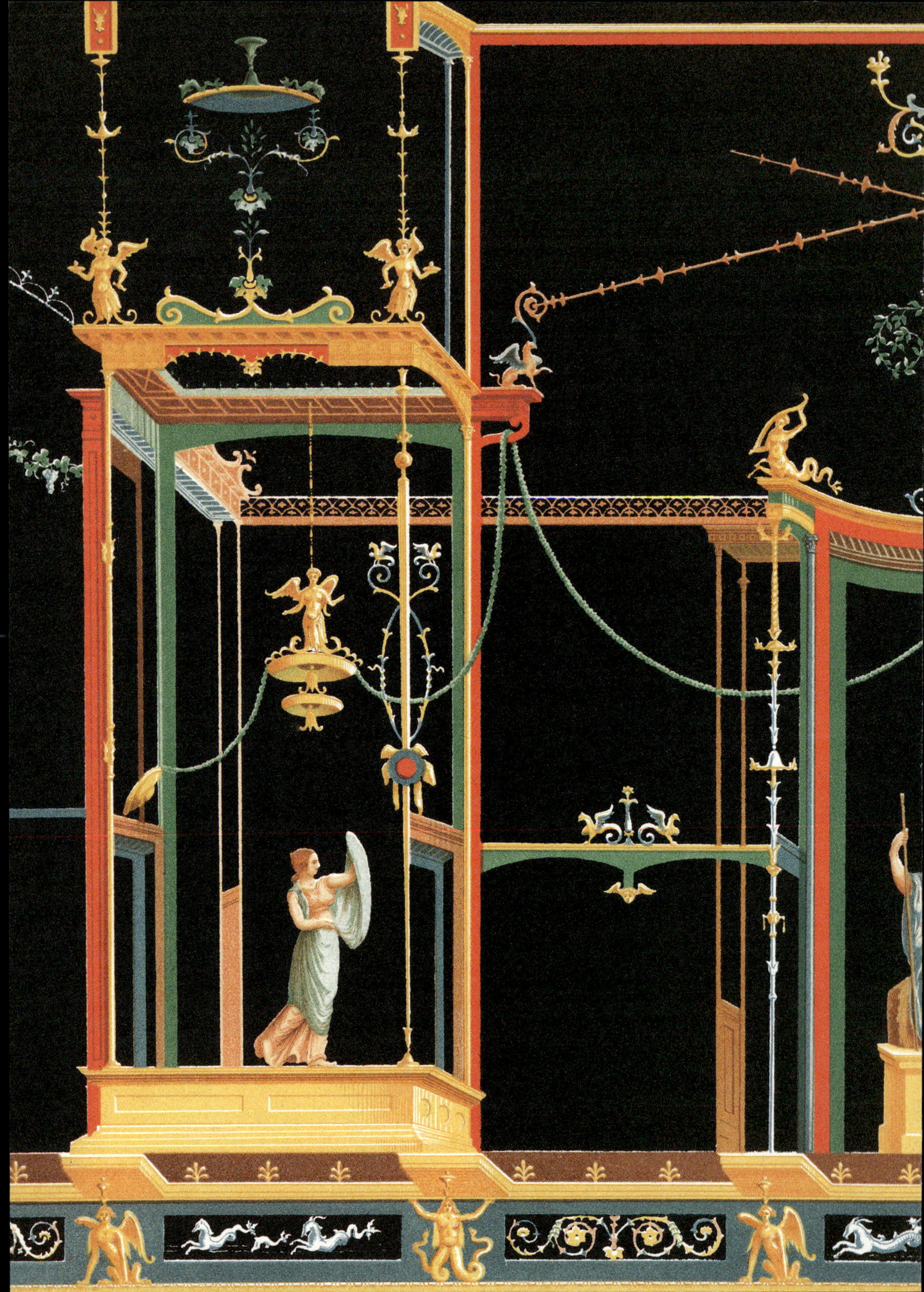

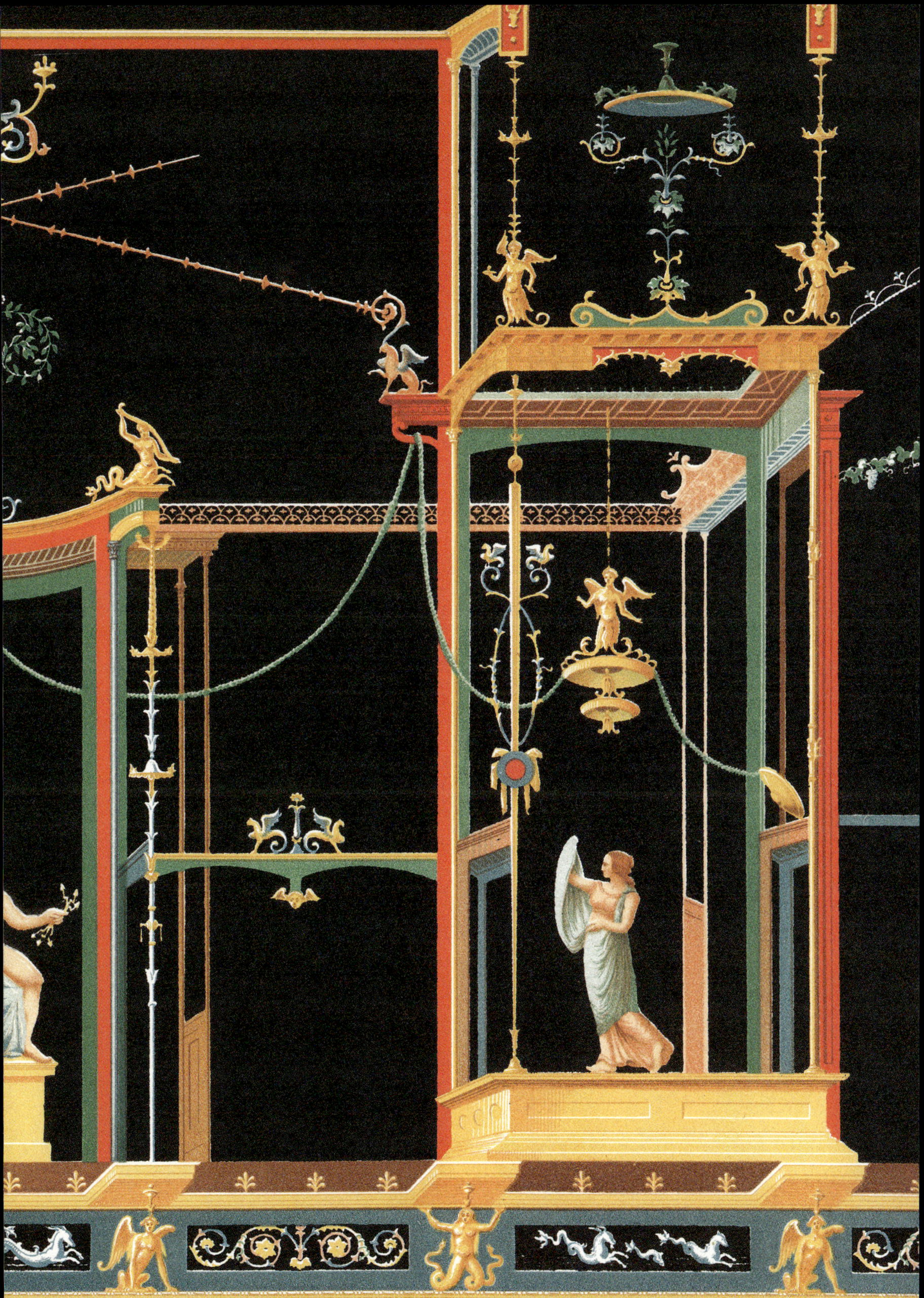

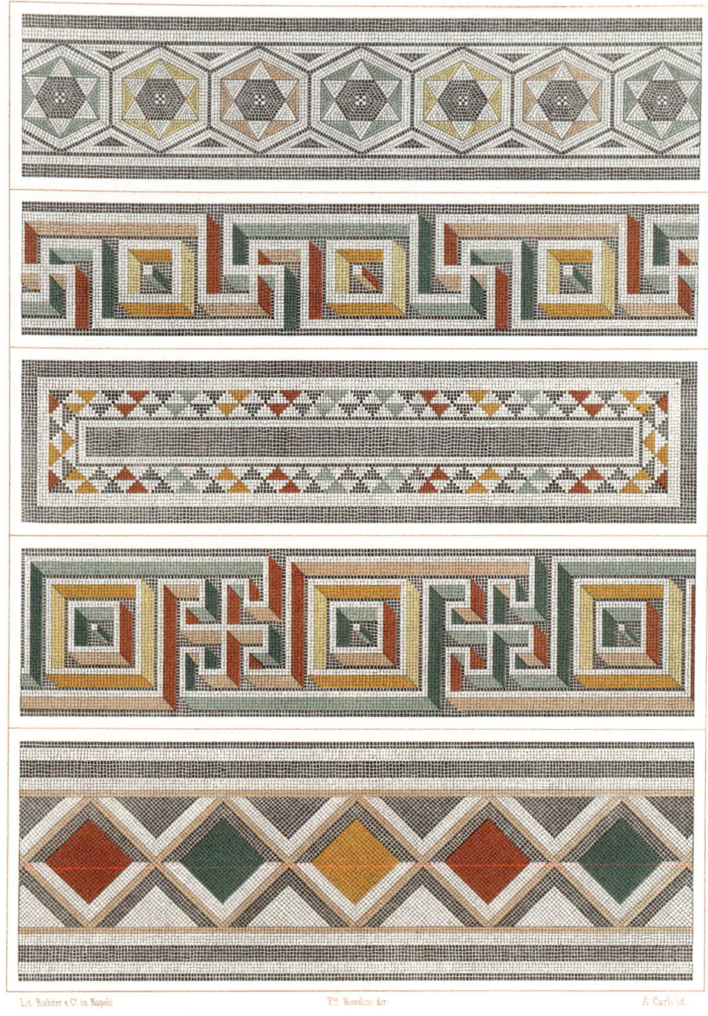

Plate 28 — *[A. Carli]*
Compilation of colourful mosaic borders from various locations, in the form of a pattern book.

❖

Plate 30 — *[V. Mollame]*
From Lucera, 1786 – With a Medusa head as its central motif. The mosaic was reused as flooring in a vase gallery in the Museo Borbonico.

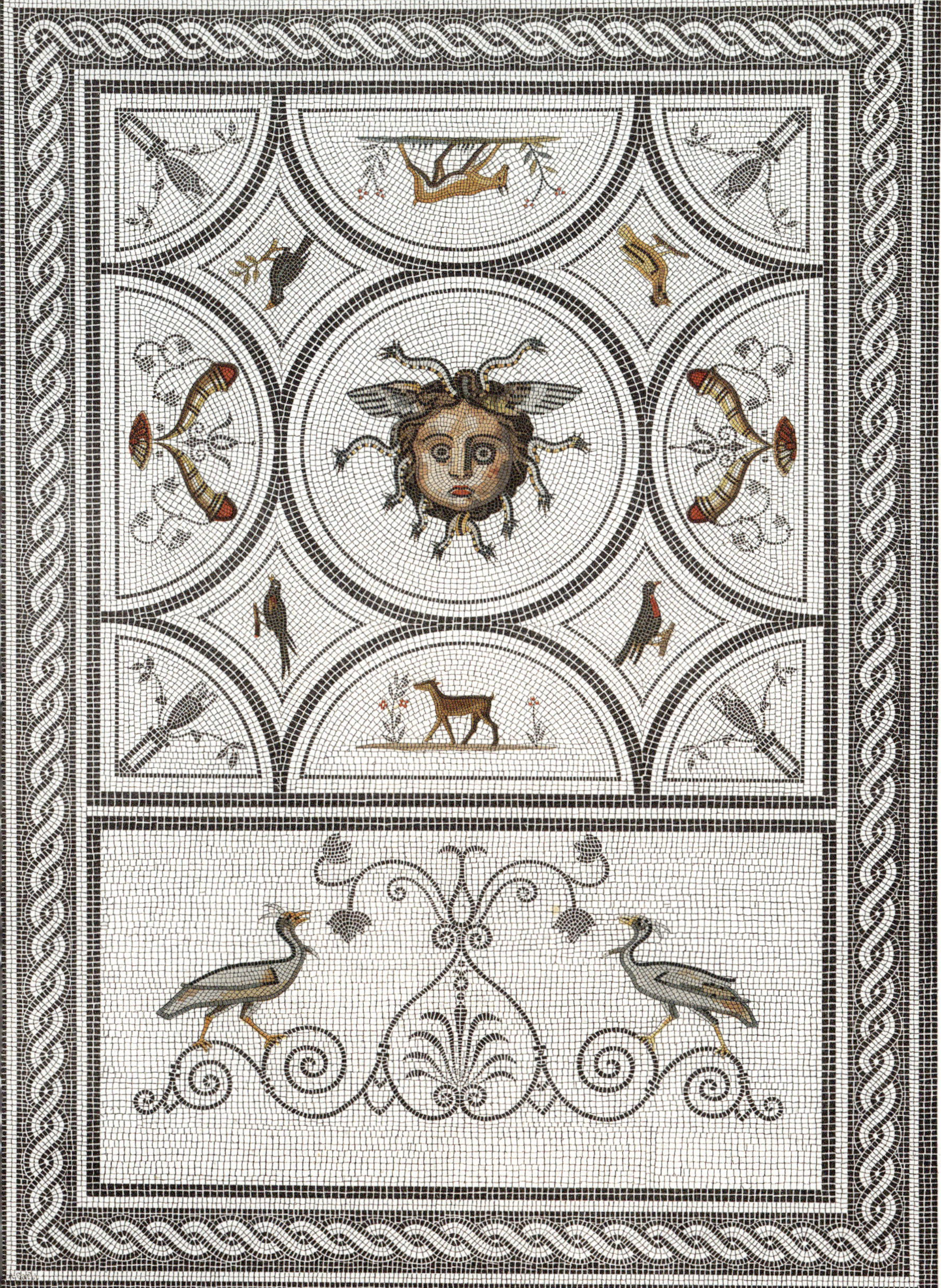

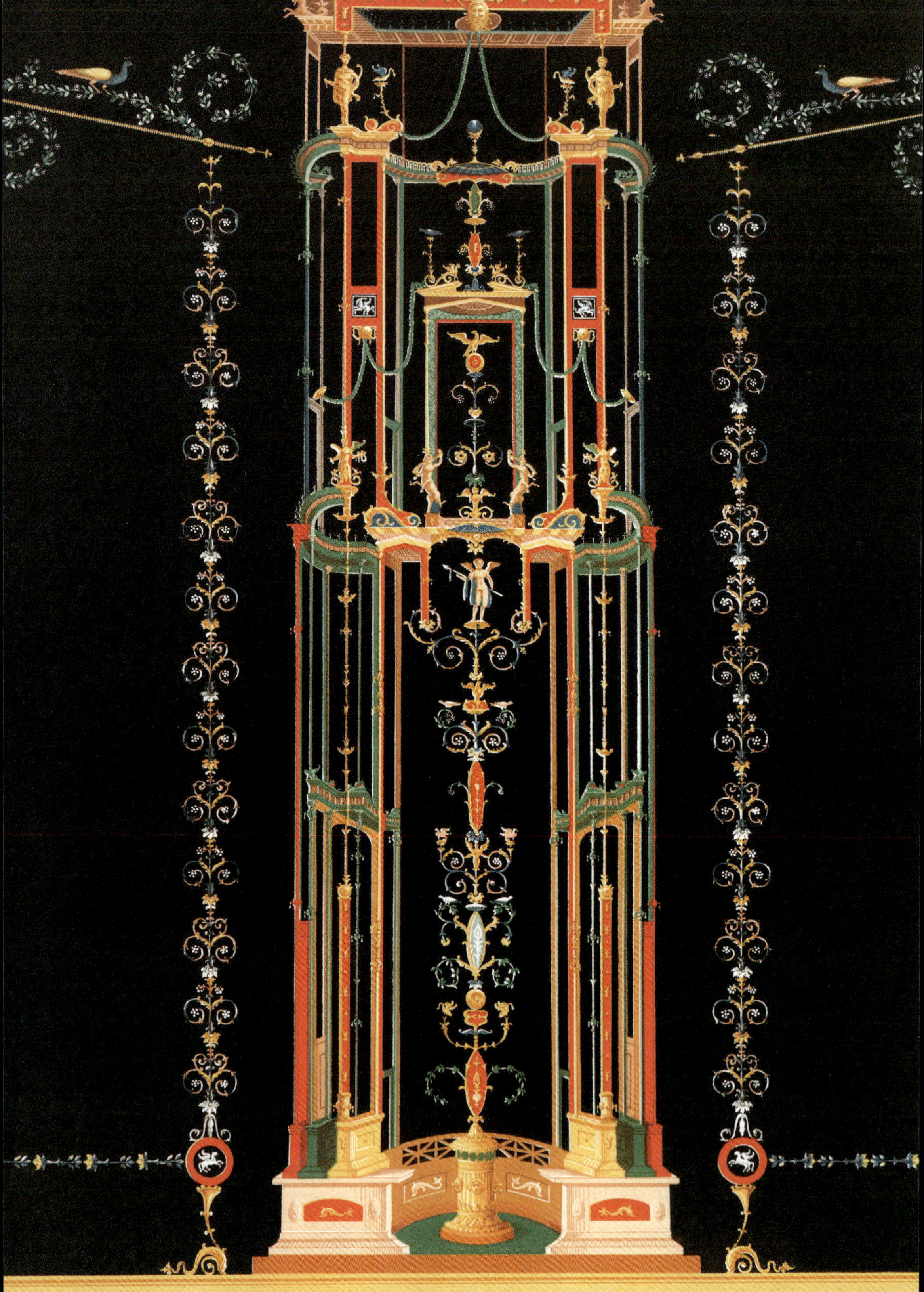

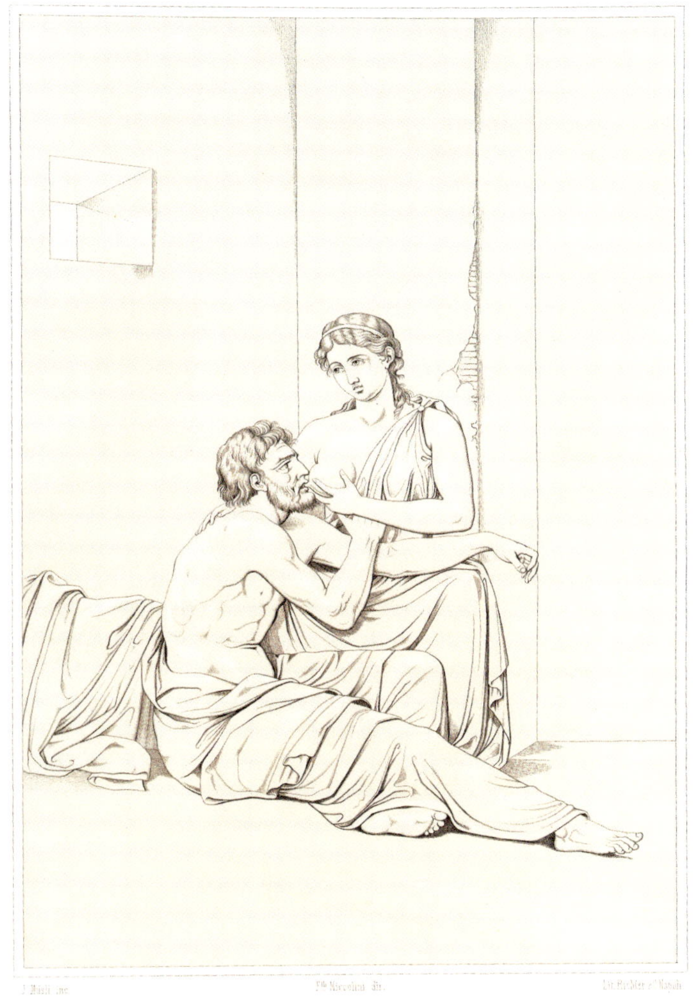

Plate 31 — *[A. Carli]*
Casa della Parete nera (Casa dei Bronzi, VII 4, 59), south wall of the exedra – Detail from the middle zone of a 3rd-style wall decoration (see pl. 27, from the same wall).

✻

Plate 32 — *[J. Müsli]*
Unknown house in Regio VI – Central picture with a representation of Pero breastfeeding her father Mikon, to prevent him from starving to death.

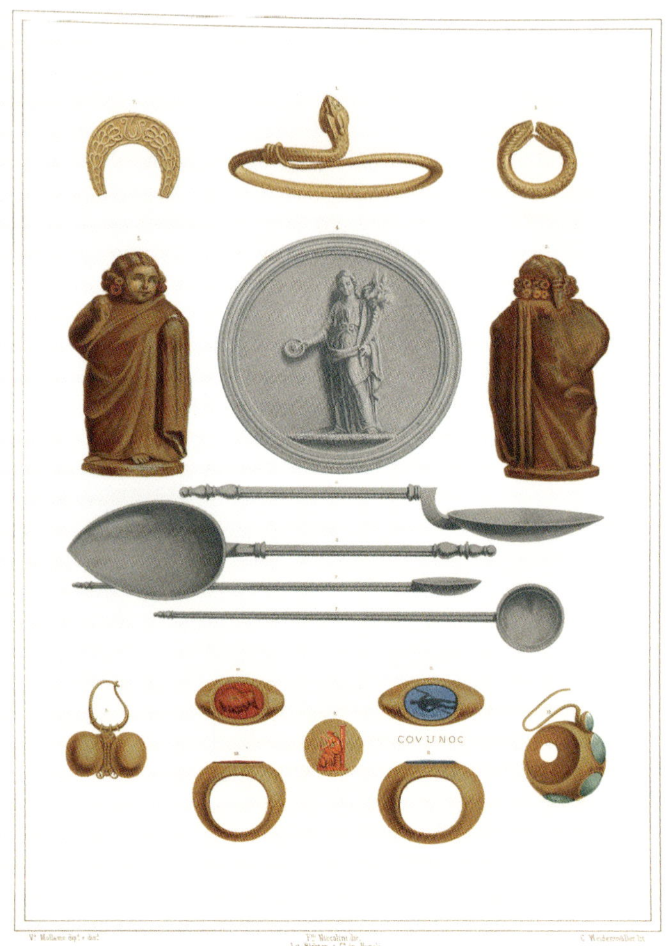

Plate 34 — *[V. Mollame]*
Jewellery and luxury items found in various locations – *5–7* Silver medallion, two spoons and an amber statuette from a small treasure trove found in 1863 in the Vicolo degli Scheletri (in front of Casa VII 13, 19), among the possessions of a family of four (for the unfortunate victims, see pl. 18).

Plate 33 — *[R. Mattej, C. Weidenmüller]*
Probably from Casa VIII 4, 12 – Money chest with decorative sheet-metal mountings and bronze nails from an atrium. Such strongboxes were used for keeping cash and other valuables in and were also intended to impress visitors who were admitted to the atrium.

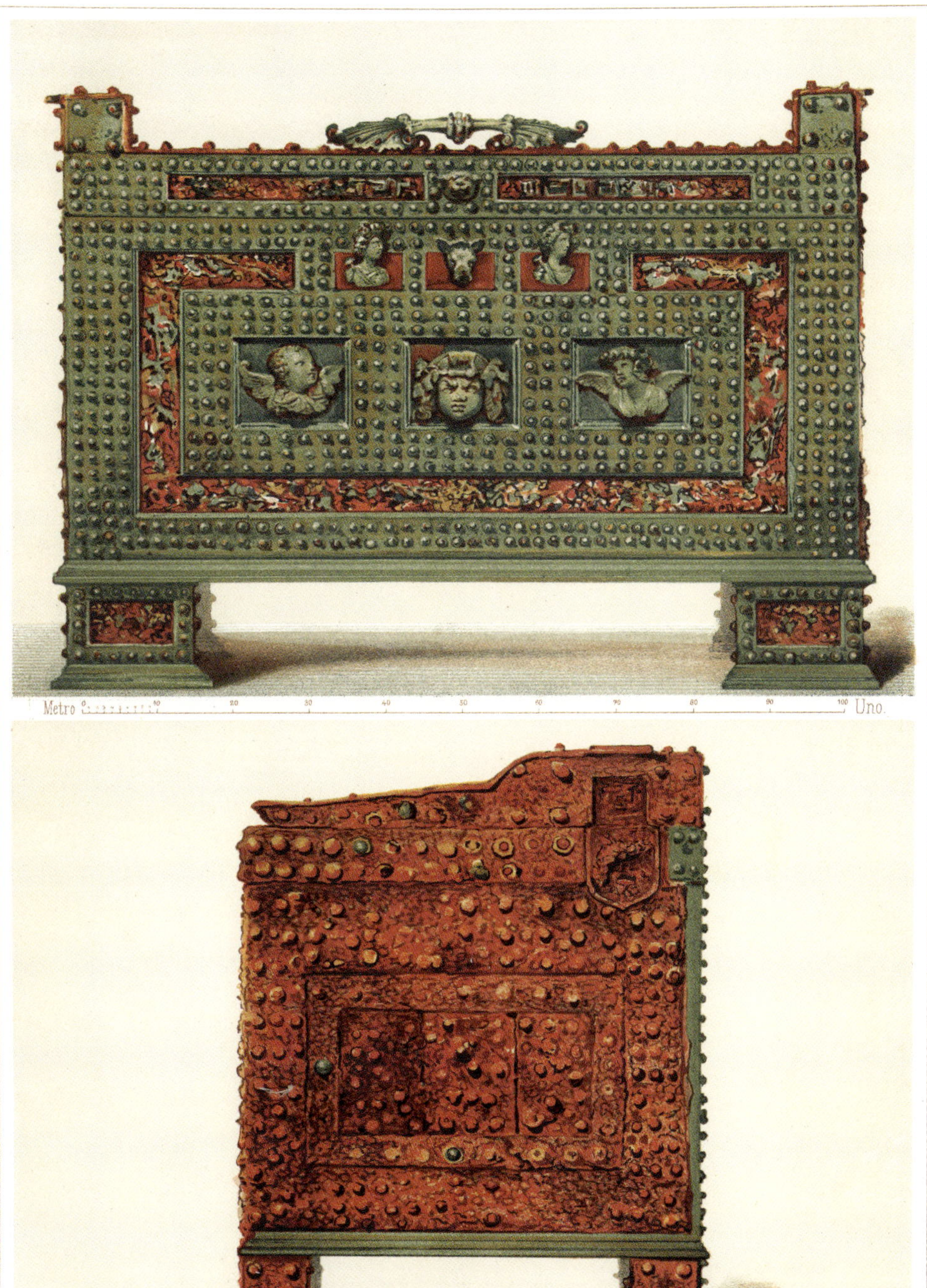

Mattej dip^e e dis^o Fr^{co} Niccolini dir C. Weidenmüller lit.
Lit. Richter & Co Napoli.

Plate 35 — *[C. Weidenmüller]*
Casa di Ganimede (VII 13, 4 and 17–18), room to the right of the triclinium – Magnificent kline with bronze fittings and silver inlay *(fulcra)*. Such couches were used during meals with invited guests. The reconstruction, for a long time exhibited in the museum, uses elements from several couches, which were apparently being stored in the as yet unpainted room of the house.

Pages 236–237
Plate 36 — *[A. Carli]*
Middle: ***Casa del Fauno (VI 12, 2)*** – Cross section and view of the impluvium, paved in a colourful lozenge pattern. Left and right: ***Elements of a floor with 20 sections in the Museo Borbonico*** – Probably found in the Casa di Championnet I (VIII 2, 1) excavated in 1798.

Pages 238–239
Plate 37 — *[A. Carli]*
Casa di Championnet I (VIII 2, 1) – Magnificent 4th-style wall decoration, with broad upright strips of scrolls and large yellow fields. Its precise original location within the house can no longer be determined. Carli based his lithograph on a reconstruction by Wilhelm Zahn, since the wall had by then already been destroyed.

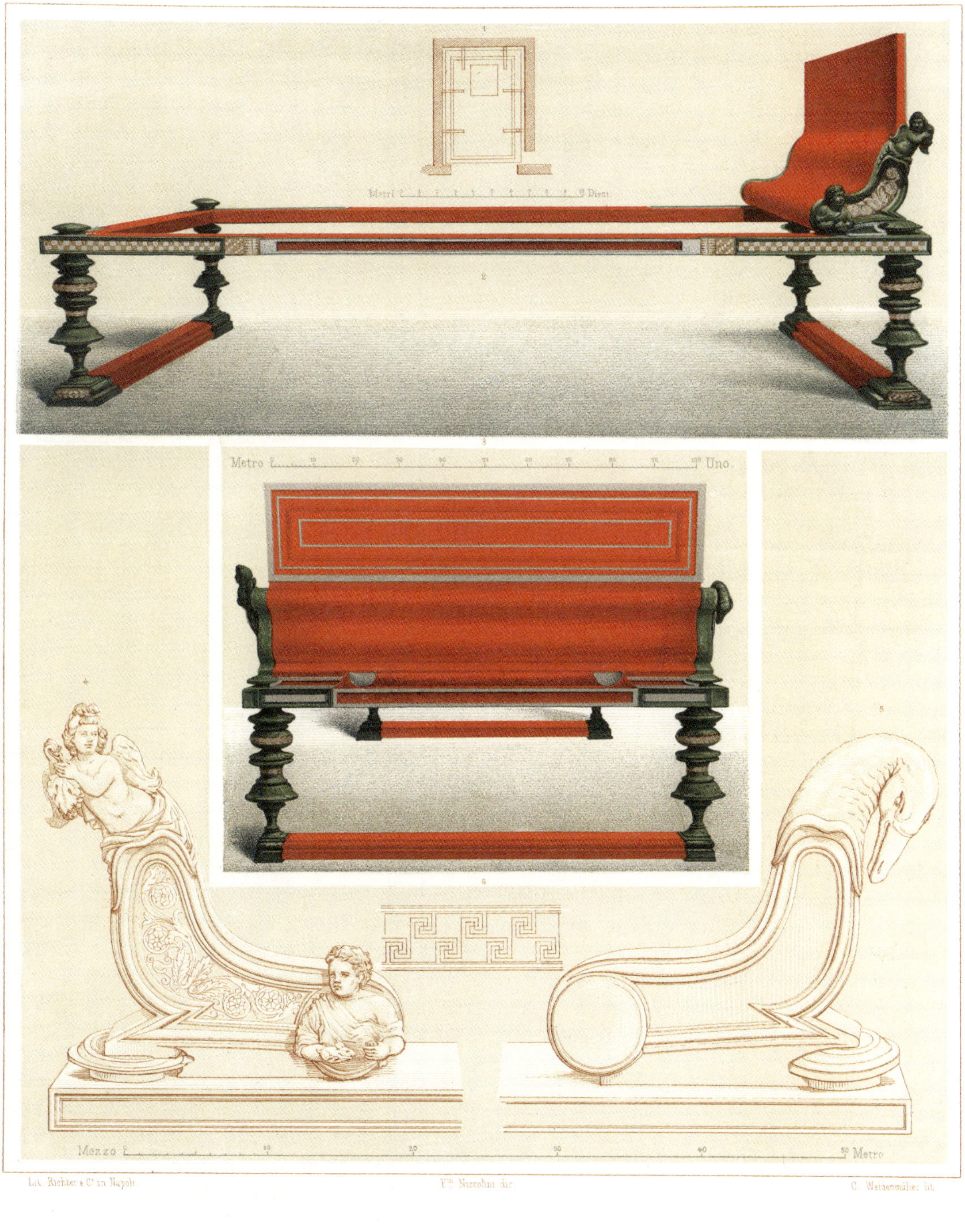

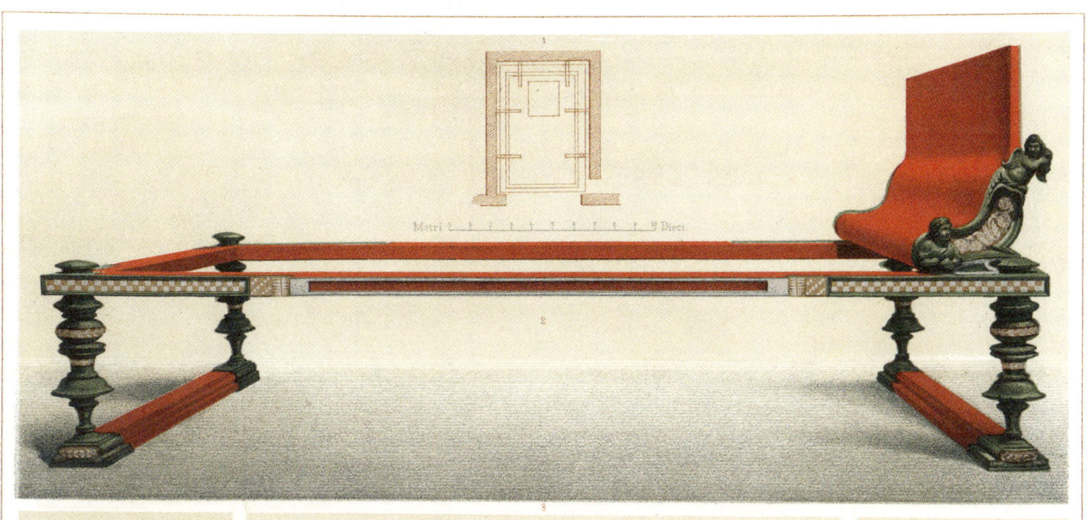

Lit. Richter e C.i in Napoli — F.lli Niccolini dir. — C. Weidenmüller lit.

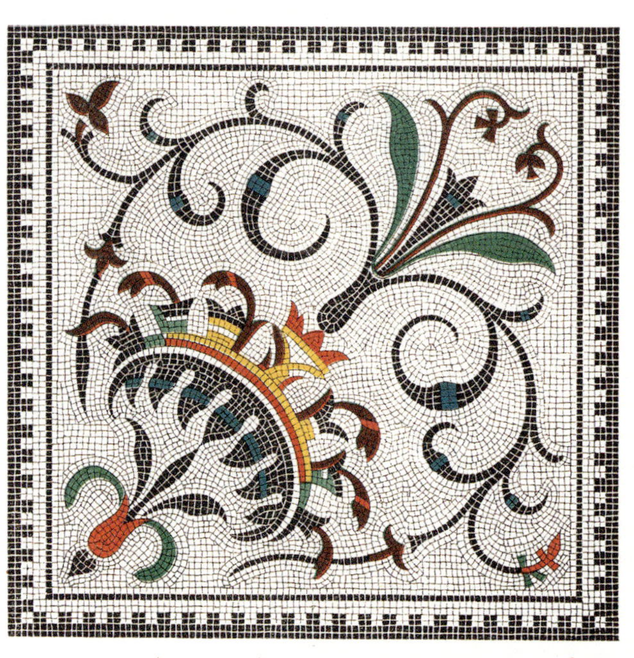

MEZZO ... METRO

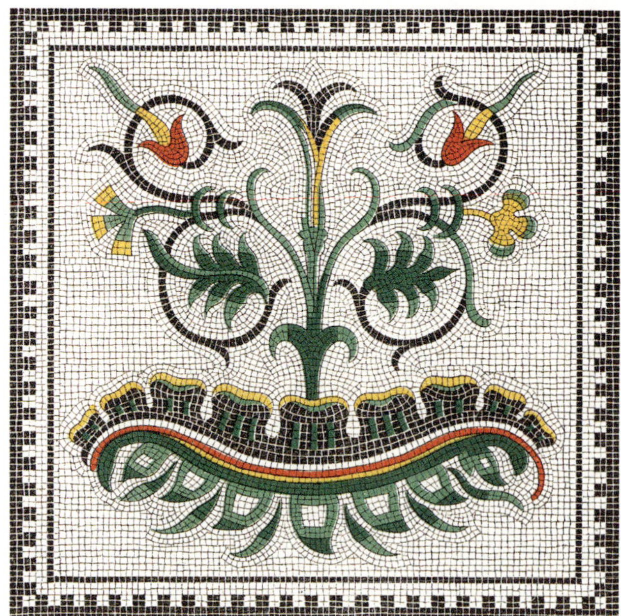

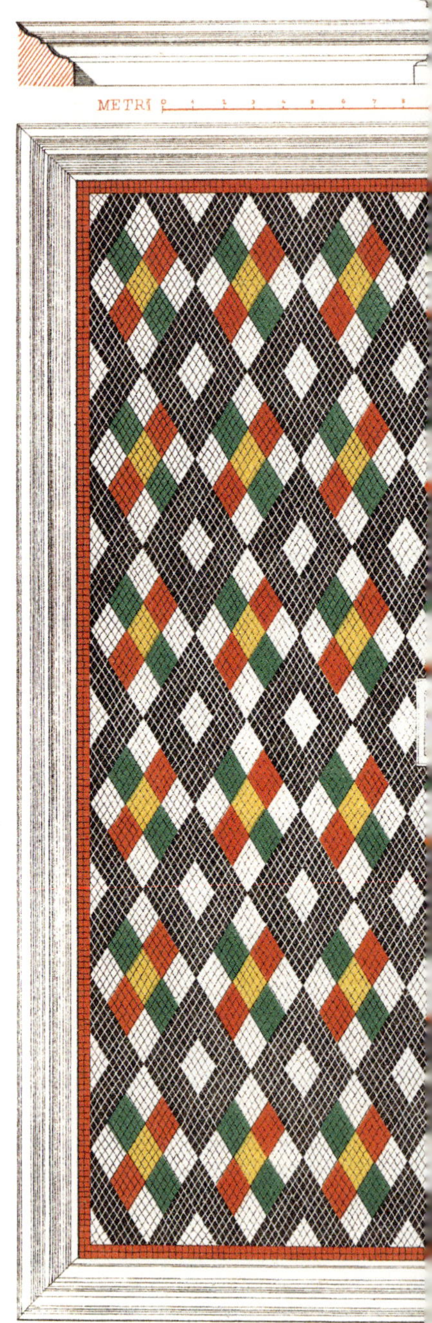

Lit. Richter & C.º in Napoli.

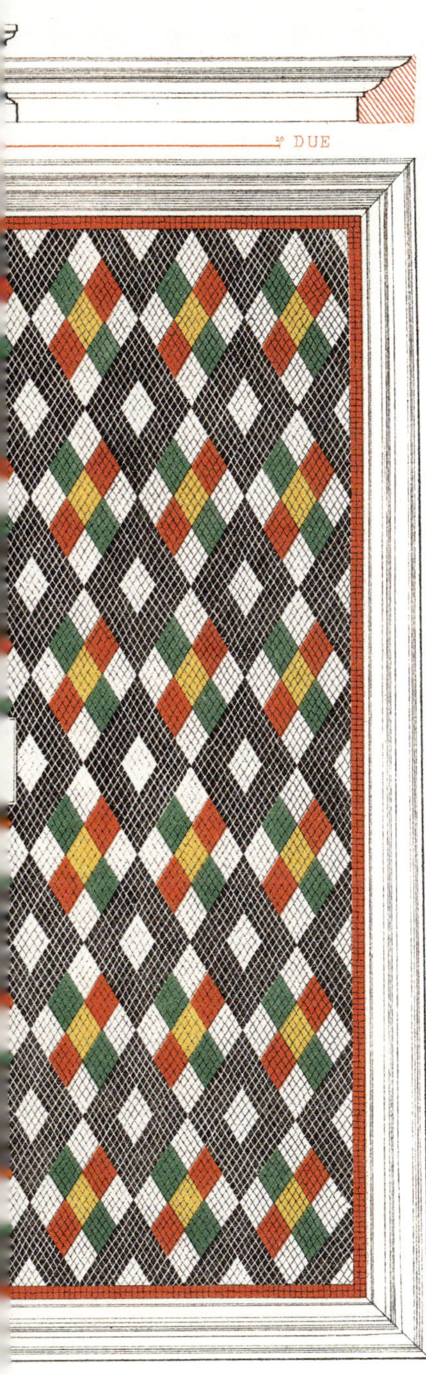

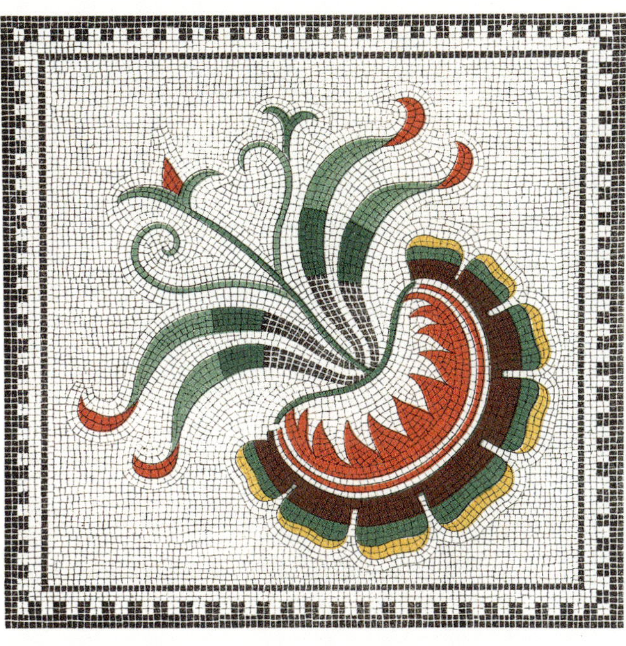

MEZZO 1 2 3 4 5 METRO

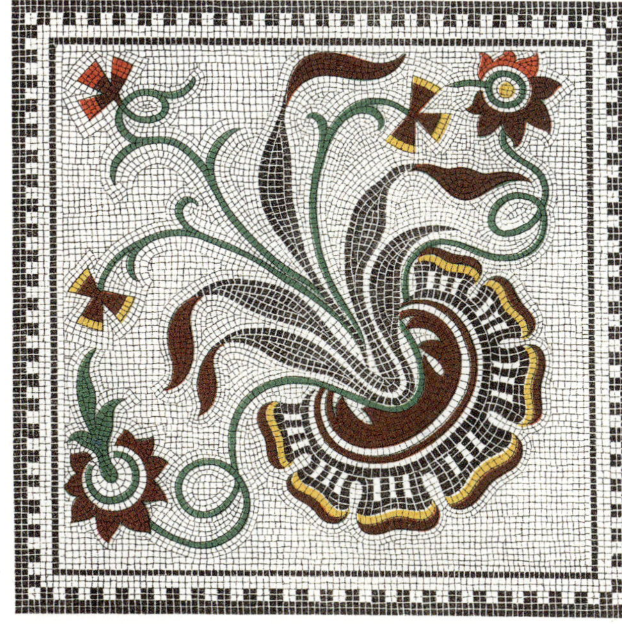

i dir.

A. Carli lit.

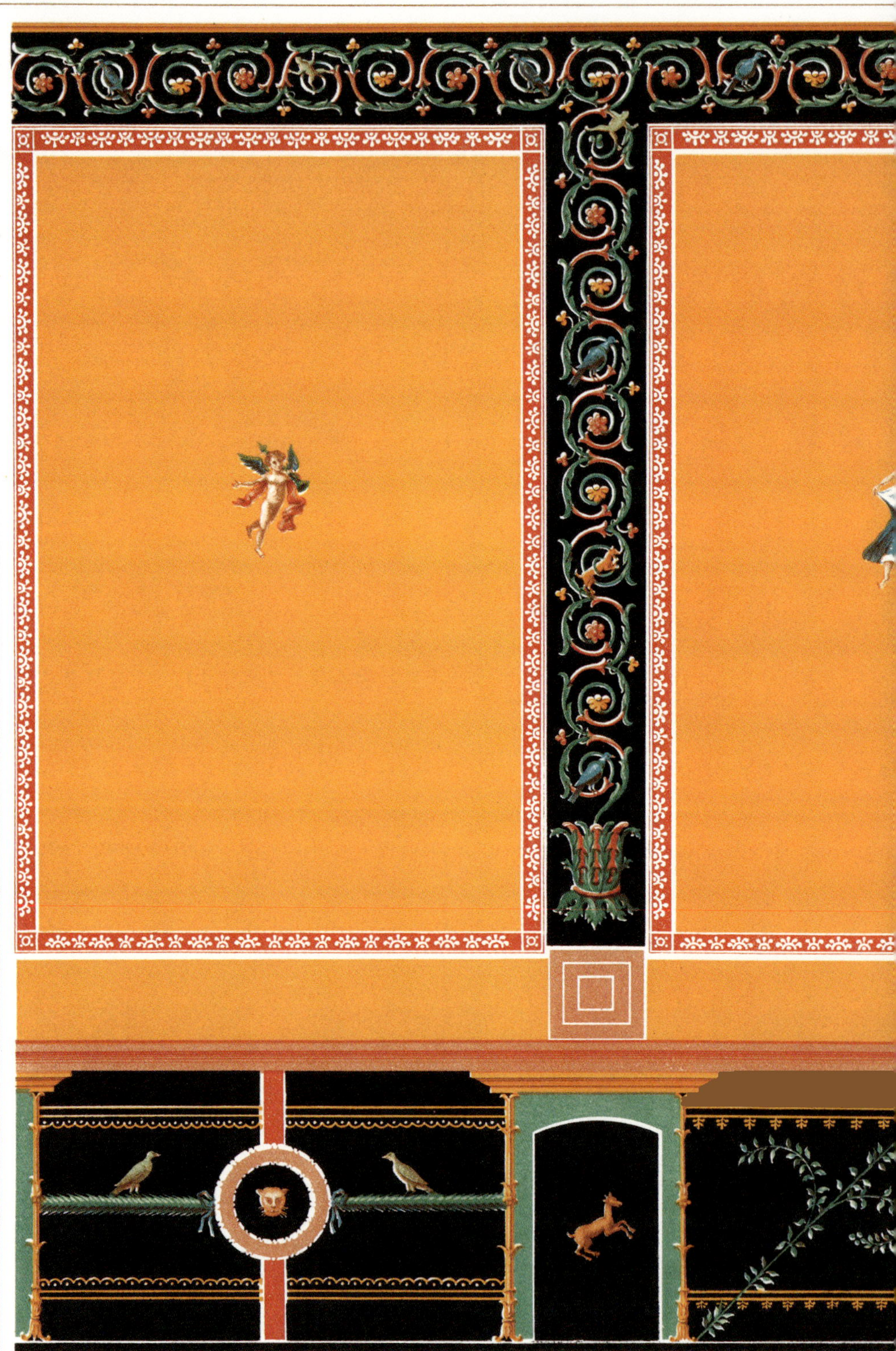

Lit. Richter & C.° Napoli.

F.lli M

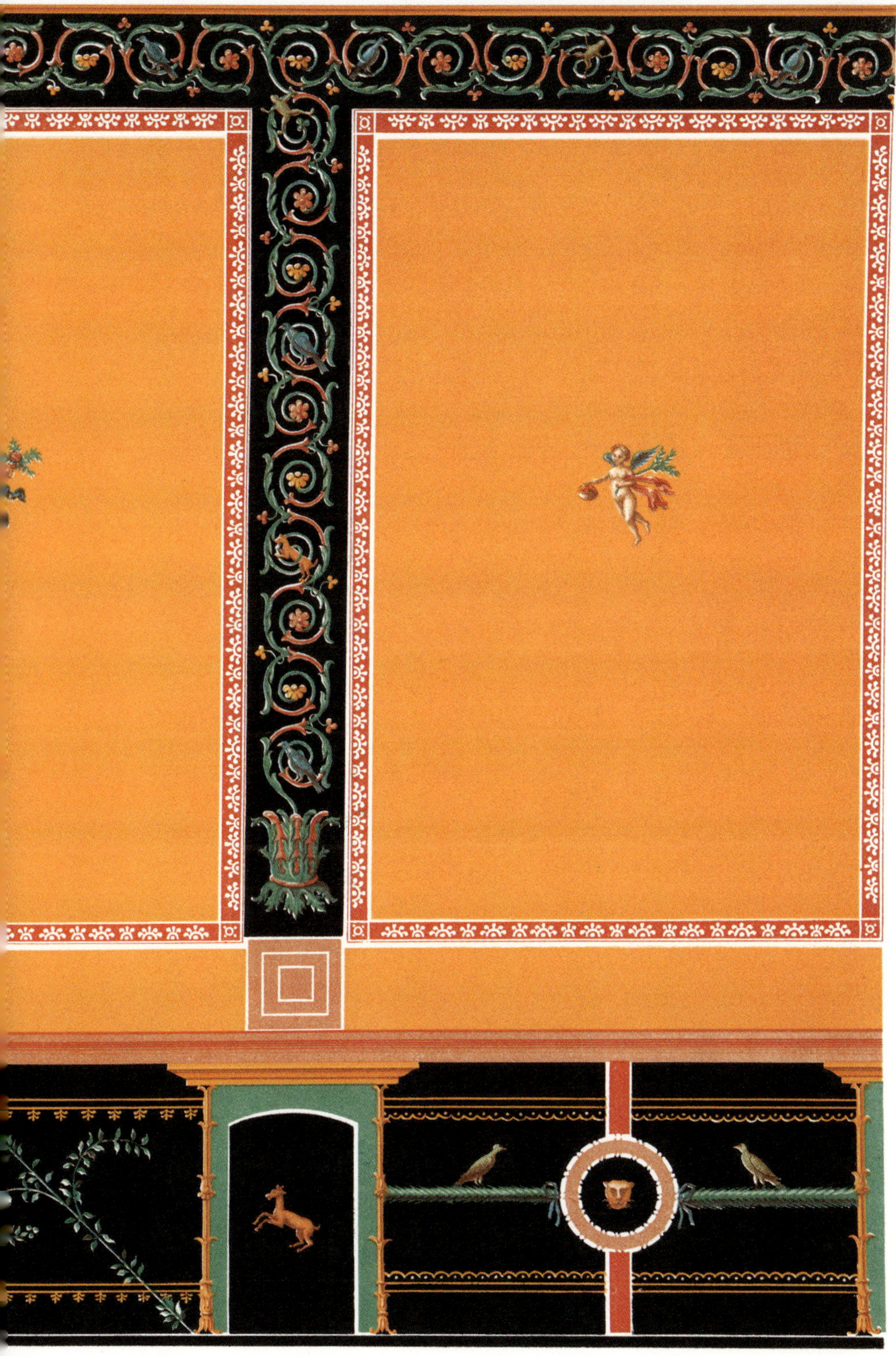

dir.

A. Carli lit.

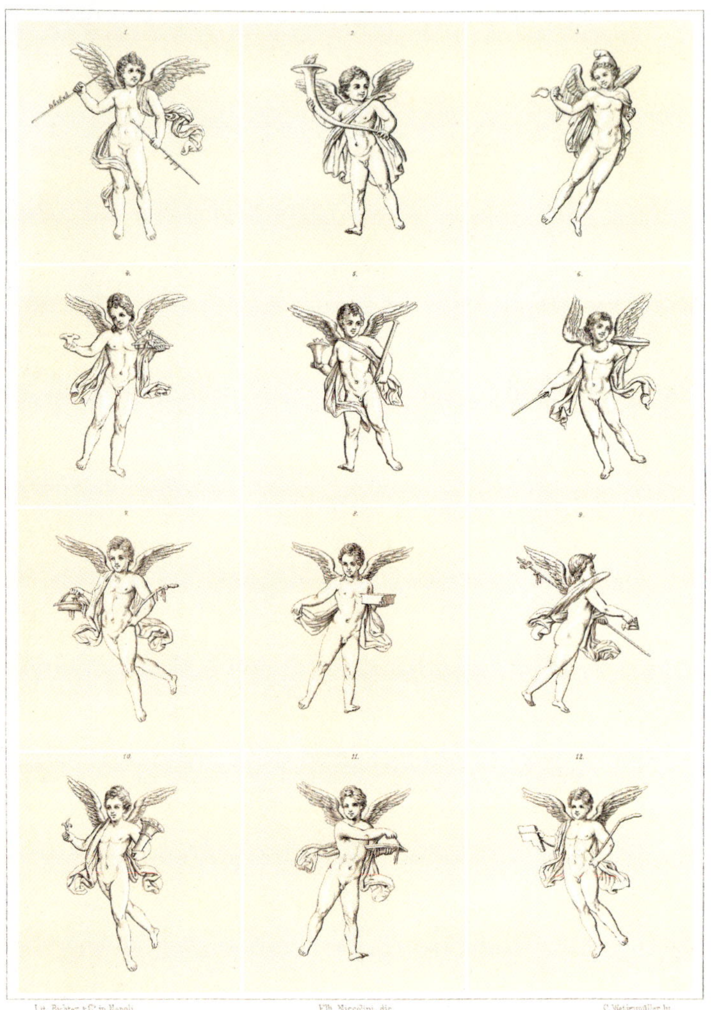

Plate 40 — *[C. Weidenmüller]*
Collection of twelve flying erotes with different attributes as a sort of specimen sheet.
From various contexts in the Vesuvian cities.

✠

Plate 38 — *[C. Weidenmüller]*
Casa della Regina Carolina (VIII 3, 14) – Fantastical 4th-style architectural scenery.
The central picture shows Hercules after defeating his rival in a fight to win the hand of Deïaneira.
He wears a victor's wreath and carries a cornucopia.

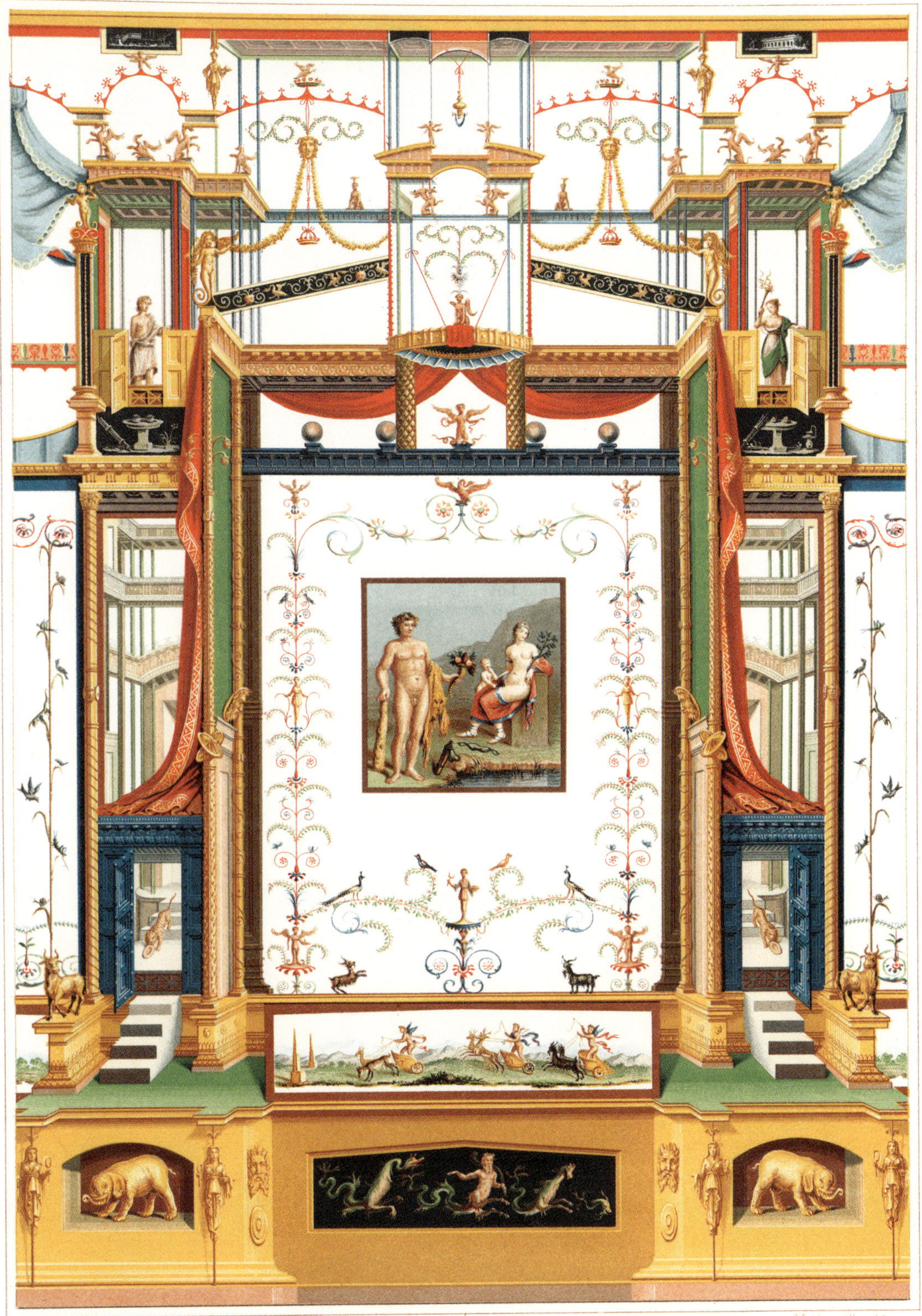

Lit. Richter & C.in Napoli — F.lli Vicceplini dir. — Weidenmüller lit.

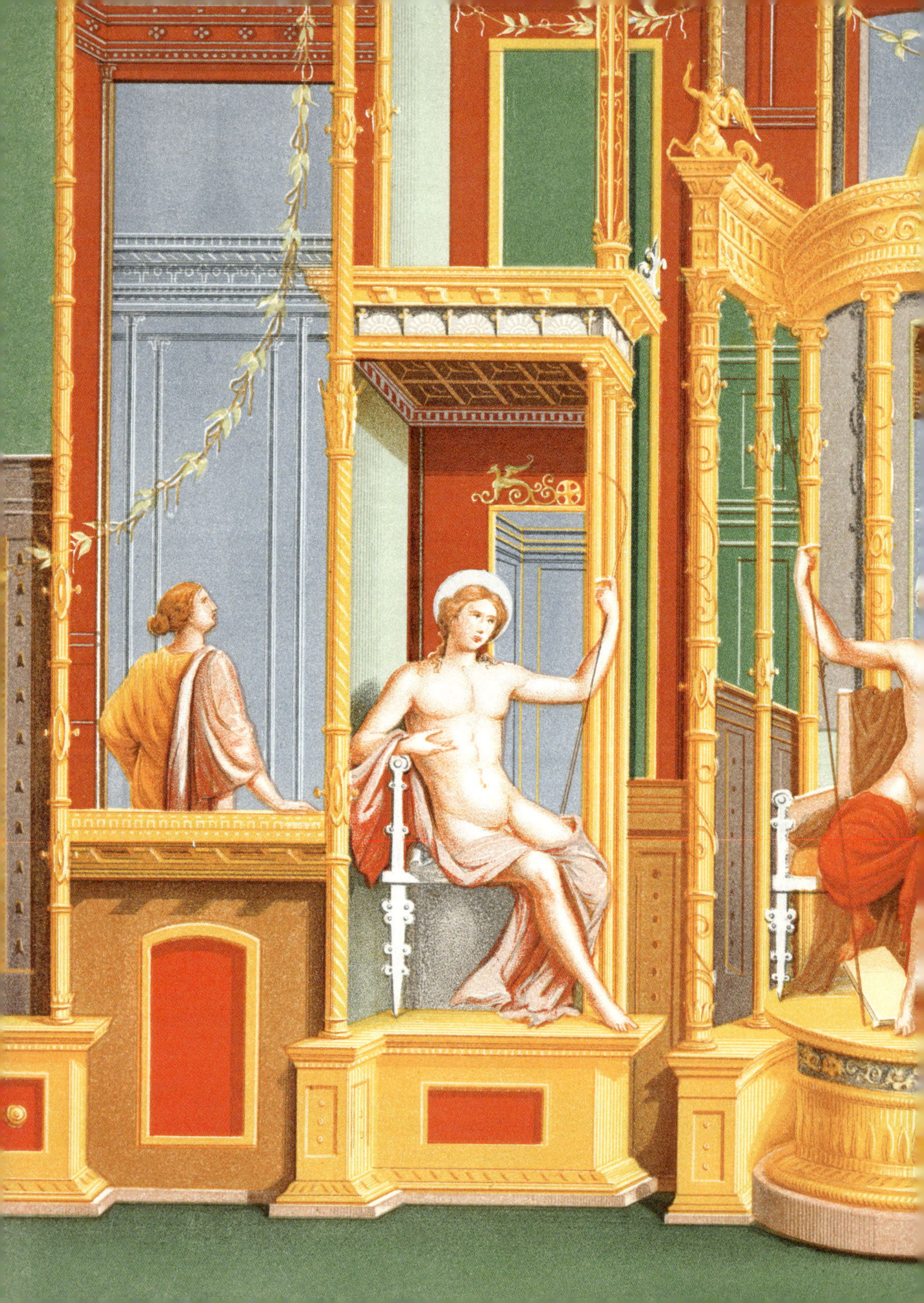

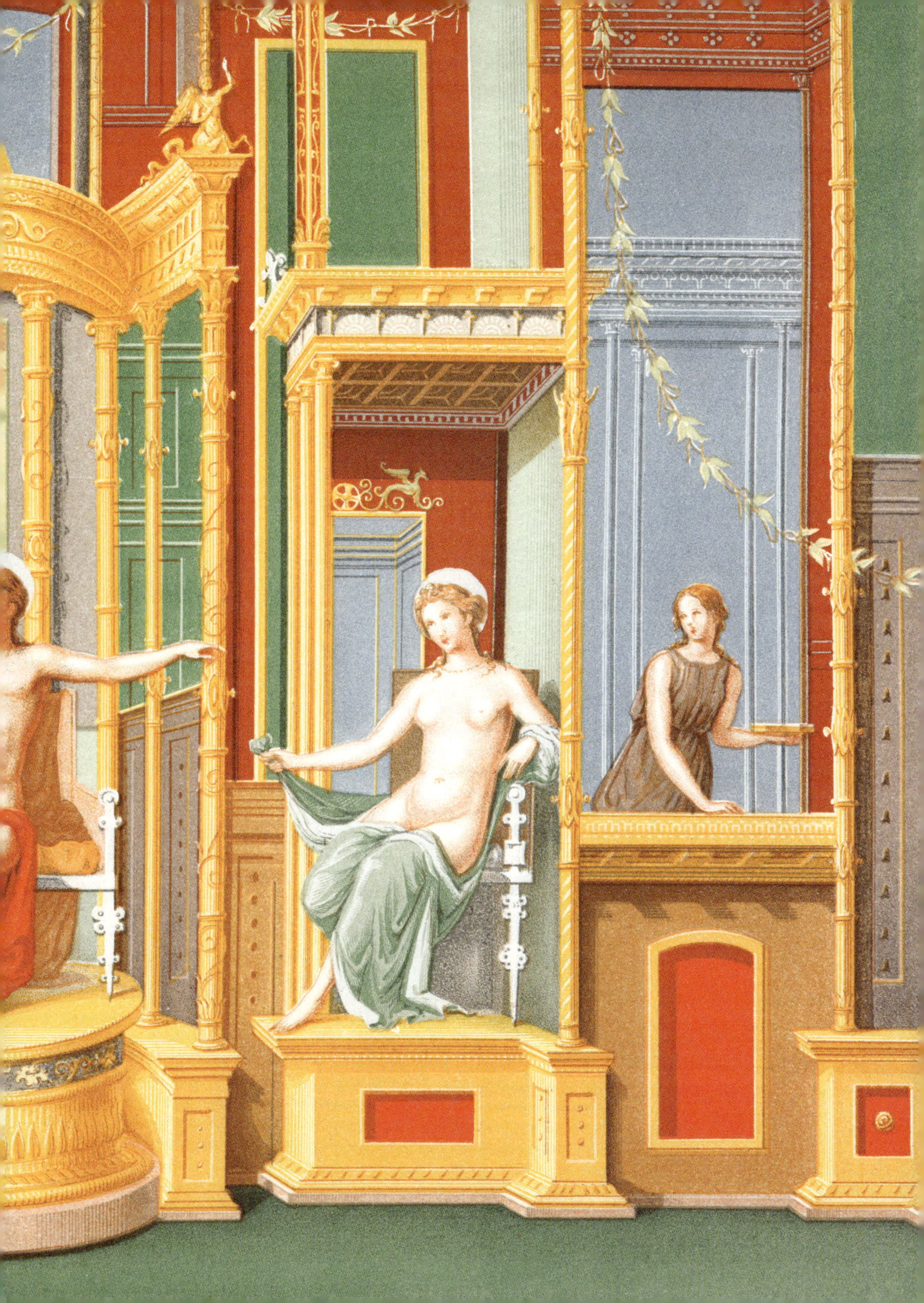

Pages 242–243

Plate 39 — *[C. Weidenmüller]*

Casa di Apollo (VI 7, 23), west wall of the alcove in the cubiculum (25) – Three divinities each with a nimbus are seated in a theatre-like architectural setting: Apollo between Adonis and Aphrodite (?). The socle zone is missing.

❖

Plate 43 — *[V. Mollame]*

Various items of glassware from Pompeii – Bowls, bottles, cups with handles, an *askos* flask and an amphora.

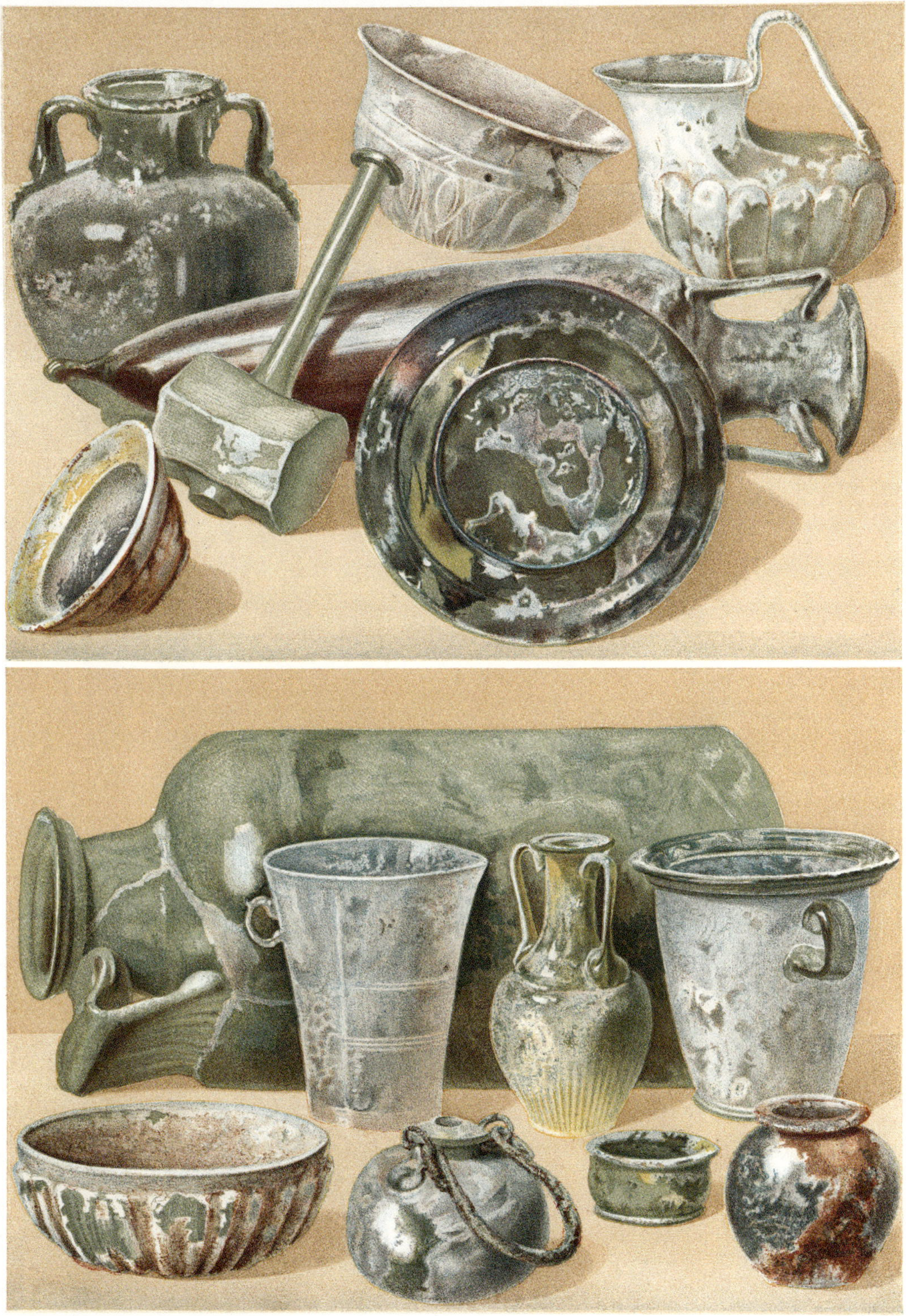

V.zo Mollame dip.e e Litog.o Flli Niccolini dir. Lit. Richter & C.i Napoli

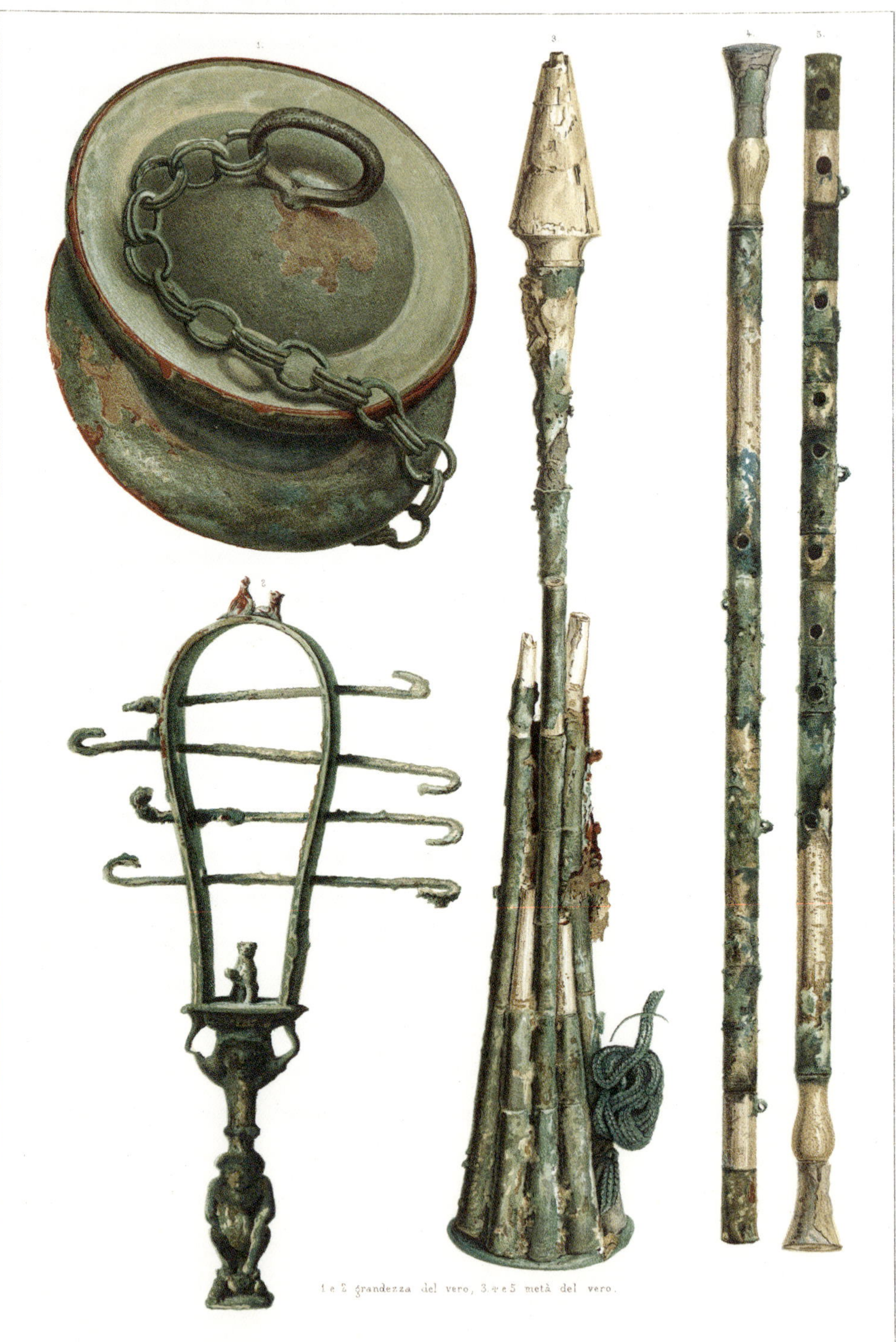

1 e 2 grandezza del vero, 3.4 e 5 metà del vero.

C. Weidenmüller lit. Fr.ni Niccolini dir. Lit. Richter e C. in Napoli

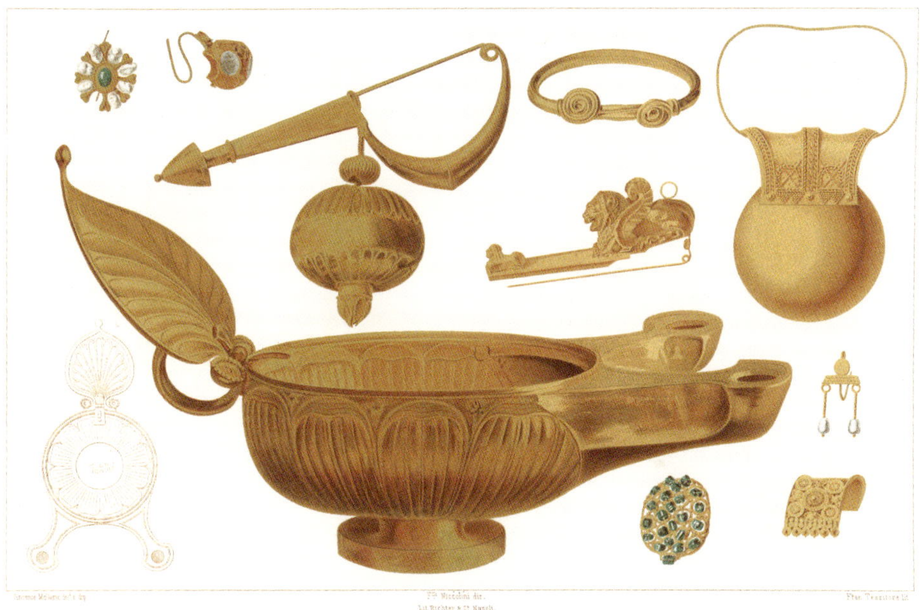

Plate 41 — *[C. Weidenmüller]*
Bronze musical instruments – Left: a *sistrum* and small cymbal *(cymbala)* for the cult of Isis (Casa del Fauno). Right: various flutes. Below: details of the scale of the different drawings.

⁂

Plate 42 — *[V. Mollame]*
Selection of various gold items, not all from Pompeii – Clothing clasps *(fibulae)*; bracelet, earrings and a *bulla* (an amulet worn around the neck by Roman boys). The oil lamp with two wick holes was placed as a consecration gift in the Temple of Venus Pompeiana, the patron goddess of Pompeii, and may have been donated by Emperor Nero. The schematic picture shows the weight incised on the discus: two Roman pounds.

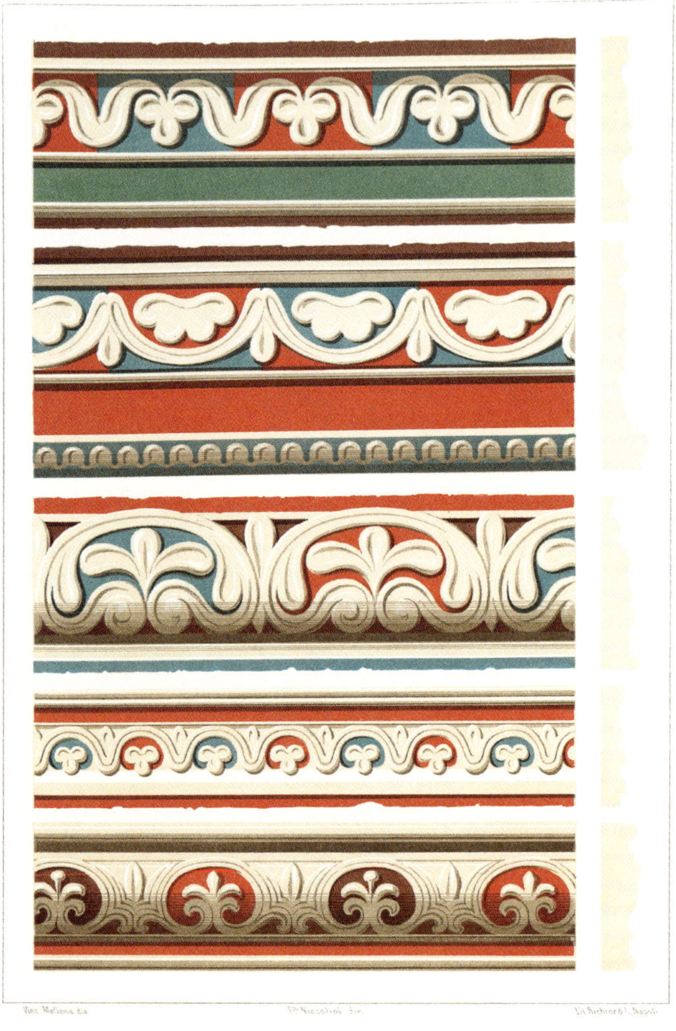

Plate 45 — *[V. Mollame]*
Examples of stucco mouldings found in various locations – The plate shows the mouldings in front view and profile in the manner of a pattern book, so that they could be copied by modern stucco artists.

Plate 44 — *[V. Mollame]*
Villa di Diomede – East wall of a room overlooking the garden peristyle on the lower level (see vol. II, Villa di Diomede).

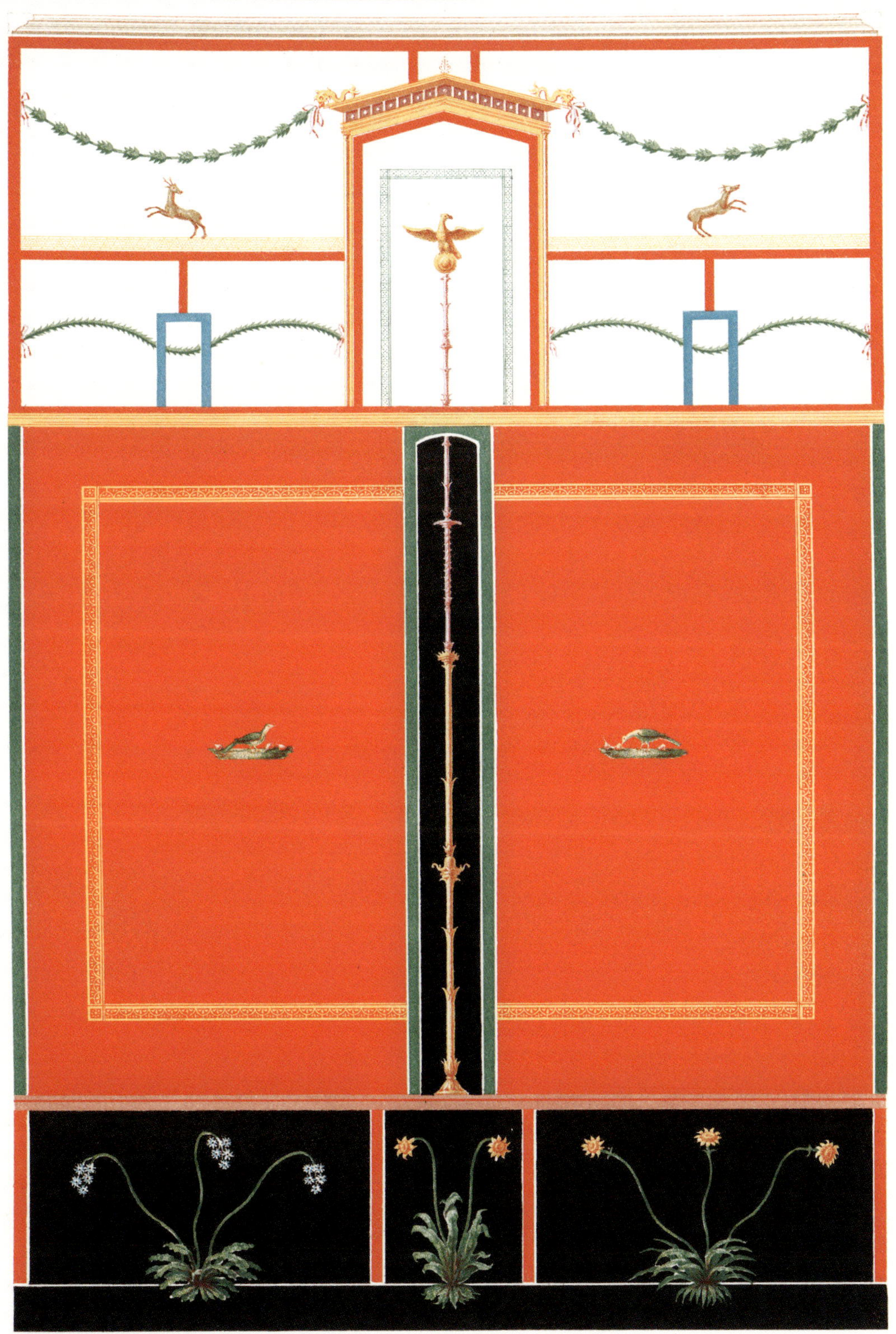

Vo Moltame lit. F.o Riccobini dis. Lit. Richter & C.o Napoli

Plate 46 — *[V. Loria]*
Casa del Gallo II (IX 2, 1), middle part of the south wall of a cubiculum – The ornamental strip in the upper zone is unusual. In the central picture, Polyphemus embraces the beautiful Galatea (see also pl. 57).

⁂

Page 252
Plate 47 — *[A. Carli]*
Mosaic floor from Pompeii – The colourful lozenge pattern lends it a seemingly three-dimensional effect. A comparable pattern can be found in the Casa del Labirinto (VI 11, 8–10), mid-1st century BC.

⁂

Page 253
Plate 48 — *[Autoriello]*
Tannery (I 5, 2), mosaic emblem from the masonry table of the triclinium in the courtyard – Memento mori: the highly unusual mosaic with an archipendulum shows that the rich man (royal sash, purple cloak and lance) and the poor man (staff, cape and bag) are both equal in the face of death; on the wheel of Fortune, a butterfly as a symbol of the soul. The mosaic encourages the viewer to make merry and enjoy life.

⁂

Pages 254–255
Plate 49 — *[V. Loria]*
Two 3rd-style wall decorations – Left: origin unknown. Right: Casa del Labirinto (VI 11, 8–10), caldarium of the house's private baths.

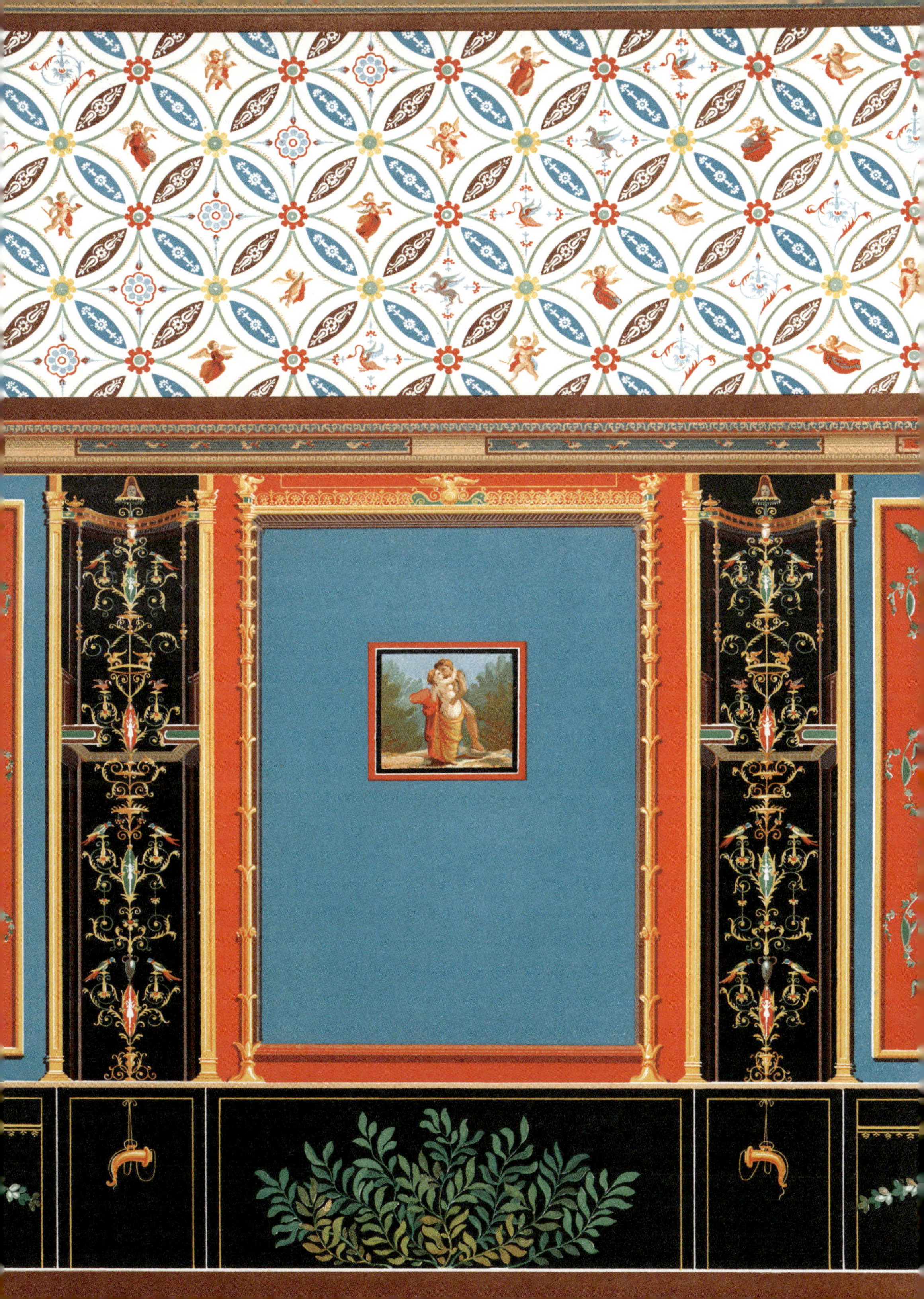

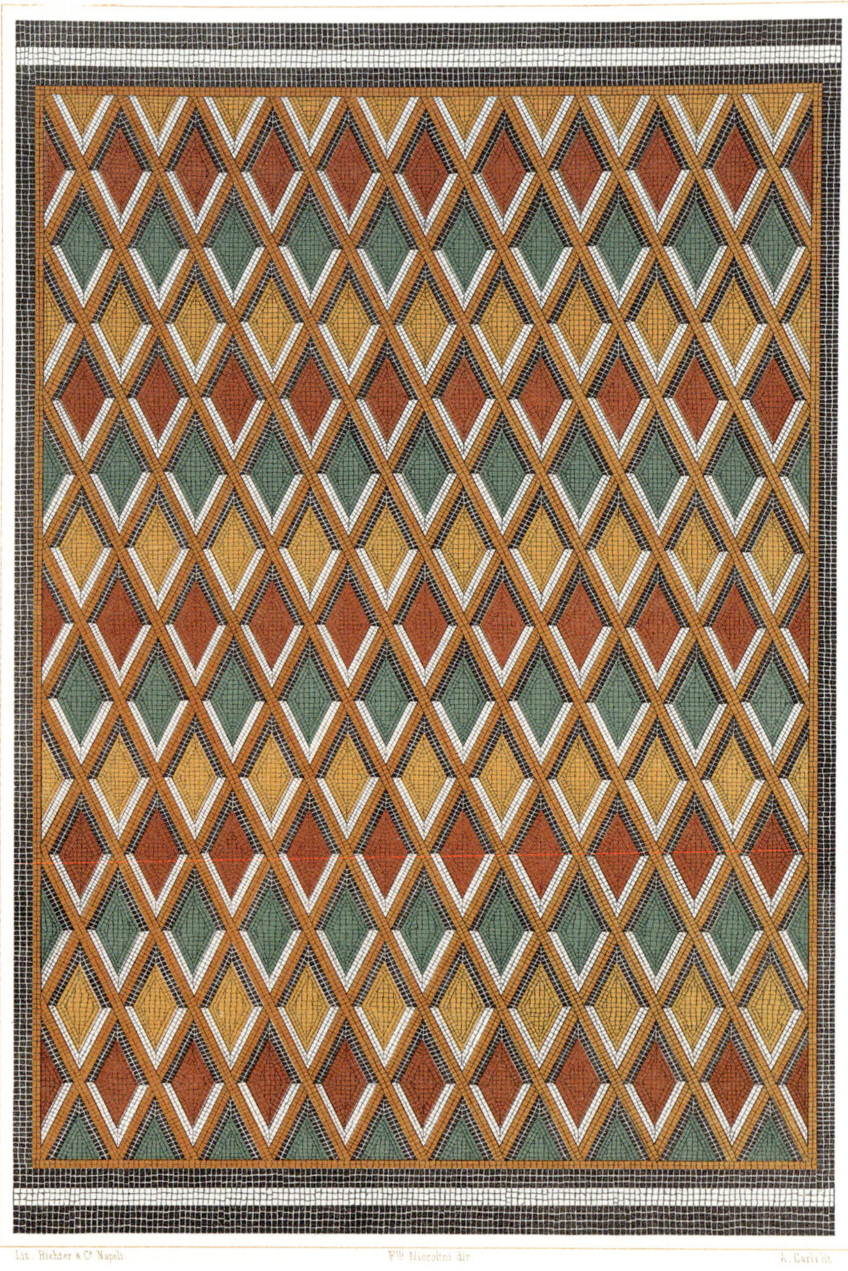
Lit. Richter e Cº Napoli
F.lli Niccolini dir.
A. Carli lit.

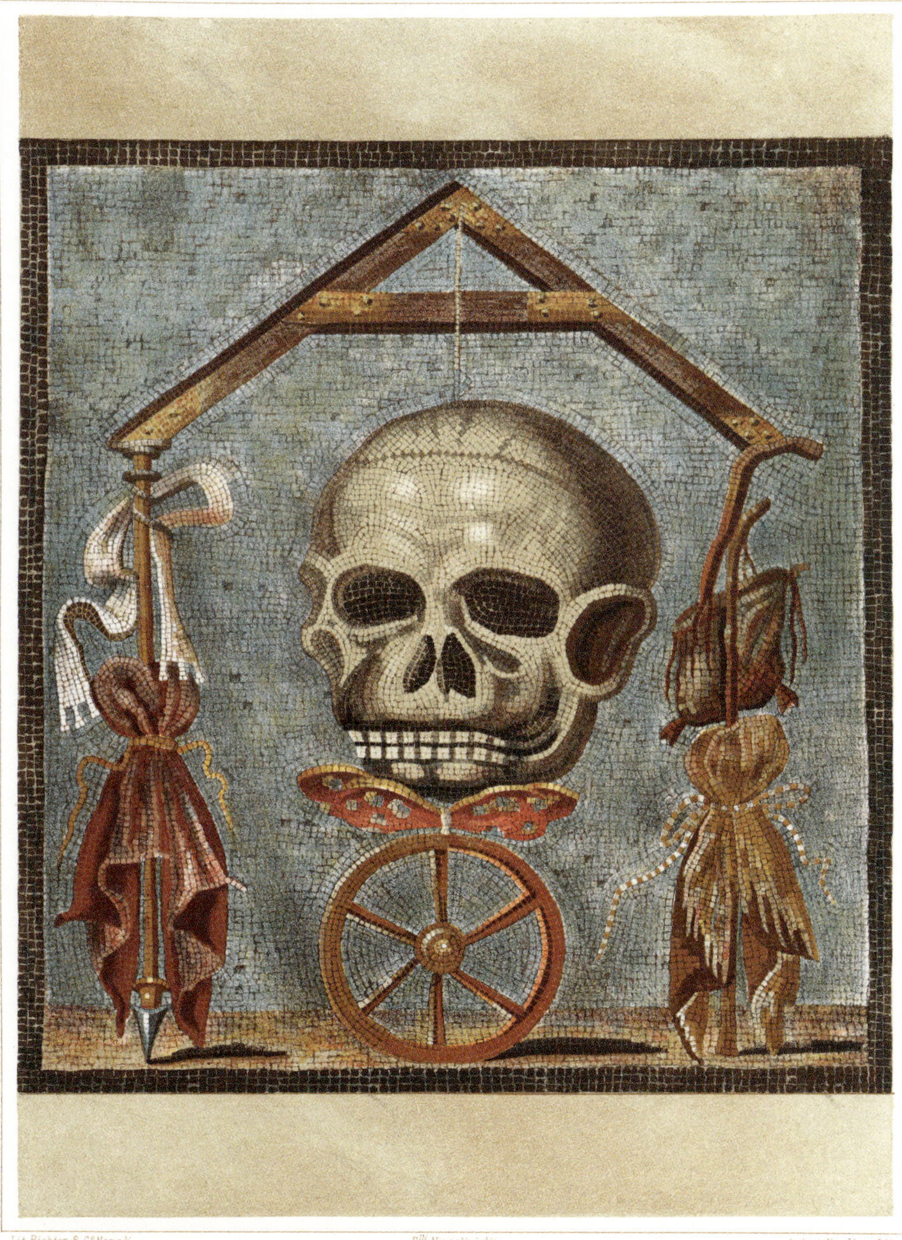

Lit. Richter & C° Napoli   F[lli] Niccolini dir.   Auforiello dis. e Lit.

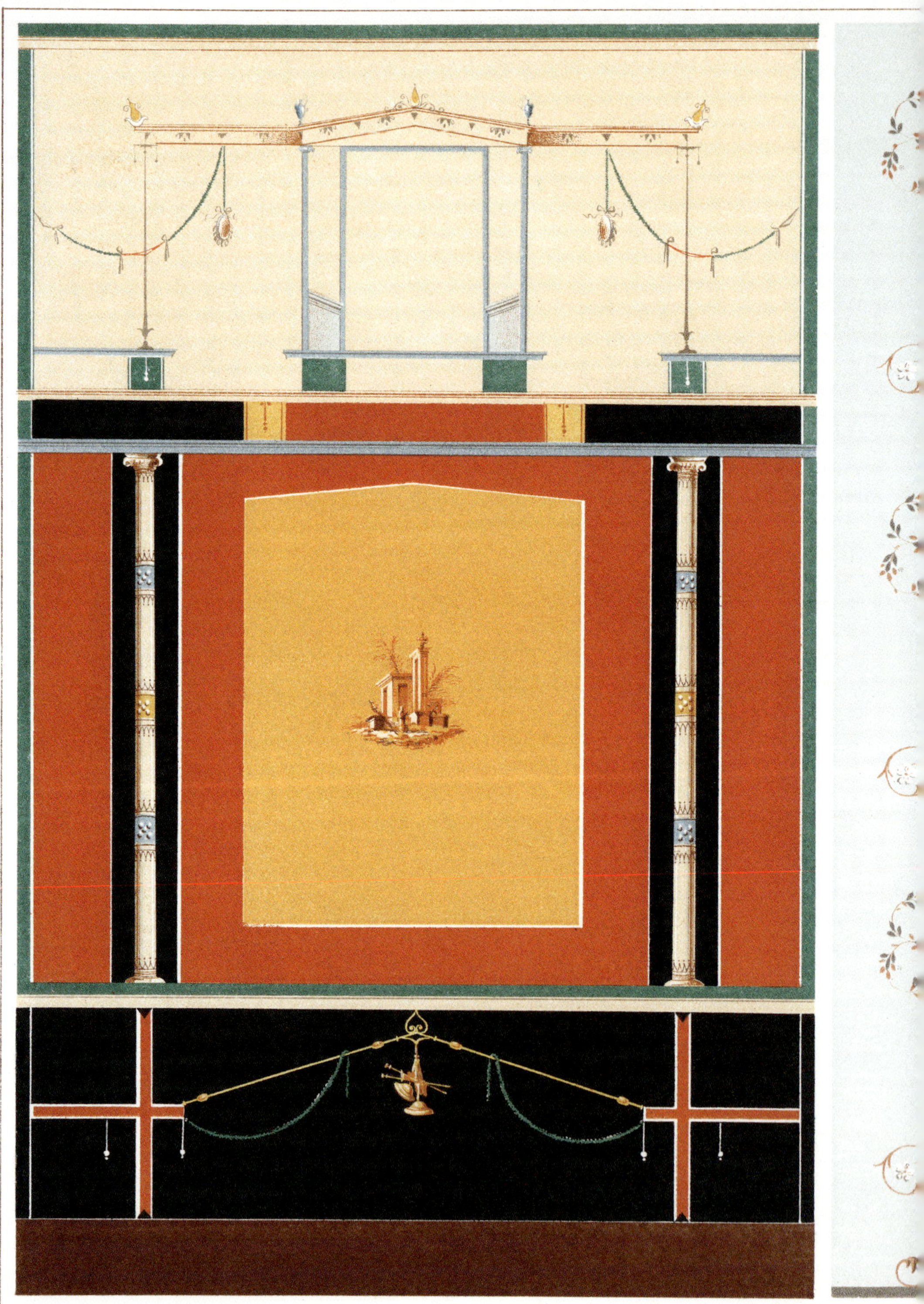

V. Loria dis.

F.lli

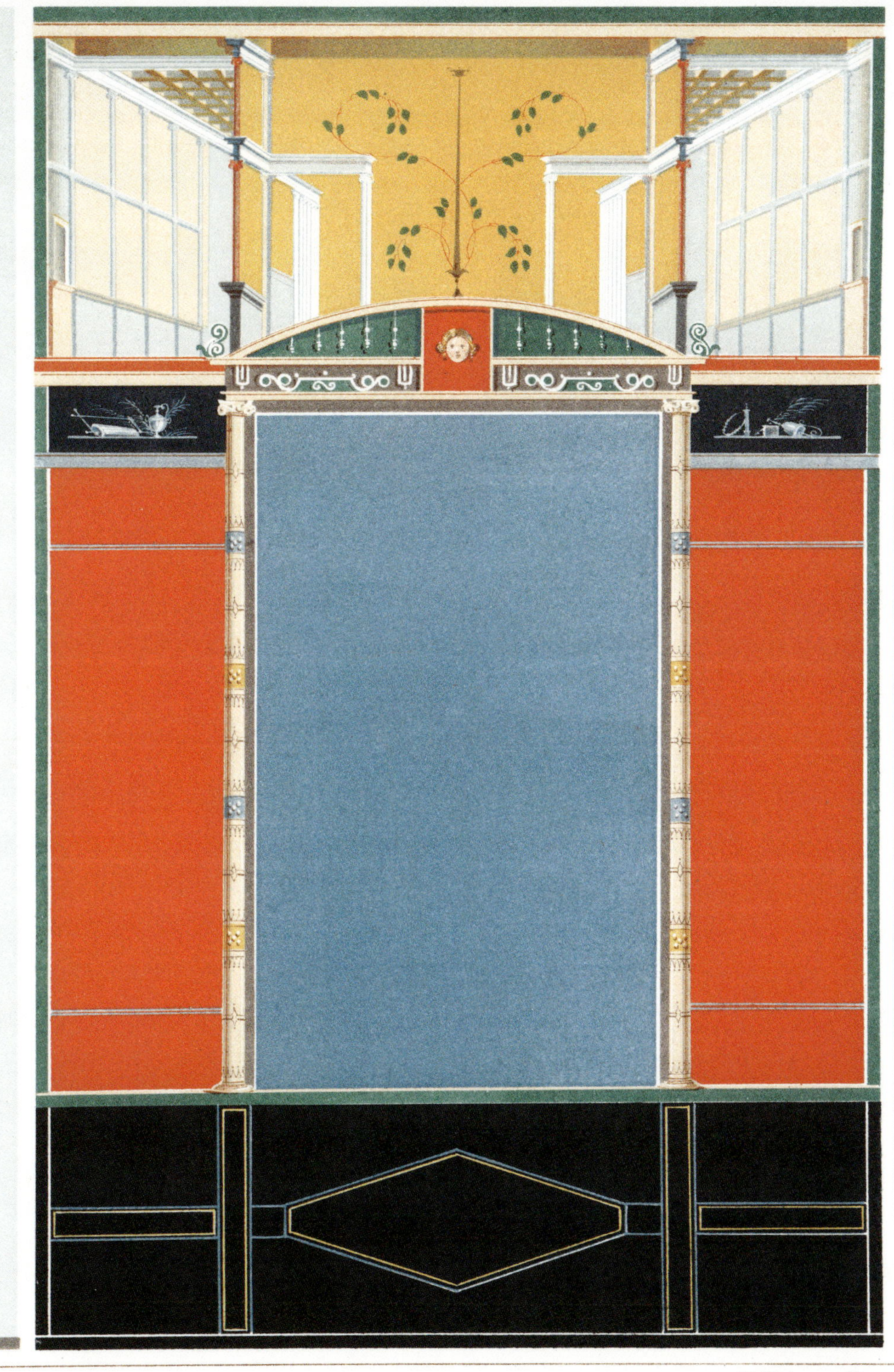

i dir.

Lit. Richter e C.o

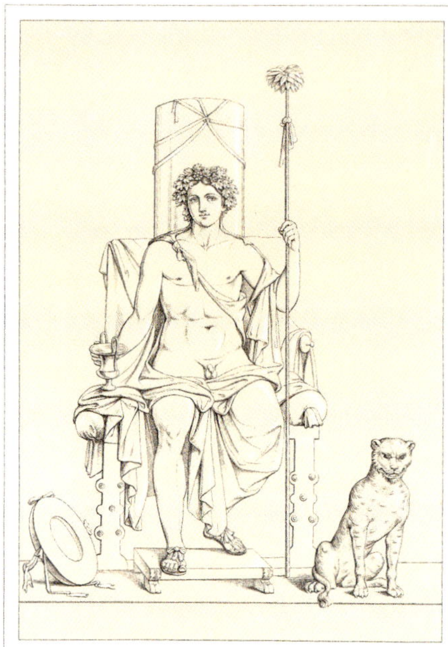

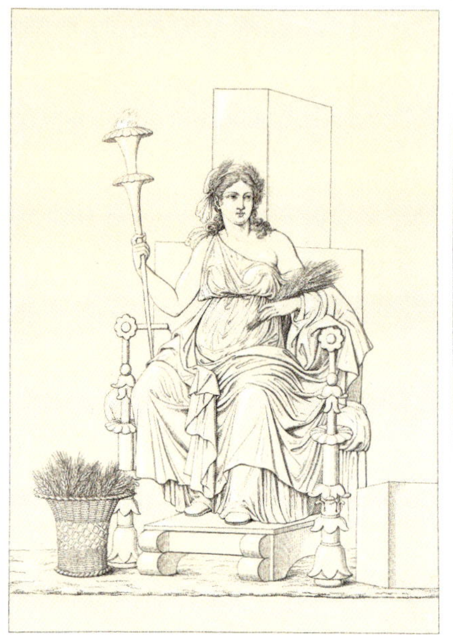

Plate 50 — *[Anonymous]*
Casa del Naviglio (VI 10, 11), atrium, south wall – Central pictures with Bacchus and Ceres, originally accompanied on the west wall by Jupiter and Juno (today destroyed; see pl. 81).

※

Plate 52 — *[V. Loria]*
Two bronze tripods – Front: sphinxes support a charcoal brazier. Behind: folding tripod.

※

Page 258
Plate 53 — *[V. Loria]*
Details of 3rd-style wall decorations from various locations – The wall detail in the top middle comes from the decoration of the caldarium in the Casa del Labirinto (VI 11, 8–10).

※

Page 259
Plate 55 — *[V. Loria]*
Decorative borders from various contexts – A collection of patterns, perhaps as a visual resource (cf. pl. 58).

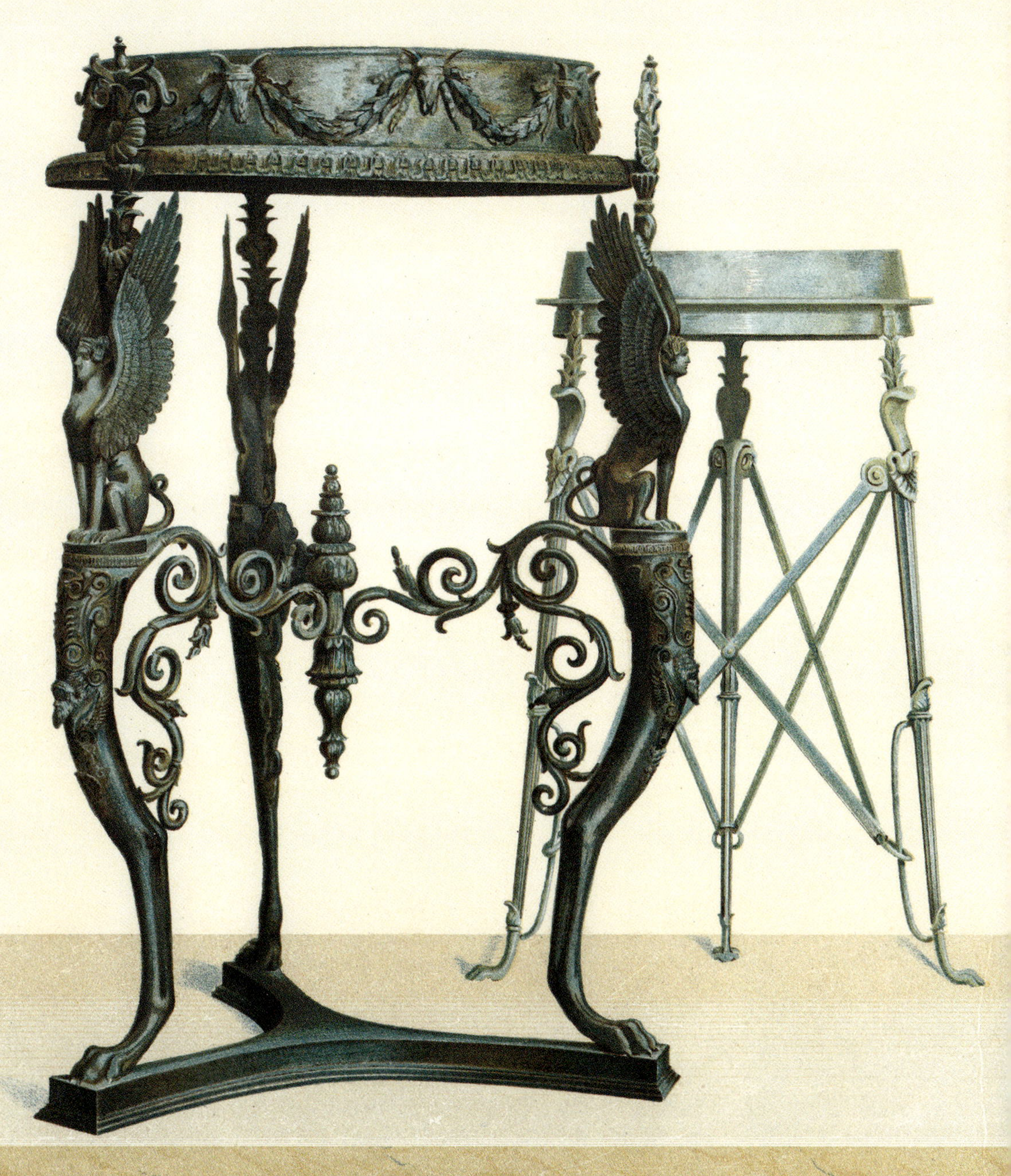

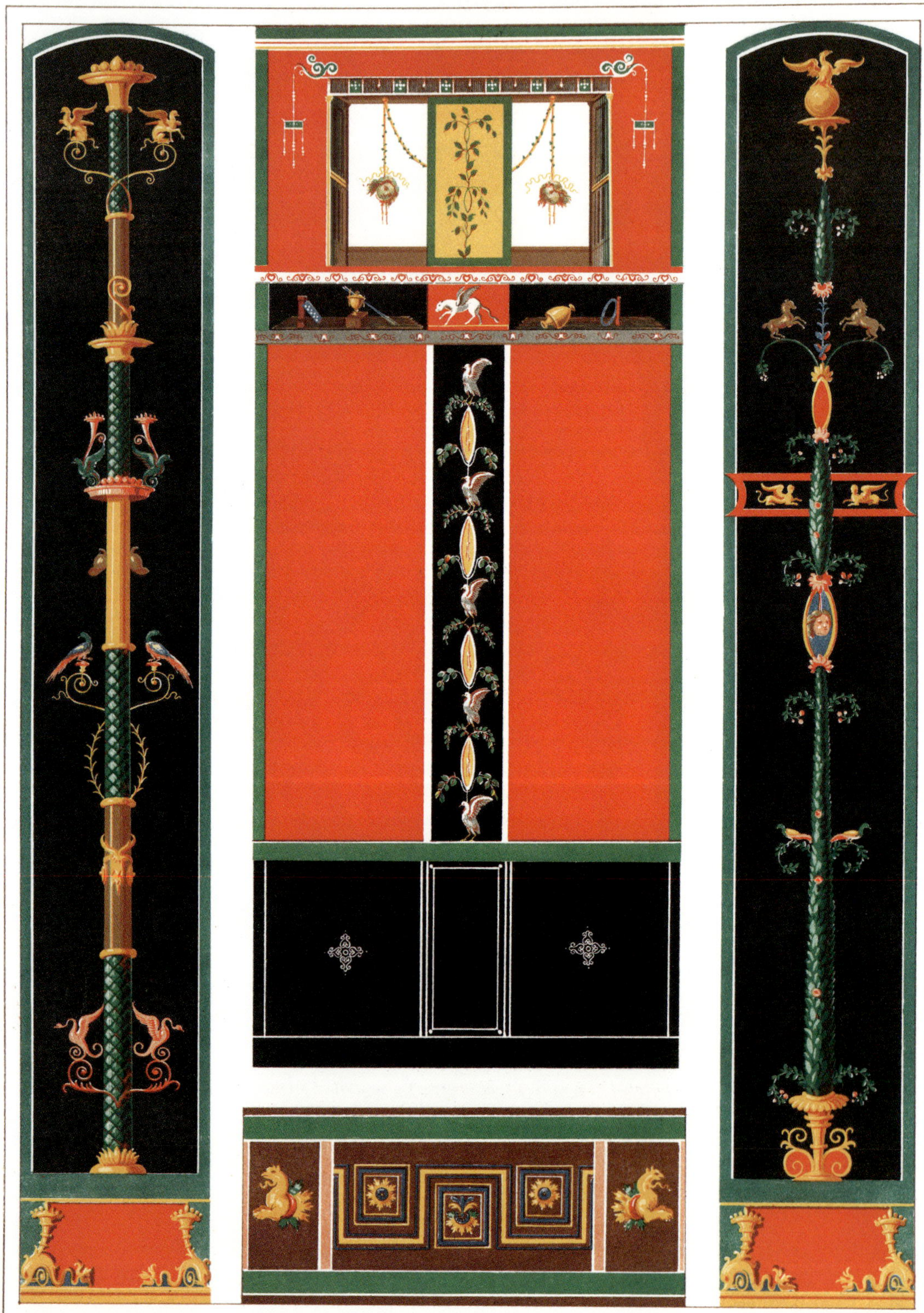

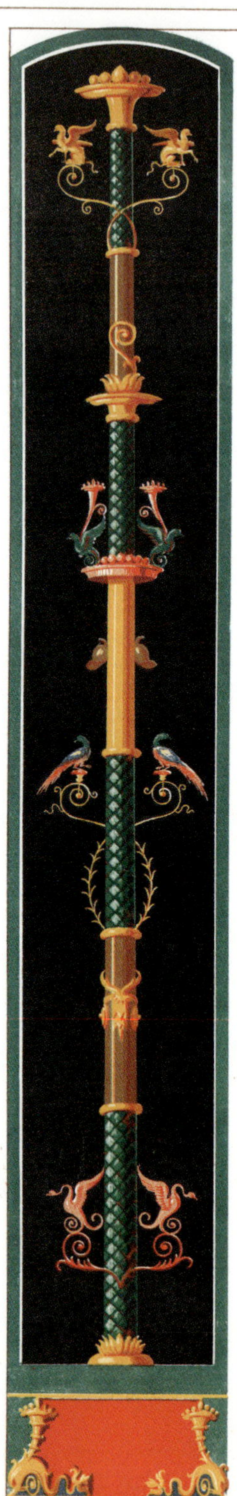

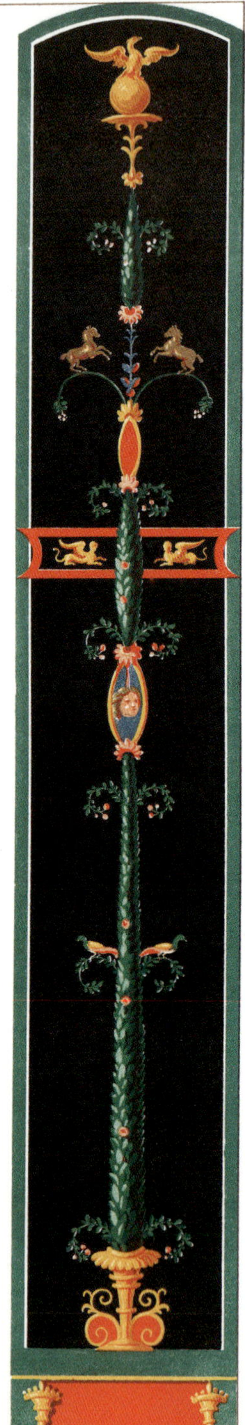

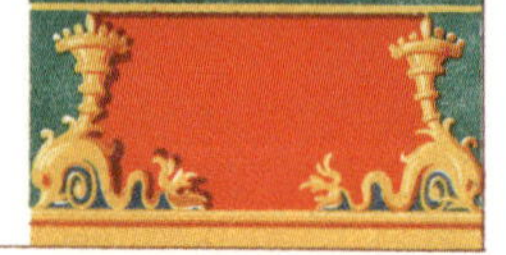

Lit. Richter & C.° Napoli F.lli Niccolini dir. Vin.° Loria dis.° e Lit.°

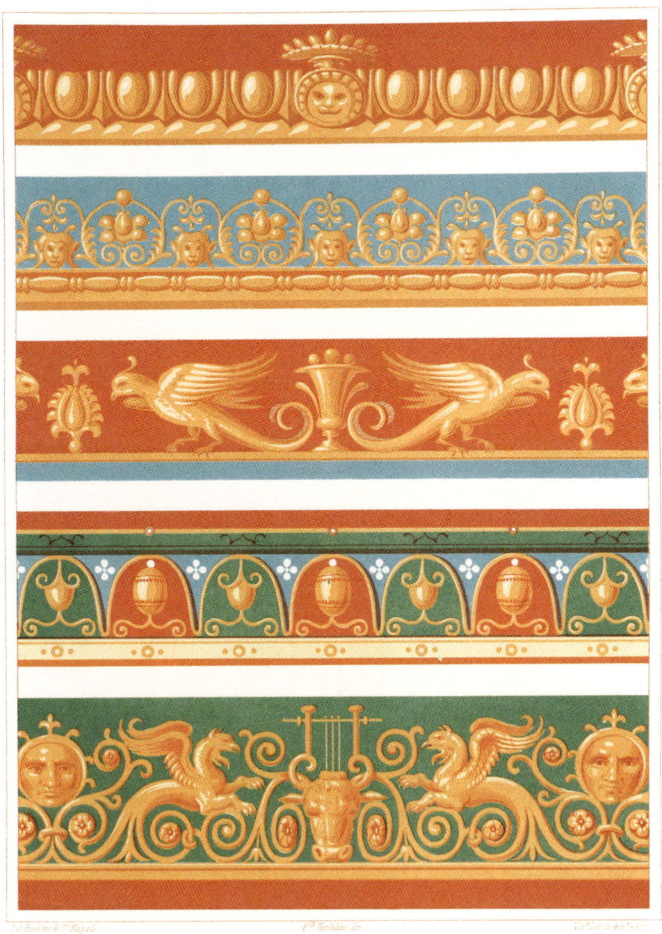

Pages 260–261

Plate 51 — *[V. Loria]*

Casa della Fontana piccola (VI 8, 23–24), tablinum (22), west wall – Details of the architectural decoration with the central picture, a still life with attributes of Zeus.

Pages 262–263

Plate 54 — *[V. Loria]*

Casa della Parete nera (Casa dei Bronzi, VII 4, 59), oecus, west wall – Details from a 3rd-style wall decoration that is today lost.

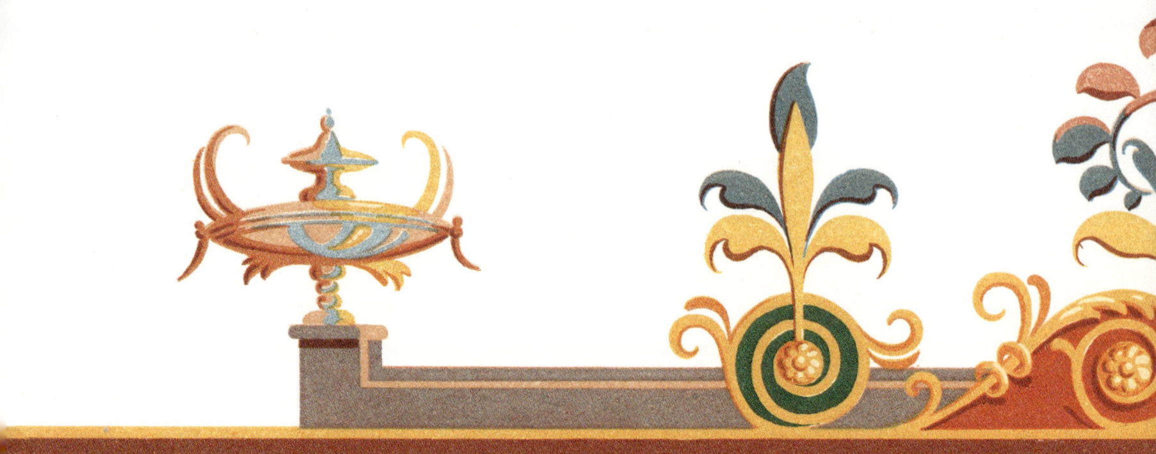

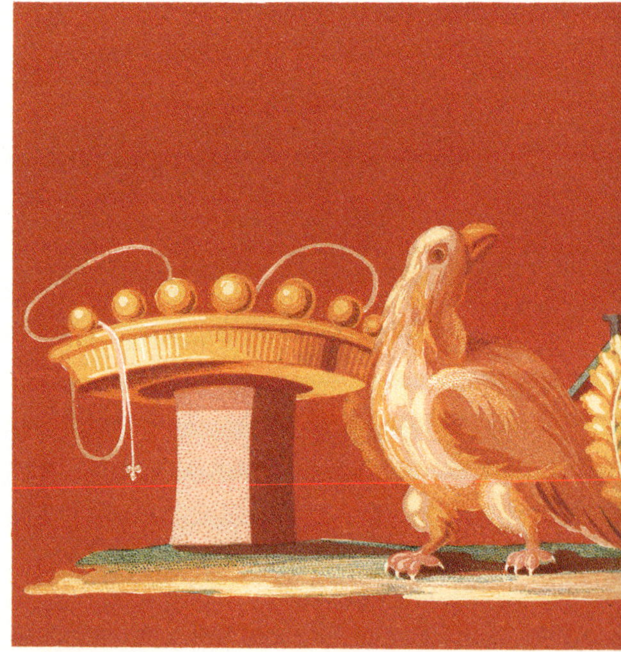

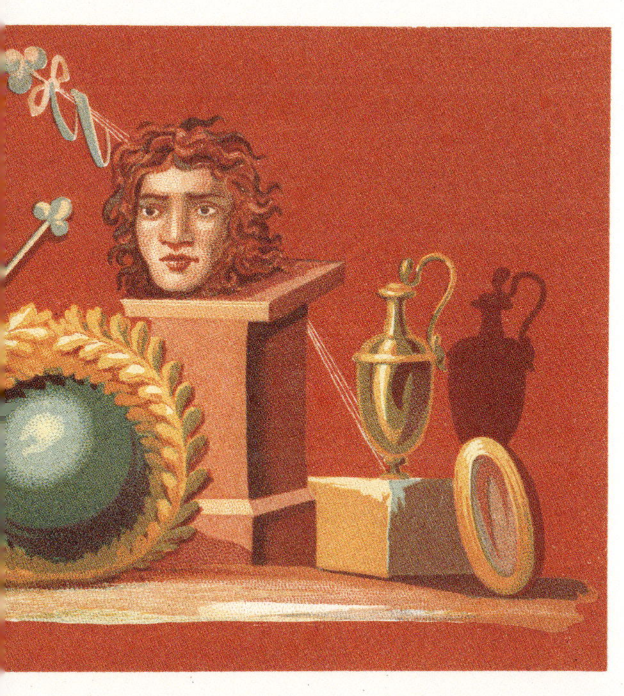

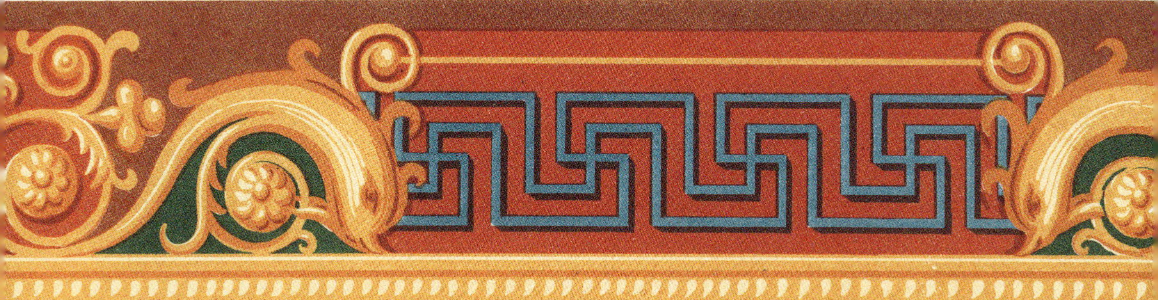

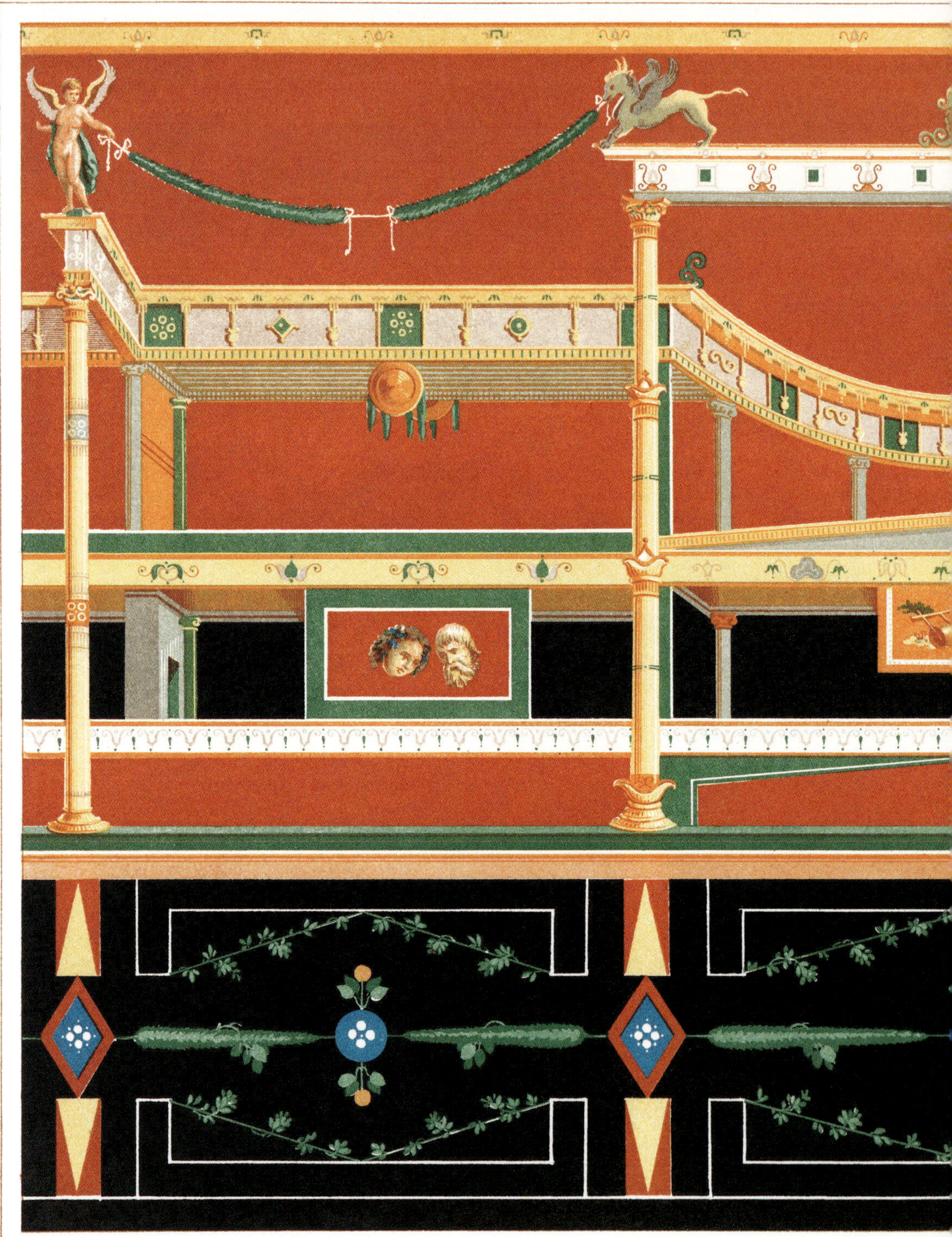

Lit. Richter & C.º Napoli.

F.lli N

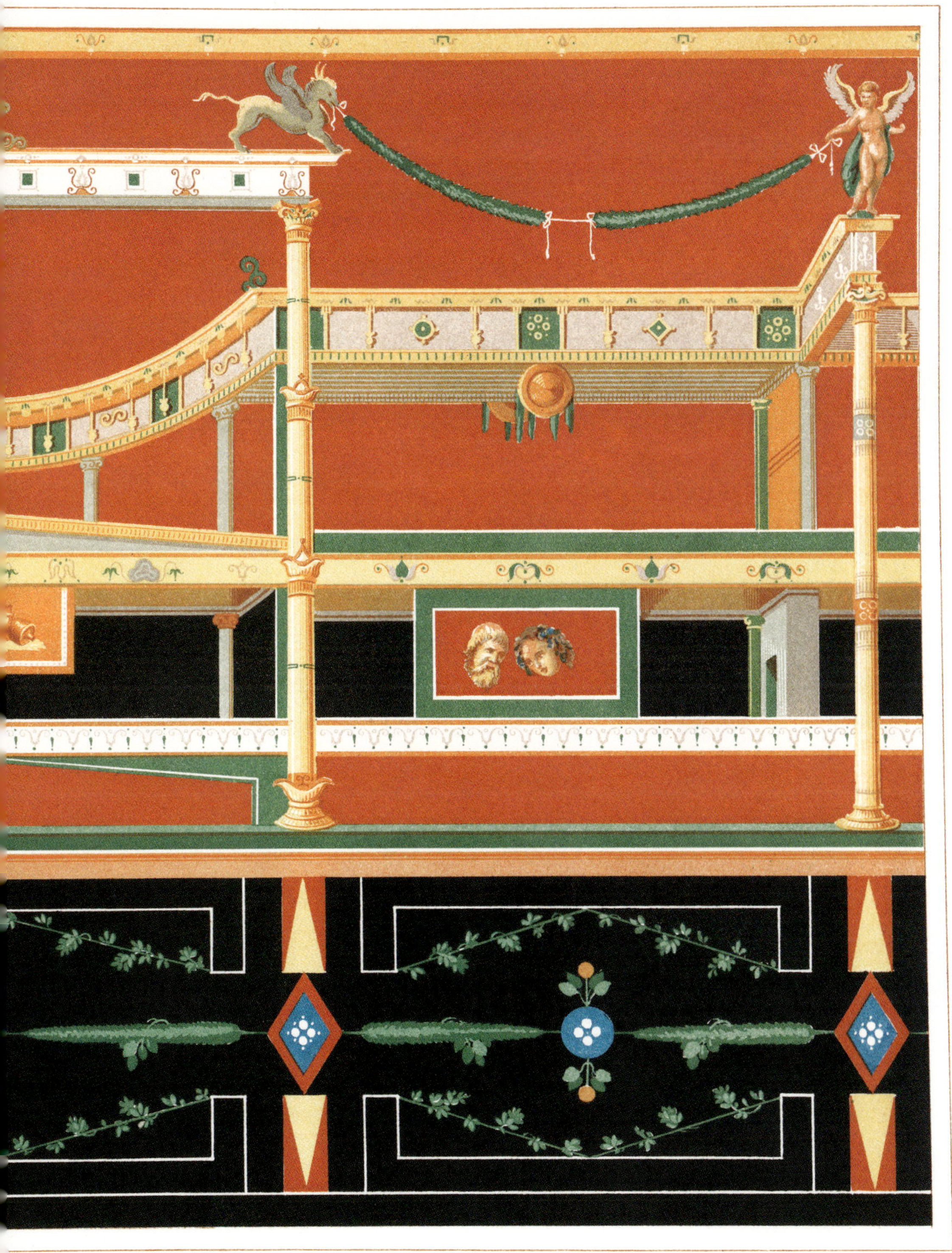

i dir.

Vin.zo Loria dis.o e Lit.o

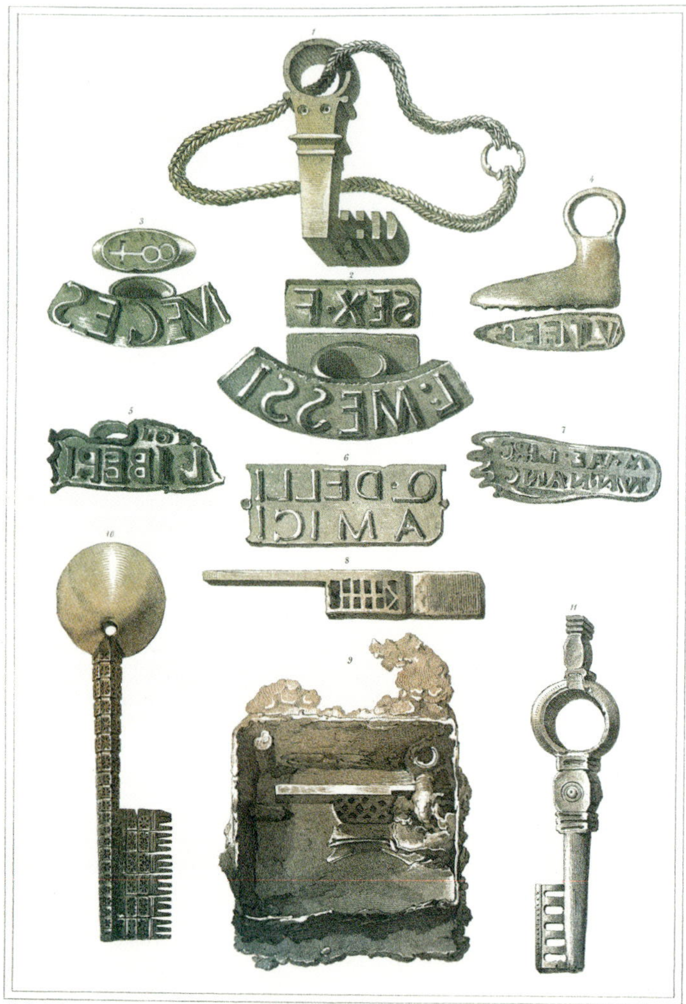

Plate 56 — *[K. Grob]*
Above and below: keys found in various locations. In between, five bronze rings with seals, some shown from both sides. Seals have occasionally been used to help determine the names of house owners.

Plate 57 — *[V. Loria]*
Casa del Gallo II (IX 2, 10), ceiling in the tablinum – Hovering eagles with Ganymede in the centre. The ceiling is still in relatively good condition today.

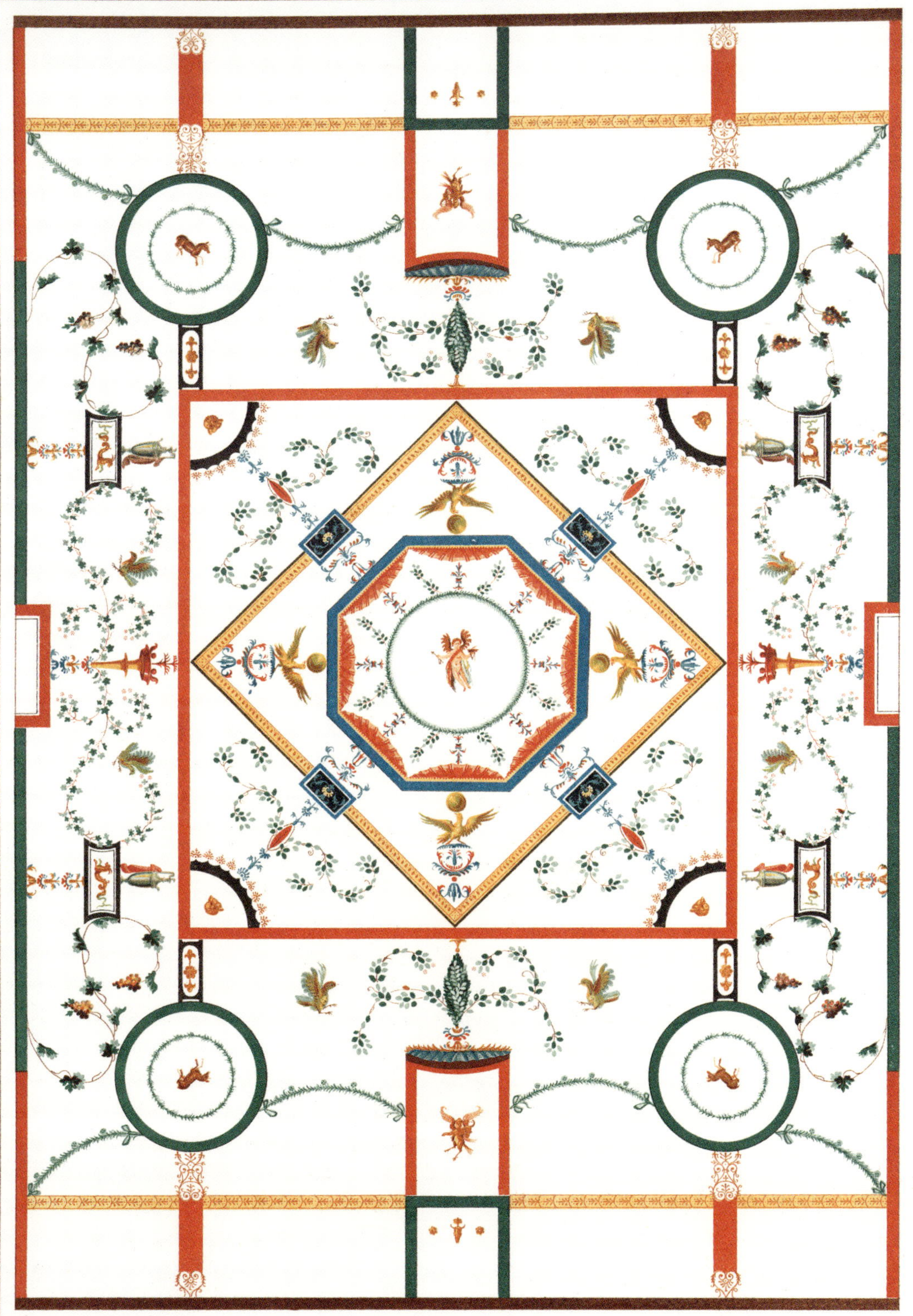

Lit. Richter & C.o Napoli — F.lli Niccolini dir. — Vin.zo Loria dis.o e Lit.o

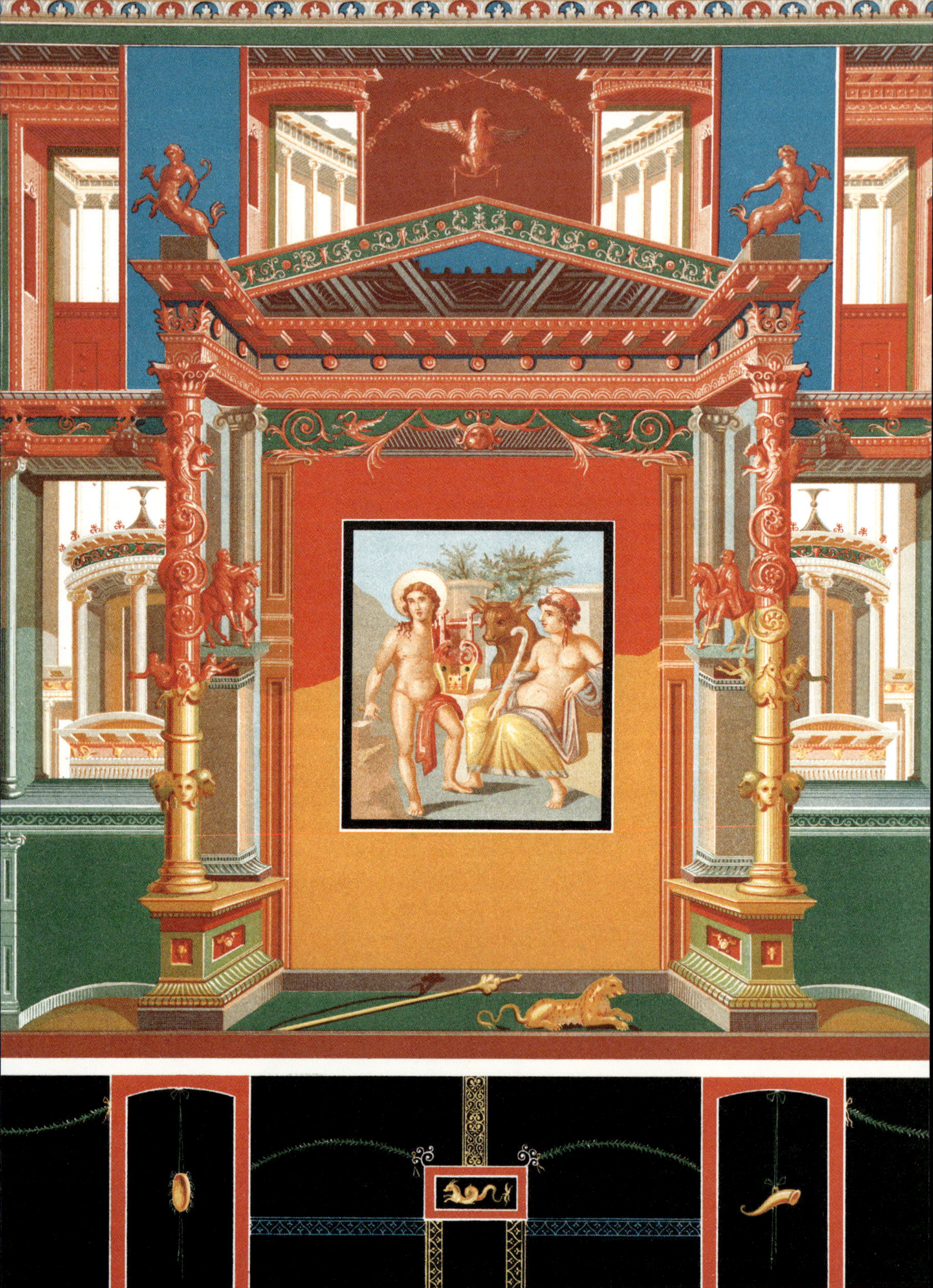

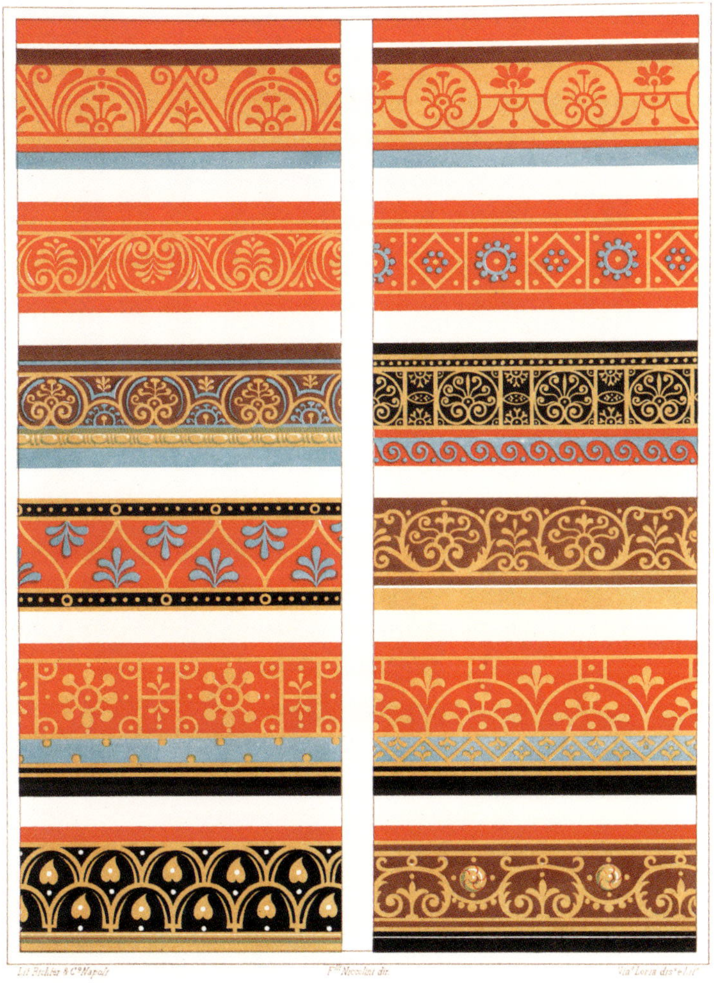

Plate 59 — *[V. Loria]*
Casa della Caccia antica (VII 4, 48 and 43), room beside the peristyle, south wall – Architectural prospect in the 4th style. In the central picture, Apollo and Branchus, a priest of the Temple of Apollo at Didyma (see vol. IV, Supplemento, pl. 16).

Plate 58 — *[V. Loria]*
Twelve ornamental borders found in various contexts, presented in the manner of a pattern book.

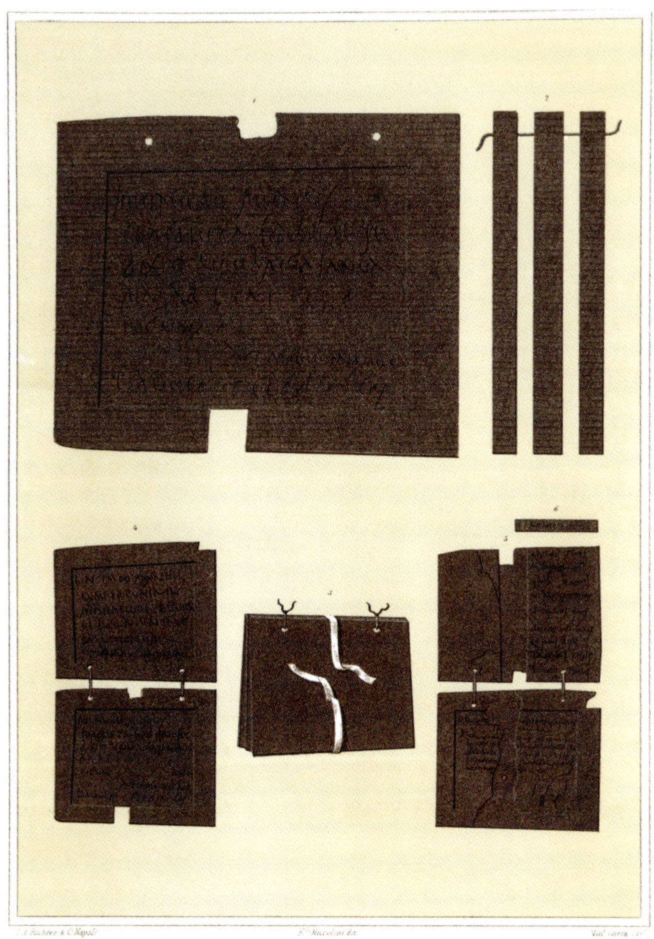

Plate 60 — *[V. Loria]*
Casa di Caecilius Iucundus (V 1, 26) – Examples of the 132 wax tablets *(tabulae ceratae)*, bound together in twos or threes (diptychs and triptychs), from the archives of the banker who owned the house. They record sales and lease contracts (for the house, see also vol. III).

Plate 62 — *[V. Loria]*
Bathing accessories, combs and a bronze bathtub from various houses – In Pompeii, excavators for the first time found private houses with their own baths, permitting the same sequence of cleansing and body care as in the large public baths, albeit on a reduced architectural scale.

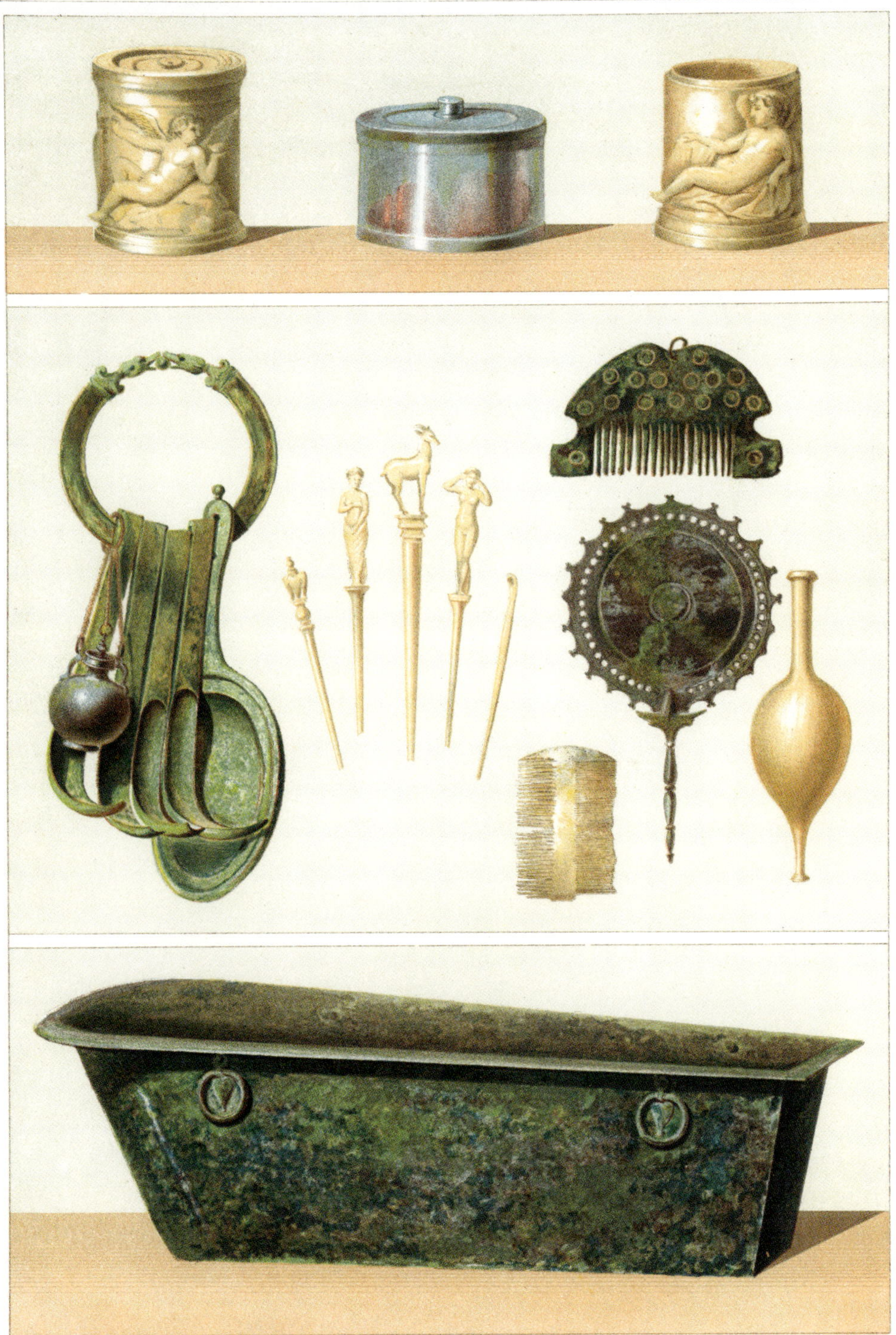

Lit. Richter & C. Napoli — F.lli Niccolini dir. — Vin.zo Loria Lit.

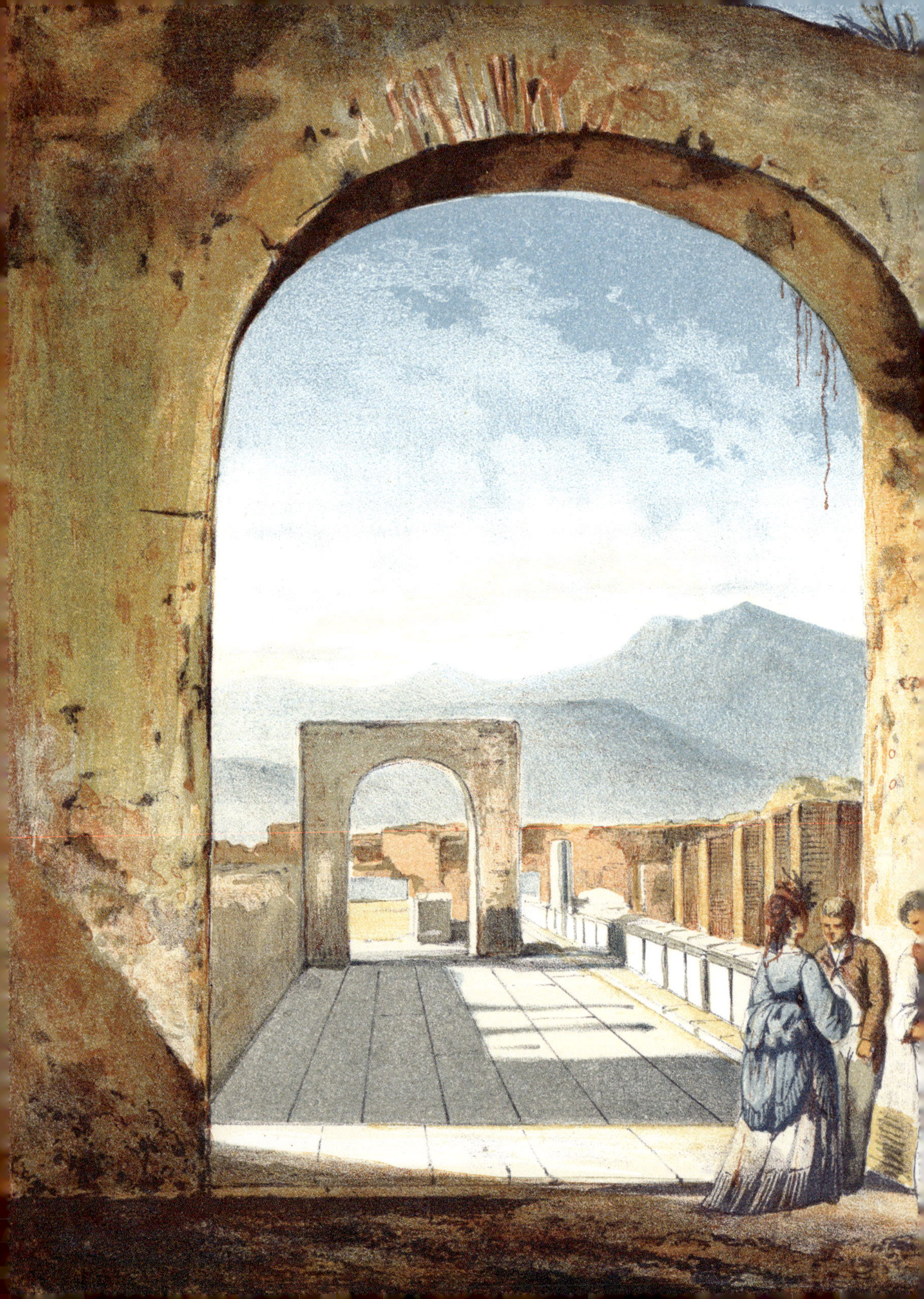

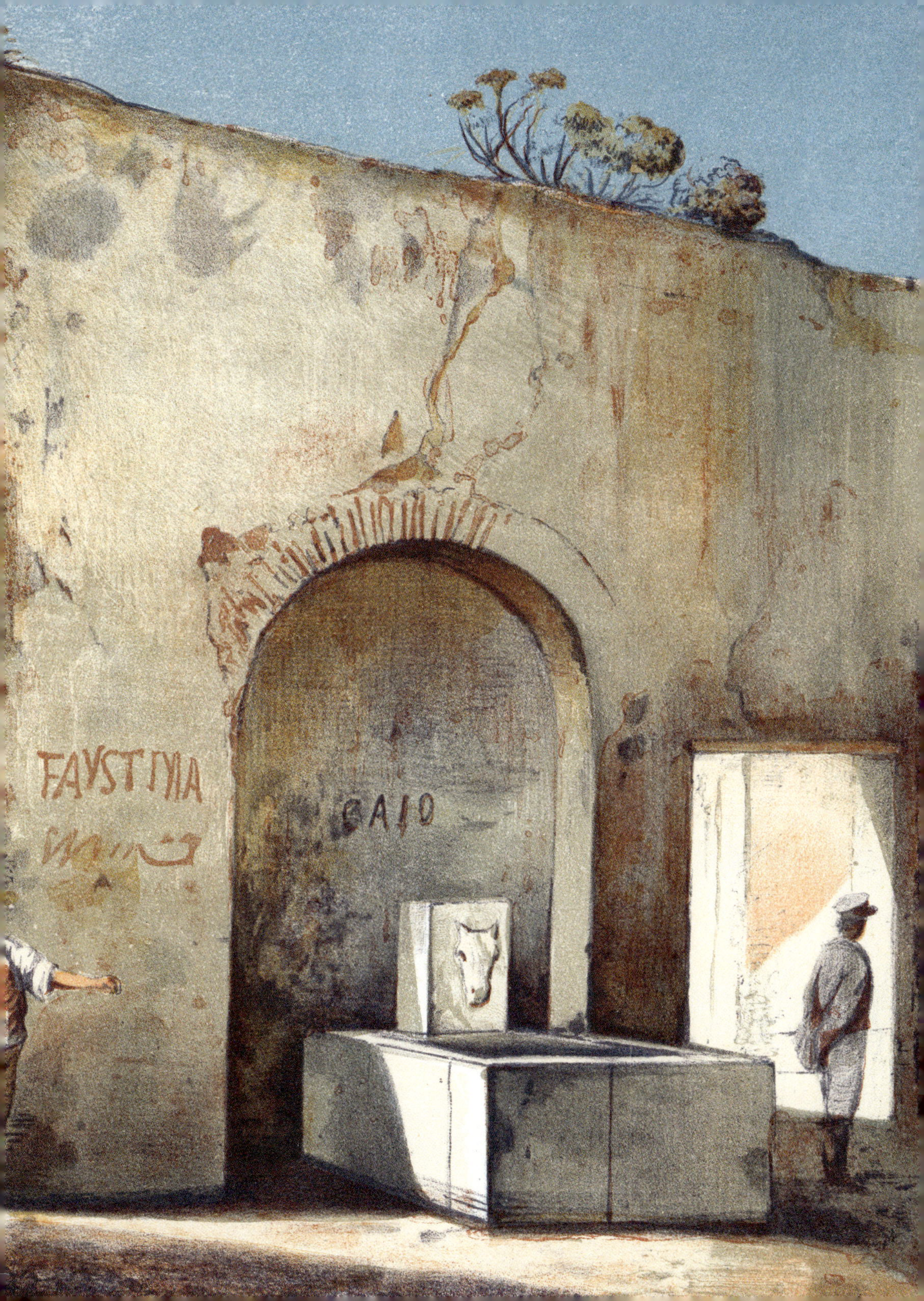
GAIO

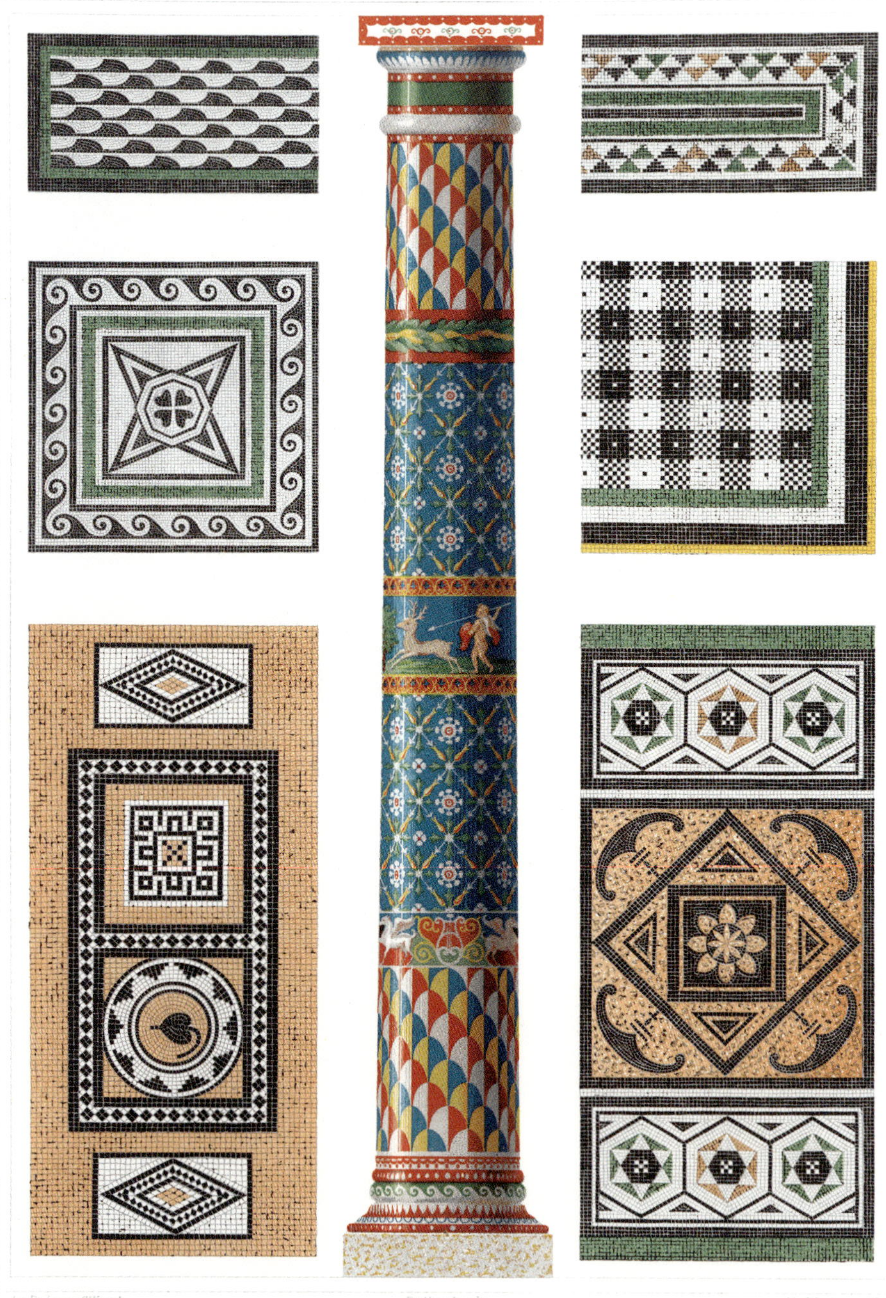

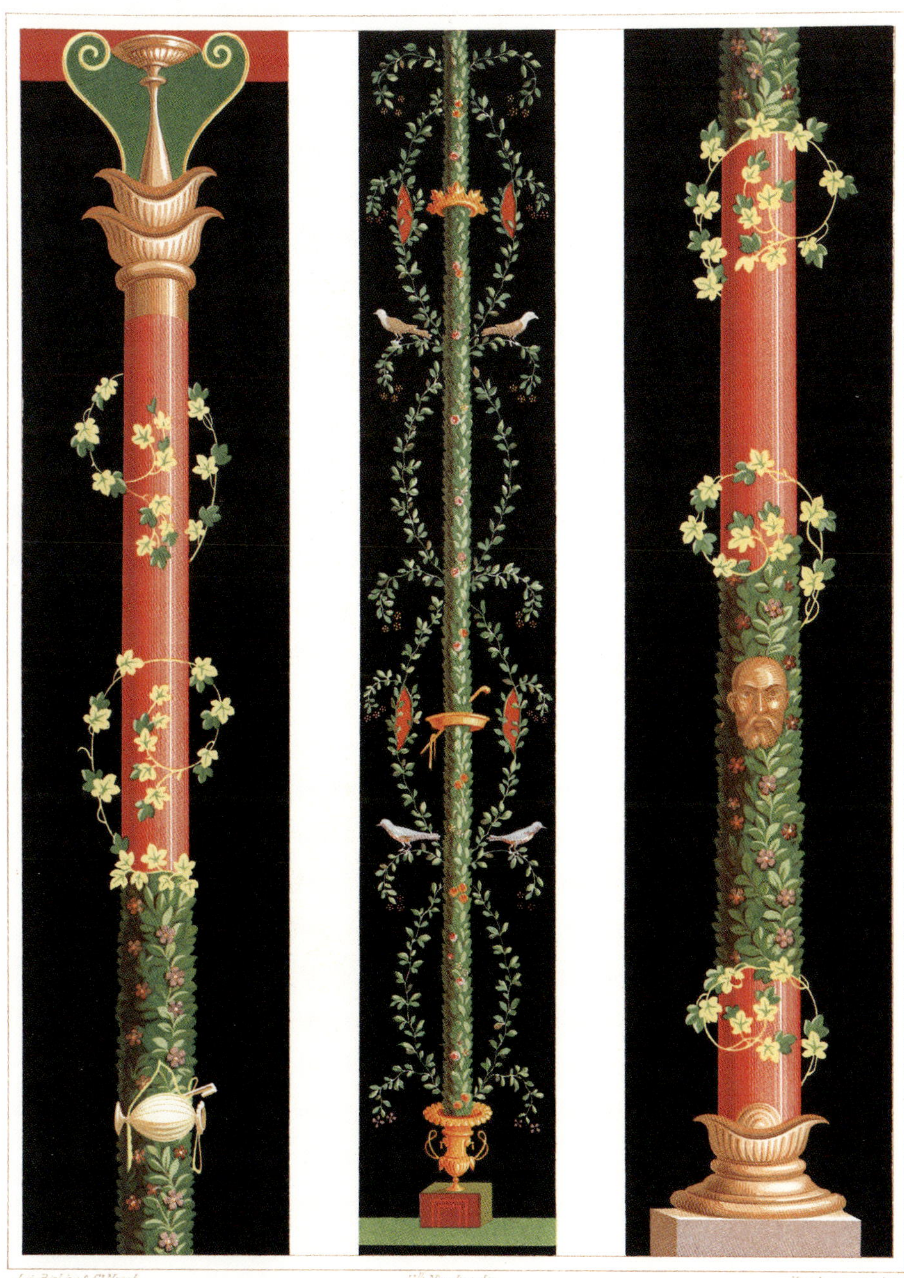

Lit. Richter & C.º Napoli   F.º Niccolini dir.   Vin.º Loria pin. e lit.

Pages 270–271

Plate 61 — *[E. Colonna, G. Gigante]*

View from Vico dei Soprastanti south through an archway over the west part of the Forum.

⁂

Page 272

Plate 63 — *[V. Loria]*

Examples of various coloured mosaic floors – The mosaic column comes from the Villa delle Colonne a Mosaico outside the Herculaneum Gate. It was copied for the interior decoration of the Neues Museum in Berlin.

⁂

Page 273

Plate 65 — *[V. Loria]*

Architectural elements from a 3rd-style wall decoration – The right- and left-hand panels show the two halves of the same column, from one wall of the tablinum in the Casa del Gruppo dei Vasi di Vetro (VI 13, 2).

⁂

Plate 66 — *[V. Loria]*

Casa di Laocoonte (VI 14, 28 and 33) – Detail from the south wall of the atrium: uncovered in 1875, the wall shows in its central picture the myth of Laocoön, who was killed by serpents because he had warned the Trojans against bringing the wooden horse into the city.

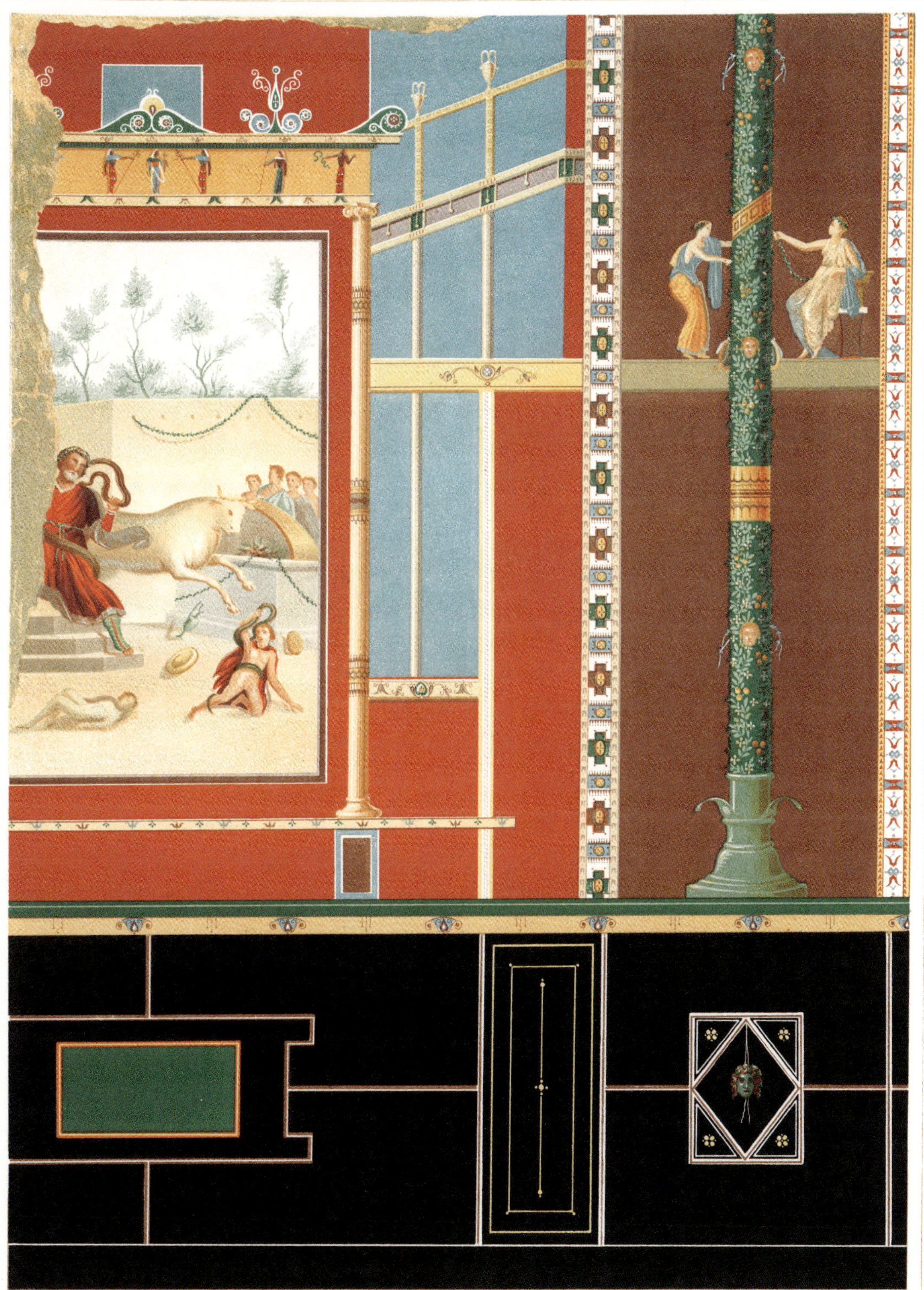

Lit. Richter & C.i Napoli F.lli Niccolini dir. Vin.o Loria pinx Lit.

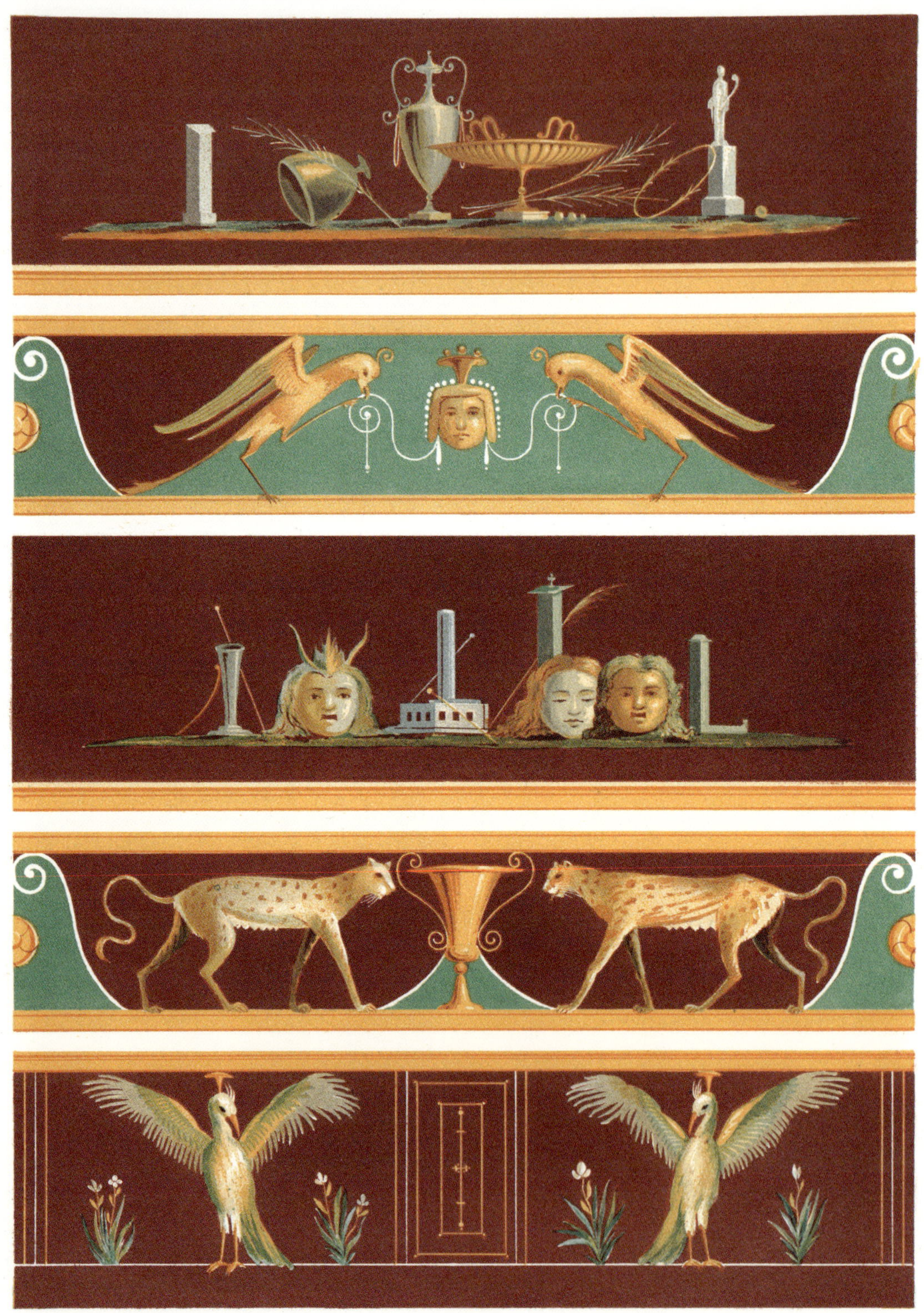

Lit. Richter e C.° Napoli　　Fr.lli Niccolini dir.　　Vin.° Loria fece e Lit.

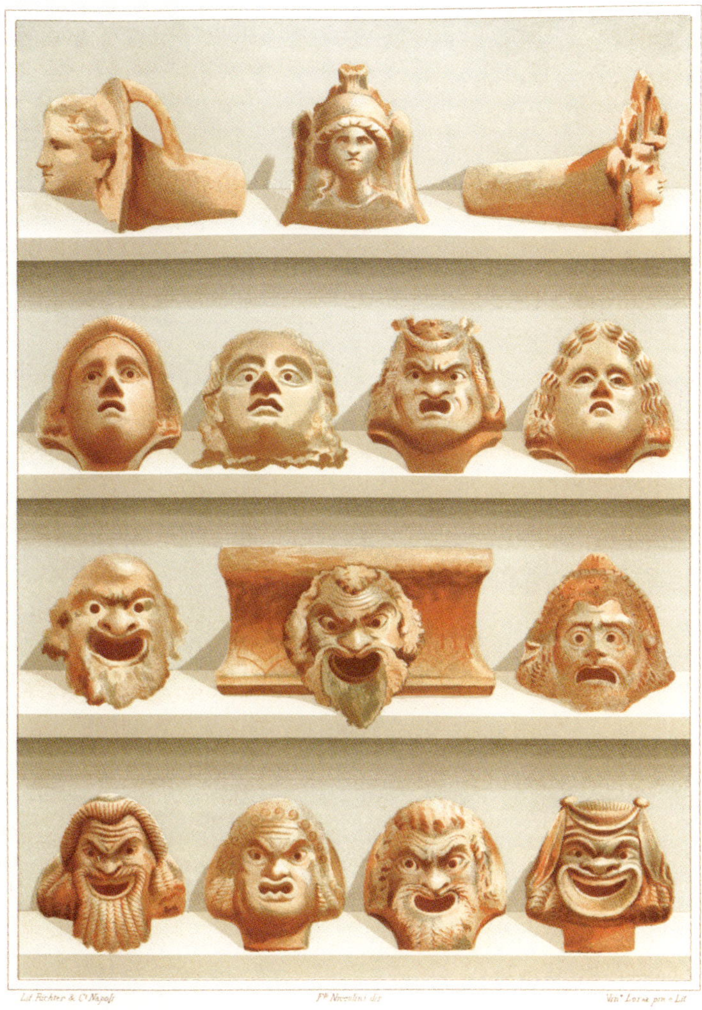

Plate 68 — *[V. Loria]*
Casa di Vesonius Primus (Casa di Orfeo, VI 14, 20), north wall in room (l) – Details from various zones, including still lifes with masks and domestic silverware (see the whole wall in pl. 70).

❖

Plate 67 — *[V. Loria]*
A selection of waterspouts and antefixae from various Pompeian houses – Here principally in the shape of theatrical masks.

Plate 69 — *[V. Loria]*

Casa dell'Ancora (VI 10, 7), west wall of the cubiculum –The central picture shows one standing and one seated woman; the significance of the scene remains unclear. Today entirely destroyed.

⁂

Pages 280–281

Plate 70 — *[V. Loria]*

Casa di Vesonius Primus (Casa di Orfeo, VI 14, 20) – The wall decoration in the 3rd style shows a so-called sacred landscape, with a temple in the middle, with Egyptian-style figures in the upper zone (see also pl. 68).

⁂

Pages 282–283

Plate 74 — *[V. Loria]*

Casa di Vesonius Primus (Casa di Orfeo, VI 14, 20), west wall of the peristyle – Orpheus tames the wild beasts with his song.

⁂

Pages 284–285

Plate 76 — *[V. Loria]*

Fullonica (VI 8, 20) – Pillar showing scenes from the different stages of woollen cloth production: cleaning in large tubs; drying, felting, checking; pressing and selling. In between, an illustration of the entire pillar, as it was when taken to the museum.

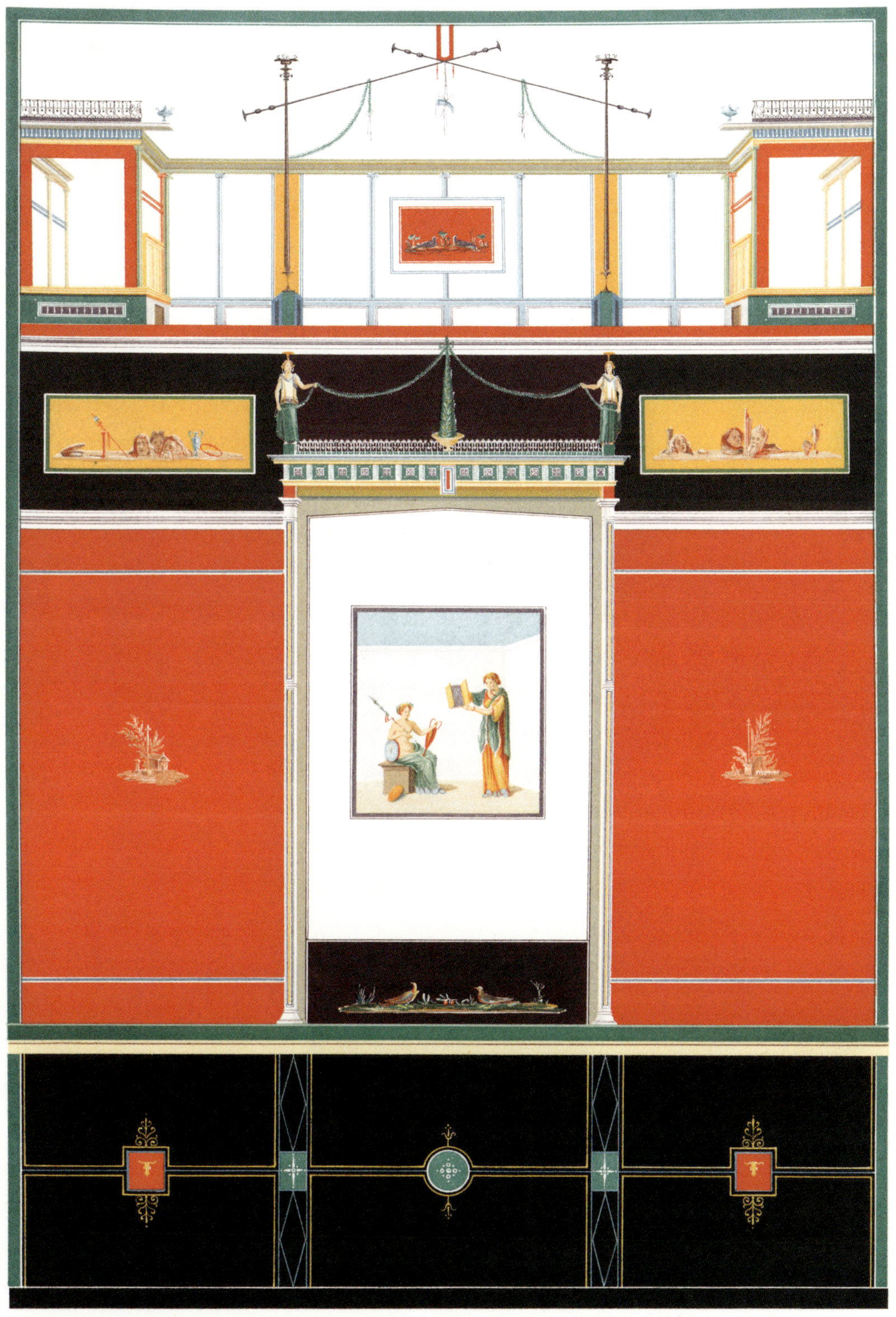

Lit. Richter & C.ⁱ Napoli F.ᶜᵒ Niccolini dir Vin. Loria Lit.

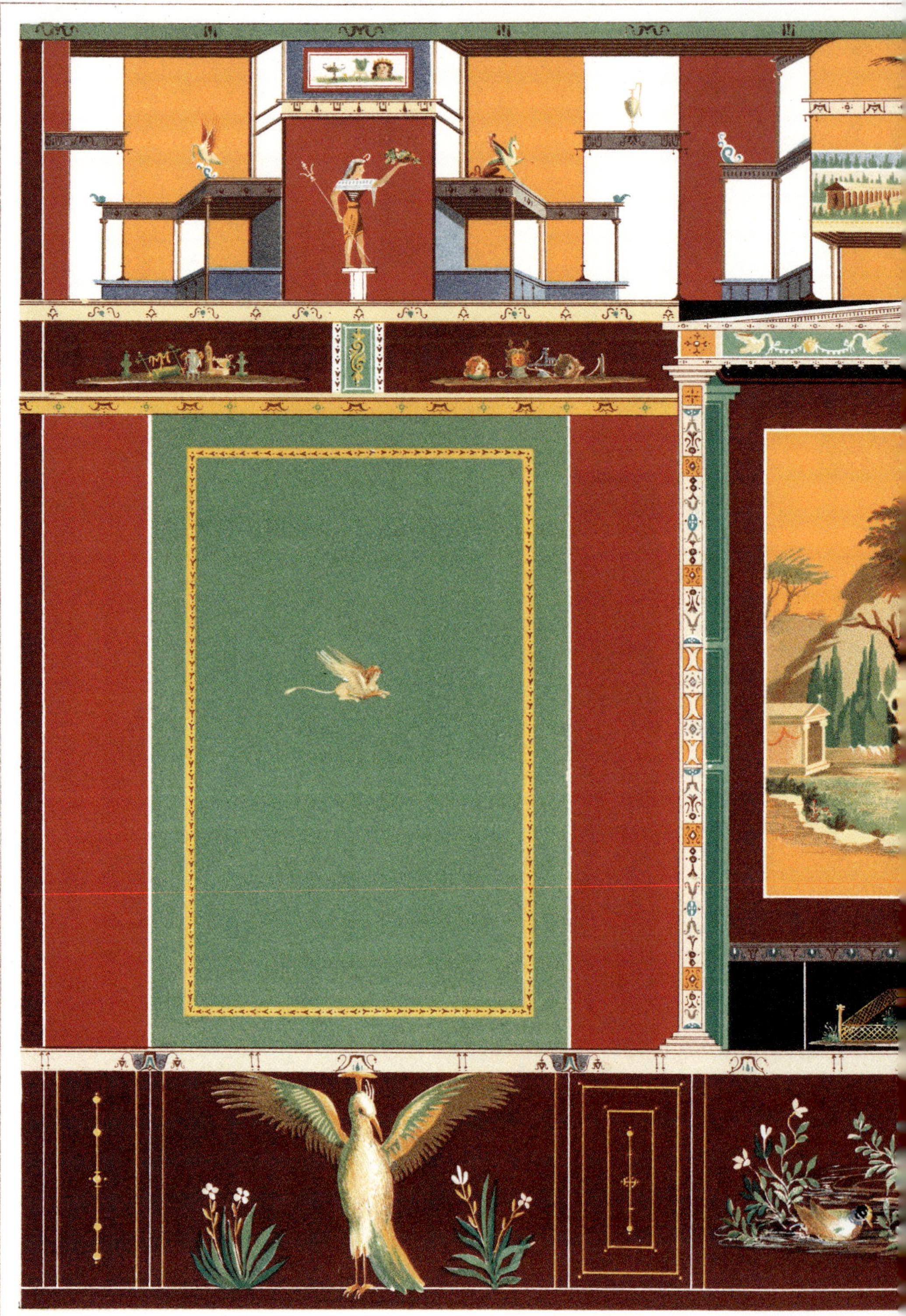

Lit. Richter & C.o Napoli

F

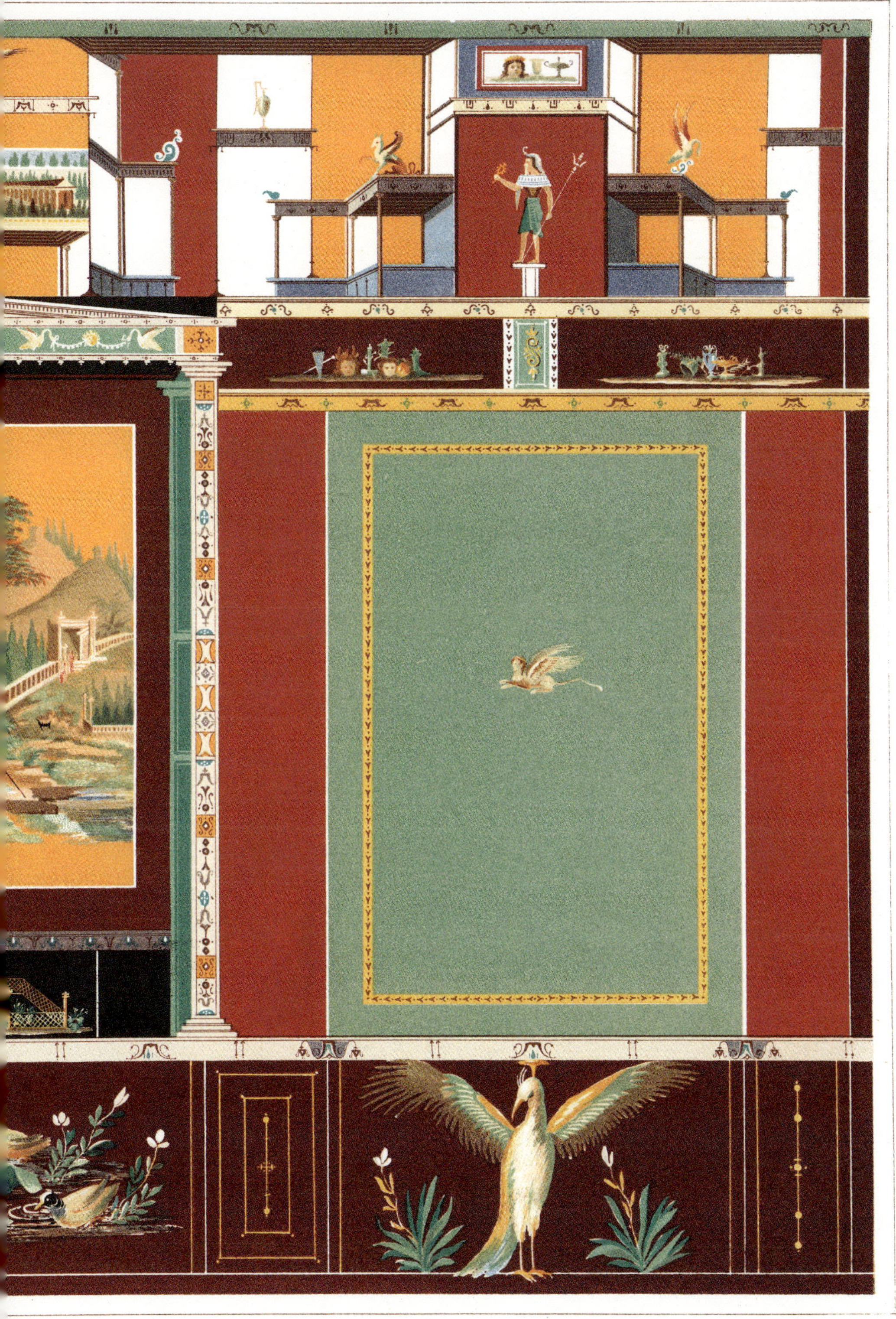

dir. Vin.° Loria pin. e Lit.

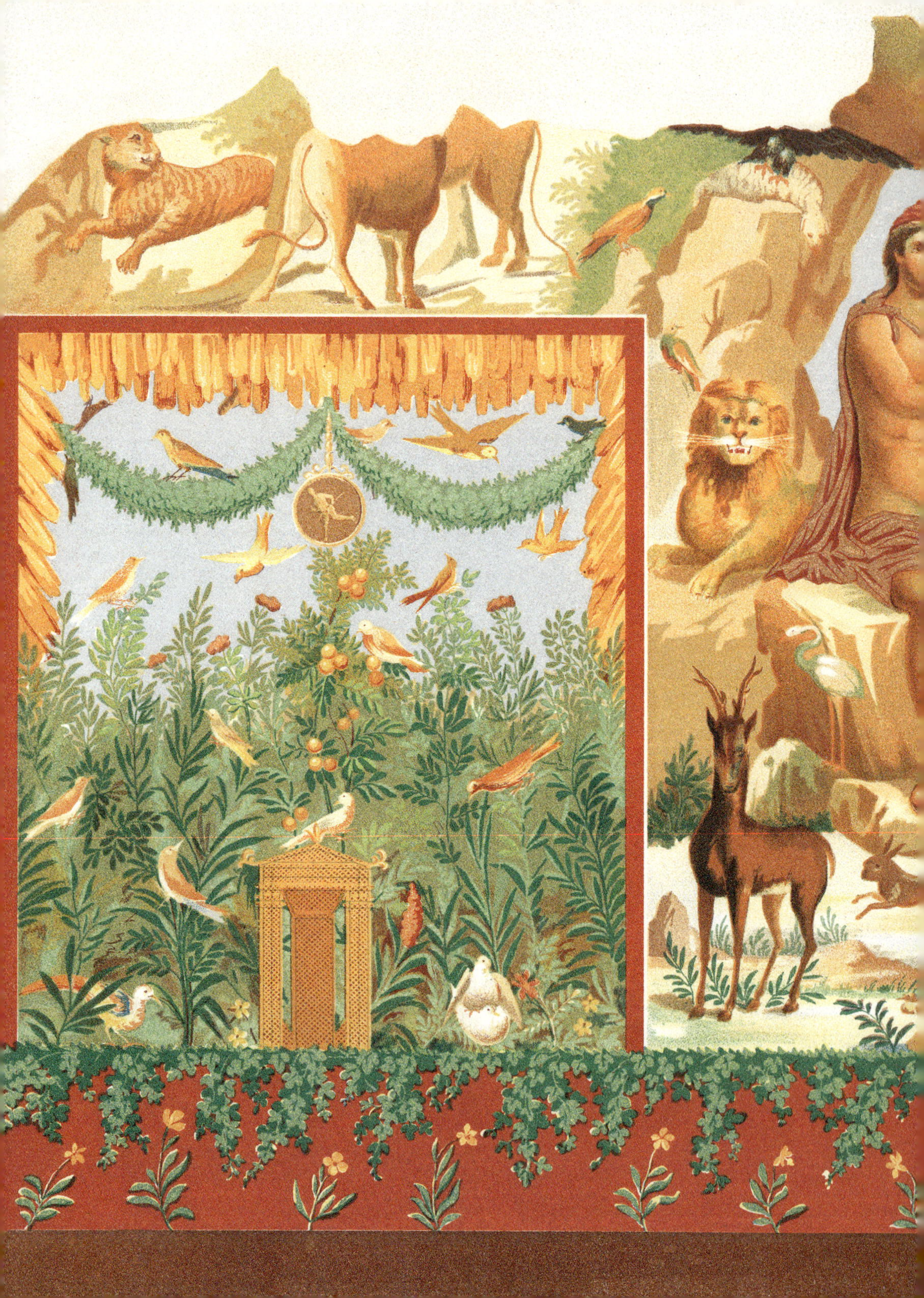

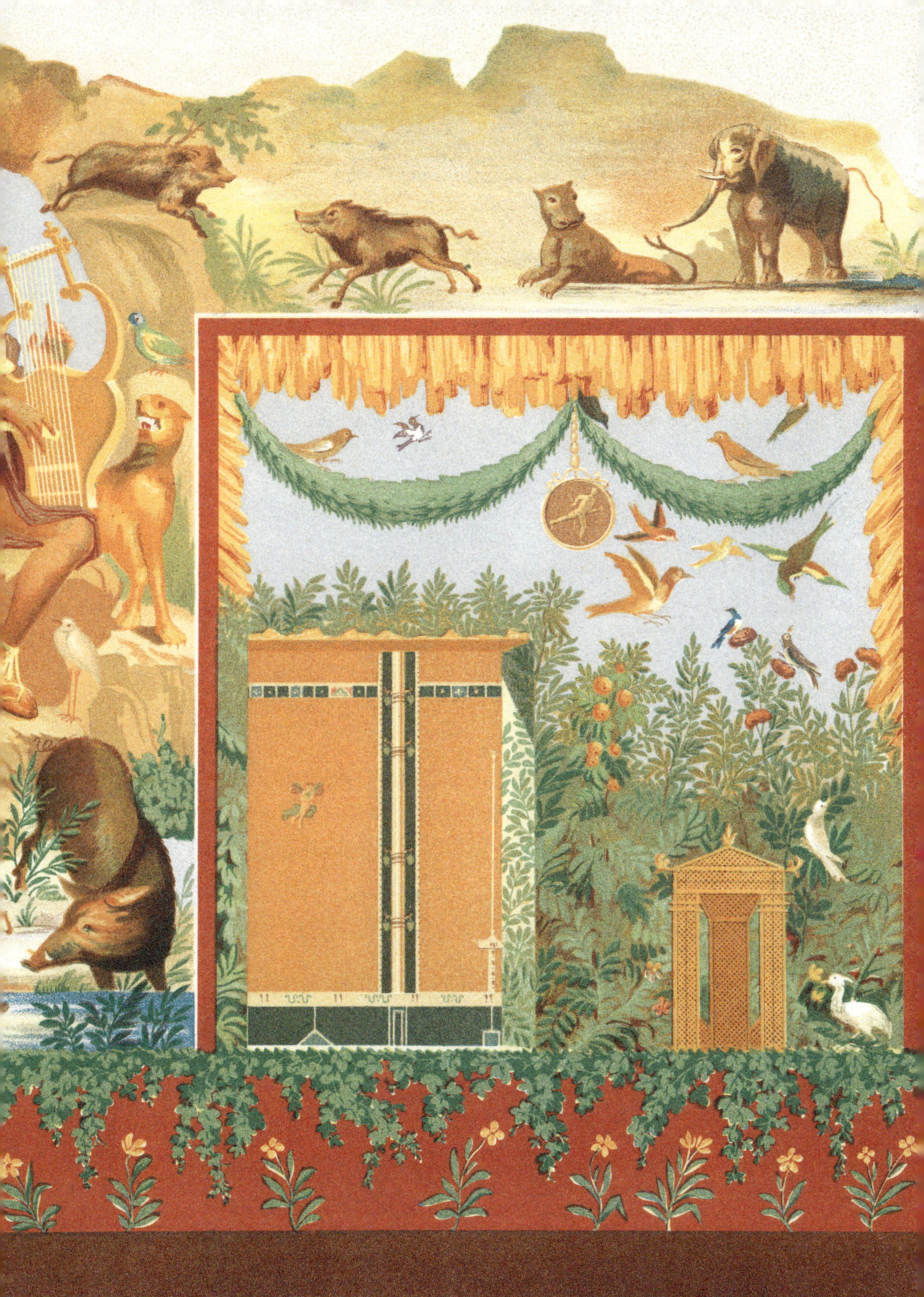

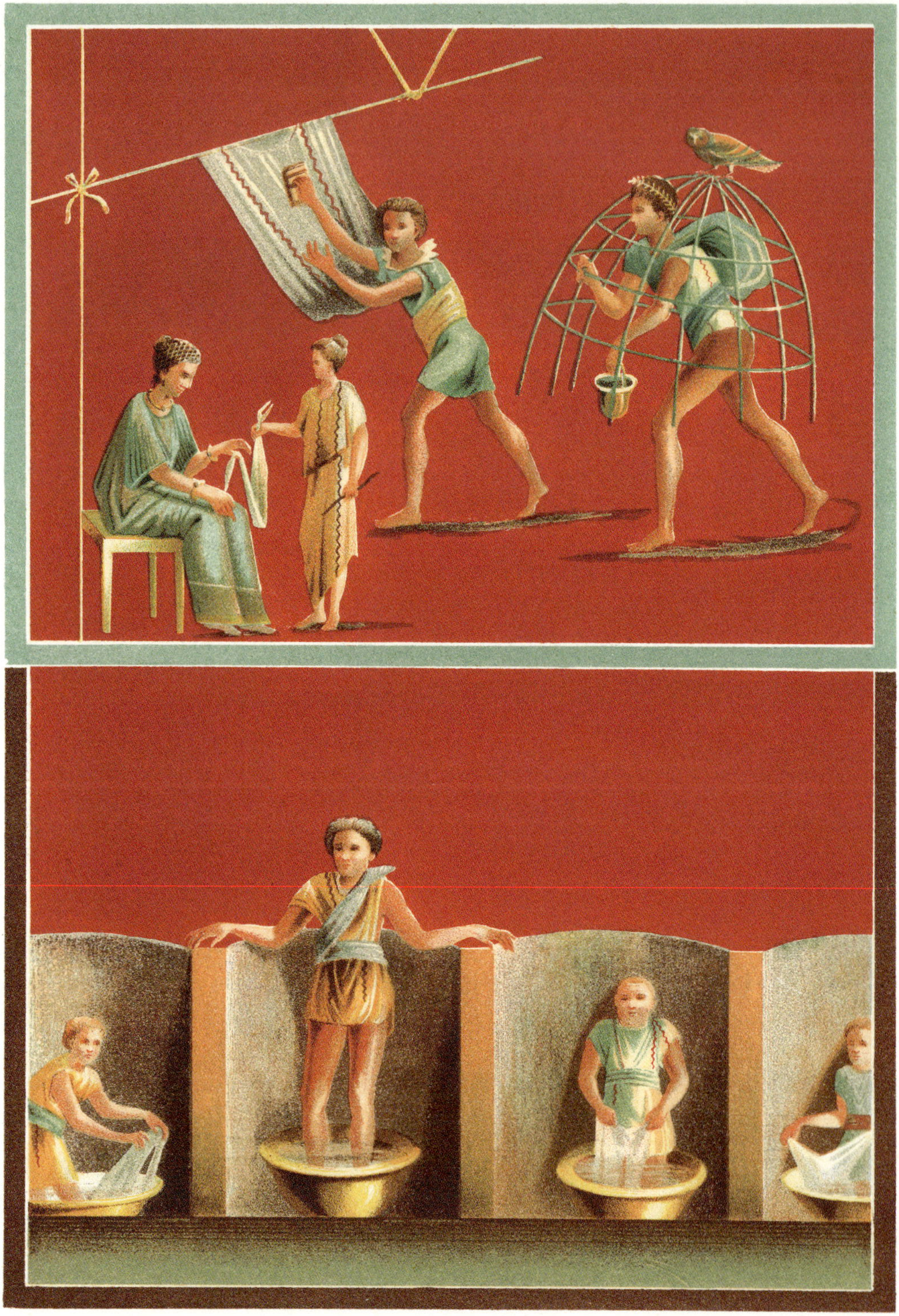

Lit. Richter & C.[o] Napoli

F.[lli] N

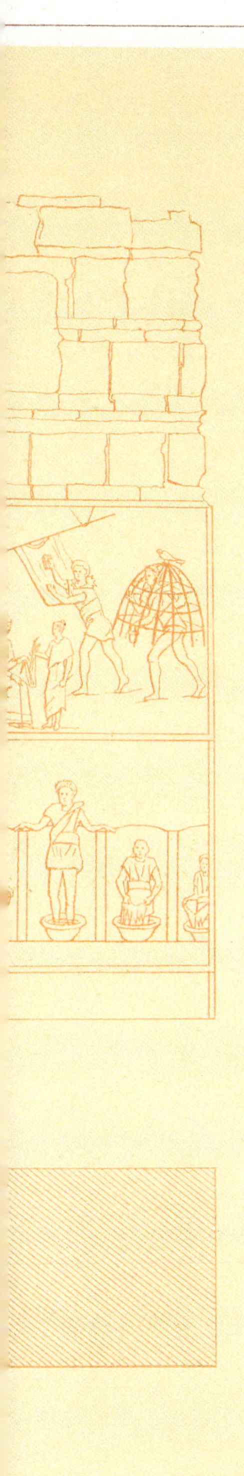

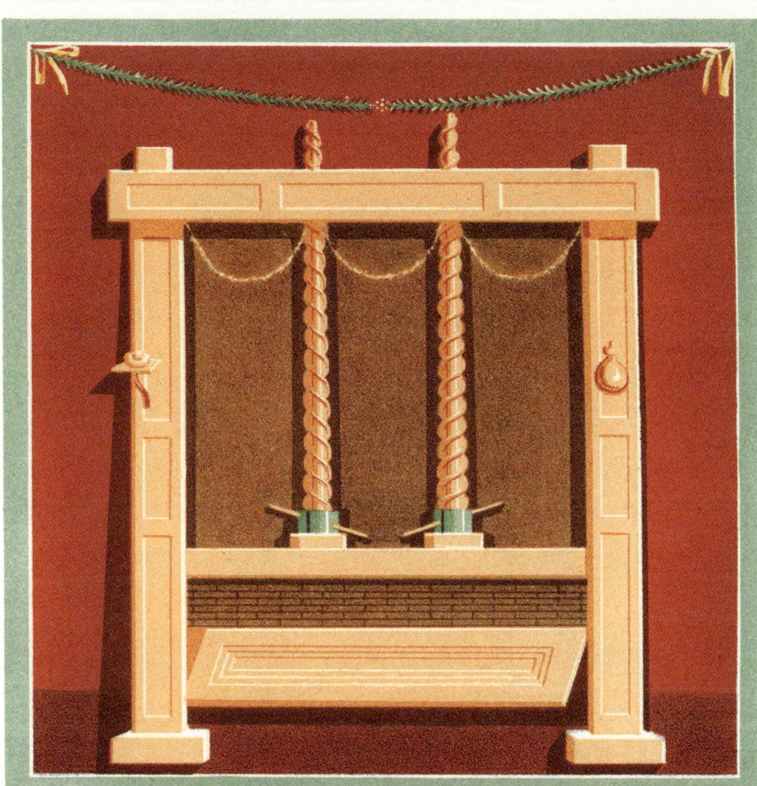

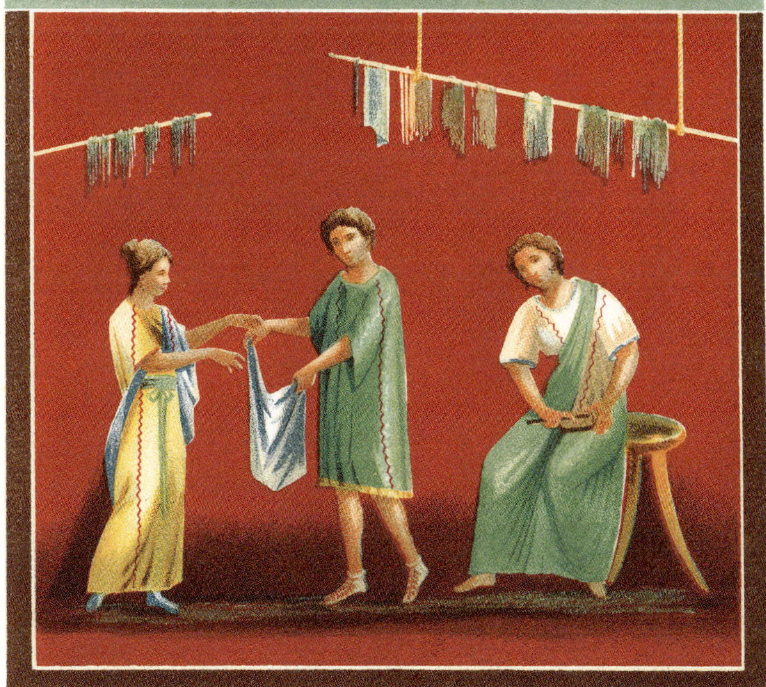

dir.

Vinᶜ Loria pin. e dis.

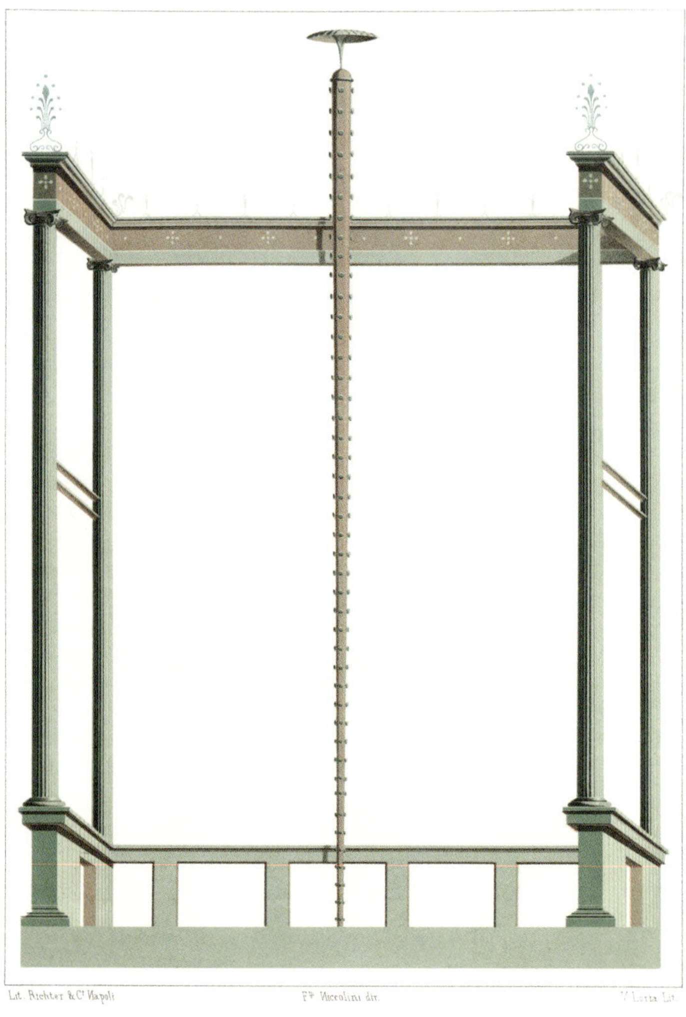

Plate 75 — *[V. Loria]*
Casa di Sallustio (VI 2, 4), cubiculum – Upper zone of a 3rd-style wall decoration.

❖

Plate 77 — *[V. Loria]*
Decorative elements from the period of the 4th style – The central motif is taken from a house excavated in 1848 "near the Casa di Marco Lucrezio".

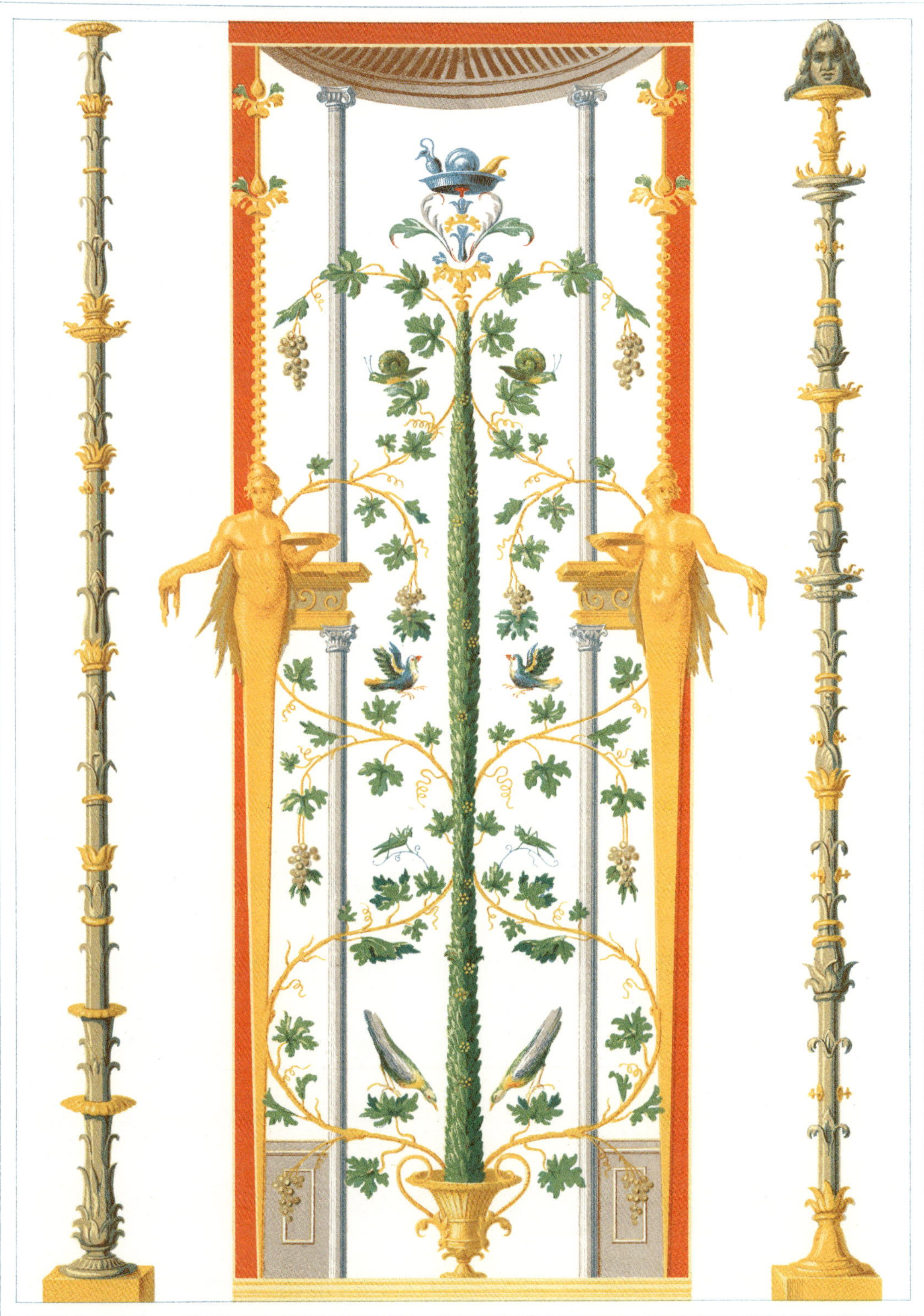

Lit. Richter e C.º Napoli F.lli Niccolini dir. V. Loria Lit.

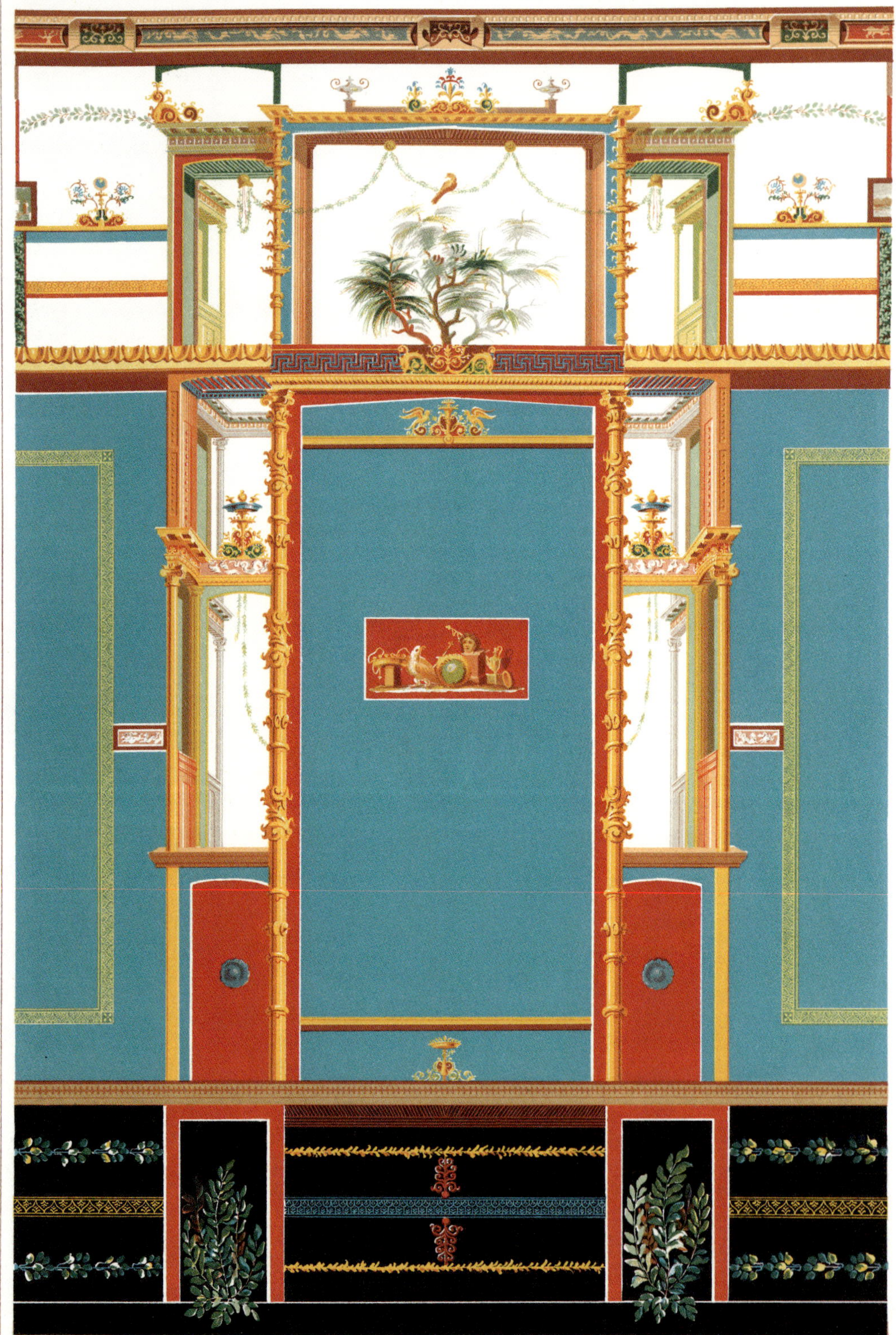

Lit. Richter e C.i Napoli Fr.lli Niccolini dir. V. Lorta Lit.

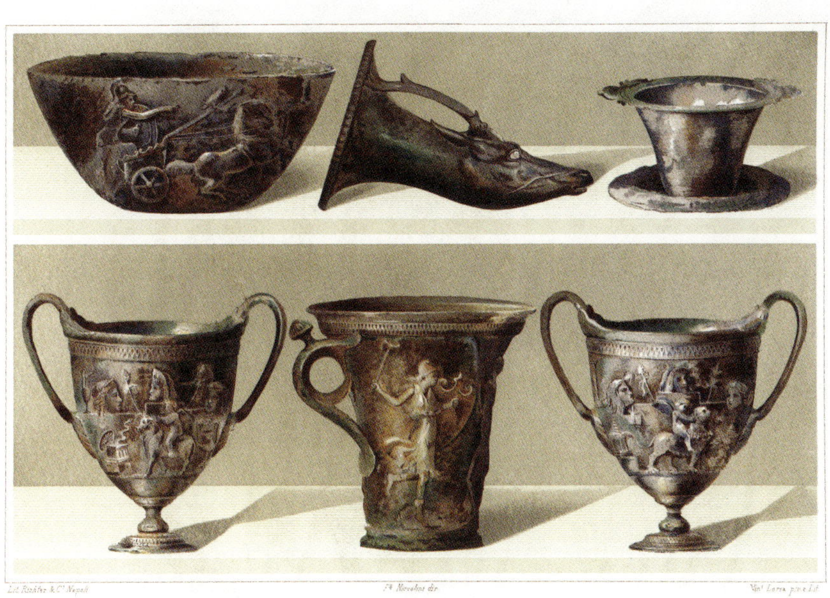

Plate 79 — *[V. Loria]*
Casa della Fontana piccola (VI 8, 23–24), tablinum (19), west wall – The sheet shows the 4th-style wall decoration trimmed on either side (see also pl. 51). The source used by Loria for his lithograph is unknown, but there are similar versions by Wilhelm Zahn and the architect Charles Garnier (1851).

Plate 72 — *[V. Loria]*
Various luxury vessels in bronze and silver – *A* Bowl from Herculaneum with two chariots driven by Athena and Ares. *B* Bronze drinking vessel in the shape of a stag's head *(rhyton)* from Herculaneum. *C* Silver sieve and saucer. *D* and *F* Two silver cups with handles *(kantharoi)* from a 64-part service from the Casa di Inaco e Io (VI 7, 19). Winged erotes ride on a bull (left) and a panther (right), with various objects associated with Dionysus behind. *E* Silver beaker with handle *(kalathos)* with a representation of the battle between Theseus and the Amazons.

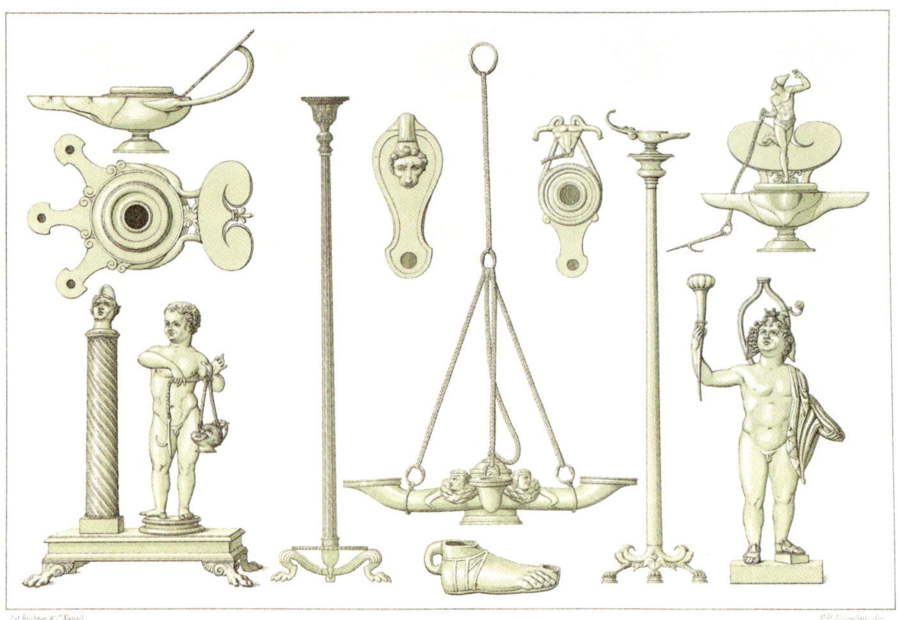

Plate 80 — *[Anonymous]*
Selection of different lamp-holders and stands together with bronze lamps.

Plate 83 — *[V. Mollame]*
Items of coloured glassware of varying origin, including from Cuma and other sites.

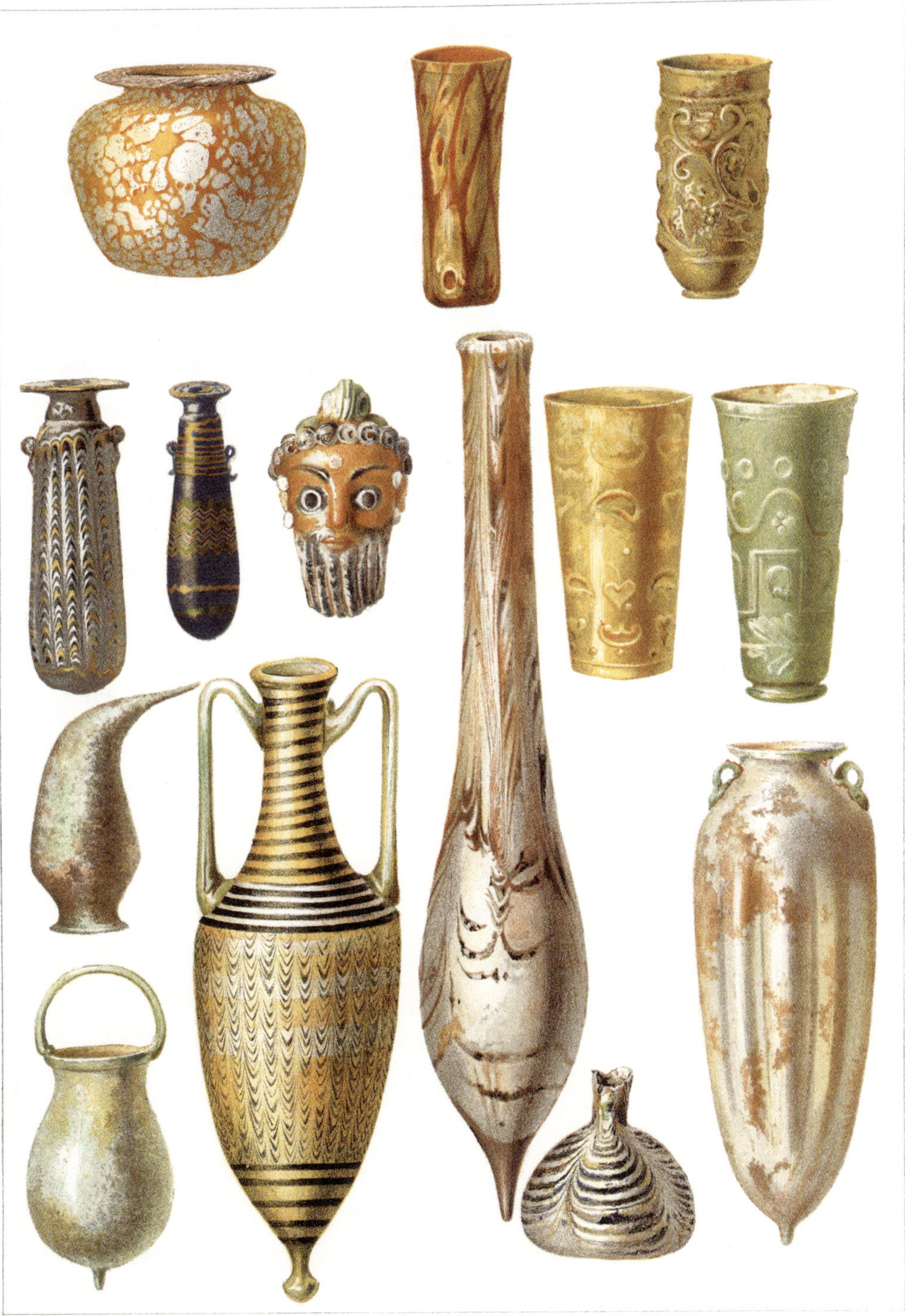

V.º Mollame dis. F.lli Niccolini dir. V.º Loria Lit.

Richter & C.º Napoli

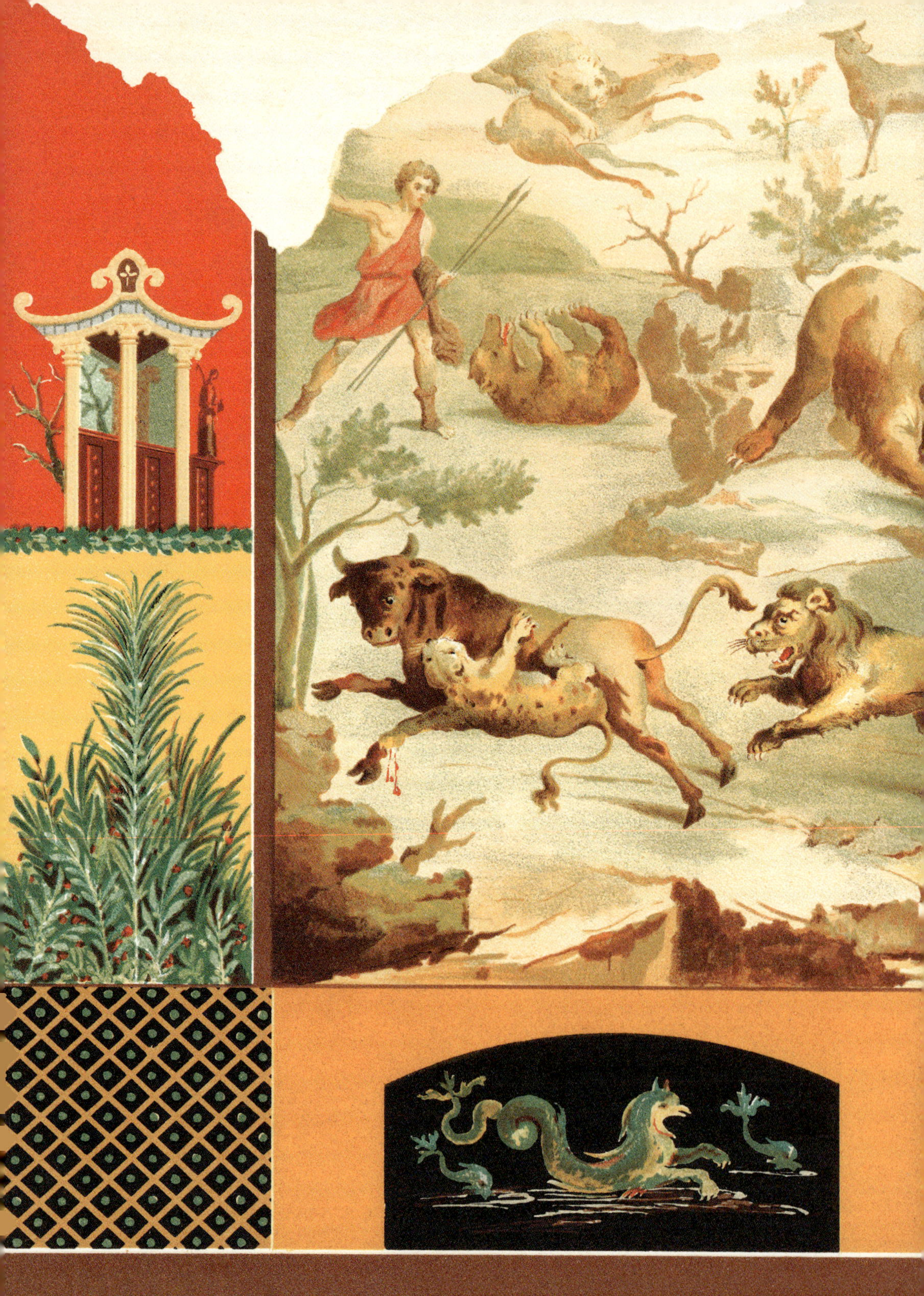

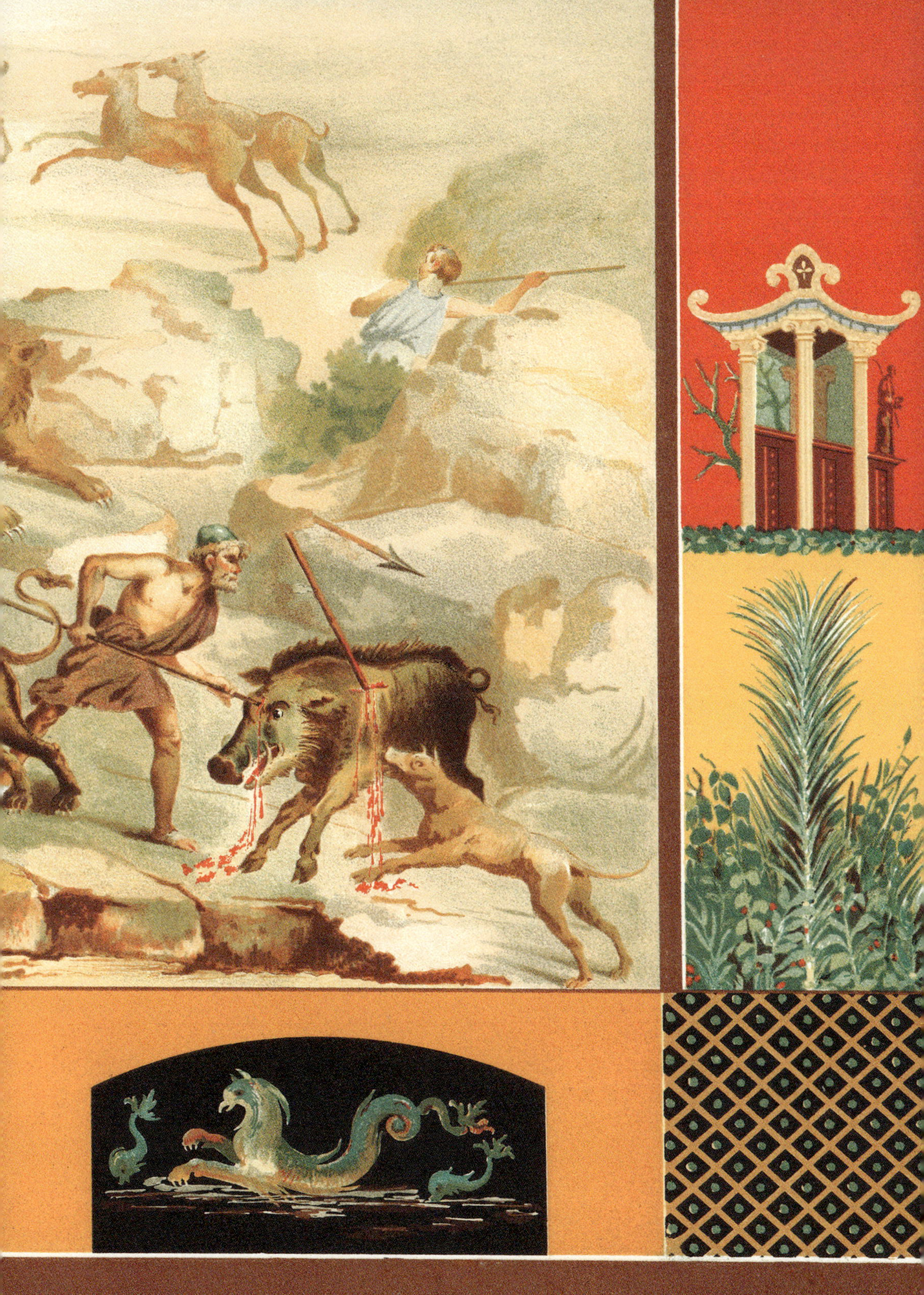

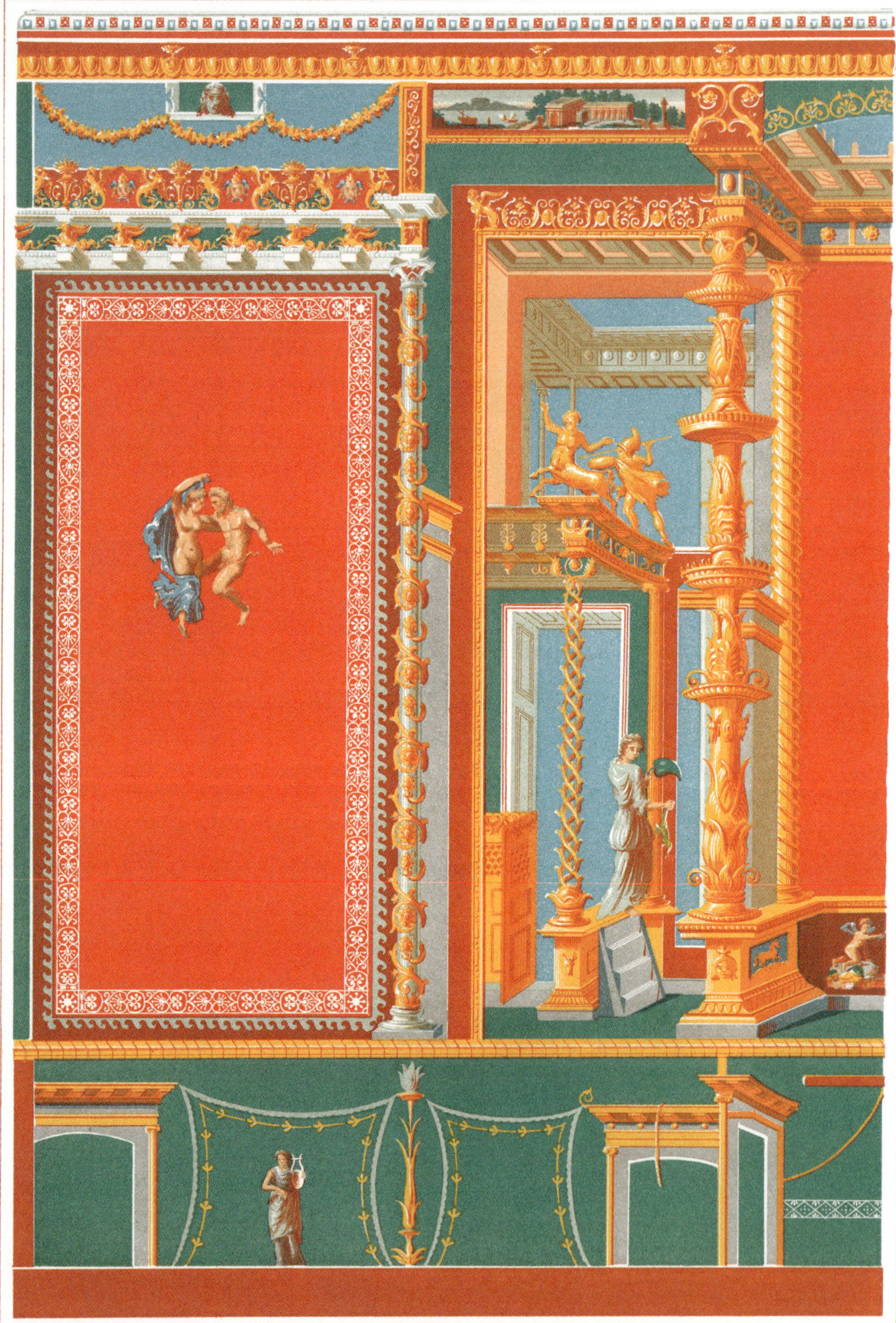

Vᵒ Loria dis. e Lit. Fˡˡⁱ Niccolini dir. Lit. Richter & Cᵒ Napoli

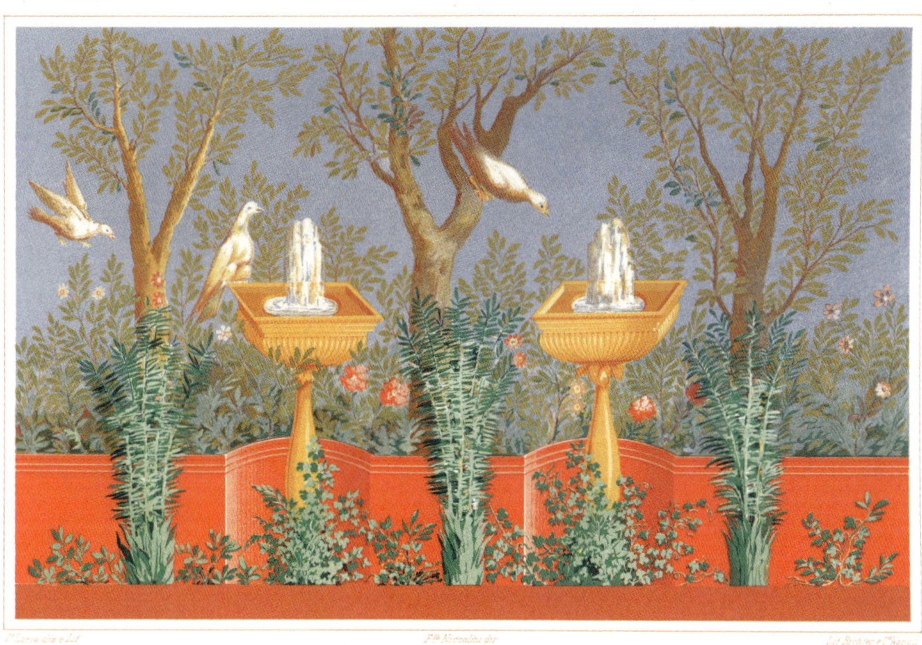

Pages 292–293

Plate 82 — *[V. Loria]*

Casa della Caccia antica (VII 4, 48), garden, south wall – In the central picture, animals are fighting in a rocky landscape; at the same time, people with lances are killing a young bear and a wild boar. The conspicuous scenery has led the picture to be interpreted as a scene from the amphitheatre.

⁂

Plate 85 — *[V. Loria]*

Casa di Adone ferito (VI 7, 18), oecus, east wall – Only half of the wall, uncovered in 1836, is shown.

⁂

Plate 88 — *[V. Loria]*

Picture of a garden from the peristyle of an unidentifiable house in Pompeii – Showing plants, basins and fountains in front of a fence, with trees behind it.

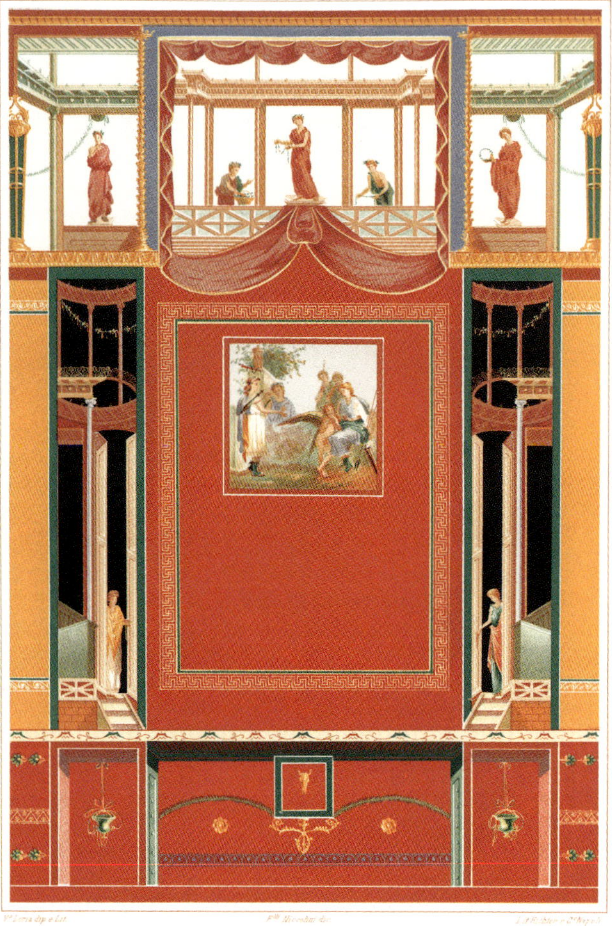

Plate 92 — *[V. Loria]*
Casa IX 5, 6 and 17, tablinum – Middle section of the east wall in the 4th style: the picture in the red central field shows Artemis banishing the pregnant Callisto from the circle of her virginal companions. In the upper zone, people who seem to be watching the scene.

Plate 89 — ***[V. Loria]***
Two black-and-white illustrations from the *Real Museo Borbonico* are here visualised in colour and combined in one sheet, with a recommendation "that decorators keep them in mind". It has so far only been possible to identify the originals to a partial extent.

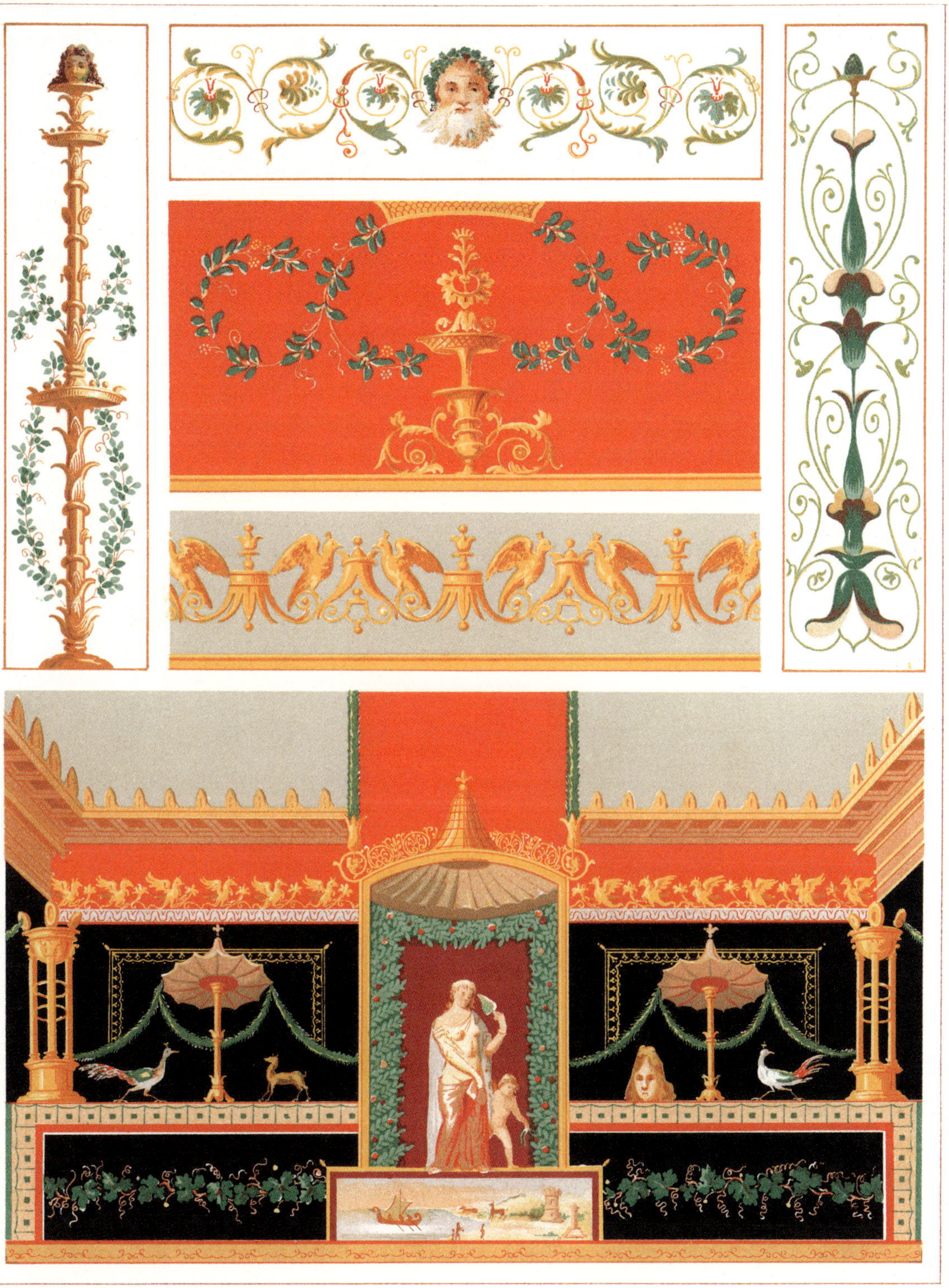

V.° Loria dis. e Lit. F.lli Niccolini dir. Lit. Richter e C.° Napoli

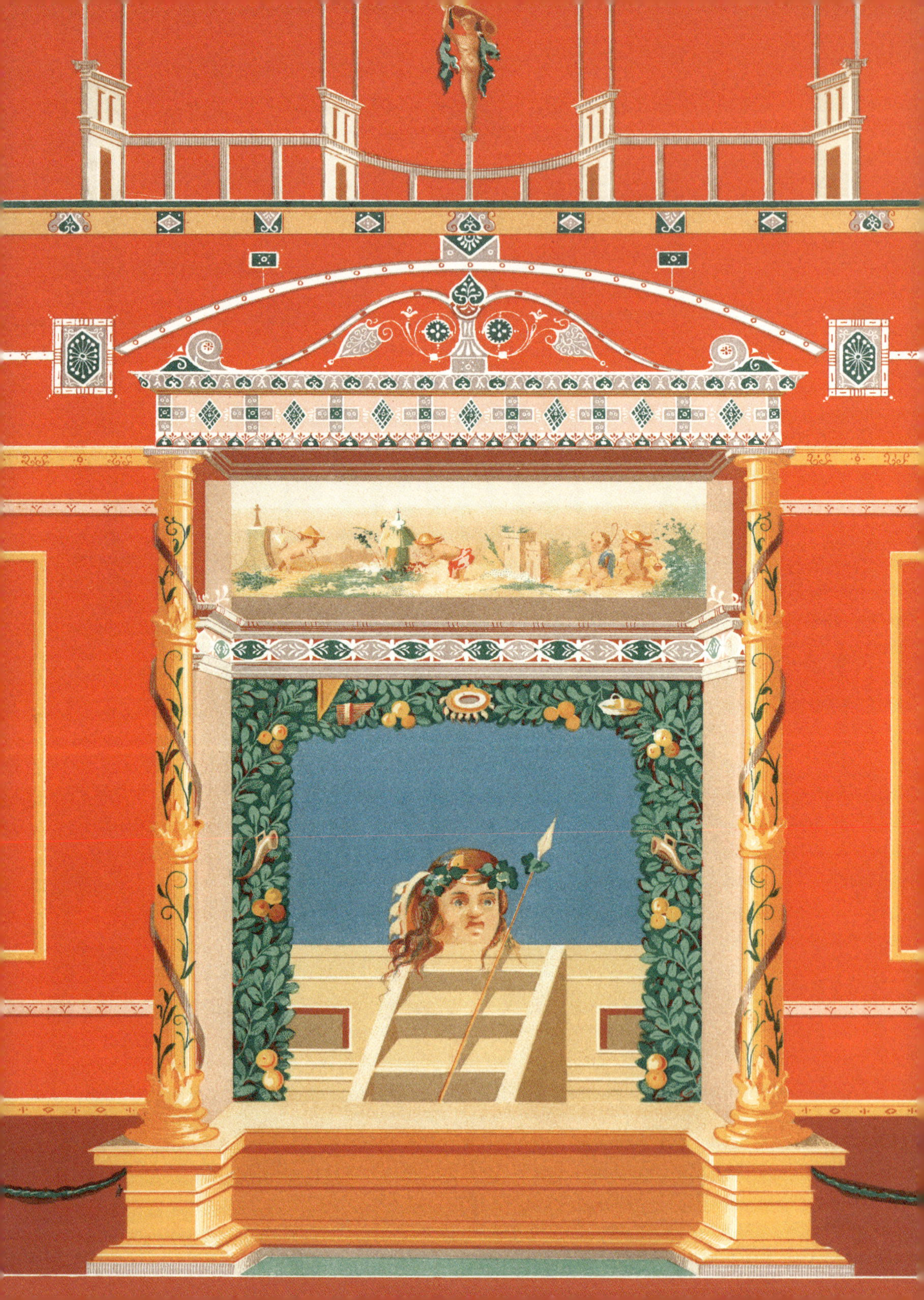

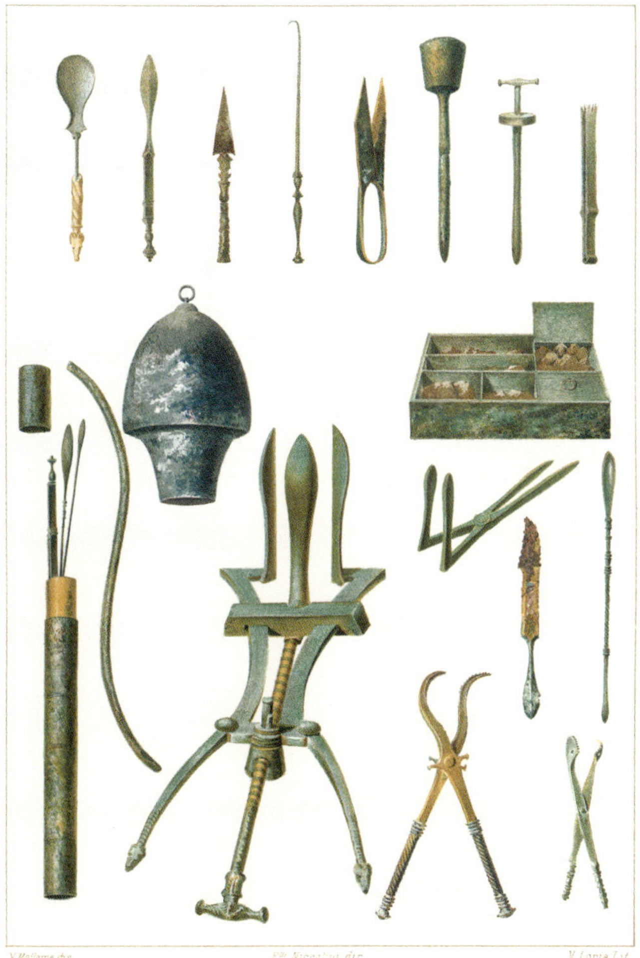

Plate 90 — *[V. Loria]*
The sheet confusingly combines different fragments of wall paintings from Herculaneum housed in the museum in Naples. Above: details from a 3rd-style decoration of very high quality. Below: *Casa dei Cervi* – Theatre mask lying on a *pulpitum* (stage) and framed by a garland. The "sopraporte" with pygmies in an Egyptian landscape goes back to an 18th-century engraving.

Plate 93 — *[V. Mollame]*
Medical equipment from the Vesuvian cities – Including a catheter, cupping glass, specula, various probes and forceps, as well as a small chest and a storage case for medical instruments.

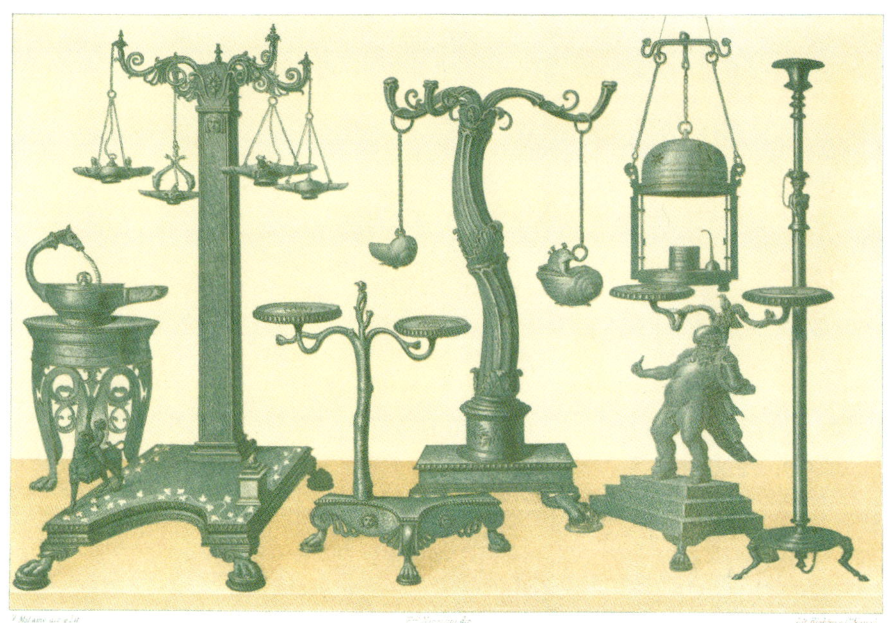

Plate 95 — *[V. Mollame]*
Various lamp-stands and bronze lamps – In part with silver inlay.
They show the quality of the manufacturing skills of the period.

Plate 94 — *[V. Loria]*
Casa del Centenario (IX 8, 3 and 7) – Bronze statuette of a satyr, who is pouring wine from a wineskin into a (lost) beaker (for the house, see also vol. III).

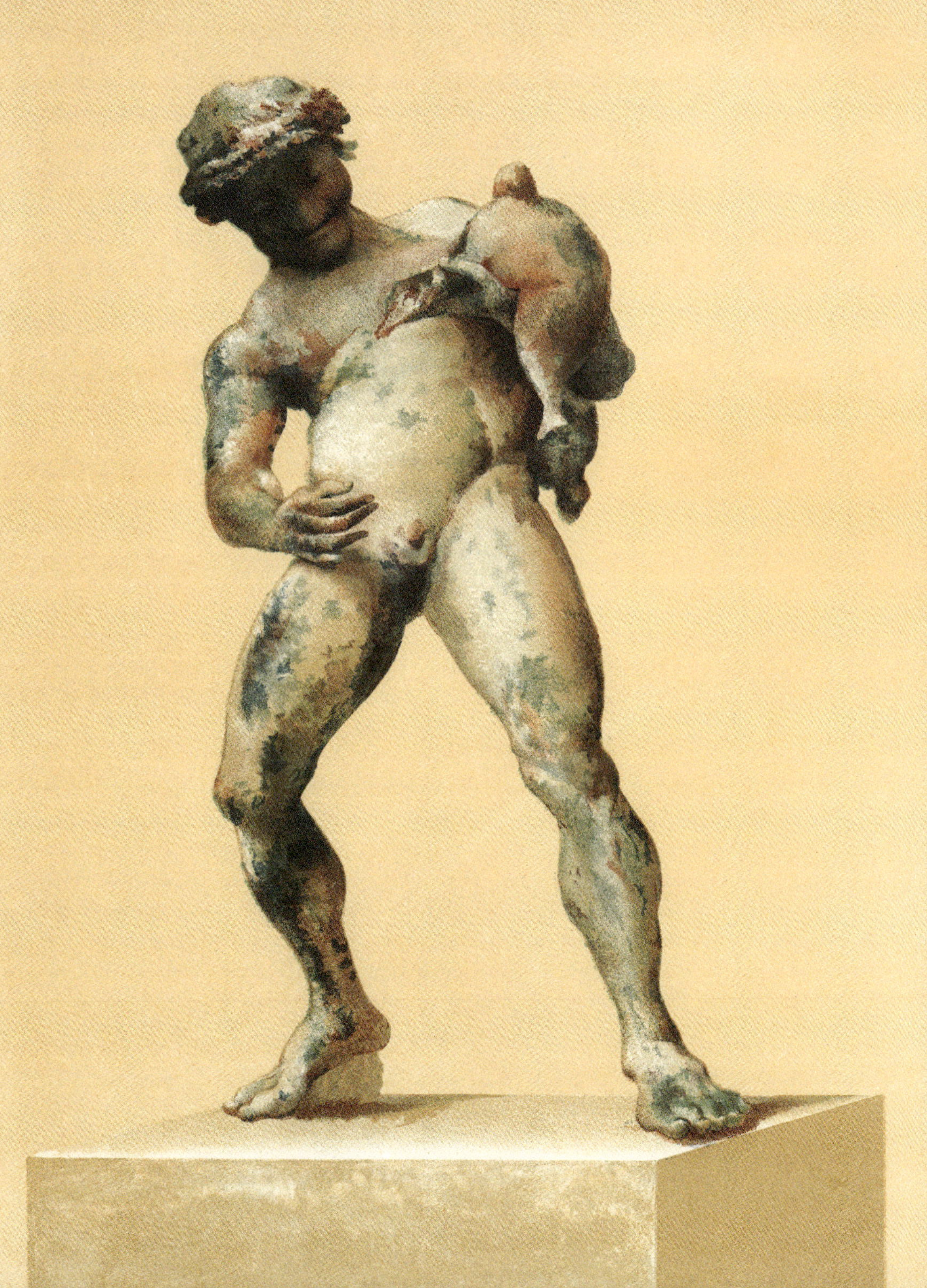

ANFITEATRO

Amphitheatre

After the eruption of Vesuvius destroyed and buried the city, the amphitheatre still remained visible as a depression in the landscape. Although excavation work began in the 18th century, it was only after 1813, under French rule, that large areas of the amphitheatre were uncovered and as far down as the floor of the arena. Frescos of gladiatorial combats, painted on the wall separating the ring from the rows of seating, were uncovered at this time – only to be rapidly destroyed by weathering. The amphitheatre is one of the major building projects financed by the Roman "colonists" after 80 BC and which profoundly changed the city's appearance. The Pompeii amphitheatre is the oldest surviving example of this type of construction. Its early date is reflected, for example, in the simple arrangement of its entrances and inner connecting passageways as compared with complexes from the imperial era, and also in its name, which is recorded in an inscription as *spectacula* rather than "amphitheatre", the Greek loanword that later became standard. Residential buildings had to be demolished to make way for the amphitheatre's construction, and its siting at one corner of the city wall and near two of the city gates allowed visitors from out of town to attend performances without having to cross the city (cf. vol. IV, Supplemento, pl. 32; IV, Saggi di Restauro, pl. 17).

❋

Plate 2 — *[C. Weidenmüller]*
Views of the amphitheatre – Above: view from the west. Below: view of the interior looking north (drawings after photographs?).

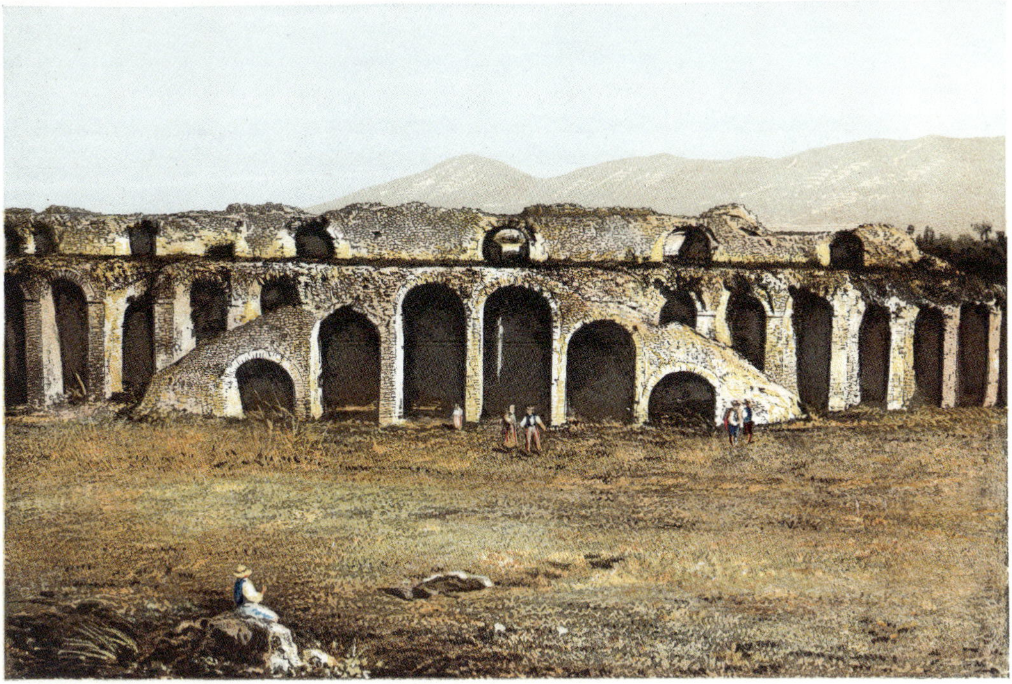

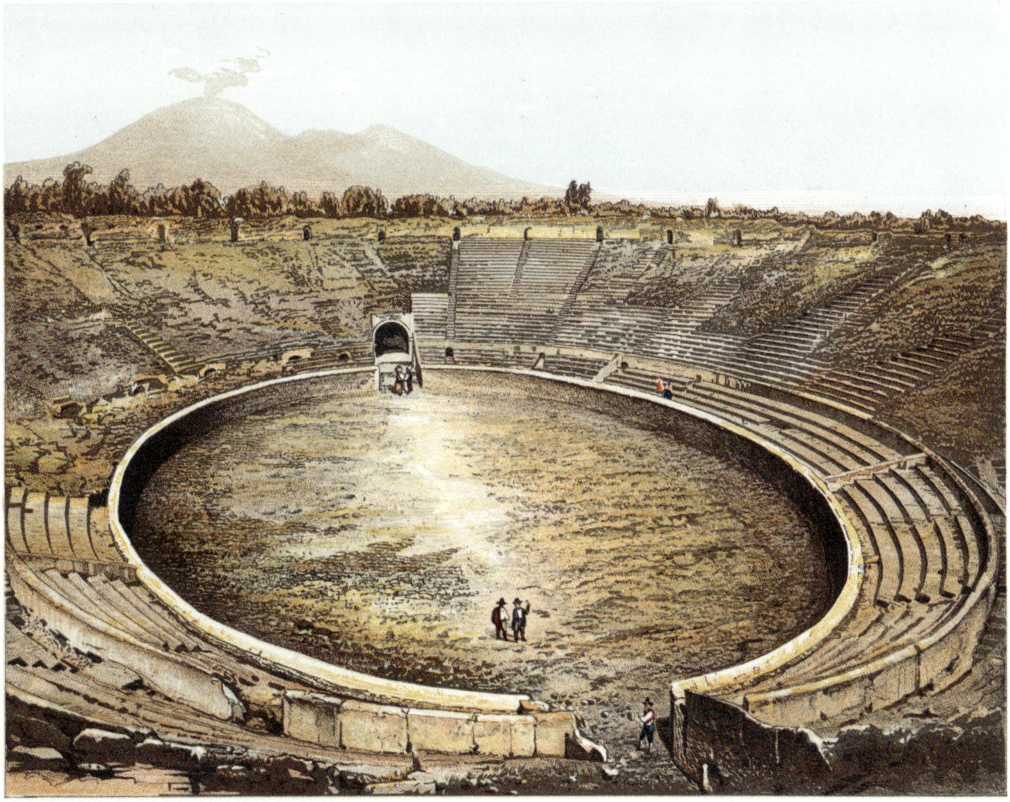

Lit. Richter a. Ci in Napoli Flli Niccolini dir. Weidenmüller. Lit.

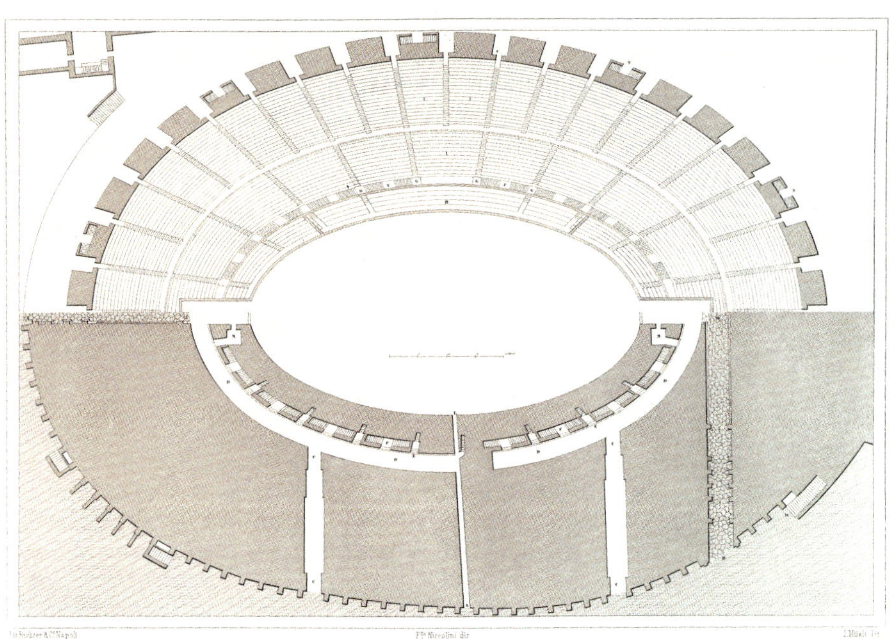

Plate 1 — *[I. Müsli]*
Plan of the amphitheatre in two levels – The lower part shows the entrances in the western part of the building, the upper part the tiers and (completed) rows of seating as well as a tower on the adjacent city wall.

❖

Plate 3 — *[V. Mollame]*
Arena wall – Details from the frescos decorating the arena wall, showing scenes of gladiatorial games. Above: trumpeter *(tibicen)*. Middle: animal baiting *(venatio)*. The paintings were destroyed by bad weather shortly after being excavated and were documented only in watercolours executed by Francesco Morelli in 1815.

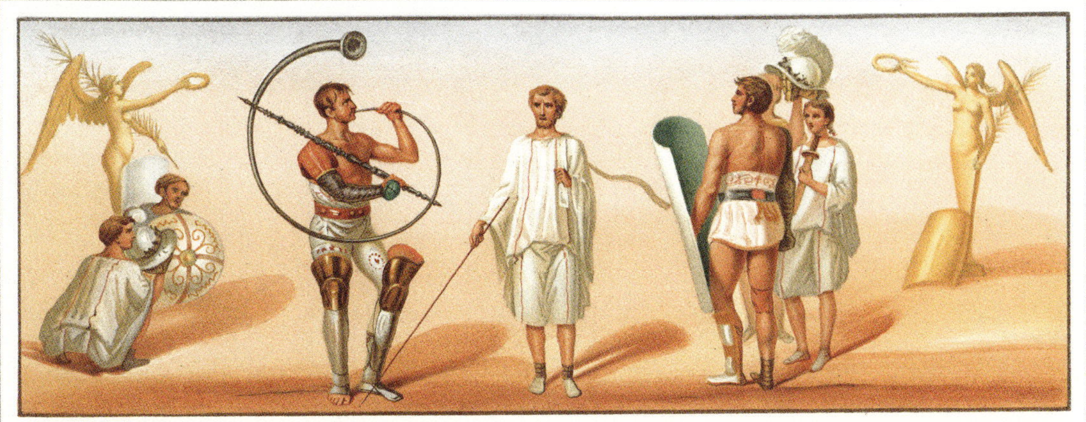

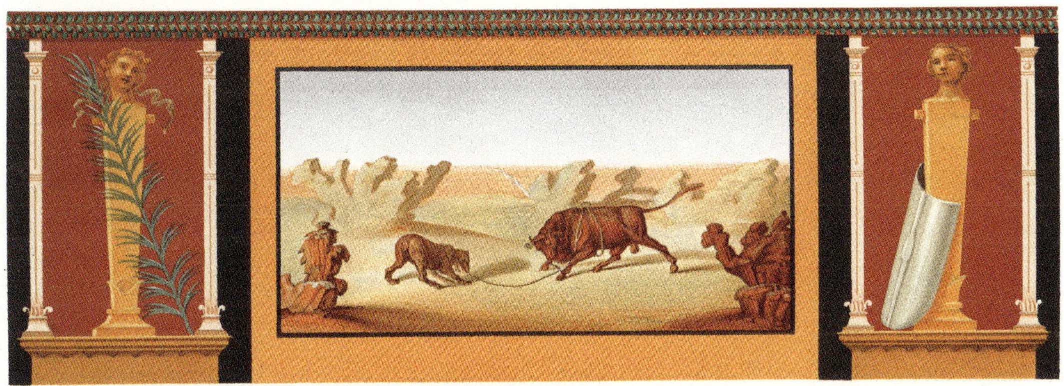

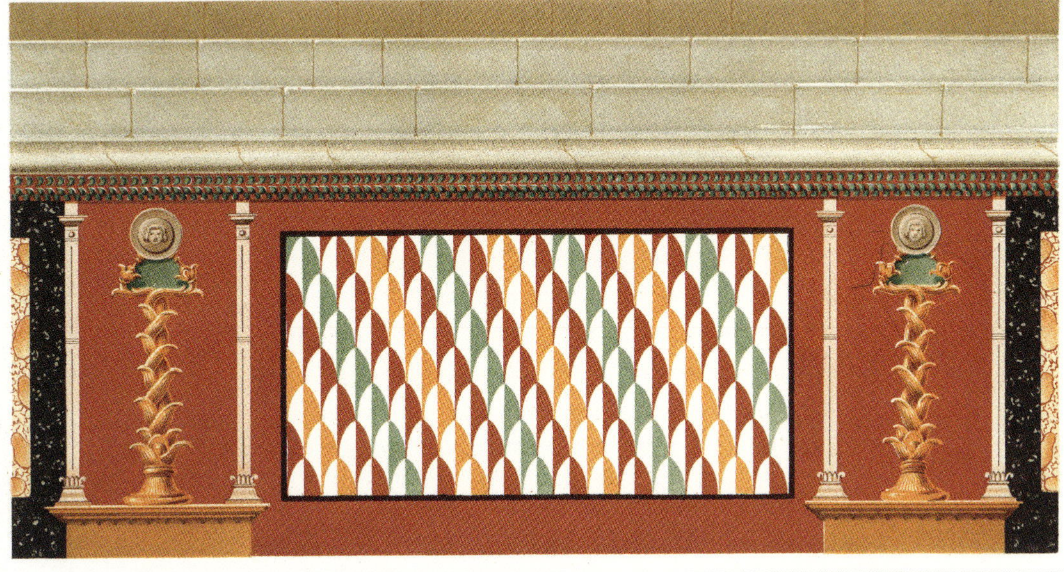

V. Mollame dis. e dip.　　　F.lli Niccolini dir.　　　C. Weidenmüller lit.

Lit. Richter & C. Napoli.

TERME PRESSO L'ARCO DELLA FORTUNA

Forum Baths

(also Terme del Foro)

In 1824, excavation of the last public building on the outside of the Forum revealed the first complex of baths to be discovered in Pompeii. Since the vaulted ceilings of the heated rooms had largely withstood the pressure of the debris on top, the baths had survived in better condition than usual. The baths "at the Arch of Fortuna", as they were initially called, were constructed soon after 80 BC and occupied an entire insula, whose previous use is unknown. The baths are bordered on three sides by two-storey tabernae. They were intended to supplement the capacities of the much older Stabian Baths (see vol. I), whose layout and heating system they adopted as their model. A men's area and a somewhat more modest women's area feature the usual sequence of a changing room followed by cold, warm and hot baths; the men also had access to a small palaestra. The position of the heating section between the two areas also copies the set up in the Stabian Baths exactly. The walls and ceilings of the Forum Baths were likewise redecorated with figural stucco reliefs shortly before the city was destroyed. Older furnishings, however, such as the bronze benches and a brazier donated by a certain Vaccula, remained in use. The discovery of the Forum Baths (VII 5, 24) was reported with unusual speed in the *Real Museo Borbonico*, which carried a description of them in 1825. Soon afterwards, the Russian architect Alexander Briullov, a brother of the more famous painter, published a small monograph on them. In 1828 Wilhelm Zahn devoted a full five plates to the Forum Baths in his first book on Pompeii. Only later did Antonio Niccolini the Younger take up the original plates and reprint them along with Guglielmo Bechi's text of 1825 in its entirety – admittedly without mentioning its author. The Forum Baths also made an appearance in 1853 when they were used by Théodore Chassériau as the setting for his well-known painting, *The Tepidarium* (see Schütze essay).

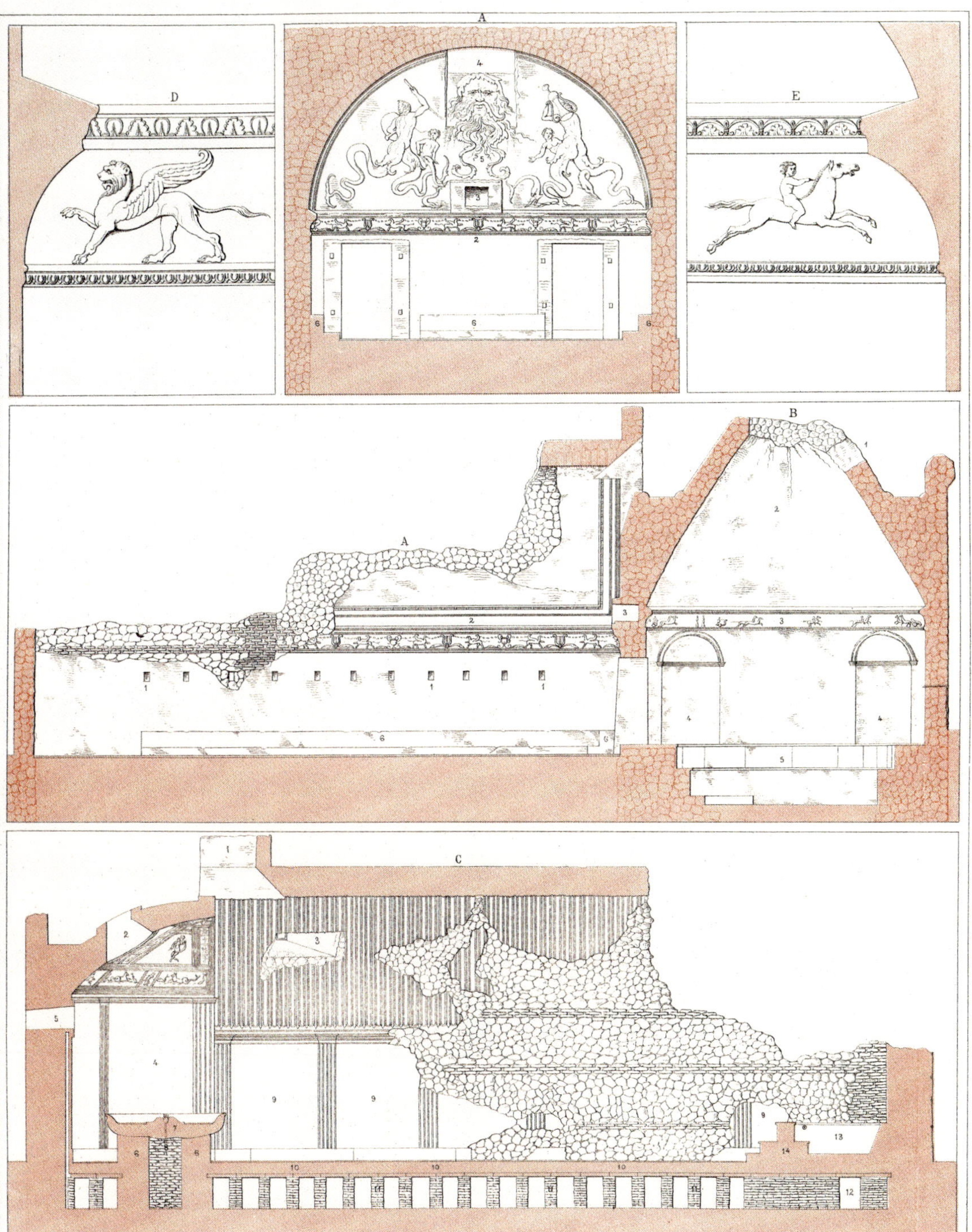

Lit. Richter & C. Napoli

F.lli Niccolini dir.

V.zo Canfora inc.

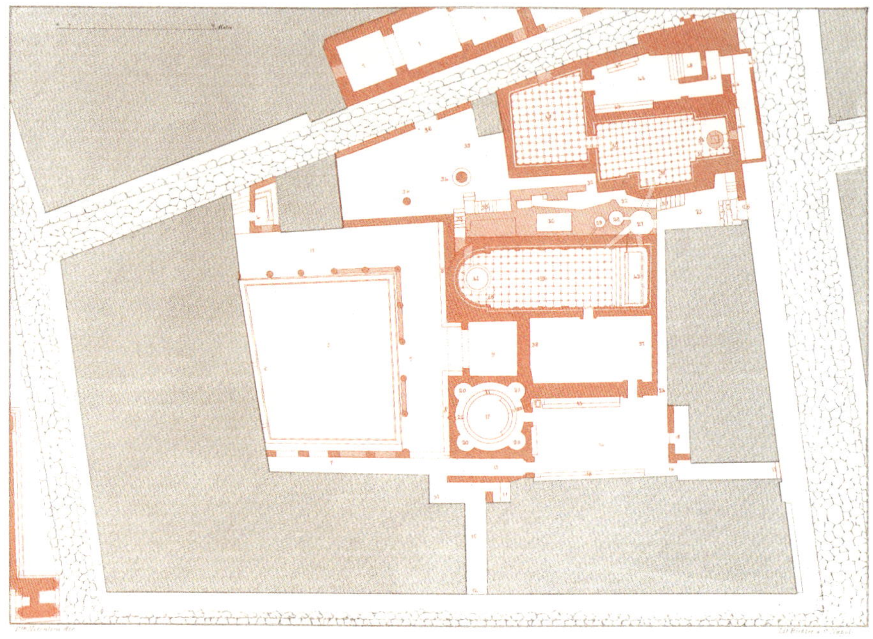

Page 307

Plate 2 — *[V. Canfora]*

Three cross sections through the rooms in the men's baths – Above: southern end-wall of the changing room (apodyterium) with a stucco relief showing Oceanus. Middle: tepidarium (A) and circular frigidarium (B). Below: caldarium with cold-water basin (7), underfloor heating (hypocausts, 10) and hot-water pool (13).

⁂

Plate 1 — *[Anonymous]*

Plan of the entire Insula VII 5 – The baths with the men's and women's areas and the heating section are marked in red, along with the neighbouring cistern. The plan also shows the heating systems within the rooms. The tabernae, here left grey, faced on to the adjoining streets and were leased in order to help finance the baths.

⁂

Plate 3 — *[R. Estevan]*

Details of the interior décor in the tepidarium – Above: two atlantes and a donation by Marcus Nigidius Vaccula (bronze bench and brazier with his cow signet; see also Stabian Baths, vol. I). Below: compilation of stucco decoration from the tepidarium; in the large areas, Eros with his bow and Apollo riding a griffin.

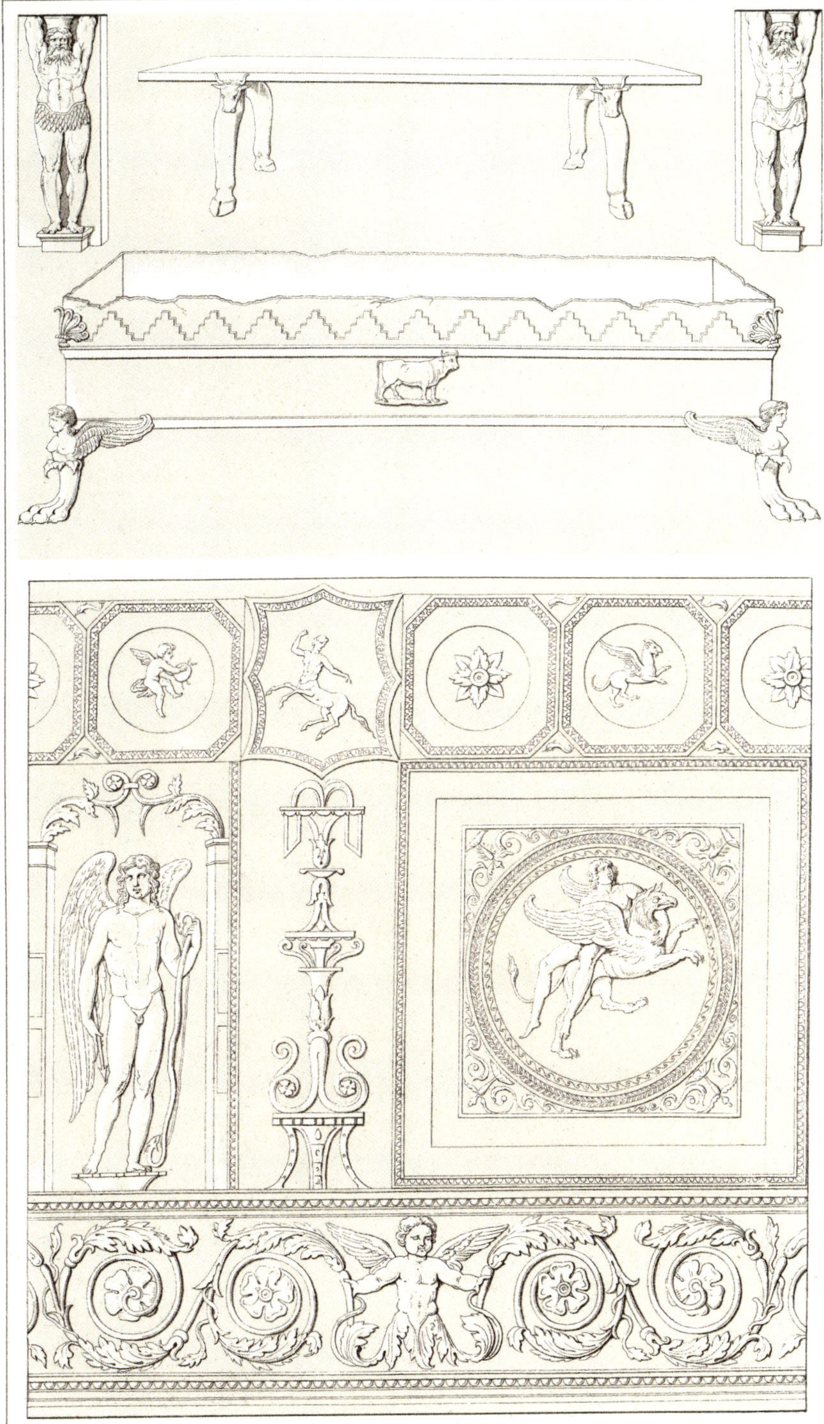

R. Estevan inc. Fth Niccolini dir. Lit. Richter & C.o Napoli

TEMPIO NEL FORO TRIANGOLARE

Doric Temple on the Triangular Forum

Pompeii's temples, at least with regard to their innermost core, rank among the city's oldest buildings. This applies both to the ancient Temple of Apollo beside the Forum and to the Doric Temple on the Foro triangolare (Triangular Forum), a lava spur slightly outside the city centre. The remains of the temple on this exposed site were first discovered in the 18th century, but it was apparent to the excavators even then that the temple had already been largely destroyed before it had been buried. Scholarly study of the Doric Temple has been seriously compromised by neglect, poor excavation work and finally by damage sustained during the Second World War. Both the plate and the text in our volume are unusual, in so far as the first shows the only cross section from the archaeological excavations while the second deals in great detail with the state of discussion concerning the site around 1891. The recent publication of the first comprehensive monograph on the Doric Temple has by no means ended the debate over its appearance, dating, name and function.

The Doric Temple takes its name from the Greek architectural order and had an arrangement of 11 x 6 or 11 x 7 Doric columns. Having undergone two distinct construction phases in the 6th century BC, its appearance was substantially modernised and modified in the 3rd century BC. It was certainly dedicated to Athena and perhaps additionally to Hercules. To what extent the temple is indebted to Greek or Etruscan influence, and in what ways its function changed after the 3rd century BC, when it was integrated into a new complex with the theatre, Foro triangolare and other buildings, are key questions that remain disputed. The entire zone may perhaps have served as a centre for the paramilitary training of Pompeii's young men.

❋

Plate 1 — *[A. Magliano]*
Plan of the Doric Temple on the Foro triangolare – The surviving parts of the step-based temple are marked in blue. The Hellenistic construction phase is shown in red and the original complex in white (with some parts completed by the artist).

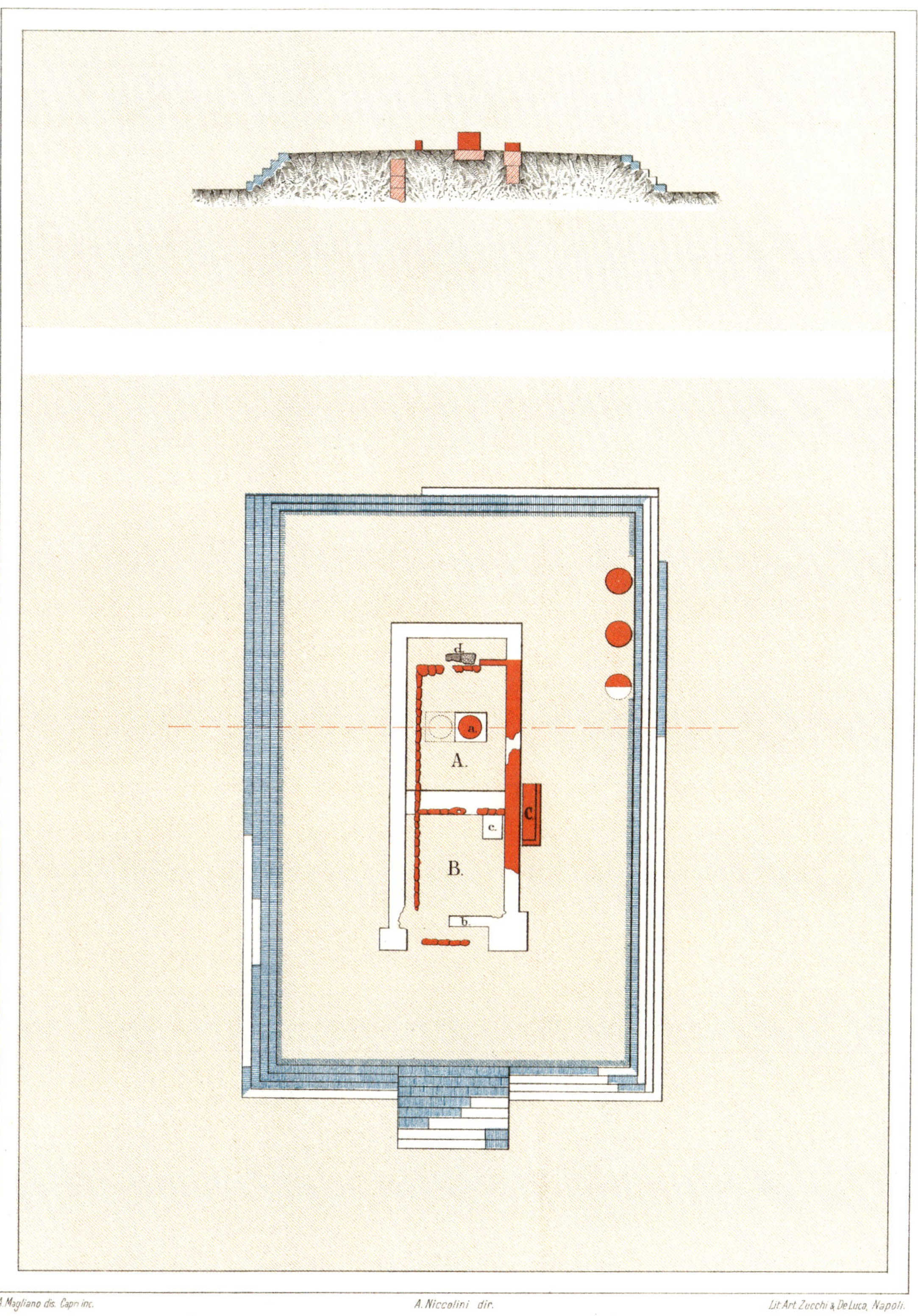
d.
a.
A.
C
c.
B.
b.
A. Magliano dis. Capri inc.
A. Niccolini dir.
Lit. Art. Zucchi & De Luca, Napoli.

CASA DI L. CAECILIUS IUCUNDUS E CASA DEL CENTENARIO

House of L. Caecilius Iucundus and House of the Centenary

These two houses, excavated in 1875 and 1879/80 respectively, are afforded a brief description in the manner of the chapters in volume I. Although only of medium size, the house belonging to the banker Caecilius Iucundus (V 1, 26; for his financial records, see vol. II, Descrizione generale, pl. 60) was painted and furnished with care just before the city was buried, as can be seen in the details of the outstanding decoration in the late 3rd style from the tablinum (pl. 2). Along with the ground plan, plate 1 shows one of the two herms with a bronze bust of the banker, which since its discovery has become a famous example of realistic portrait sculpture. The much larger House of the Centenary (IX 8, 3 and 7) derives its name from the fact that it was excavated exactly 1,800 years after the eruption in AD 79. It is one of the rare large residences in Pompeii that boasts a double atrium, an extended peristyle and private baths. Plates 3 and 4 attest to the excellent quality of its 4th-style wall decoration. Among the finds in both houses were important visual sources for the last years of Pompeii. Along the top of a panel, decorated with the artistically unremarkable reliefs of the marble cladding in the shrine to the household gods (lararium) in the banker's atrium, there is a representation of the north side of the Forum with the Capitolium during the earthquake of AD 62, depicted here in a manner unique in antiquity (pl. 1). An equally unique image was found in one of the subsidiary areas of the Casa del Centenario, again as part of a lararium (pl. 2): above a representation of a snake in front of an altar (a common motif in these household shrines) rises a steep-sided rocky mountain whose slopes are planted with vines. Beside it stands the god of wine, Dionysus/Bacchus. This representation is popularly interpreted as an image of the "peaceful" Vesuvius before the eruption. Overall, however, the few illustrations assembled in these plates fail to do justice to the importance of these two houses.

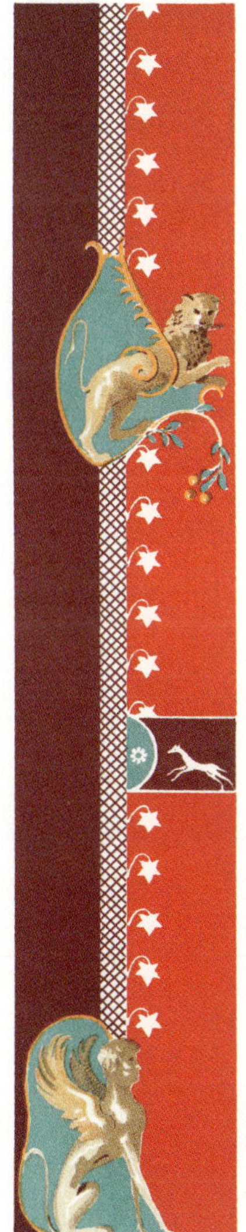

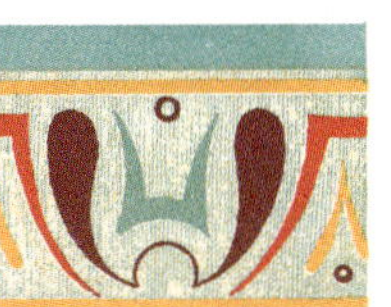
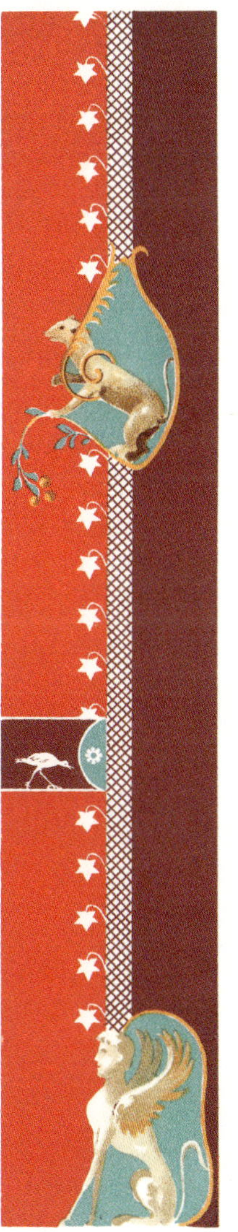

V. Loria dis. e Lit. F.lli Niccolini dir. Lit. Richter & C.o Napoli.

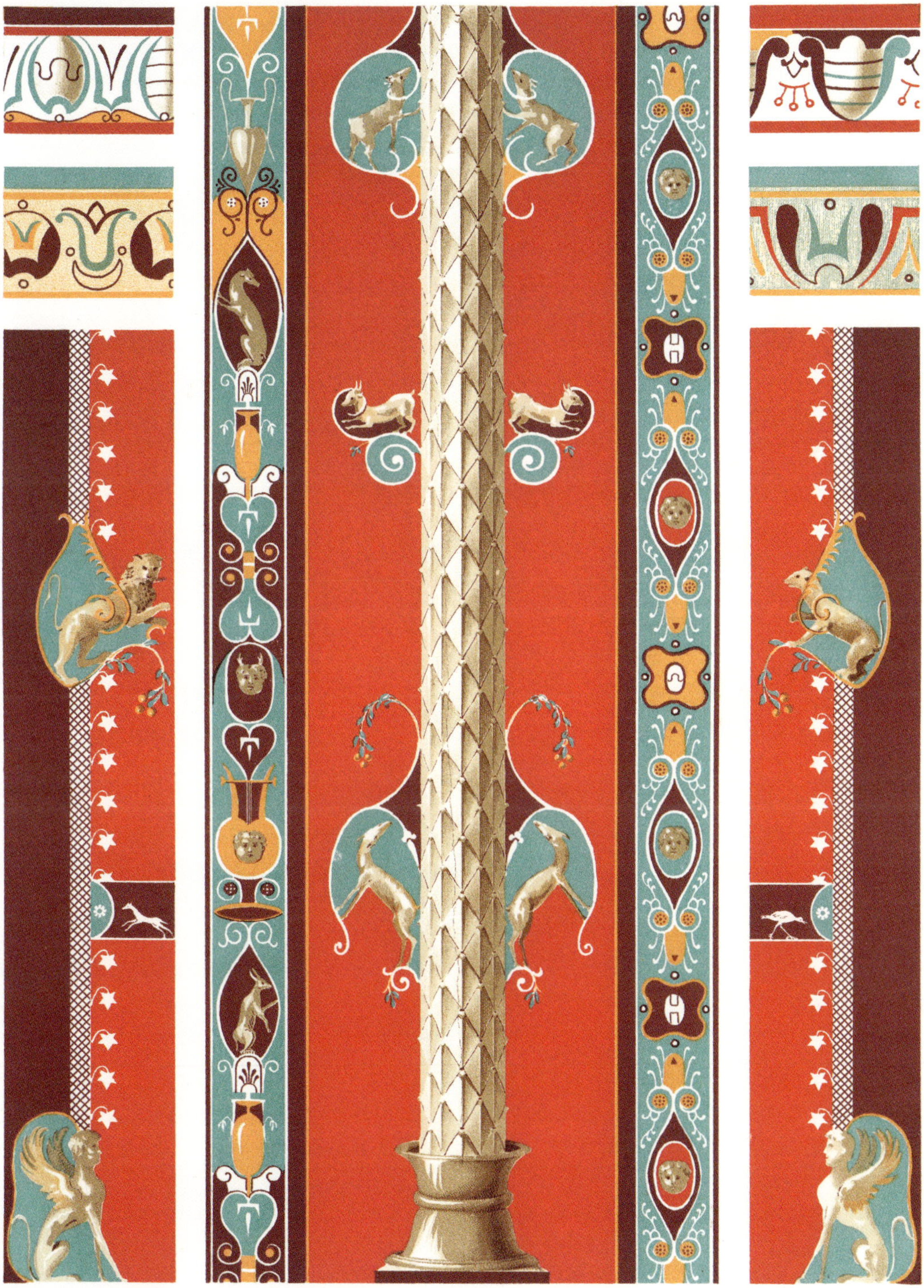

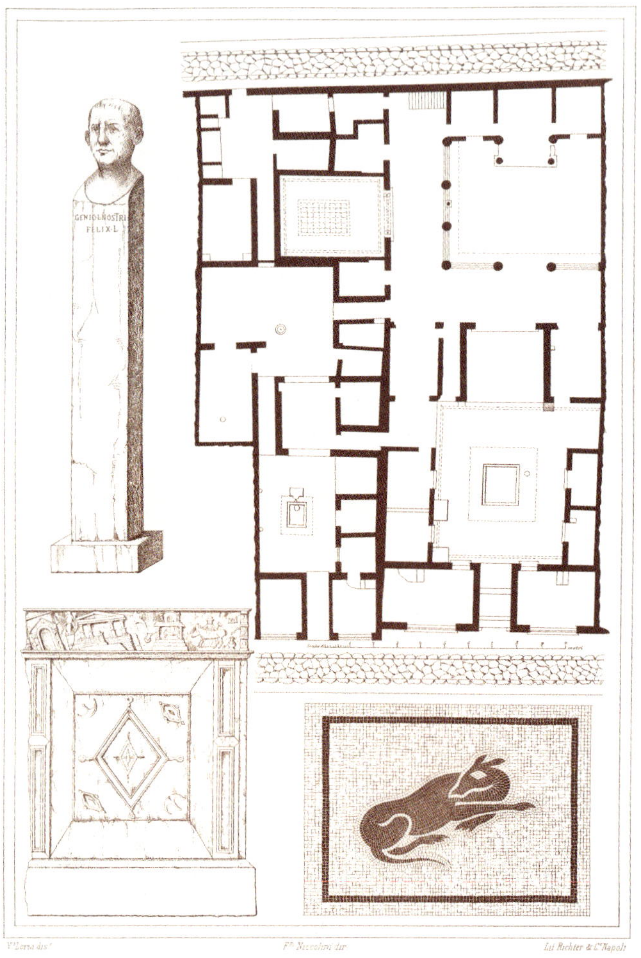

Page 313

Plate 2 — *[V. Loria]*

Tablinum – Various details from the outstanding architectural painting in the late 3rd style.

✠

Plate 1 — *[V. Loria]*

Above right: ground plan of the house showing the main area.
Above left: herm with the bust of the banker Caecilius Iucundus. Below left: lararium in the north-west corner of the atrium, with a relief depicting the earthquake of AD 62.
Below right: mosaic of a sleeping dog in the main entrance.

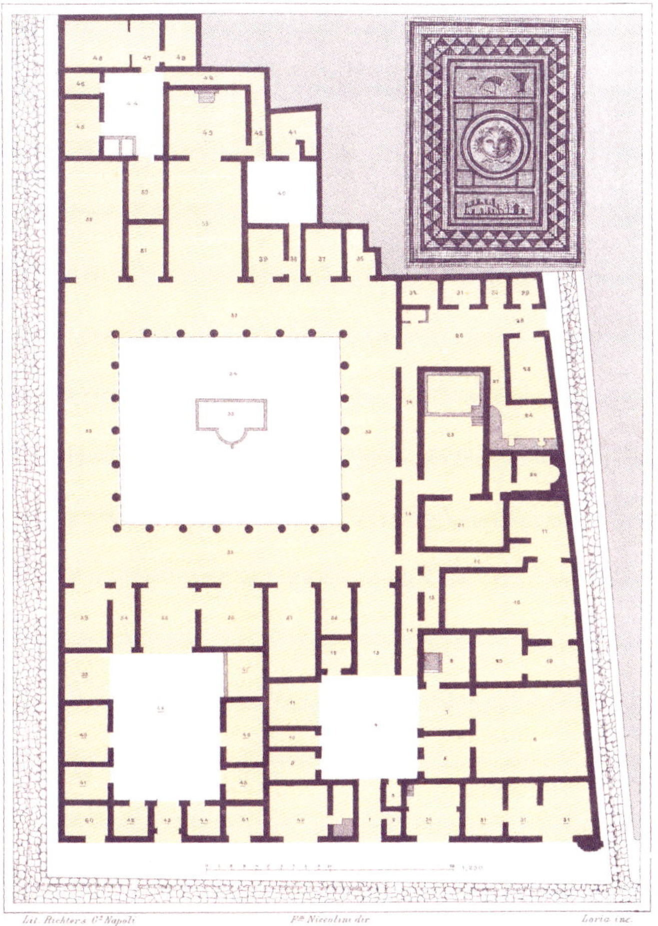

Plate 1 — *[V. Loria]*

Ground plan of the house – The house comprised two atria, a large peristyle and a sumptuous fountain complex. The mosaic with the Gorgoneion was found in room (58) and subsequently removed and taken to the museum.

✖

Pages 316–317

Plate 3 — *[V. Loria]*

Triclinium (56), west wall – An unusually elegant mural decoration from the period of the 4th style. Delicate, playful garlands of leaves are arranged against the white background of the wall. The room presented a deliberate contrast to the neighbouring "black salon" (53) (vol. IV, Supplemento, pl. 29).

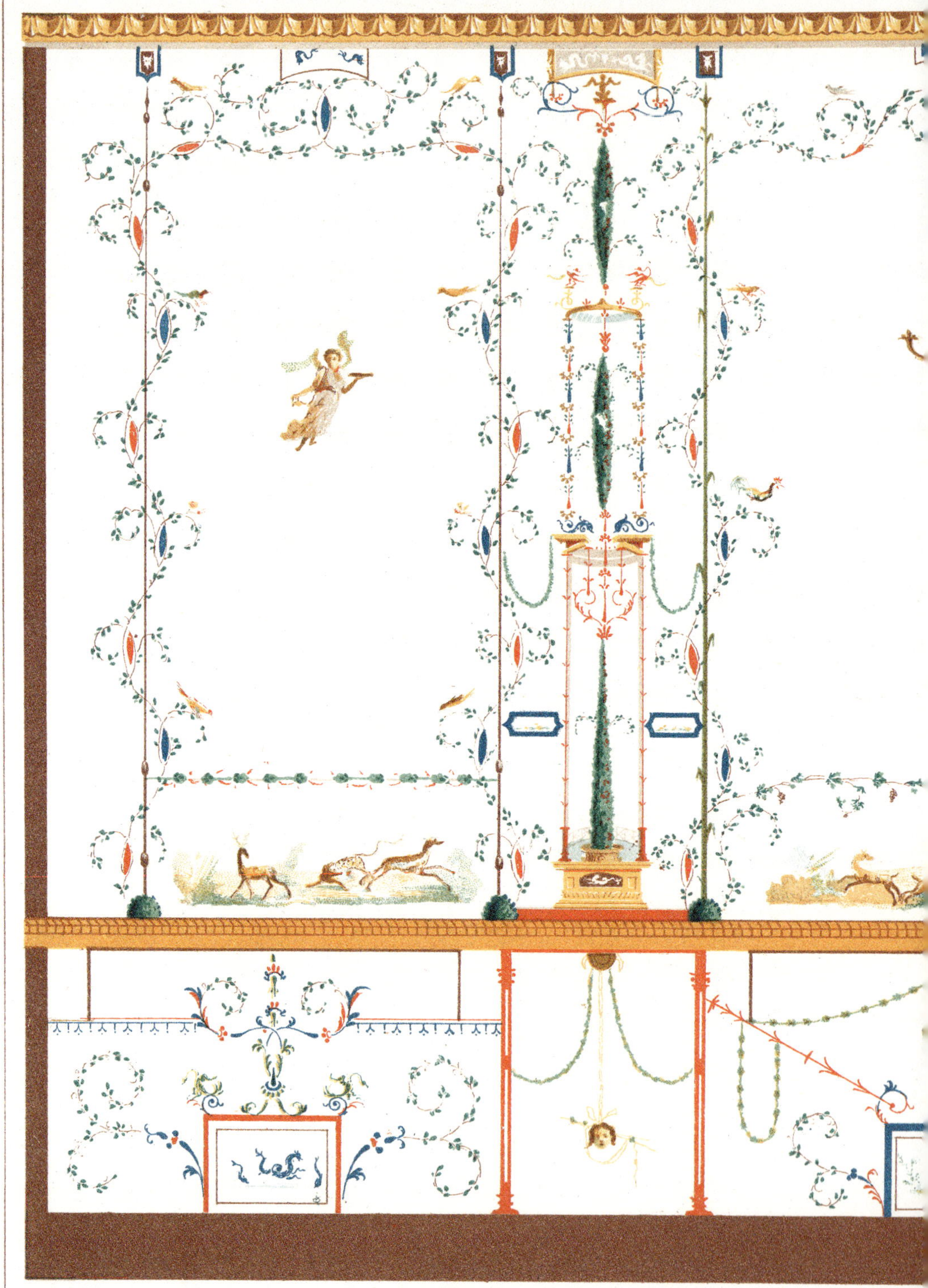

V. Loria dis. e lit. F.lli M

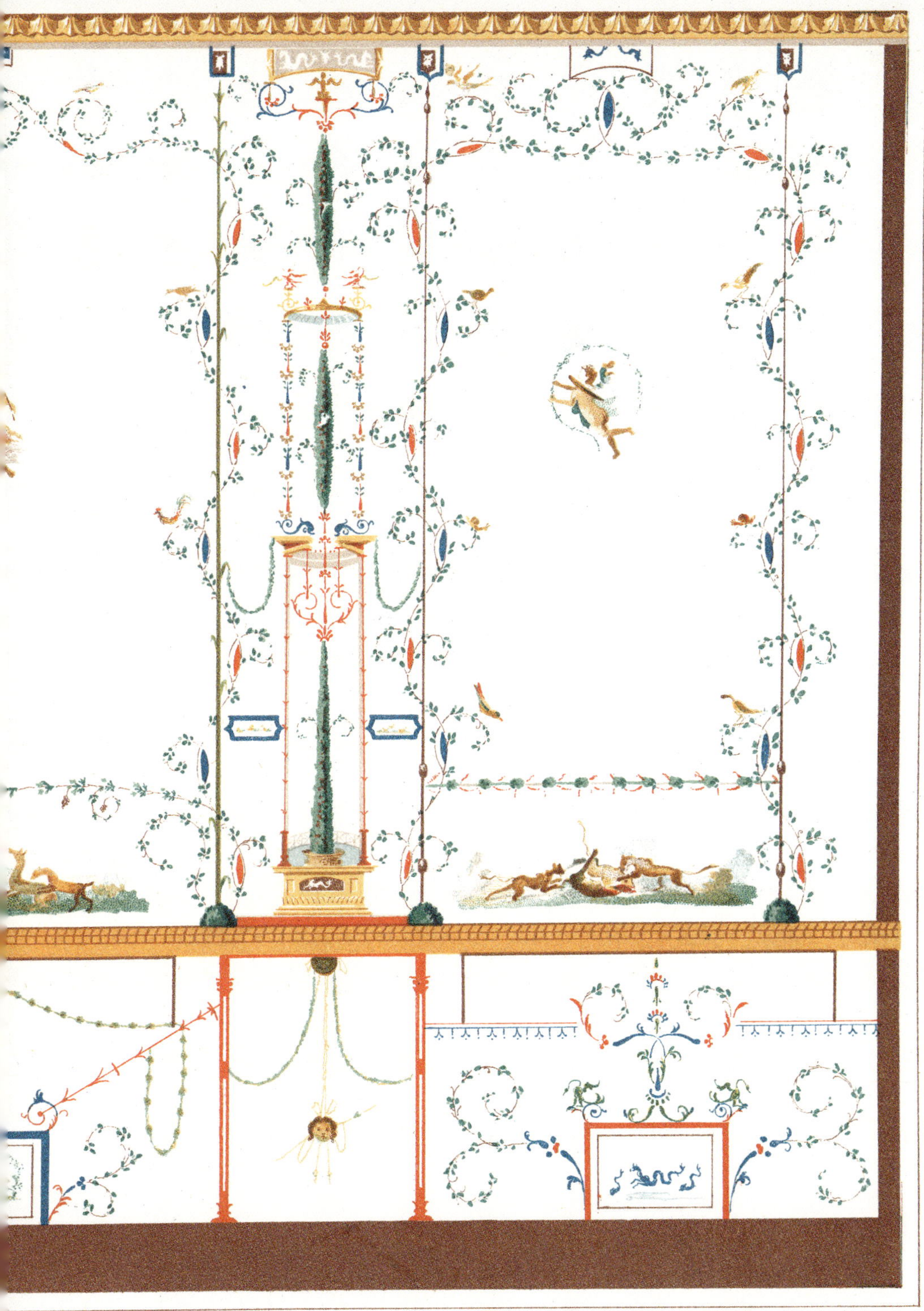

dir.

Lit. Richter & C. Napoli

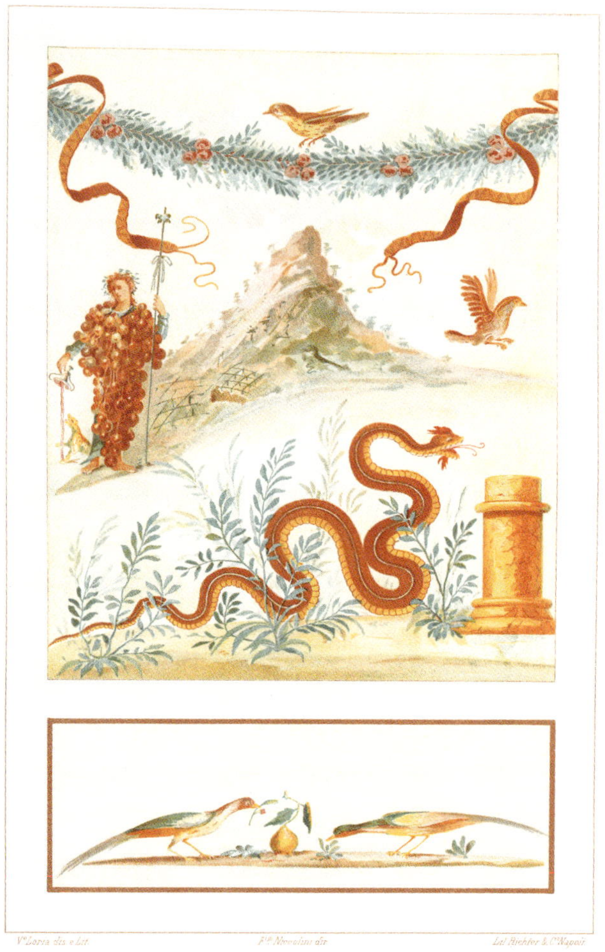

Plate 2 — *[V. Loria]*

Domestic service wing, so-called atrium (26), east wall – The famous painting comes from an unusually large lararium decorated with painted garlands. Dionysus, accompanied by a panther and wearing a robe made out of grapes, stands in front of a rocky, wooded mountain. In the lower section, a snake – part of the household cult – approaches an altar. Although we may be tempted to interpret the mountain as Vesuvius, this cannot be proven.

✲

Plate 4 — *[V. Loria]*

Two details from a frieze with pygmies from room (56) – The small figures are shown in caricatured fashion, standing on stilts and an upturned basket as they struggle to pick the grapes growing on vines high overhead.

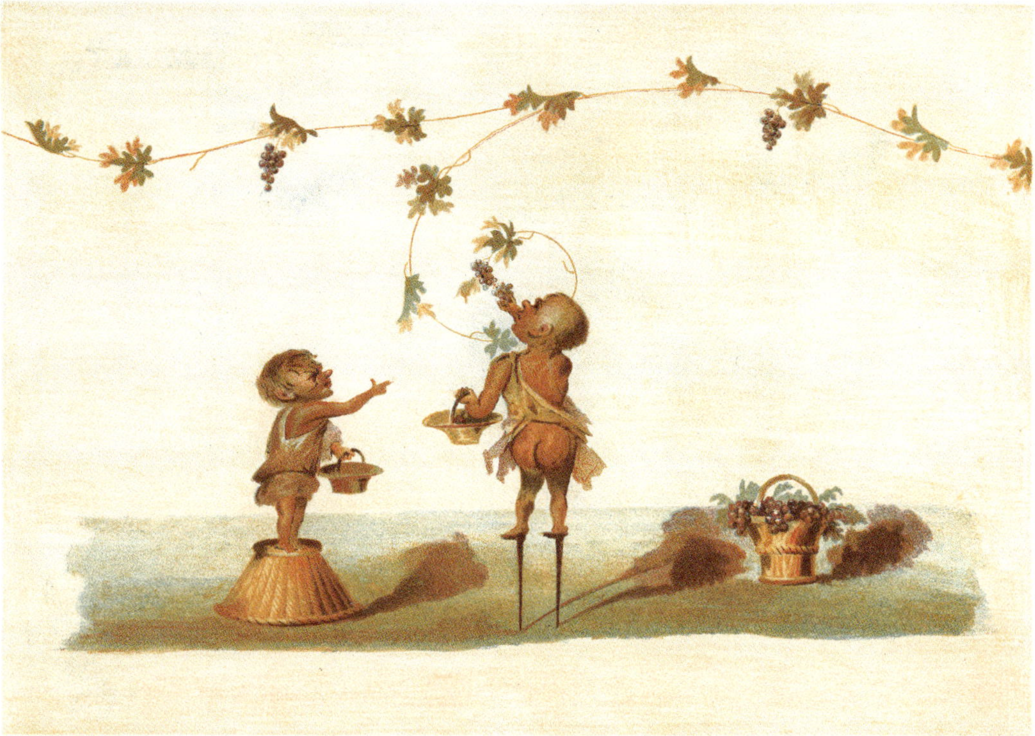

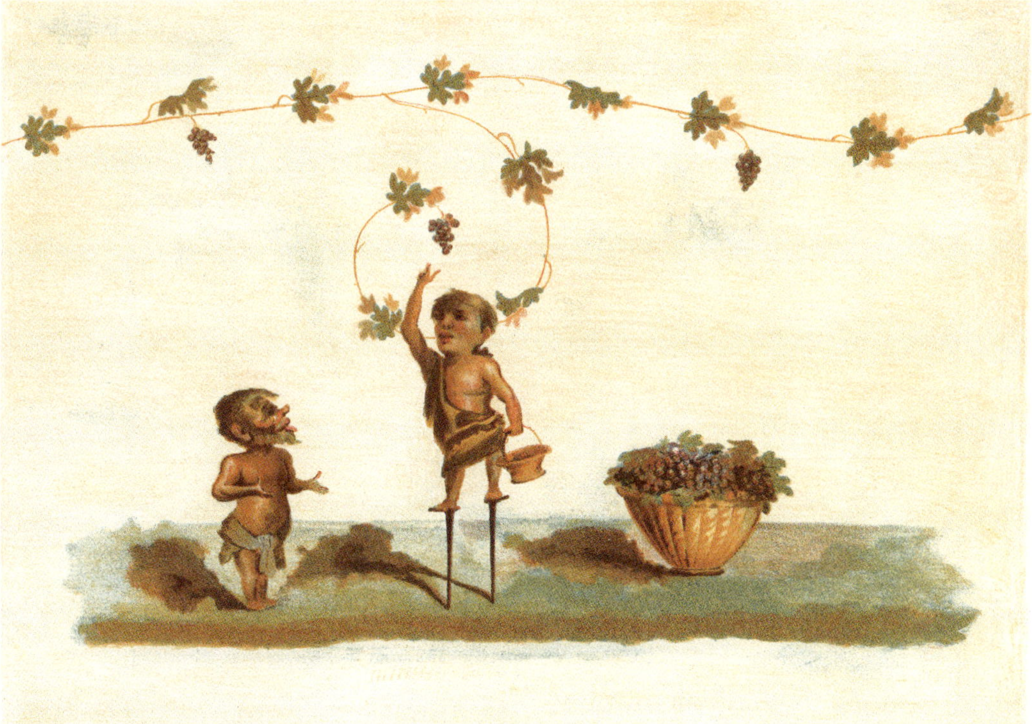

V. Loria dis. e lit. | F.lli Niccolini dir. | Lit. Richter & C. Napoli.

CASA DELLA FORTUNA

House of Fortuna

The medium-sized Casa della Fortuna (IX 7, 20), which was uncovered at the end of 1880, was situated then as now at the edge of the excavated area. It suffered bomb damage during the Second World War and lies off the path usually taken today by visitors to Pompeii. Its atypical ground plan is probably the result of a complicated history of construction and conversion (pl. 1, below). The design of the peristyle colonnade as a row of arcades is also unusual (pl. 1, above). The finds include a full set of bronze statuettes that originally furnished a small household shrine (lararium) in the shape of a temple (pl. 1 above, on the right). In addition to the usual figurines of dancing household gods (lares) a larger statuette of extremely high quality was found, representing the seated Empress Livia in the form of the goddess Concordia. With her cornucopia in her left hand, she is enthroned on a magnificent chair, whose backrest is ornamented with two small tritons (pl. 2). The attribute in her right hand is missing. Plate 3 shows the middle section of the western longitudinal wall in the oecus (22) with a small central picture the subject of which is uncertain (Adonis riding?). The two other mythological pictures in this room show Ares and Aphrodite, and Dionysus and Ariadne, who join a series of other mythological lovers in room (21): Poseidon and Amymone, Ariadne and Theseus and once again Ariadne and Dionysus.

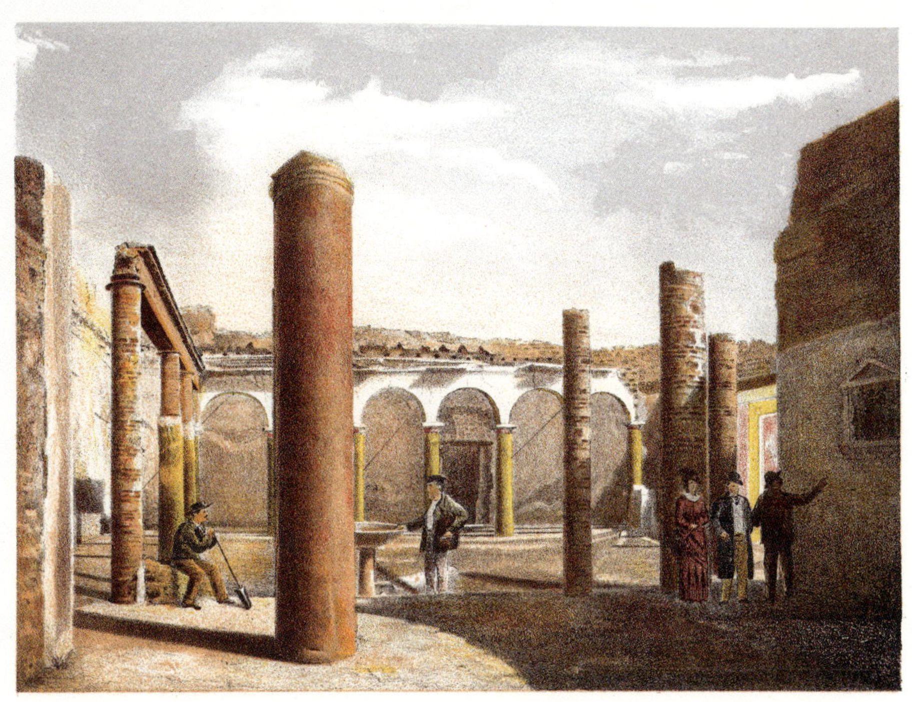

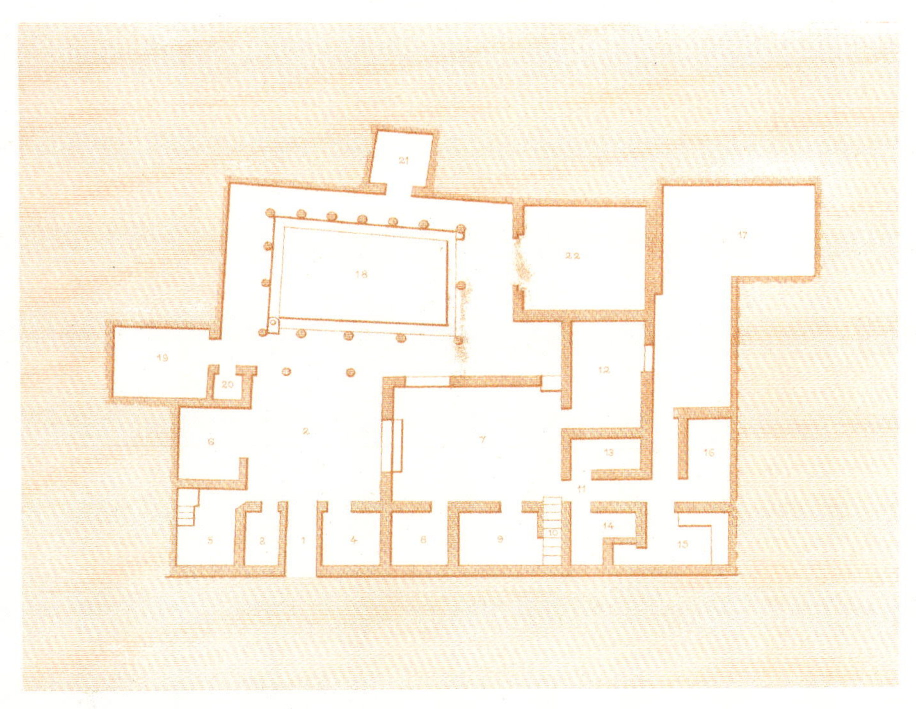

Vto. Loria dis. e Lit. | Flli Niccolini dir. | Lit. Richter & C. Napoli.

Page 321

Plate 1 — *[V. Loria]*

Above: view from the entrance of the house into the peristyle, with the lararium above the group of visitors on the right. Below: ground plan of the house.

✻

Plate 2 — *[V. Loria]*

Shrine of the household gods (lararium) in the atrium (3) – View and ground plan. The enthroned goddess – probably Concordia Augusta – is flanked by two lares. A lamp in the shape of a shod foot hangs overhead.

✻

Pages 324–325

Plate 3 — *[V. Loria]*

Middle section of the west wall in the large oecus (22) – The interpretation of the central motif is unclear: Adonis (?) sets off hunting on horseback, accompanied by a person in Persian dress.

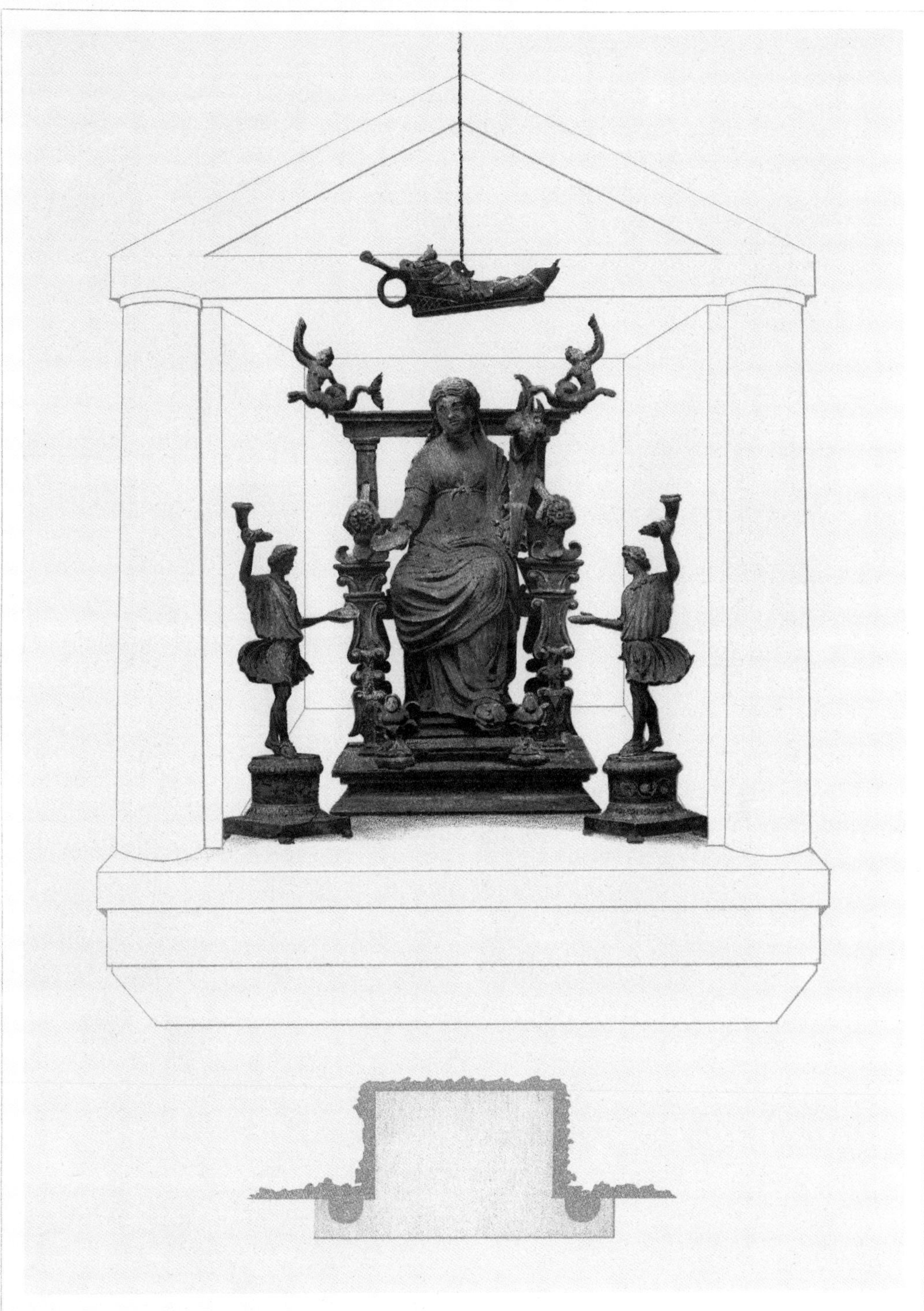

V.to Loria dis. e Lit. F.lli Niccolini dir. Lit. Richter & C. Napoli

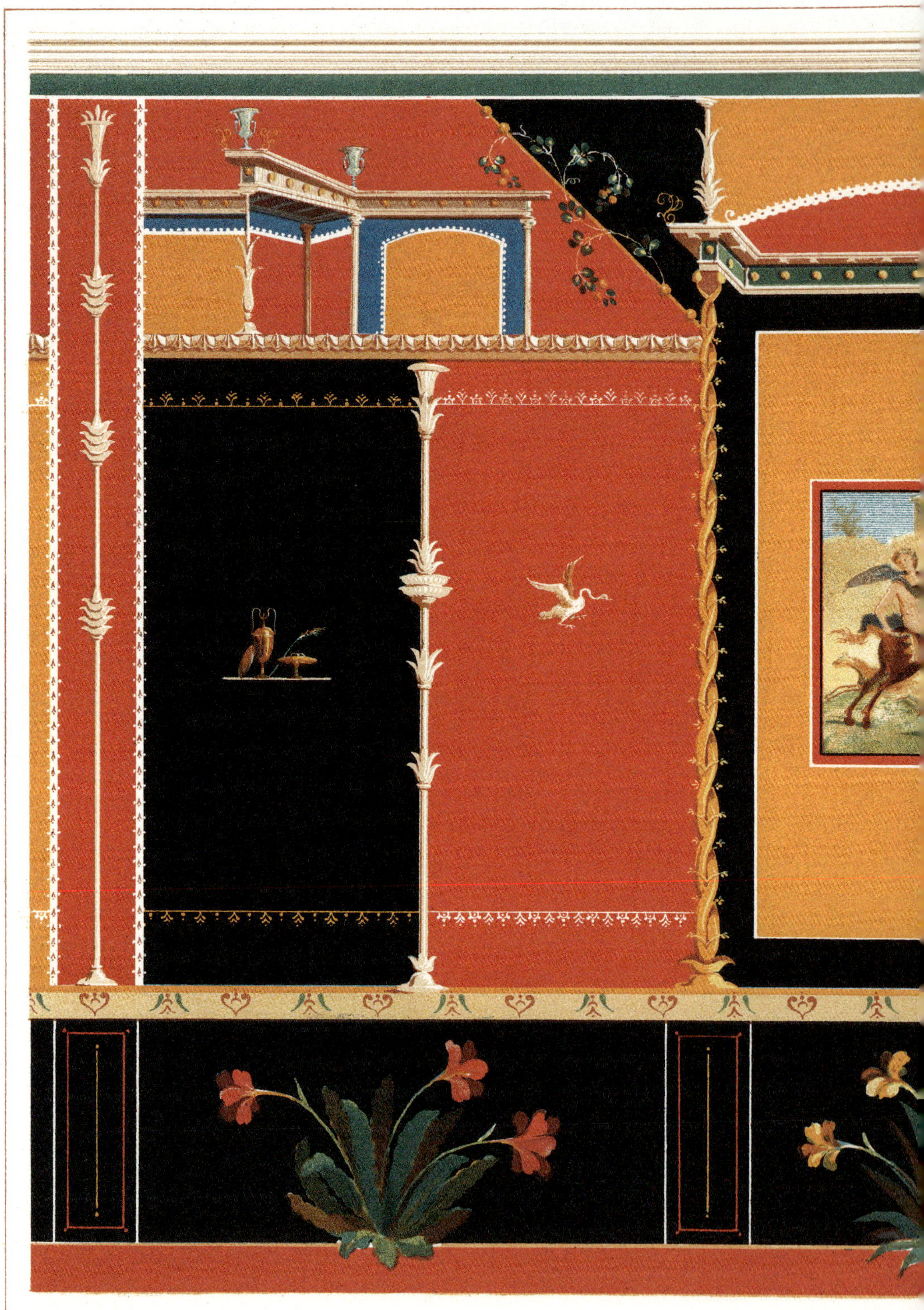

V.zo Loria dis. e Lit.

F.lli Ni

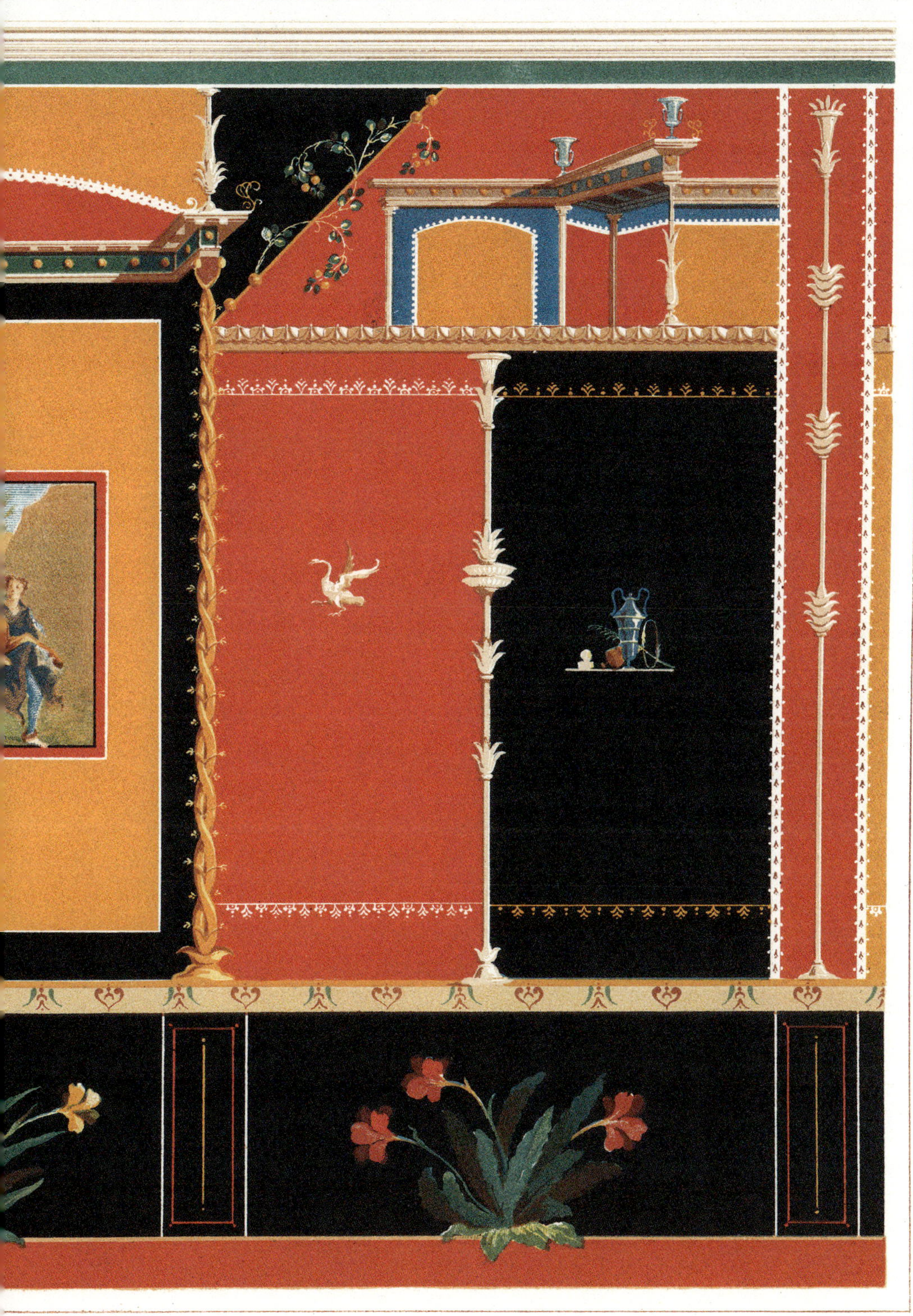

dir.

Lit. Richter & C.o Napoli

CASA DI SALLUSTIO

House of Sallust

The Casa di Sallustio (VI 2, 4) is the first imposing residence visitors see upon entering the city and it lies on a small square. Its splendid façade of tufa ashlars once included capitals with figural decorations at the main entrance. Behind this was concealed an atrium house, largely symmetrical at its core but with the later addition, during a phase of remodelling, of a garden to the east and a peristyle with a large dining room to the south. Dating from the house's early period (2nd century BC) are the substantial remains of a wall decoration in the 1st style, the great abundance of whose variations can be observed throughout the house. From the ground plan, François Mazois recognised early on the systematic nature of its layout, and consequently the Casa di Sallustio entered archaeology textbooks as a "typical" Roman house. While the old decoration around the atrium was clearly retained on purpose, the remodelled parts of the house were newly painted in the 3rd and 4th style. In the last years of the city, the originally rather elite residence was converted into a sort of hotel, with a number of shops along its street front.

The house was uncovered at the start of the 19th century and has been much documented since, with attention being chiefly focused on the areas of 4th-style decoration. However, all the walls were meticulously reproduced in a cork model on a scale of 1:50, made in 1838 for King Ludwig I of Bavaria, in conjunction with his Pompejanum villa project in Aschaffenburg. Antonio Niccolini made reference in his description to the findings of the scholars of his day, in so far as he used terms such as "Tufa Period" and "First Style", which had been introduced by Heinrich Nissen and August Mau. The house was badly damaged by allied bombing in 1944 and restored with little sensitivity in 1970.

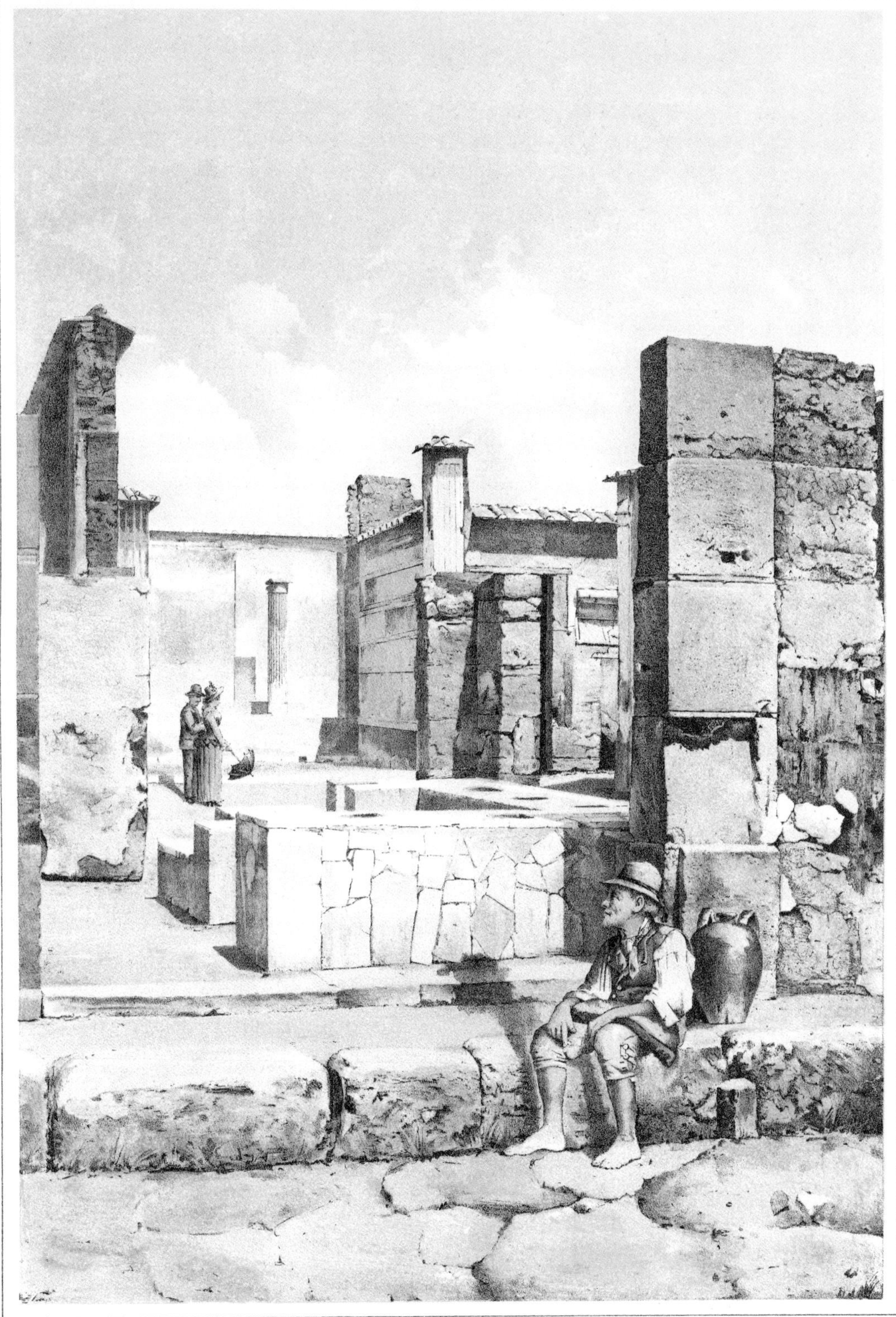

V.º Loria dis e Lit. | Niccolini dir. | Lit. Artis. Zucchi e De Luca Napoli

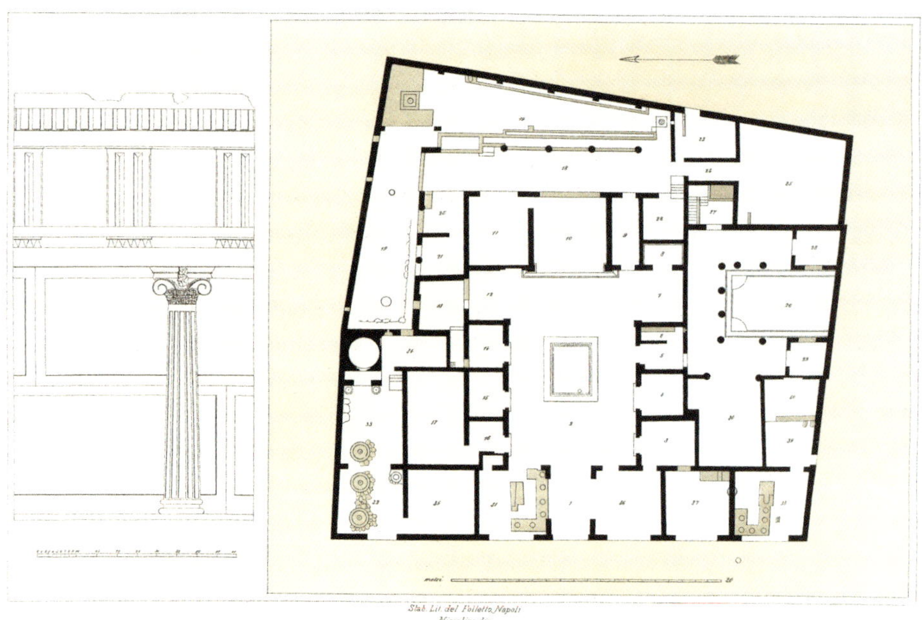

Page 327

Plate 1 — *[V. Loria]*

View into the house from the Via Consolar – In the foreground, a sales counter. The ancient ruins are enlivened by a water seller and a couple of visitors. The lithograph may have been based on a photograph.

❖

Plate 2 — *[Anonymous]*

Ground plan of the house – The oldest parts of the house are grouped around the atrium (2). Rooms were later built around the garden (18) and a peristyle (26) added on one side. The detail shows a section of 1st-style stucco decoration from the upper zone of room (4). The sections converted for use as a bakery (32–34) and two bars (31 and 38) in the city's final years can be easily recognised.

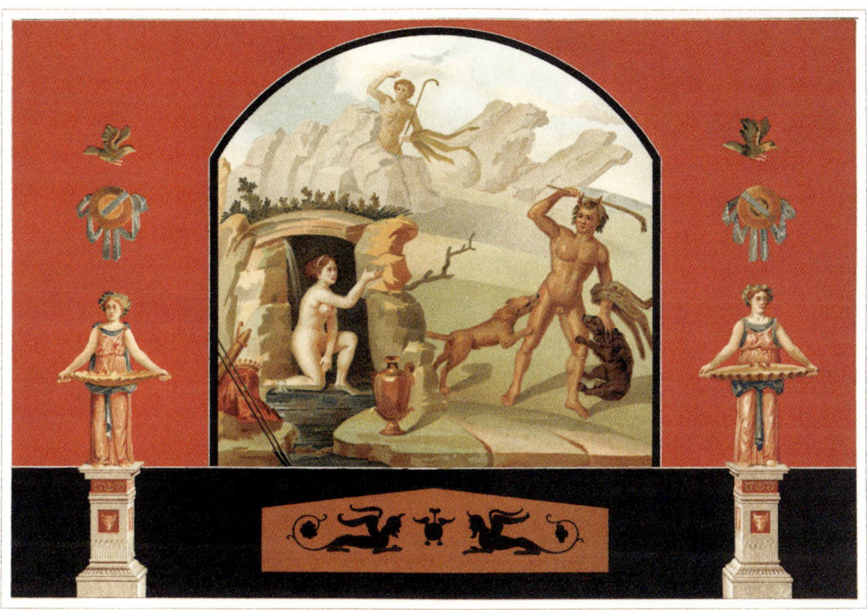

Plate 3 — *[V. Loria]*
Rear wall of the small peristyle (26) – The central picture shows the hunter Actaeon, who surprises Diana while she is bathing, and to punish him she causes his own dogs to take him for a deer and tear him to pieces. The picture gave the house its original name of Casa di Atteone (House of Actaeon).

I MESTIERI E LE INDUSTRIE DEI POMPEIANI

The Trades and Industries of the Pompeians

The new editor Antonio Niccolini the Younger began volume III in the same manner as volume I, by compiling short chapters on individual public buildings and private residences. With the ninth section, however, he introduced a new category into the classification system: "Trade and Industry". This section is devoted to an area of life in ancient Pompeii for which the city offers a great variety of sources of all different kinds. Even if individual objects which correspond to this heading had already been presented elsewhere, with this chapter Niccolini for the first time followed a trend in late 19th-century positivism, namely to document antiquity not just in terms of its art and myths, but also the everyday world of work and so too the pursuit of pleasure in bars and brothels. Similar sections had indeed already appeared in books by scholars from around the world. In the person of Antonio Sogliano (1854–1942), who had worked in Pompeii for many years and would serve as director of excavations from 1905 to 1910, Niccolini was able to secure a highly knowledgeable author for the accompanying text. In his essay, which was fully up to date with the state of scholarship at the time, Sogliano characterised Pompeii as a city of trade and labour, in which only a few were able to make their living "from their estate". He systematically described the different professions as documented by literary and in particular epigraphic sources (the majority in the form of inscriptions painted on plastered façades), and whose work premises had in some cases also been uncovered. The activities of gold- and silversmiths, bakers, fishermen, fullers, carpenters and innkeepers, and lastly even farm labourers, are described and "illustrated" in nine plates. These show plans of workshops, ancient paintings with scenes from working life, as well as examples of the products from these trades – albeit without raising the question of how many of them may have been imports.

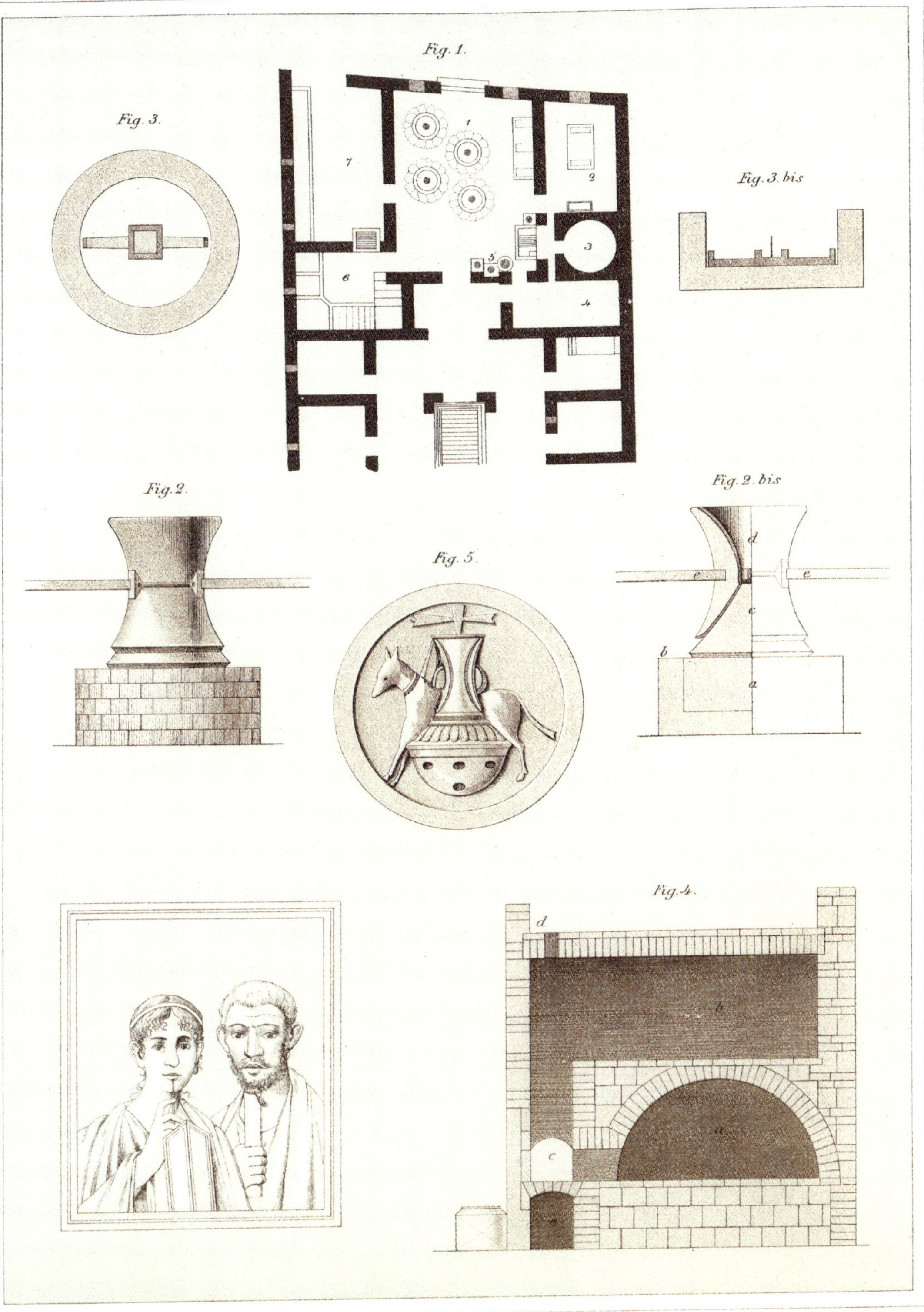

Lit Art Zucchi & De Luca Napoli — A Niccolini dir — V Loria dis ed inc

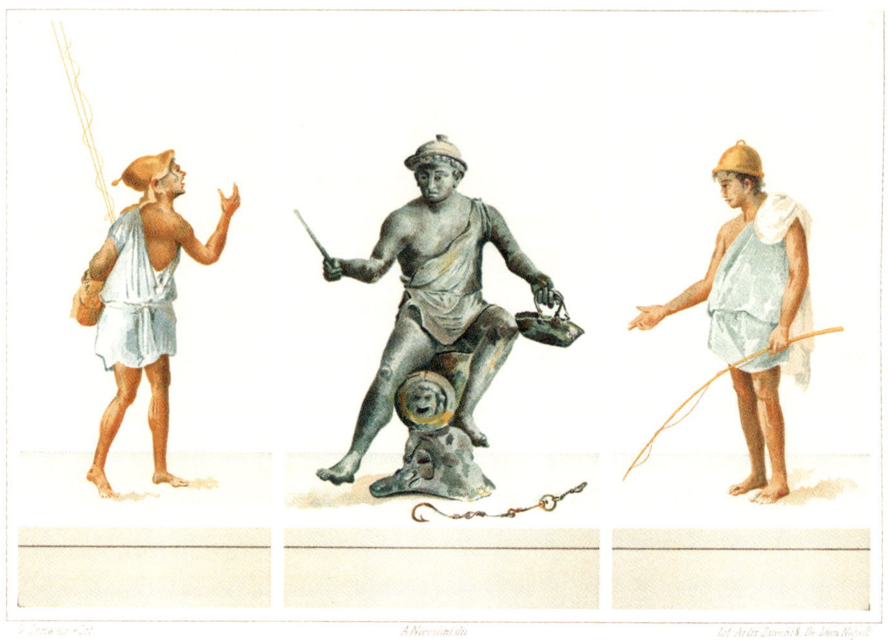

Page 331

Plate 1 — *[V. Loria]*

Milling and baking – Fig. 1: plan of the bakery VI 3, 3 (the front half of the house is not shown): four mills (1), oven (3). Figs. 2–3 bis: view and cross sections of a typical Pompeii mill constructed from porous lava. Fig. 4: cross section through the bread oven. Fig. 5: discus of a clay lamp with the representation of a donkey turning a mill. Fig. 6: married couple with diptych and scroll along with writing utensils. They are thought to be the owners of another bakery (VII 2, 3)

Plate 3 — *[V. Loria]*

Fishing – In the centre, the bronze angler from the fountain in the Casa della Fontana piccola (see vol. I). On either side, two painted fishermen with rods and felt hats. The large fishing hook "lying" beneath the statuette does not belong to it and is for illustration purposes only.

Plate 2 — *[V. Loria]*

Selling or distributing bread – Casa VII 3, 30, Tablinum: free distribution of bread on the orders of a magistrate? A man dressed in a tunic is seated on a high podium made of boards nailed together and is handing a loaf of bread to two plainly dressed men and a boy. Loaves with similarly notched patterns on top were found numerous times in the Vesuvian cities.

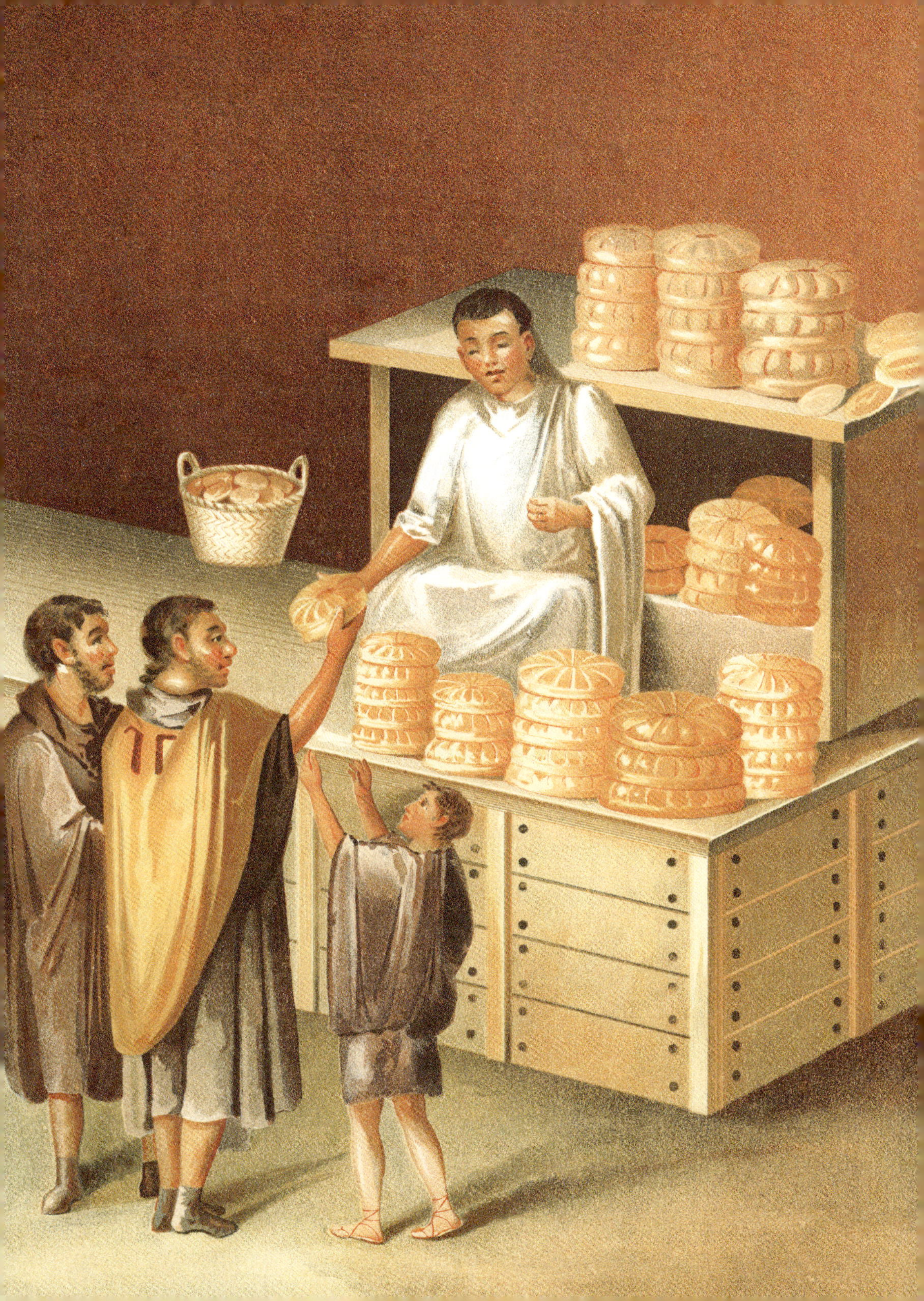

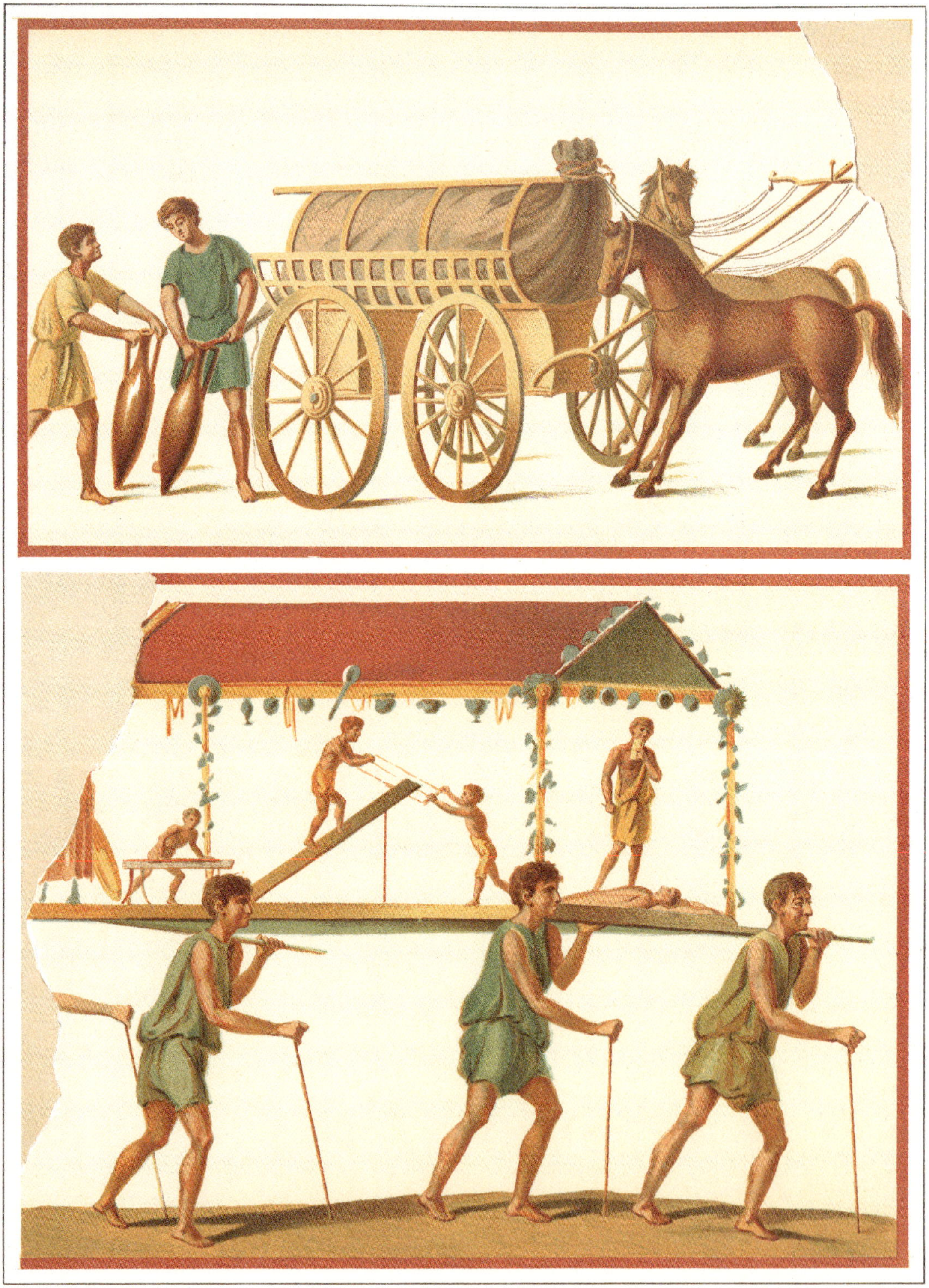

G. Discanno dis D. Capri Lit.

A. Niccolini dir.

Lit. Art. Zucchi & De Luca, Napoli.

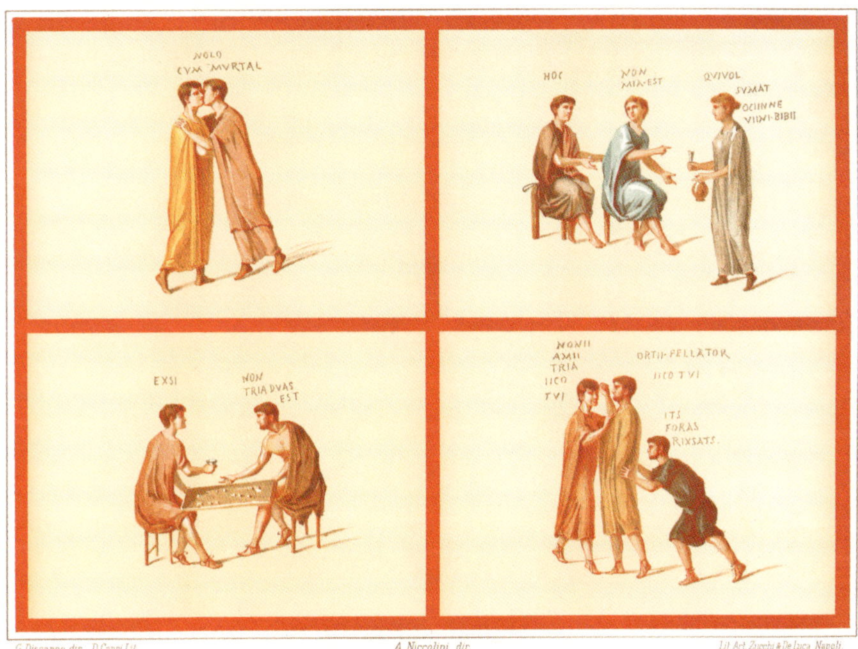

Plate 5 — *[G. Discanno]*

Above: ***Wine being delivered to a caupona (pub; VI 10, 1)*** – Two men are filling amphorae from a large wineskin transported in a four-wheeled cart. Below: ***Joiners and carpenters*** – So-called Workshop of the Perfume-seller (VI 7, 8), shop sign. Men with sticks are carrying a litter *(ferculum)* in a procession. Beneath its roof are scenes relating to the joiners' trade: at the front, the statue of Daedalus, the patron of carpenters, beside his dead nephew Perdix.

Plate 4 — *[G. Discanno]*

Tavern scenes – *Caupona* (pub) of Salvinus (VI 14, 36): four scenes from a tavern with explanatory captions. An argument breaks out over a game of dice, which ends with the landlord pushing the guests out of his pub with the words: "Go and fight outside!" (below right).

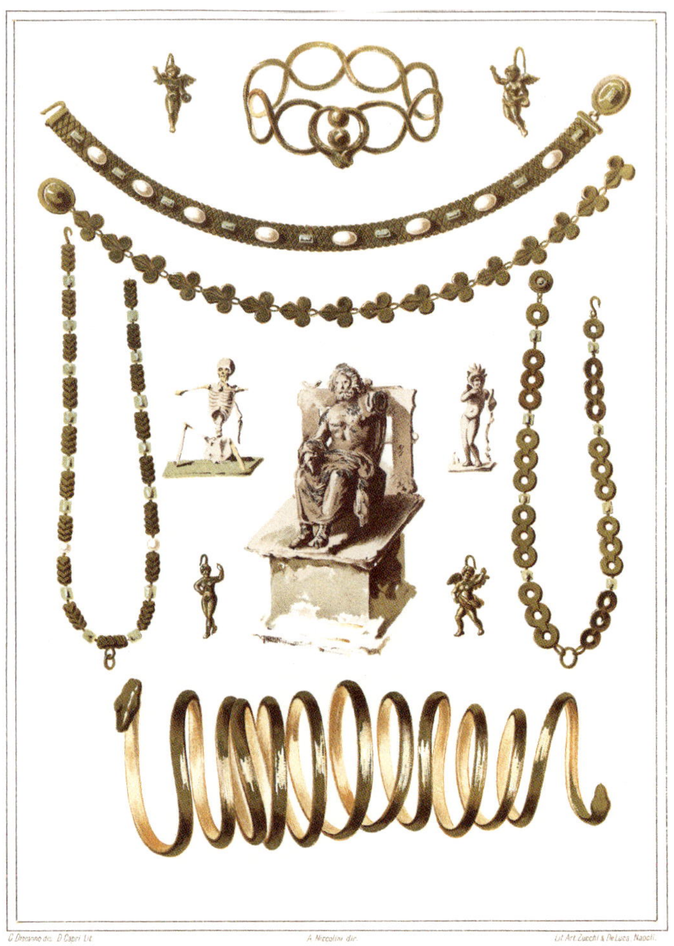

Plate 7 — *[G. Discanno]*
Gold jewellery of varying origin, together with silver statuettes – Whether, as the accompanying texts suggests, these works were all made in Pompeii, cannot be verified.

Plate 6 — *[D. Capri]*
Textiles: Fullonica VI 8, 20 – Above: ground plan of the complex, excavated in 1825/26. The furnace for heating the water (14) can clearly be made out, along with the basins (19) in which the wool was trampled. Below: four pictures illustrating aspects of the wool-processing trade (see also vol. II, Descrizione generale, pl. 76).

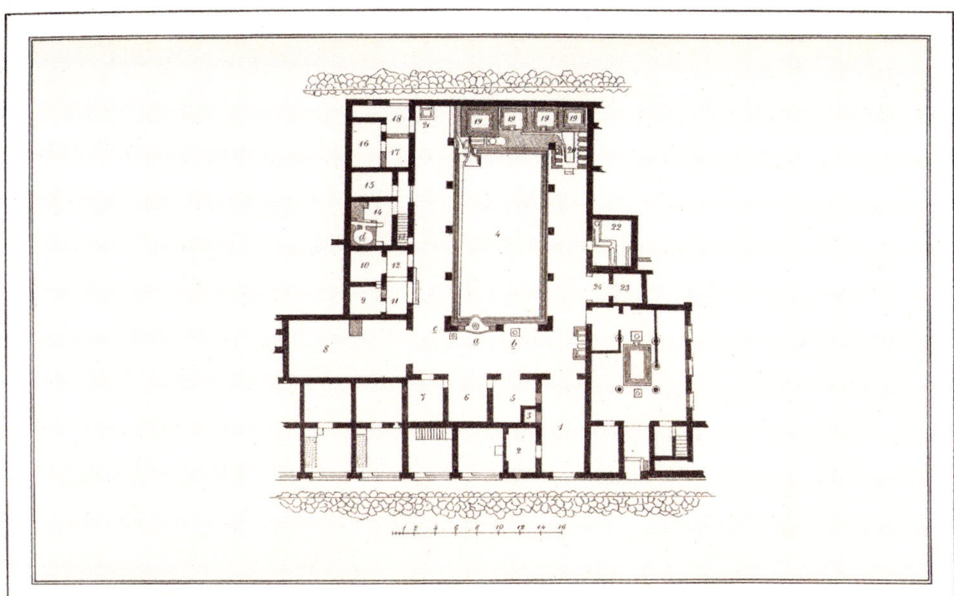

2

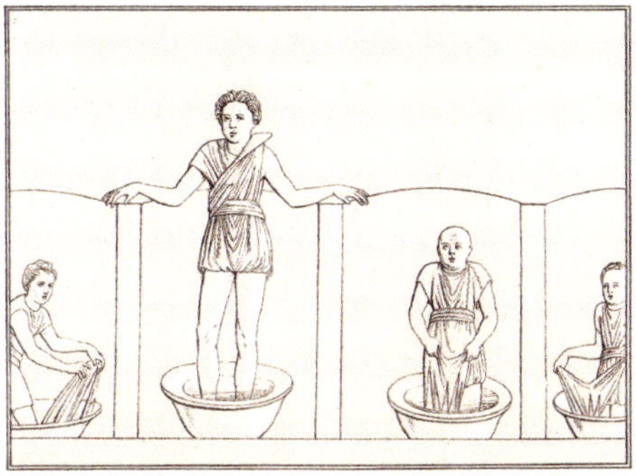

3

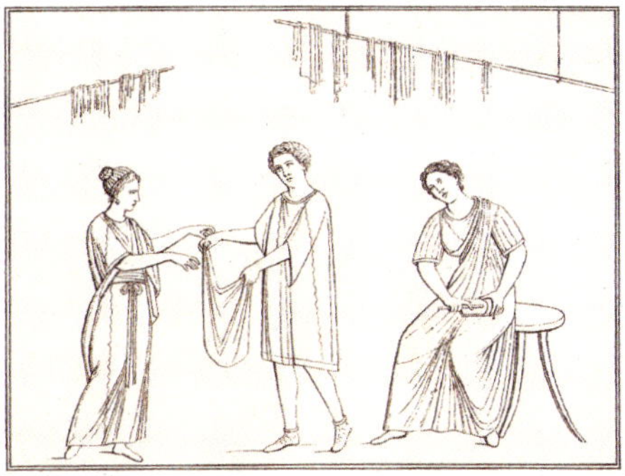

1.

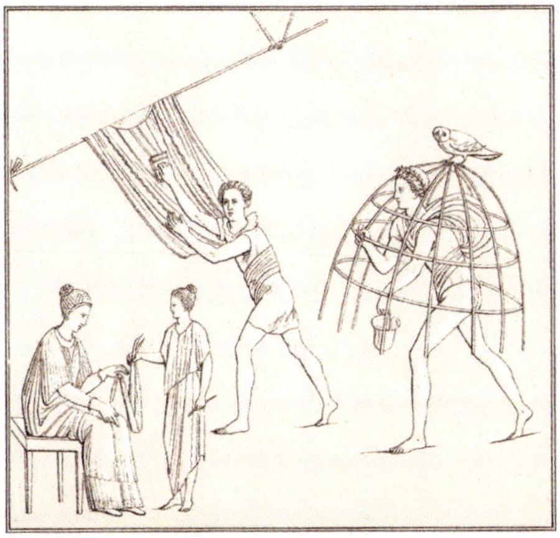

4.

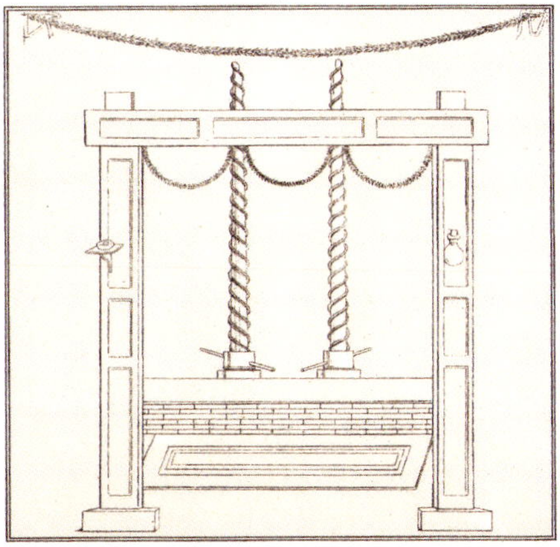

Lit. Art. Zucchi & De Luca - Napoli.   A. Niccolini dir.   D. Capri dis.

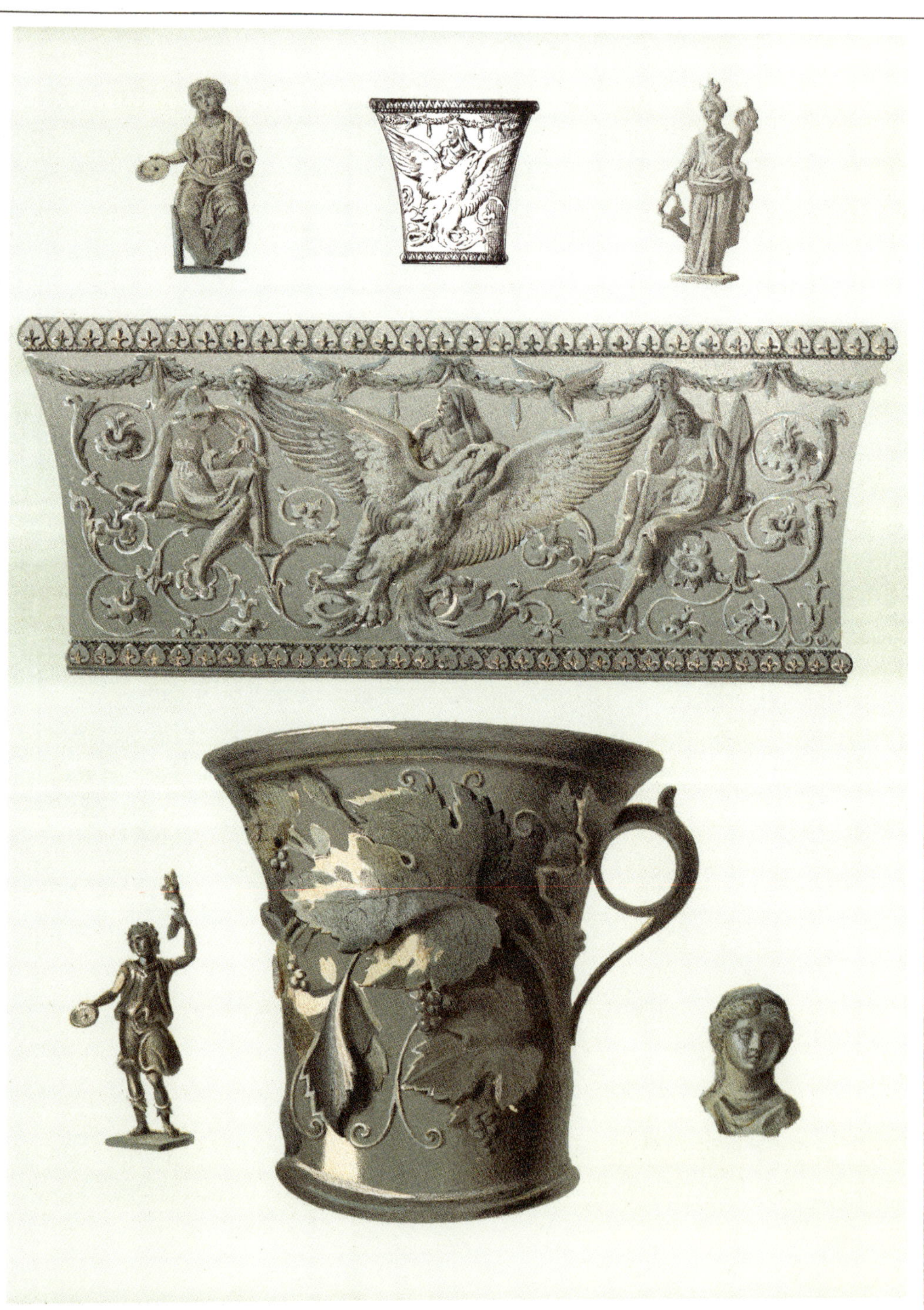

G. Discanno dis. e lit. A. Niccolini dir. Lit. Art. Zucchi & De Luca Napoli.

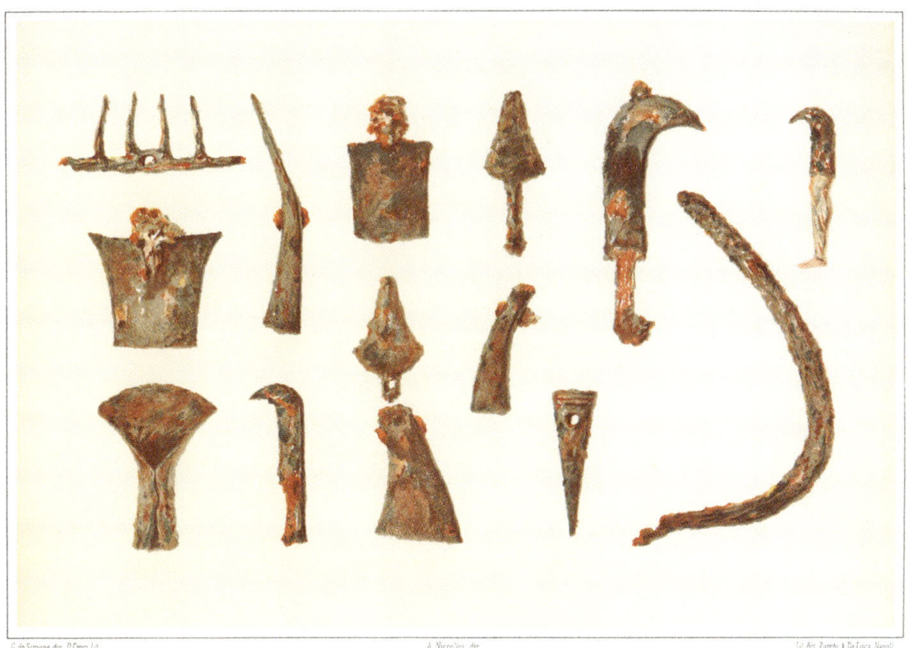

Plate 8 — *[G. Discanno]*

Silver beakers from Pompeii – The flat view shows the deification of Homer being borne aloftby an eagle, accompanied by personifications of the *Iliad* (left) and the *Odyssey* (right). A second cup is decorated simply with vine leaves and was found amongst a large treasure trove in the Casa di Inaco e Io (VI 7, 19). The plate also shows three statuettes (a goddess dispensing bounty, an Isis-Fortuna and a dancing lar) together with a female bust.

Plate 9 — *[G. Discanno]*

Iron agricultural implements of varying origin – The rake, pick and scythe (all missing handles, which have rotted away over time) resemble tools still in use in the last century. These objects had only very recently gone on display at the Museo Nazionale, not having previously been deemed worthy of exhibition.

FORME IN GESSO

The Victims of the Vesuvian Eruption

None of Giuseppe Fiorelli's archaeological achievements caused such an instant and at the same time lasting sensation as the casts he made from the body-shaped cavities found where victims of the Vesuvian eruption had perished. Since 1748 excavators had found skeletons in Pompeii on a regular basis and, from observing their position, deduced the dramatic fate of the city's inhabitants. Most impressive of all was the discovery, in 1772, of the remains of 18 bodies in the basement of the Villa di Diomede. The volcanic ash had hardened sufficiently to preserve the imprints left by their bodies, so that it was possible to cut these out in sections and transport them to the museum. The presence of these "negatives" is explained by the fact that Pompeii was buried first by a layer of fine pumice and then by sodden ash, which solidified around the organic material and, after this had decayed, left behind a matching hollow. Not until the 1850s, however, did anyone go ahead and pour liquid plaster into the hollows left behind, starting with wooden doors, and thereby make them visible again. On February 3, 1863 Giuseppe Fiorelli then had the idea of making such a cast from one of the cavities left by a human body. Even if not quite perfect from a technical point of view, the result was the sight of a young woman lying on her back as she was dying. The sense of immediacy with which every visitor to Pompeii feels confronted by the past now assumed an extra and more vivid dimension: the tragedy of the city's destruction was materialised in its people, and we could now be present immediately in their death throes. Fiorelli's "invention" was quickly reported across the whole of Europe, and soon documented in early photographs by Giorgio Sommer. By 1890 plaster casts of 16 victims had been made in this manner, with many more since right up to the present. The Niccolinis reproduced 13 of them here and in the Descrizione generale (vol. II), in illustrations based on photographs. The casts were amongst the most important exhibits at the local antiquarium. They make a moving impression on visitors to Pompeii exhibitions, and their emotional impact extends all the way to modern sculpture (see Schütze essay).

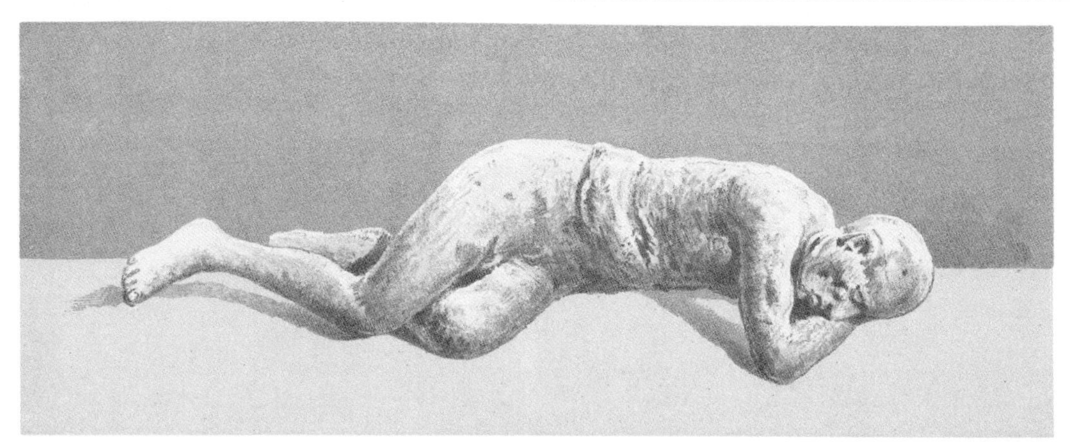

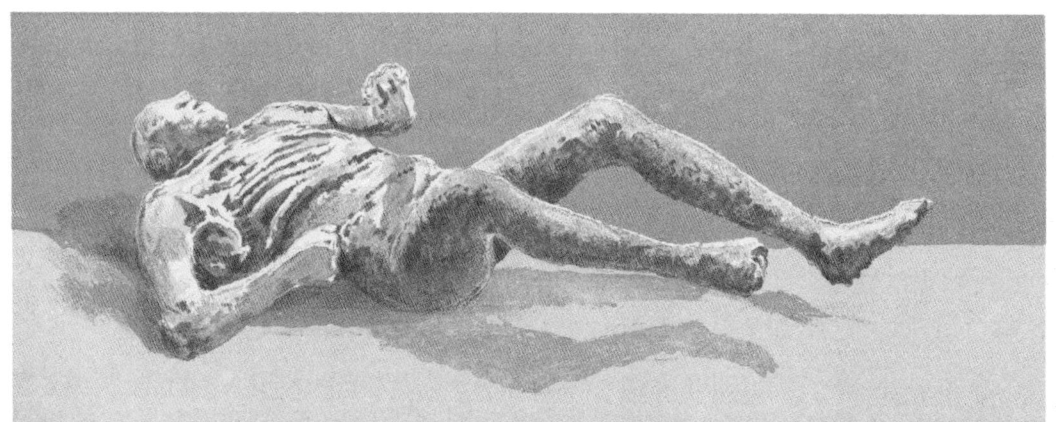

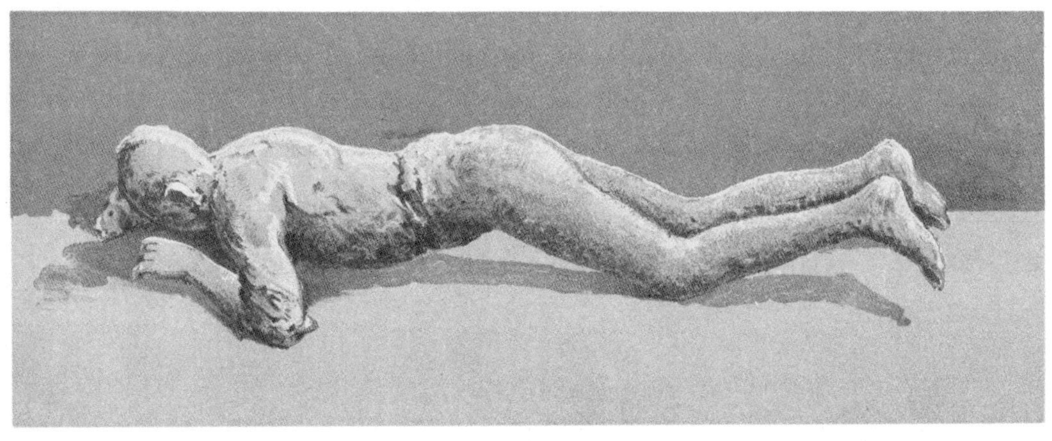

G. Discanno dis. D. Capri Lit. A. Niccolini dir. Lit. Art. Zucchi & De Luca, Napoli.

Page 341

Plate 1 — *[G. Discanno]*

Above: Casa I 5, 3, so-called sick man. Middle and below: from the Via Stabiana, in front of Casa VI 14, 30 (?). The cast of a woman's body (below) was considered the most successful, since it also partly reproduced the victim's facial features.

⁂

Plate 4 — *[G. Discanno]*

Above: young man, found in front of the Porta Stabiana. His upper garment, some kind of underwear and one shoe can all very clearly be made out. Below: casts of parts of a door (left) and the trunk of a laurel tree (right) lso made here.

⁂

Page 344

Plate 2 — *[G. Discanno]*

Above: Casa di Vesonius Primus (VI 14, 20); the guard dog was chained to a door post and tried in vain to escape the mounting layer of debris. Middle: in front of the Casa di Acceptus e Euhodia (VIII 5, 39); the sick child died with its mother, whose body, however, could not be cast. Below: Casa di Gavius Rufus (VII 2, 16); man from a group of seven victims.

⁂

Page 345

Plate 3 — *[G. Discanno]*

These three victims were found in August and October 1889 in front of the Porta Stabiana. Above: older woman lying on her stomach with outstretched arms (turned face up in the photo). Middle: man lying on his side. Below: man lying on his back.

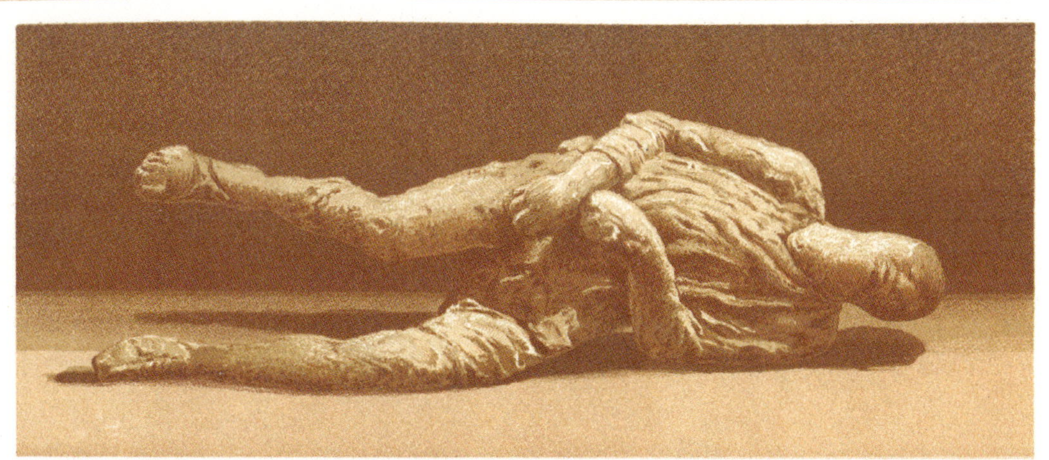

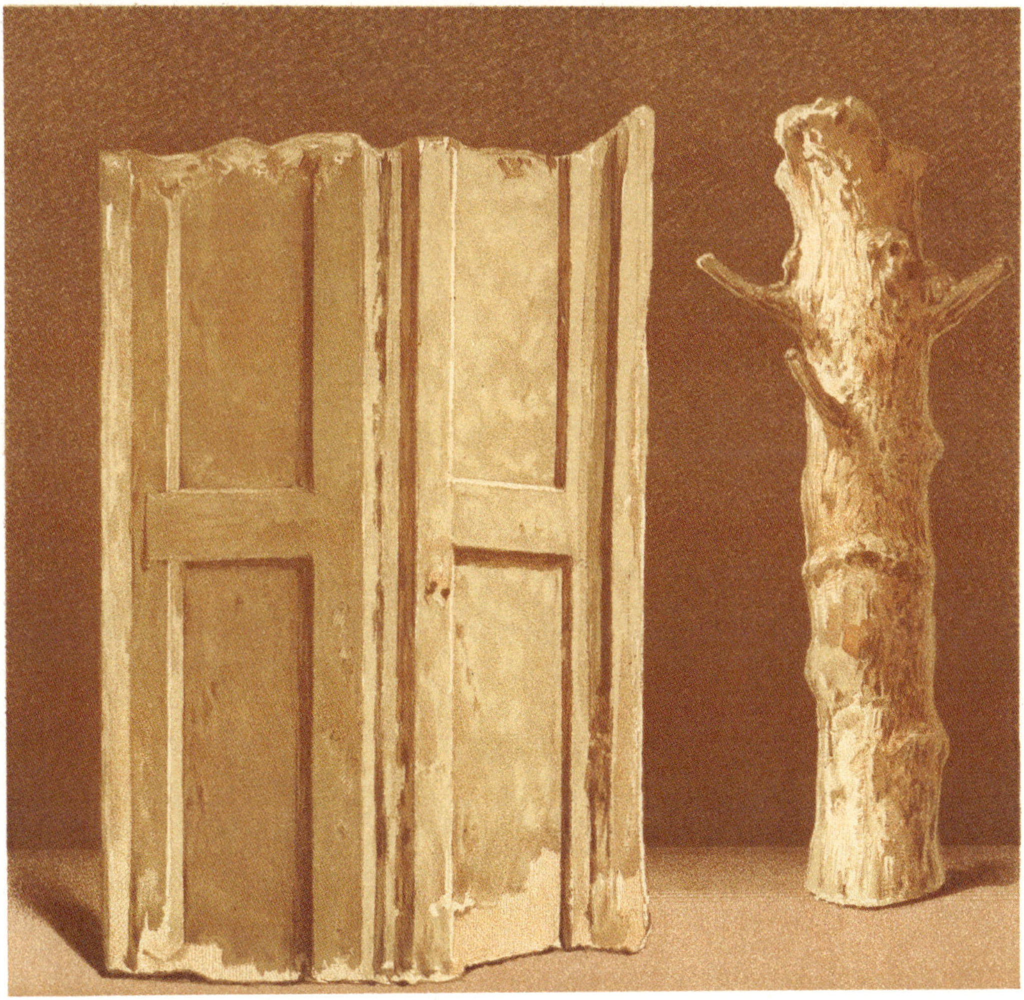

G. Discanno dis. D. Capri Lit. | A. Niccolini dir. | Lit. Art. Zucchi & De Luca, Napoli.

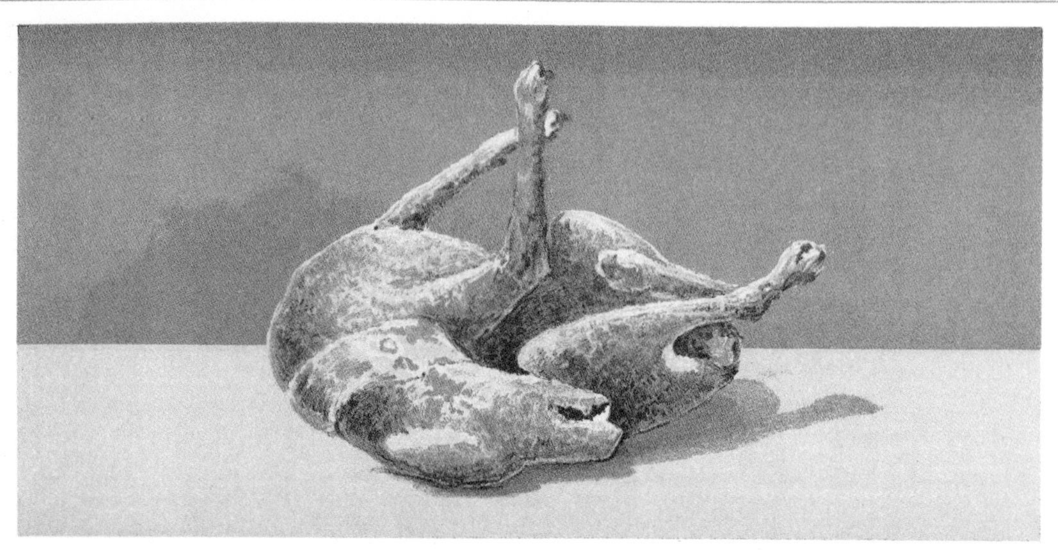

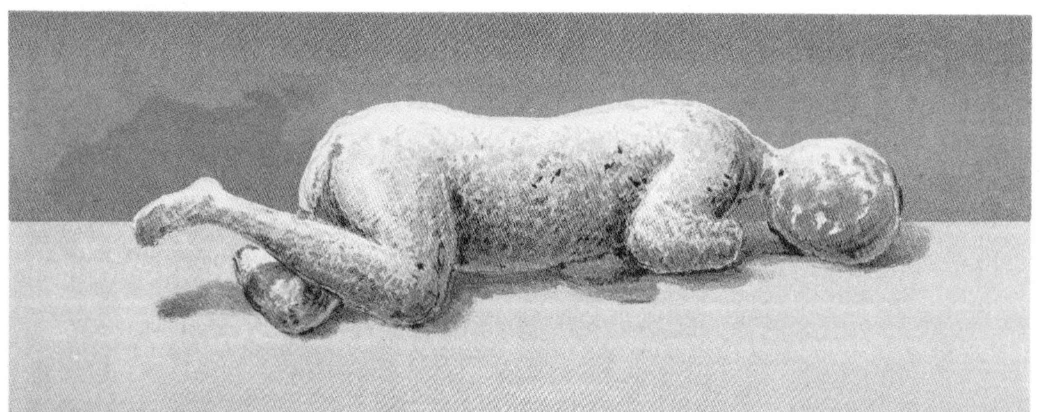

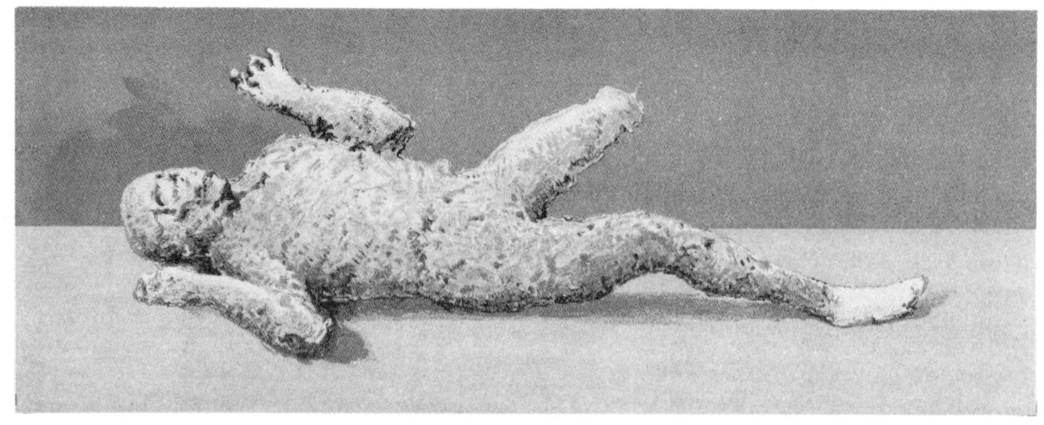

G. Discanno dis. D. Capri lit. A. Niccolini dir. Lit. Art. Zucchi & De Luca, Napoli

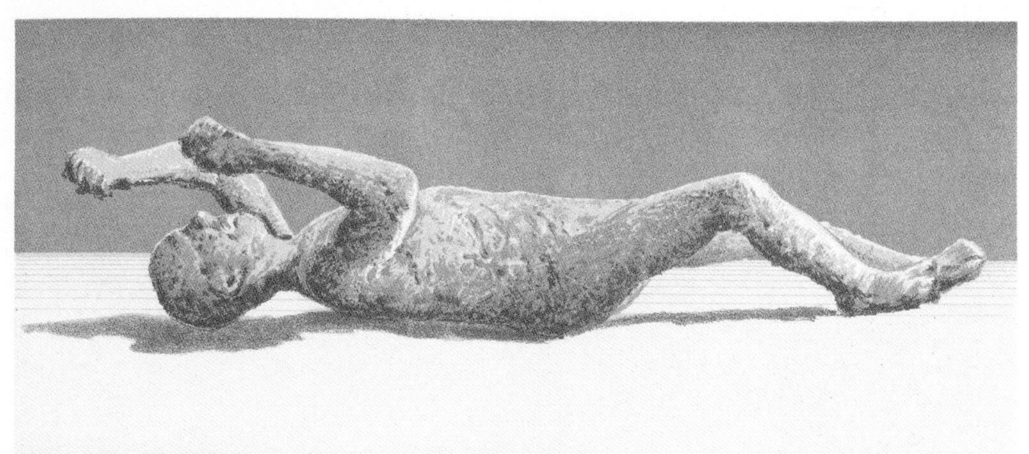

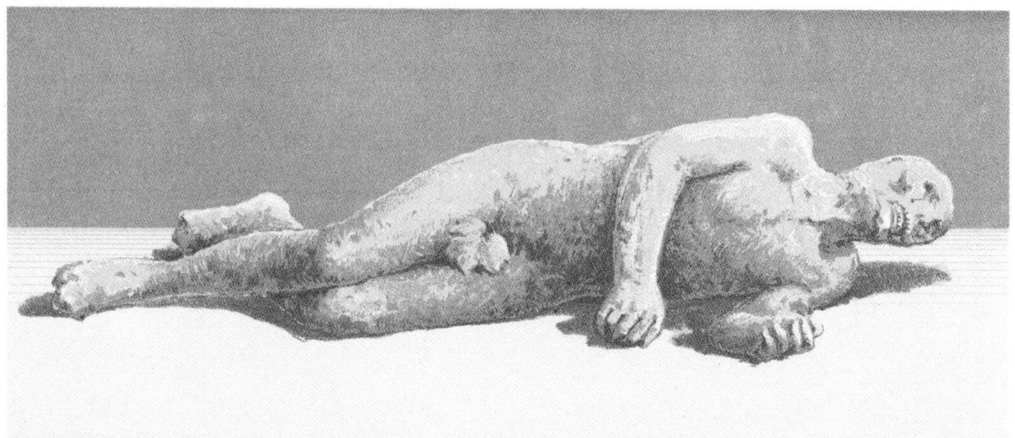

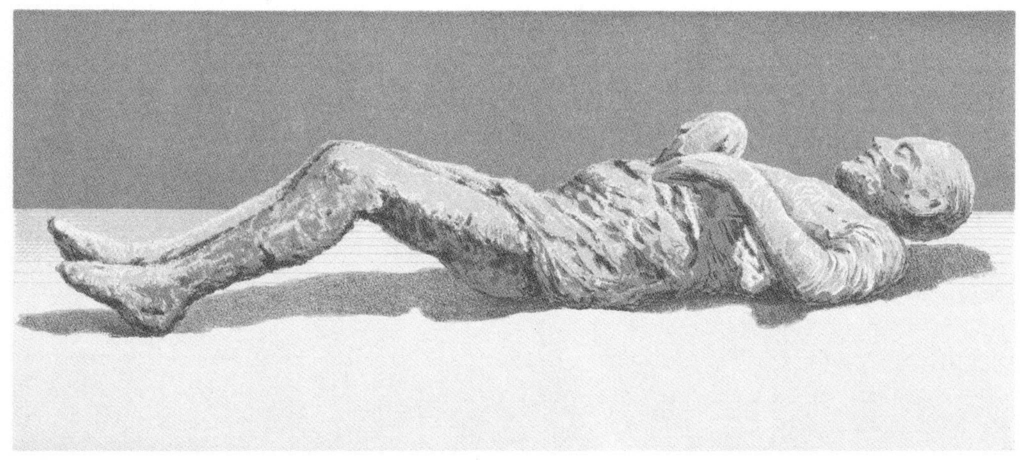

G.Discanno dis D.Capri Lit A. Niccolini dir Lit Art Zucchi & De Luca Napoli

L'ARTE IN POMPEI

The Arts in Pompeii

This chapter too, with its extensive text and illustrations, took up a topic that was a common feature in the international literature on Pompeii at the time. The section in question, to which specific reference was made in the Proemio (preface), is nothing less than a coherent – albeit not original – presentation of Pompeii's importance for the understanding of ancient, and more accurately Roman art. This importance, according to Niccolini, lies not in the city herself; only as a consequence of its "premature death" and later excavation does Pompeii become so significant for us. The text discussed different genres of ancient art – architecture, painting and sculpture – in their public and private manifestations. It thereby made reference not only (although also) to the 56 plates in this section, but equally to numerous other illustrations in the first two volumes and even the final volume (see Supplemento).

Antonio Niccolini the Younger – if he was indeed the author of this text – started with an overview of Pompeian architecture, which he presented in terms of its historical development as had first been done by Giuseppe Fiorelli, Heinrich Nissen and others. This development reached its high point with Oscan tufa architecture, whereas the Augustan architecture was described as decadent on account of its non-canonical use of entablature orders. Domestic architecture was of particular significance given the unparalleled wealth of surviving examples in Pompeii.

More important, however, was Pompeii's contribution to an understanding of the history of painting. Here the author explicitly followed the two "dotti tedeschi" (German scholars) Wolfgang Helbig and August Mau. Niccolini, with Mau, saw a historical development that can be traced above all through Pompeian forms of decoration, which also had its phase of decadence in the shape of "exaggerations" during the Imperial age (4th style). With regard to figurative paintings, he named two categories: 1. pictures dealing with "ideal" themes such as myths, which belong to the common cultural heritage of the Greco-Roman world and

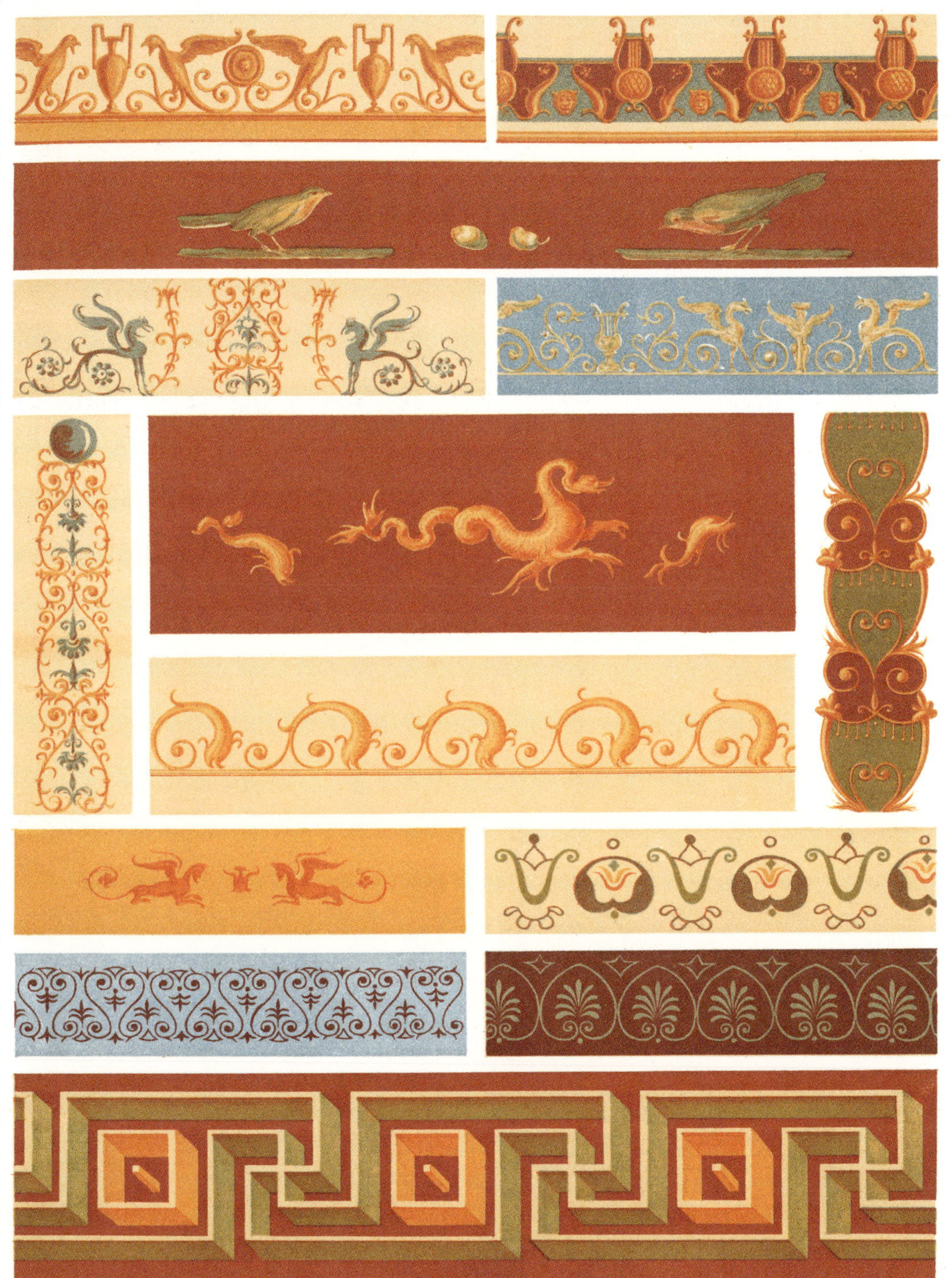

Lit. Art. Zucchi & De Luca-Napoli *A. Niccolini dir.* *G. Discanno dis. – S. Longobardi Lit.*

which in Pompeii are found in the shape of "copies", in some cases of only very average quality; 2. pictures conceived and executed in Pompeii and which often do not follow the "laws of aesthetics" – a genre, that scholarship for a long time labelled "folk art". The mythological subjects were classified according to whether they showed the key moment of a certain episode, whether they simply radiated an atmosphere of blissful happiness or formulated visual content in the manner of an epigram. This use of literary categories is altogether striking. Next came a discussion of sculpture, whose importance again lay not so much in its quality as in the contexts in which it was found and any evidence for polychrome painting, gilding etc. Alongside statues being set up in shrines and on public squares, their use as decoration within houses and villas played a major role. The text then discussed portraits, before turning lastly to small decorative objects and examples of the applied arts, whose influence upon the art of the 18th and 19th century was significant.

Overall the author shows himself to be very well acquainted with the current state of scholarship and makes reference to its findings (which of course are not necessarily still valid today). In particular, his assessment of Pompeii's modest role in its ancient context is circumspect and aimed at the interested reader. It repeatedly becomes clear that he understands the heritage of Pompeii not as a homogeneous whole but as the result of a historical process, thereby responding to the new interest in archaeology in the second half of the 19th century of the immanent historicity of the object of its research. The text thus dissociates itself from the long-dominant Neapolitan antiquarian tradition, so called, in which the individual object is decontextualised and objects are viewed as illustrations of antiquity's rich literary heritage. In comparison with this essay, intended for a more general public, the 35 pages given over to a description of the individual plates are of clearly inferior quality. It is hard to imagine that both texts could have been written by the same author.

In this chapter, the connection between text and plates is closer than in the Descrizione generale in volume II. For the first time too, comparative illustrations of the iconography of specific themes are brought together. Nevertheless, by no means all the plates are mentioned explicitly or even incorporated into the main argument, while once again a number of pictures from the editors' own archives seem to have been introduced for no obvious reason.

Page 347

Plate 2 — *[G. Discanno]*

Details of ornamental friezes "popularly used by modern decorators", compiled from Pompeian wall decorations found in various locations.

⁂

Plate 7 — *[G. Discanno]*

Villa di Cicerone – The acrobatic satyrs on a black background are among the earliest (1748) and subsequently most copied figures to have been found in Pompeii.

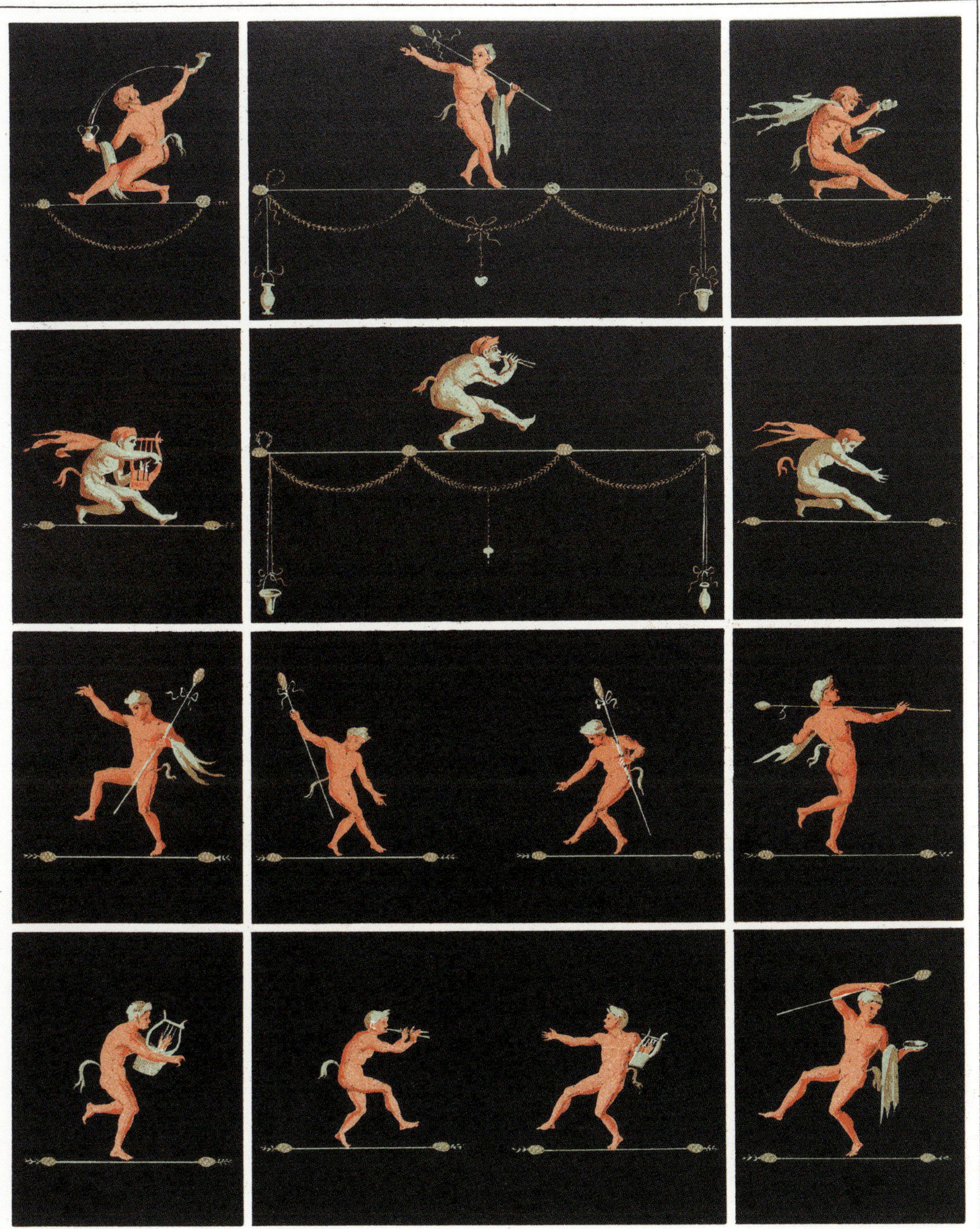

G. Discanno dis. D. Capri Lit. A. Niccolini dir. Lit. Art. Zucchi & De Luca, Napoli.

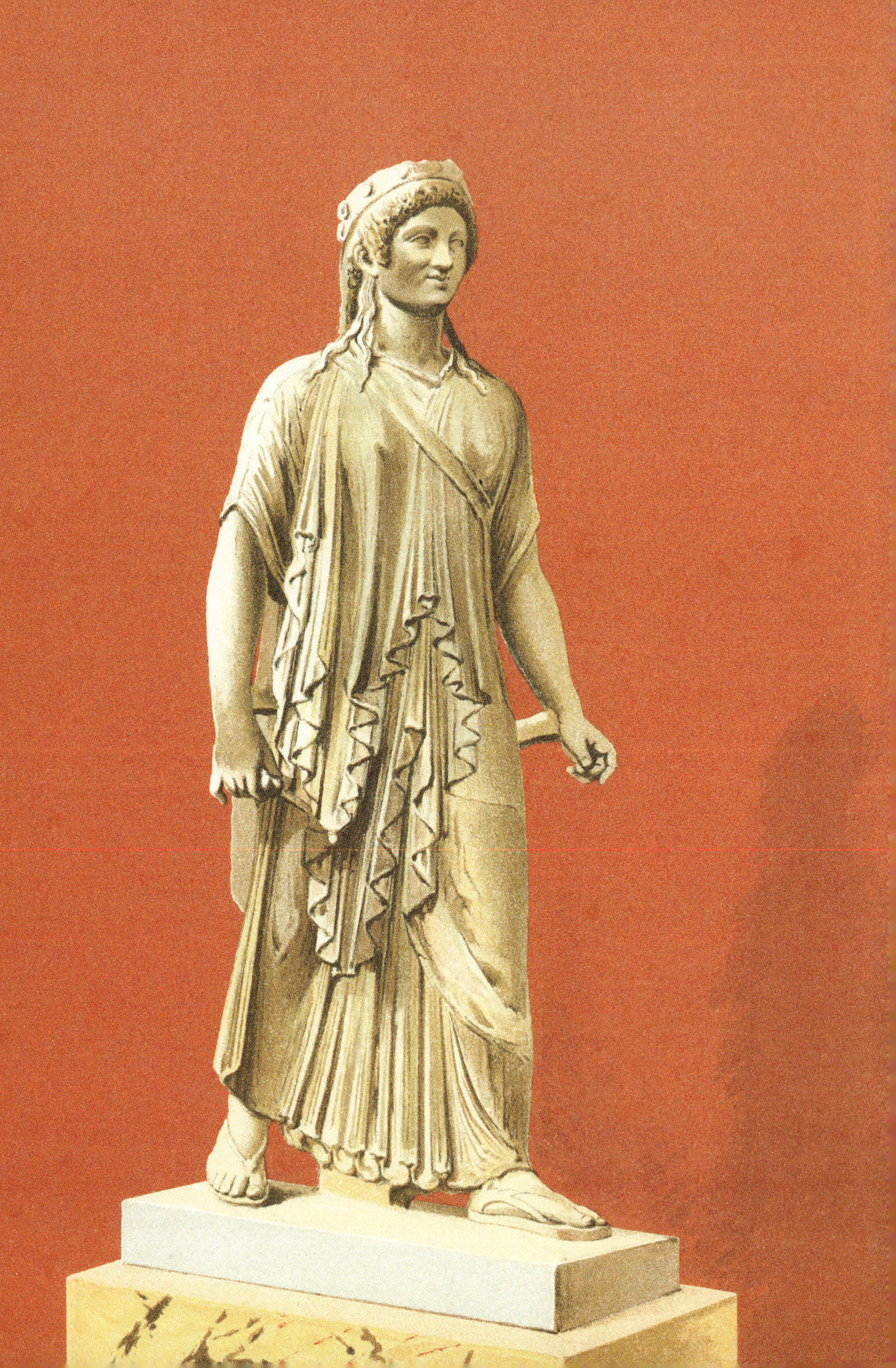

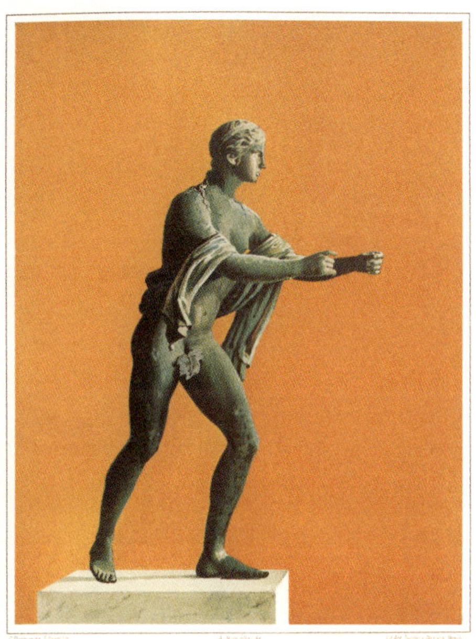

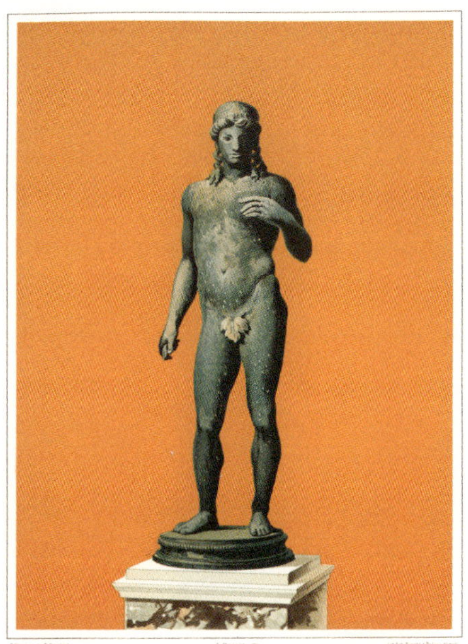

Plate 3 — *[G. Discanno]*
Casa di Diana (VII 6, 3) – Marble statuette of a striding Artemis in an archaistic style, found in 1760. The figure exhibited clear traces of colour, which prompted Winckelmann to embark on a study of the polychrome painting of ancient sculpture.

Plate 8 — *[G. Discanno]*
Temple of Apollo – The bronze statues of siblings Apollo and Artemis shooting their bows were found here in 1817. They rank among the most important large bronzes uncovered in Pompeii.

Plate 5 — *[G. Discanno]*
Casa del Citarista (I 4, 5. 25 and 28) – Bronze statue of Apollo. Whether the statue originally carried a cithara in its left hand, or a lamp and thus functioned as a kind of inanimate servant, remains disputed.

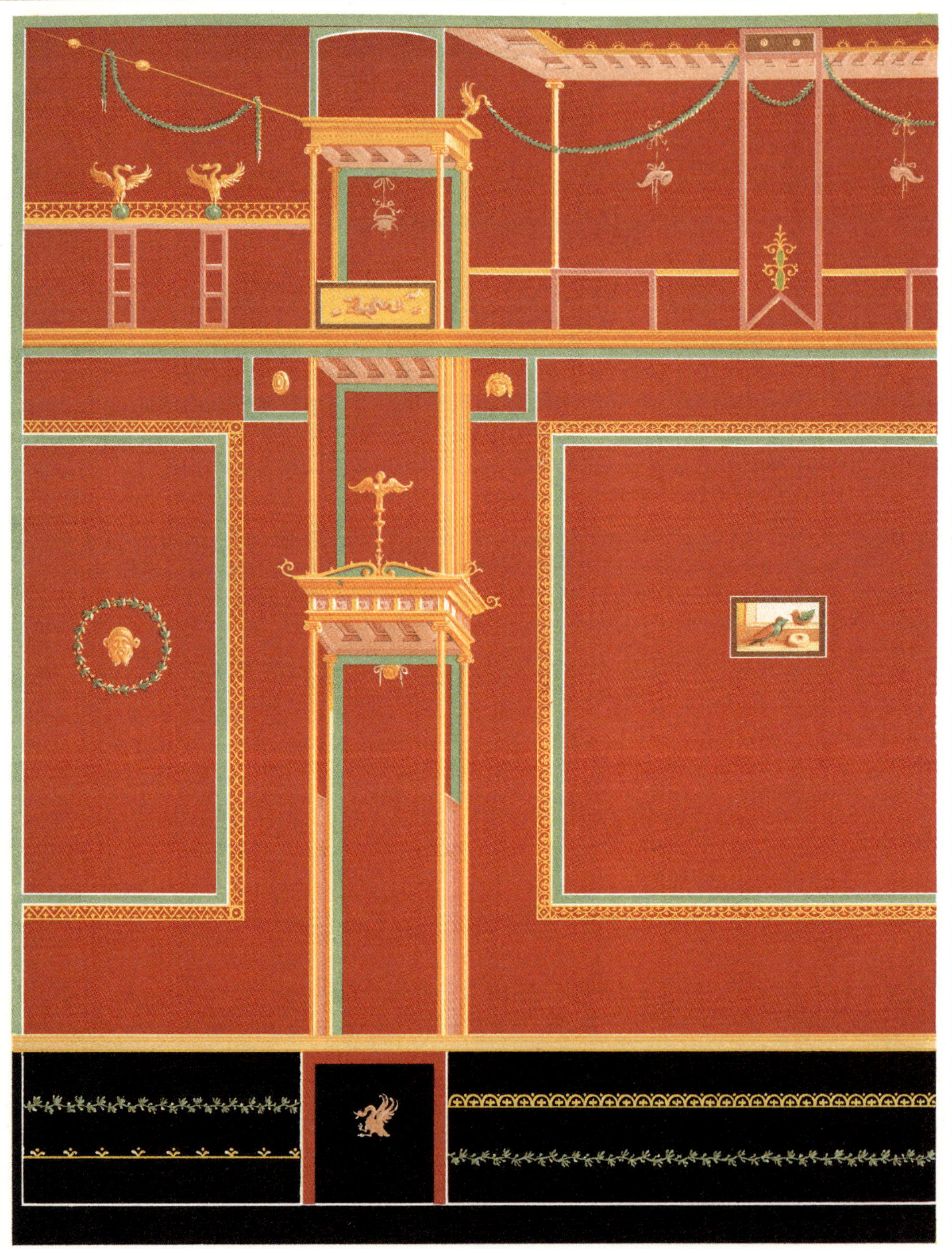

G. Discanno dis. D. Capri Lit. A. Niccolini dir. Lit. Art. Zucchi & De Luca, Napoli.

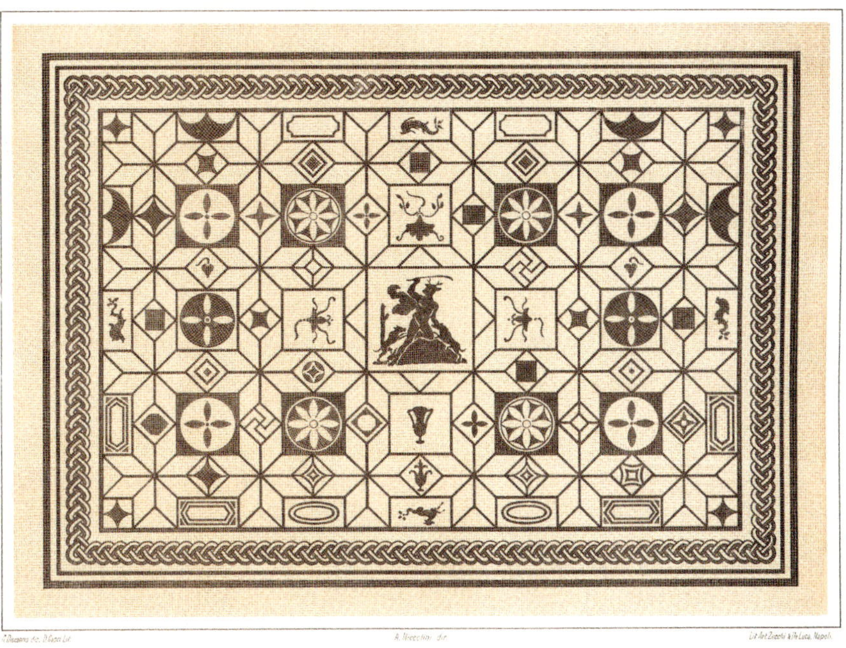

Plate 12 — *[G. Discanno]*
Villa di Diomede – Detail from the east or west wall of the caldarium in the villa's baths. The lithograph perhaps goes back to a watercolour by Francesco Morelli now in the museum's collection.

Plate 13 — *[G. Discanno]*
The large black-and-white mosaic was found in the Insula occidentalis in Regio VI and drawn by Francesco Morelli in 1808. The central picture shows Actaeon being torn apart by his dogs.

Page 354
Plate 14 — *[G. Discanno]*
Casa I 2, 17 – Marble statuette of a Venus, leaning on an archaistic statuette of a girl (kore). The lithograph reproduces the clear traces of the ancient painting.

Page 355
Plate 11 — *[G. Discanno]*
Palaestra – This marble statue is a Roman copy of one of the most famous Greek bronzes of the 5th century BC, the so-called Doryphoros (Spear-Bearer) by the sculptor Polykleitus of Argos. It probably served not just a decorative purpose in the palaestra, the exercise area where young men assembled, but according to one attractive hypothesis could be crowned by the victors at competitions.

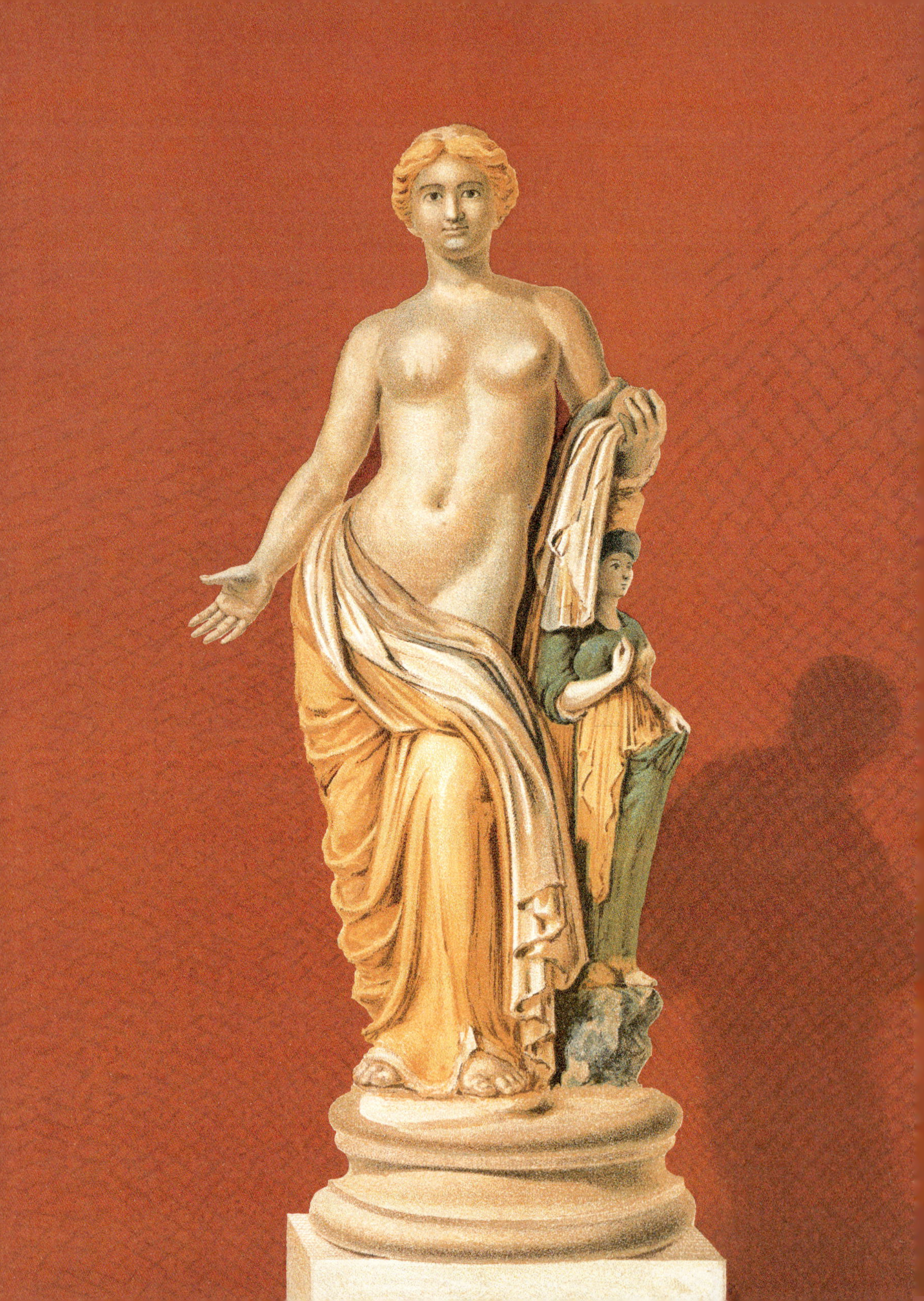

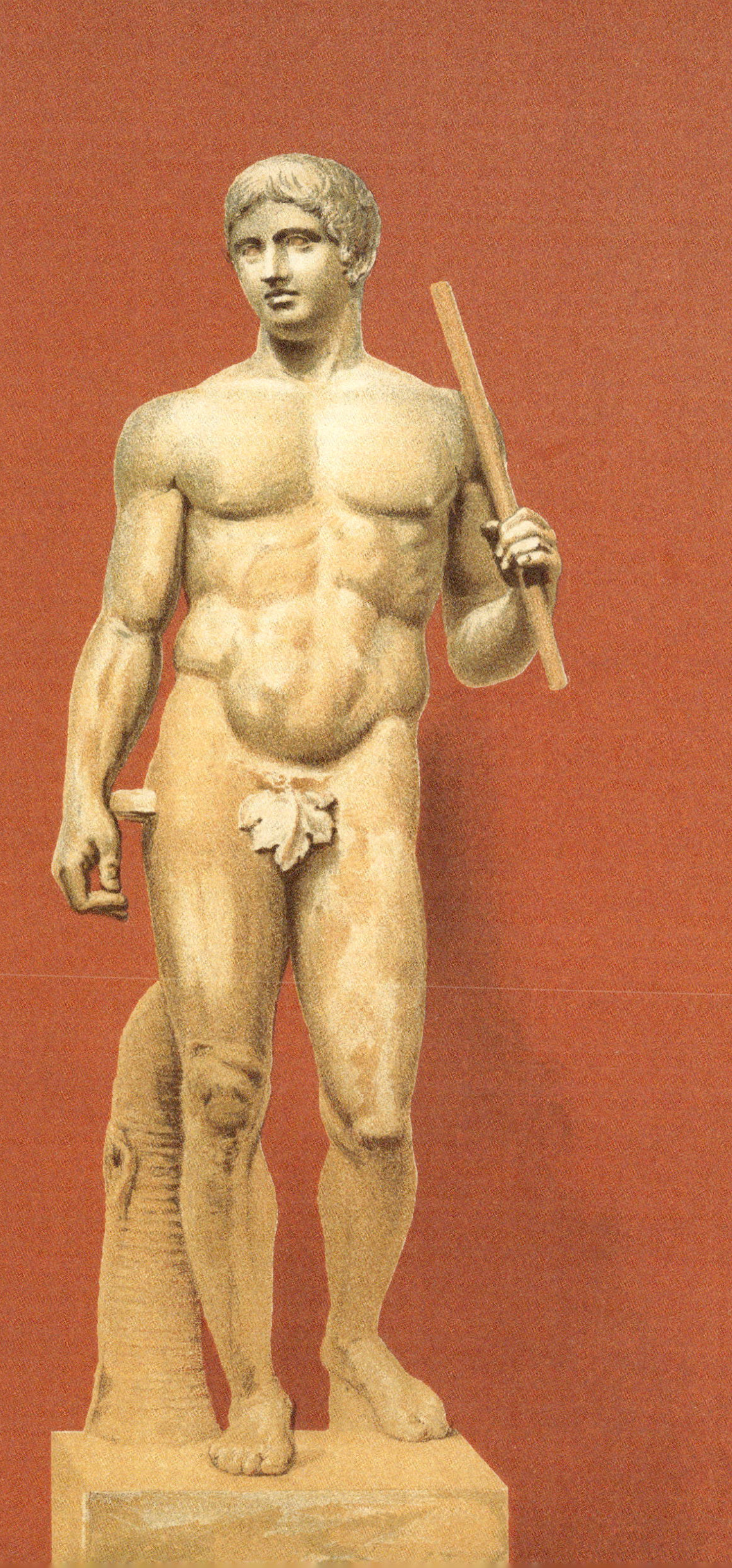

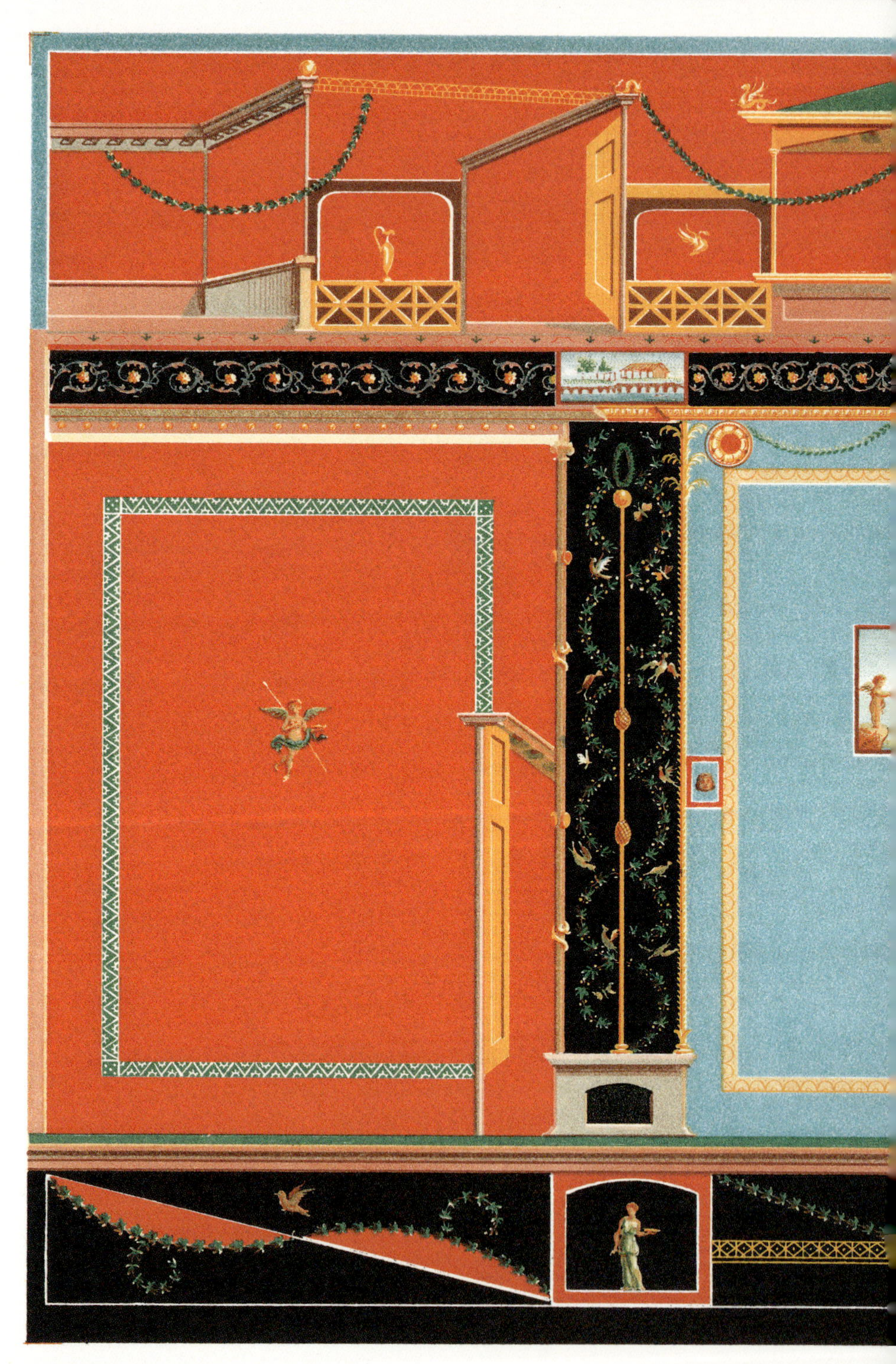

G. Discanno dis. D. Capri Lit.

A.N.

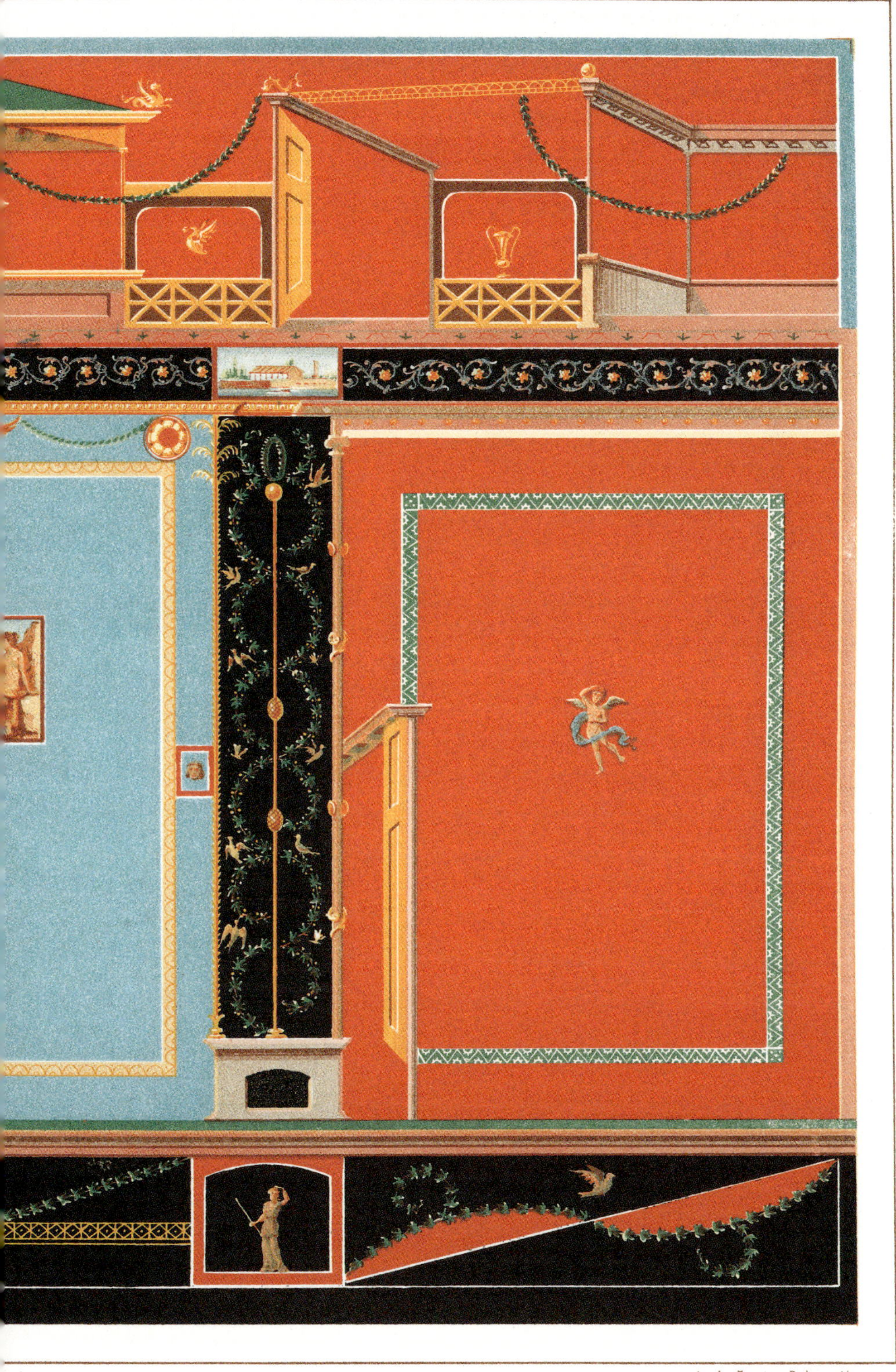

dir.

Lit. Art. Zucchi & De Luca, Napoli.

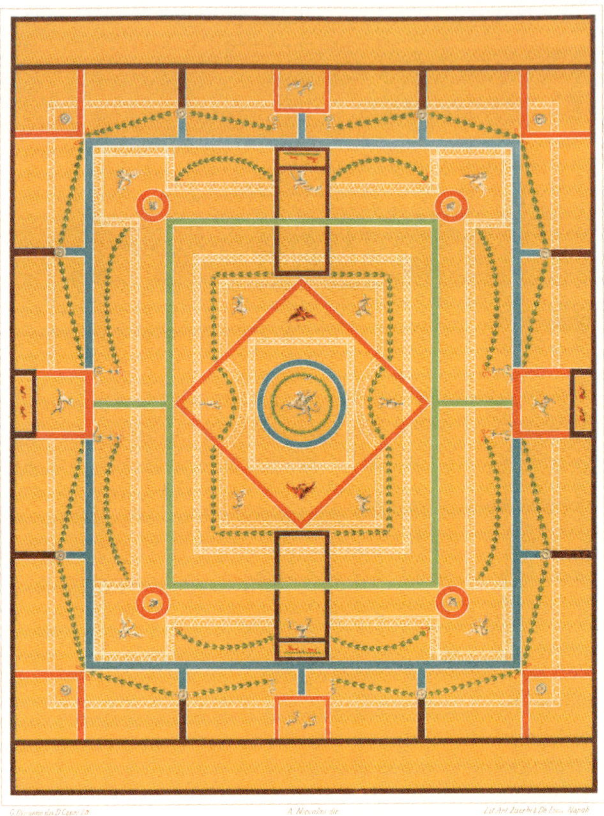

Page 356-357

Plate 15 — *[G. Discanno]*

Casa delle Amazzoni (VI 2, 14), triclinium, north wall – 3rd style; in the central picture, the popular motif of Venus fishing. The wall, uncovered in 1811, survives only in the form of a watercolour by Francesco Morelli, on which this plate is probably also based.

Plate 16 — *[G. Discanno]*

Villa di Diomede – Ceiling decoration of a room in the lower peristyle. Here too the Niccolinis' design is based on an earlier visual source.

Plate 18 — *[G. Discanno]*

Casa della Caccia antica (VII 4, 48. 43 and 44) – Large architectural prospect in the 4th style.

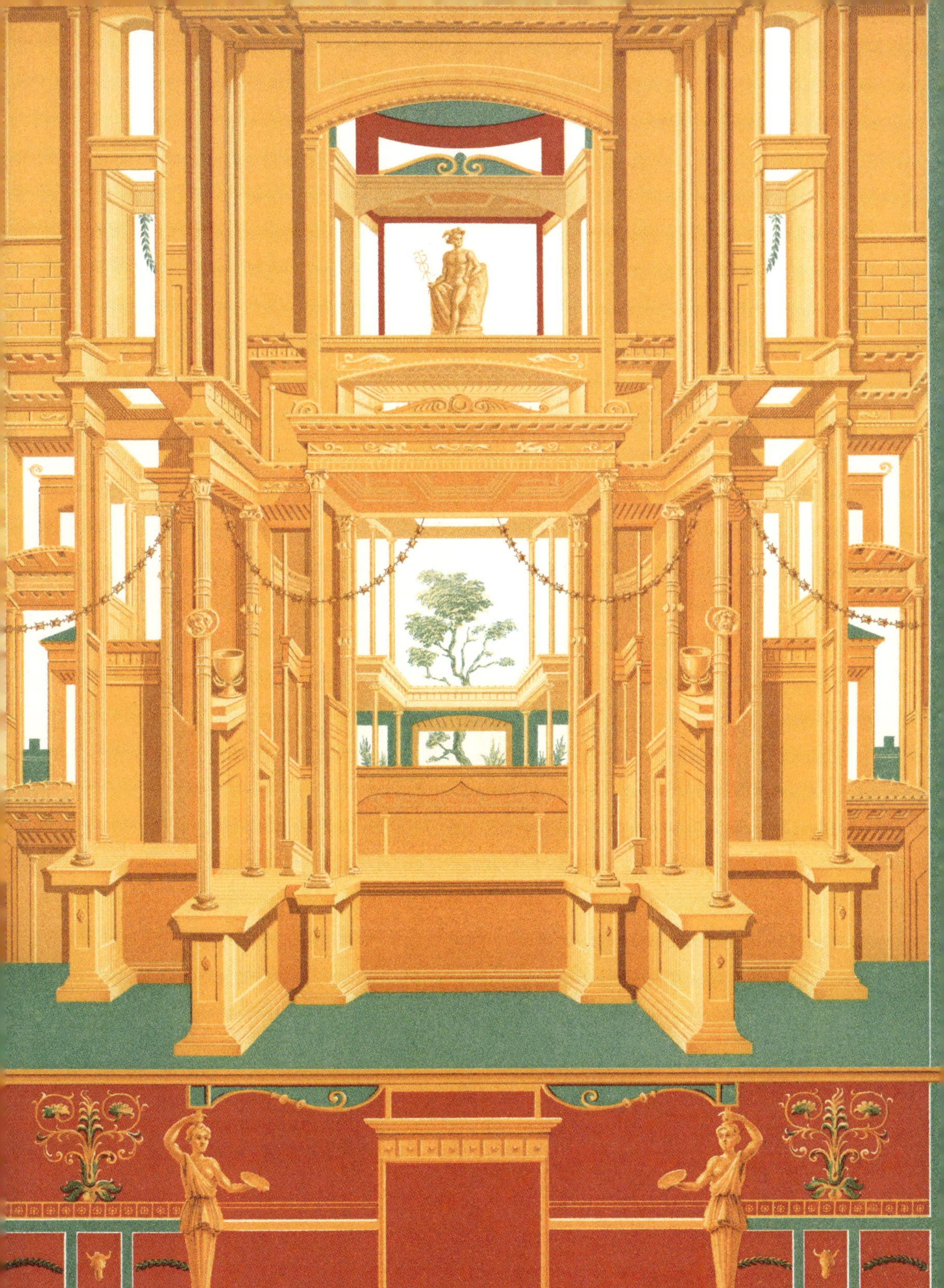

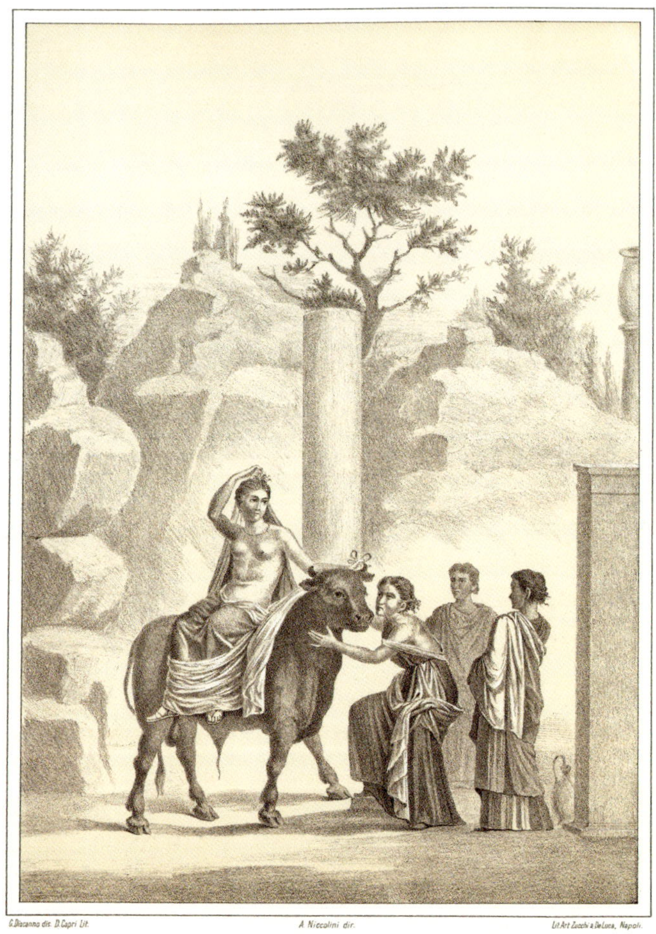

Plate 19 — *[G. Discanno]*
Casa di Giasone (IX 5, 18–21) – Central picture of a wall decoration in the 3rd style. Europa is sitting on a bull, which is being stroked by a female companion.

Plate 17 — *[G. Discanno]*
Casa di Sirico (VII 1, 25. 46 and 47), central picture in an exedra – The drunken Hercules lies helpless on the ground in front of an altar, while a group of erotes appropriate his weapons. Omphale is seated with her female companions on the left, and in the right-hand background Dionysus can be seen with his retinue. His power has vanquished the hero (vol. I, Casa di Sirico).

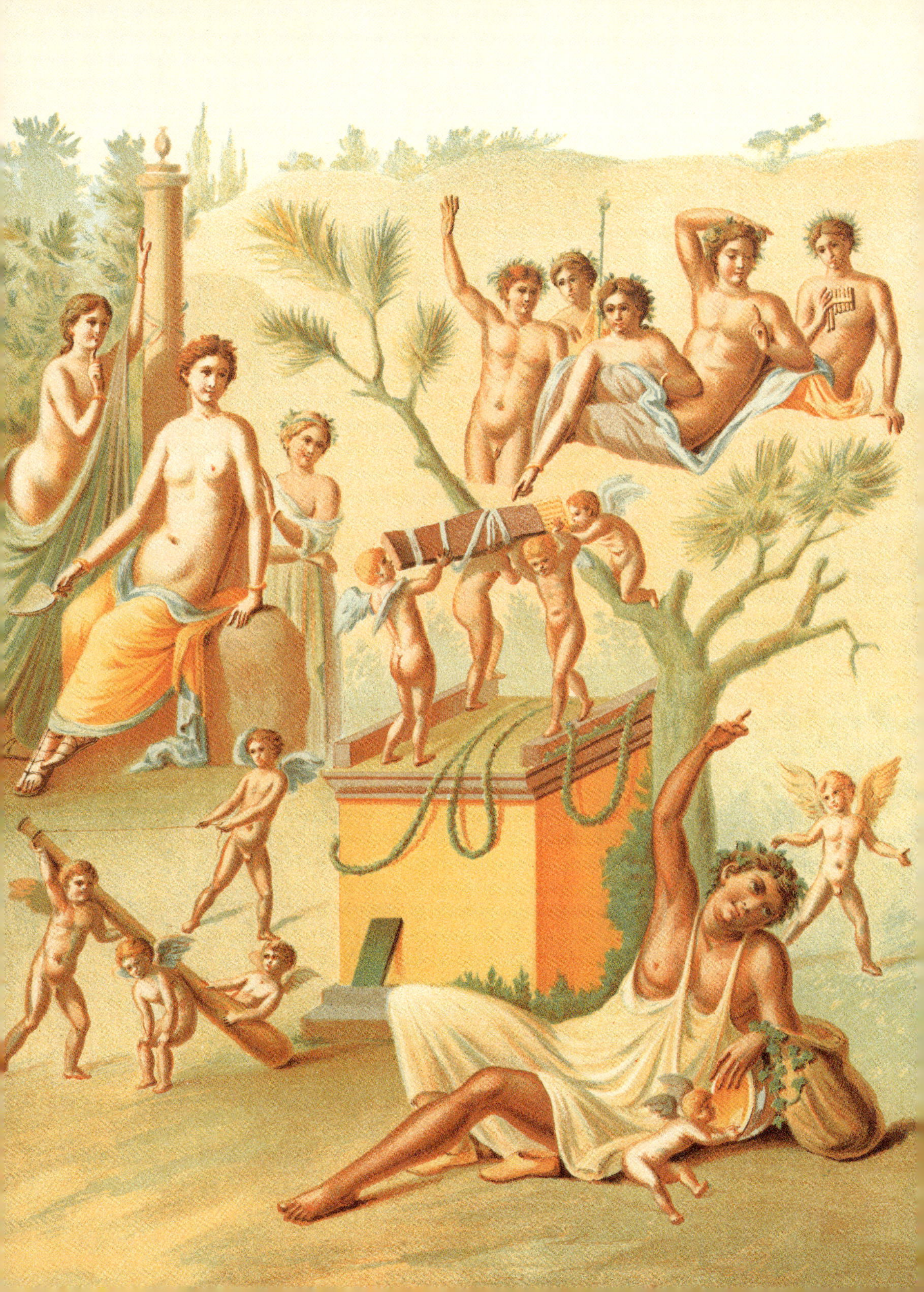

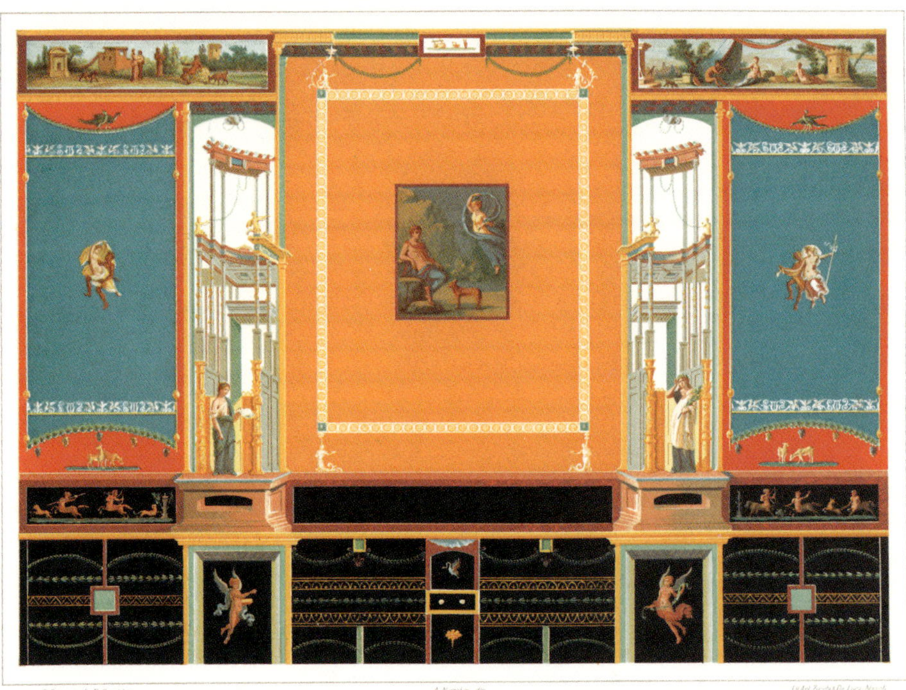

Plate 20 — *[G. Discanno]*
The original location of this decoration is not recorded and the plate perhaps represents a compilation of different elements. The central picture shows the myth of Endymion and Selene.

Plate 21 — *[G. Discanno]*
Casa di M. Caesius Blandus, Oecus (VII 1, 40) – Socle zone of a decoration in the late 2nd style with winged supporting (?) figures.

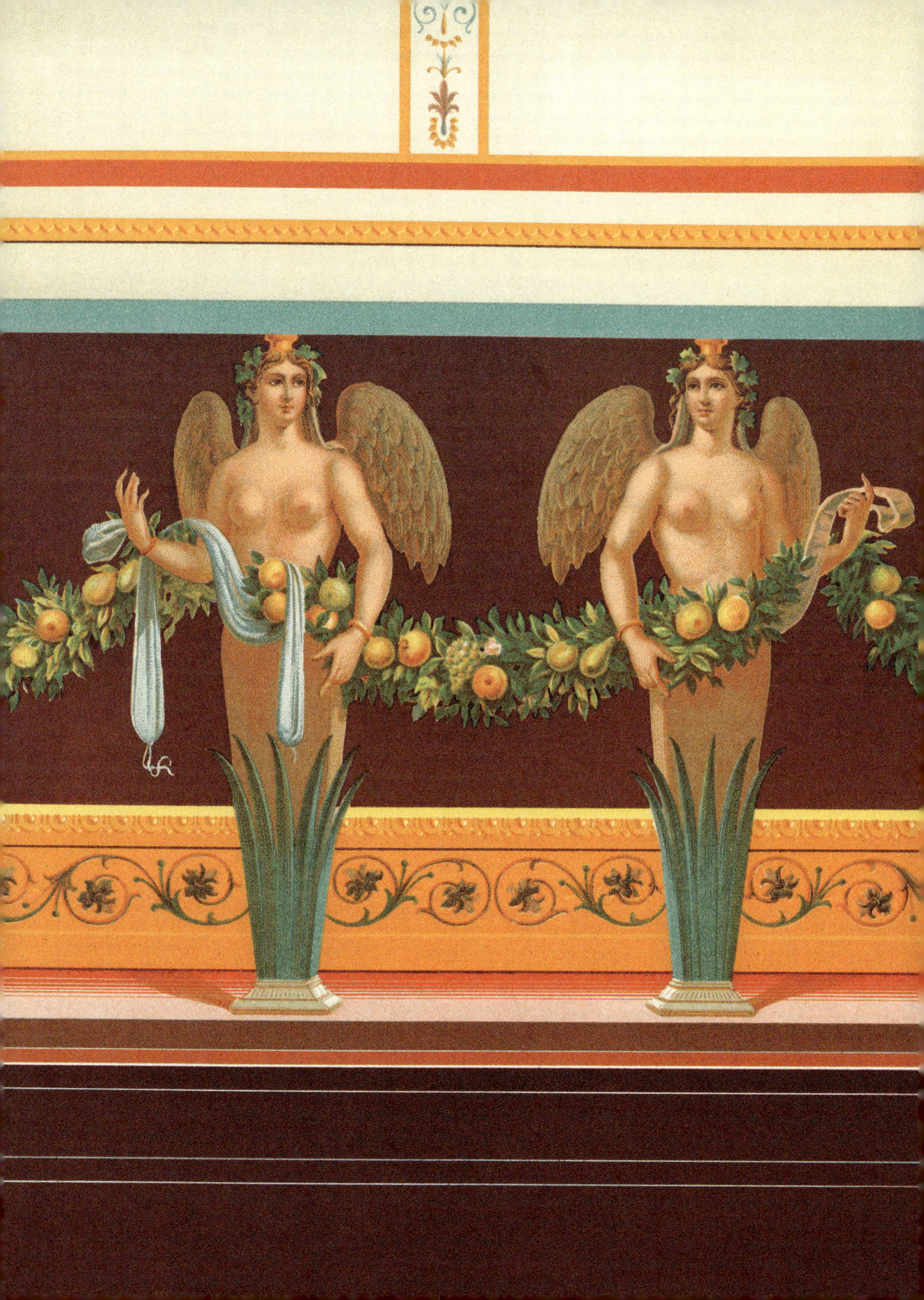

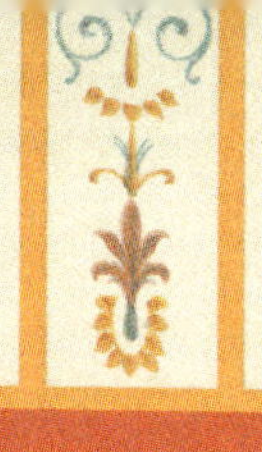

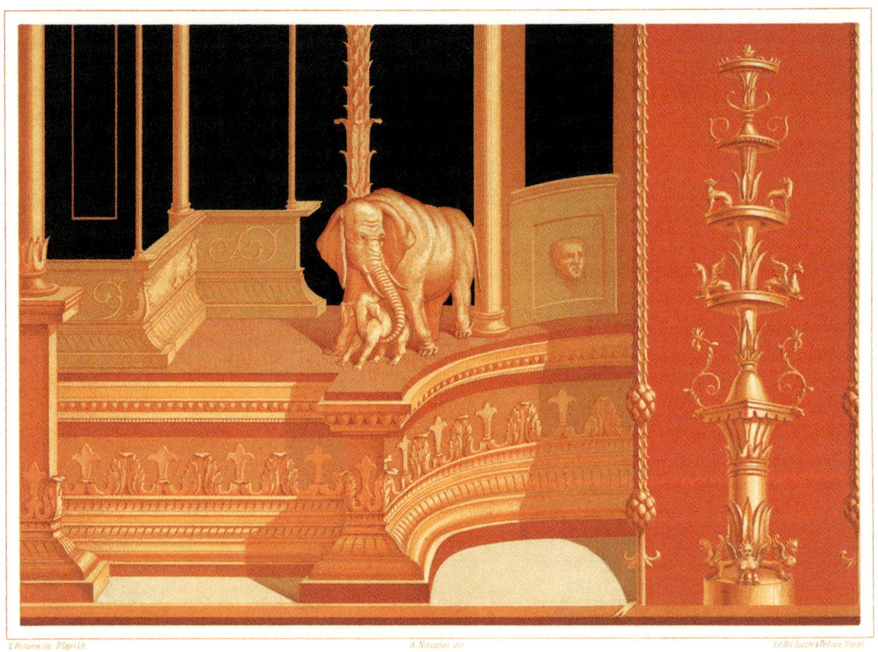

Plate 25 — *[V. Mollame]*
Herculaneum – Detail of a 4th-style wall decoration that was discovered and cut out in the 18th century.

Plate 22 — *[V. Mollame]*
Herculaneum, palaestra in the Insula occidentalis – The large fragment, which was cut out at the early date of 1743, shows the upper zone of a large architectural prospect in the 4th style. It was frequently reproduced in illustrations.

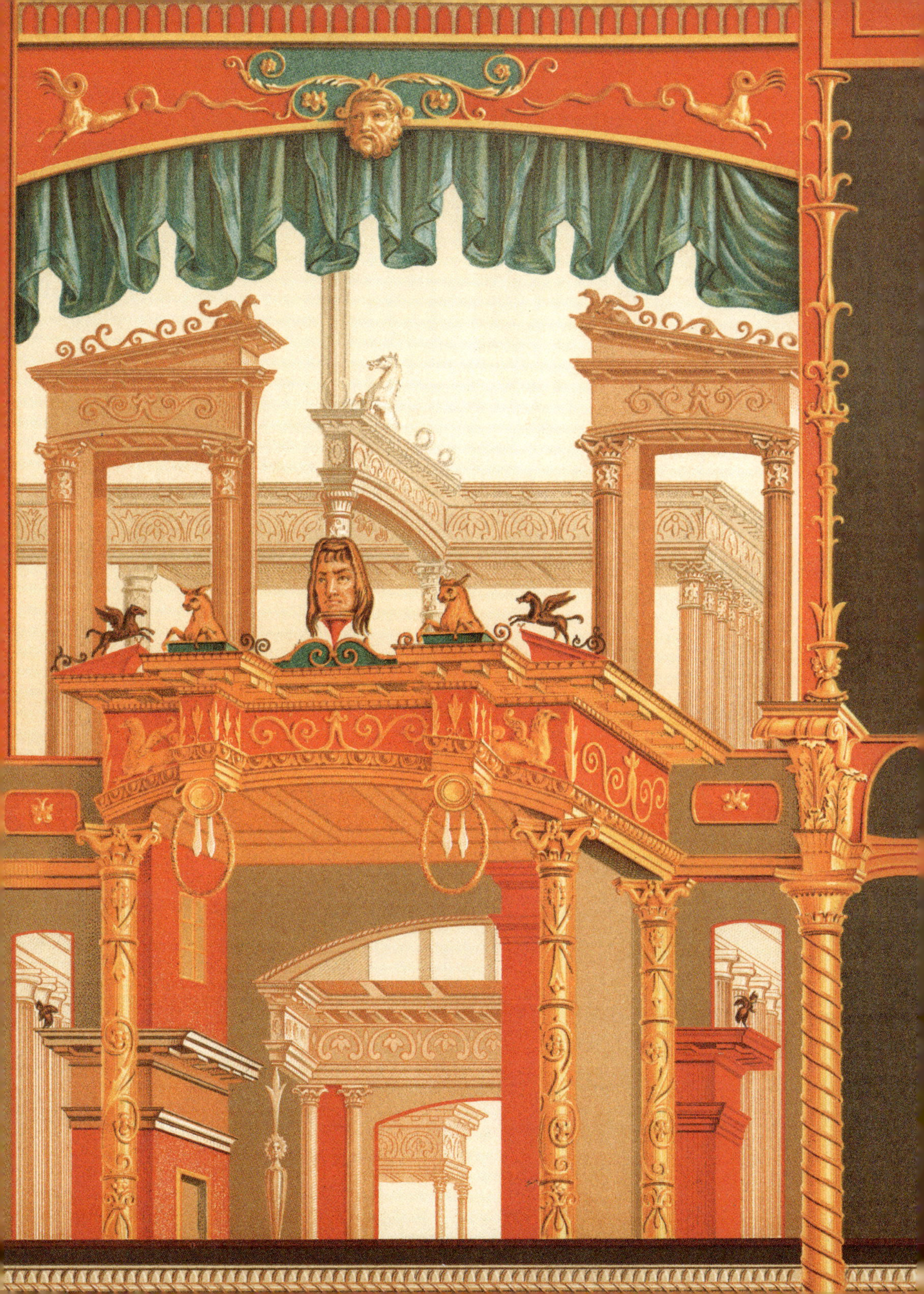

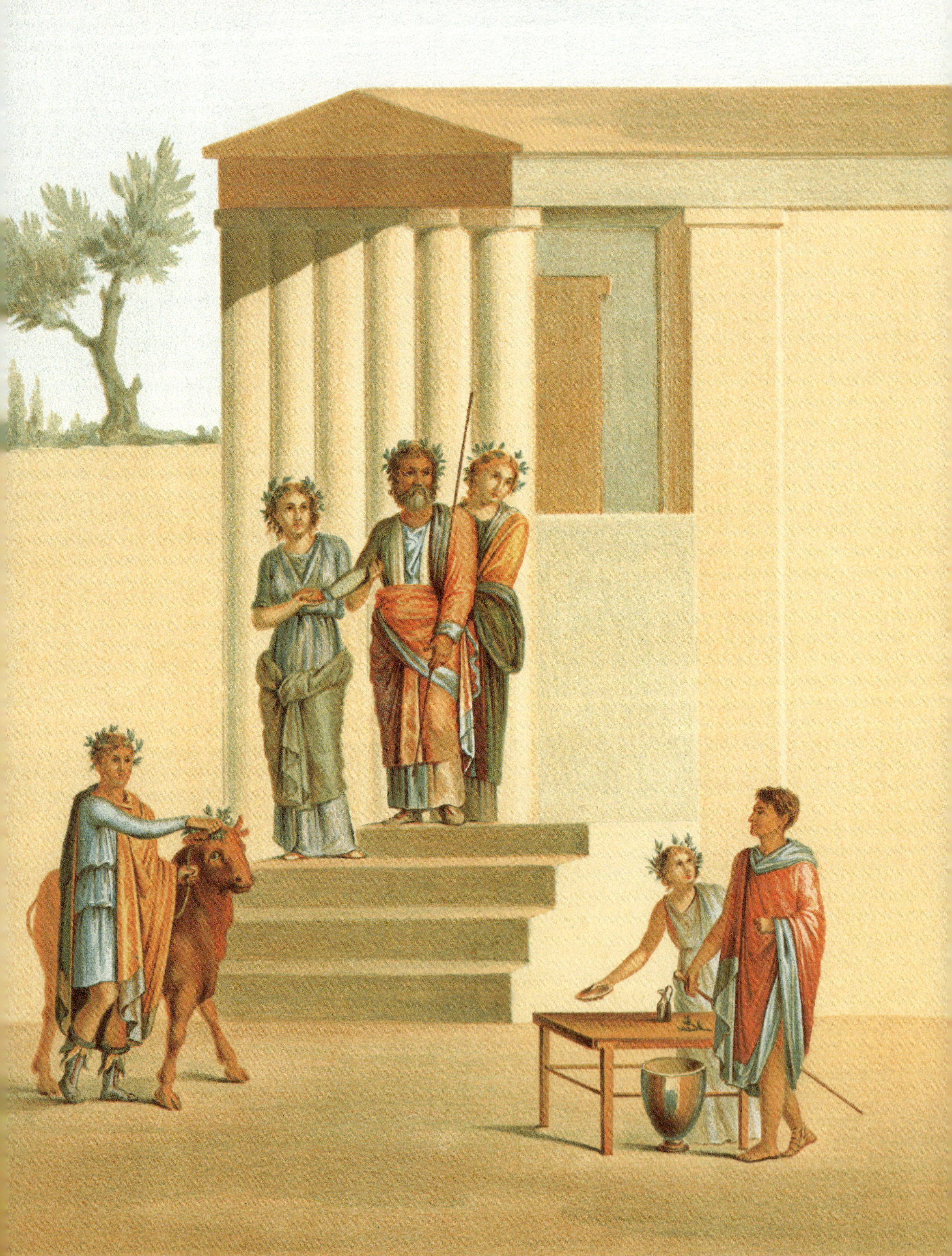

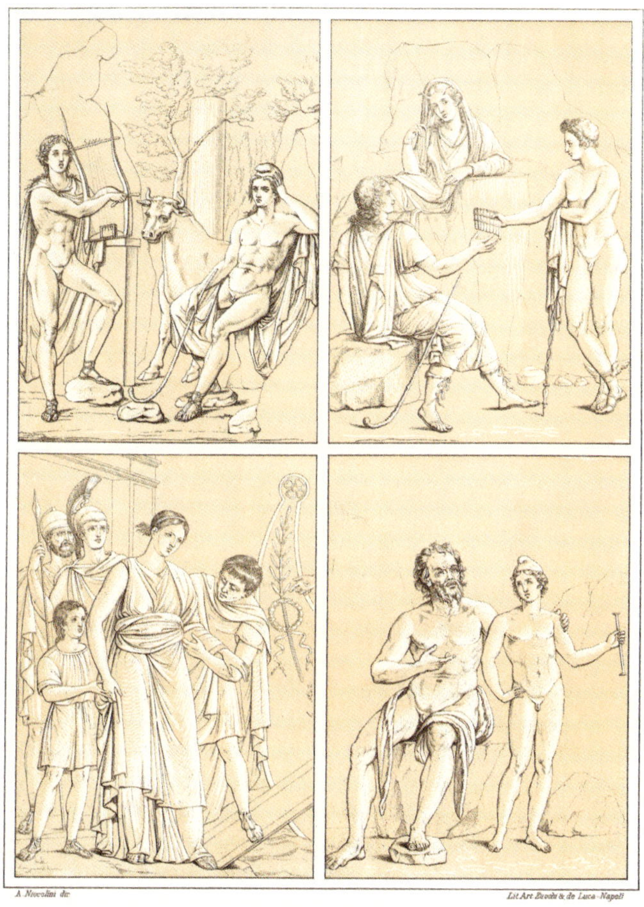

Plate 23 — *[G. Discanno]*
Casa di Giasone, triclinium (IX 5, 18–21) – Scene from the legend of the Argonauts: Jason before the high priest Pelias.

✲

Plate 24 — *[Anonymous]*
Four mythological pictures of different subjects, found in different locations – Above left: from the Casa dei Dioscuri (VI 9, 6–9); Apollo and a shepherd (Laomedon, Admetus or Branchus, the priest of the oracle at Didyma). Above right: from the Casa del Citarista (I 4, 5); Hermes hands Argus, who is guarding Io, a set of panpipes (syrinx). Below left: from the Casa del Poeta tragico (VI 8, 3–5), atrium; abduction of Helen (?). Below right: from the Casa di Meleagro (VI 9, 2 and 13); Marsyas teaches Olympus to play the flute.

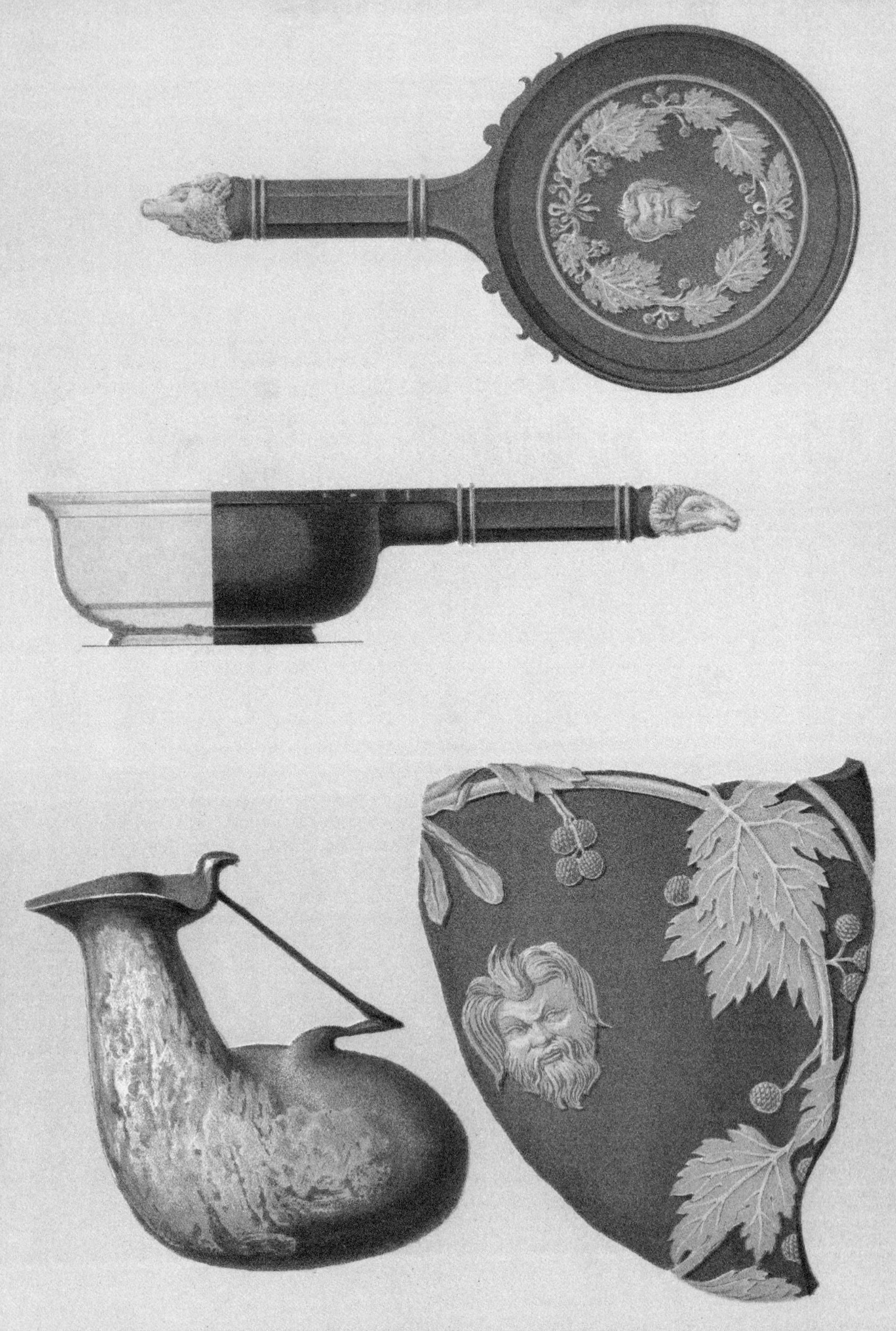

Plate 26 — *[V. Mollame]*

Casa dei Bronzi (VII 4, 59) – Fragment and reconstruction of a dish with a handle, made of two-layered glass (so-called cameo glass). The central motif shows a satyr's head encircled by vine leaves. Below left: wine jar made of blue glass.

✠

Page 370

Plate 35 — *[D. Capri]*

Casa di Epidius Sabinus (IX 1, 22 and 29) – Detail of a 3rd-style wall decoration. The socle zone is missing.

✠

Page 371

Plate 33 — *[V. Mollame]*

Accademia di Musica (VI 3, 7), triclinium – Middle section of a wall in the 3rd style. The central picture shows the grieving Dido with a sword in her lap.

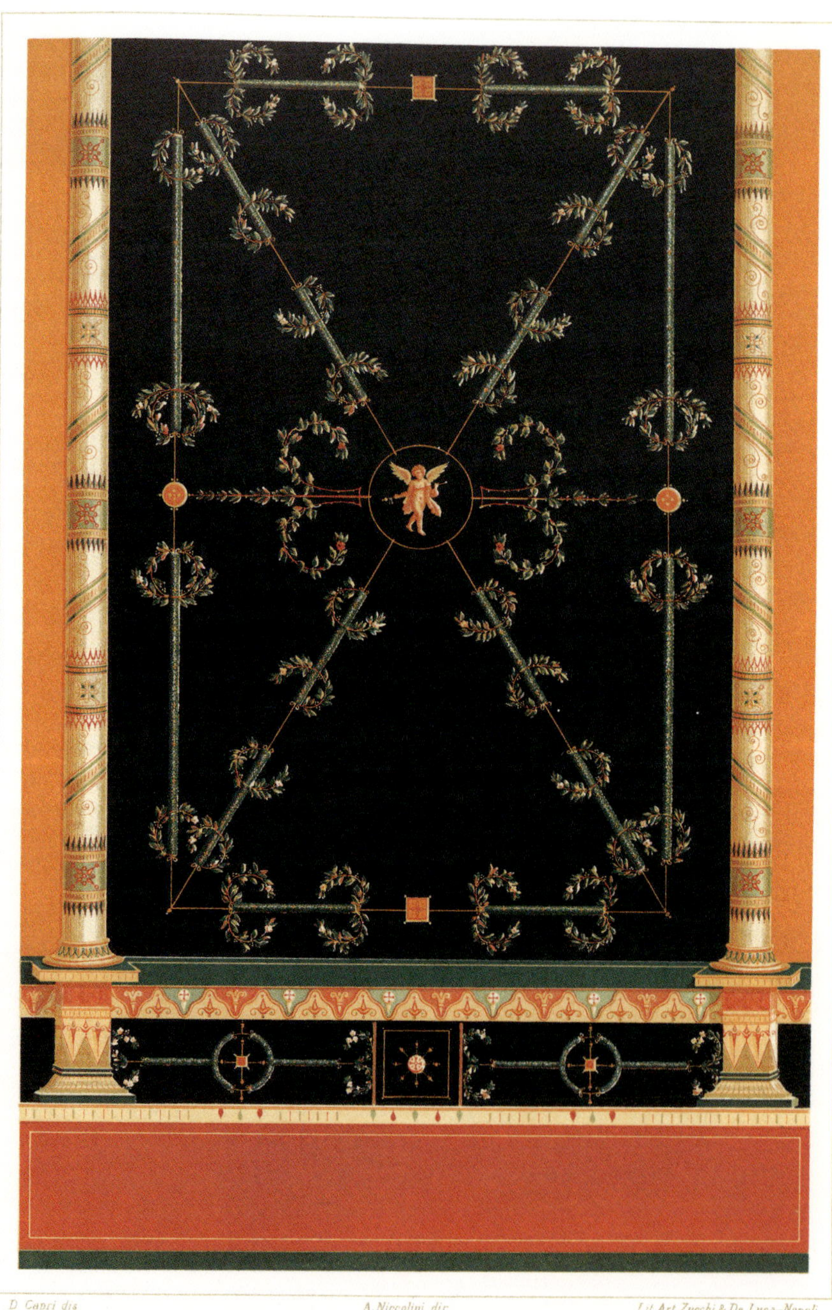

D. Capri dis A. Niccolini dir. Lit. Art. Zucchi & De Luca–Napoli

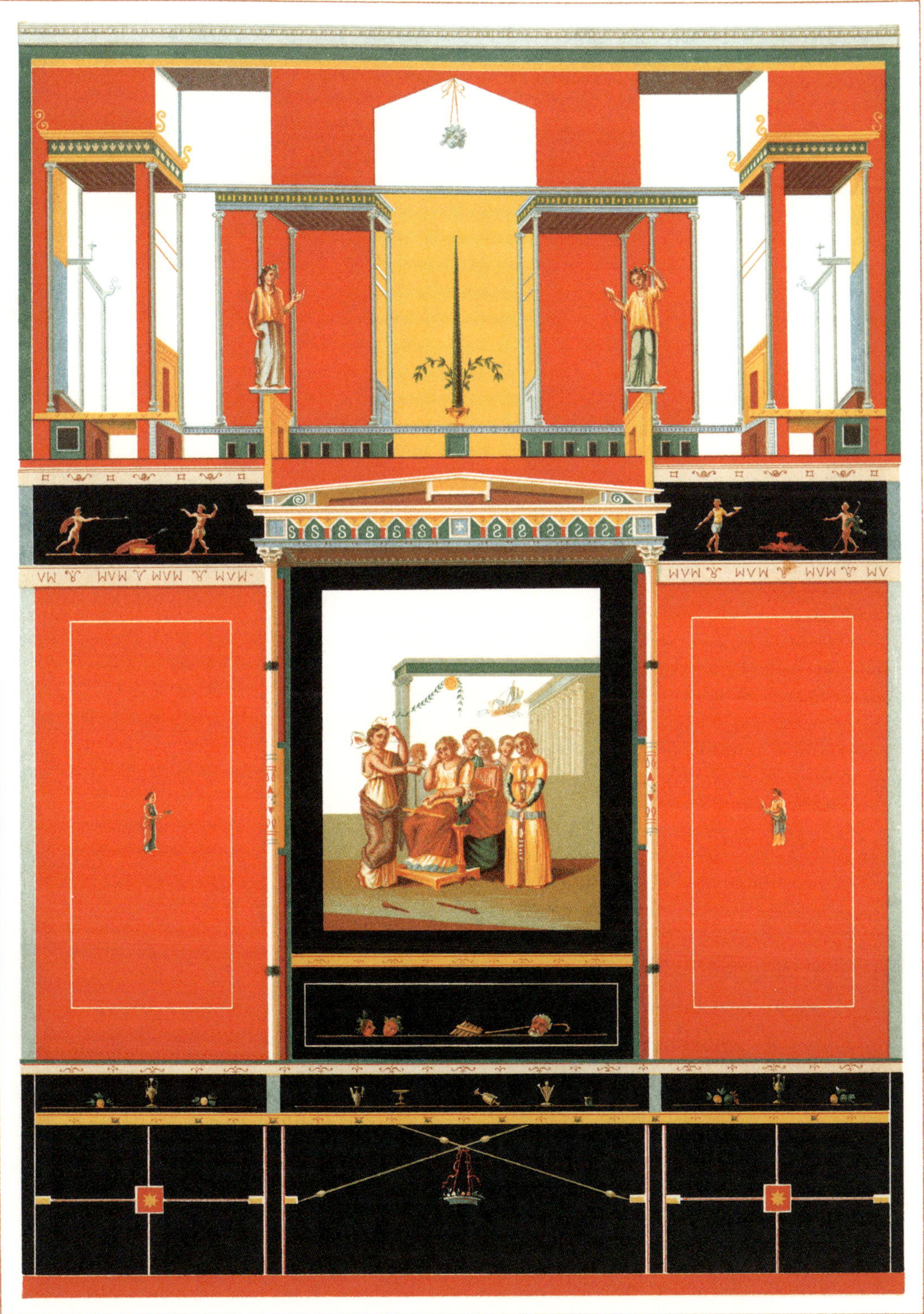

V. Mollame dis. D. Capri Lit. A. Niccolini dir. Lit. Art. Zucchi & De Luca, Napoli.

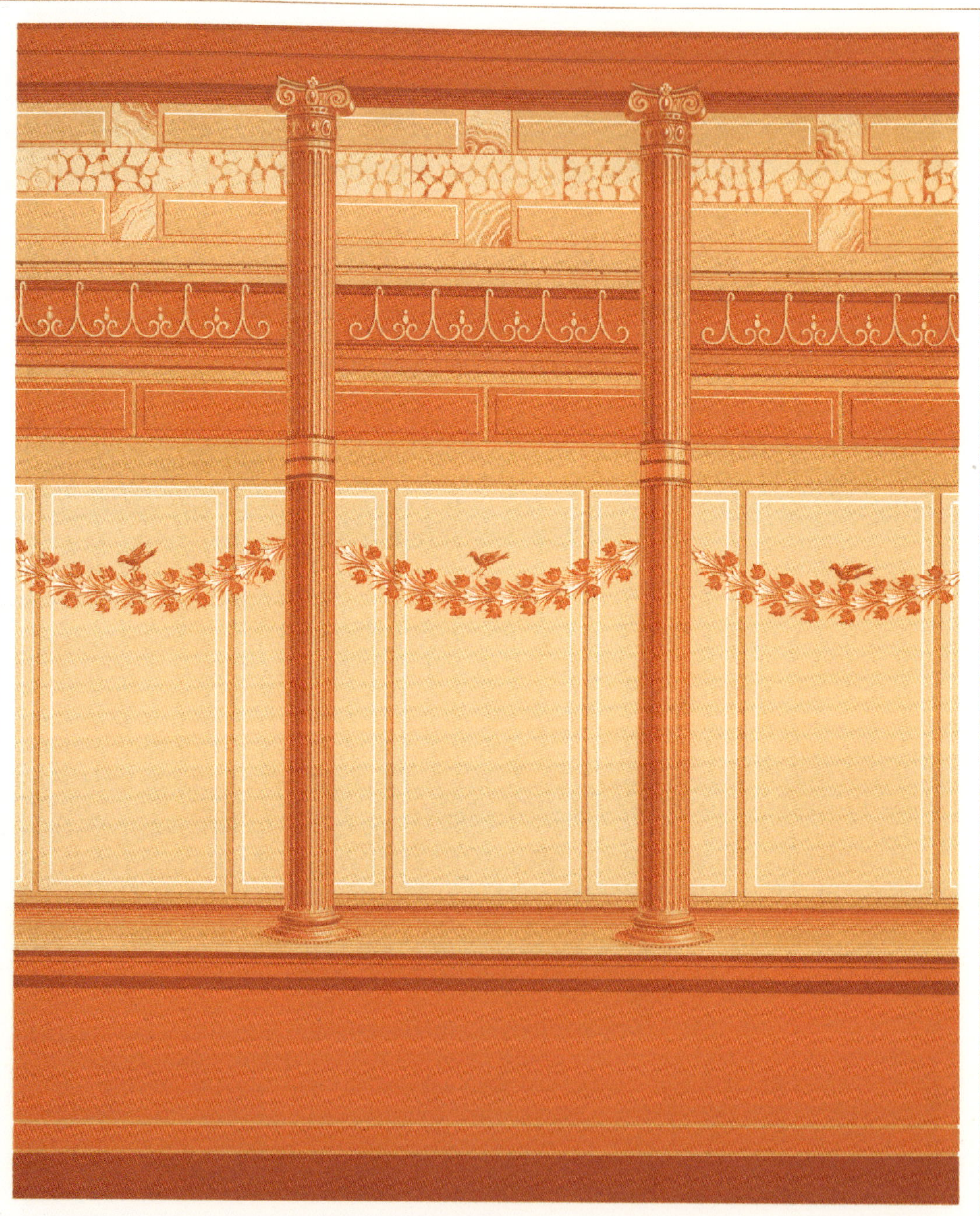

A. Magliano dis. D. Capri Lit. A. Niccolini dir. Lit. Art. Zucchi & De Luca, Napoli.

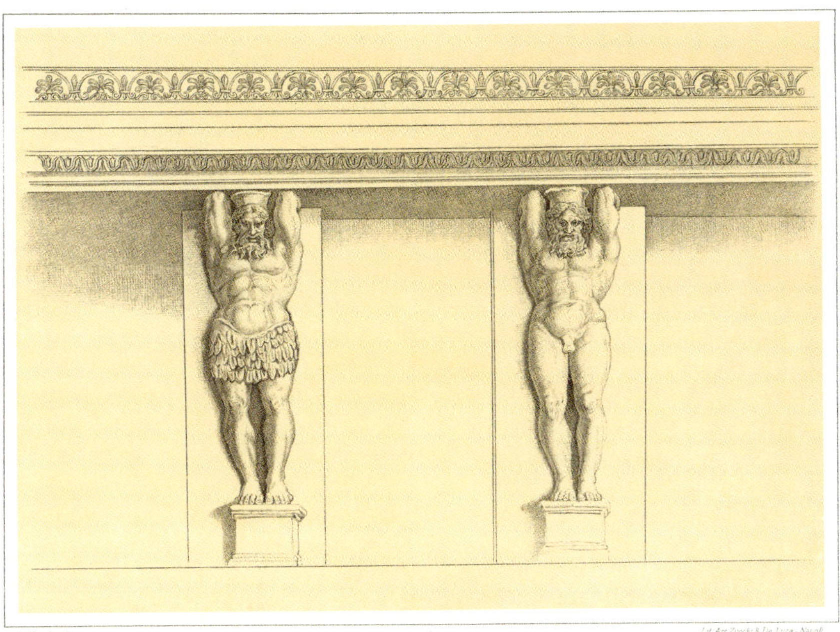

A. Niccolini dir. Lit. Art. Zerchi & De Luca - Napoli

Plate 36 — *[A. Magliano]*
Casa degli Epigrammi greci (V 1, 18), triclinium – Wall decoration in the 2nd style, here making its first appearance in the Niccolini repertoire. The monochrome palette does not correspond to the lost original, however.

Plate 37 — *[Anonymous]*
Forum Baths, caldarium – Terracotta male supporting figures on a wall cornice. Niccolini's description made particular mention of the traces of colour originally clearly visible on the beard and hair (black), cornice and background (gold and porphyry red).

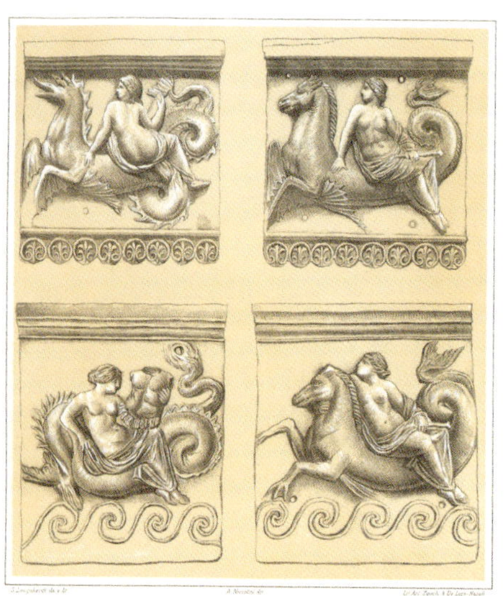

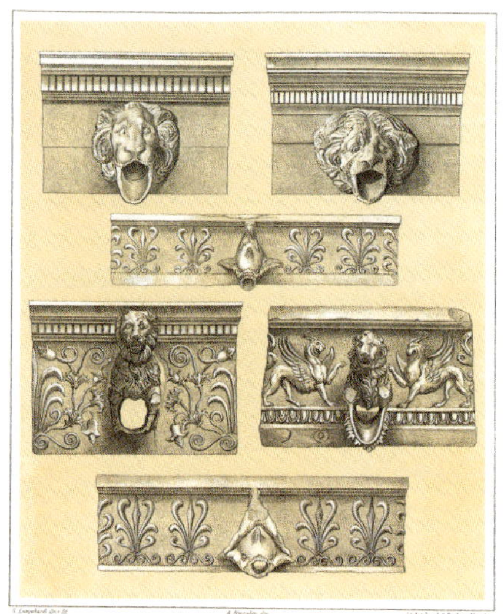

Plate 39 — *[S. Longobardi]*
Terracotta friezes from roof claddings in Pompeii – Above: origin unknown; Nereids on a sea dragon and a sea horse. Below: Casa del Fauno (VI 12, 2), peristyle; a Nereid on the back of a sea monster carrying a breastplate across the sea.

✥

Plate 42 — *[S. Longobardi]*
Various terracotta decorations from roof lines and water containers – Found in different houses and in some cases preserved in the museum depository in Pompeii.

✥

Plate 38 — *[V. Mollame]*
Casa del Centauro (VI 9, 3 and 5) – Mosaic with the representation of a lion being tamed by erotes. Below: *Casa dei Capitelli colorati (VII 4, 31–51)* – From a wall decoration (?) in the upper storey. Marble intarsia *(crustae)* on a slate panel. This rare and costly piece shows a maenad and a satyr dancing in front of a small temple of Dionysus.

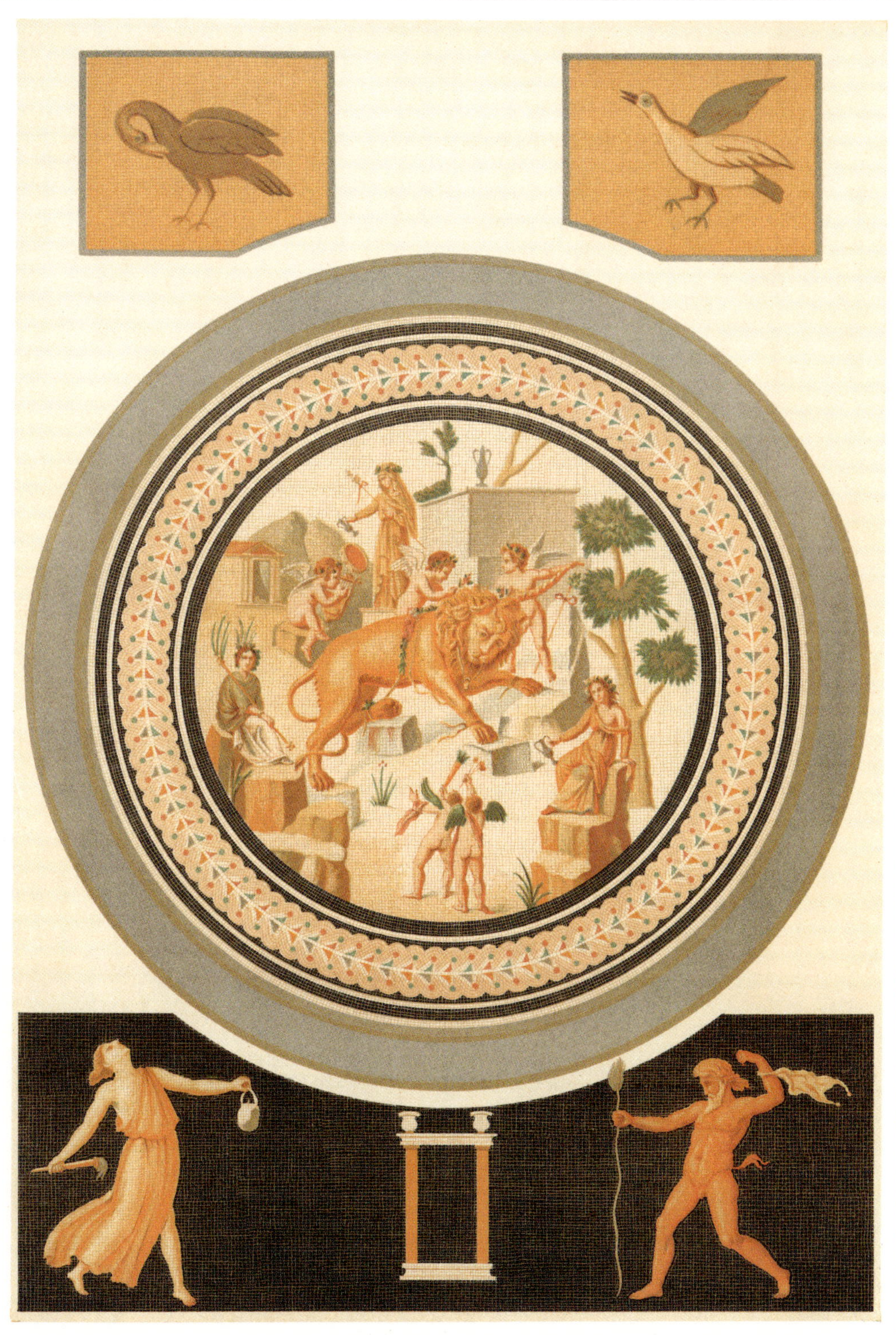

V. Mollame dis. D. Capri Lit. A. Niccolini dir. Lit. Art. Zucchi & De Luca, Napoli.

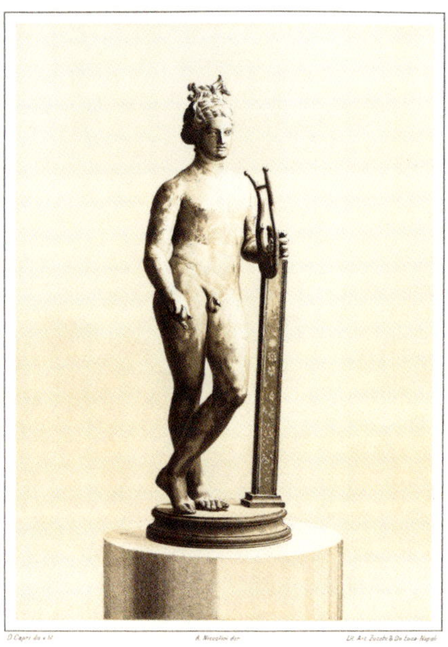

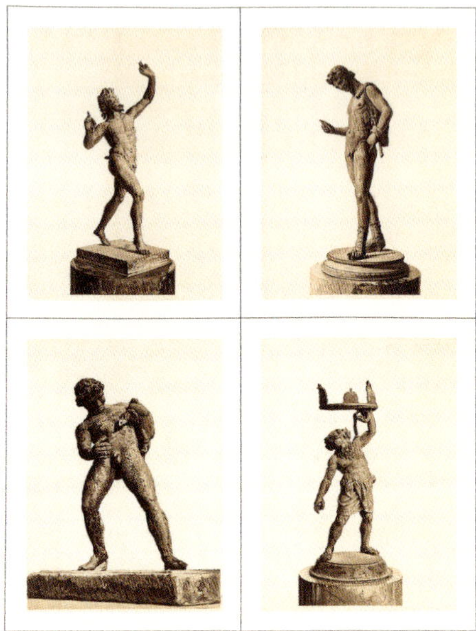

Plate 46 — *[D. Capri]*
Casa delle Danzatrici (VI 2, 15 and 21) – Bronze statuette of Apollo playing the cithara. The statuette, actually found in March 1811, was reburied and then "officially" discovered in April in the presence of Queen Caroline Murat.

Plate 41 — *[D. Capri]*
Composite picture of four famous bronze statuettes – Already reproduced in other plates (vol. I, Casa del Fauno, pl. 5; vol. II, Descrizione generale, pl. 15, 94 and 19) and here shown again "for the convenience of the reader".

Plate 40 — *[A. Magliano]*
Casa degli Epigrammi (V 1, 18. 11 and 12), exedra – Detail from a wall decoration in the 3rd style. The central picture shows Aphrodite, Ares and erotes. The upper part of the all, which was destroyed by bombing in the Second World War, survives only in the form of this lithograph.

Pages 378–379
Plate 44 — *[A. Magliano]*
Casa IX 5, 11 and 13, tablinum – This 4th-style wall decoration, uncovered in 1877, is otherwise only documented in a black-and-white photograph taken around 1880.

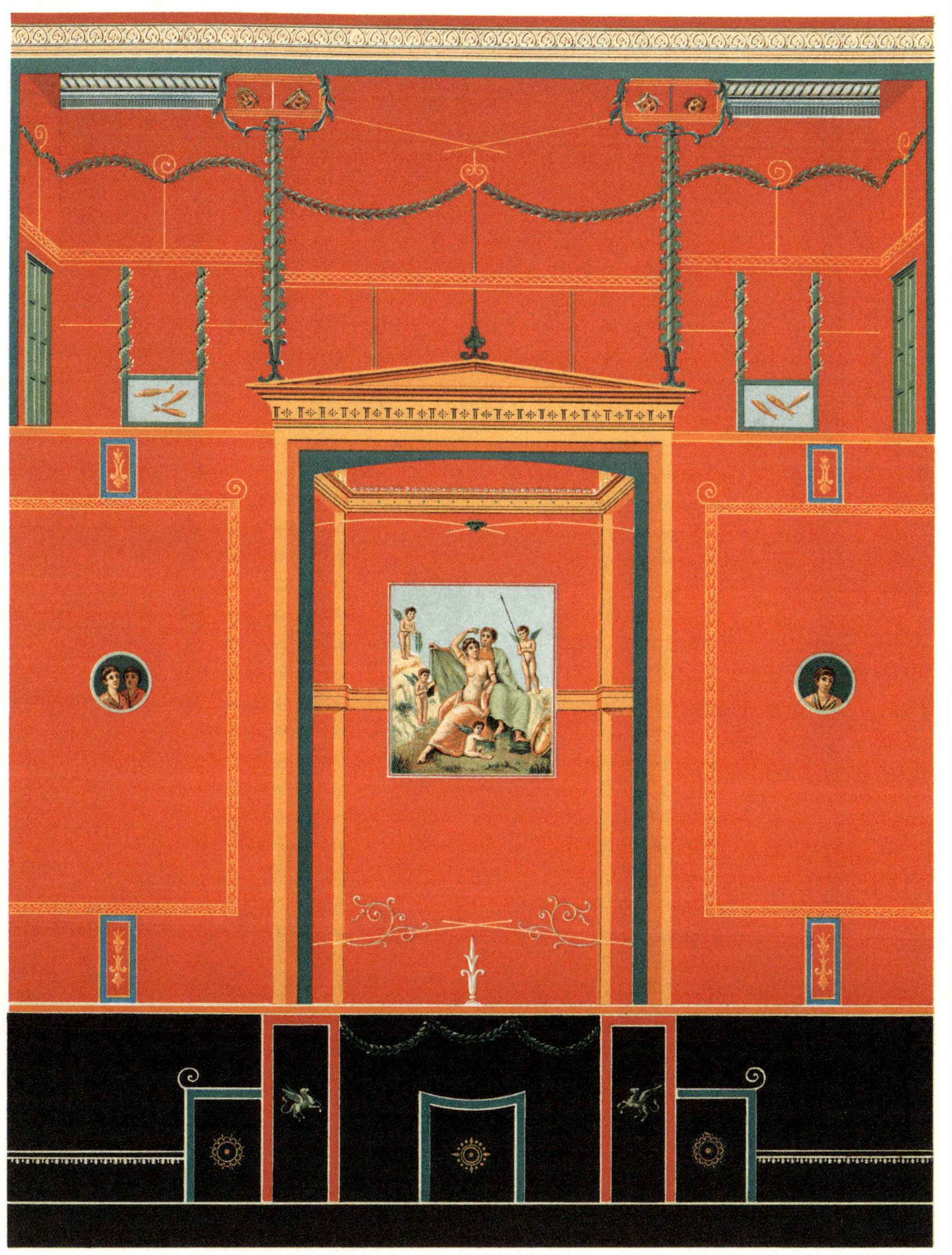

A. Magliano dis. D. Capri Lit. A. Niccolini dir. Lit. Art. Zucchi & De Luca, Napoli.

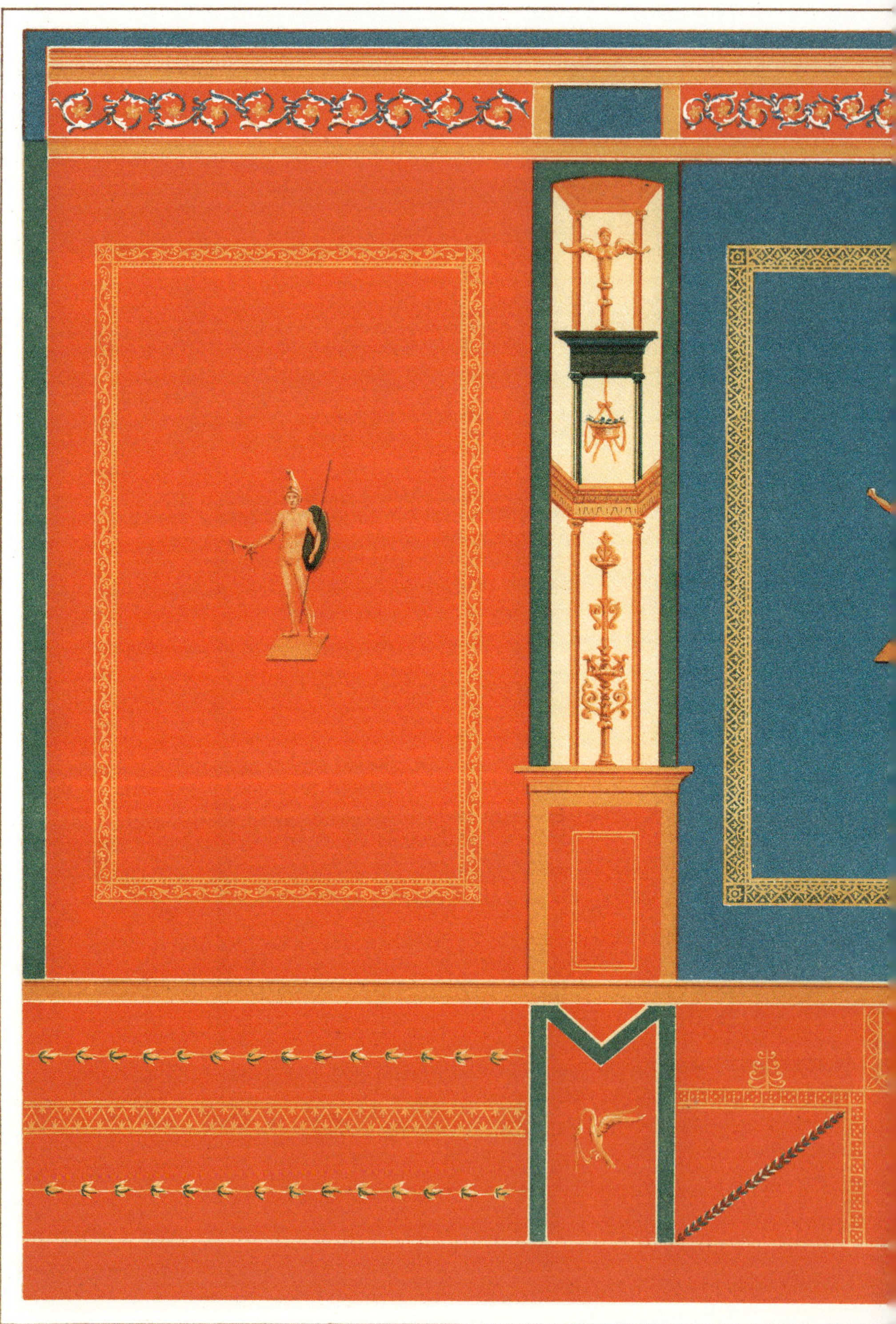

A. Magliano dis. D. Capri Lit. A. Nicc

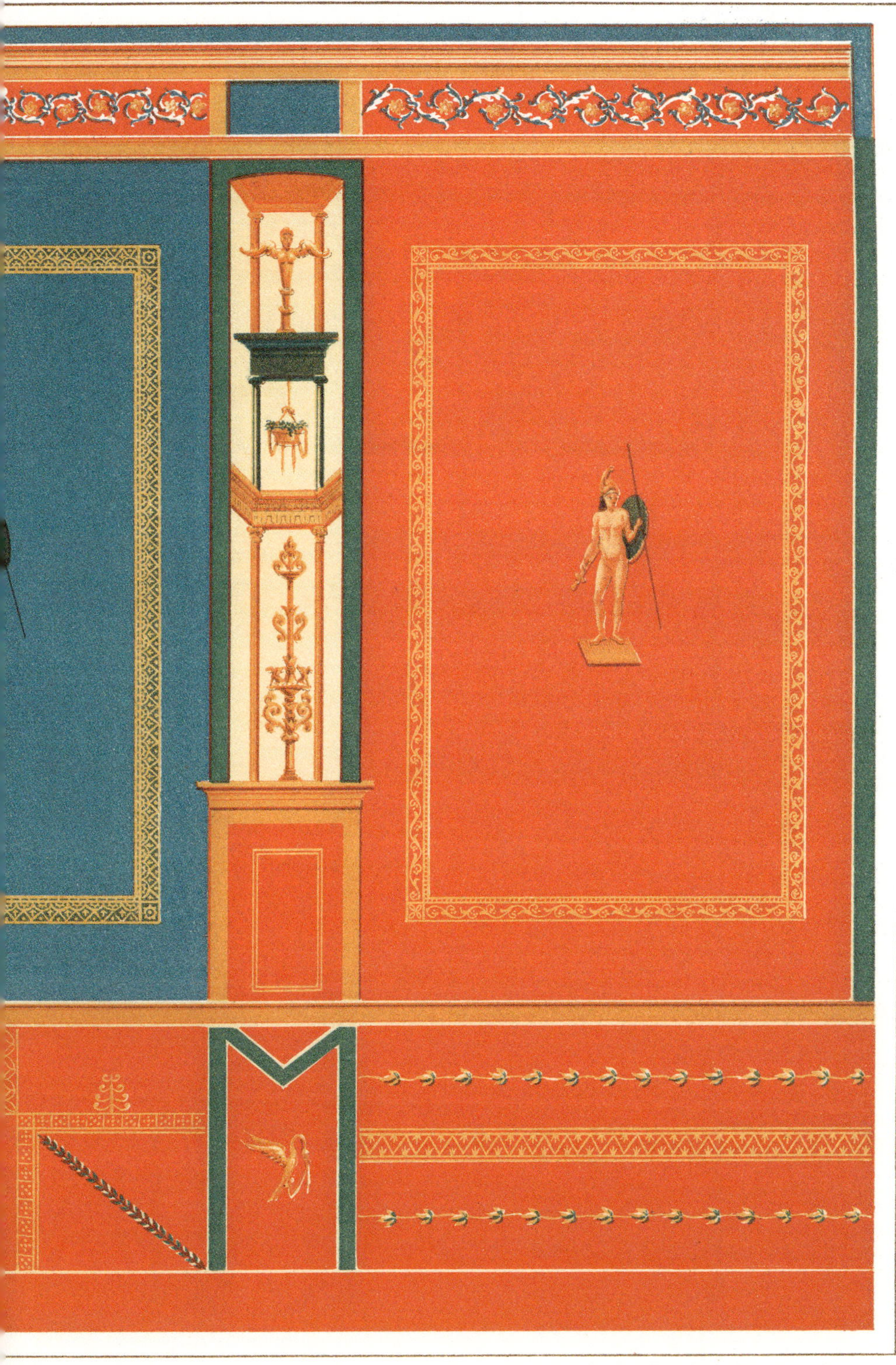

r.

Lit. Art. Zucchi & De Luca–Napoli

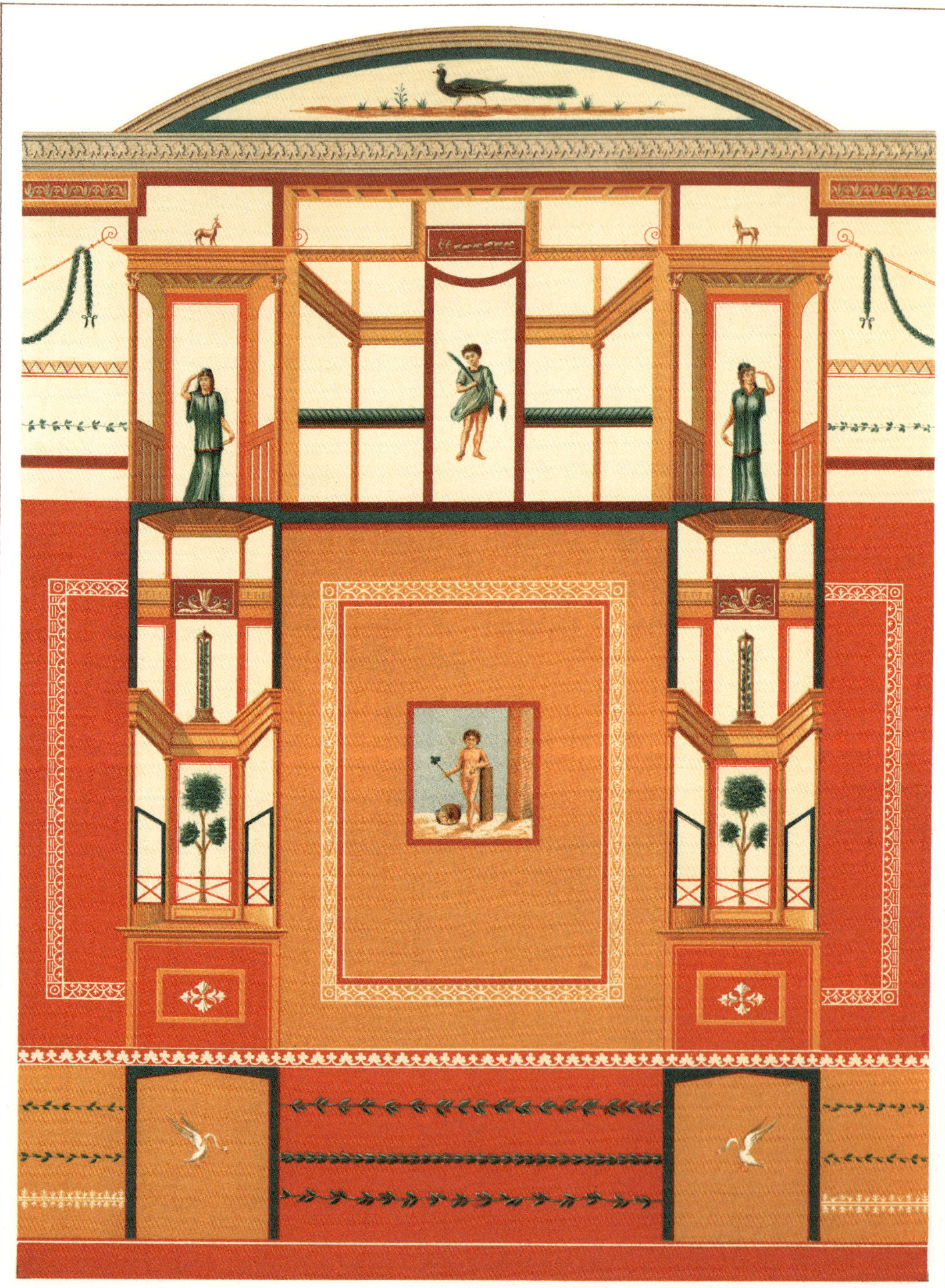

A. Magliano dis. Capri Lit. A. Niccolini dir. Lit. Art. Zucchi & De Luca, Napoli.

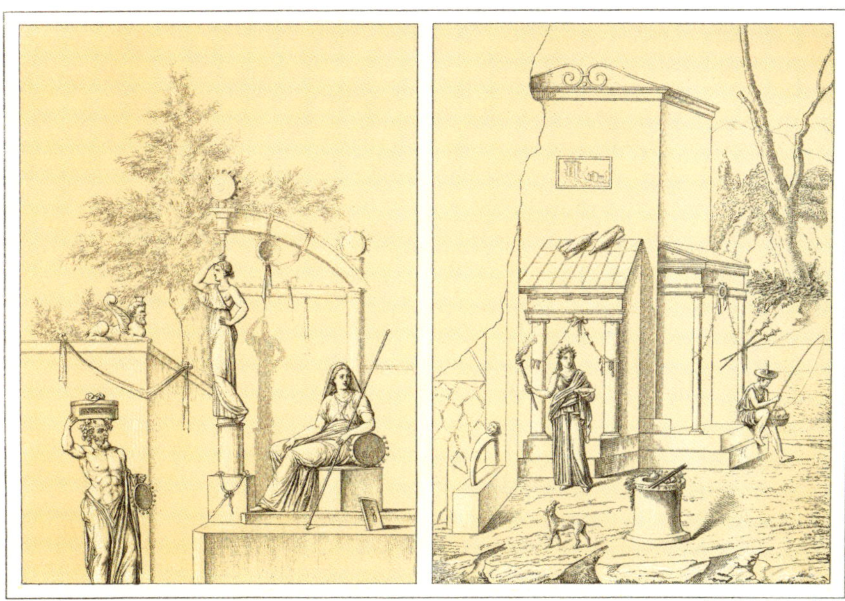

A. Niccolini dir. Lit. Art. Zucchi & De Luca-Napoli

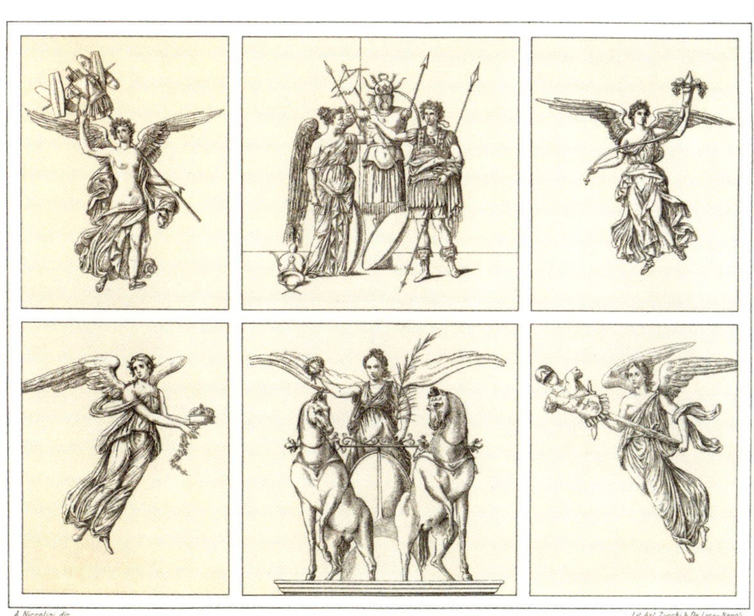

A. Niccolini dir. Lit. Art. Zucchi & De Luca-Napoli

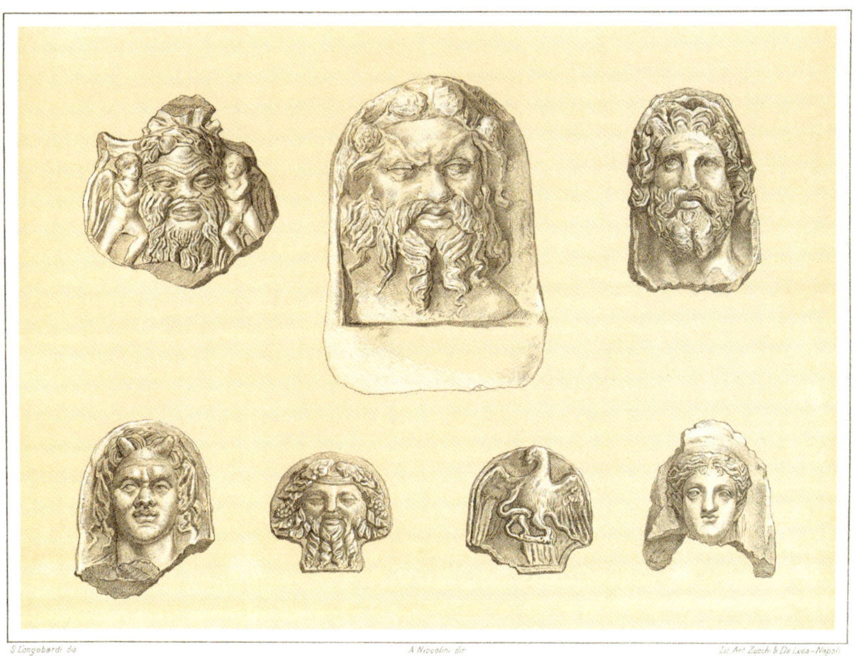

Page 380

Plate 43 — *[A. Magliano]*

Casa IX 5, 11 and 13 – Today largely lost wall decoration in the 4th style.

Page 381

Plate 51 — *[Anonymous]*

Two pictures in the 3rd style showing landscapes with temples (so-called sacro-idyllic landscapes) – Left: Casa VII 6, 28, cubiculum. Right: Casa dei Dioscuri (VI 9, 6 and 7) (?).

Page 381

Plate 52 — *[Anonymous]*

Various representations of the goddess Victory from Pompeii – With a cornucopia, a victor's crown, in a chariot and with a warrior crowning a tropaion.

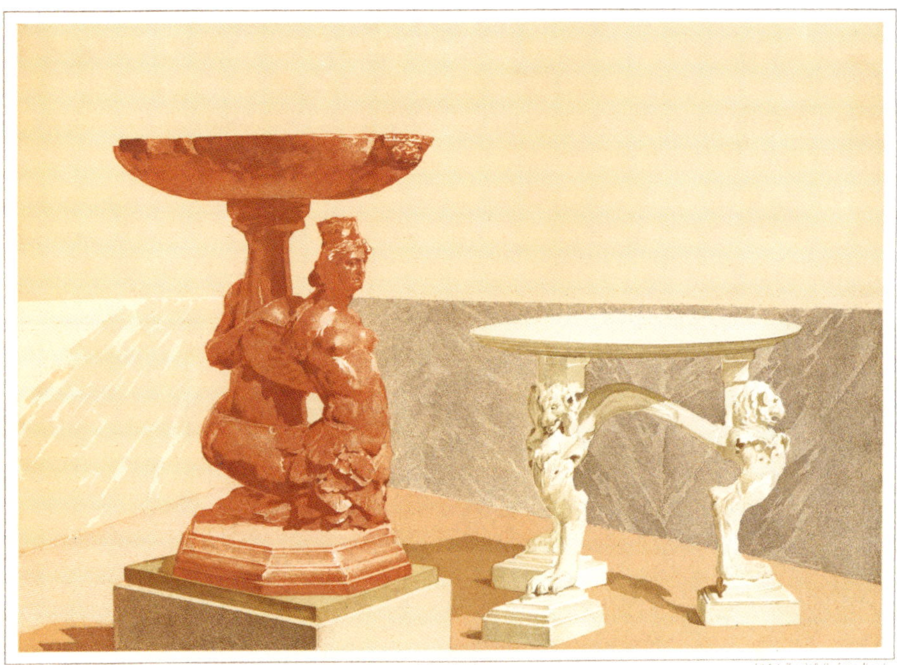

Page 382

Plate 47 — *[S. Longobardi]*

Terracotta antefixae (ornamental blocks concealing the ends of roof tiles) with various motifs, found in different locations.

Plate 48 — *[A. Carelli]*

Casa delle Amazzoni (VI 2, 14), Atrium – In 1812 the red marble basin found in Pompeii was combined, in the royal palace in Naples, with a modern pedestal in the shape of the sea monster Scylla. The marble table in the background likewise once furnished an atrium and comes from Herculaneum.

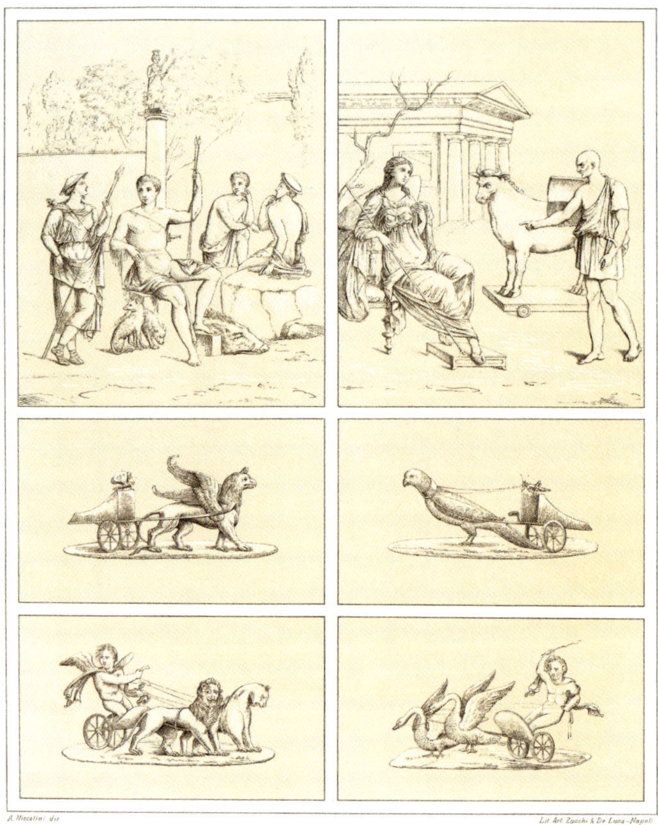

Plate 55 — *[Anonymous]*
The sheet combines two mythological pictures and representations of unusual chariots. Above left: Casa del Centauro (VI 9, 3 and 5), tablinum; the lovers Atalanta and Meleager. Above right: Casa della Caccia antica (VII 4, 48. 43 and 44); Daedalus presents Queen Pasiphae with the wooden cow in which she conceals herself in order to mate with Zeus, in the form of a bull, and so conceives the Minotaur. Below: young erotes driving chariots.

❖

Plate 53 — *[A. Carelli]*
Casa di Sallustio (VI 2, 4), peristyle, west wall – Niccolini emphasised that this decoration survives only in the form of a watercolour in his own archive.

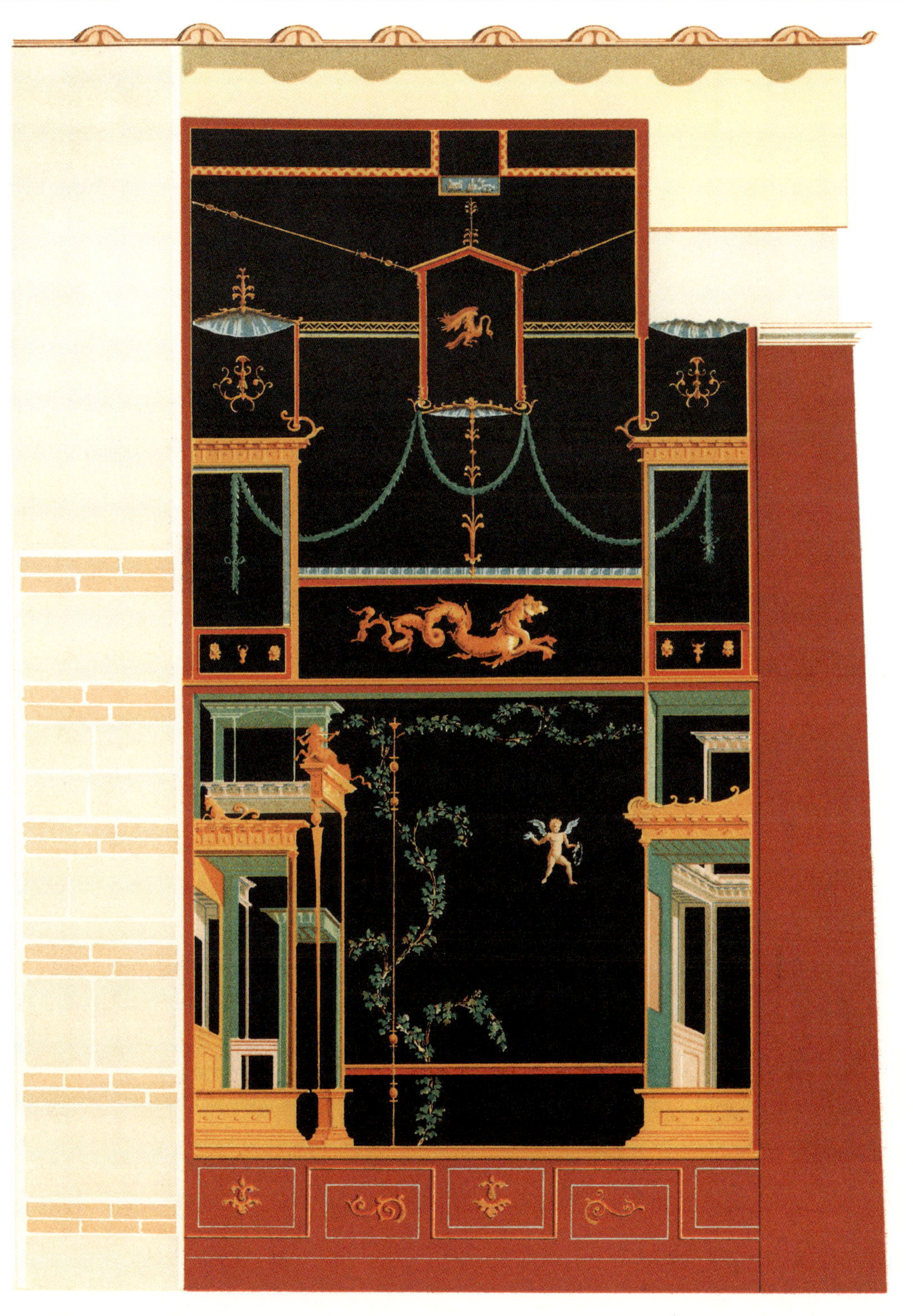

A. Carelli dis. D. Capri Lit. A. Niccolini dir. Lit. Art. Zucchi & De Luca, Napoli.

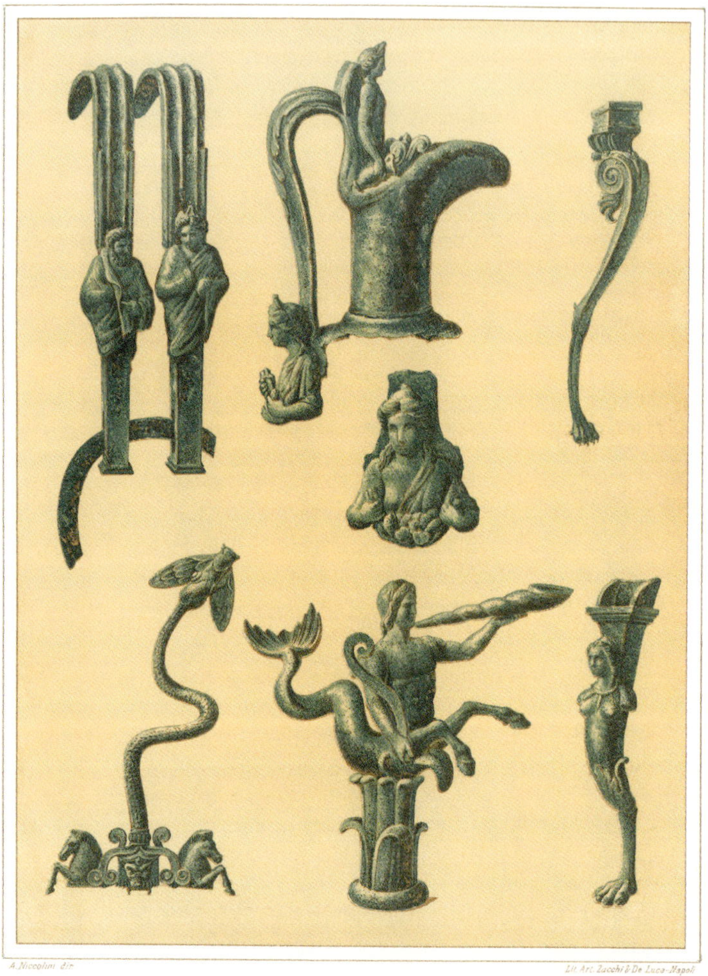

A. Niccolini dir. Lit. Art. Zucchi & De Luca-Napoli

Plate 56 — *[Anonymous]*
Parts of various utility items made of bronze – Two *strigiles* and the spout and handle of a jug, as well as table legs and a table decoration in the shape of a triton. Niccolini underlined the artistic quality of these pieces, evident even in the details of these fragments.

Plate 54 — *[A. Magliano]*
Casa dei Capitelli colorati (VII 4, 31 and 51), tablinum – Wall decoration in the 4th style.

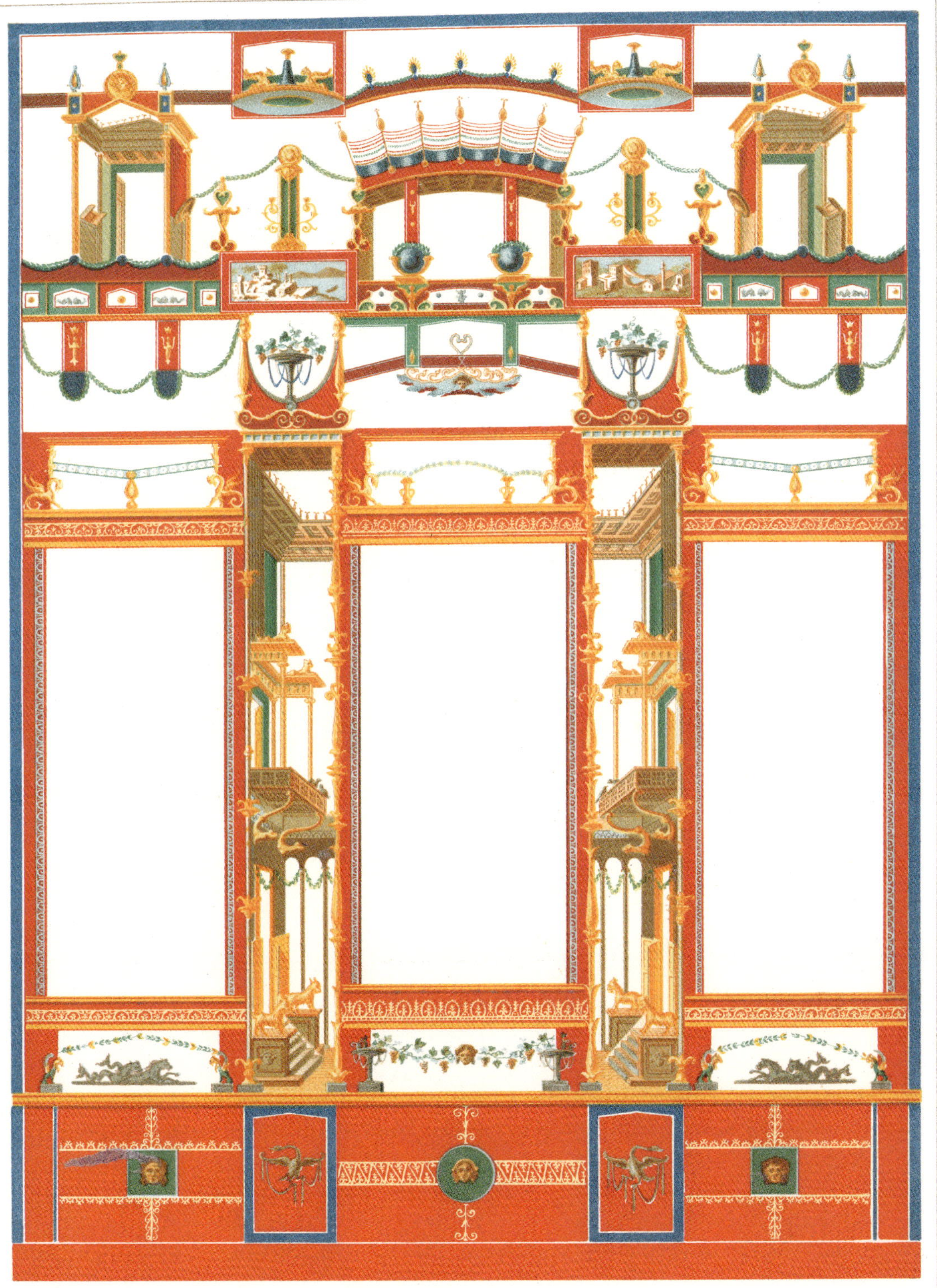

A. Magliano dis. D. Capri Lit. | A. Niccolini dir. | Lit. Art. Zucchi & De Luca, Napoli.

SUPPLEMENTO

Supplement

The chapter devoted to the wall inscriptions is followed by another topographical section, entitled Appendice (Appendix), which describes in 21 pages the excavations between 1874 and 1882. It continues the Descrizione generale of volume II and discusses finds in Insula 1 of Regio V, Insulae 13 and 14 of Regio VI and Insulae 4 and 5 of Regio IX. The text follows the house numbers but refers only rarely to the plates accompanying this volume. The next chapter, the Supplemento, makes up for this, in so far as it includes descriptions of the 50 plates compiled under this heading. These descriptions provide very differing amounts of information, such that in some cases the objects illustrated can only be identified with difficulty. Sadly it is not possible here again to reconstruct the order in which the individual fascicles were published or the individual plates and texts produced. Although the subtitle gives the year as 1896, the fascicles fall into the period during which editorship was passing from the brothers Fausto and Felice Niccolini (died 1886; pl. 1–26, 29) to their nephew Antonio (pl. 27, 28, 30–50). The Niccolinis' collaboration with the firm Litografia E. Richter (pl. 1–26, 29), and with Vincenzo Loria, their most important artist/printer up to that point (pl. 1–35), also came to an end at this time.

The plates present a wide variety of subjects, ranging from gold rings to panoramic views of the city. In addition to five vedute of houses and public buildings, many plates are devoted to small bronze sculptures, bronze utensils and other items of daily life. These show how much the editors endeavoured to present Pompeii not just as a monument to ancient architecture or as a gallery of mythological pictures, but as an example of a city in which every aspect of life in antiquity had been preserved. Even so, the objects are only very rarely depicted in context. An exception are the statuettes from a lararium (pl. 7), which convey an overall impression of such a domestic shrine. Other objects, by contrast, are organised strictly by type: measuring devices, scales, ladles and jugs, sieves and buckets, jewellery and tokens. Most plates show the objects in orthogonal view, but some of them introduce an unexpected dynamism into their representation of simple utility items, which is startling even to the modern eye (pl. 25, 45, 46; see also vol. II, Descrizione generale, pl. 43, 83). The illustrations were frequently taken from

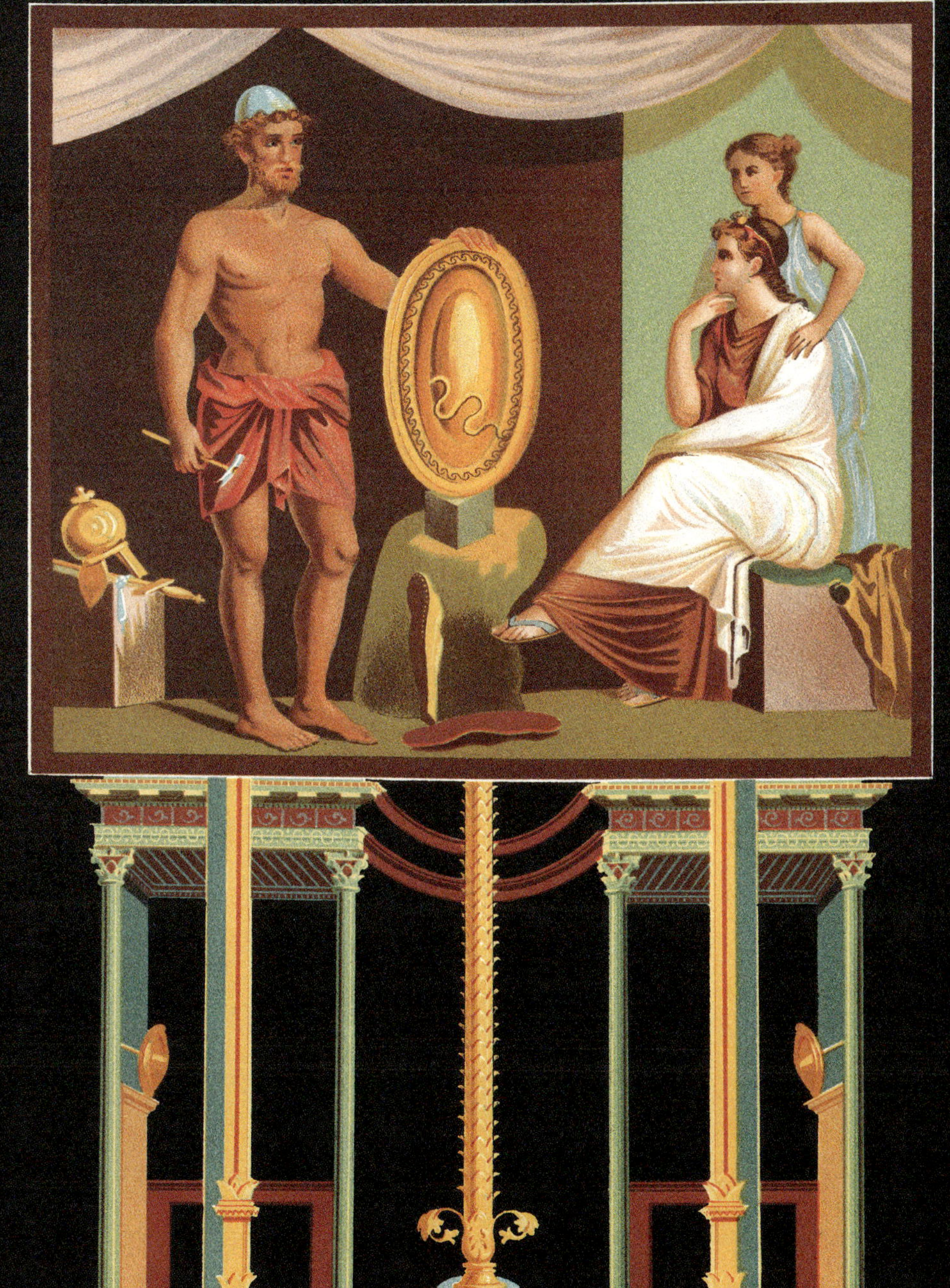

engravings from the 16 volumes of the *Real Museo Borbonico* and even from copper engravings made in the 18th century, but never published, for the volumes of the *Antichità di Ercolano*. The Niccolinis clearly had access to these works while professionally engaged at the Museo Nazionale in Naples. They were thus catering to a strong, positivist interest in such real-life objects that was a feature of the relevant publications on Pompeii and the corresponding reference works of the day. The museum's first illustrated catalogues, for example, were organised along these lines. Only in the last few decades has this aspect again attracted strong interest, as for example in the travelling exhibition *Homo faber: natura, scienza e tecnica nell'antica Pompei*, whose venues included the Los Angeles County Museum of Art (*Pompeii: Life in a Roman Town*, 1999–2000).

Pompeian life is also the subject of plates 12 and 32. The first shows two banqueting murals from a triclinium, in which the house owner's guests are encouraged to eat, drink and be merry. The second, by contrast, appears to show Pompeians and residents of neighbouring Nuceria involved in a bloody brawl inside and outside the amphitheatre. Among the reproductions of wall paintings are a number of compilation plates which bring together individual pictures treating the same theme – a practice already noted in volume III in the section devoted to the arts in Pompeii, and which was intended to encourage comparative study. These pictures are often reduced to an almost monochrome spectrum, which not only approaches the aesthetic of line engravings but was also simpler and hence cheaper to print.

Page 389

Plate 1 — *[V. Loria]*

Casa di Meleagro (VI 9, 2 and 13), atrium – Above: Thetis in the workshop of Hephaestus, who is showing her the arms he has made for Achilles. The strong colours do not correspond to the badly damaged original. Below: detail from a 4th-style wall decoration.

Plate 4 — *[V. Loria]*

Bronze weighing and measuring instruments – Along the top: dividers, plumb bobs and rules; below: various types of scales. According to the inscription engraved on it, one of the sets of scales was calibrated in AD 77.

Pages 392–393

Plate 2 — *[G. Discanno]*

Casa del Medico (VIII 5, 24), viridarium, partition wall facing the garden – Two pictures from a series of caricature paintings of pygmies, probably based on the Alexandrian tradition. Above: the pygmies battle wild beasts from the Nile, including crocodiles and a hippopotamus. Below: this unusual picture offers an ironic treatment of the biblical story of the Judgement of Solomon, here transferred into the world of the pygmies.

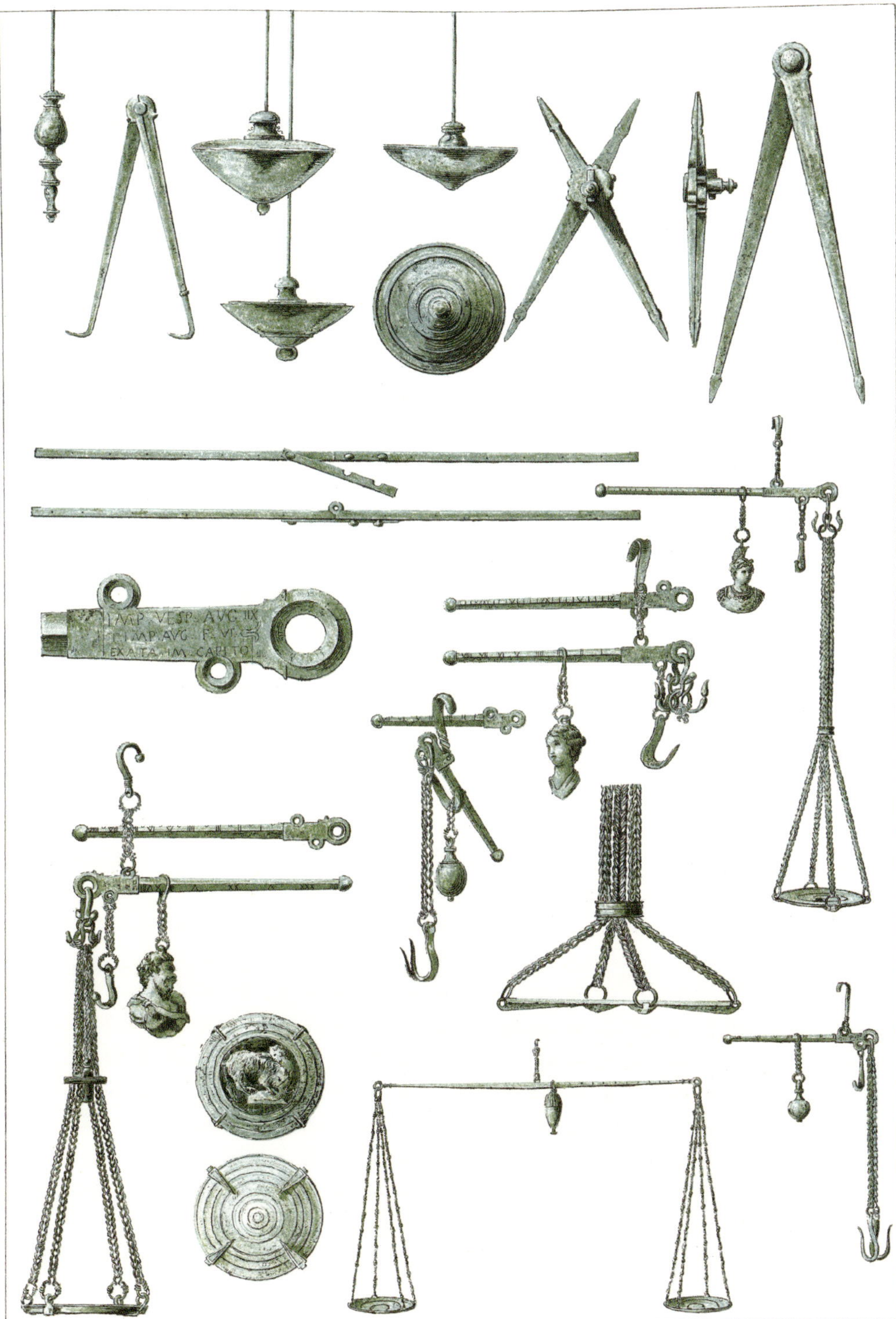

Lit Richter e C. Napoli — Fr.lli Niccolini dir. — V.zo Lorze dis. e Lit.

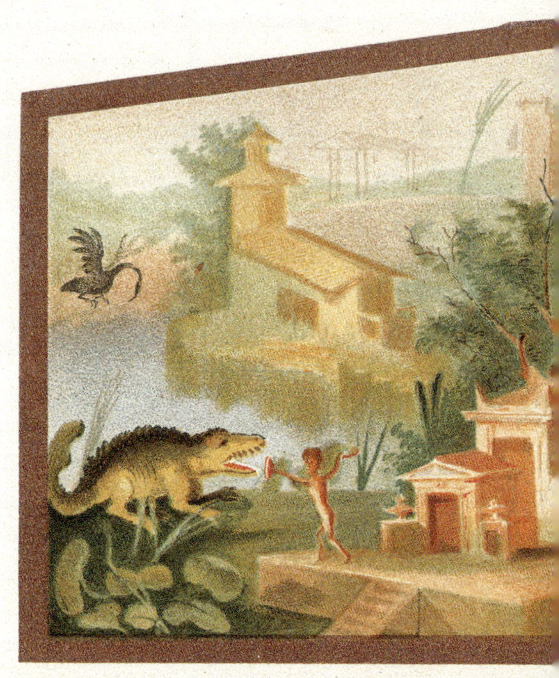

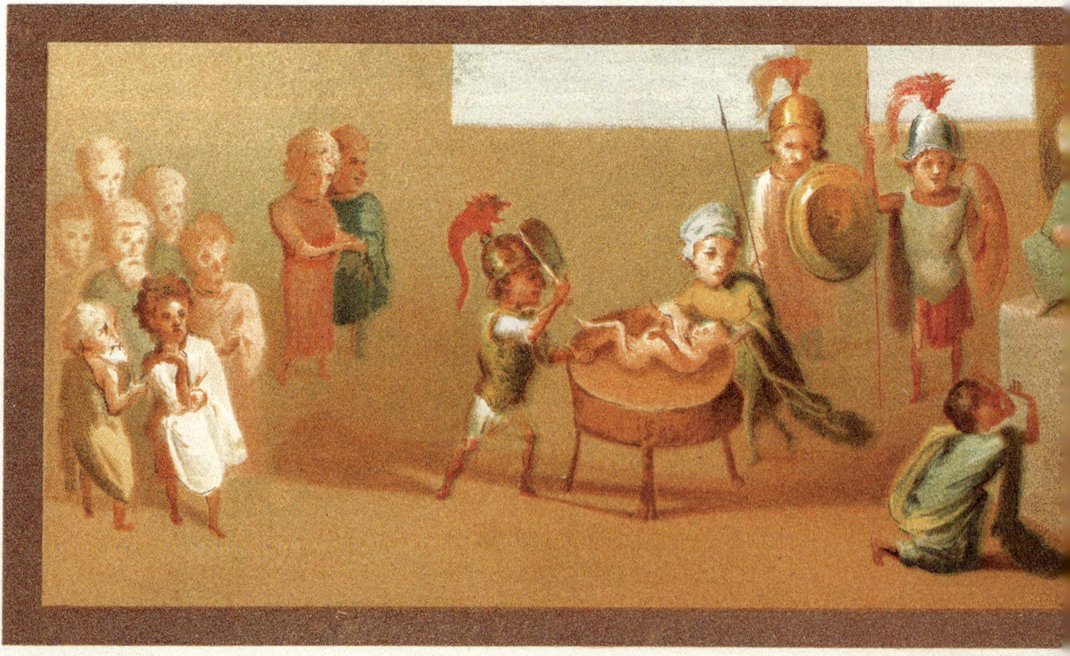

G. Discanno dip.

F.lli M

Lit.Ric

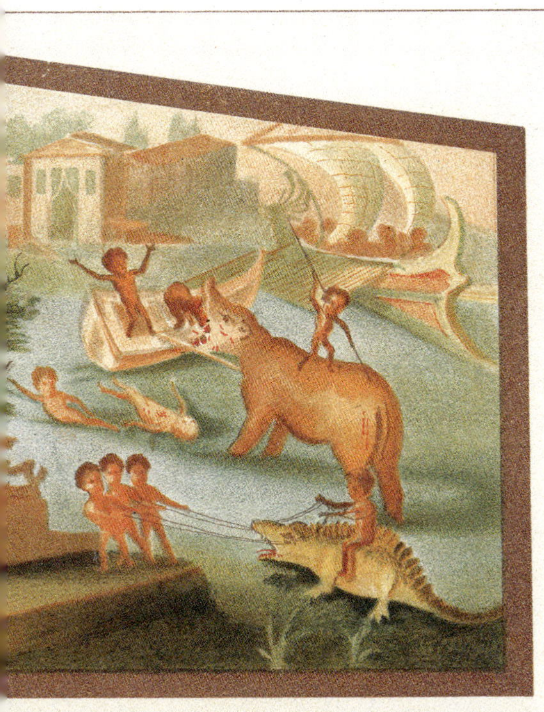

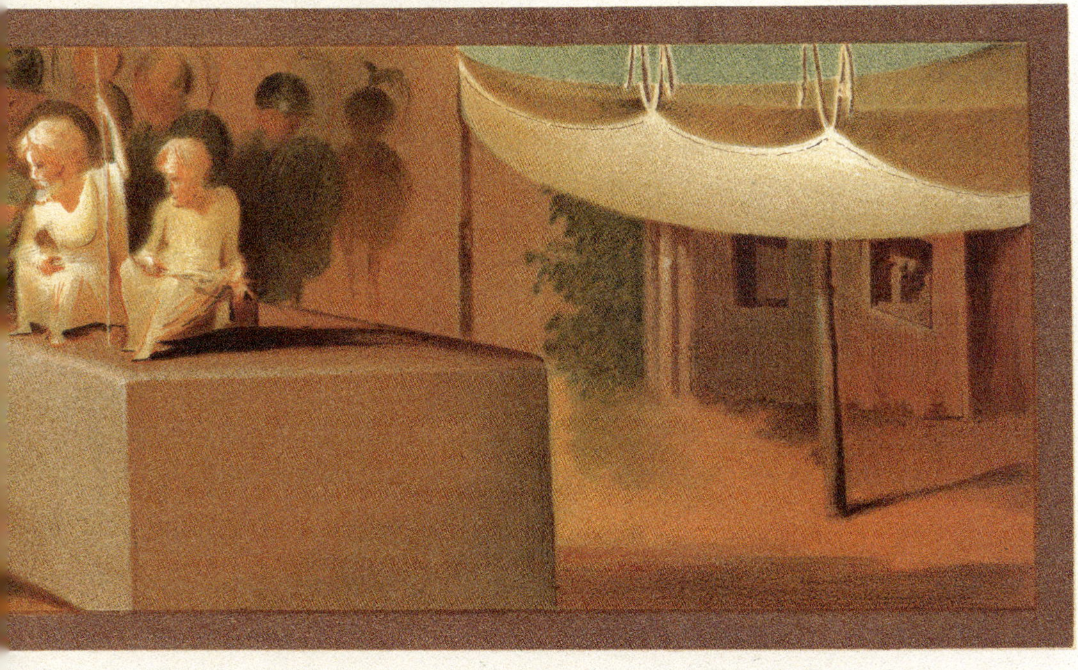

i dir.
Napoli

V. Loria lit.

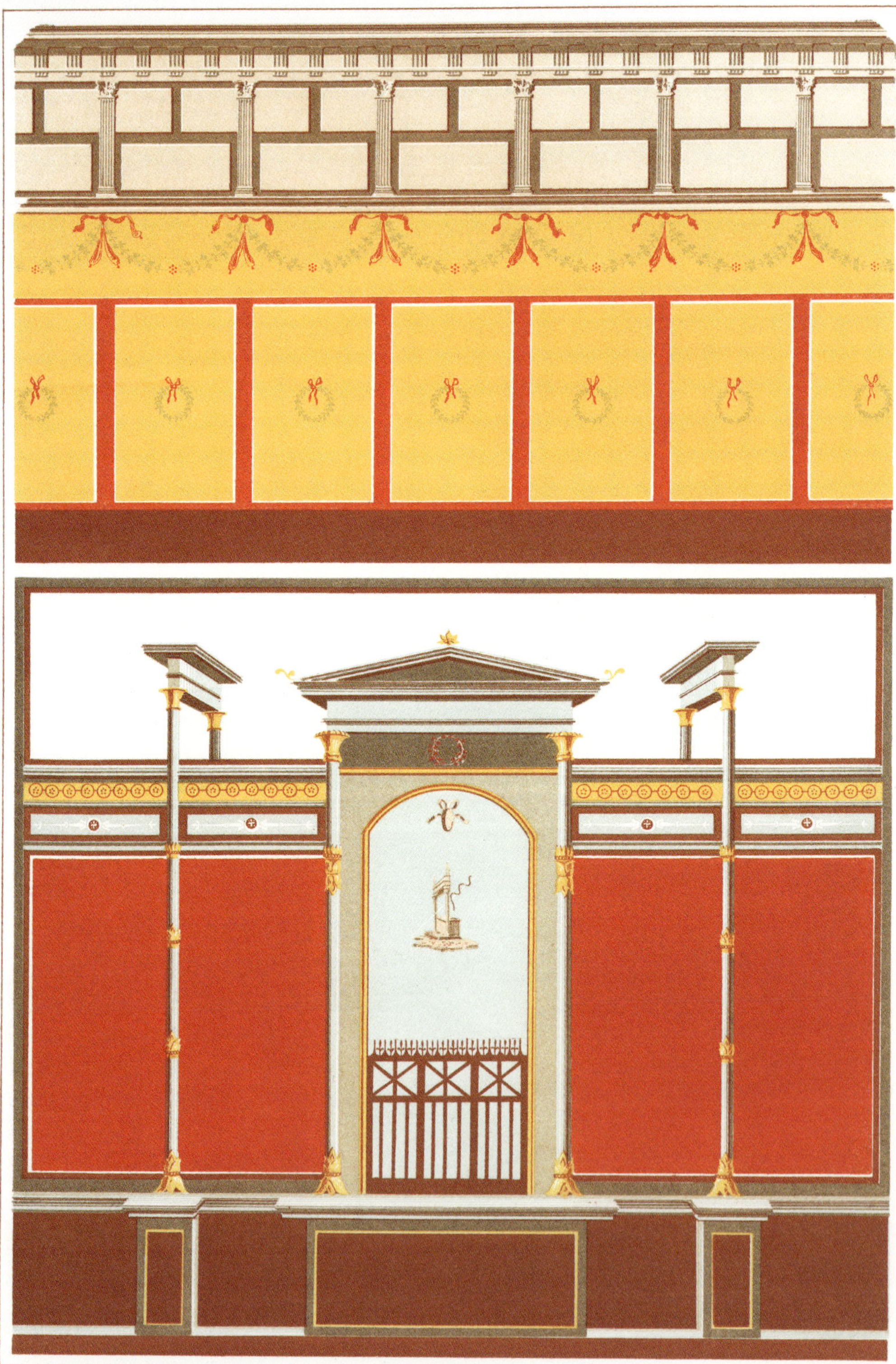

Lit. Richter & C. Napoli   Fr[co] Niccolini dir.   V. Loria dis. e lit.

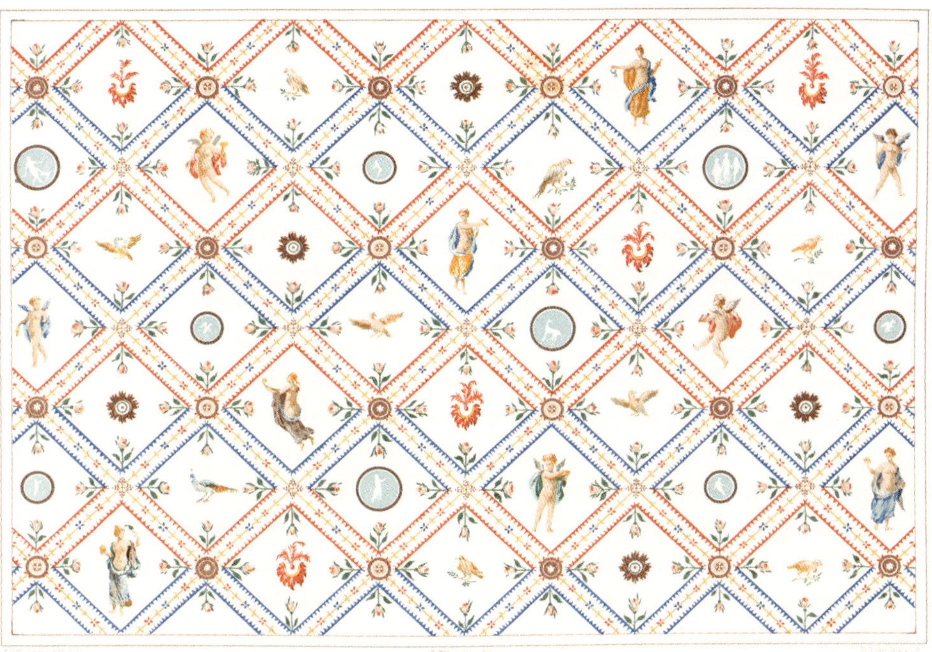

Plate 6 — *[V. Loria]*
Above: *Casa di Sallustio (VI 2, 4), cubiculum* – Upper zone with decoration in the 1st style.
Below: *Fullonica (VI 8, 20) (?)* – Wall decoration in the 3rd style.

Plate 8 — *[V. Loria]*
Stabia, Villa di Arianna – Unusual "wallpaper" décor from a wall in the 4th style.
The details include floating figures, small medallions and floral motifs.

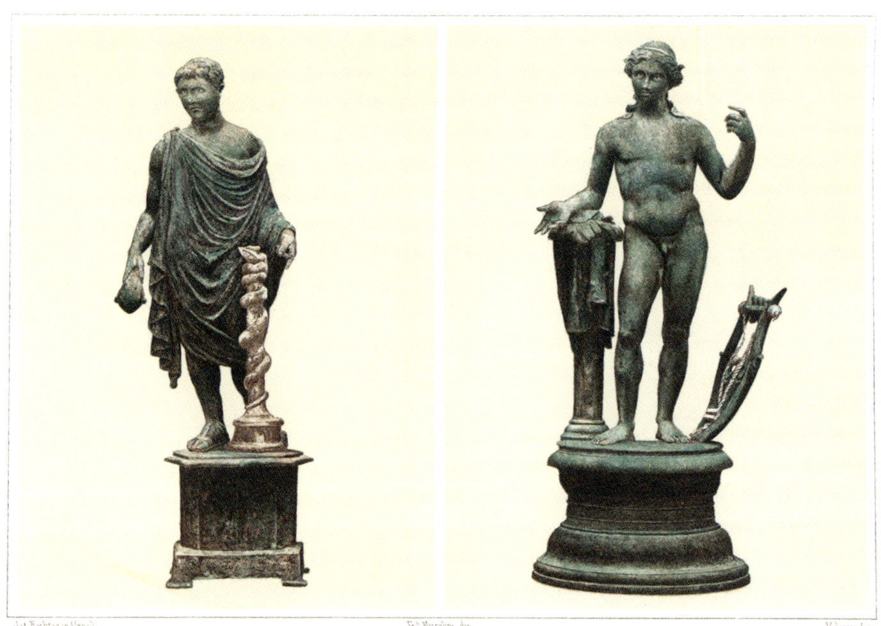

Plate 7 — *[V. Loria]*

Apollo with cithara and "Mercury" – Two statuettes from the lararium in plate 5: "Mercury" is holding a money-bag in his right hand but has been transformed into an Asclepius figure through the addition of a silver column with a snake. These figures are clearly represented on a larger scale than the other two statuettes of gods in plate 5, Hercules and Mercury with their usual attributes.

⁂

Plate 9 — *[V. Loria]*

Casa degli Argenti (VI 7, 20–22) – Silver *kantharos* with relief decoration of erotes mounted on female and male centaurs. This *kantharos* was part of a treasure trove of 14 vessels.

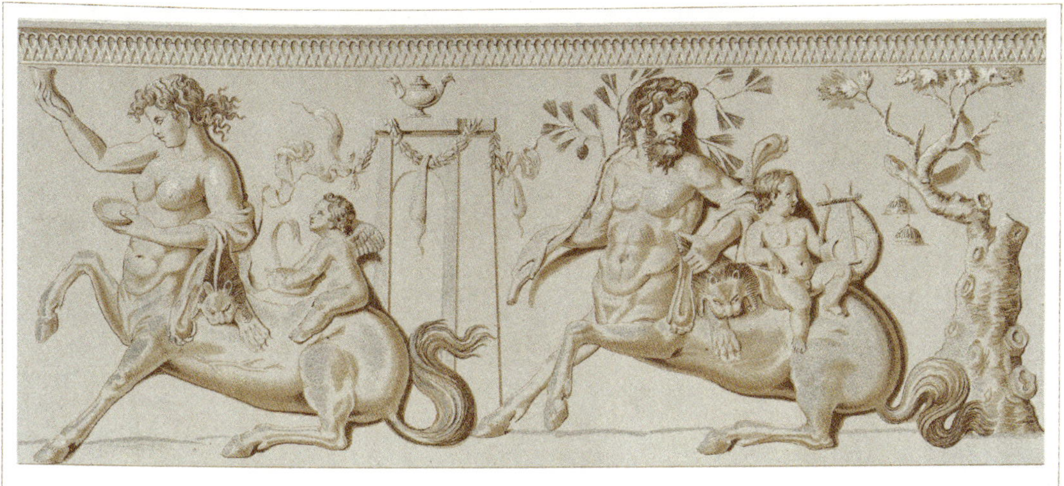

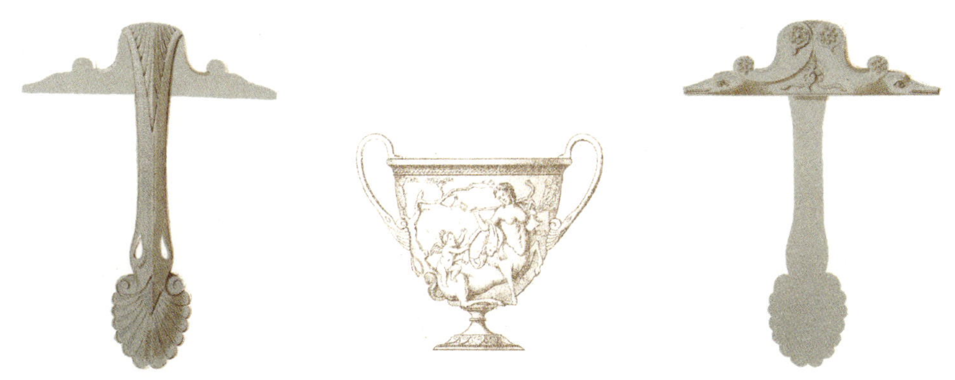

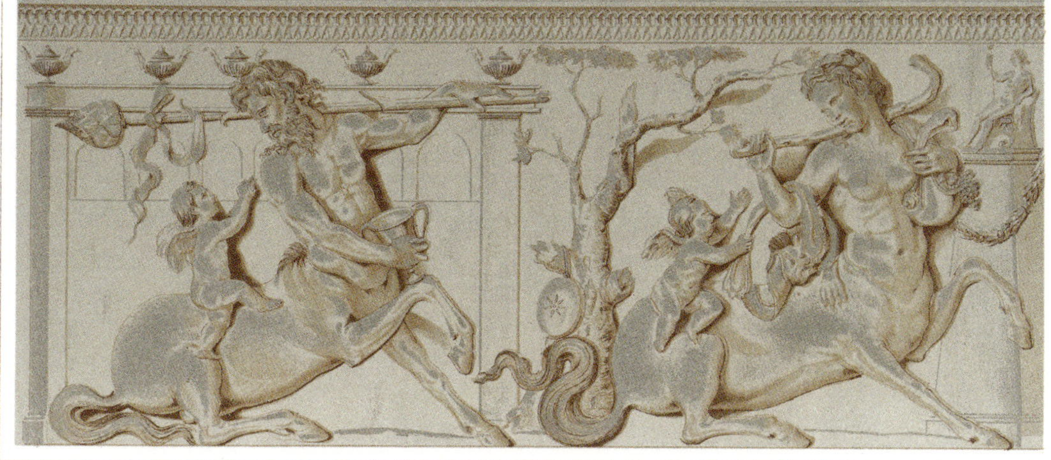

Lit. Richter in Napoli — Fr.lli Niccolini dir. — V. Loria pin. e lit.

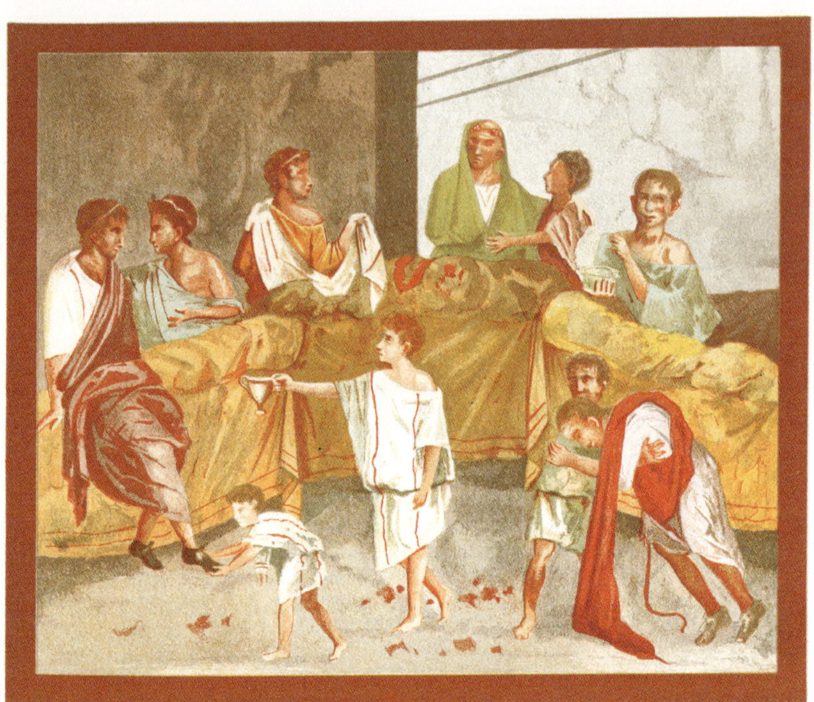

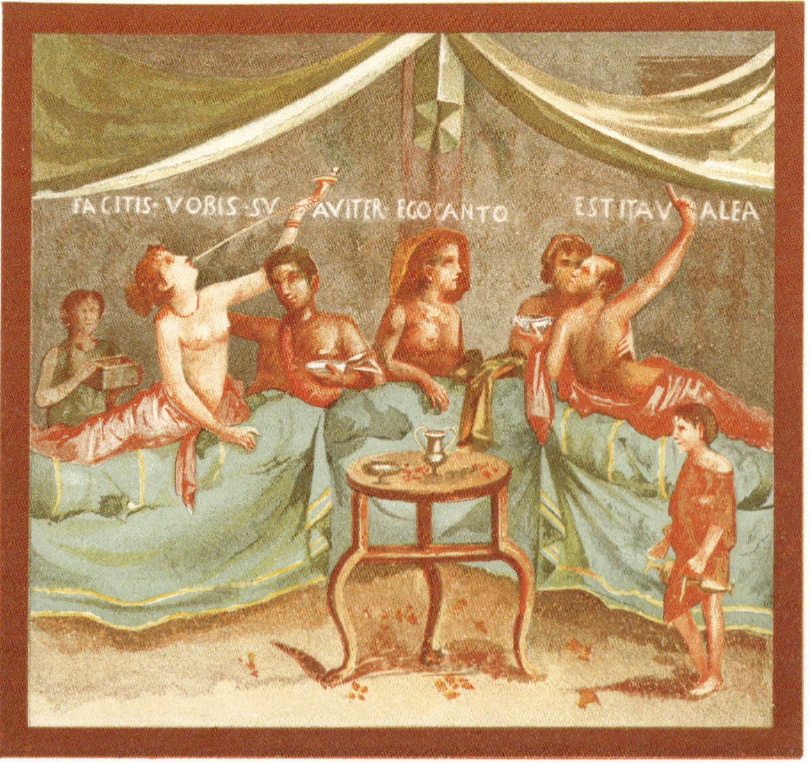

Lit. Richter & C° *Fr.lli Niccolini dir.* *Napoli.*

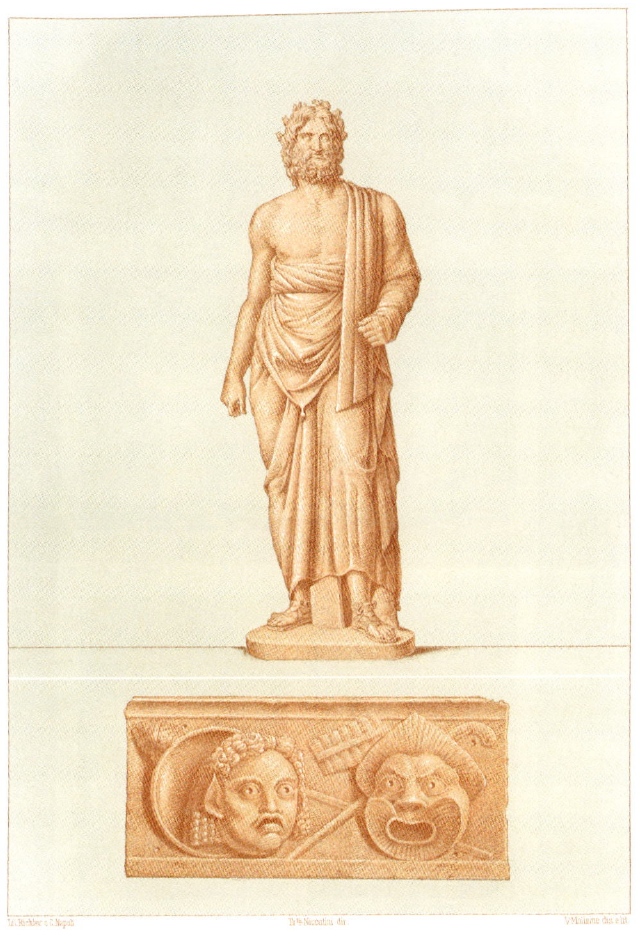

Plate 12 — *[Anonymous]*
Casa del Triclinio (V 2, 4), triclinium – Two banqueting scenes from the period before the earthquake of AD 62. Above: banquet in an enclosed room. Some of the exclusively male guests have just arrived; one is having his shoes taken off. Another, by contrast, is having to be propped up and is in the course of vomiting. Below: banquet outdoors under an awning. Men and women are feasting together. Painted inscriptions reproduce common phrases: "Make yourself comfortable", "I am singing", "So it is" and "Your health".

Plate 11 — *[V. Mollame]*
Casa VIII 8, 3 – Terracotta statue of Asclepius ("Zeus Meilichios") from his temple near the theatre (3rd–2nd century BC).

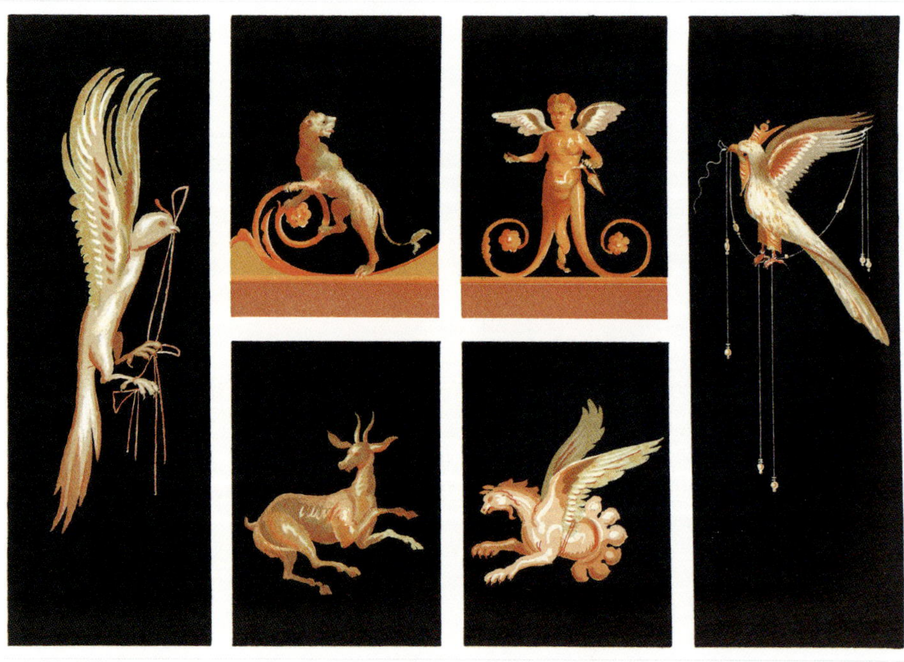

Plate 14 — *[V. Loria]*
Casa di M. Fabius Rufus (VII 16, Insula occidentalis, 22) (?) – Decorative elements from a 4th-style wall decoration on a black background.

Plate 10 — *[V. Loria]*
Casa del Granduca (VII 4, 56) – Mosaic fountain in the viridarium. With its gleaming mosaics and appliqué scallops and conches, the nymphaeum conveys the concept of this decorative element of Pompeian houses particularly well. Water bubbled up from the basin in front and out of the vessel held by Silenus.

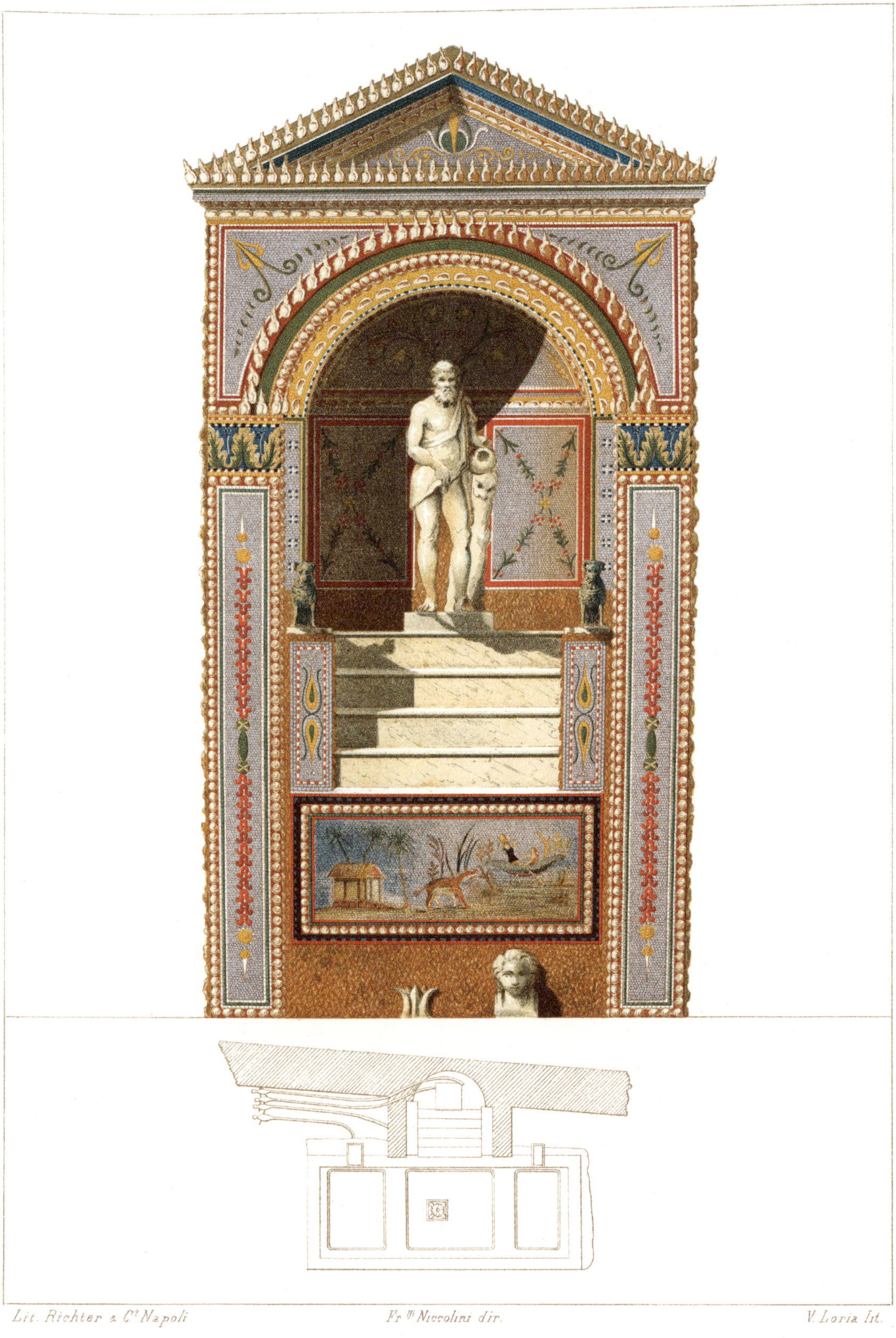

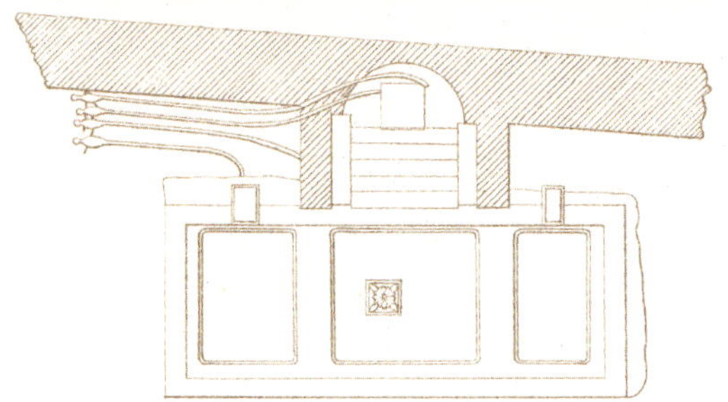

Lit. Richter e Cº Napoli | *Fr.lli Niccolini dir.* | *V. Loria lit.*

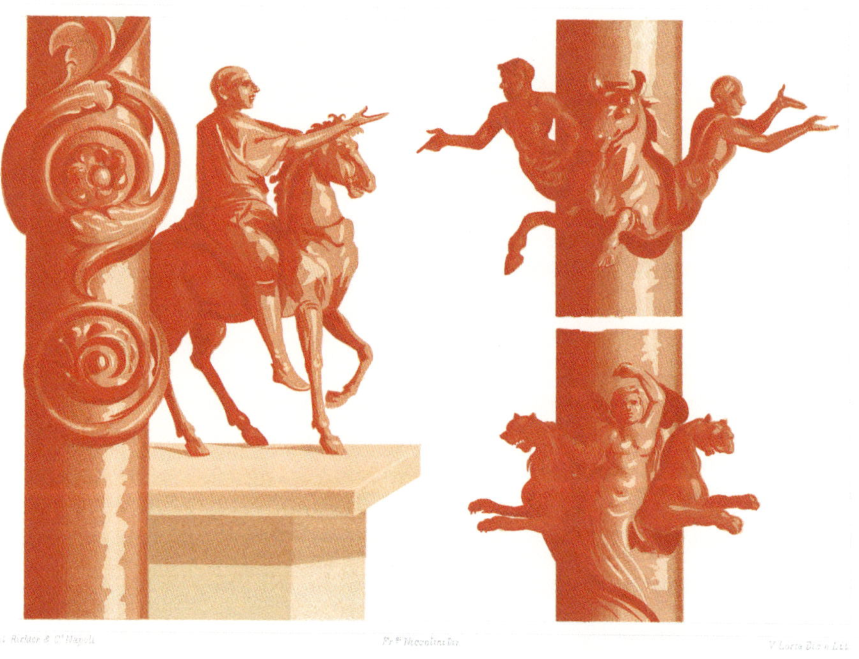

Plate 16 — *[V. Loria]*
Casa della Caccia antica (VII 4, 48) – Framing of a central aedicule with an equestrian statue and protomes of fabulous beasts.

❖

Plate 15 — *[V. Loria]*
Praedia of Julia Felix (II 4, 3), small courtyard – Aedicule with the floating figure of a lion.

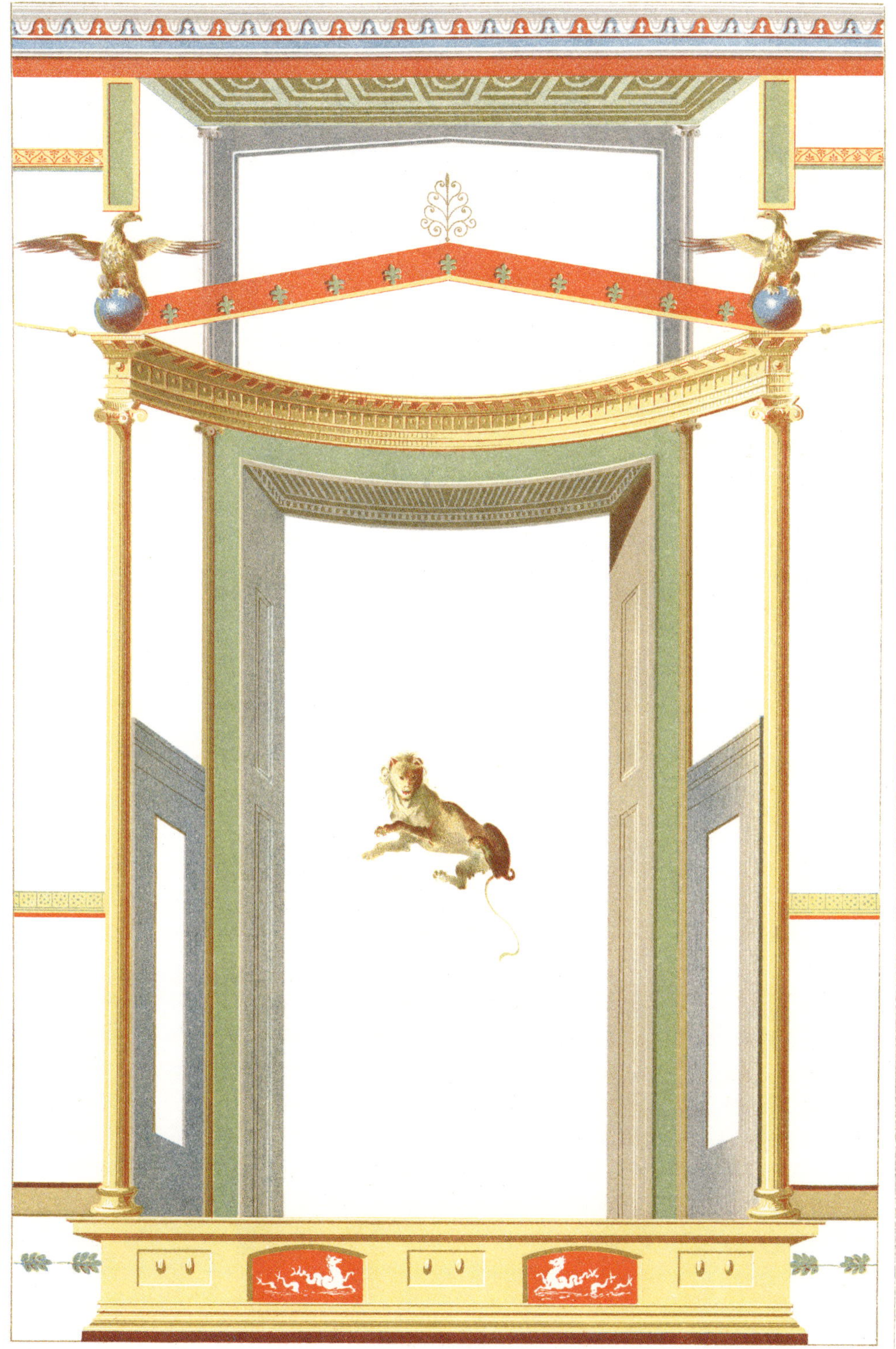

Lit. Richter Napoli   Fr.[lo] Niccolini dir.   V. Loria fec. e Lit.

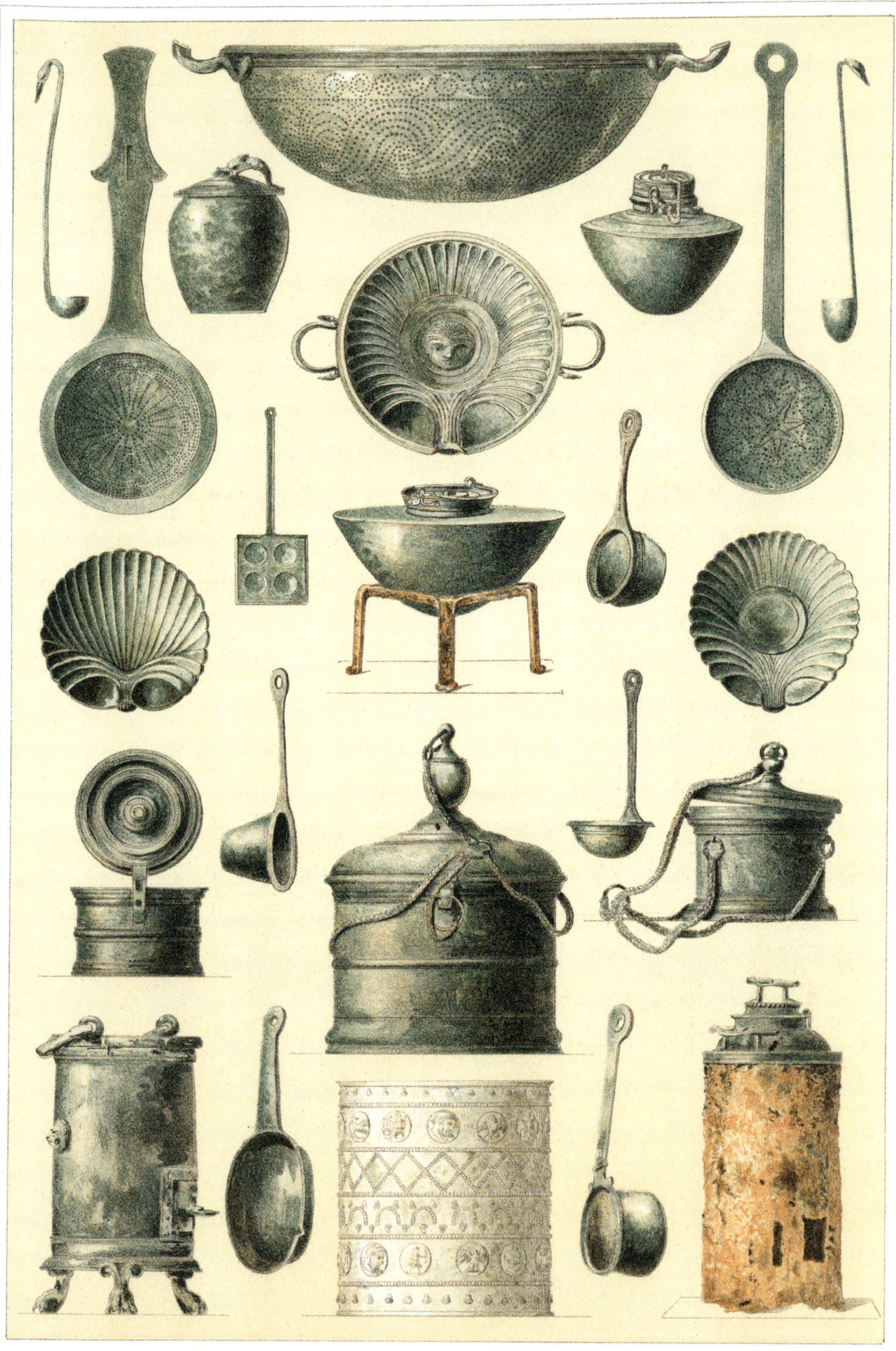

Lit. Richter & C° Napoli   Fr^{lli} Niccolini Dir.   V. Loria Dis. e Lit.

Plate 17 — *[V. Loria]*

Bronze utensils – Various origins: bowls, sieves, ladles and containers for keeping things warm, along with a lead water-tank (cf. pl. 50).

Page 406

Plate 19 — *[Anonymous]*

Casa della Parete nera (Casa dei Bronzi, VII 4, 59) – Two of three surviving pictures with erotes and a psyche from the exedra. Left: in front of attributes of Hera. Right: in front of attributes of Ares/Mars.

Page 406

Plate 21 — *[Anonymous]*

Apollo and the Muses – Left: Herculaneum or Stabia – Female figure with a wreath and lyre. Middle: Casa dei Capitelli colorati (VII 4, 51 and 53) – Achilles playing the cithara in his tent, with Patroclus on the left and two women listening in front of him. Right: Casa della Parete nera (Casa dei Bronzi, VII 4, 59), triclinium – Muse (?) with a lyre in her left hand.

Page 407

Plate 20 — *[V. Loria]*

Casa IX 5, 11 and 13, atrium – Wall decoration in the 4th style with a personification of spring, carrying a goat kid on her shoulders.

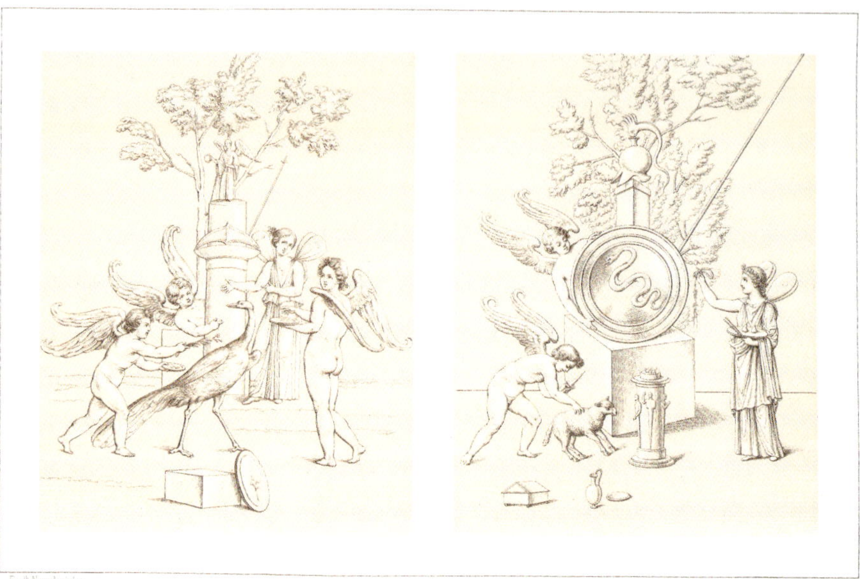

Fra.co Niccolini dir. Lit. Richter & C. Napoli

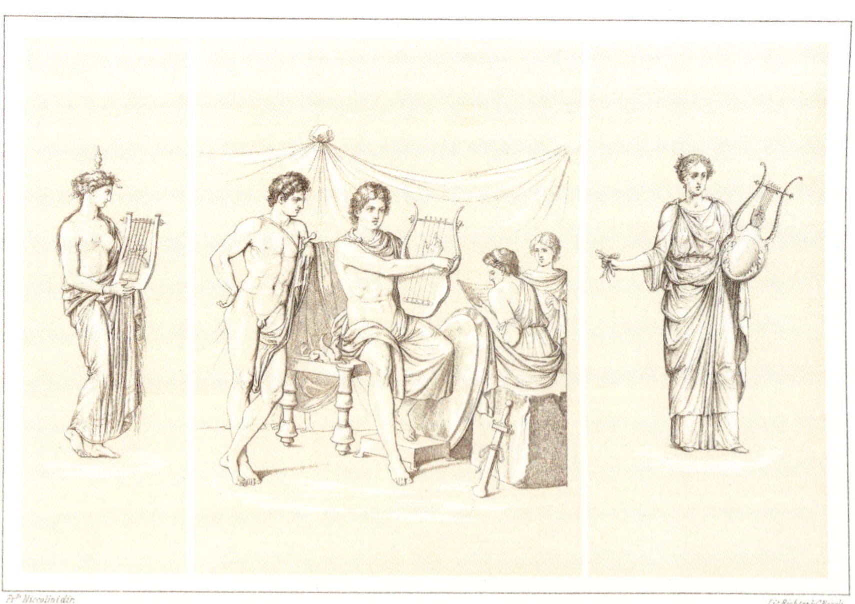

Fr.co Niccolini dir. Lit. Richter & C. Napoli

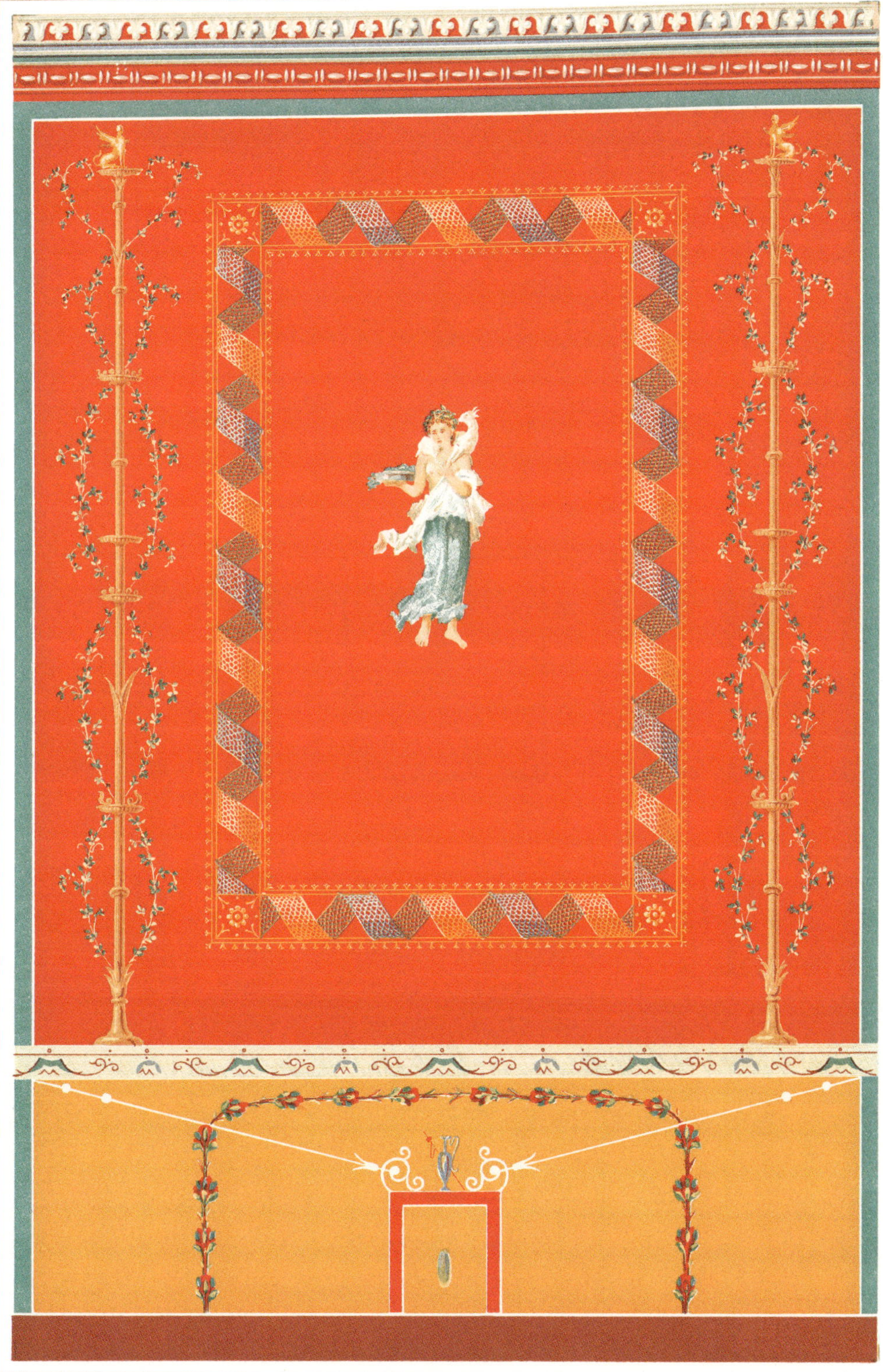

V. Loria pin. e lit. | Fr.lli Niccolini dir. | Lit. Richter & C.i Napoli

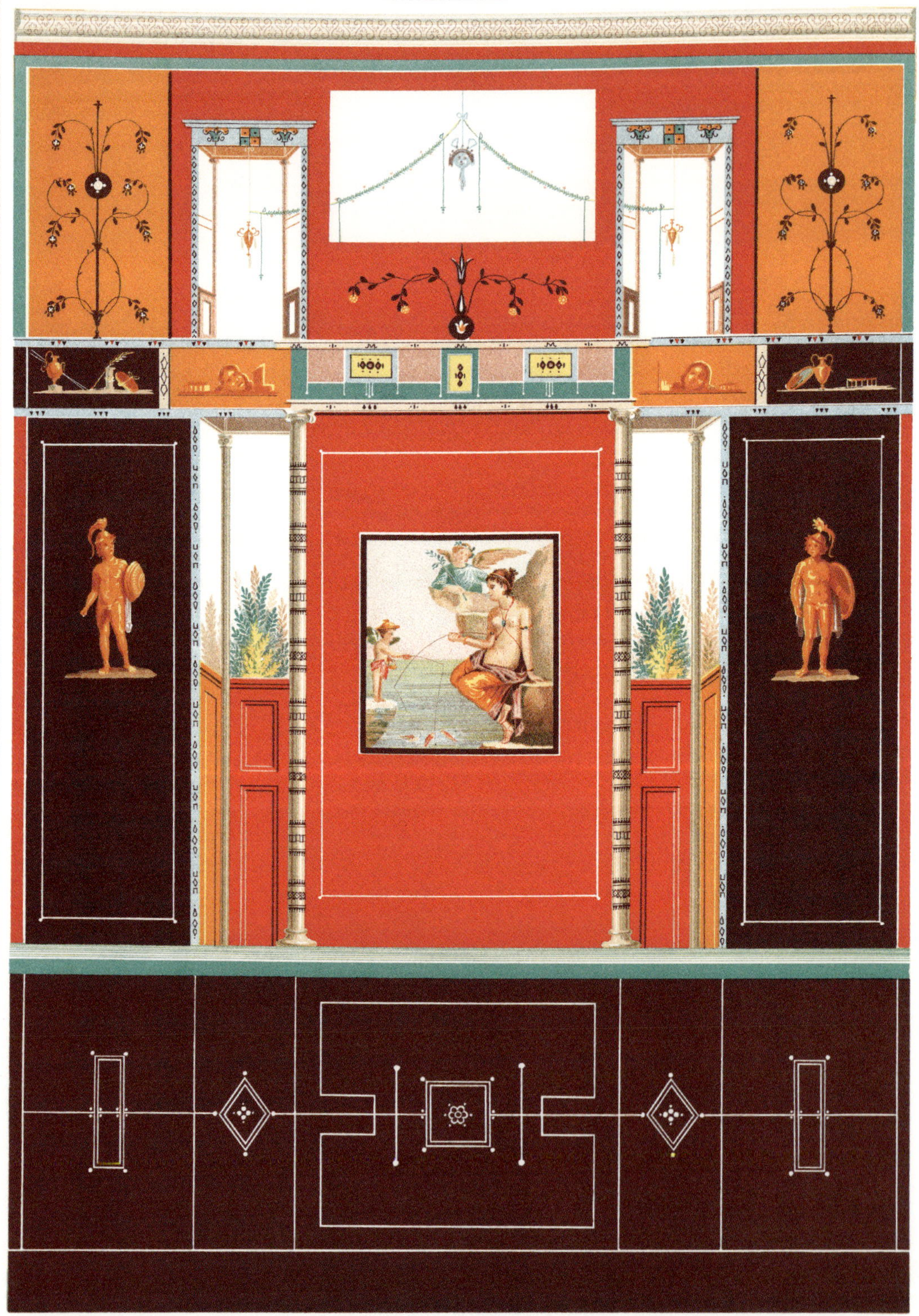

V.o Loria dis. e Lit. F.lli Niccolini dir. Lit. Richter & C.o Napoli

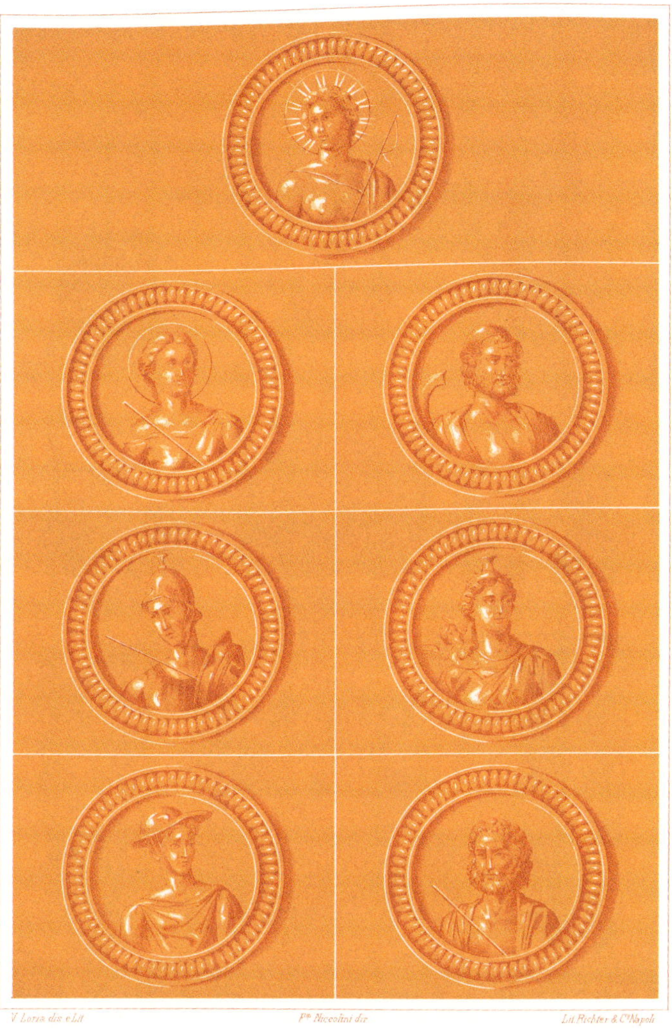

Plate 24 — *[V. Loria]*
Casa di Laocoonte (VI 14, 28) – The plate shows a large wall decoration in the late 3rd style.

❖

Plate 26 — *[V. Loria]*
Seven tondi with personifications of the days of the week – Further tondi from the same context show personifications of the months and seasons.

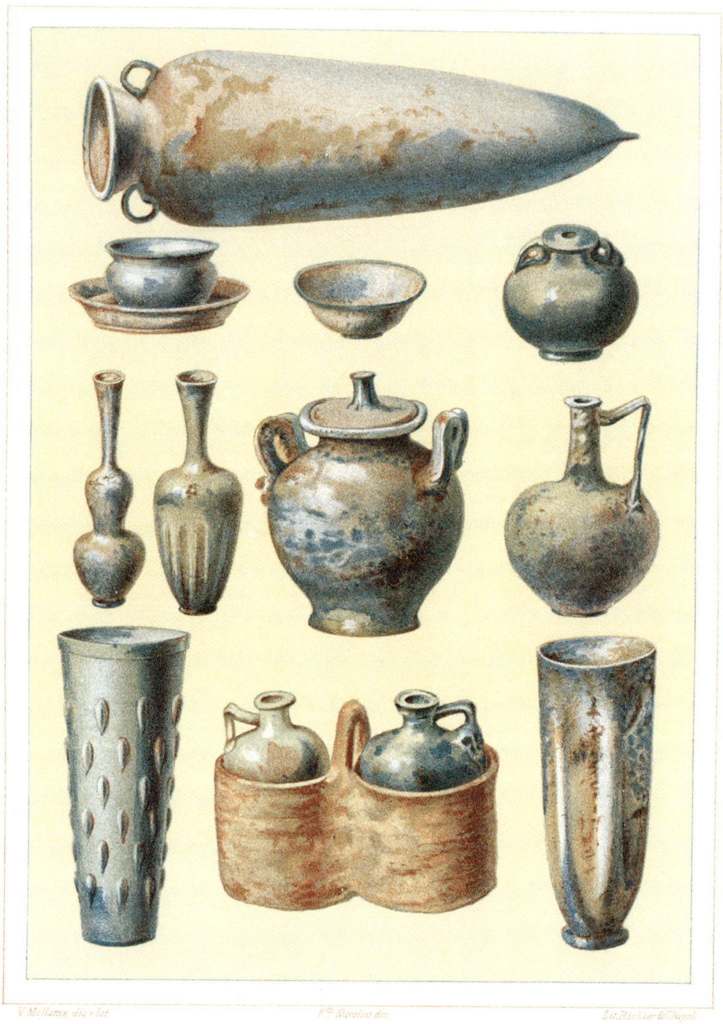

Plate 25 — *[V. Mollame]*
Glassware of different shapes and functions – Drinking glasses, jugs, dishes and an amphora.
In the middle, a funerary urn; below, a "bottle carrier" with a bronze handle, for transporting two glass bottles.

Plate 27 — *[V. Loria]*
Casa degli Epigrammi (V 1, 18) – Detail of the garden decoration. In the main picture framed by half-columns, a leopard is attacking a bull. Underneath, a grisaille painting of a river god; above, a sea scene.

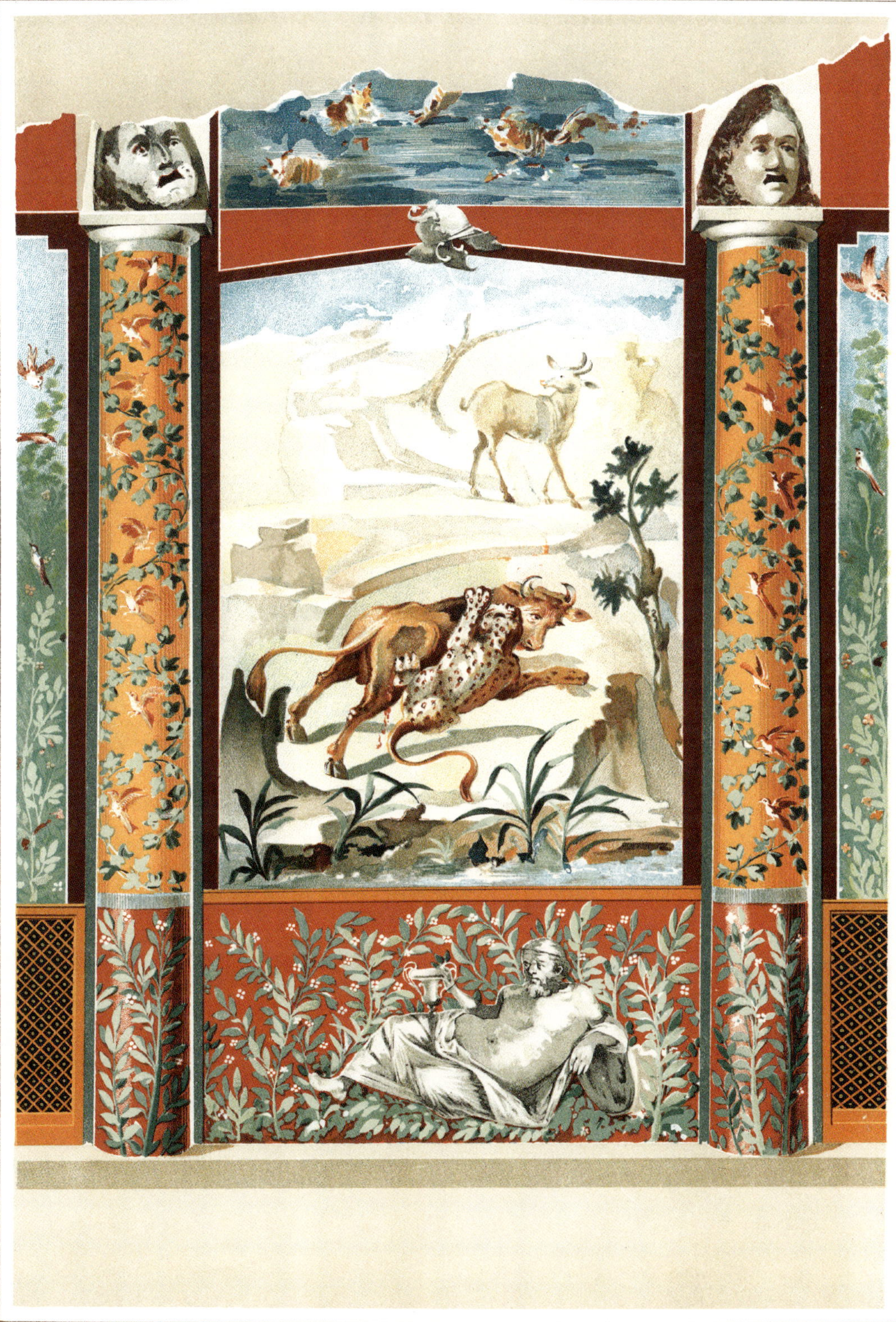

V. Loria dis.

Stab. Lit. del Folletto, Napoli
Niccolini dir.

E. Bocchino Lit.

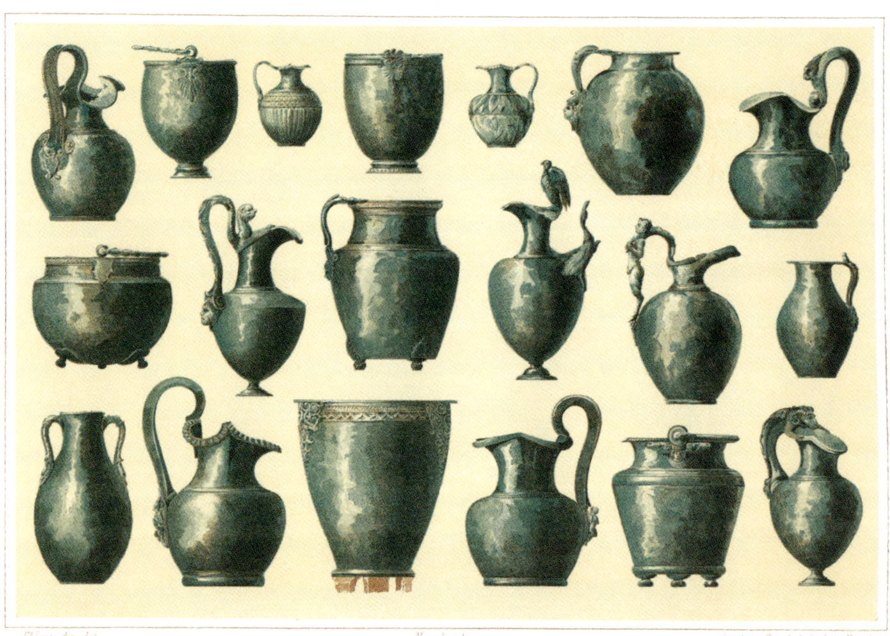

Plate 30 — *[V. Loria]*

Bronze vessels – For carrying, mixing and serving liquids, in most cases probably wine. The style of the illustration recalls sheets of design samples published by industrial manufacturers or more recent archaeological catalogues organised by types.

Plate 28 — *[V. Loria]*

Gold jewellery of various origins – Necklaces, rings, earrings, bracelets. Of particular interest, top right, is a gold *bulla*, a capsule containing an amulet that was worn around the neck by free-born boys. In their 17th year, when they officially reached adulthood, it would have been placed in the lararium.

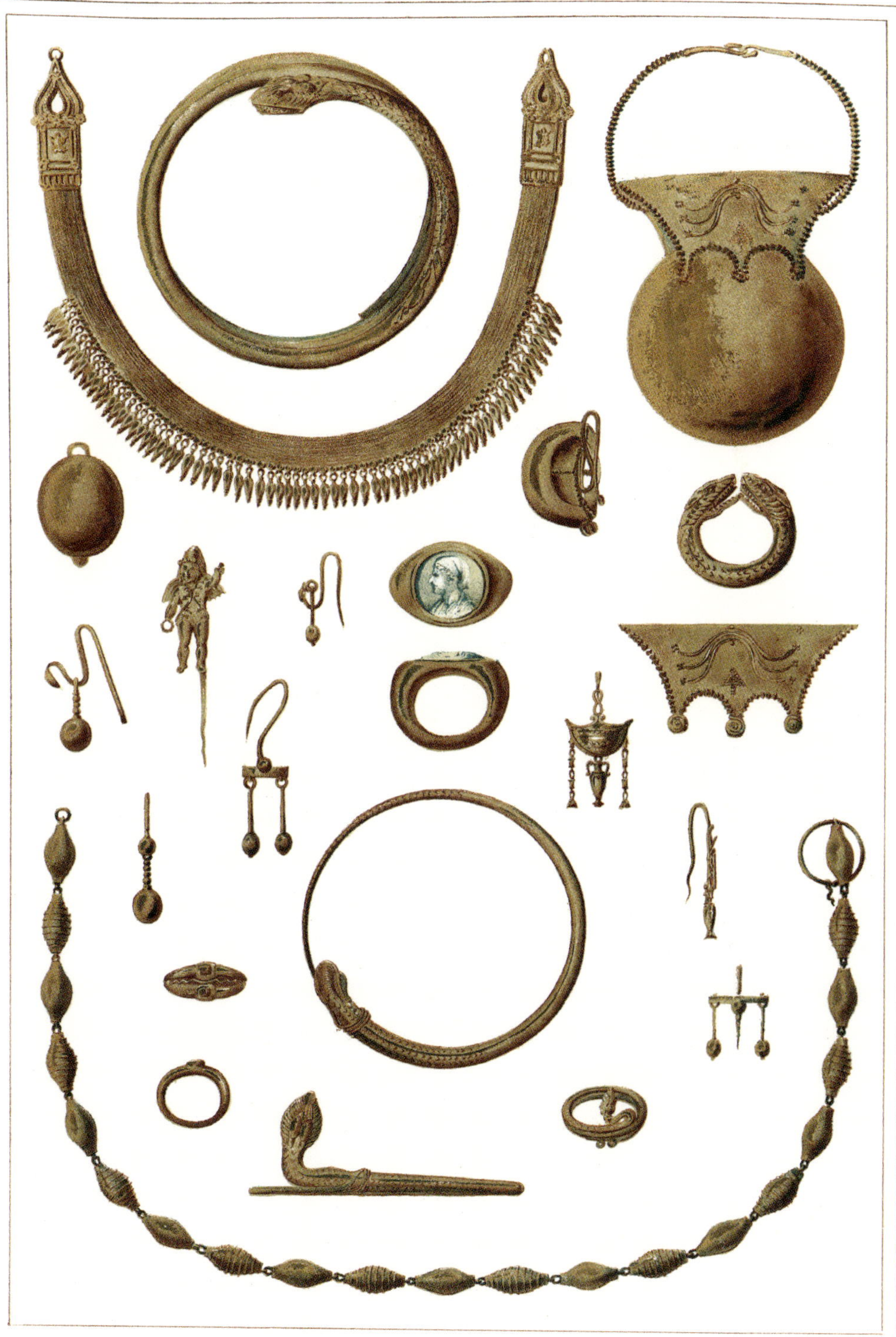

V. Loria dis. — *Stab. Lit. del Folletto, Napoli* — *Niccolini dir.* — *E. Bocchino Lit.*

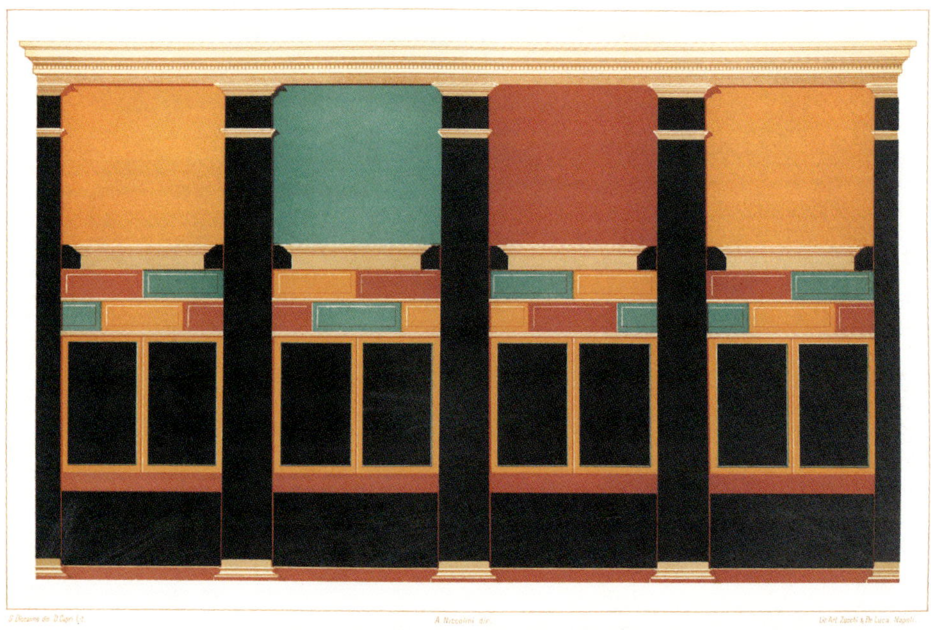

Plate 38 — *[G. Discanno]*
Fabbrica di Prodotti chimici (IX 3, 2), garden courtyard – Wall decoration in the 1st style, the oldest style of wall decoration in Pompeii. The painted stucco in sculptural relief imitates rusticated walls. One of the few examples of this early style of decoration in the Niccolinis' work.

Plate 29 — *[V. Loria]*
Casa del Centenario (IX 8, 3 and 7), triclinium (53), north wall – A particularly elegant wall with a completely black background but without a central picture, from the period between AD 62 and 79. Pendant to the white decoration of room (56) (see vol. III, Casa del Centenario, pl. 3).

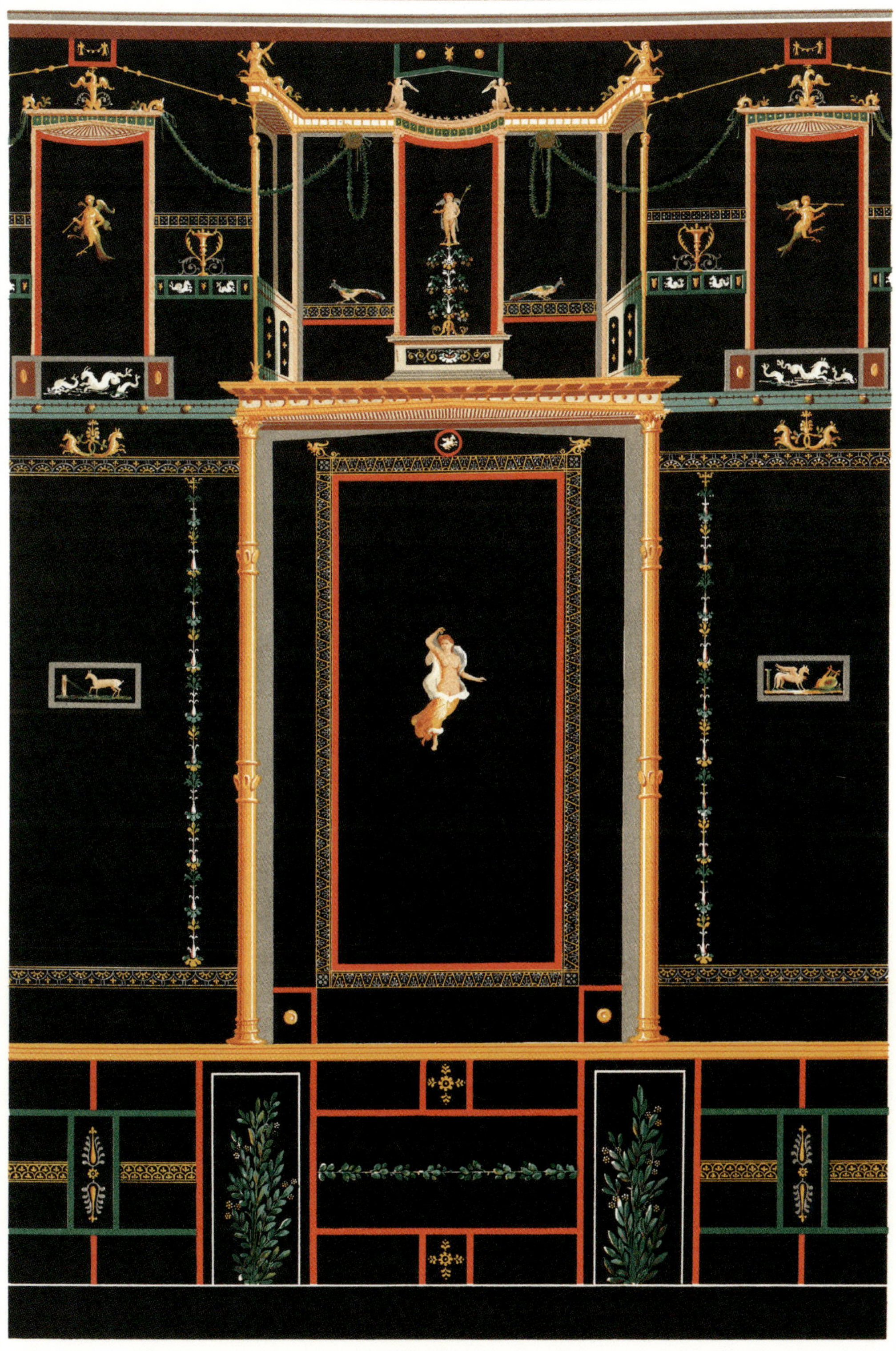

V. Loria dis e Lit

F.lli Niccolini dir.

Lit. Richter & C.o Napoli

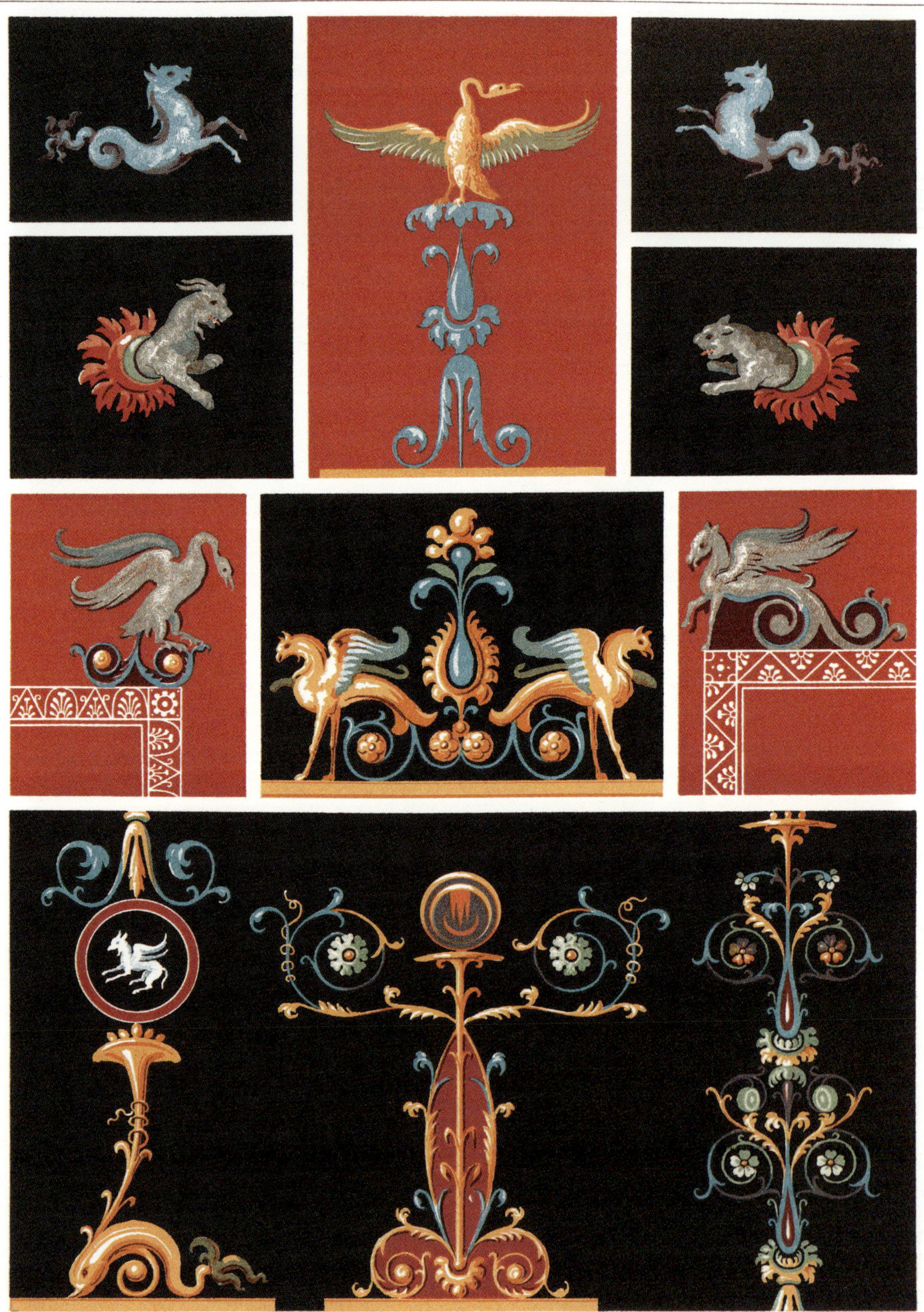

Lit Art Zucchi & De Luca-Napoli A.Niccolini dir. V.Loria dis. e Lit.

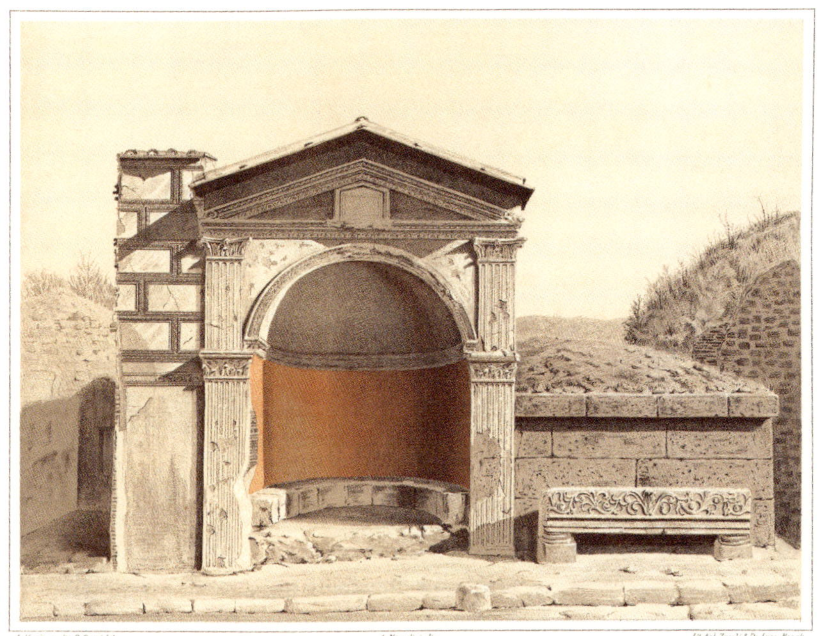

Plate 31 — *[V. Loria]*
Details of ornaments and fabulous beasts on 4th-style walls with black and red grounds.
Niccolini described them as "fine specimens".

⁂

Plate 47 — *[A. Magliano]*
Street of Tombs in front of the Herculaneum Gate, north side – View of the tomb exedra here.
Immediately to the left lies the Villa delle Colonne a Mosaico, on the right another tomb.

⁂

Pages 418–419
Plate 40 — *[D. de Simone]*
The lower half of the view shows the southern part of the Via di Mercurio looking south, with the so-called Arch of Caligula at its end. The upper zone of the picture, however, faces north towards Vesuvius.

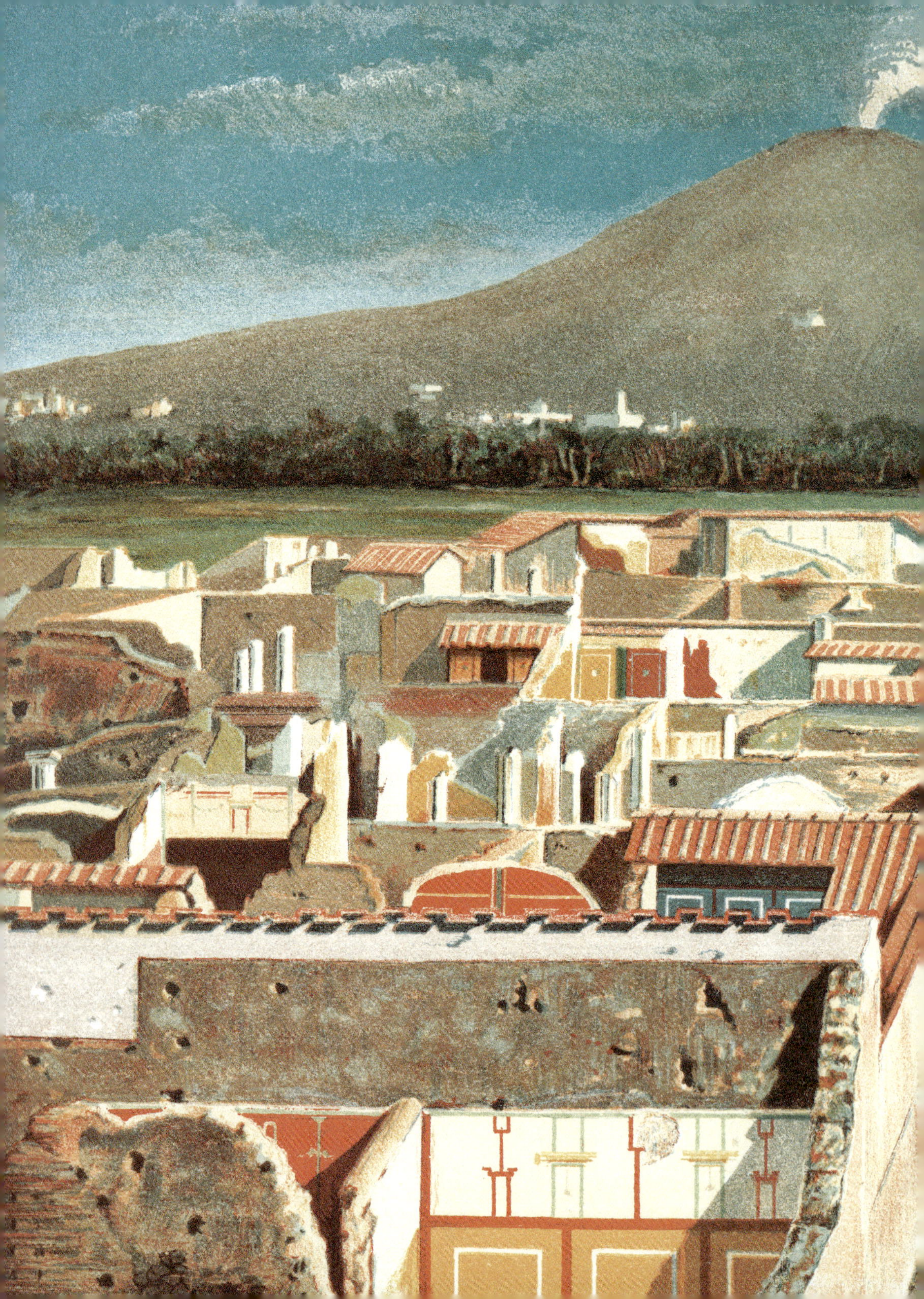

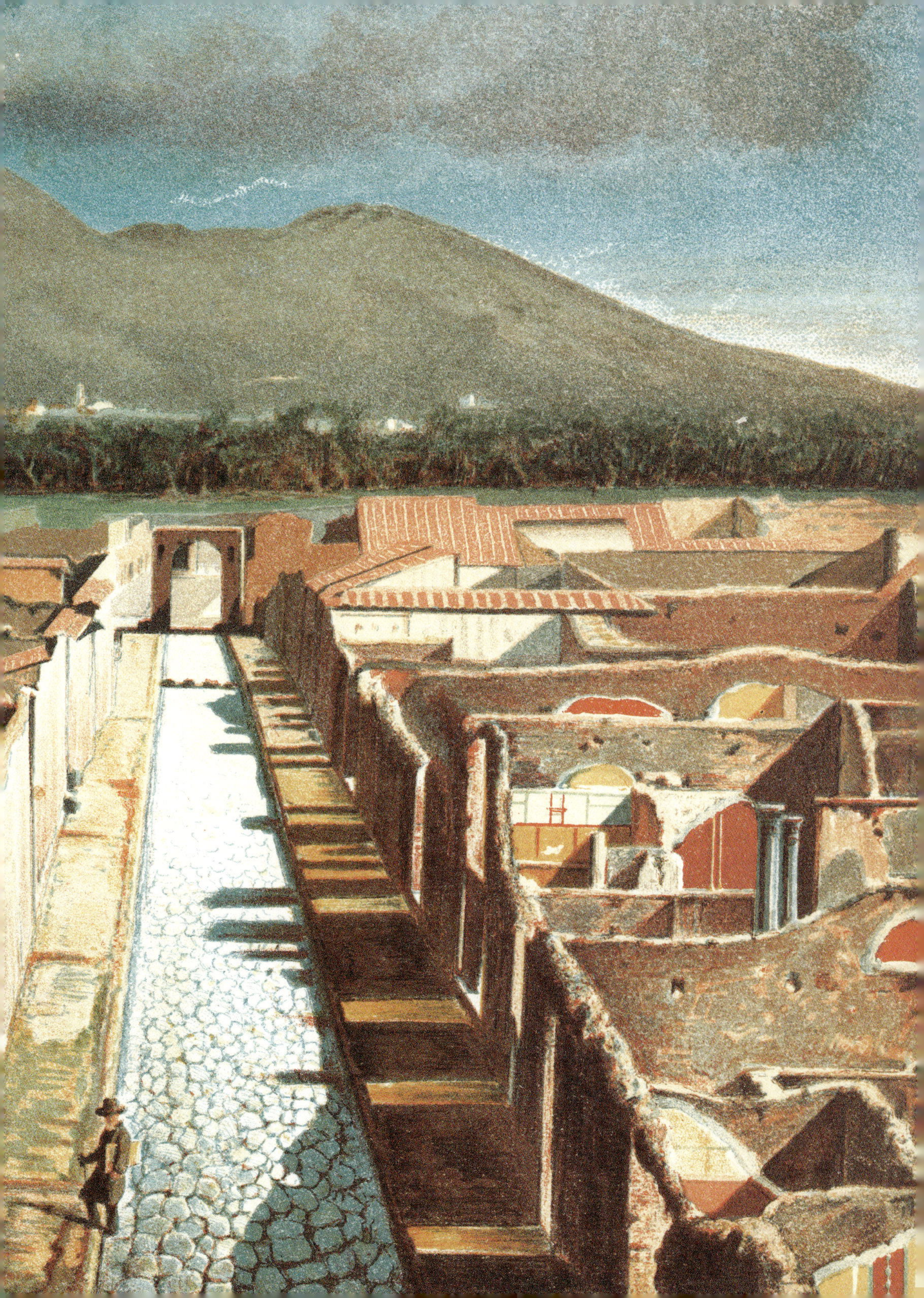

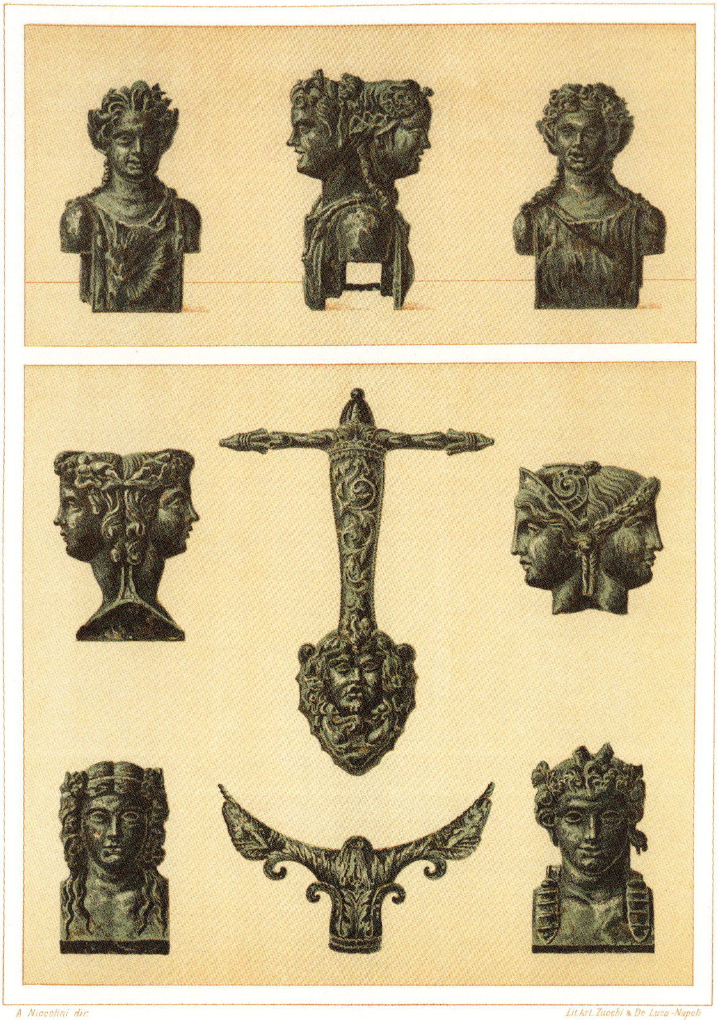

A Niccolini dir.

Lit.Art. Zucchi & De Luca-Napoli

Plate 43 — *[Anonymous]*

Bronze and marble objects – Above: ***Casa della Parete nera*** (Casa dei Bronzi, VII 4, 59) – One of three bronze double herms found here. Middle and below: double herms and herms made of marble; handles of bronze utensils. The greenish tone in the illustrations erroneously suggests that all the pieces are made of bronze.

Plate 41 — *[Anonymous]*

Various bronze lamps and lamp-holders from Pompeii and Herculaneum.

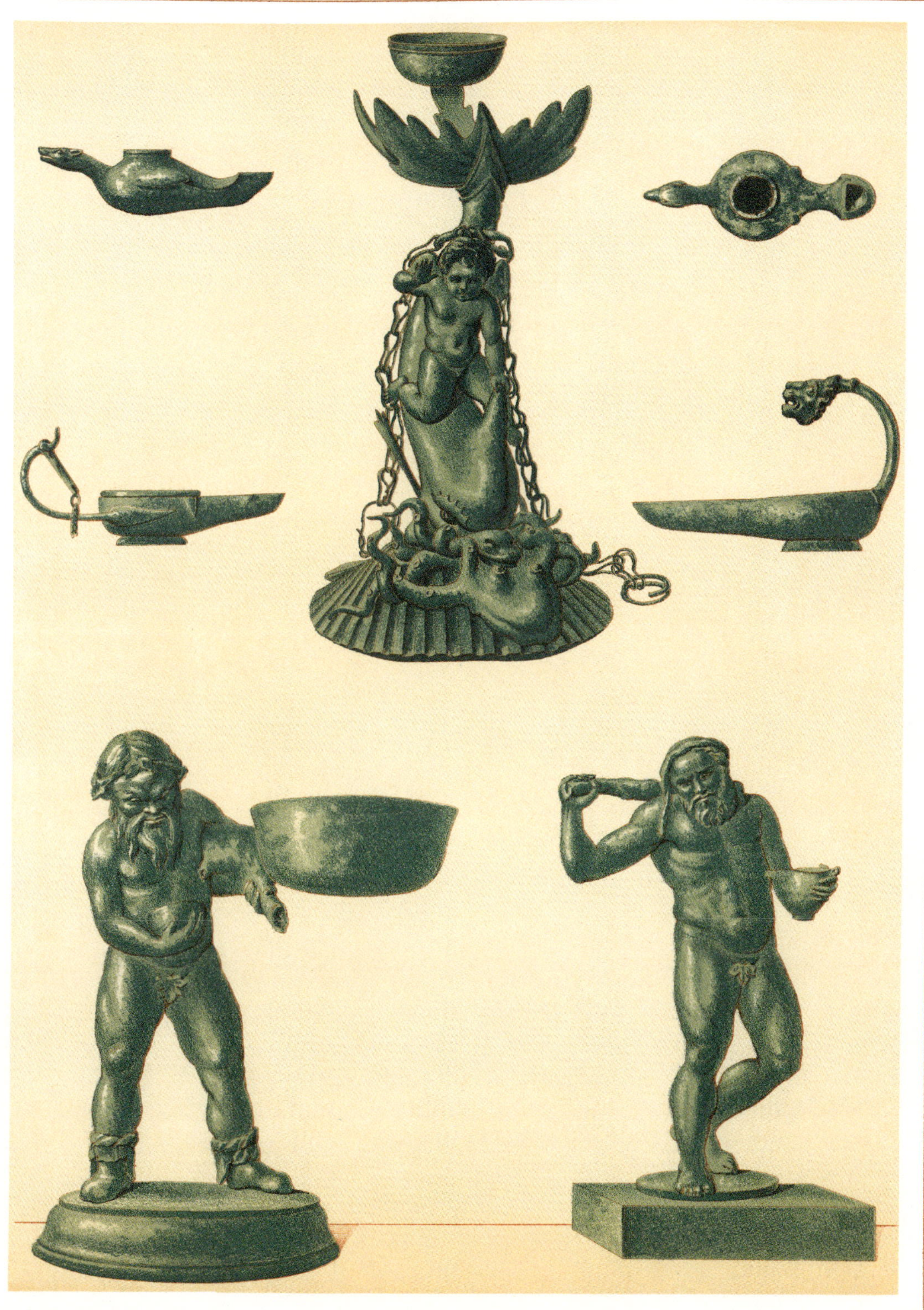

Lit. Art. Zucchi & De Luca, Napoli.

A. Niccolini dir.

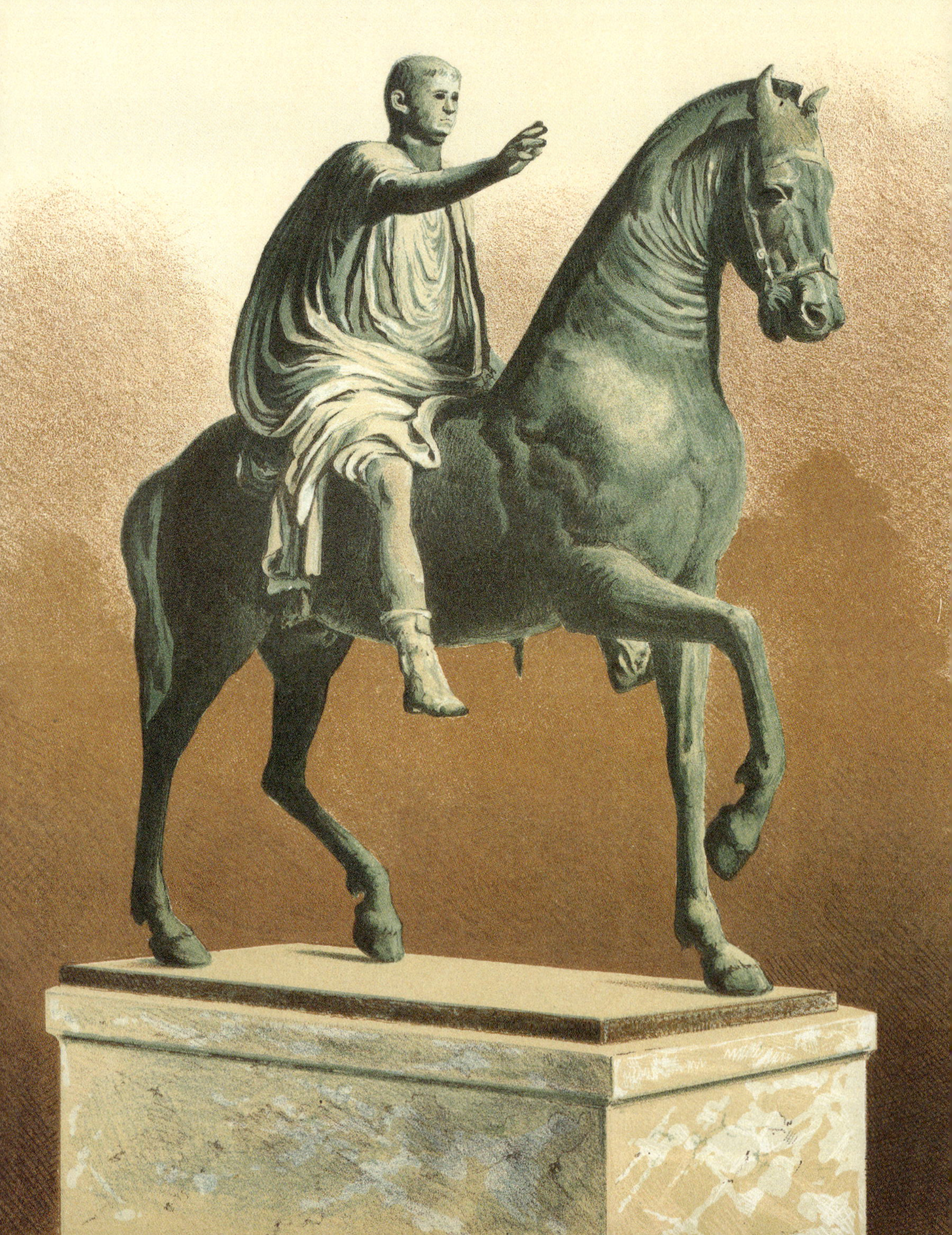

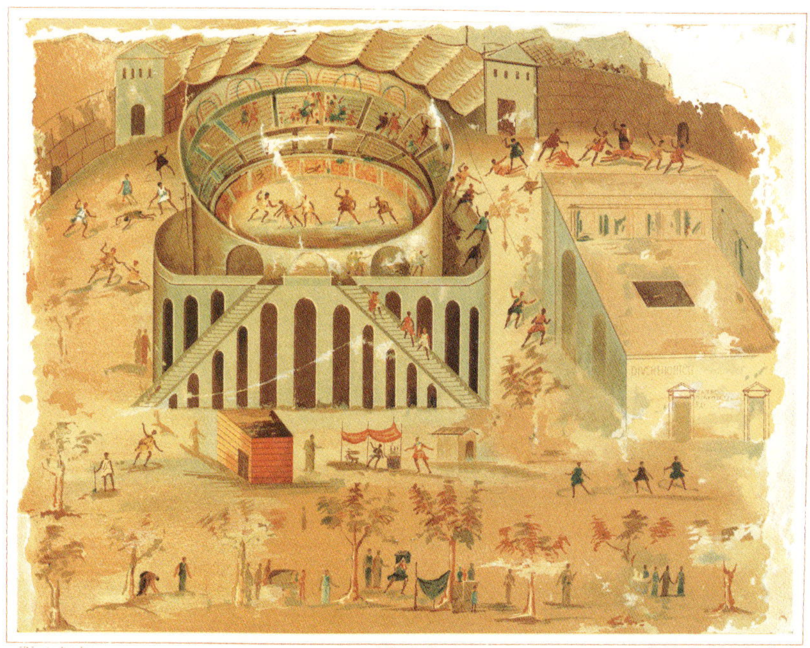

Plate 39 — *[G. Discanno]*
Equestrian statue – Made up out of fragments of various origins. The rider and parts of the horse stood at the start of the Via di Mercurio on the so-called Arch of Caligula. The figure represents a member of the local upper class. Similar equestrian statues stood in large numbers on Pompeii's Forum.

Plate 32 — *[V. Loria]*
Casa I 3, 23 – Bloody riot between the inhabitants of Pompeii and Nuceria. The picture, which is unusual in many respects, probably shows – in a sort of bird's-eye view – a local event that occurred in AD 59 and which even found its way into the *Annals* of Tacitus. As a consequence of the disturbance, gladiatorial games were banned in Pompeii for ten years.

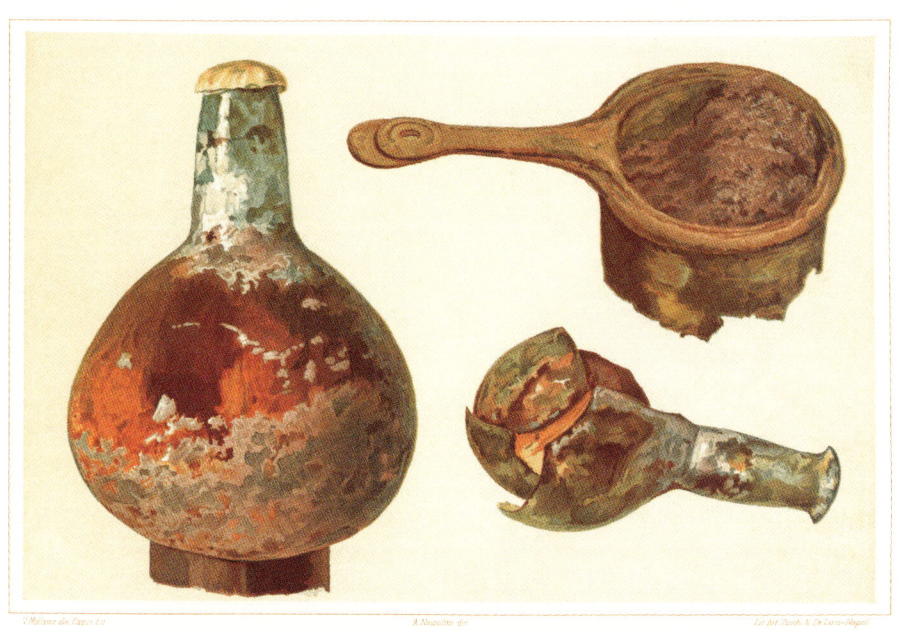

Plate 45 — *[V. Mollame]*
Glass vessels containing organic materials – In an Academy paper published in 1868, the chemist Sebastiano de Luca identified the rancid contents of the container below right as linseed oil and wax.

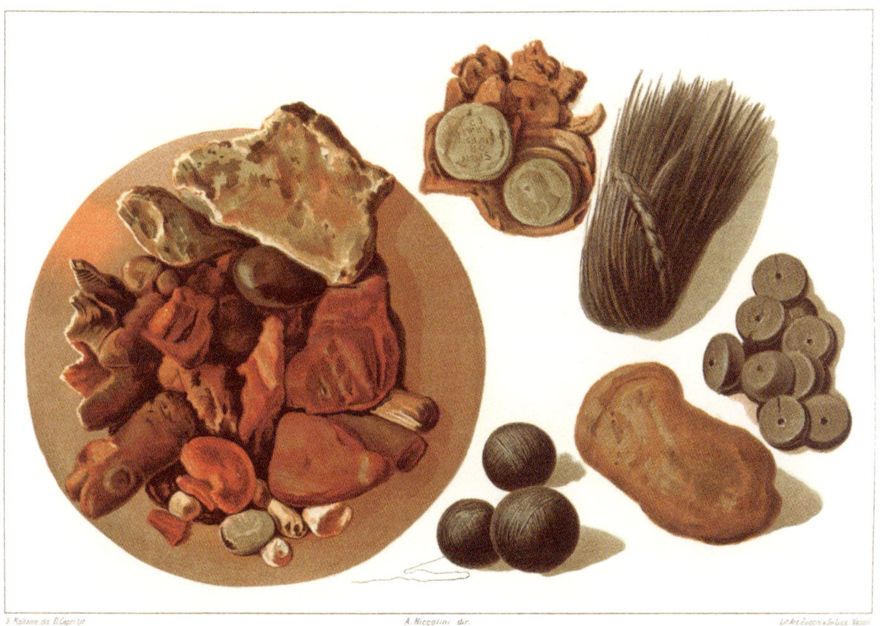

Plate 46 — *[V. Mollame]*
Organic finds from Pompeii – Amber, a fabric purse, a bundle of willow twigs, a cleaning cloth, three balls of thread and some buttons.

Pages 426–427
Plate 48 — *[A. Carelli]*
Various tokens and games pieces (tesserae) made of bone – These were used for various purposes, including admission- and money-tokens. Their forms are highly diverse.

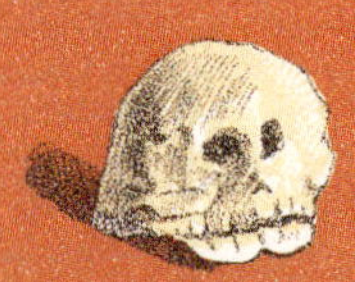
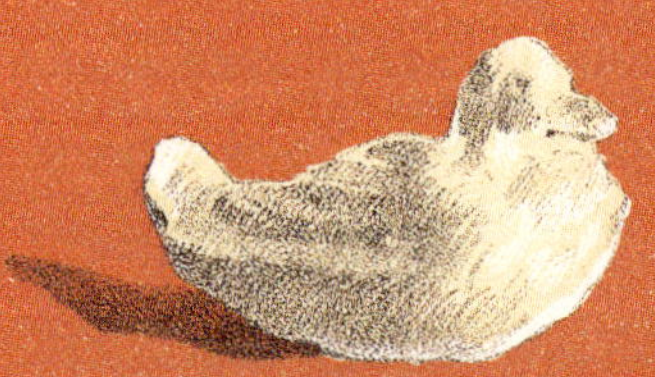
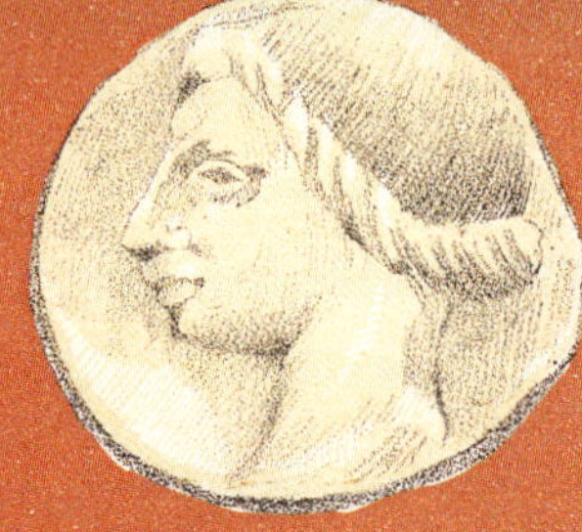
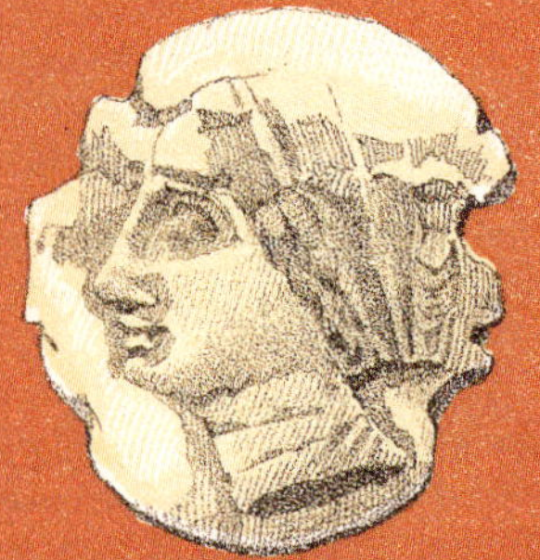
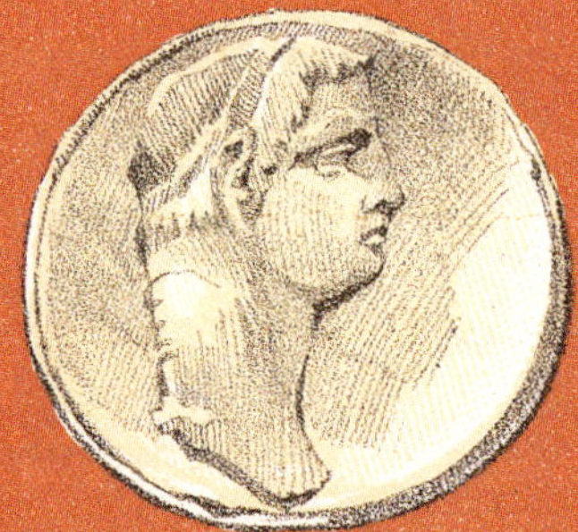
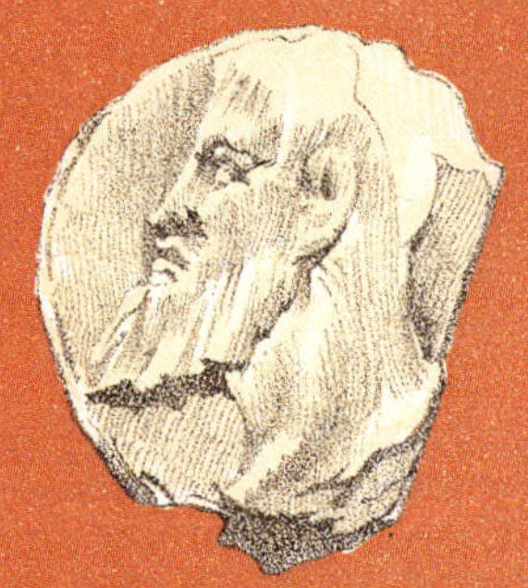
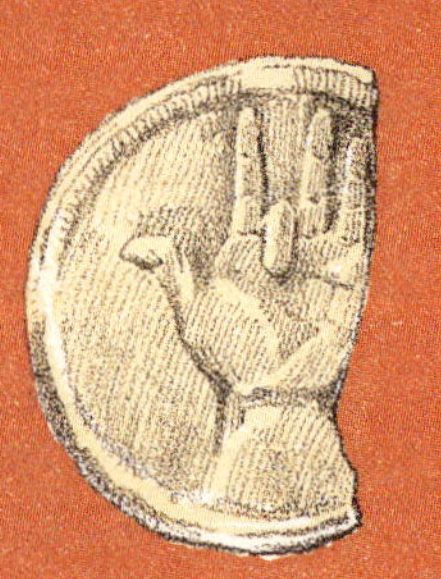
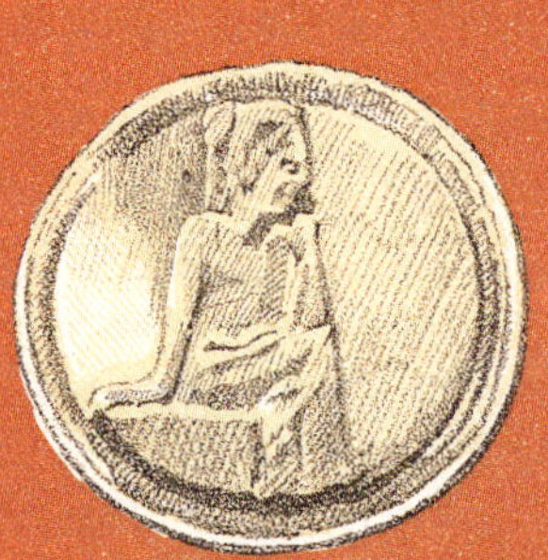
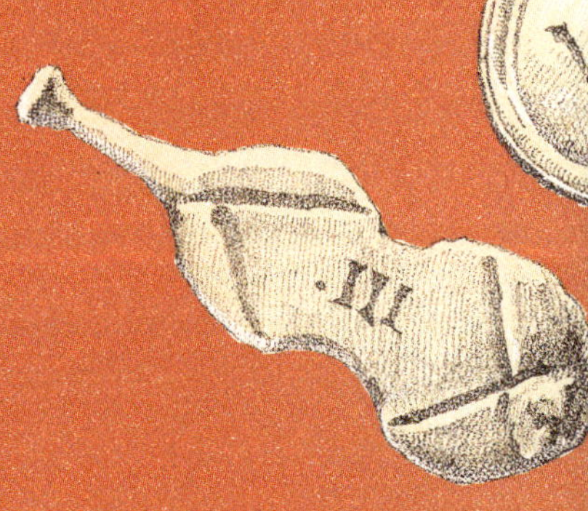

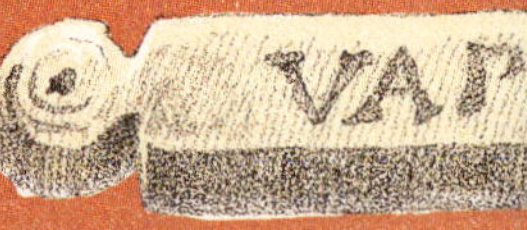

HILARVS
TVRPILIN
PHILOXENVS-METEL
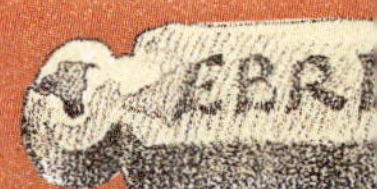

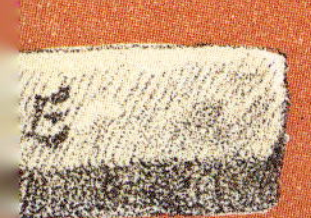

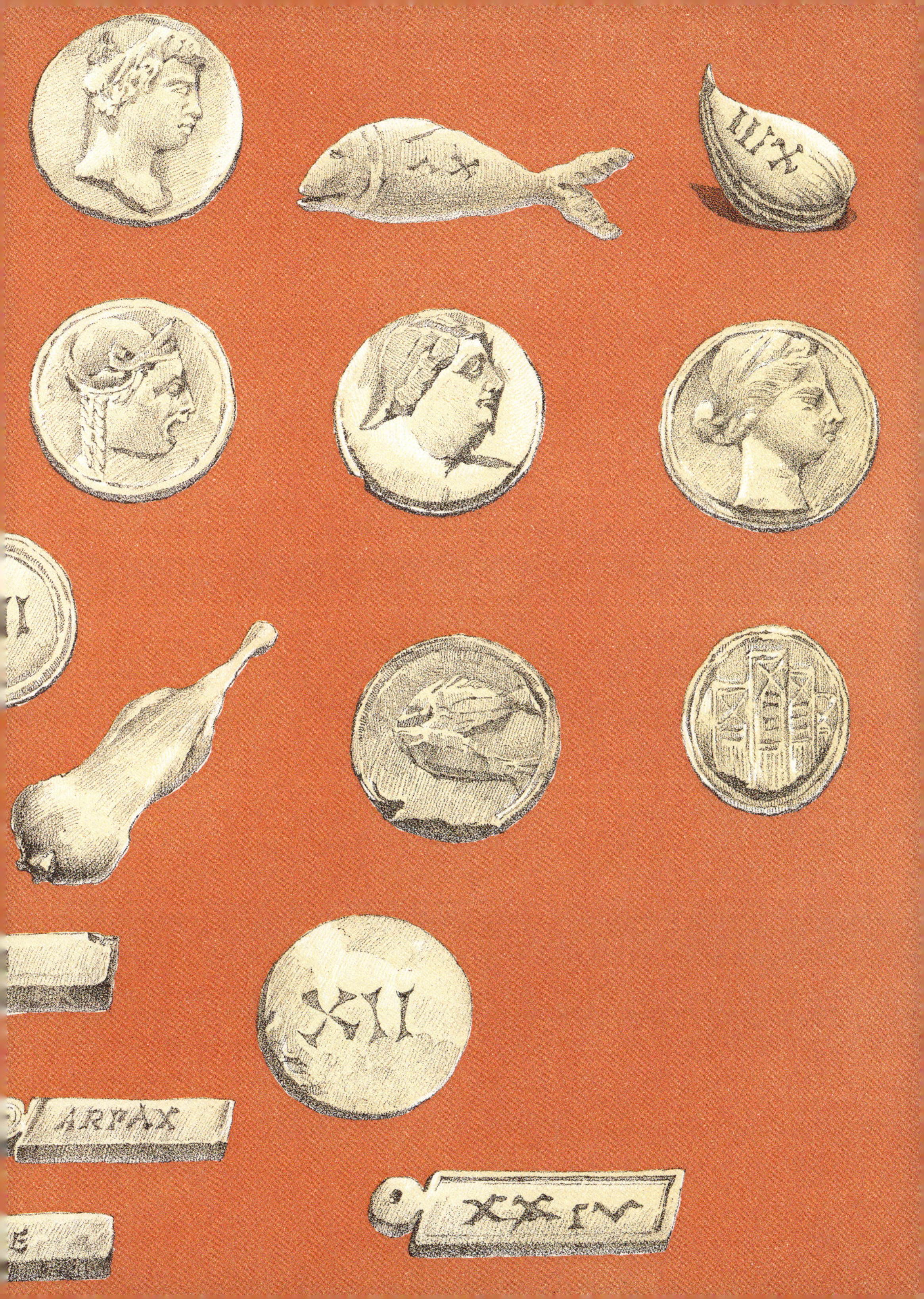

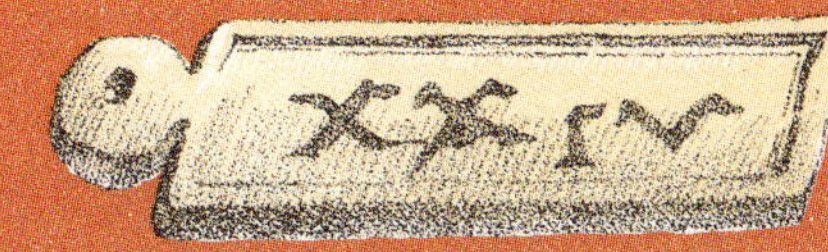
XXIV

SAGGI DI RESTAURO

Reconstructions

The well-preserved ruins of Pompeii have inspired artists since the 18th century to visualise them in their original form. Alongside the somewhat sober (but from today's perspective, scholarly) drawings made by architects, right from the start artists produced perspective illustrations, often embellished with scenic details, of the city's streets and squares, and above all its houses. The works by François Mazois and William Gell from the early 19th century were particularly successful, and in later years were regularly re-used and revised. The Niccolini plates, which show public and private buildings and areas of the city, also follow in this tradition. A distinctive feature here is the way in which two reconstructions are in each case accompanied by a third plate with pictures presenting a view of the same buildings as ruins. This juxtaposition was intended to prove the accuracy of the reconstructions, not unlike the illustrated booklets, for a long time popular at archaeological sites, in which a picture of the ruins was overlaid by a transparent sheet with a view of the reconstruction. It is difficult to say how much of each reconstruction is the work of the artist credited in each case. In some instances designs by Gell and Mazois have simply been appropriated, coloured in and occasionally augmented. Other sheets are less derivative but were in some measure executed with little knowledge of ancient domestic architecture. Scenes of temple sacrifices, gladiatorial combat in the amphitheatre and theatrical performances take up motifs of the salon painting of the day. Precisely on account of their anecdotal character, these pictures are today again being used as illustrations. Only at the end of the 19th century, in the drawings by Carl Weichhardt and August Mau, was there a resurgence of academically "more correct" reconstructions oriented towards Pompeian finds and the latest research.

Plate 3 — *[G. Discanno]*
Reconstruction of the atrium in the Casa del Poeta tragico (VI 8, 3 and 5) –
There is no archaeological evidence for the roof construction, the painting of the upper wall zone or the wooden walkway for the upper storey (for the house see vol. I).

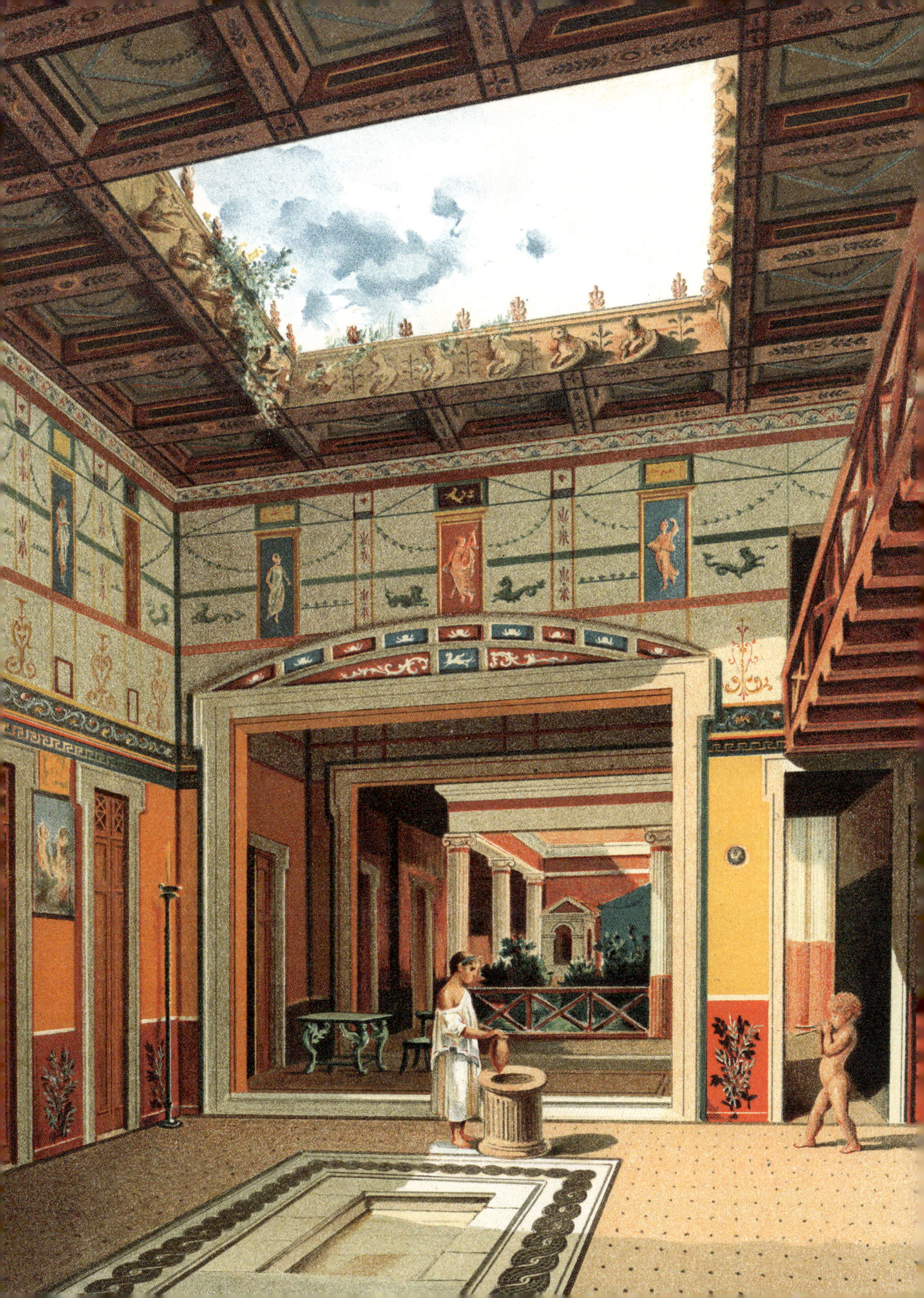

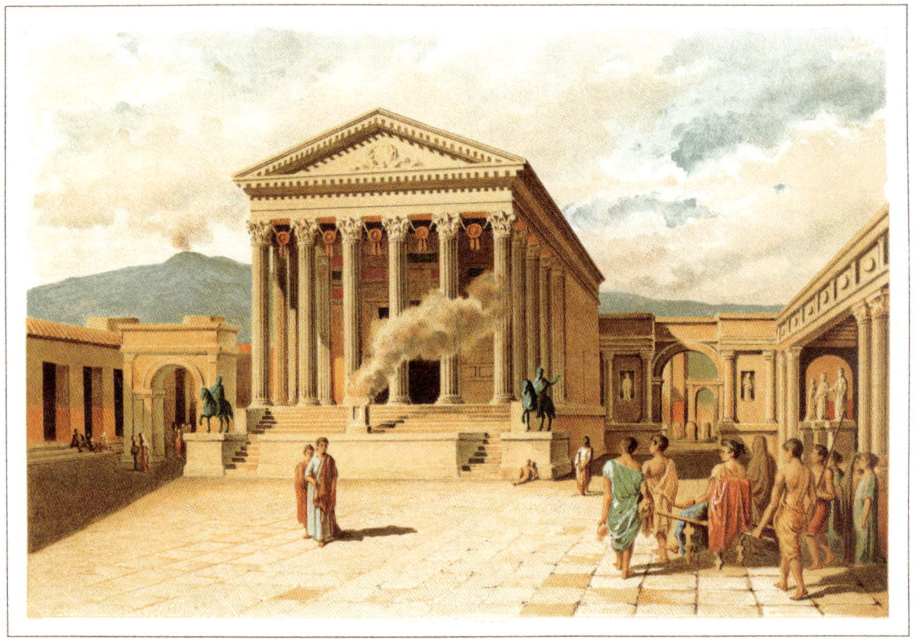

Plate 1 — *[G. Discanno]*
Reconstructed view of the north side of the Forum – With the city's main temple (Capitolium), honorary arches and porticos. In the foreground, a litter.

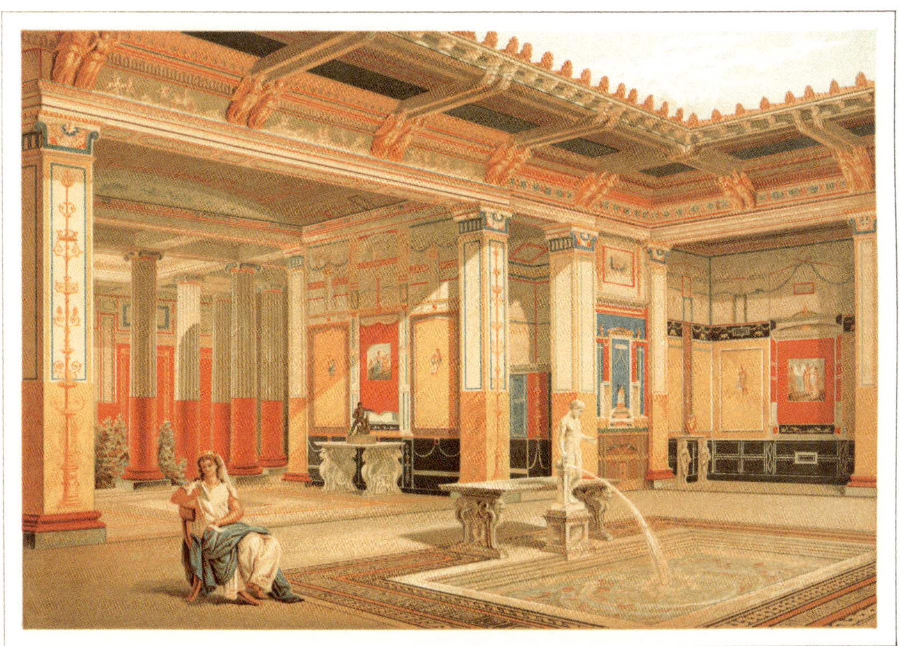

Plate 5 — *[Anonymous]*

This "reconstruction" does not show any Pompeian house that actually existed, but is based on a photograph of the so-called Pompeian Court at the Crystal Palace in Sydenham (1854). This replica of a Pompeian interior was designed by the architect M. D. Wyatt, with Giuseppe Abbate contributing the designs for the wall decorations. The furnishings combined objects from various contexts: the Hercules group, for example, comes from the Casa di Sallustio, the table legs from the Casa di Cornelius Rufus etc.

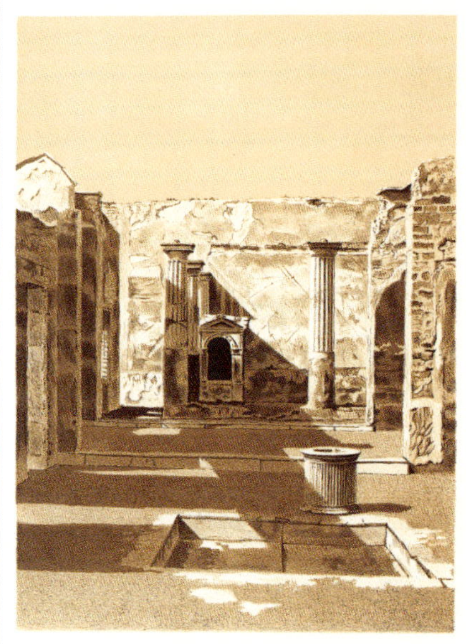

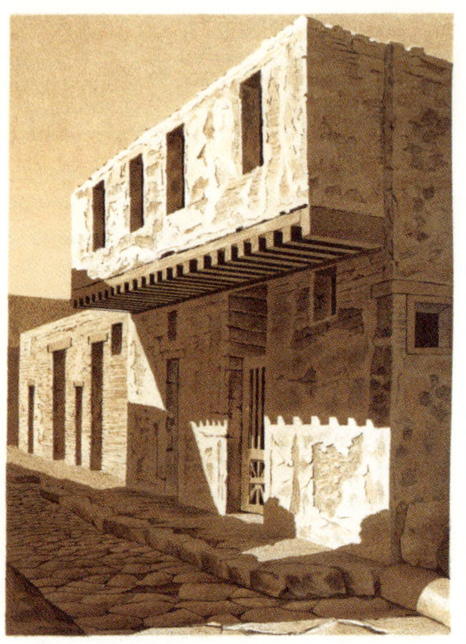

G. Autoriello dis. A. Niccolini dis. Lit. Art. Zucchi & De Luca–Napoli

Plate B — *[G. Autoriello]*

View of the ruins of the Casa del Poeta tragico and the Casa del Balcone pensile (VII 12, 28) – In the latter house, archaeologists for the first time succeeded in conserving and reconstructing parts of an upper storey in situ. The balcony overhanging the house's plain front entrance will have served as the inspiration for the illustration in plate 4.

Plate 4 — *[G. Discanno]*

Reconstruction of a street scene – With an overhanging balcony above a "bottega". Even if the arrangement of the various elements (lararium, Mercury, inscription, decoration of the upper wall, partly taken from pl. 8) seems a little arbitrary, the atmosphere is convincing.

Pages 434–435

Plate 7 — *[V. Mollame]*

So-called Building of Eumachia on the Forum – The lithograph shows a niche in the rear section of the extensive complex, in which was found the statue of the female donor, a priestess. The sheet only reconstructs the colouring of the wall, but does not complete the missing parts of the niche's architecture.

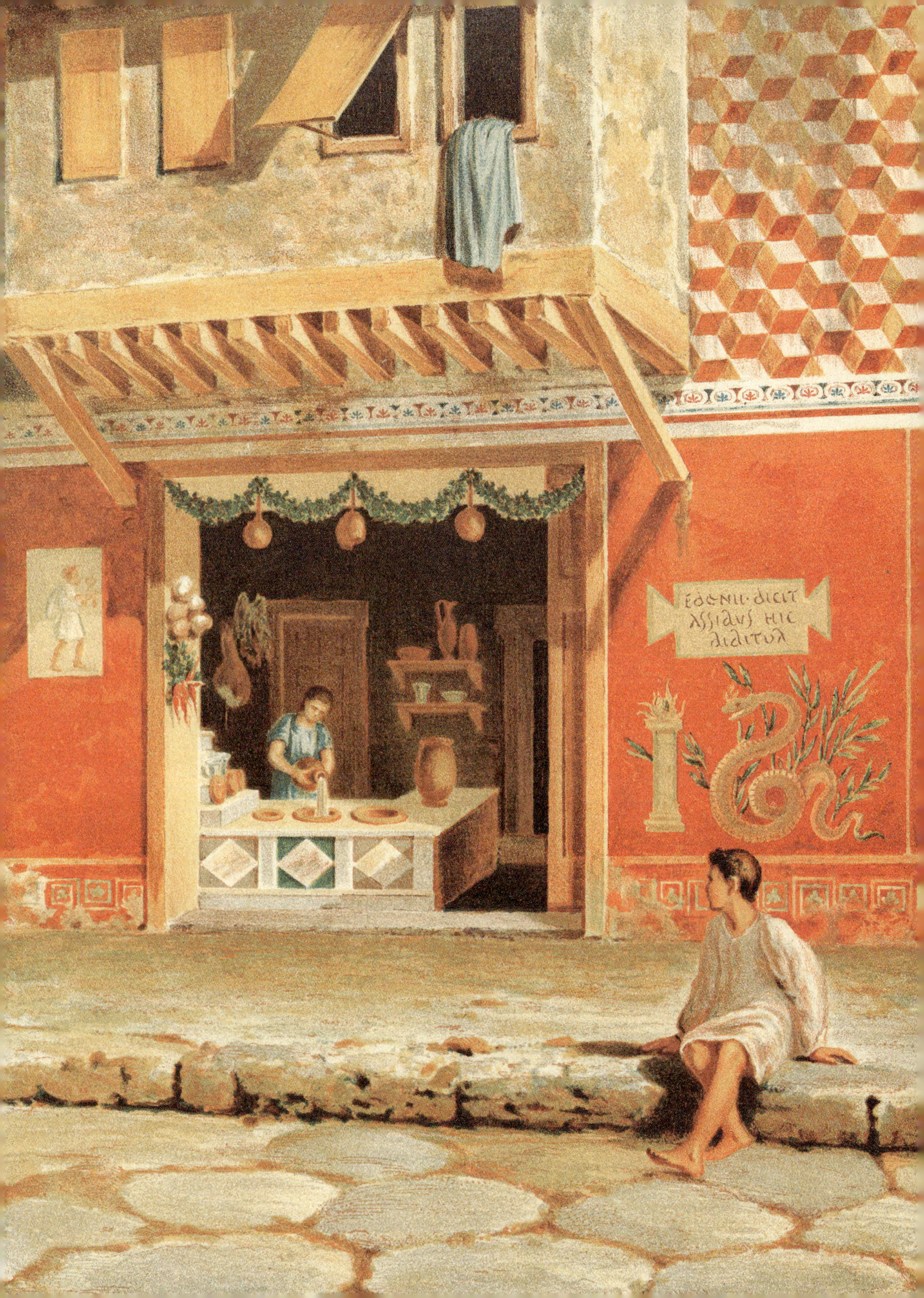
EDONE · DICIT
ASSIBUS HIC
BIBITUR

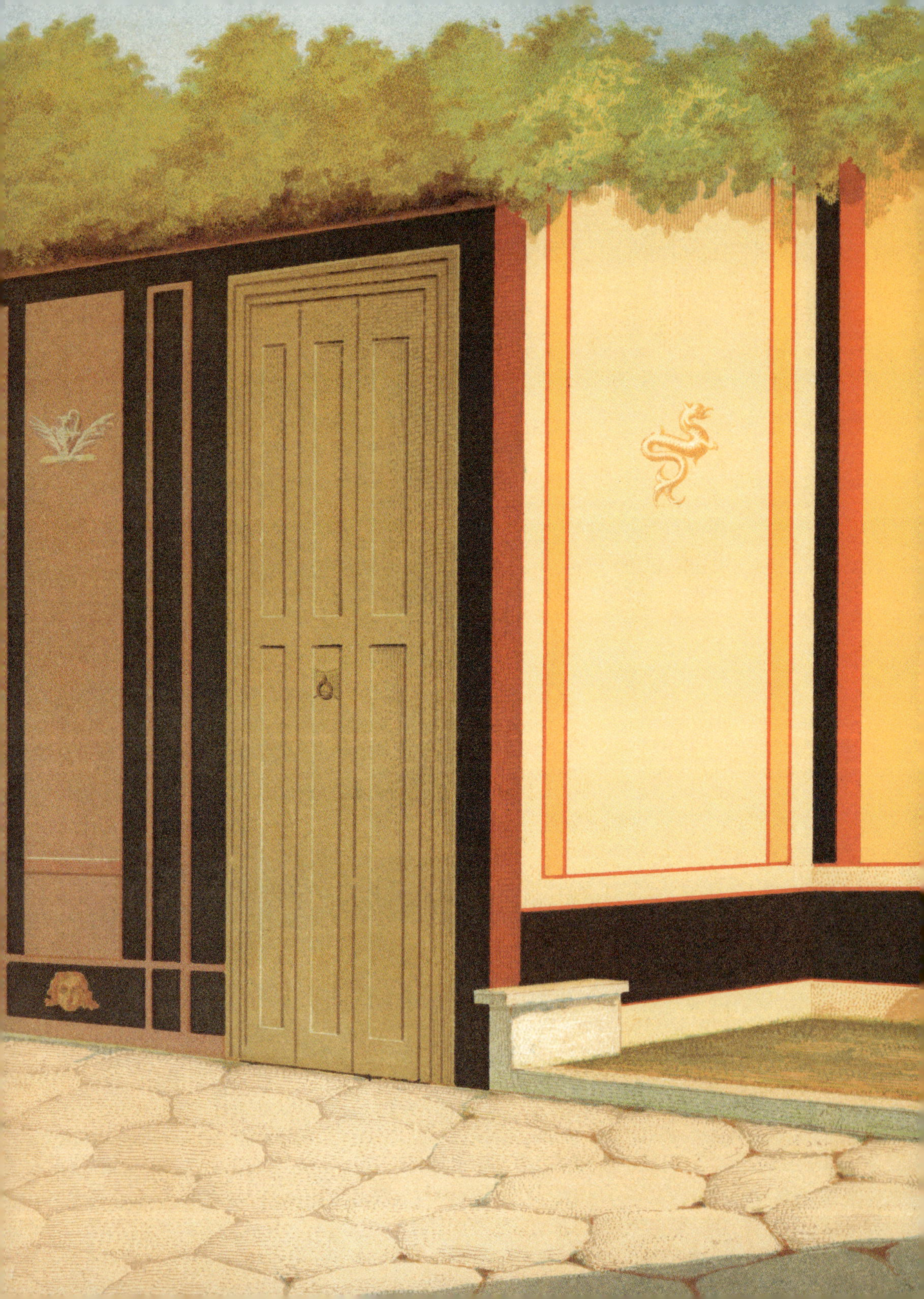

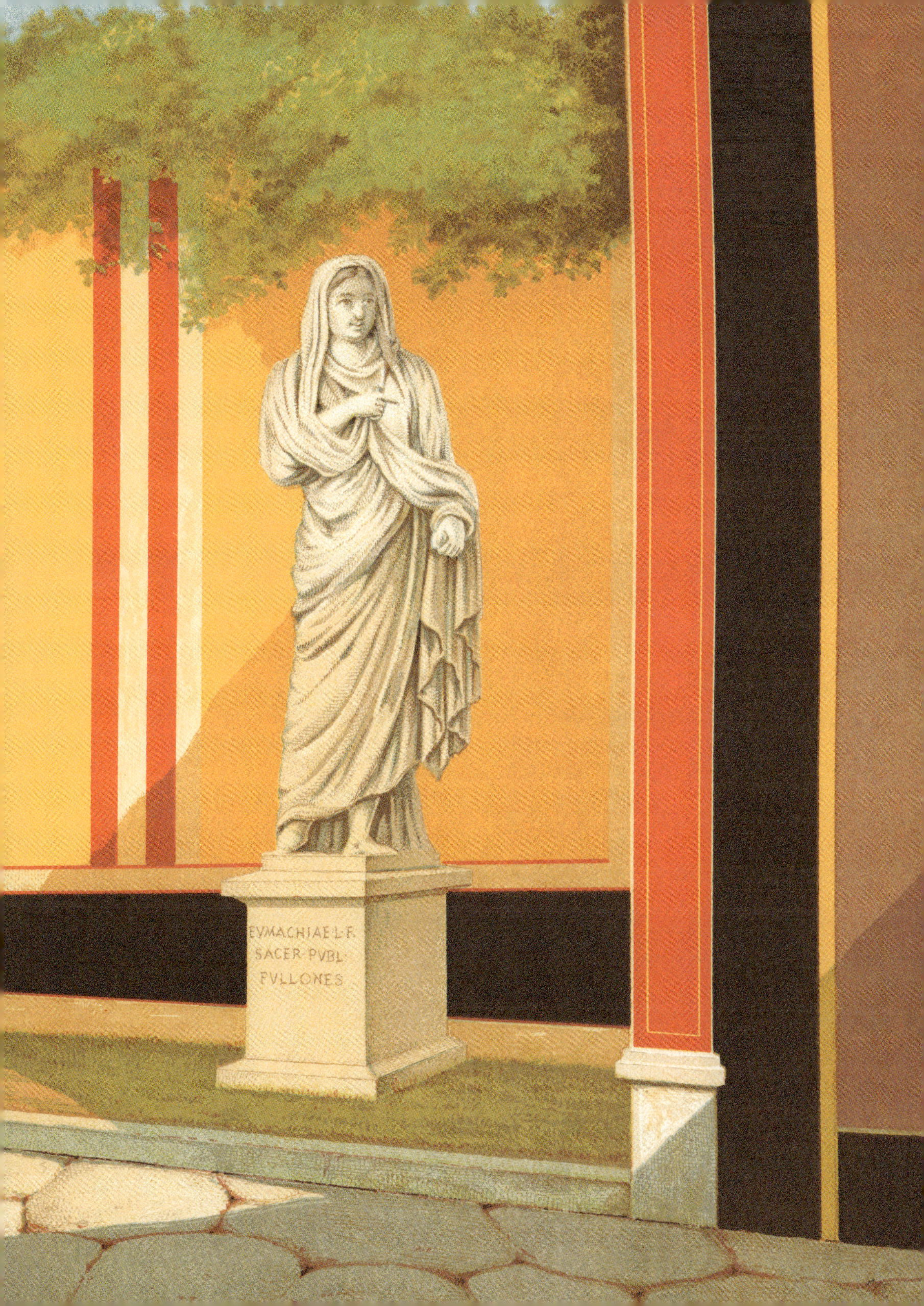
EVMACHIAE·L·F·
SACER·PVBL·
FVLLONES

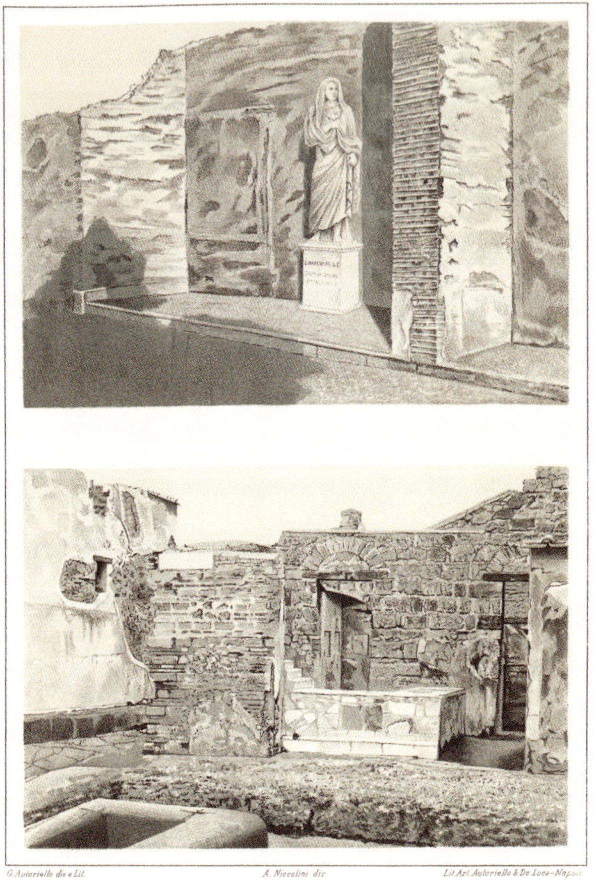

Plate D — *[G. Autoriello]*
Views of the state of the buildings reconstructed in plates 7 and 8. Lithographs after photographs (?).

✱

Plate 8 — *[Oscar Dressler]*
"Bottega" near the Fountain of Mercury in the Via di Mercurio (VI 10, 1) – The reconstruction is based on the frontispiece of volume 10 of the *Real Museo Borbonico*.

✱

Pages 438–439
Plate 9 — *[A. Magliano]*
Atrium in the Casa di Marcus Lucretius (IX 3, 5 and 24) – The view of the sculpture garden is well captured, but the wall decoration is reduced to plain surfaces (for the house see vol. I).

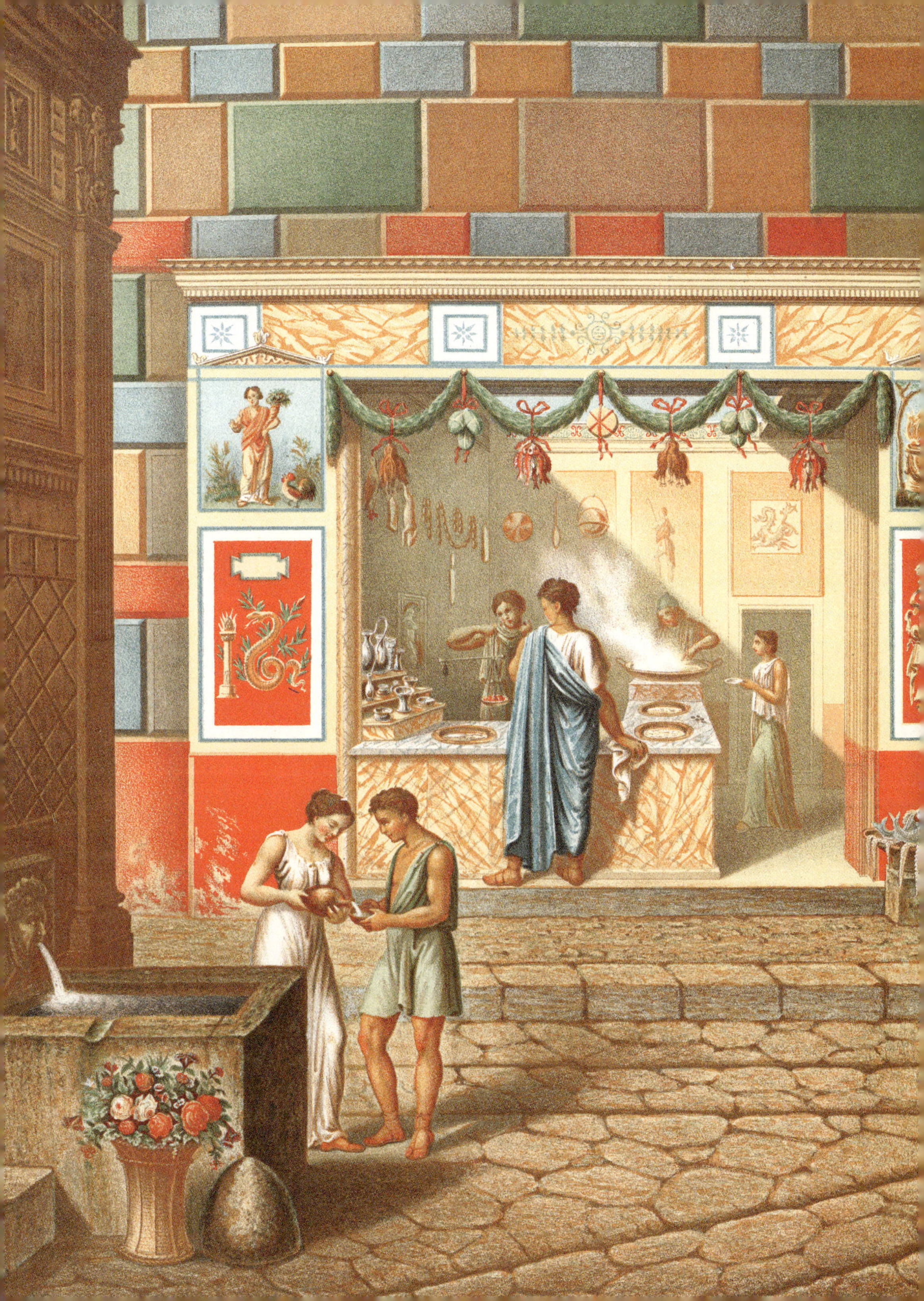

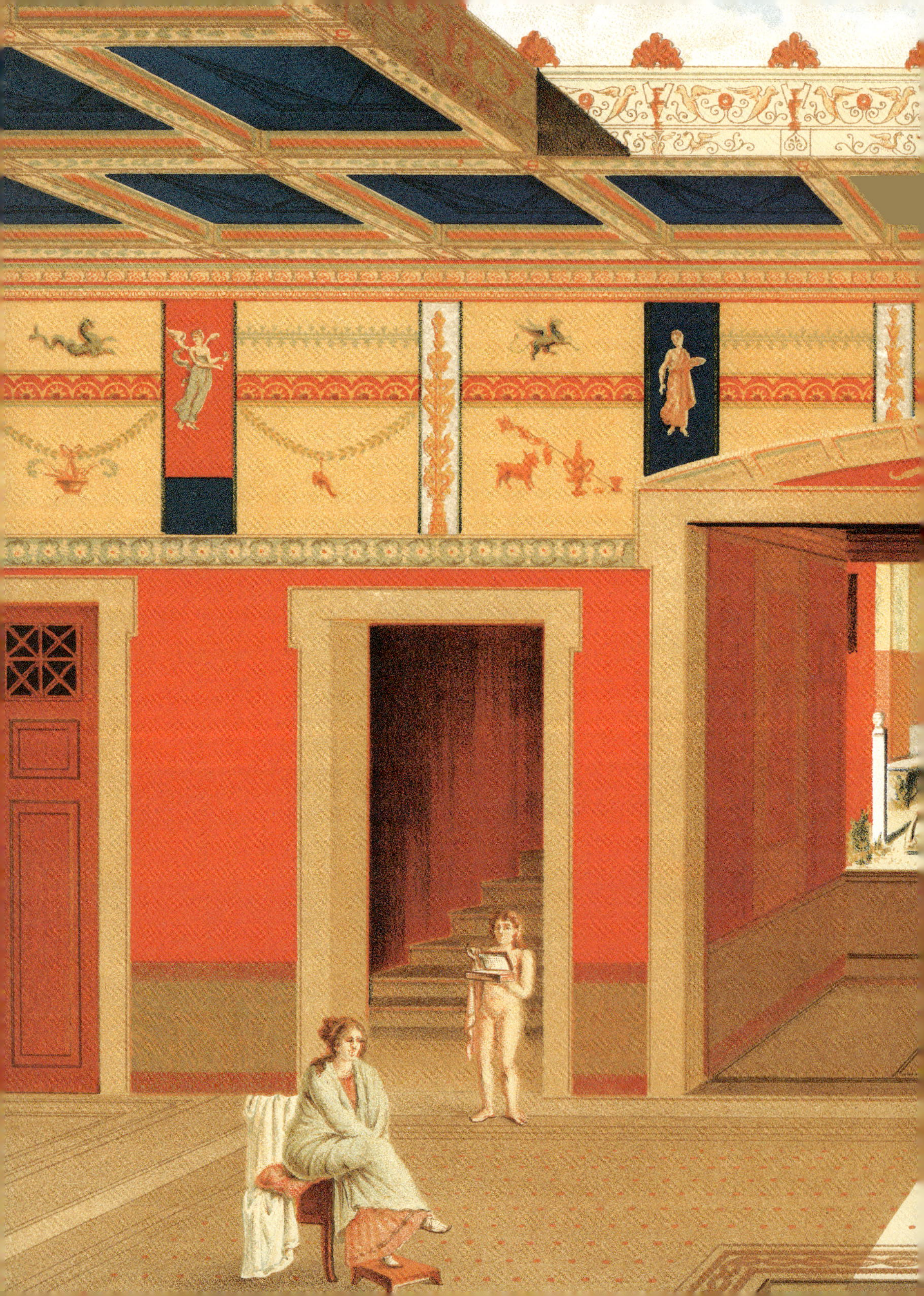

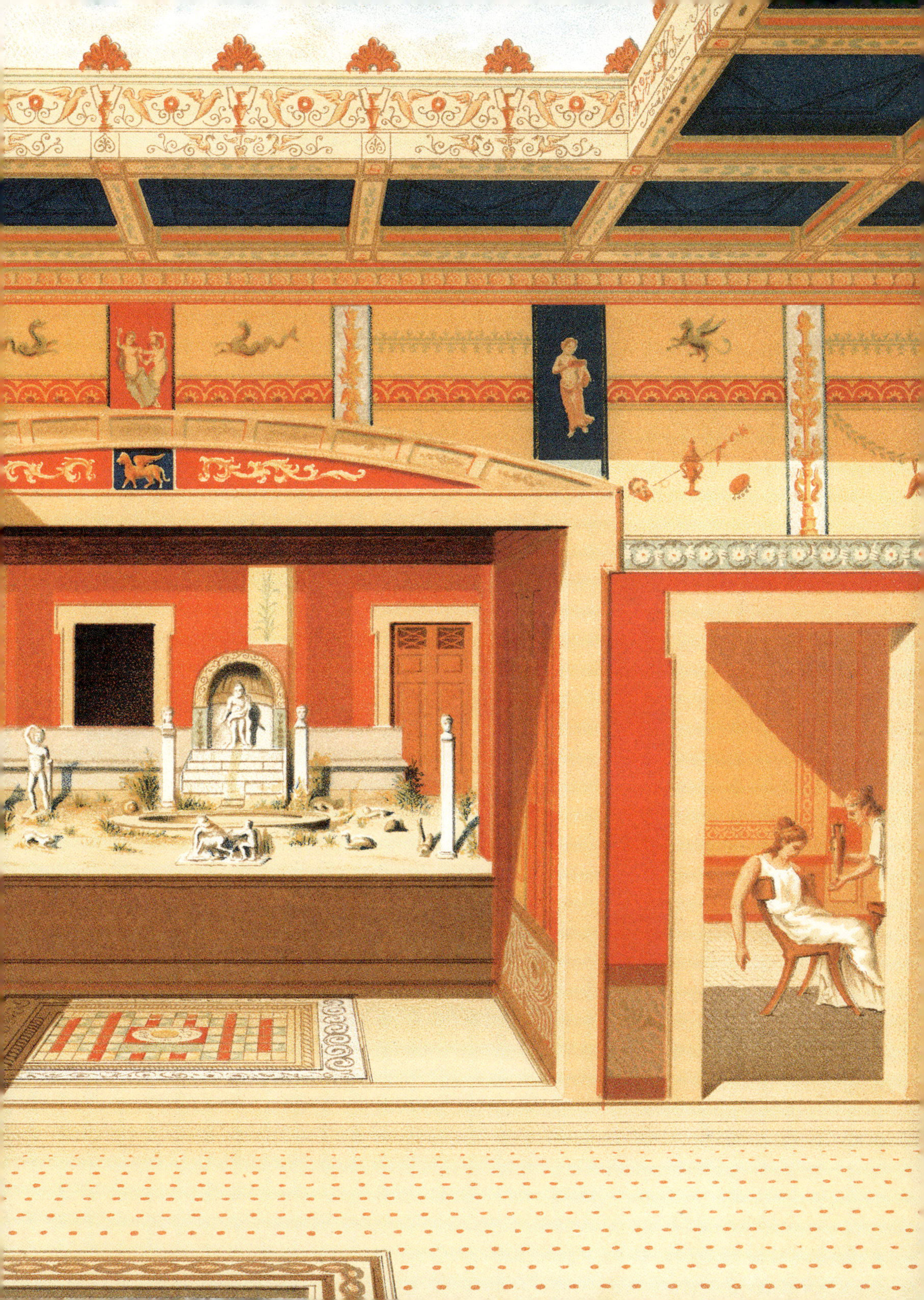

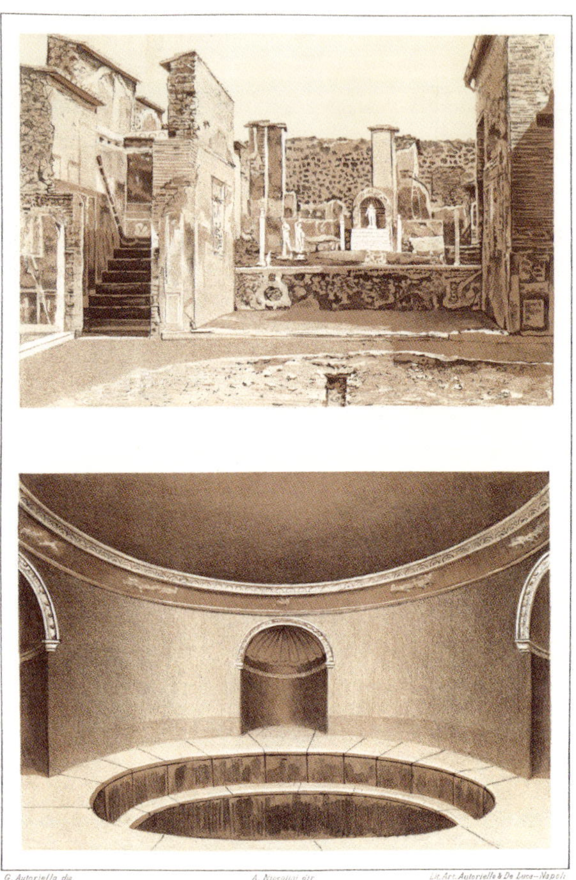

Plate E — *[G. Autoriello]*
Views of the state of the buildings reconstructed in plates 9 and 10.
Lithographs after photographs (?).

⁂

Plate 10 — *[O. Dressler]*
Circular room (frigidarium) in the Stabian Baths – Dressler copied the angle and lighting from William Gell and added figures (for the Stabian Baths see vol. I).

⁂

Pages 442–443
Plate 12 — *[C. de Simone]*
Religious activity at the Temple of Fortuna Augusta – On the left, the arch at the entrance to the Via di Mercurio. The picturesque reconstruction is based very closely on a drawing by William Gell.

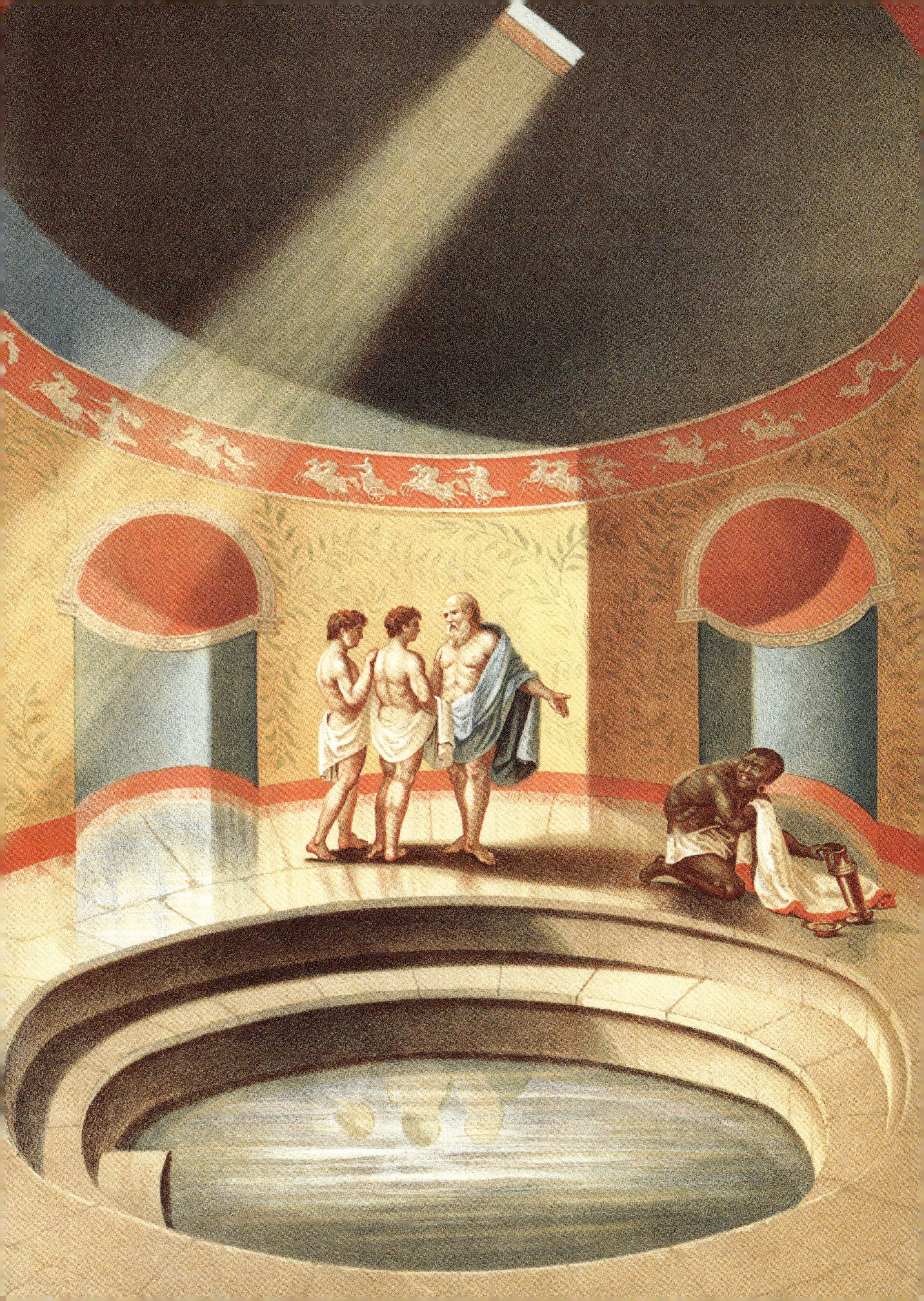

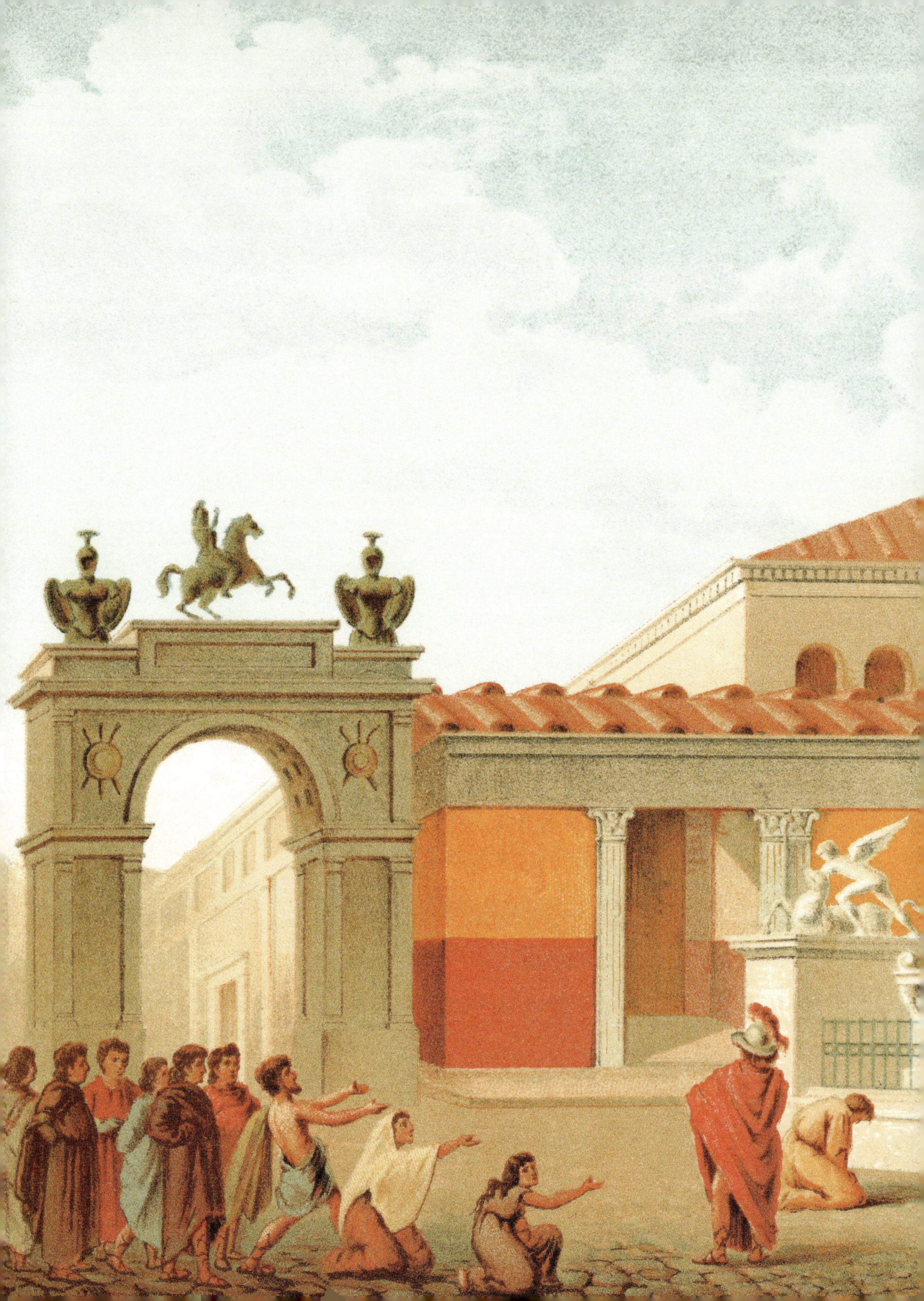

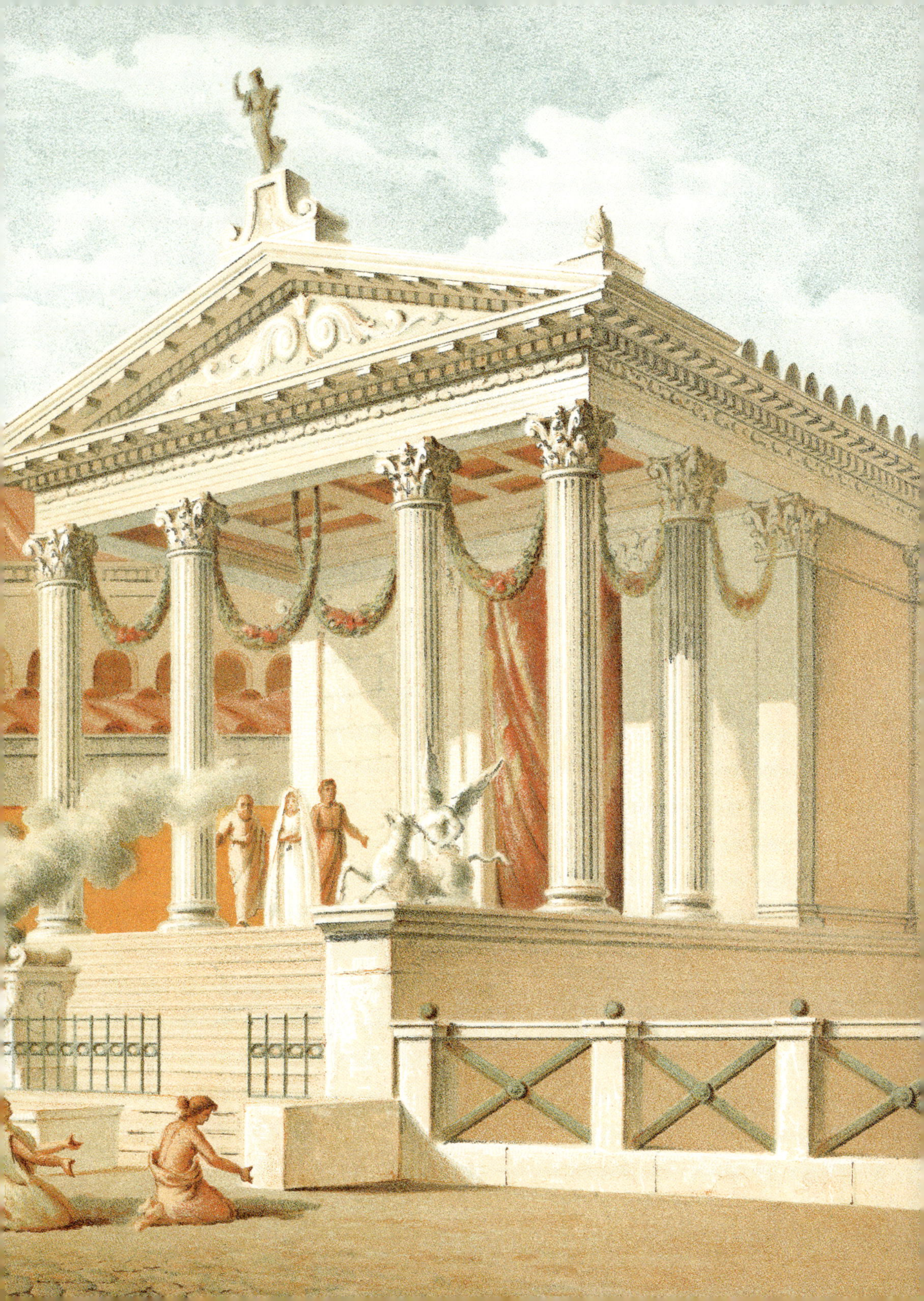

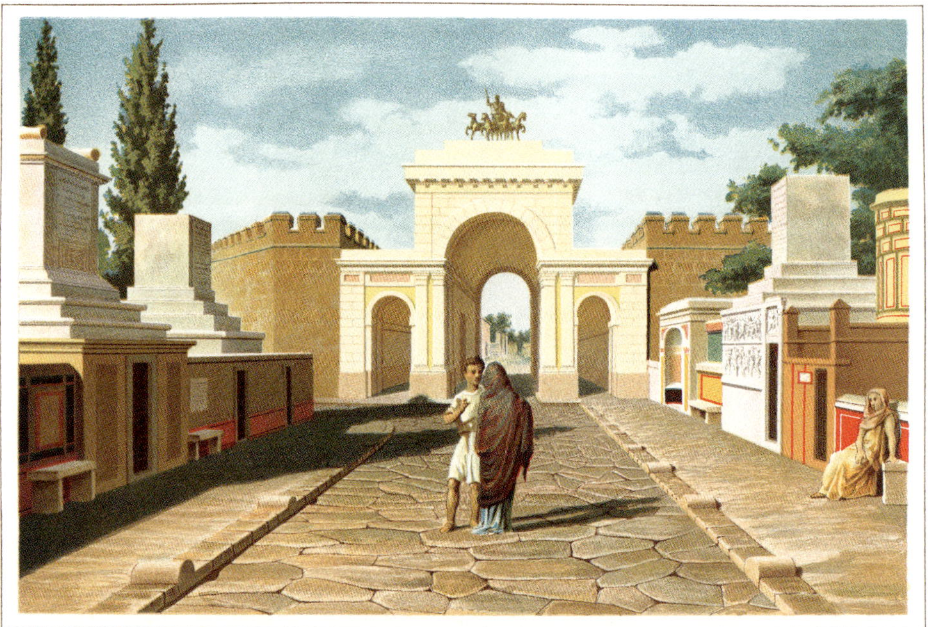

Plate 14 — *[G. Autoriello]*
Street of Tombs with the Herculaneum Gate – The plate was taken from a drawing by François Mazois, but modified its perspective and proportions to produce a highly distorted reconstruction.

Plate 15 — *[G. Autoriello]*
Peristyle of the Casa dei Capitelli colorati (VII 4, 31–33, 50 and 51) – The reconstruction misunderstands the ancient architectural concept, in so far as it leaves the columned hall open to the skies and places a roof over the garden area (for the house see vol. 1).

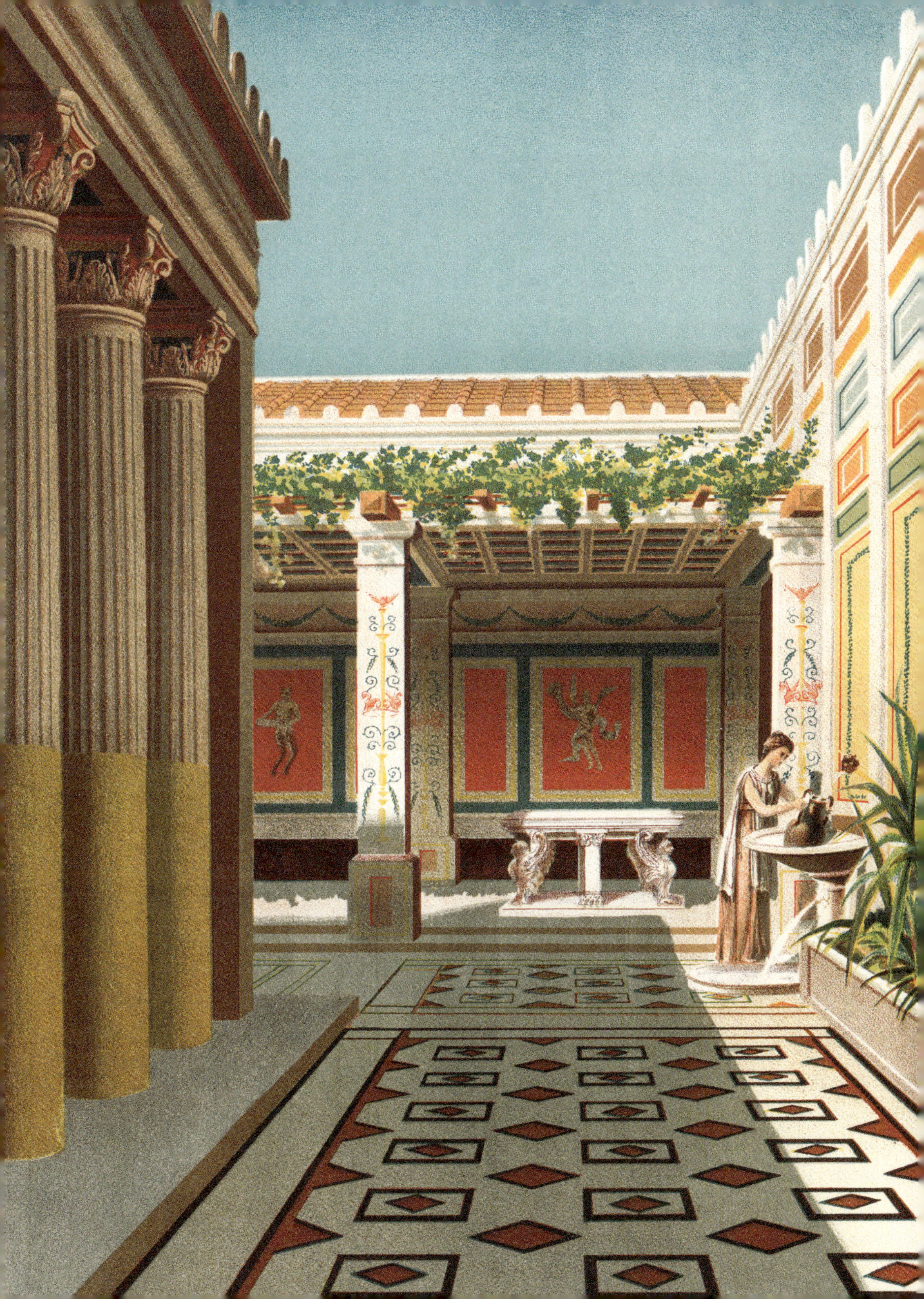

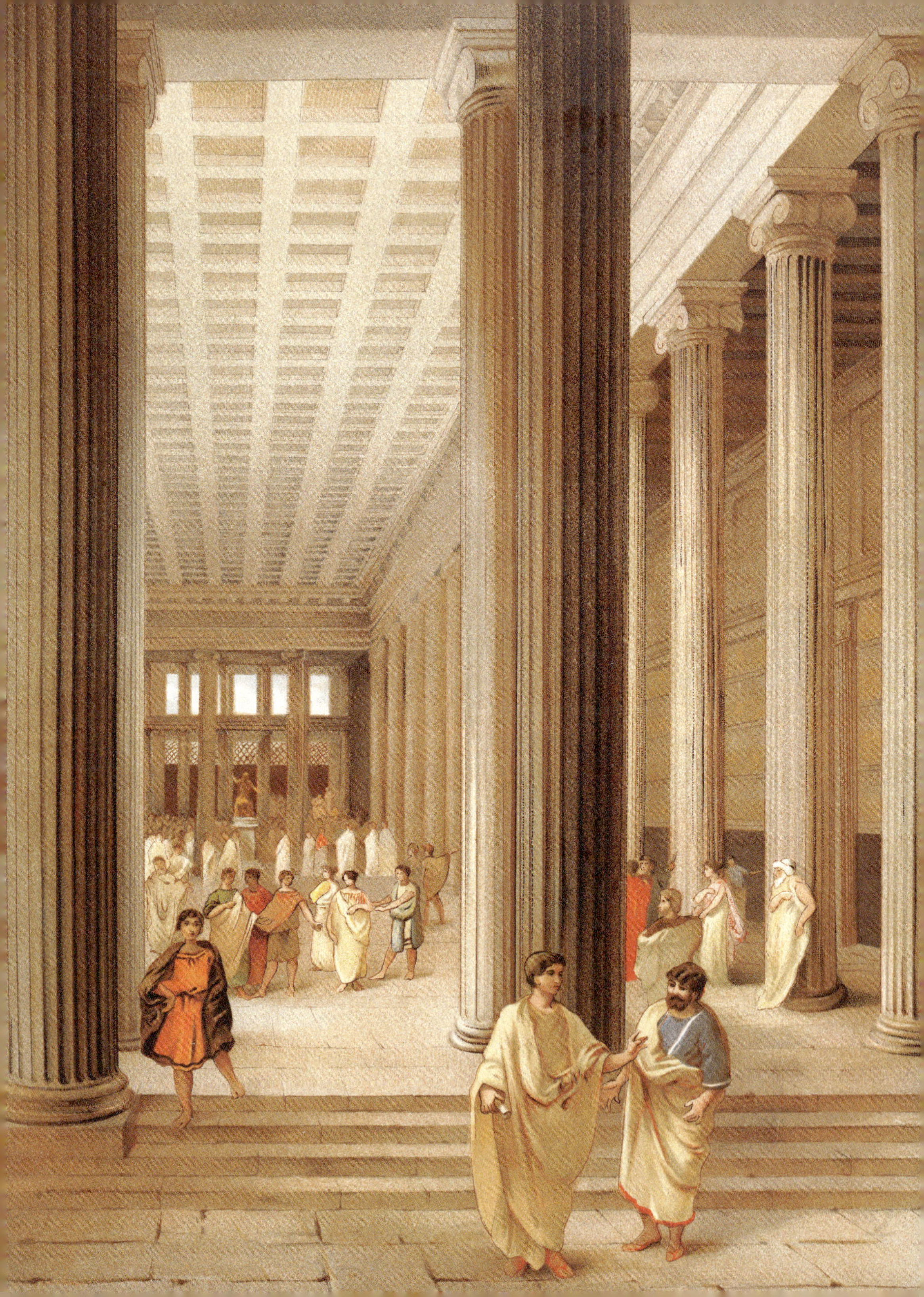

Plate 16 — *[G. Cel.]*

Interior of the Basilica – The great hall on the Forum served as a meeting point for wholesalers and for court proceedings.

Pages 448-449

Plate 17 — *[G. Cel.]*

Pompeii amphitheatre – On a day with gladiatorial games. Visible at the top of the arena are the awnings *(vela)* that are always mentioned in announcements as ensuring the particular comfort of the audience.

Page 450

Plate J — *[S. De Stefani]*

Two views of the amphitheatre.

Page 451

Plate K — *[S. De Stefano]*

View of the large theatre seen from the Forum triangolare and interior view of the *theatrum tectum* (cf. vedute in vol. I, Teatri, pl. 3).

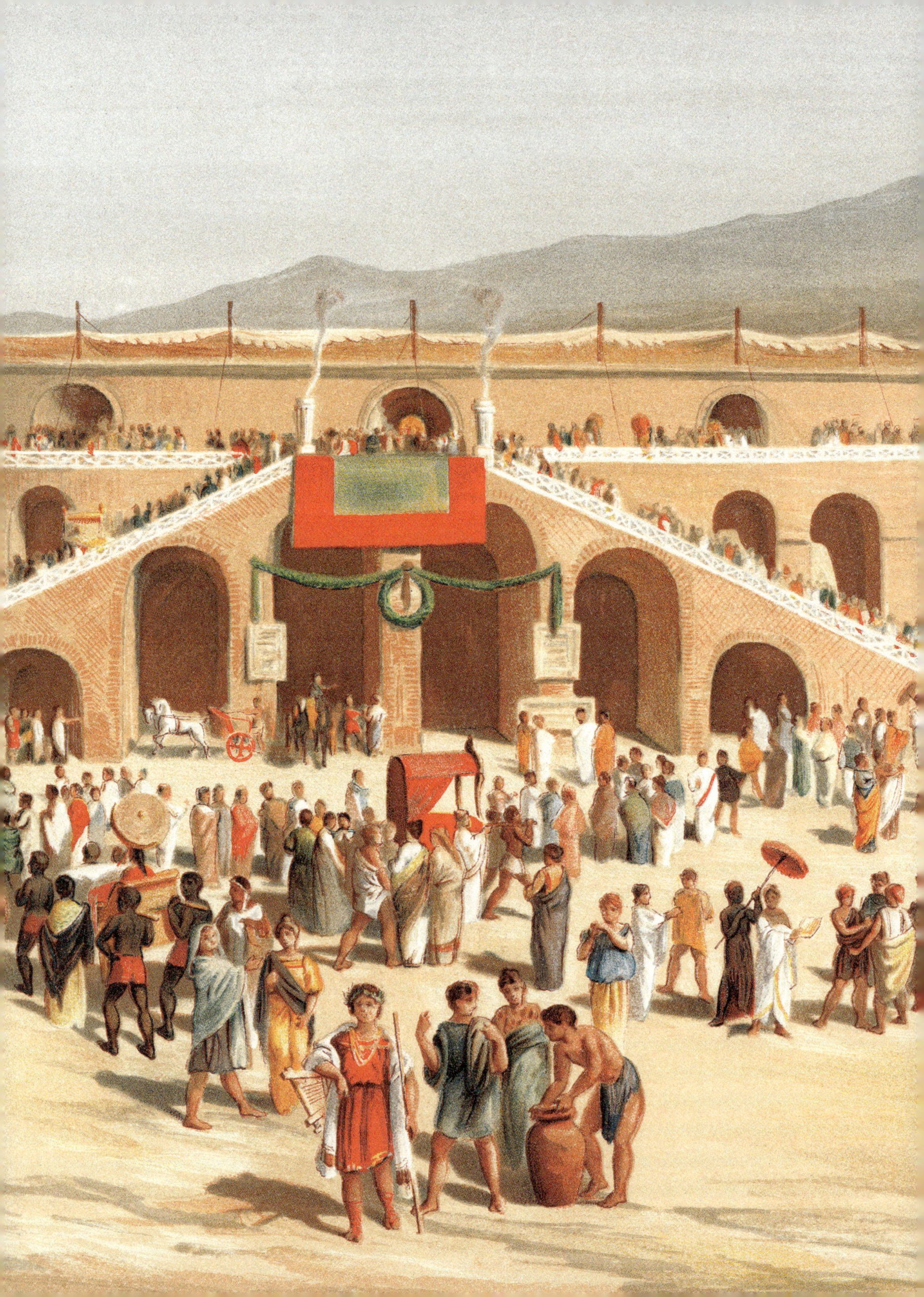

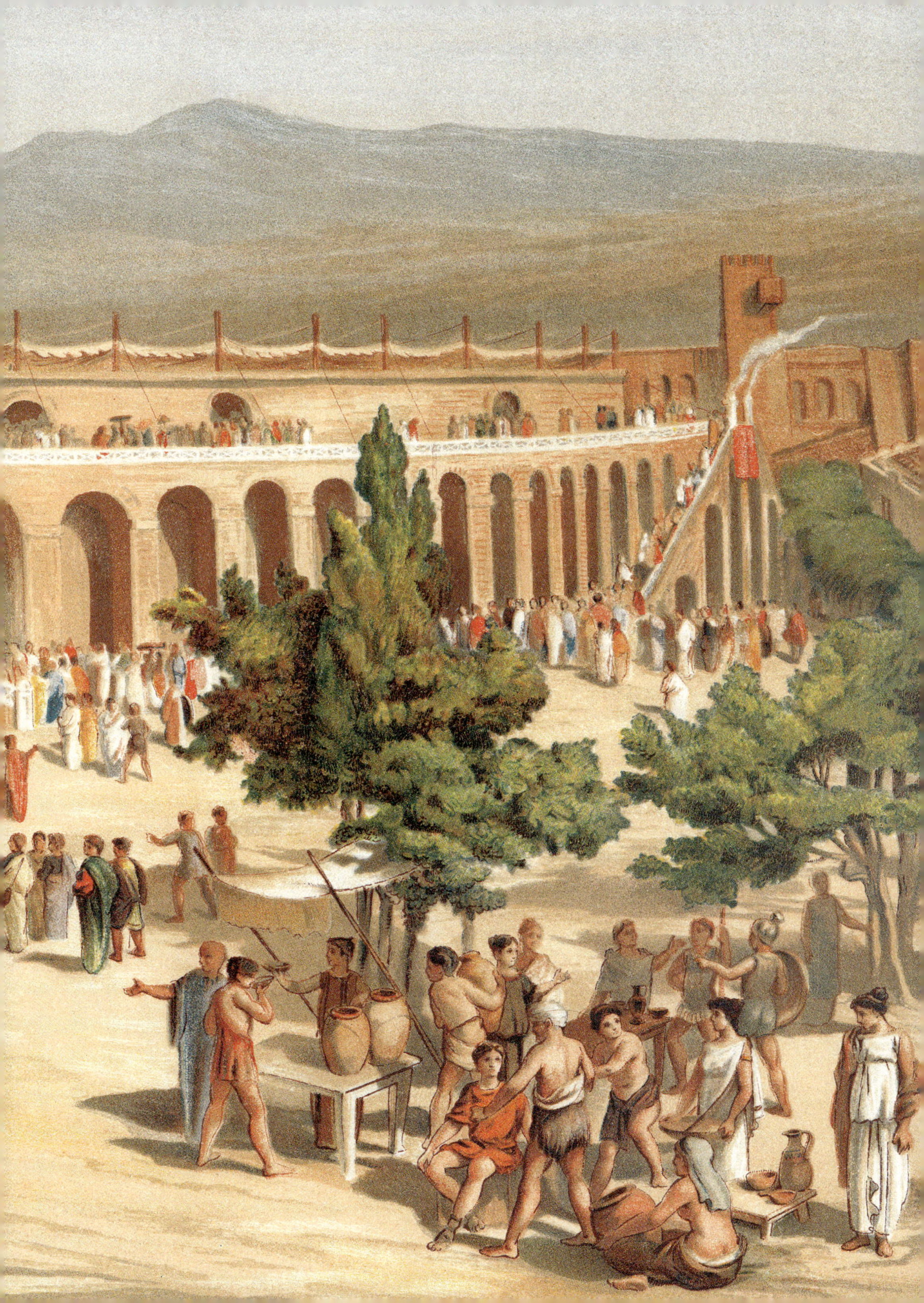

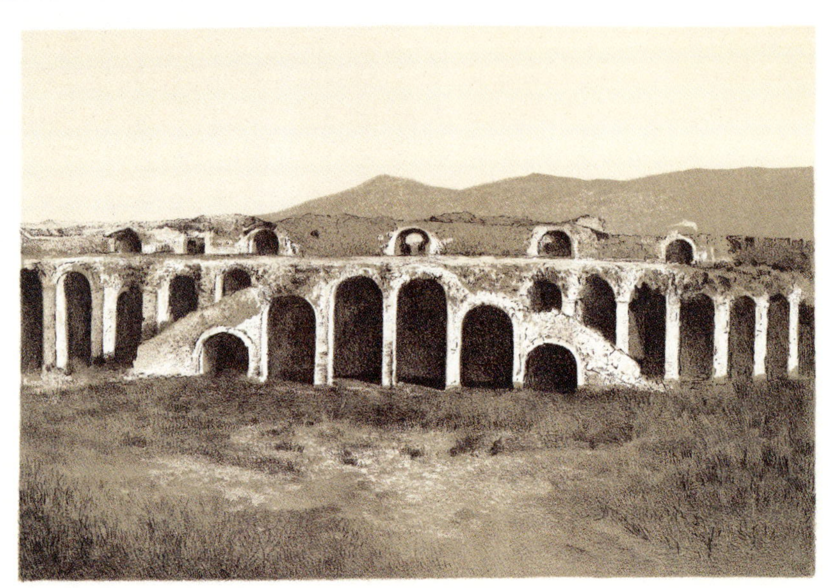

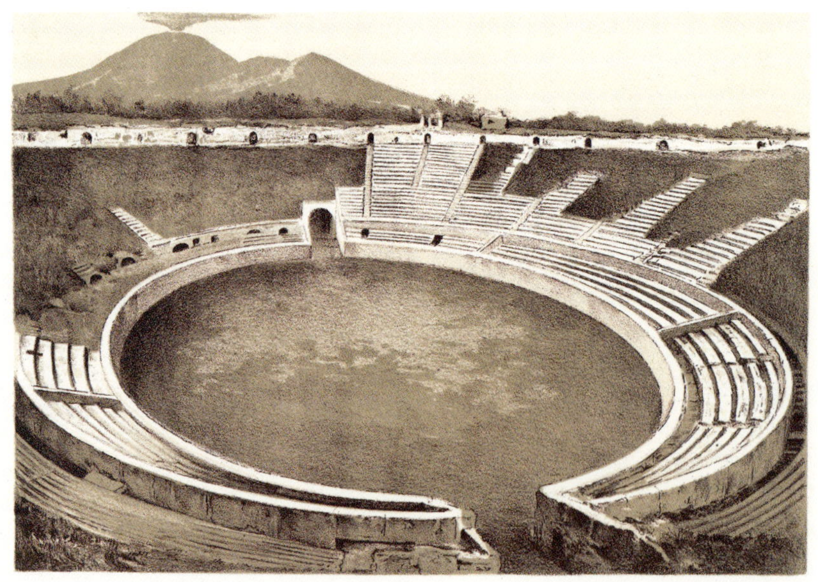

S.De Stefani dis. A.Niccolini dir. Off.Lit.Casa Edit.Fausto Niccolini, Napoli

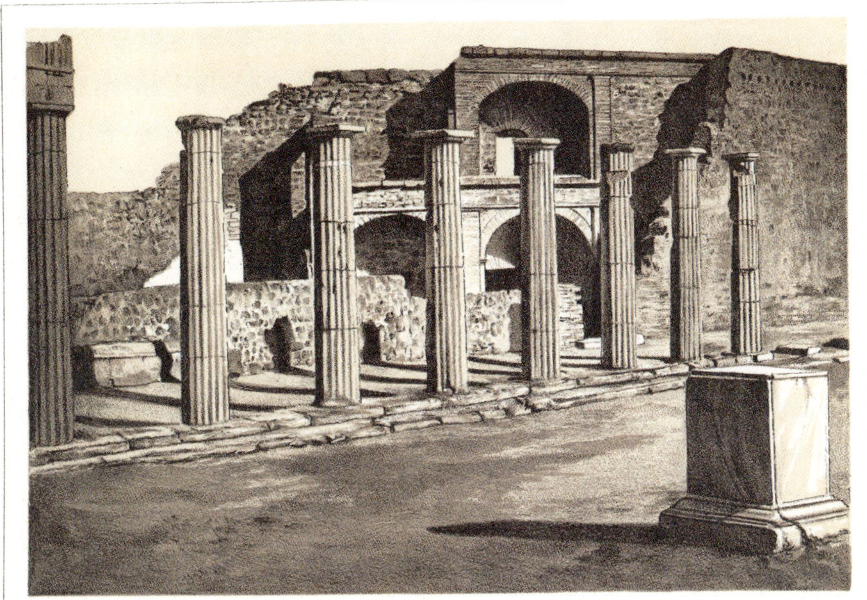

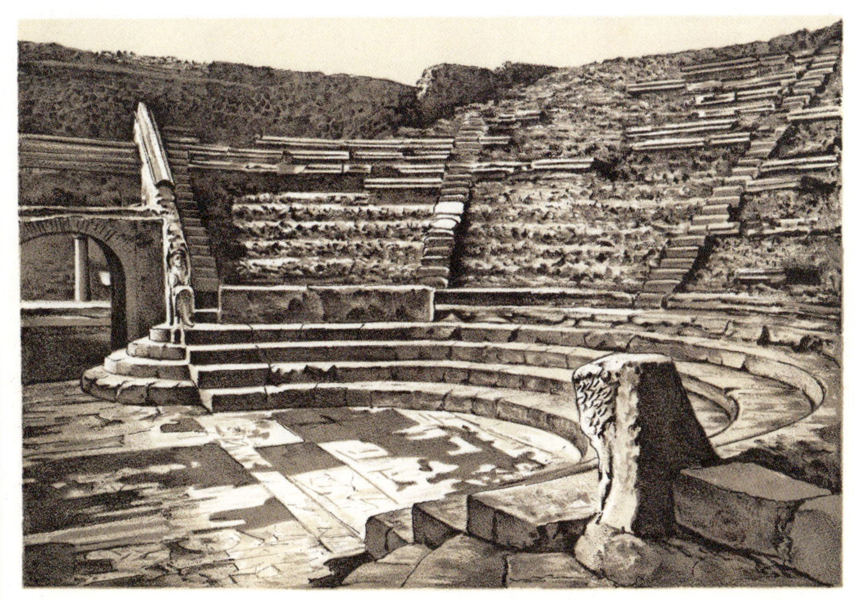

S. De Stefano dis. A. Niccolini dir. Off. Lit. Casa Edit. Fausto Niccolini. Napoli.

Plate 19 — *[C. Gel.]*
Exterior view of the large theatre, seen from the Forum triangolare – In the foreground stands a commemorative statue of Marcellus, a nephew of Augustus, the pedestal of which was found here.

Page 454
Plate 20 — *[C. Gel.]*
Interior view of the small roofed theatre *(theatrum tectum)* during a performance.

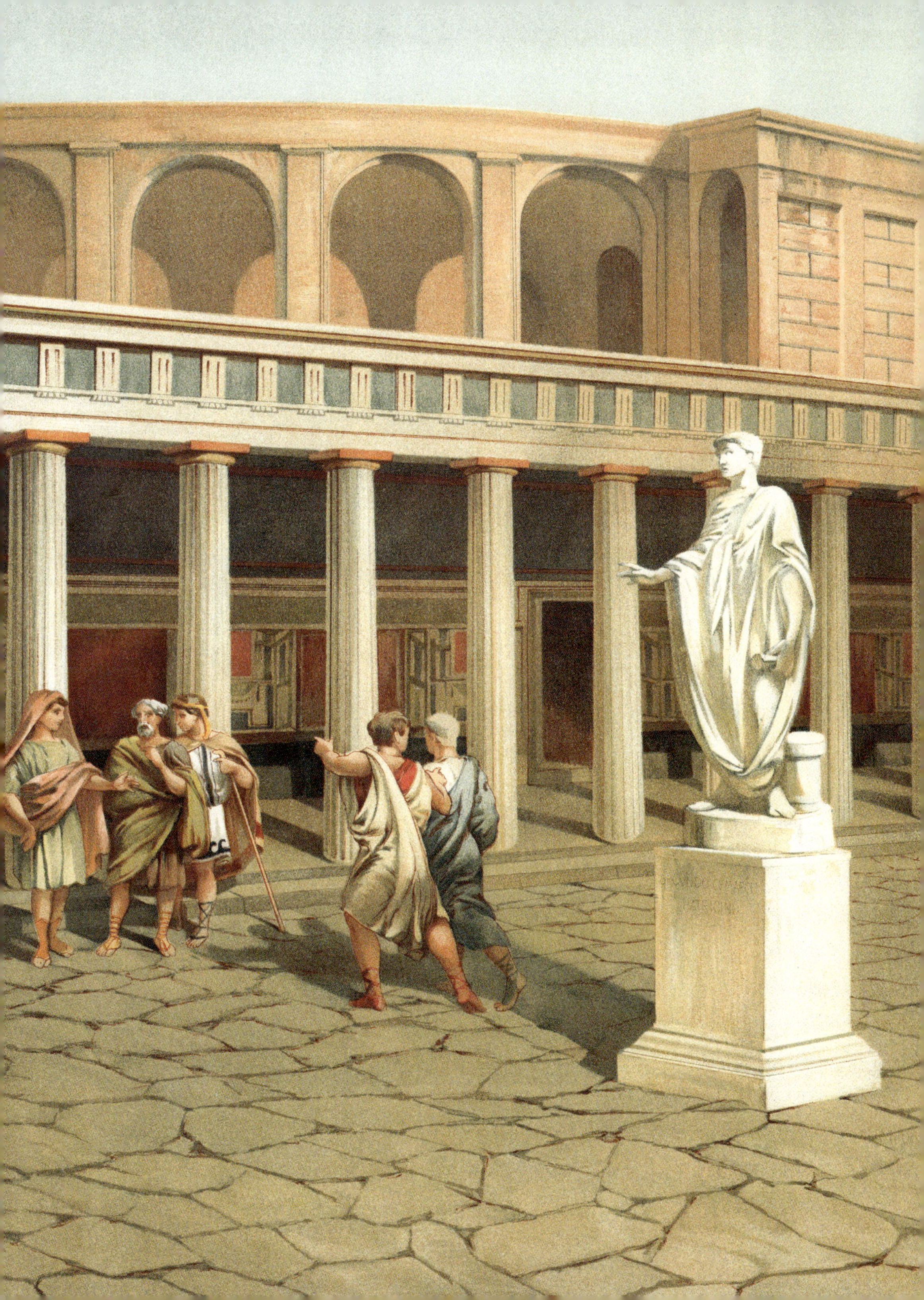

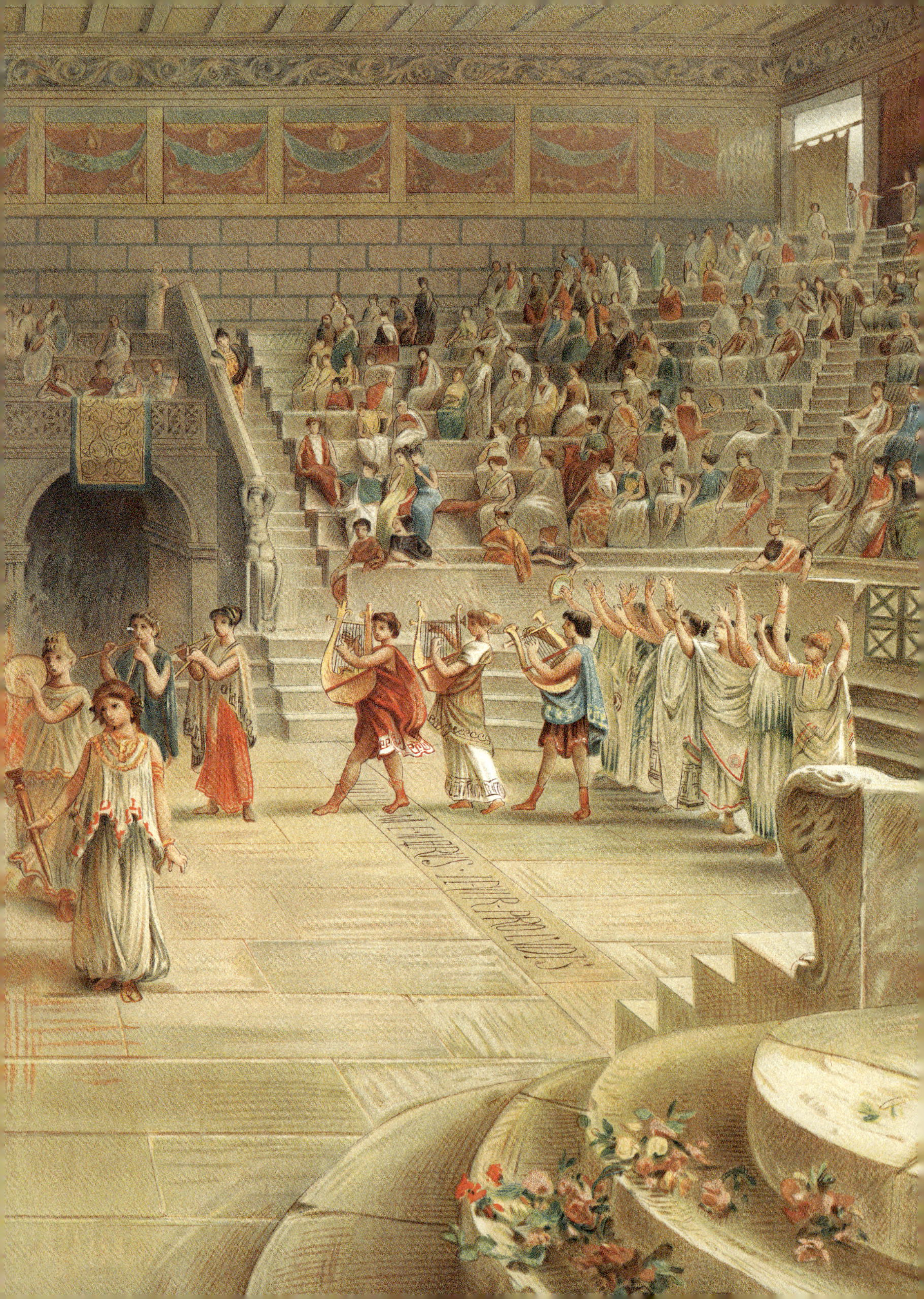

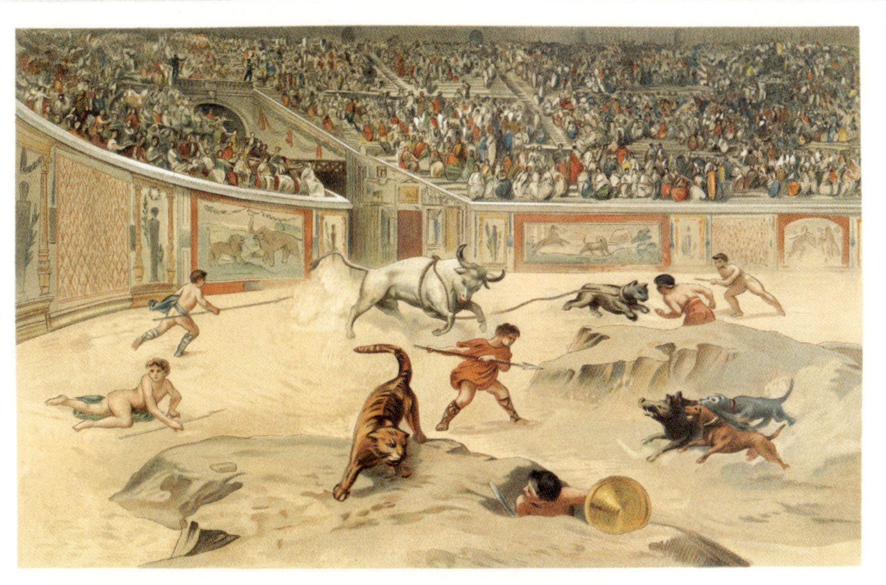

Plate 18 — *[G. Gel.]*
Animal baiting (venatio) in the amphitheatre – Ancient authors tell us that artificial landscapes were constructed for such games in Rome. In the reconstruction, the artist has applied this information to Pompeii.

✠

Pages 456–457
Plate 21 — *[C. Gel.]*
Pompeii's theatre district during the eruption of Vesuvius –
The draughtsman has perhaps been inspired in this reconstruction by Felice Padiglione's large architectural model of the city in the Naples museum.

✠

Pages 458–459
Plate L — *[S. De Stefano]*
Architectural model of Pompeii – Detail showing the theatre district, seen from the south.

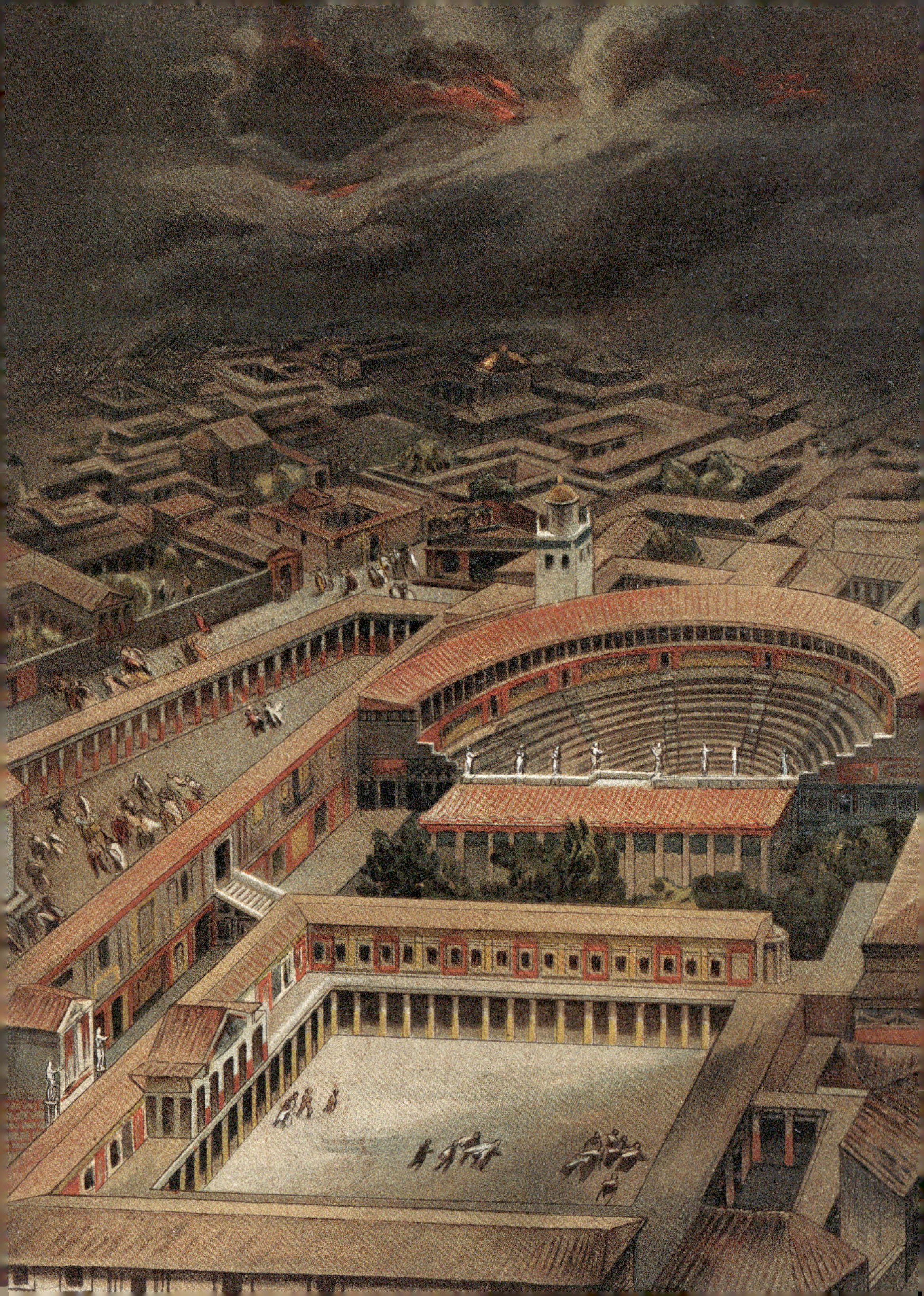

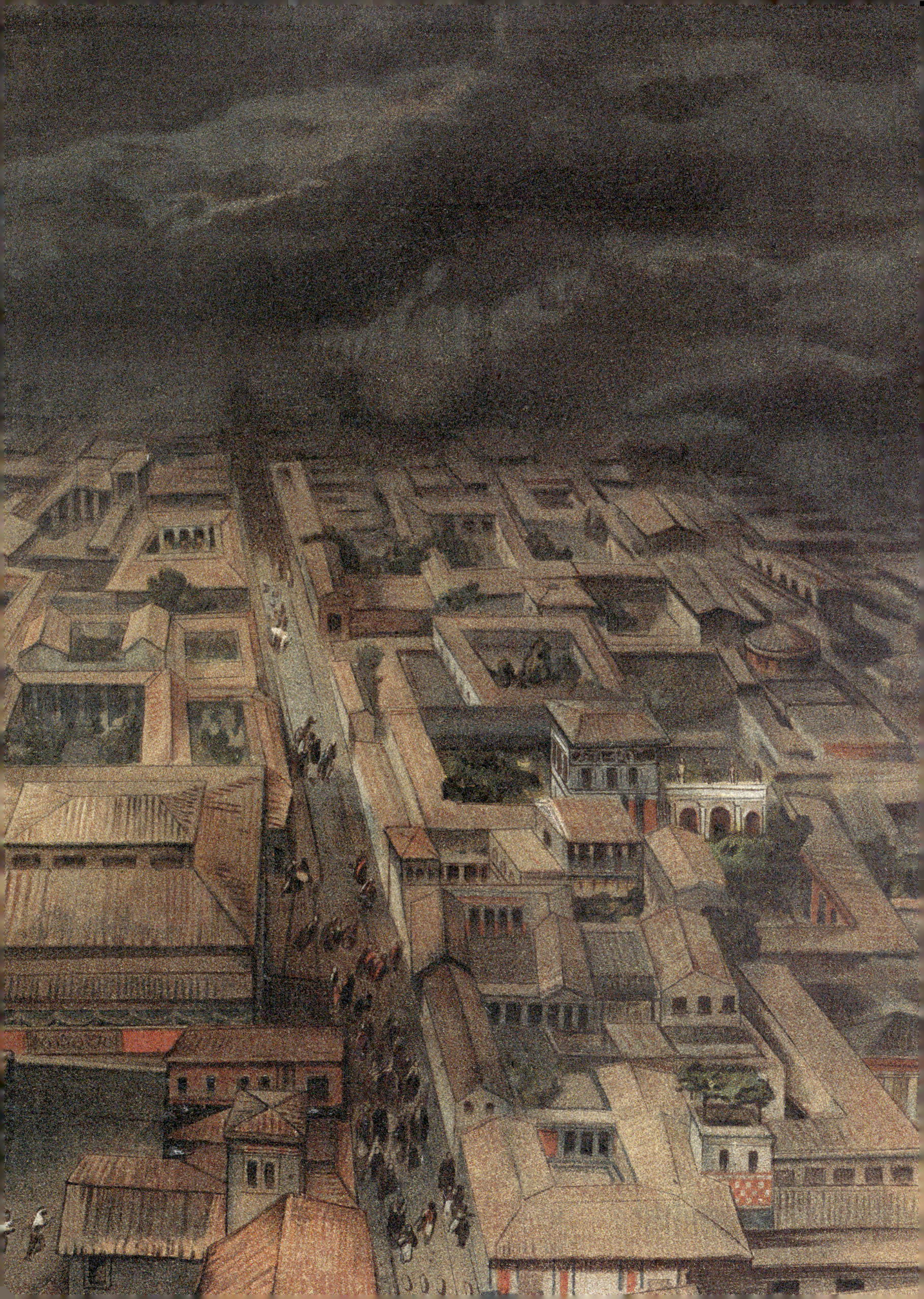

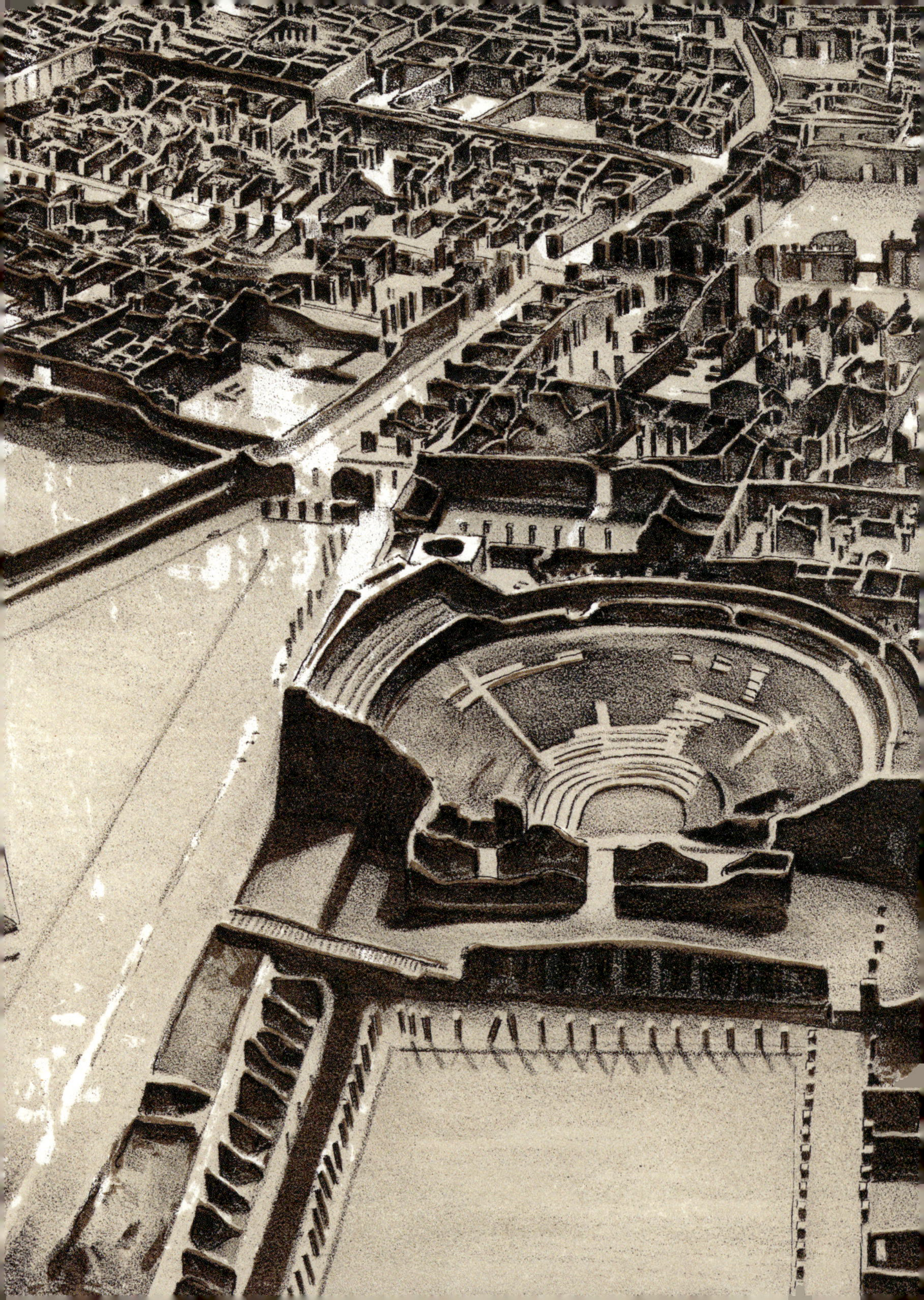

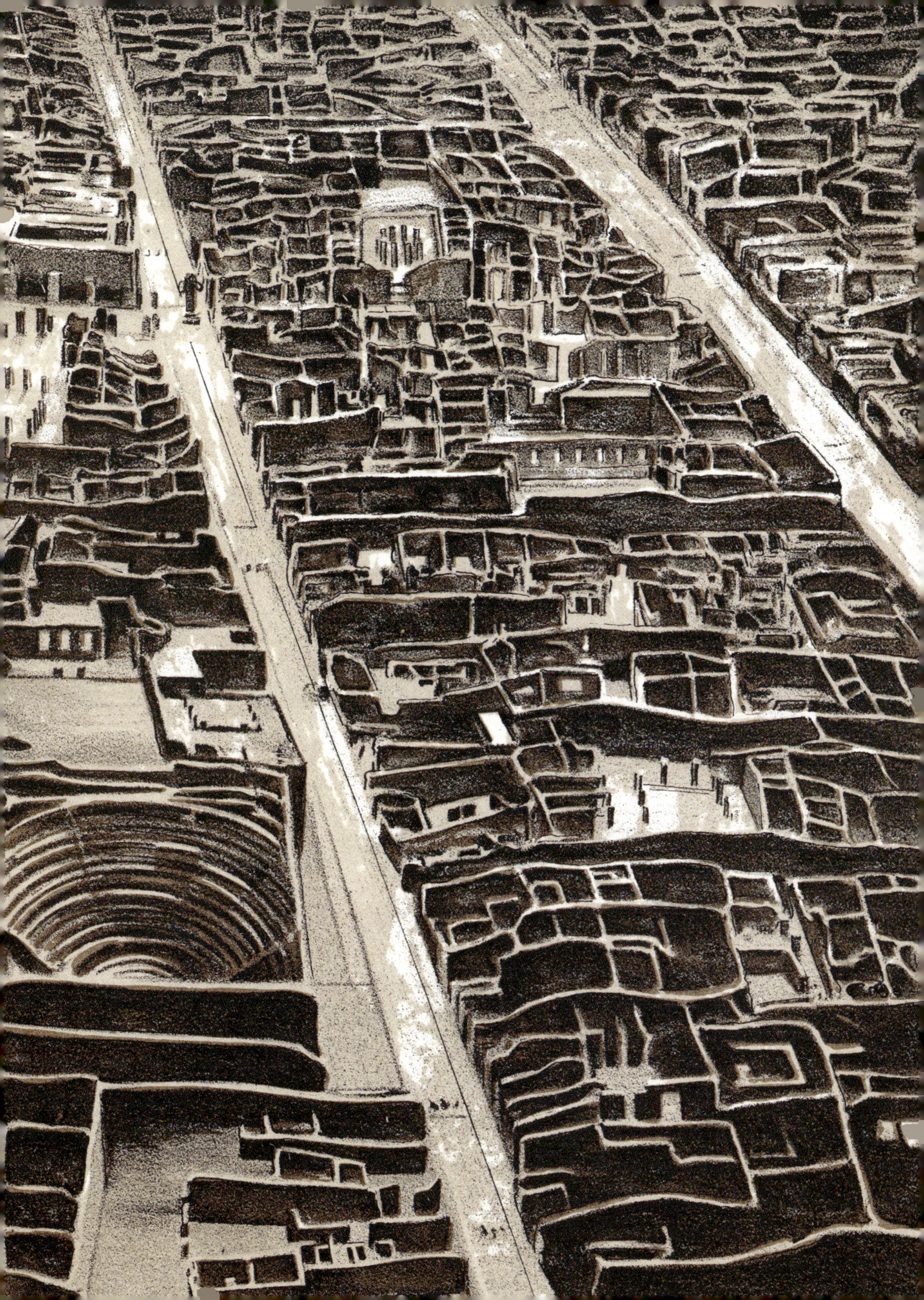

NUOVI SCAVI

New Excavations

In this last section, A. Niccolini the younger returned once again to the records from recent excavations, the Nuovi Scavi, and continued the "appendix" from the beginning of volume IV (see Supplemento). He described the new finds uncovered since 1883 up until January 1896, the year in which *Case e monumenti* was finally completed. The text (78 pages) was largely based, as before, on the official excavation reports that appeared regularly in the *Notizie degli Scavi di Antichità* edited by Giuseppe Fiorelli. Apart from a few interpolations, the description is organised chronologically and follows the course of excavations area by area. The scholarly reports were abridged for a general audience, as Niccolini himself stated. However, in the text, explicit links to the plates are limited to only a few references.

Outside the city, in particular to the south, new sections of the necropolises had been uncovered (pl. 9), whilst within the walls, digging work had concentrated above all on three zones. The excavation of Insula 2 of Regio V was dominated by the discovery of the spacious House of the Silver Wedding (Casa delle Nozze d'Argento), named after the silver wedding anniversary celebrated by the Italian royal couple in 1893. The house was largely rebuilt and roofed at this time and consequently today remains one of the buildings in Pompeii giving the best impression of an upper-class residence in the 1st century BC. It offered Niccolini the opportunity to show, for the first time, the full range of examples of Pompeian decoration in the so-called 2nd style, in which the walls are covered with large *trompe l'œil* paintings of architecture that create a convincing illusion of spatial depth (pl. 13, 16 and 28). Further excavations were carried out in Insula 2 of Regio VIII, which occupies the southern slope of the city hill. This exceptionally attractive location with its fine views was a popular site after 80 BC for properties with multiple storeys (pl. 2–3, 5–8, 11–12, 19), the most prominent being the so-called Sarno Baths, a large complex that had coalesced out of individual elements and

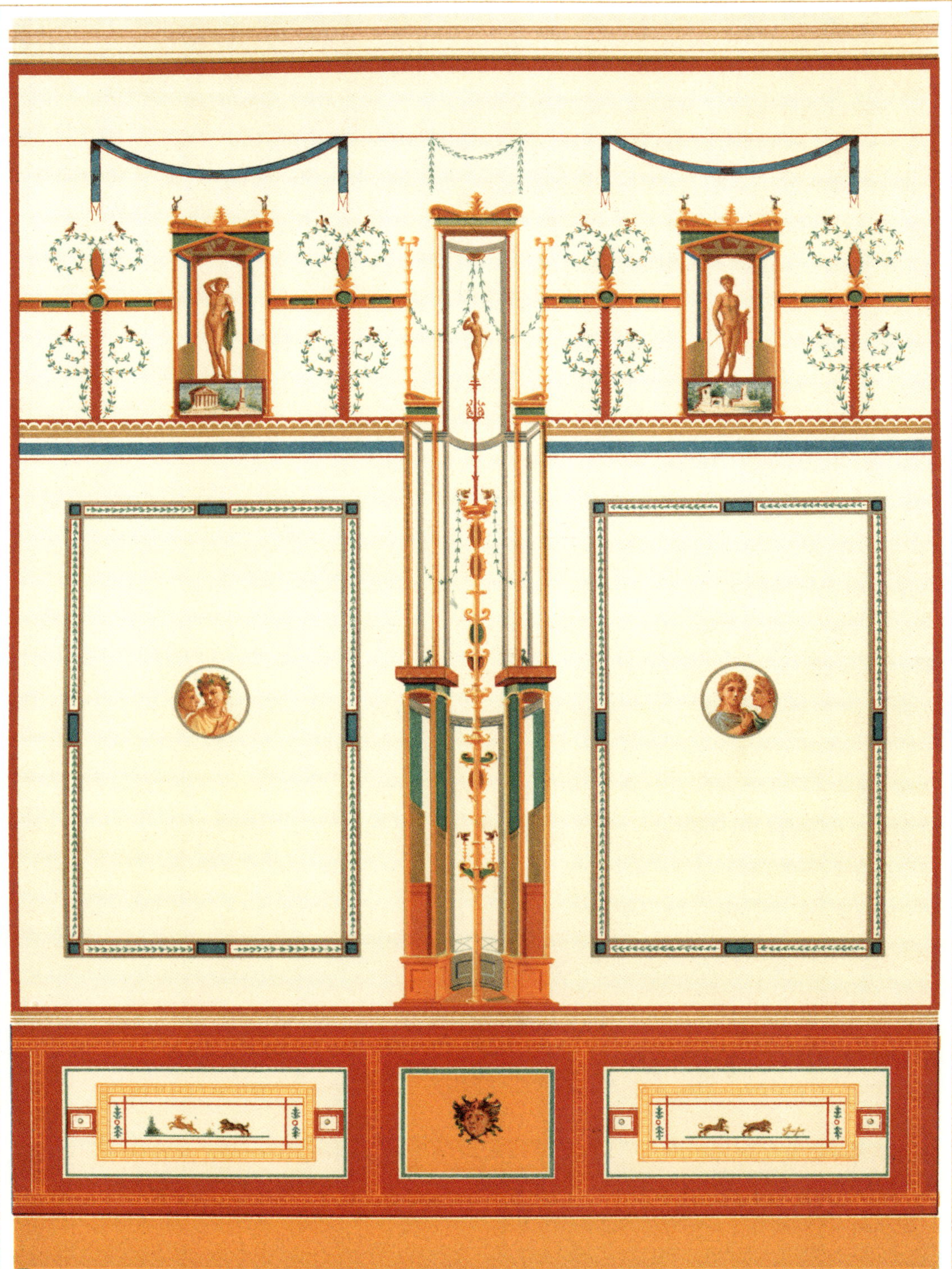

G. Discanno dis. D. Capri Lit. A. Niccolini dir. Lit. Art. Zucchi & De Luca Napoli which included a luxuriously appointed, privately run baths section. Plates 4, 10, 15 and 17 document important rooms with very high-quality paintings in the 3rd style from the Casa di Sulpicius Rufus (IX 9, 18). The last plates (20–33) are devoted to the Casa dei Vettii (VI 15, 1), whose owners were freed slaves who had risen to prosperity. The house had been completely repainted shortly after the earthquake of AD 62, and excavations brought to light a large number of fresh-looking walls with mythological pictures in very good condition. It was therefore decided to conserve the house in its ancient form and to restore its paintings with due care and attention. The Casa dei Vettii consequently became the most famous house in Pompeii. Alongside the mythological pictures from the triclinia (pl. 24, 25, 29, 31), the friezes of erotes at their labours are among the most popular pictorial motifs from the city (pl. 28, 30). Niccolini succeeded one more time here in presenting a complete picture of a house, as in volume I, in so far as he brought together in a total of 14 plates a ground plan, view, wall decoration and inventory of the garden. These could also be sold as a separate set.

The Casa dei Vettii had already been fully documented in photographs, still a new medium at this time. In the case of many other illustrations in this final section, however, and in particular those relating to regions VIII and IX, Niccolini's plates remain important visual sources for then recent finds which were otherwise only inadequately recorded and are today lost.

Page 461
Plate 8 — *[G. Discanno]*
So-called Terme del Sarno (VIII 2, 17–21), connecting room on the first lower storey – Wall decoration in the 4th style on a white ground, with medallions as central motifs.

⁂

Plate 4 — *[C. de Simone]*
Casa di Sulpicius Rufus (IX 9, c), cubiculum, west wall – Wall decoration in the 3rd style. The central picture shows a satyr from behind, accompanied by dogs.

⁂

Pages 464–465
Plate 2 — *[G. Discanno]*
So-called Terme del Sarno (VIII 2, 17–21), ground floor – Outstanding 4th-style painting on a black ground. The "Sarno Baths" are a complex extending over several levels on the southern slope of the city, which included among other things a private suite of baths (see pl. 8, 11–12, 19).

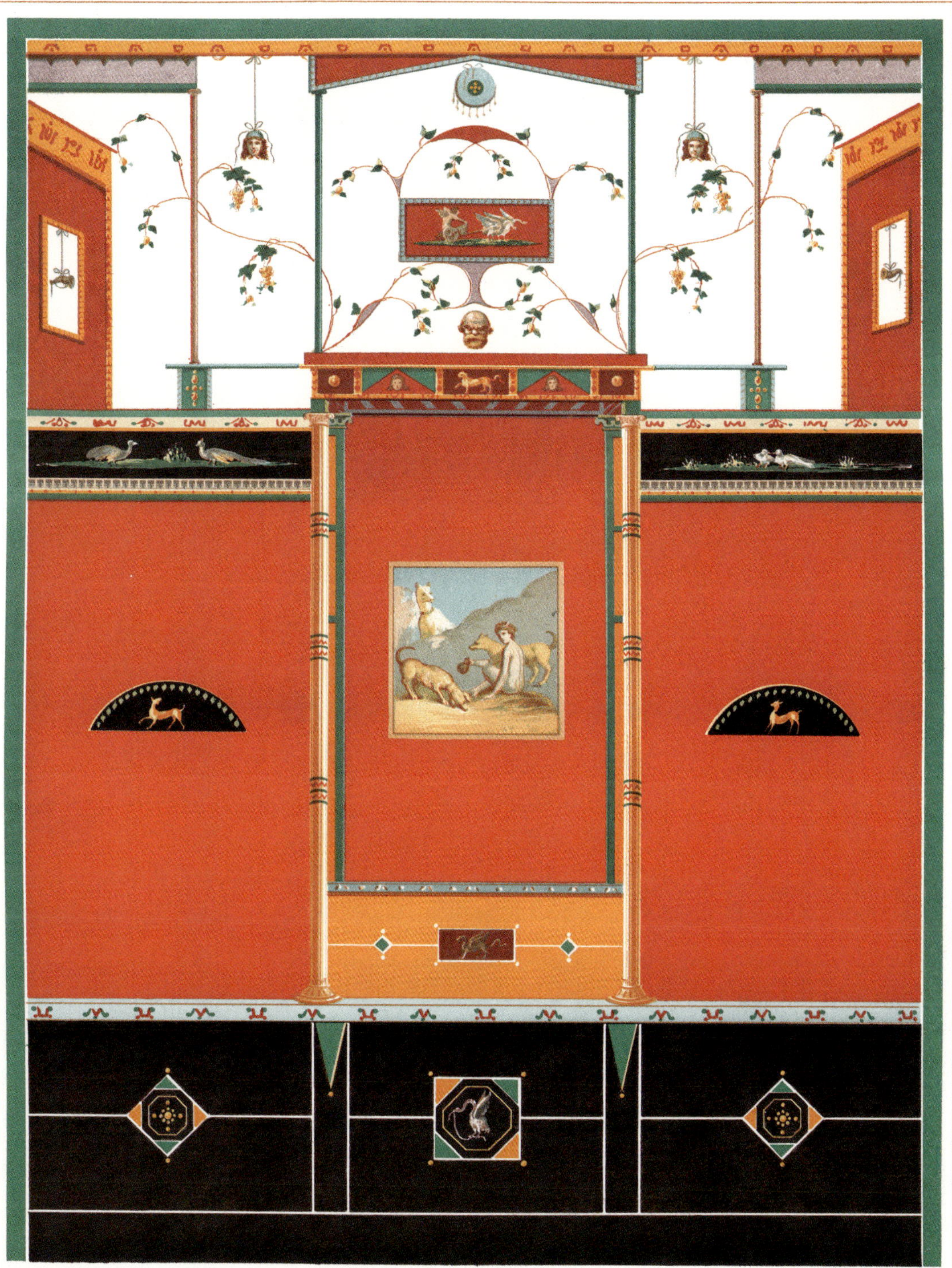

C. de Simone dis. D. Capri Lit. A. Niccolini dir. Lit. Art. Zucchi & De Luca- Napoli.

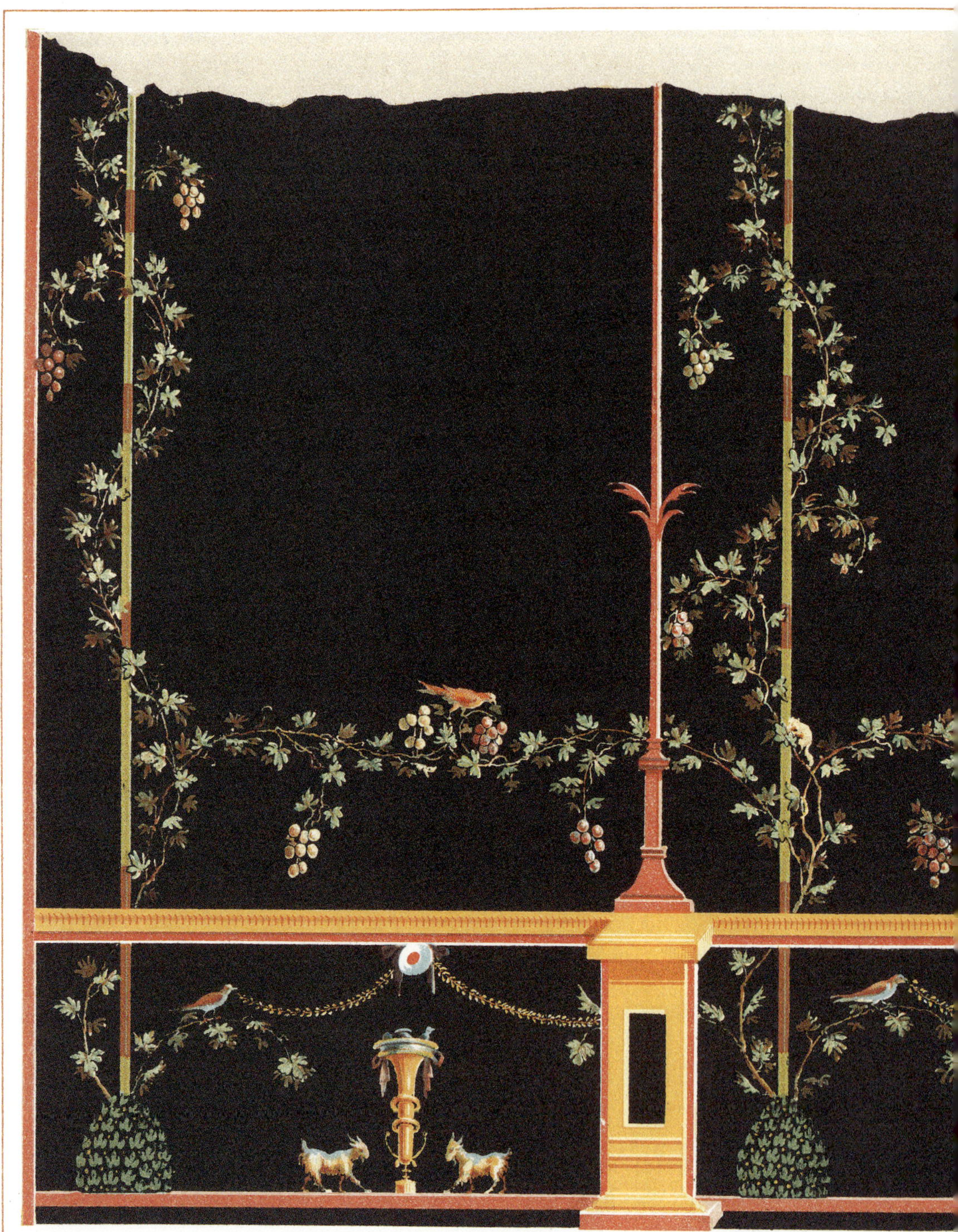

G Discanno dis. D Capri Lit.

A. Nic

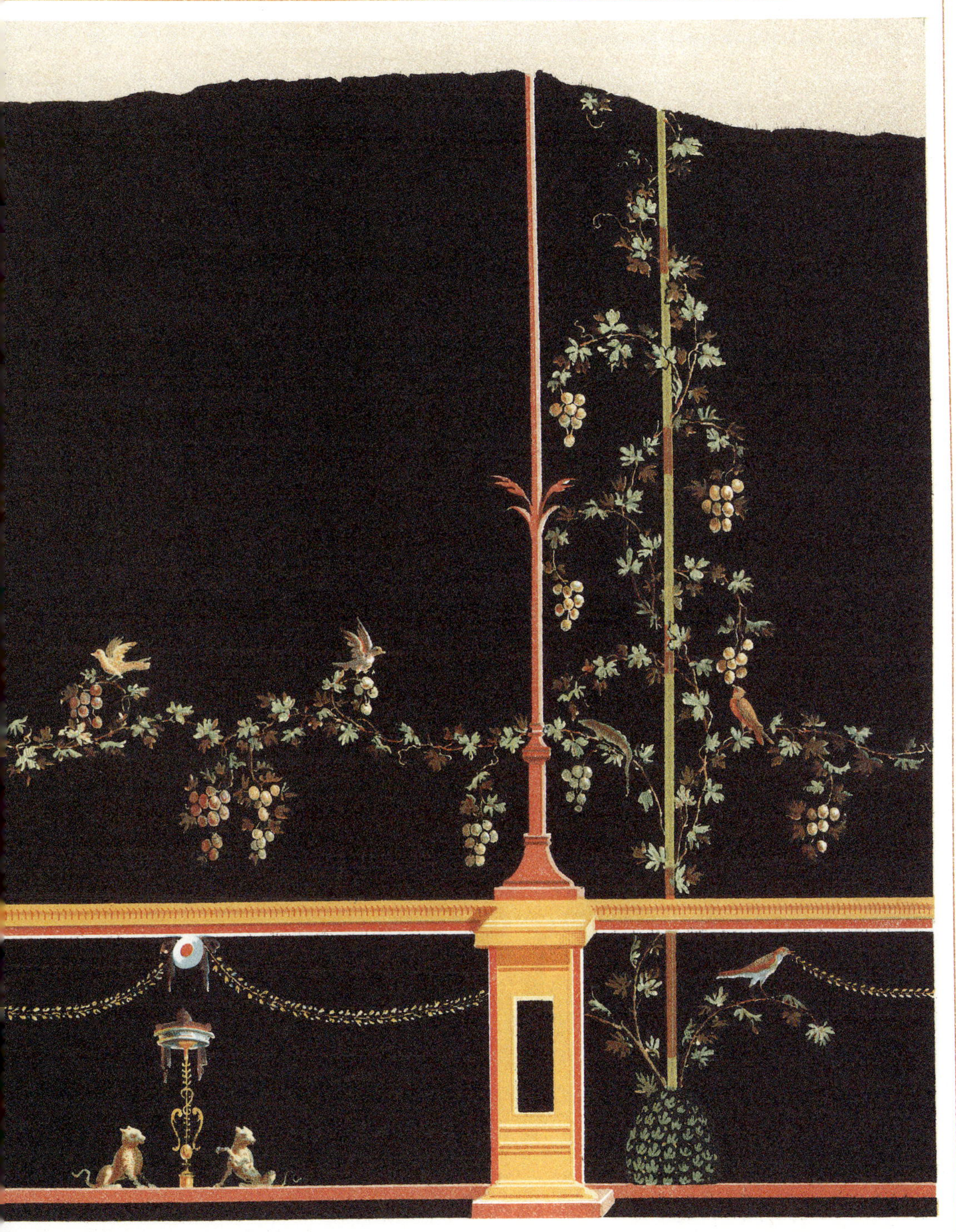

ni dir.

Lit. Art. Zucchi & De Luca, Napoli

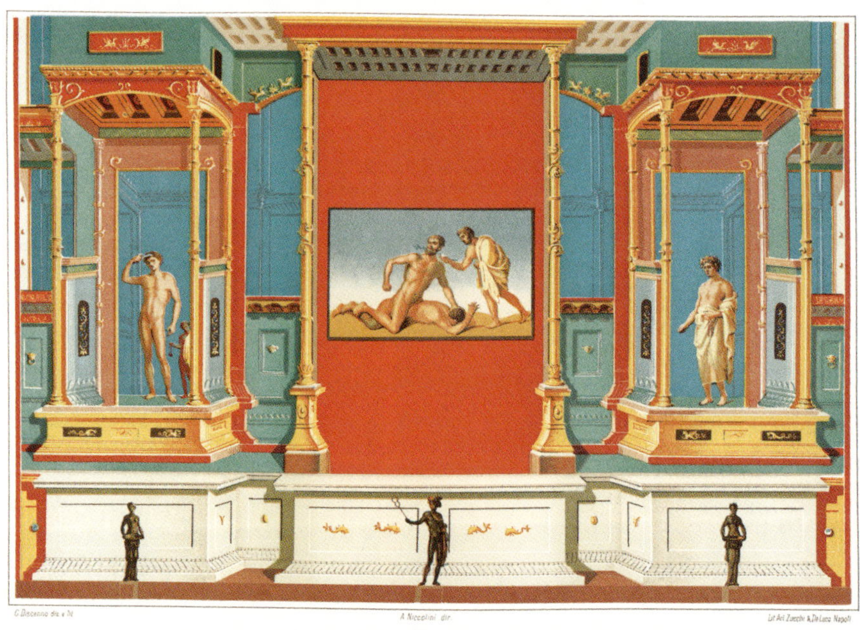

Plate 3 — *[G. Discanno]*
Casa VIII 2, 23–24, palaestra on the ground floor, east wall – In this architectural prospect, the mythological pictures are replaced by scenes from the palaestra: left and right, victor and judge, in the centre, the end of a boxing match.

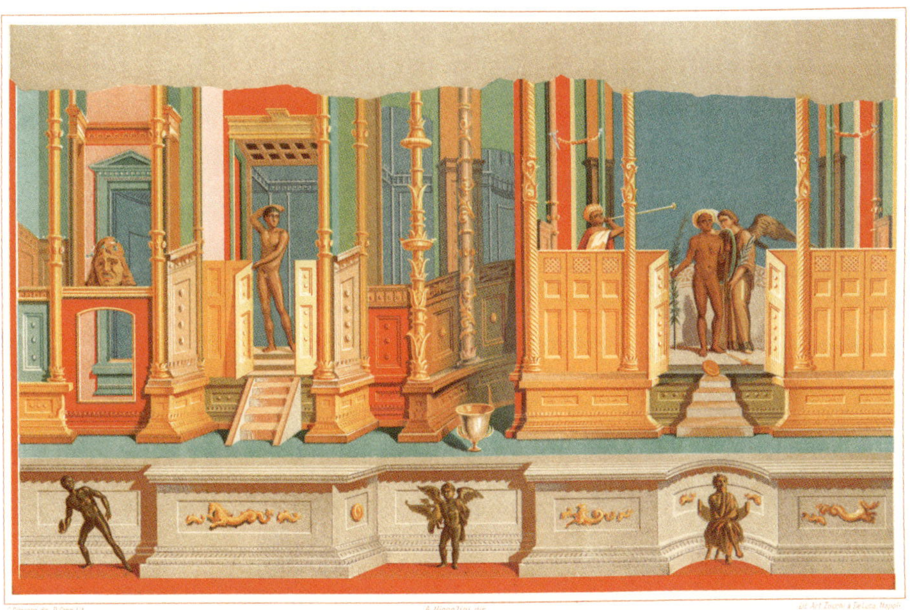

Plate 6 — *[G. Discanno]*
Casa VIII 2, 23–24, palaestra on the ground floor, south wall – Large view of theatre architecture. In front of the plinth zone, a discus thrower and the patron of the games sitting on a chair.

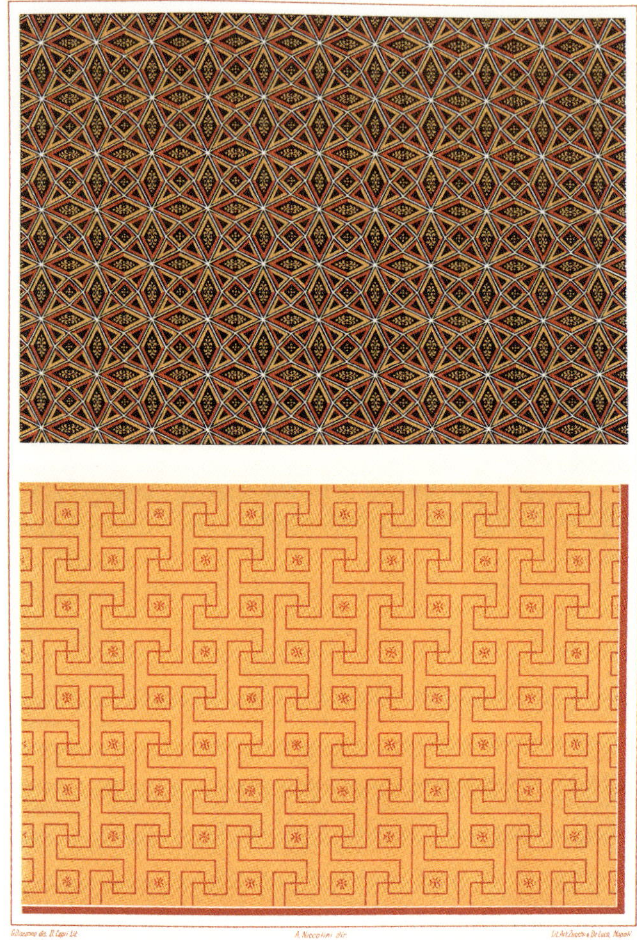

Plate 7 — *[G. Discanno]*
Above: ***Casa del Cinghiale II (VII 2, 26-27), triclinium on the lower floor*** – Ceiling decoration with squares, triangles and lozenges in red and yellow on a black ground. Below: ***Casa VIII 2, 29–30, lower floor*** – eometrical wall decoration that falls outside the usual Pompeian styles.

Plate 5 — *[G. Discanno]*
Casa delle Colombe a Mosaico (VIII 2, 34–35), triclinium on the ground floor – The mosaic emblema shows doves drinking from a large bronze vessel. This popular motif probably goes back to a famous mosaic by Sosos of Pergamon.

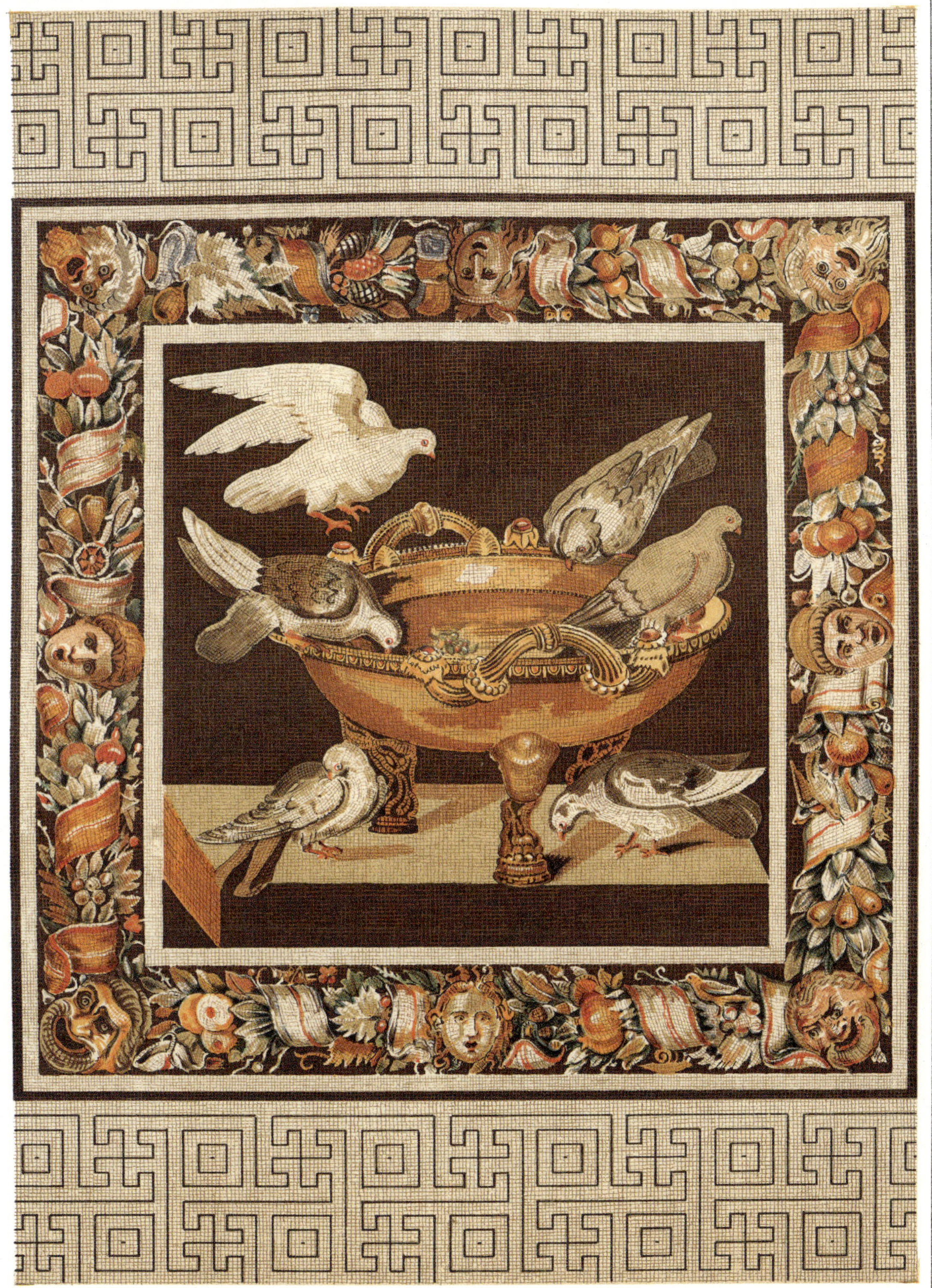

G. Discanno dis. D. Capri Lit. A. Niccolini dir. Lit. Art. Zucchi & De Luca, Napoli.

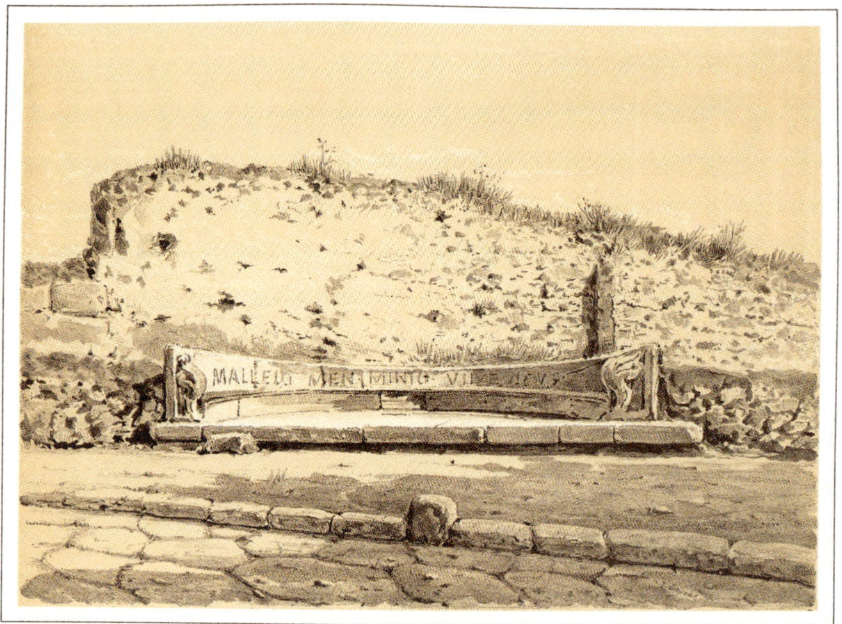

Plate 9 — *[G. Discanno]*
Exedra of the tomb of Marcus Alleius Minius outside Porta Stabiana – Benches of a similarly plain design were found in front of all the city gates (see vol. II). They were installed by the city council in honour of worthy dignitaries.

Plate 10 — *[G. Discanno]*
Casa di Sulpicius Rufus (IX 9, c), cubiculum, west wall – Wall decoration in the 3rd style. In the centre, standing in front of a wall, probably Paris wearing a Phrygian cap.

Pages 472–473
Plate 11 — *[G. Discanno]*
So-called Terme del Sarno (VIII 2, 17–21), third lower storey, frigidarium and apodyterium – Stucco decoration painted in colour. In the fields, fabulous beasts, erotes along with Hylas and the Nymphs.

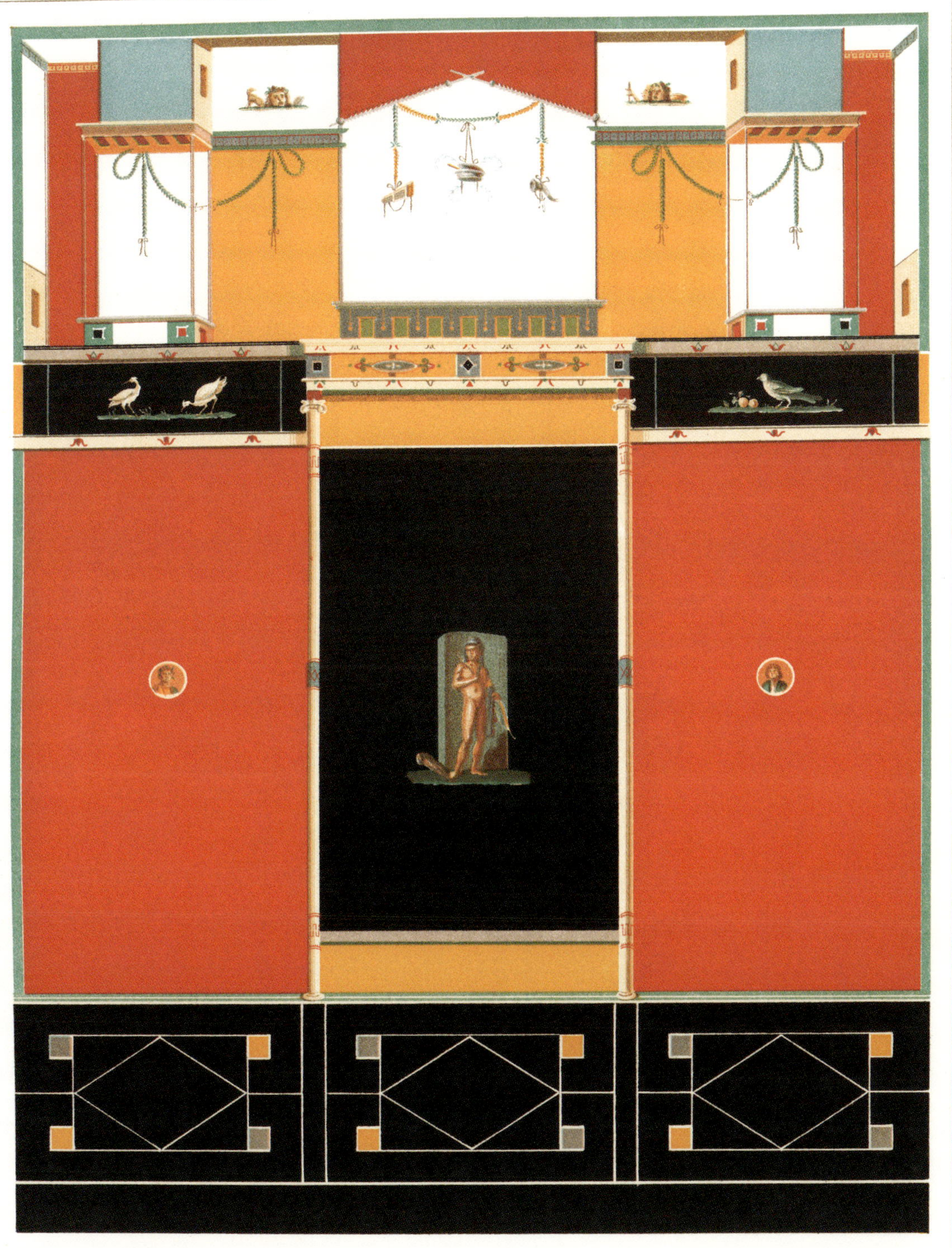

G. Discanno dis. D. Capri Lit. — Niccolini dir. — Lit. Art. Zucchi & De Luca-Napoli

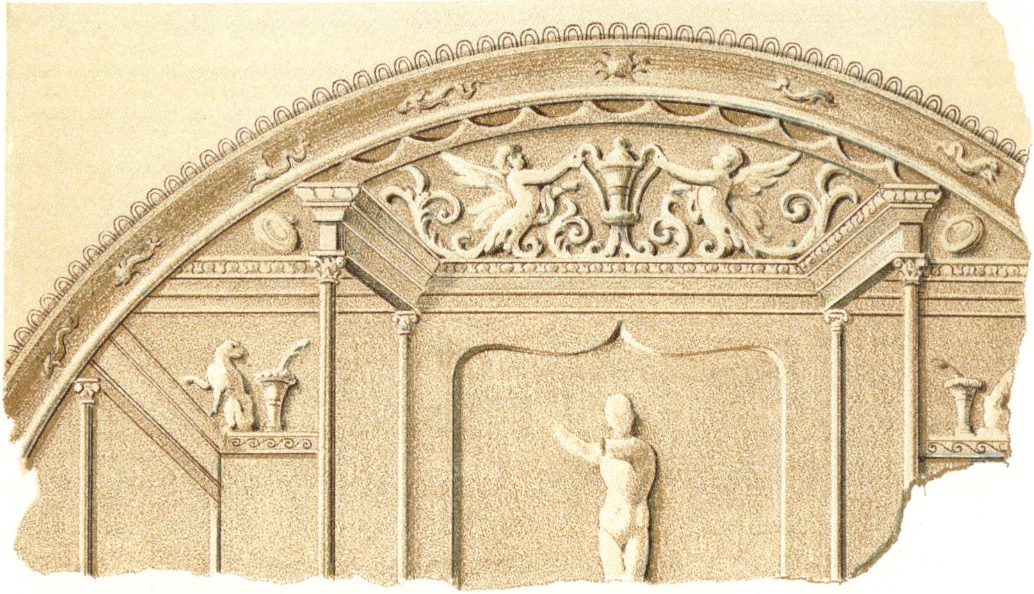

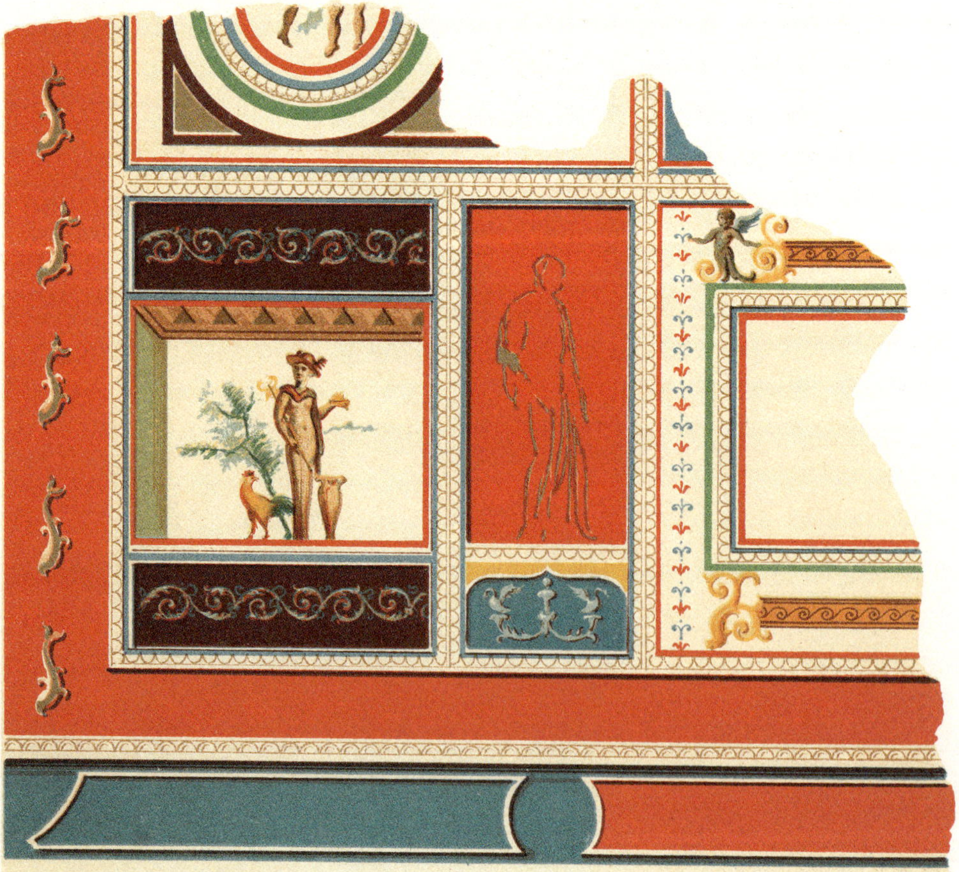

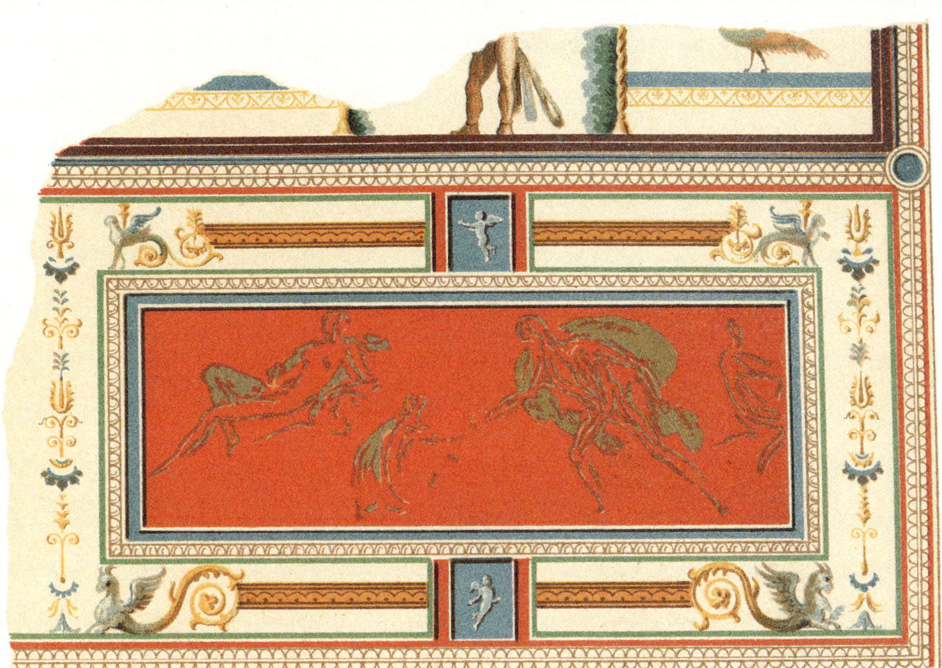

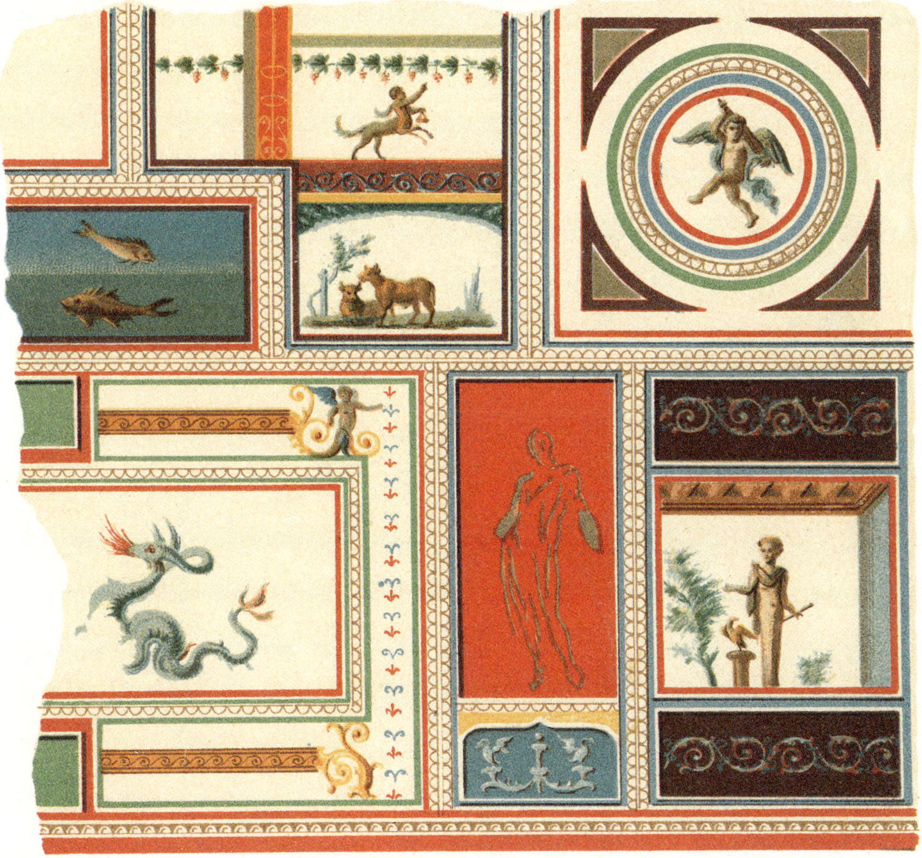

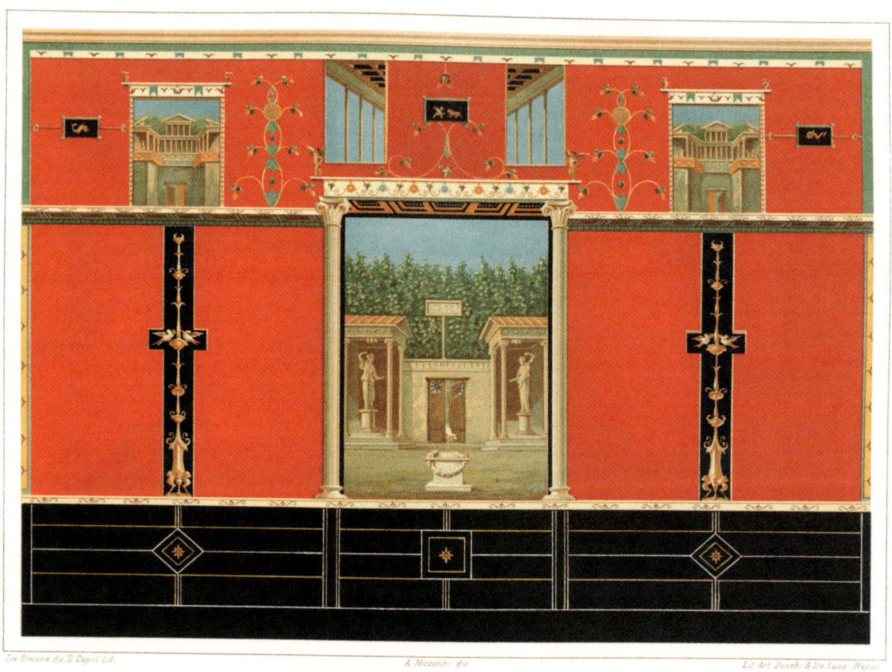

Plate 15 — *[C. de Simone]*
Casa di Sulpicius Rufus (IX 9, c), triclinium, south wall – Decoration in the 3rd style, in the middle picture, the interior view of a sanctuary seen from the temple. Behind the altar in the foreground, a white donkey with its tongue hanging out is entering through the half-open entrance gates.

Plate 12 — *[G. Discanno]*
So-called Terme del Sarno (VIII 2, 17–21), third lower storey, frigidarium, back wall – Decoration in the 4th style. In the socle zone, an Egyptian landscape with pygmies; top centre, perhaps a personification of the river Sarno, which flows into the sea near Pompeii.

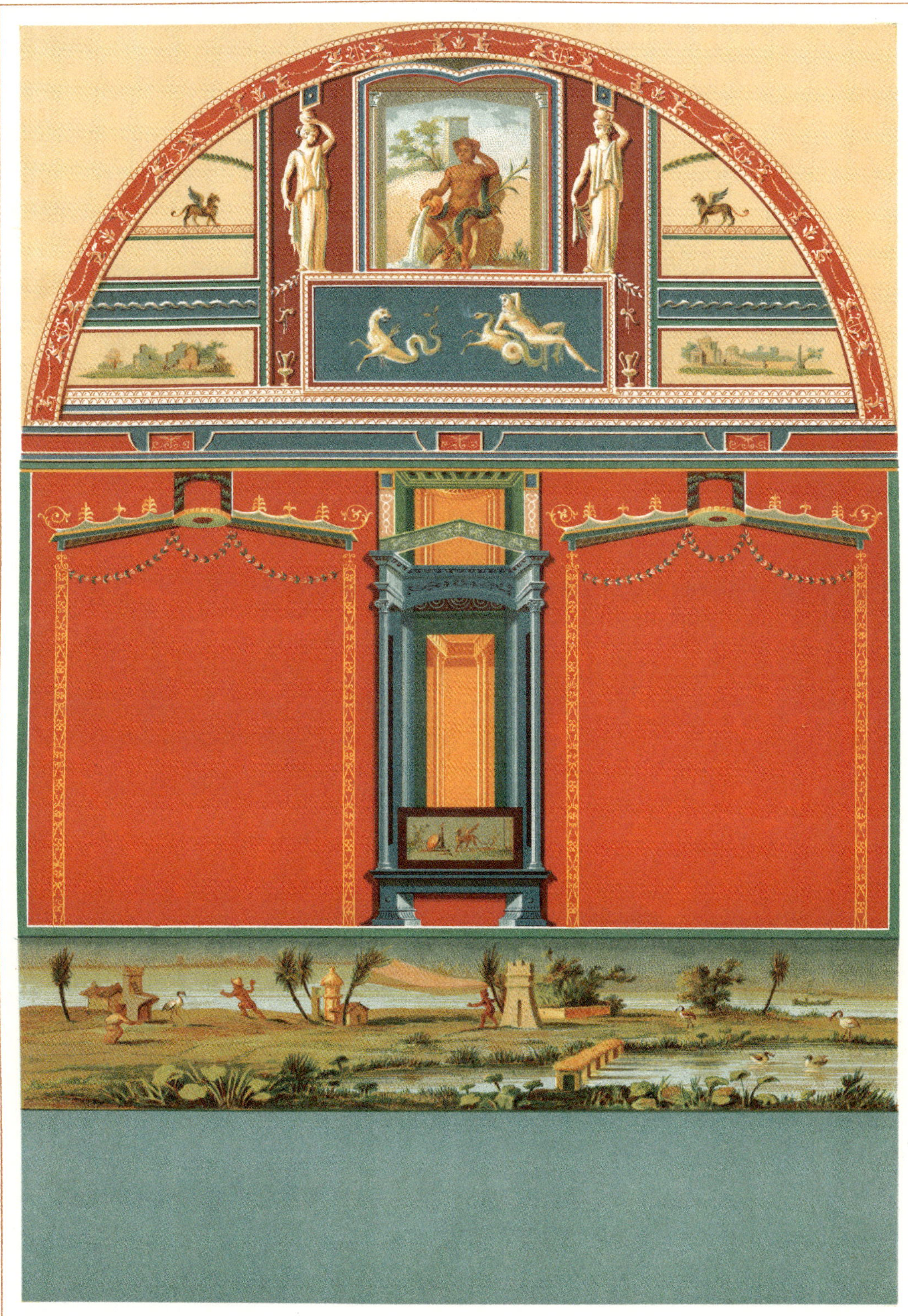

G. Discanno dis. D. Capri Lit.

A. Niccolini dir.

Lit. Art. Zucchi & De Luca, Napoli.

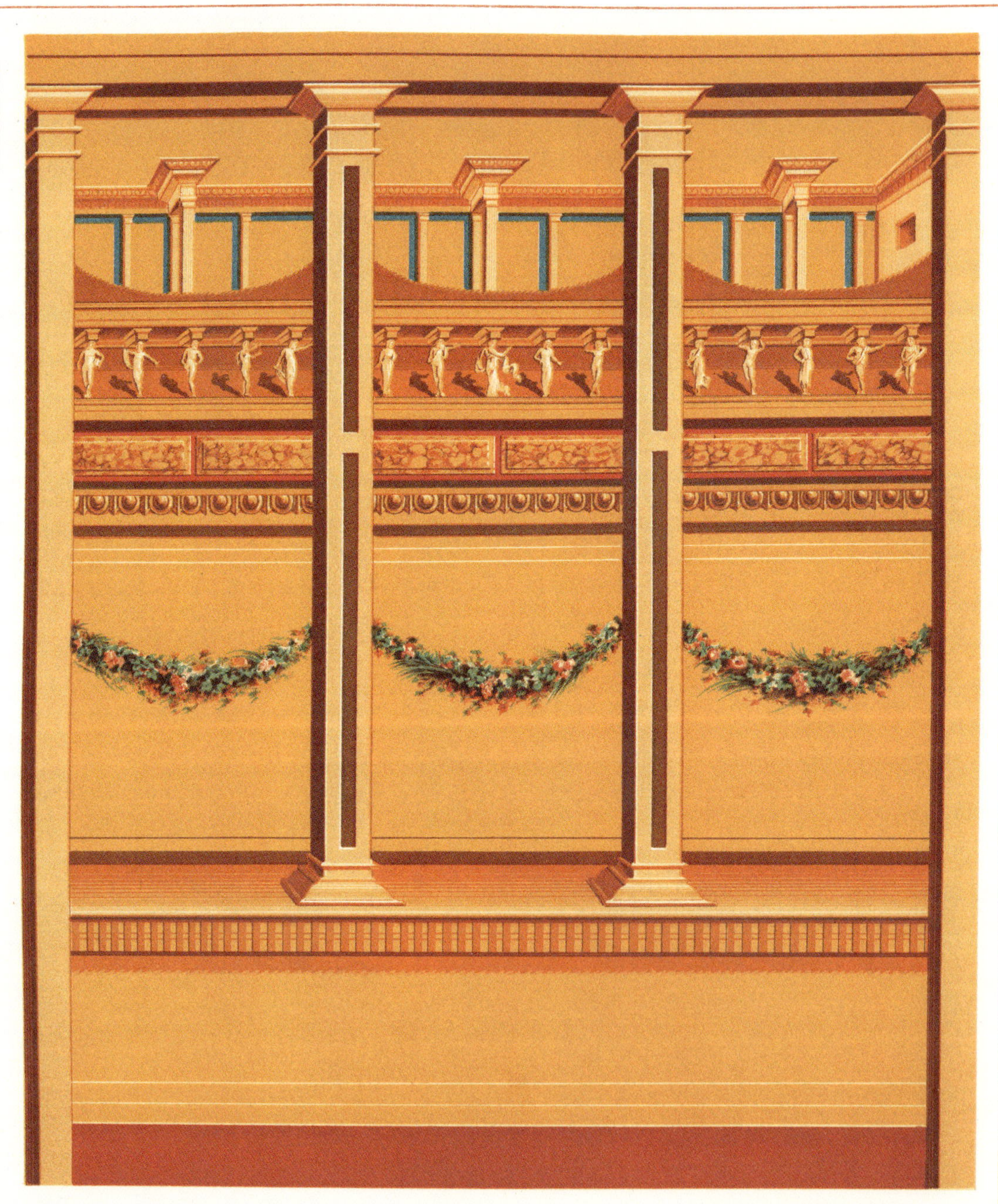

De Simone dis. D. Capri Lit. A. Niccolini dir. Lit. Art. Zucchi & De Luca-Napoli

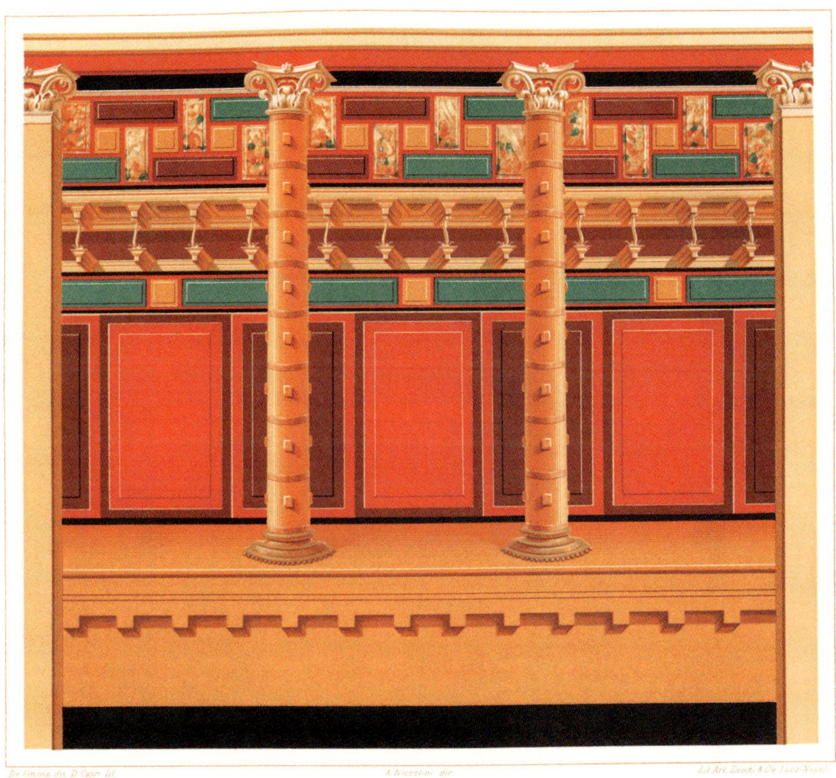

Plate 13 — *[C. de Simone]*
Casa delle Nozze d'Argento (V 2, I), room beside the peristyle, west wall –
The golden-brown 2nd-style wall decoration shows two rows of pillars, one behind the other, with a shear wall between them, whose coping is carried by "mythical" supporting figures.

❋

Plate 16 — *[C. de Simone]*
Casa delle Nozze d'Argento (V 2, I), room beside the peristyle, south wall – Decoration in the 2nd style. Two embossed columns stand on a continuous plinth. Behind them, a continuous wall with different-coloured ashlars and a strange console entablature.

❋

Pages 478–479
Plate 18 — *[C. de Simone]*
Casa delle Nozze d'Argento (V 2, I), south wall of the triclinium beside the peristyle – Wall decoration in the 4th style on a black ground. In the central field, a floating female figure; in the lateral fields, tondi with personifications of the seasons (?).

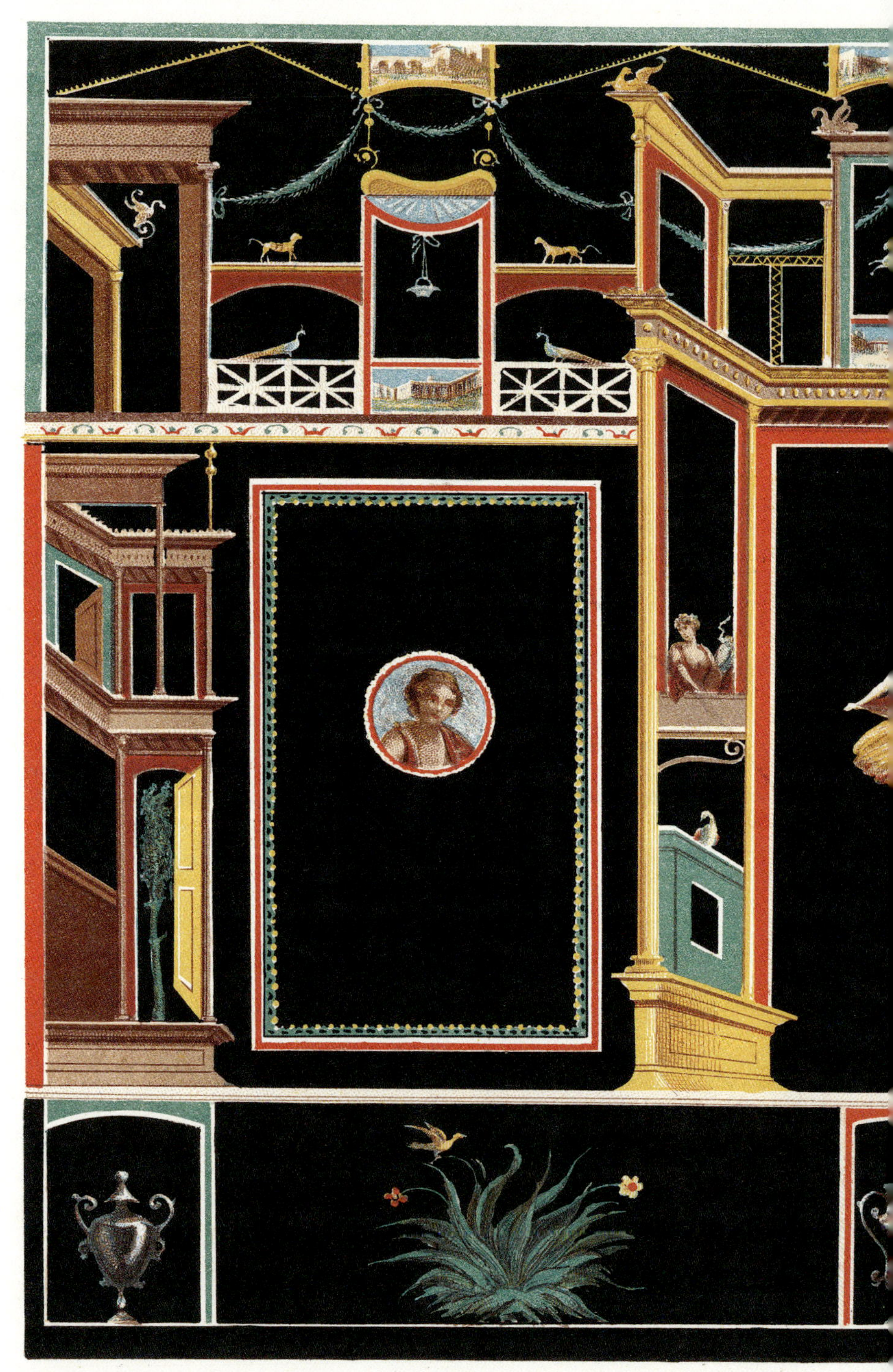

De Simone dis. - G. Autoriello Lit.

A. N

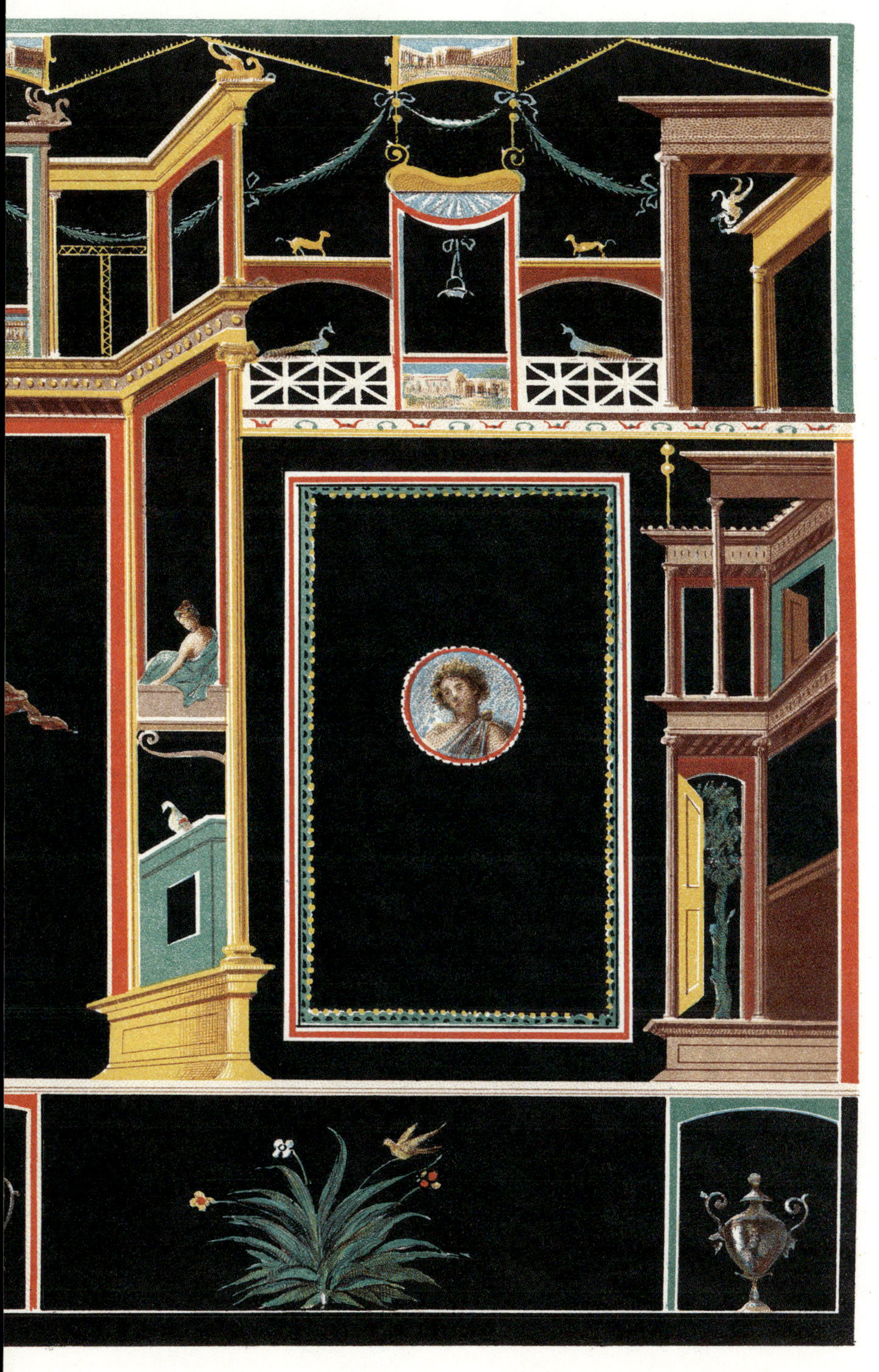

lini dir

Lit. Art. Autoriello & De Luca-Napoli

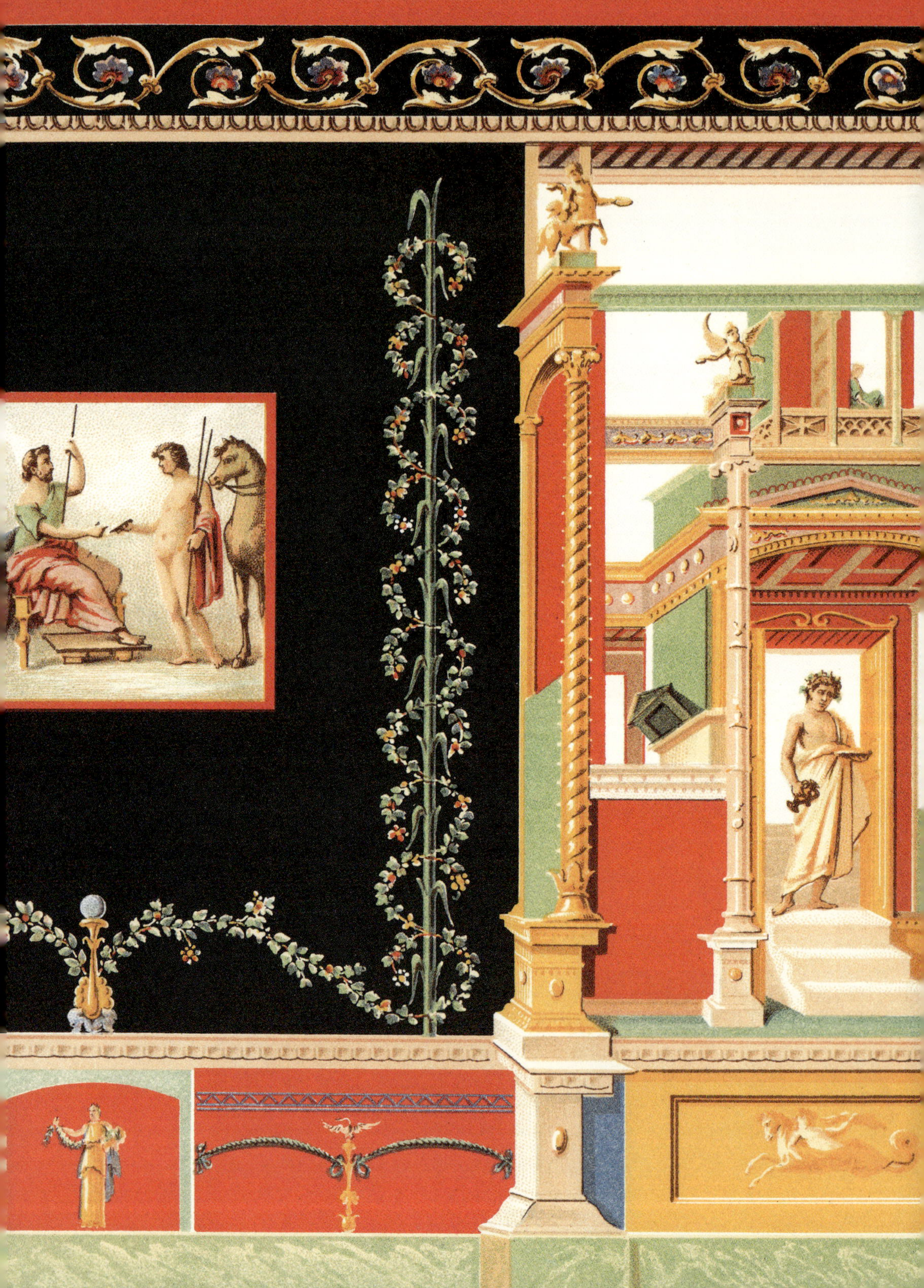

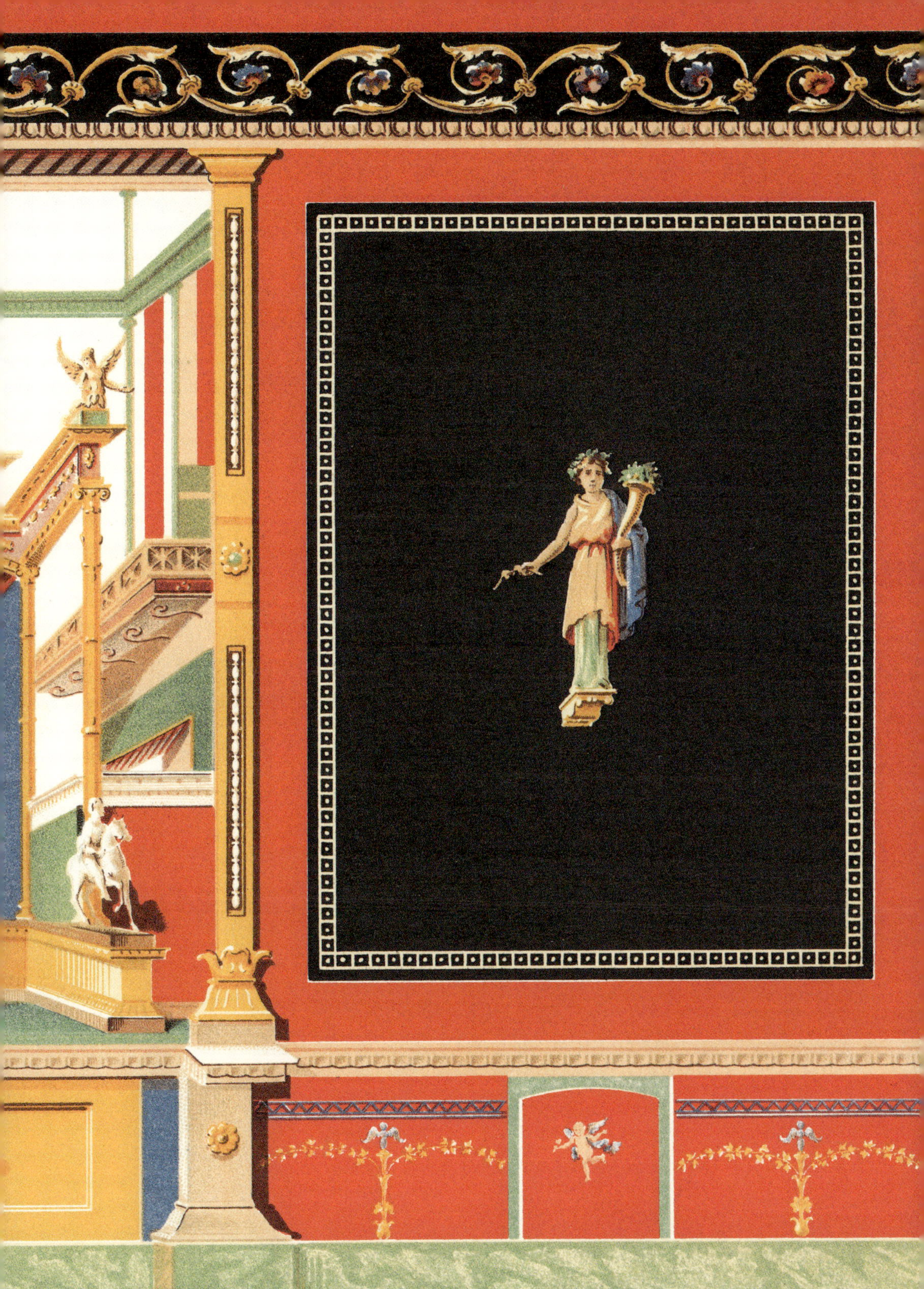

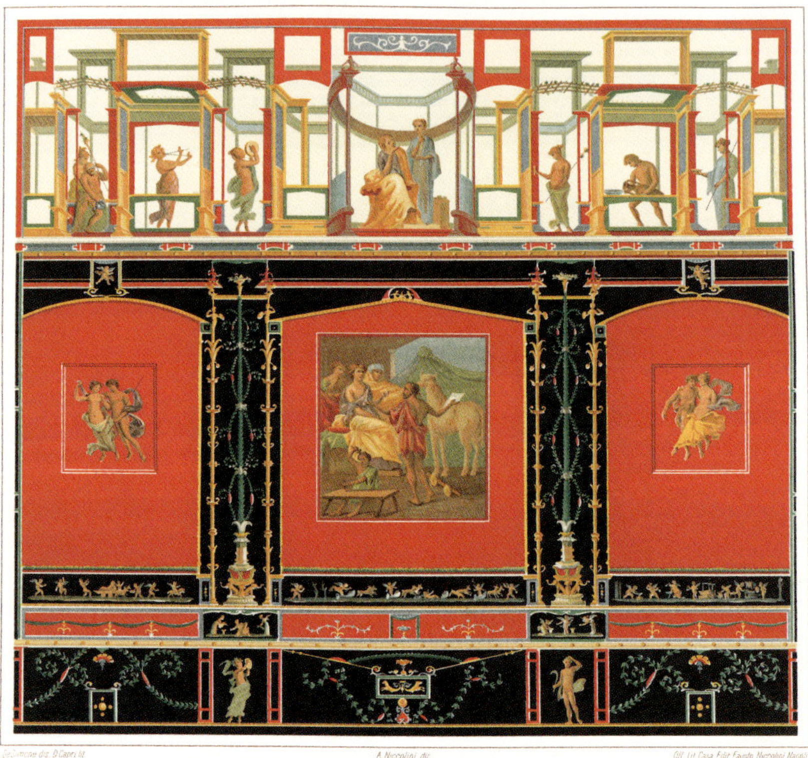

Pages 480–481

Plate 19 — *[C. de Simone]*

So-called Terme del Sarno (VIII 2, 17–21), atrium of entrance (18) on the ground floor, part of the north wall – The scene with Bellerophon in the central field (shown here on the left) does not match any descriptions and may have been a creative addition by the artist (C. de Simone).

✠

Plate 29 — *[C. de Simone]*

Casa dei Vettii (VI 15, 1), triclinium (13), north wall – Decoration in the 4th style. In the central field, Daedalus shows Pasiphae the wooden cow. In the lateral fields, floating pairs of gods. In the pale upper zone, Dionysian figures. (The wall decorations shown in pl. 24 and 31 also come from this room.)

✠

Plate 20 — *[C. de Simone]*

Casa dei Vettii (VI 15, 1), atrium (4) – Elements of the decoration on the narrow walls between the doorways.

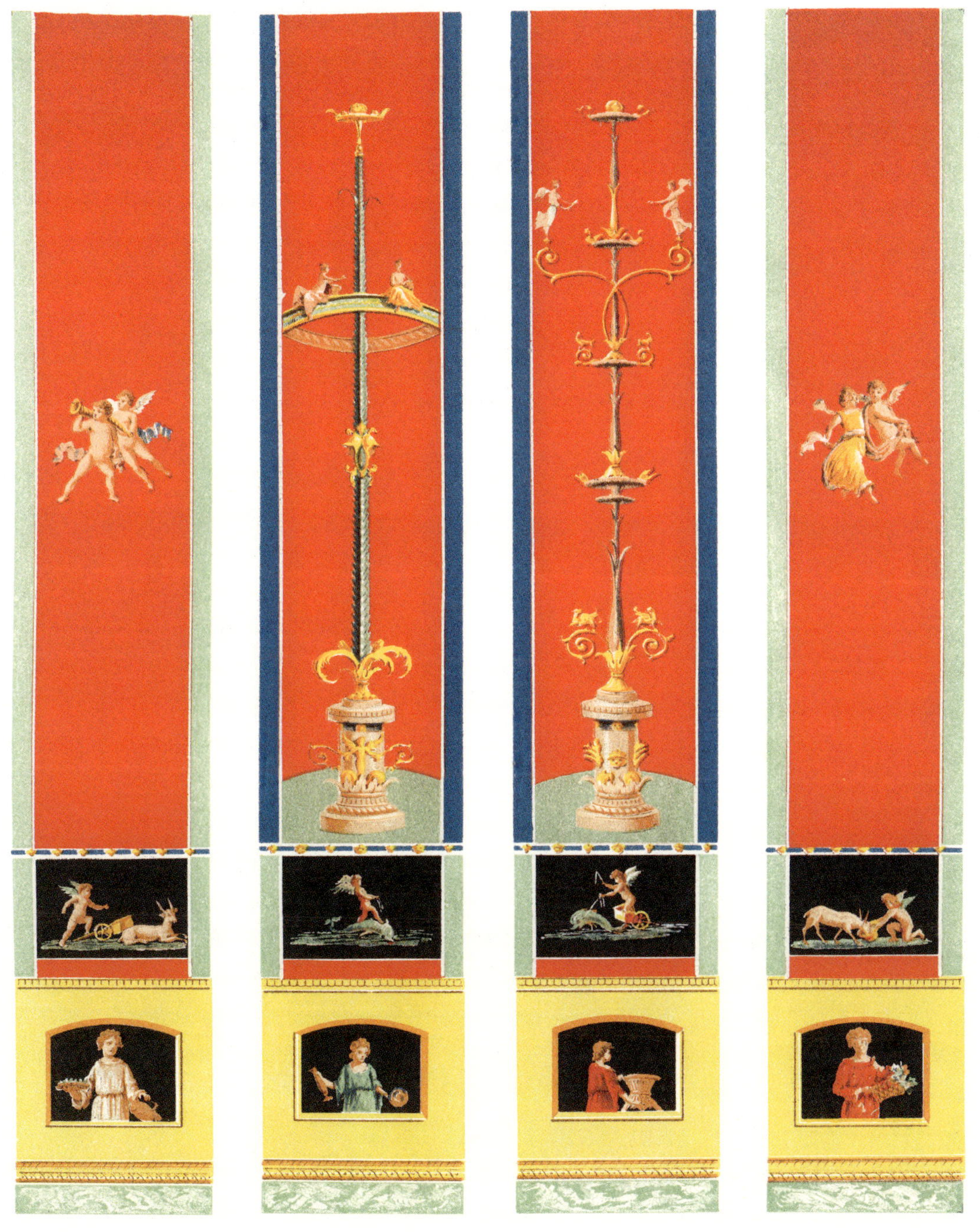

G. De Simone dis. D. Capri Lit. A. Niccolini dir. Stab. Lit. F. Niccolini_ Napoli.

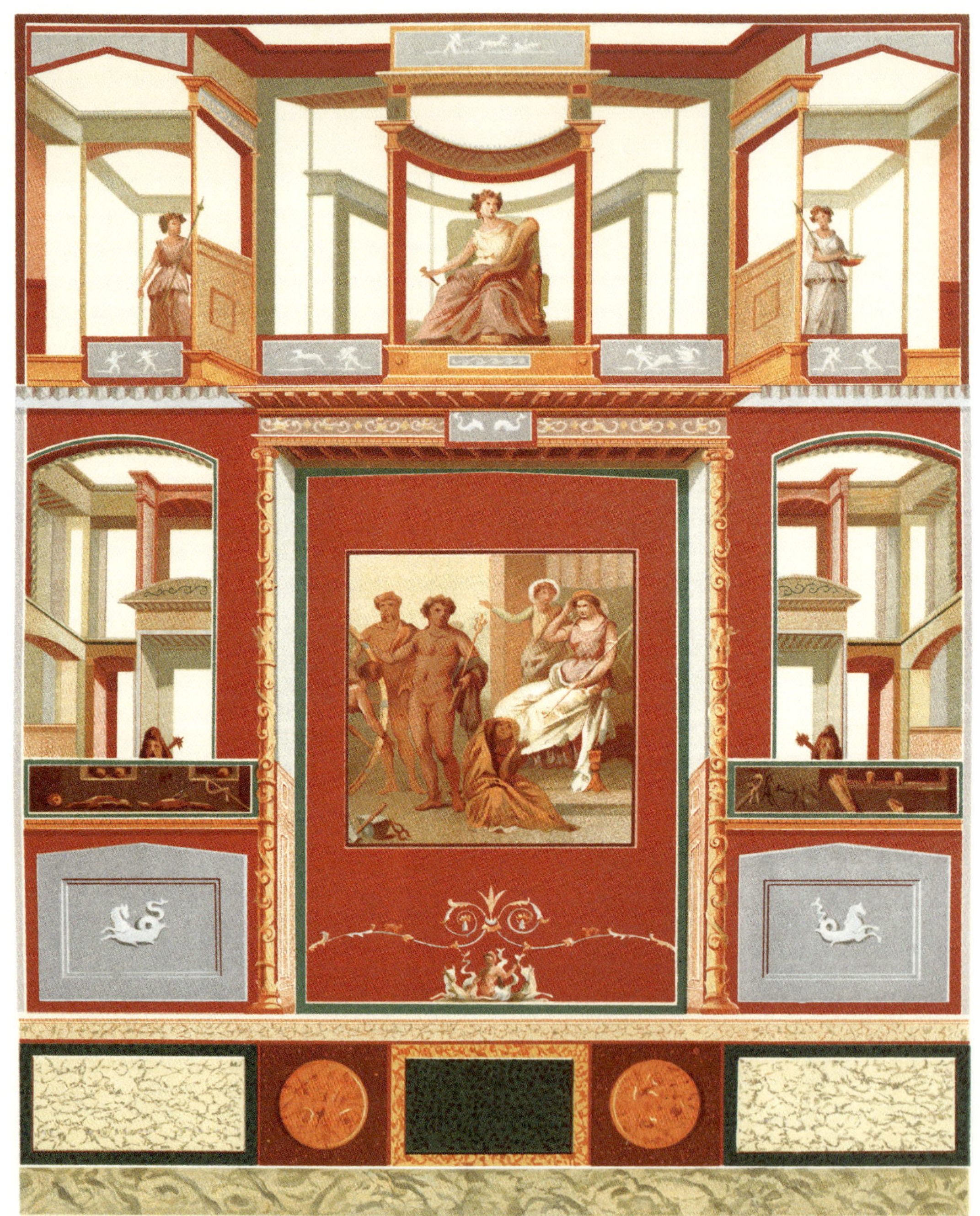

De Simone dis. Friedrich Lit. A. Niccolini dir. Off. Lit. Casa Edit. Fausto Niccolini, Napoli

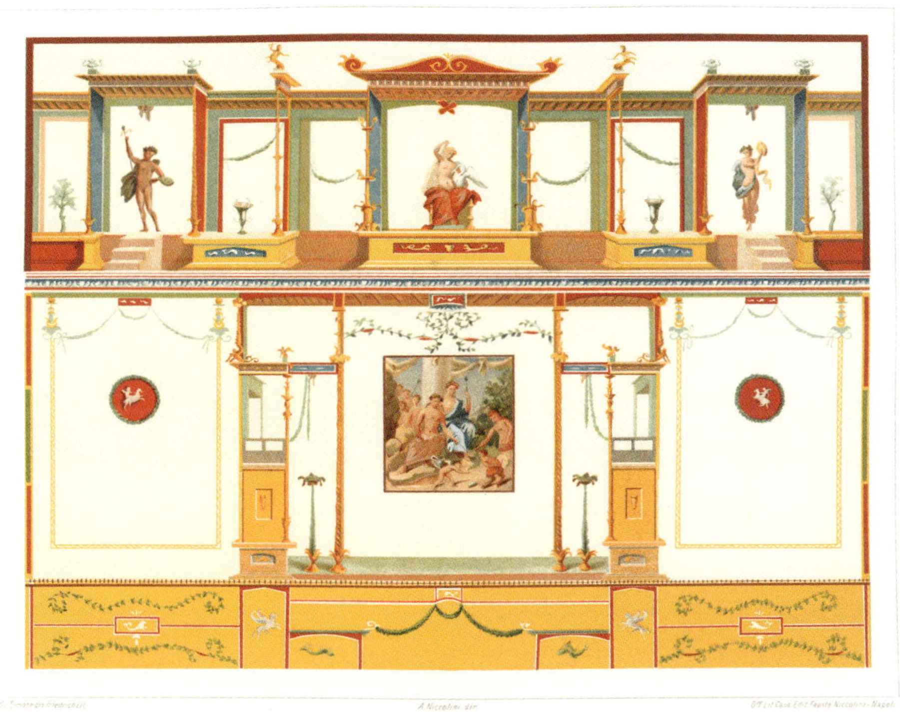

Plate 24 — *[C. de Simone]*
Casa dei Vettii (VI 15, 1), triclinium (13), rear wall – Decoration in the 4th style. The central field shows the rare mythological representation of the punishment of Ixion, who was bound to a wheel. (The wall decorations shown in pl. 29 and 31 also come from this room.)

Plate 25 — *[C. de Simone]*
Casa dei Vettii (VI 15, 1), oecus (5), south wall – Wall in the 4th style on a white ground. Above centre, Leda and the swan. In the central field of the main zone, a cupid and a satyr are fighting with each other while Dionysus and Ariadne look on.

Plate 23 — *[C. de Simone]*
Casa dei Vettii (VI 15, 1), peristyle (10) – Marble and bronze elements of the garden furnishings: basins, water-spouting fountain figures and columns with winding vine reliefs supporting herms. For a long time the original figures remained in situ, but have today been replaced by replicas.

Pages 488–489
Plate 28 — *[C. de Simone]*
Casa dei Vettii (VI 15, 1), frieze from the east wall of the large hall (15) – Above: scenes from the myth of Iphigenia (after Euripides): the sacrifice of Iphigenia by Agamemnon in Aulis; Apollo and Artemis watching a bull being sacrificed in Tauris. Middle and below: psyches and erotes at work (making perfume, goldsmithery, cloth fulling) and at play (chariot-racing).

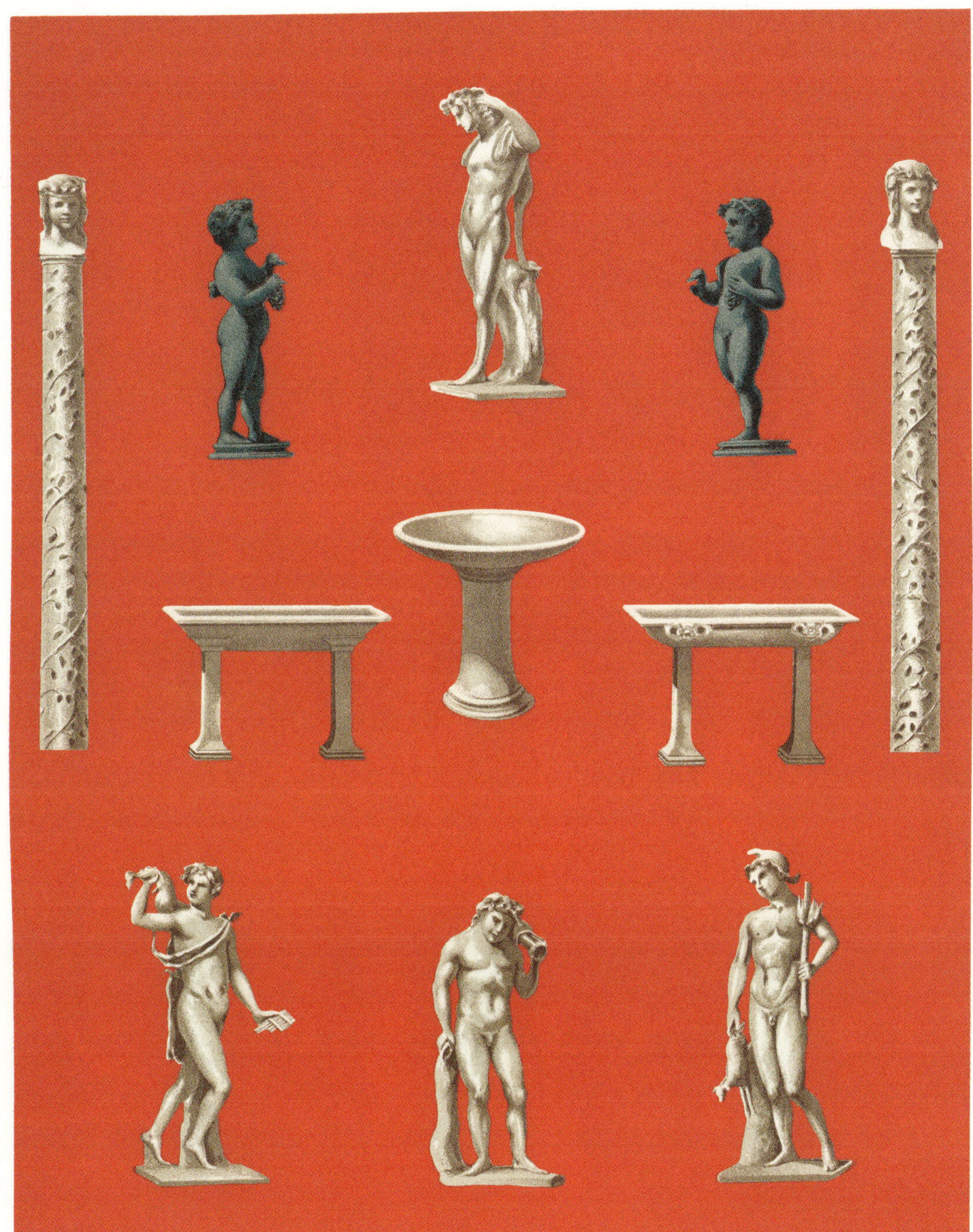

De Simone dis. De Stefani Lit. *A. Niccolini dir.* *Off. Lit. Casa Edit. Fausto Niccolini Napoli.*

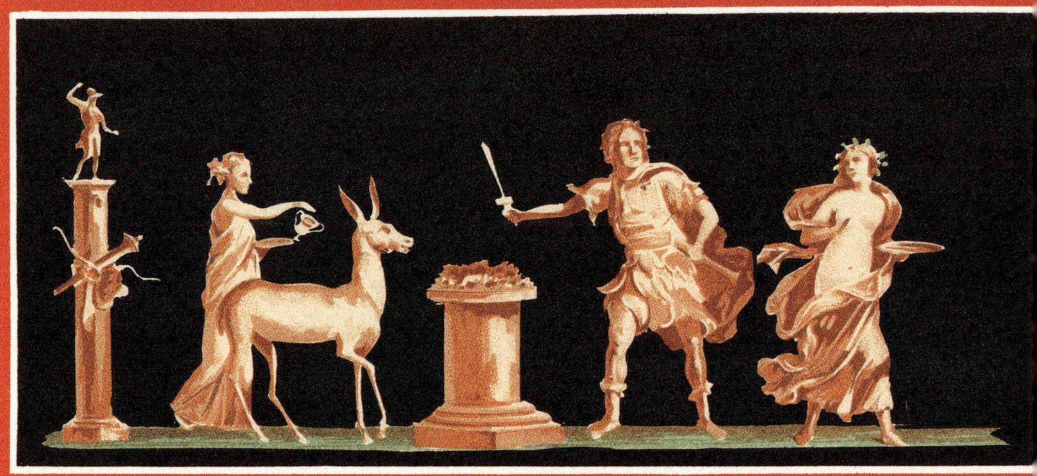

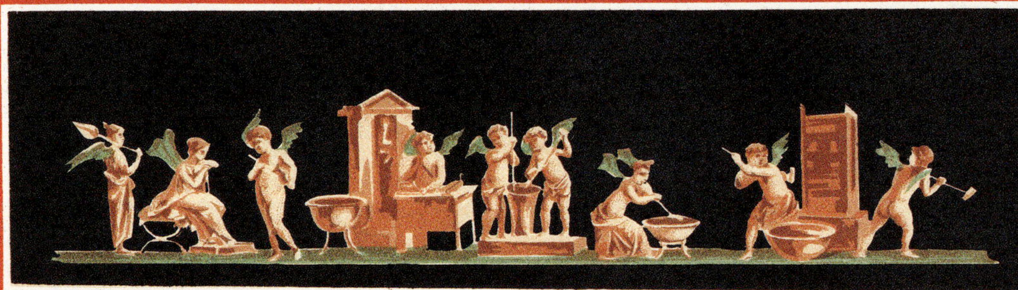

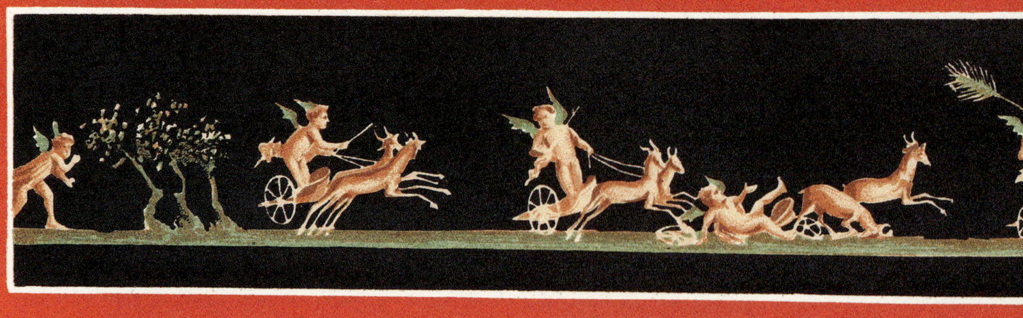

De Simone dis. De Stefano lit.

A.Ni

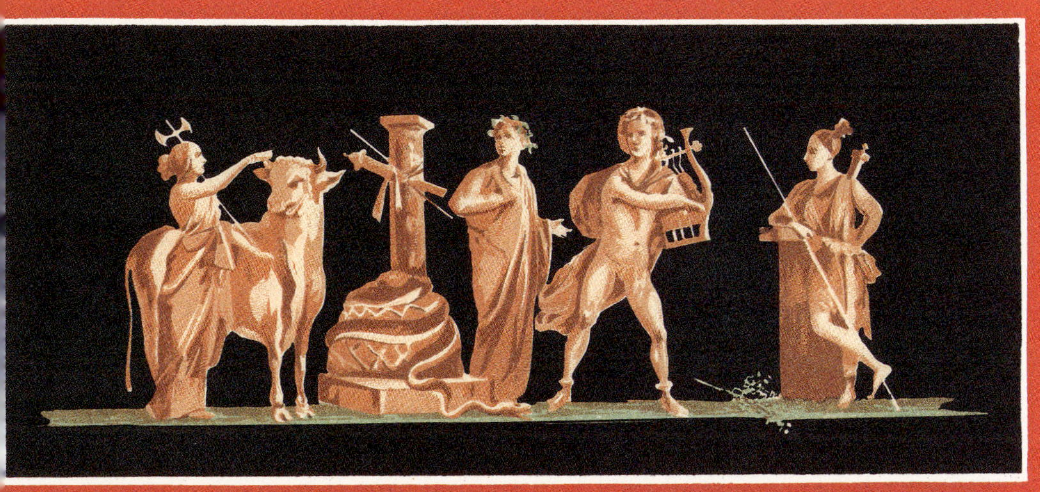

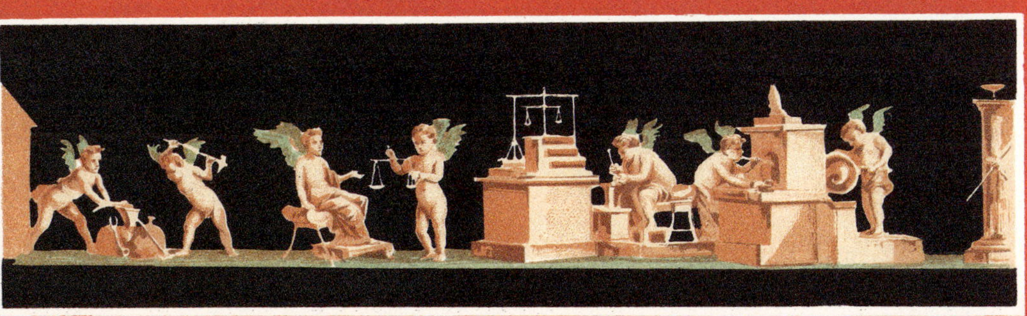

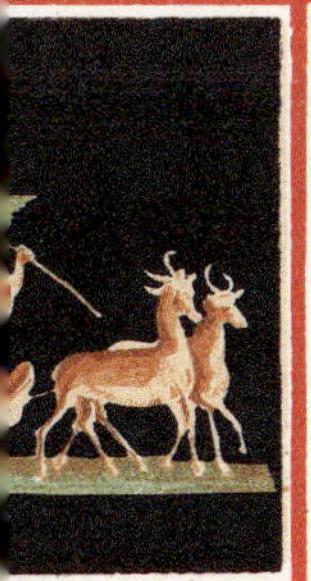

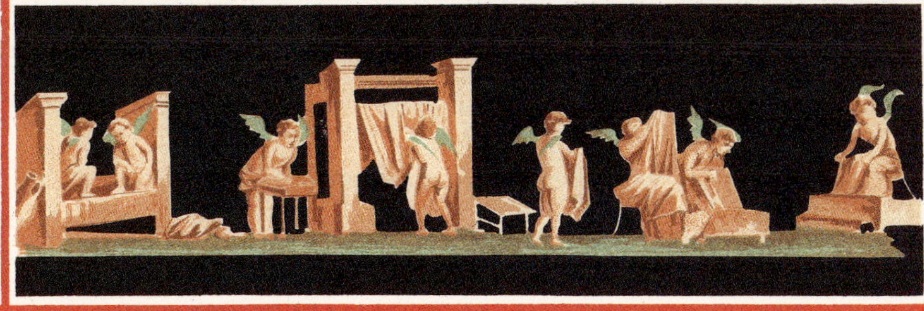

[...]ini dir.

Off. Lit. Casa Edit. Fausto Niccolini-Napoli

Plate 27 — ***[Anonymous]***
Casa dei Vettii (VI 15, 1), peristyle (10) – Two marble double herms on their column bases.

Pages 492–493
Plate 30 — ***[C. de Simone]***
Casa dei Vettii (VI 15, 1), details from the east wall of the large hall (15) –
Predella paintings of industrious psyches.

Pages 494–495
Plate 31 — ***[C. de Simone]***
Casa dei Vettii (VI 15, 1), triclinium (13), south wall – Decoration in the 4th style.
In the central field, Dionysus discovers Ariadne abandoned on Naxos by Theseus.

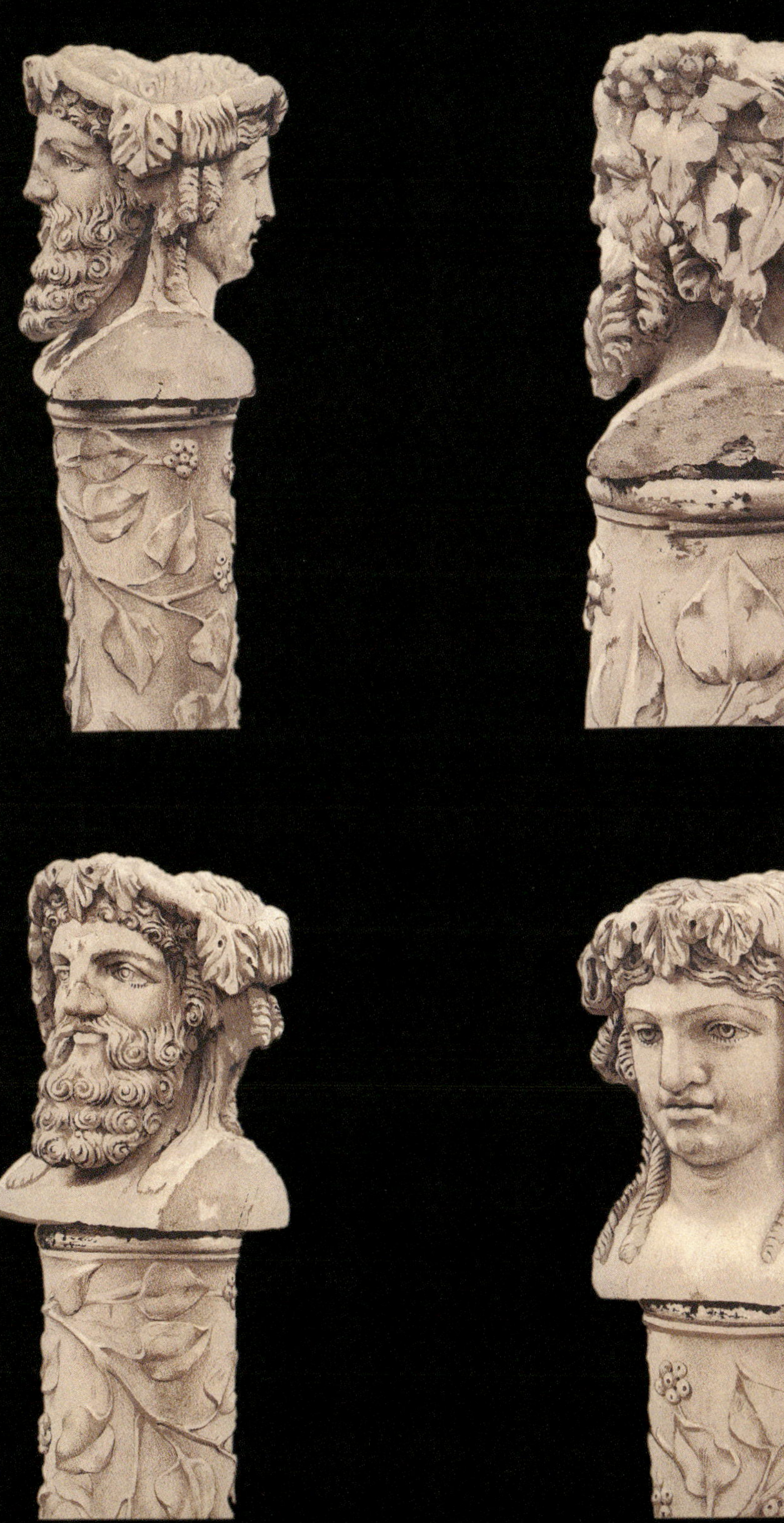

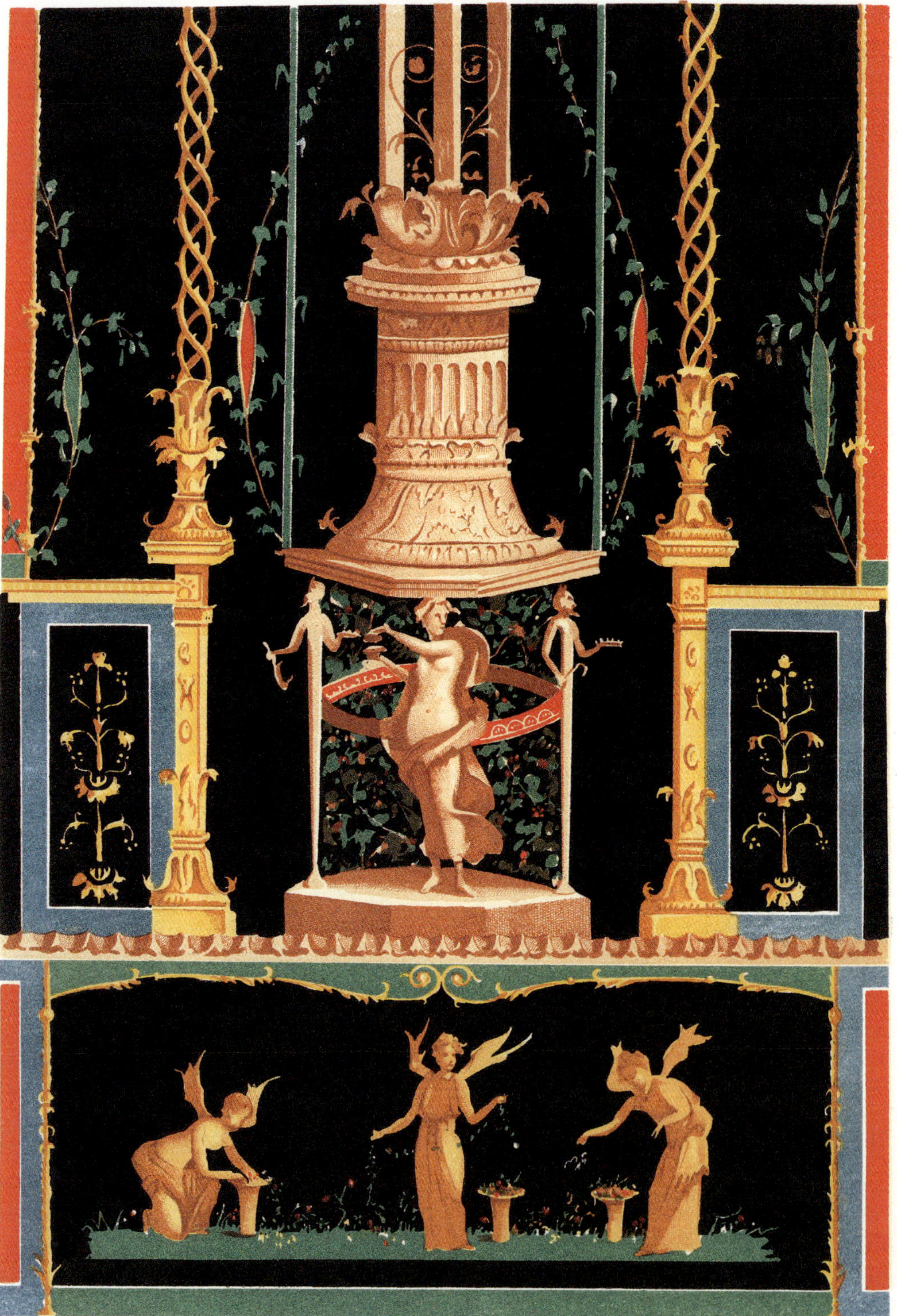

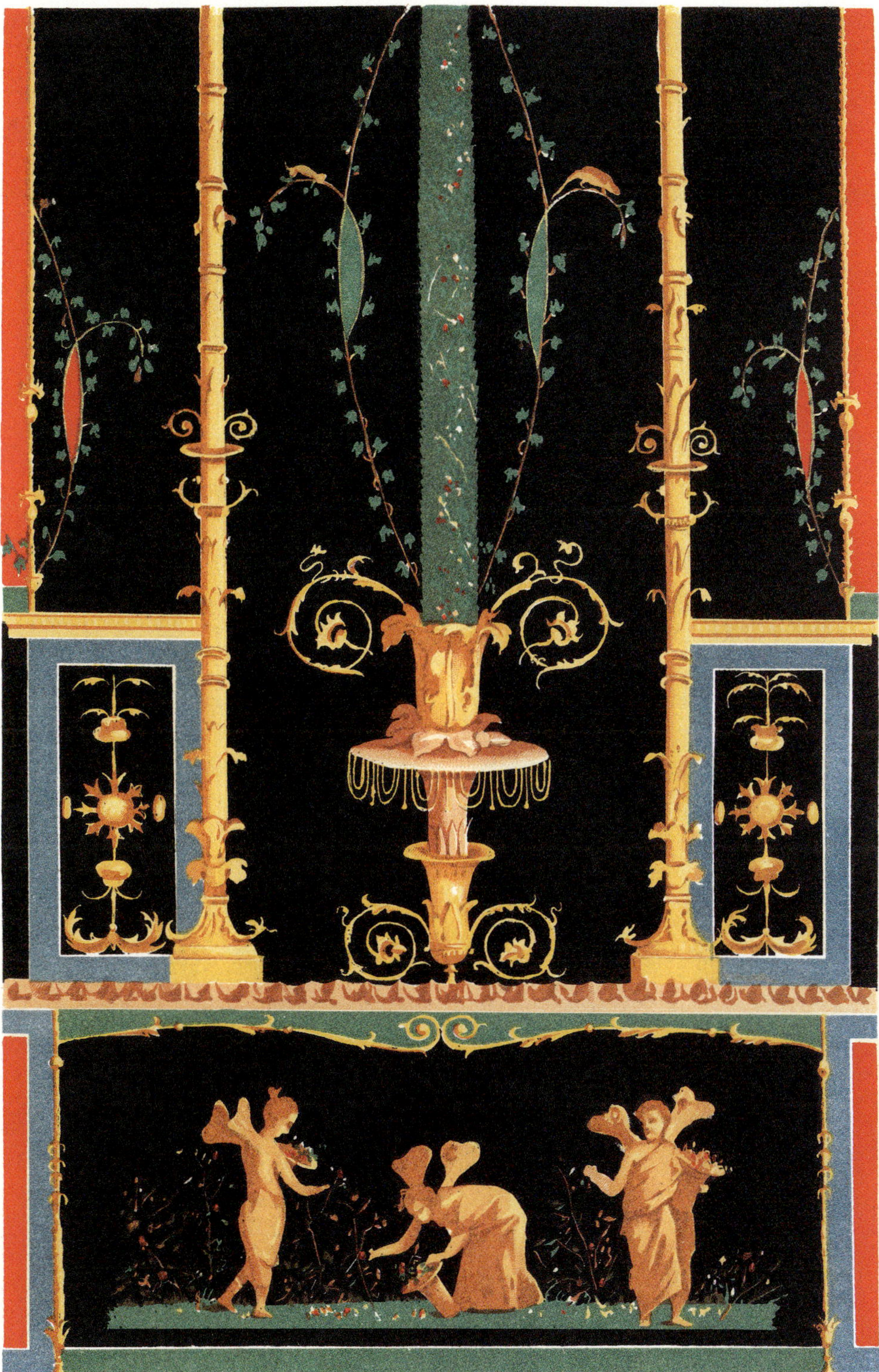

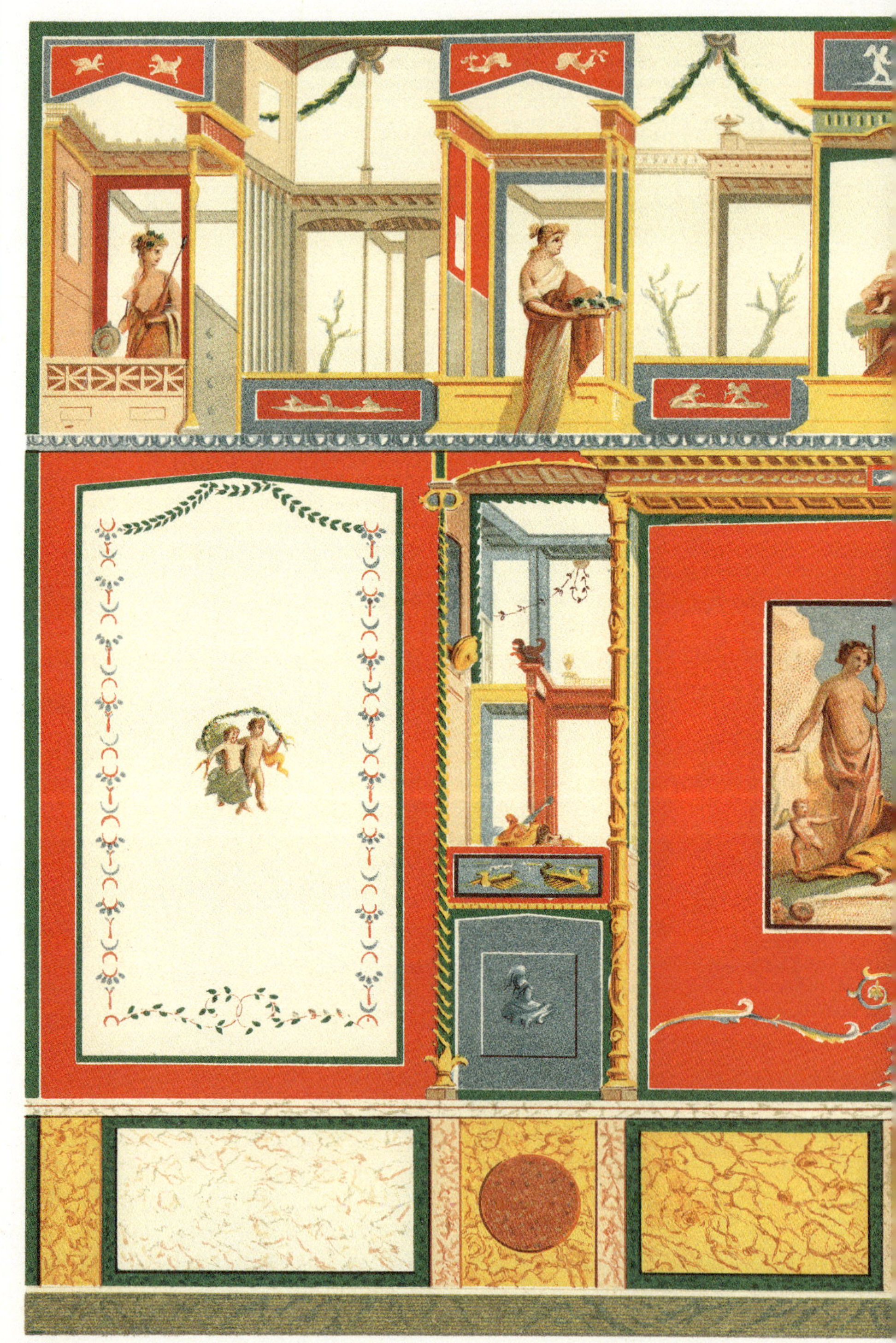

De Simone dis. D.Capri lit.

A. N

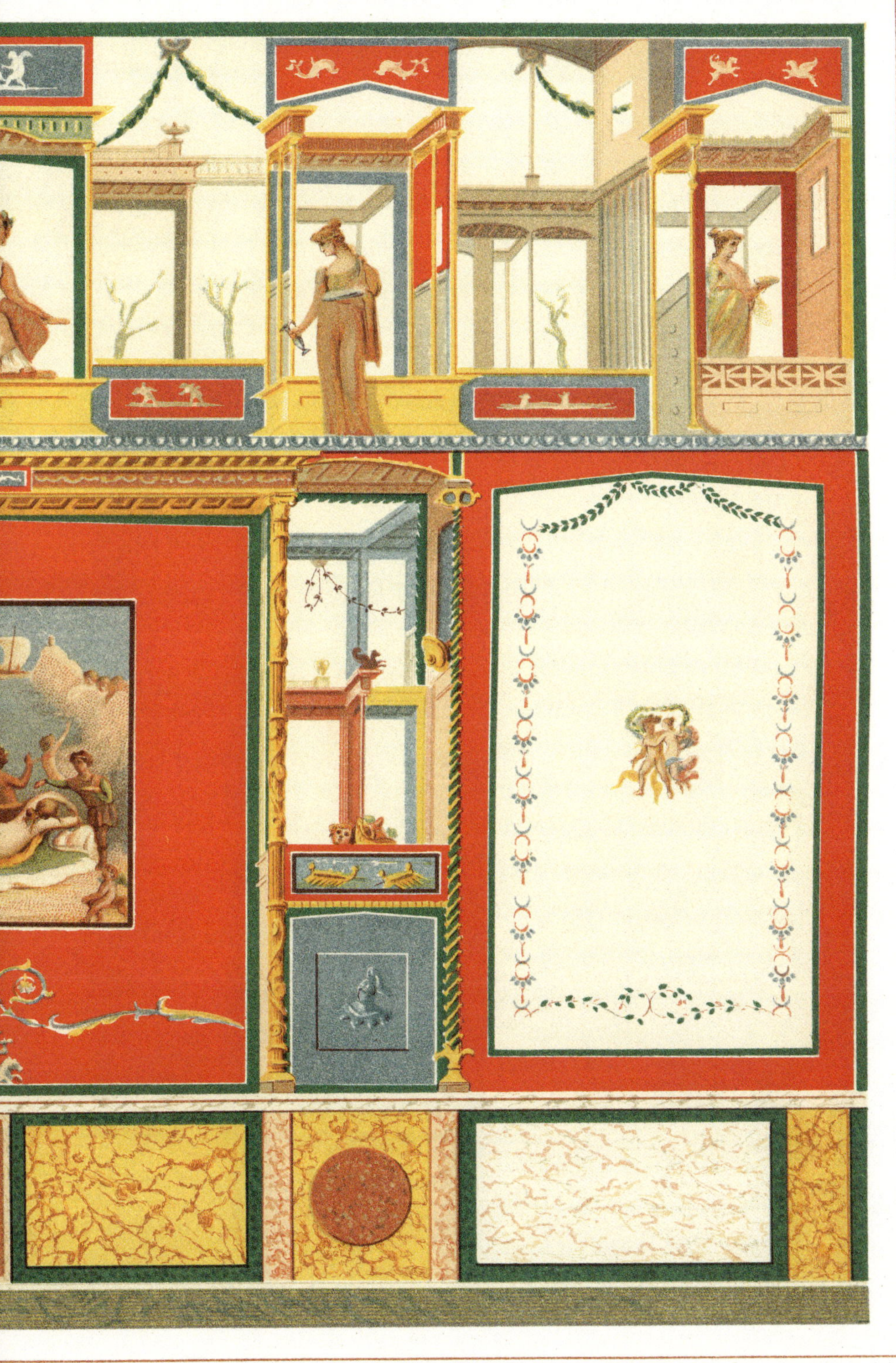

…olini dir.

Off. Lit. Casa Edit. Fausto Niccolini. Napoli.

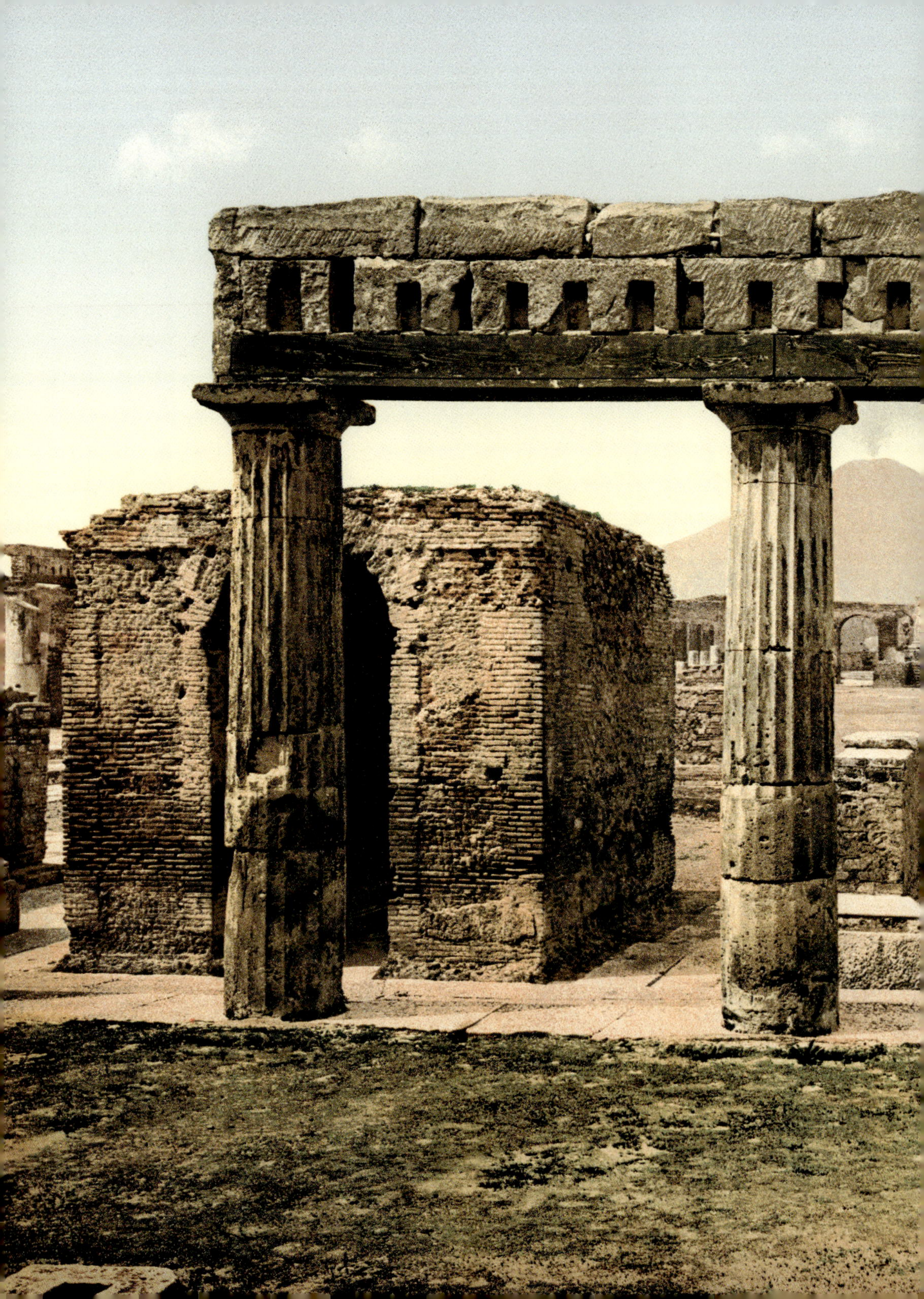

APPENDIX

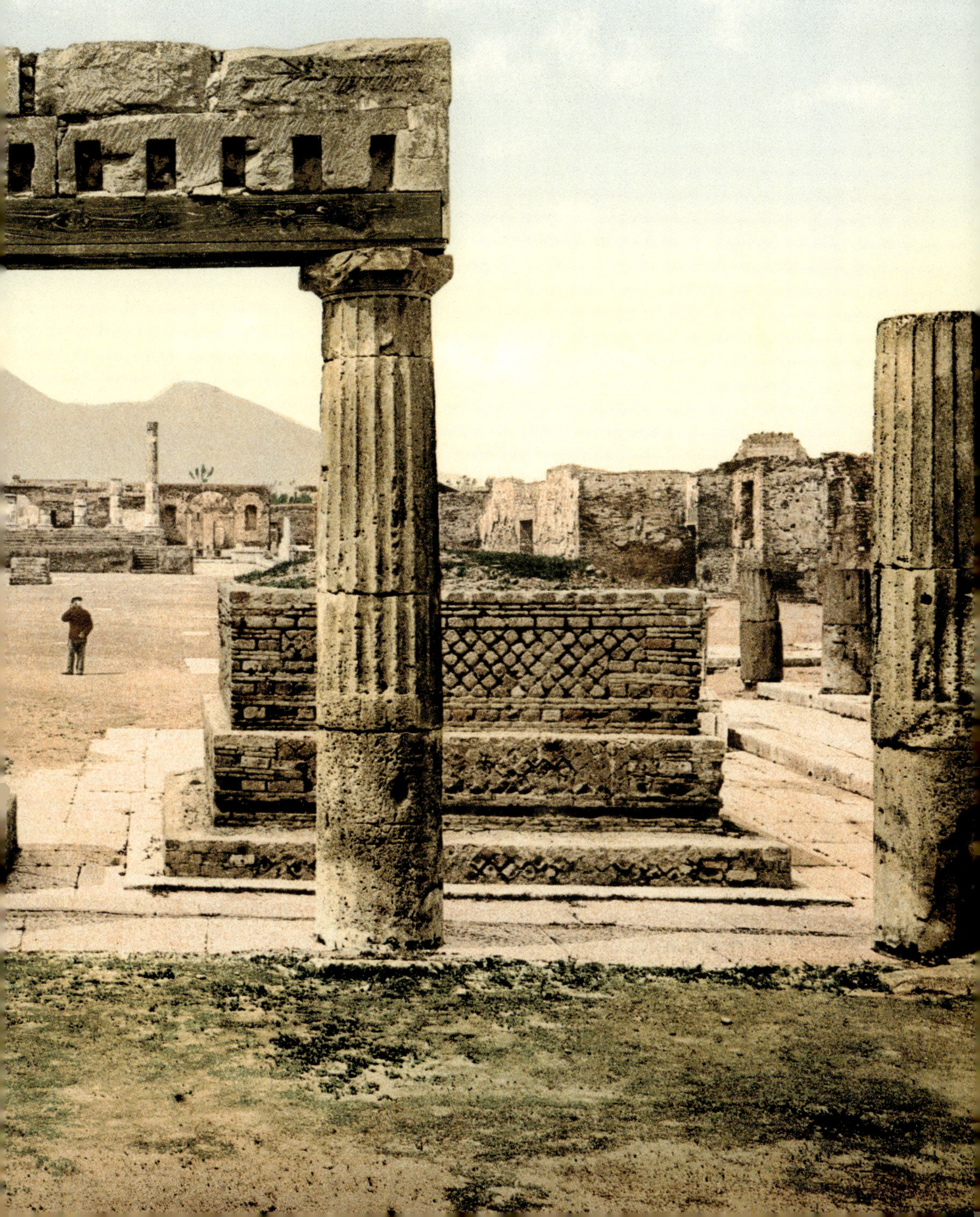

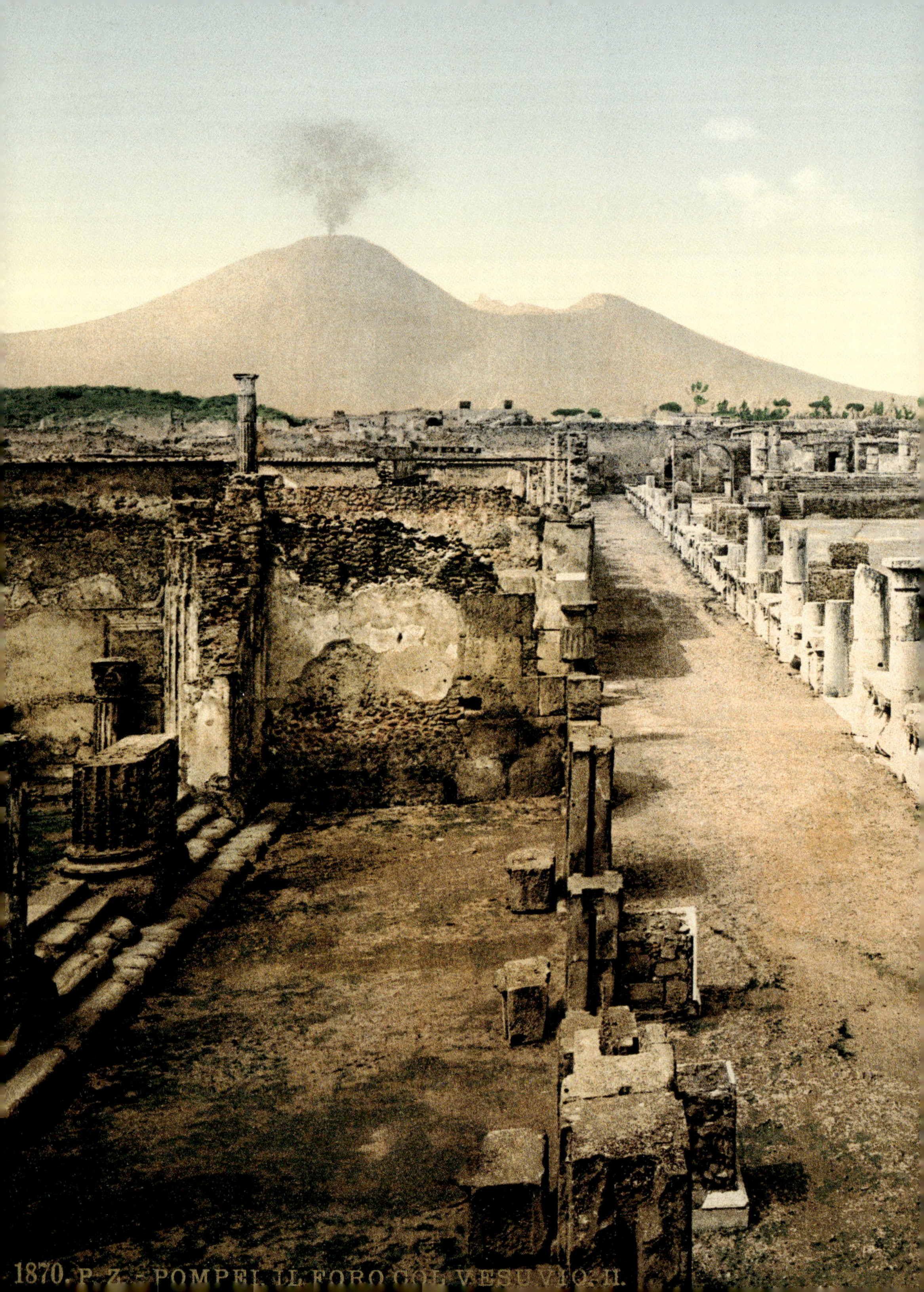
1870. P. Z. - POMPEI. IL FORO COL VESUVIO. II.

BIBLIOGRAPHY

Original edition

Fausto Niccolini – Felice Niccolini, *Le case ed i monumenti di Pompei. Disegnati e descritti*, 4 vols., Naples 1854–1896

Reprint

Stefano De Caro (ed.), Fausto e Felice Niccolini, *Le Case e i monumenti di Pompei, disegnati e descritti.* Saggio introduttivo di Stefano De Caro. 4 vols., Facsimile edition, Sorrento – Naples 2003–2006

E-book: DOI: https://doi.org/10.11588/diglit.3925

Selected editions

Roberto Cassanelli – Pier Luigi Ciapparelli – Enrico Colle – Massimiliano David, *Le case e i monumenti di Pompei nell'opera di Fausto e Felice Niccolini*, Novara 1994 (also Engl. and Fr. editions)

Roberto Cassanelli – Pier Luigi Ciapparelli – Enrico Colle – Massimiliano David, *Houses and Monuments of Pompeii. The work of Fausto and Felice Niccolini*, Los Angeles 2002

Fausto Niccolini – Felice Niccolini, *Houses and Monuments of Pompeii. Essays by Valentin Kockel and Sebastian Schütze*, Köln 2016 (texts Eng., Ger. and Fr.) [This edition of all plates served as the basis for the present, slightly abridged volume.]

Abbreviations

AKLONLINE Allgemeines Künstlerlexikon, online version

CIL Corpus Inscriptionum Latinarum (Berlin, as from 1862)

MANN Museo Archeologico Nazionale di Napoli

NBP Laurentino García y García, Nova Bibliotheca Pompeiana, 2 vols., Rome 1998

PAH Giuseppe Fiorelli (ed.), Pompeianarum Antiquitatum Historia, 3 vols., Naples 1860–1864

PPM Documentazione Giovanni Pugliese Carratelli – Ida Baldassarre (eds.), Pompei. Pitture e Mosaici. Unnumbered volume [11]: La documentazione nell'opera di disegnatori e pittori dei secoli XVIII e XIX, Rome 1995

RMB Antonio Niccolini the Elder (ed.), Real Museo Borbonico, vol. 1–16, Naples 1824–1857

General literature

Alix Barbet, *Les cités enfouies du Vésuve: Pompéi, Herculanum, Stabies et autres lieux*, Paris 2001

Mary Beard, *Pompeii. The Life of a Roman Town*, London 2008

Joan Berry, *The complete Pompeii*, London 2007

Filippo Coarelli (ed.), *Pompeii*, New York 2002 (Eng.); *Pompeji*, Munich 2002 (Ger.); *Pompéi, la vie ensevelie*, Paris 2002/2005 (Fr.)

Jens-Arne Dickmann, *Pompeji. Archäologie und Geschichte*, Munich ²2010

John J. Dobbins – Pedar W. Foss (eds.), *The World of Pompeii*, London and New York 2007

Harald Meller – Jens-Arne Dickmann (eds.), *Pompeji – Nola – Herculaneum. Katastrophen am Vesuv*, exhibition cat. Halle 2011/2012, Munich 2011

Paul Roberts, *Life and Death in Pompeii and Herculaneum*, London 2013

Valeria Sampaolo – Andreas Hoffmann (eds.), *Pompeji. Götter, Mythen, Menschen*, exhibition cat. Hamburg 2014/2015, Munich 2014

William Van Andringa, *Pompéi. Mythologie et histoire*, Paris 2013

Paul Zanker, *Pompeii. Public and Private Life*, Cambridge (Mass.) and London 1998 (Eng.); *Pompeji. Stadtbild und Wohngeschmack*, Mainz 1995 (Ger.)

Historical sources (up to 1908)

Antichità d'Ercolano 1757–1792

Le antichità di Ercolano esposte, 8 vols., Naples 1757, 1760, 1762, 1765, 1767, 1771, 1779, 1792. See also: *Pitture d'Ercolano*

Brunn 1859

Heinrich Brunn, "Rezension zu W. Ternite, Wandgemälde aus Herculaneum", in: B*ullettino dell'Instituto di Corrispondenza archeologica* 1859, 234-236

Cochin – Bellicard 1754

Charles Nicolas Cochin – Jérôme Charles Bellicard, *Observations sur les antiquités de la ville d'Herculanum*, Paris 1754 (with new editions and an English translation in 1765)

Curtius 1849

Ernst Curtius, "Rezension zu: W. Ternite, Wandgemälde aus Herculaneum, issue 1–5", in: *Morgenblatt für gebildete Stände. Kunstblatt* 1849, Nr. 18, 69–71

D'Amelio 1888

Pasquale D'Amelio, *Dipinti murali di Pompei*, text by Eduardo Cerillo, Naples 1888

D'Amelio 1899

Paquale D'Amelio*, Pompei. Nuovi scavi. Casa dei Vetti*, text by Antonio Sogliano, Naples 1899

Fiorelli, GdS 1861ff
Giuseppe Fiorelli, *Giornale degli Scavi di Pompei*, Naples 1861–1865
Fiorelli 1873
Giuseppe Fiorelli, *Gli scavi di Pompei dal 1861 al 1872. Relazione al Ministro della Istruzione Pubblica*, Naples 1873
Fischetti 1882
Luigi Fischetti, *Pompei com'era e com'è*, Naples 1882 (with many further editions in various languages and formats)
Furchheim 1891
Friedrich Furchheim, *Bibliografia di Pompei, Erconao e Stabia*, Naples 1891
Gell – Gandy 1817–1819
William Gell – John Peter Gandy, *Pompeiana*, 2 vols., London 1817–1819
Gell 1832
William Gell, *Pompeiana: the Topography, Edifices and Ornaments of Pompeii, the Result of Excavations since 1819*, 2 vols., London 1832
Gerhard 1828
Eduard Gerhard, "Rezension zu Zahn 1828 und Zahn I, 1828-29, issue 1 - 2", in: *Morgenblatt für gebildete Stände. Kunstblatt*, no. 75, September 1828, 297–299
Helbig 1868
Wolfgang Helbig, *Wandgemälde der vom Vesuv verschütteten Städte Campaniens*, Leipzig 1868
Jones 1856
Owen Jones, *The Grammar of Ornament*, London 1856 (further new editions and translations, Ger.: *Grammatik der Ornamente*, London 1856)
Mau 1882
August Mau, *Die Geschichte der decorativen Wandmalerei in Pompeji*, Leipzig 1882
Mau 1896
August Mau, "Der Tempel der Fortuna Augusta in Pompeji", in: *Mitteilungen des Deutschen Archäologischen Instituts, Römische Abteilung*, 11, 1896, 269–284
Mazois 1, 1812–1824; 2, 1824; 3, 1829; 4, 1838
François Mazois, *Les ruines de Pompéi*, 4 vols., Paris 1812–1838. (The two final volumes were published after Mazois' death in 1826 by François Gau and partly updated with the latest news)
Niccolini 1832
Antonio Niccolini, "Musaico scoperto in Pompei", *RMB* 8, 1832, pl. 36–45
Ornati 1796/1829/1838
Gli ornati delle pareti ed i pavimenti delle stanze dell'antica Pompei, 2 vols., Naples, Stamperia Reale, 1796 (reprints in 1829 and 1838 with, in places, different or no numbering)
Overbeck 1856/1866
Johannes Overbeck, *Pompeji in seinen Gebäuden, Alterthümern und Kunstwerken*, Leipzig 1856; 2nd edition in 2 vols., Leipzig 1866
Overbeck – Mau 1884
Johannes Overbeck – August Mau, *Pompeji*, Leipzig [4]1884
Piranesi 1804
Francesco Piranesi, *Antiquités de la Grande Grèce. Antiquités de Pompeia*, vol. I and II, Paris 1804
Piranesi 1807
Francesco Piranesi, *Les Antiquités de la Grande Grèce* (vol. III). *Tables des usages civiles et militaires trouvés à Pompeia et Herculaneum*, Paris 1807
Pitture d'Ercolano
Le Pitture d'Ercolano e contorni, vol. 1–5, Naples 1757, 1760, 1762, 1765, 1779 (= *Antichità d'Ercolano*, vol. 1–4 and 7)
Presuhn 1877
Emil Presuhn, *Die pompejanischen Wanddekorationen für Künstler und Gewerbeschulen, sowie Freunde des Alterthums*, Leipzig 1877 (also Eng., It. and Fr.)
Presuhn 1878
Emil Presuhn, *Pompeji. Die neuesten Ausgrabungen von 1874–1876*, Leipzig 1878 (also It. and Fr.)
Presuhn 1882
Emil Presuhn, Pompeji. *Die neuesten Ausgrabungen von 1878 bis 1881* (supplementary volume to Presuhn 1878), Leipzig 1882
Raoul-Rochette 1828
Désiré Rochette, known as Raoul-Rochette, *Pompéi. Choix de monuments inédits. Ière partie: Maison du Poète tragique à Pompei, publiée avec ses peintures et ses mosaiques fidèlement reproduites et un texte explicatif par Raoul Rochette, antiquaire, et J. Bouchet, architecte*, Paris 1828
Raoul-Rochette 1844–1853
Désiré Raoul-Rochette, *Choix de Peintures*, Paris 1844
Rohden 1880
Hermann von Rohden, *Die Terrakotten von Pompeji* (= *Die antiken Terrakotten*, vol. 1), Stuttgart 1880
Roux – Barré 1837–1841
Henri Roux – Louis Barré, *Herculanum et Pompéi. Recueil général des peintures, bronzes, mosaiques etc.*, Paris 1837–1841

Ruesch 1908
Arnold Ruesch (ed.), *Guida illustrata del Museo Nazionale di Napoli*, Naples 1908
Saint-Non 1782
Jean-Baptiste Claude Richard, *Abbé de Saint-Non, Voyage pittoresque ou description des royaumes de Naples et de Sicile*, vol. II, Paris 1782
Schasler 1863
Max Schasler, "Wilhelm Zahn (Studien zur Charakteristik bedeutender Künstler der Gegenwart 32)", in: *Die Dioskuren. Kunst-Zeitung*, vol. 8, 1863, 209 f., 217–219, 225–227, 233–235, 241–243, 249 f., 255 f., 261 f.
Ternite 1839–1858
Wilhelm Ternite, *Wandgemäde aus Pompeji und Herculanum nach den Zeichnungen und Nachbildungen in Farben.* With an explanatory text by C. O. Müller and F. G Welcker (as from issue 2), Berlin 1839–1858. 11 issues with altogether 88 plates
Winckelmann 1762
Johann Joachim Winckelmann, *Sendschreiben von den Herculanischen Entdeckungen*, Dresden 1762
Winckelmann 1764
Johann Joachim Winckelmann, *Nachrichten von den neuesten Herculanischen Entdeckungen*, Dresden 1764 (recent annotated edition of the two letters of 1762 and 1764: Stephanie-Gerrit Bruer – Max Kunze, *Johann Joachim Winckelmann. Schriften und Nachlass*, vol. 2. *Herkulanische Schriften Winckelmanns*, part 1 and 2, Mainz 1997)
Zahn 1828
Wilhelm Zahn, *Neu entdeckte Wandgemälde in Pompeji*, Munich, Stuttgart and Tübingen 1828
Zahn 1, 1828–1829; 2, 1842–1844; 3, 1849–1859
Wilhelm Zahn, *Die schönsten Ornamente und merkwürdigsten Gemälde aus Pompeji, Herculanum und Stabiae, nebst einigen Grundrissen und Ansichten nach den an Ort und Stelle gemachen Originalzeichnungen*, vol. 1, Berlin 1828–1829; vol. 2, Berlin 1842–1844; vol. 3, Berlin 1849–1859 (each with 10 fascicles and 100 plates)
Zahn 1843
Wilhelm Zahn, *Ornamente aller klassischen Kunst-Epochen nach den Originalen in ihren eigenthümlichen Farben*, Berlin 1843 (and later editions)

Secondary literature (as from 1909)

Antichità di Ercolano 1988
Banco di Napoli (ed.), *Le Antichità di Ercolano*, texts by R. Ajello; F. Bologna; M. Gigante; F. Zevi, Naples 1988
Adamo Muscettola 2001
Stefania Adamo Muscettola, "Problemi di tutela a Pompei nell'ottocento: il fallimento del progetto di esproprio murattiano", in: Pietro Giovanni Guzzo (ed.), *Pompei. Scienza e società*, Milan 2001, 29-49
Allroggen-Bedel 1996
Agnes Allroggen-Bedel, "Archäologie und Politik. Herculaneum und Pompeji im 18. Jahrhundert", in: *Hephaistos*, 14, 1996, 217–252
Allroggen-Bedel 2008
Agnes Allroggen-Bedel, "L'antico e la politica culturale dei Borboni", in: R. Cantilena – A. Porzio (eds.), *Herculanense Museum*, Naples 2008, 53–72
Andreae 1977
B. Andreae, *Das Alexandermosaik aus Pompeji*, Recklinghausen 1977
Andreae 2003
Bernard Andreae, *Antike Bildmosaiken*, Mainz 2003
Aßkamp et al. 2007
Rudolf Aßkamp et al. (ed.), *Luxus und Dekadenz. Römisches Leben am Golf von Neapel*, exhibition cat., Haltern et al. 2007
Betzer 2011
Sarah E. Betzer, "Archaeology meets fantasy. Chassériau's Pompeii in nineteenth-century Paris", in: Shelley Hales – Joanna Paul (eds.), *Pompeii in the public imagination from its rediscovery to today*, Oxford 2011, 118–135
Blix 2009
Göran Blix, *From Paris to Pompeii. French Romanticism and the Cultural Politics of Archeology*, Philadelphia 2008
Bologna 1990
Ferdinando Bologna, "La riscoperta di Ercolano e Pompei/The Rediscovery of Herculaneum and Pompeii", in: *Rediscovering Pompeii*, exhibition cat. New York 1990, Rome 1990, 78–91 (Ger.: "Die Wiederentdeckung von Herculaneum und Pompeji", in: *Pompeji wiederentdeckt*, Rome 1993, 78–91)
Borriello – D'Ambrosio – De Caro – Guzzo 1996
Mariarosaria Borriello – Antonio d'Ambrosio – Stefano De Caro – Pietro Giovanni Guzzo (eds.), *Pompei. Abitare sotto il Vesuvio*, Ferrara 1996
Bouquillard 2000
Jocelyn Bouquillard, *Le résurrection de Pompéi. Dessins d'archéologues des XVIIIe et XIXe siècles*, Paris 2000
Bragantini 2003
Irene Bragantini, "La documentazione degli affreschi antichi", in: Maria Ida Catalano – Gabriella Prisco

(eds.), *Storia del restauro dei dipinti a Napoli e nel Regno nel XIX secolo*, Rome 2003, 85-95

Bragantini – Sampaolo 1995
Irene Bragantini – Valeria Sampaolo, "Le pitture di Pompei nei disegni dell'Archivio della Soprintendenza di Napoli", in: *PPM Immagine*, 17–24

Bragantini – Sampaolo 2009
Irene Bragantini – Valeria Sampaolo, *La pittura pompeiana*, Milan 2009

Cahen 1999
Antoine Cahen, "Nicolas-Hubert Roux l'aîné et a chromolithographie. Le livre illustré dans les années 1840", in: Claude Albore-Livadie (ed.), *Peintures à Pompéi – peintures en Gaule*, Blanc 1999

Cassanelli et al. 1997
Roberto Cassanelli – Pier Luigi Ciapparelli – Enrico Colle – Massimiliano David, *Le case e i monumenti di Pompei nell'opera di Fausto e Felice Niccolini*, Novara 1997 (also Eng. and Fr. editions)

Cassanelli et al. 2002
Roberto Cassanelli – Pier Luigi Ciapparelli – Enrico Colle – Massimiliano David (eds.), *Houses and Monuments of Pompeii. The works of Fausto and Felice Niccolini*, Los Angeles 2002

Ciapparelli 1997
Pier Luigi Ciapparelli, "L'avventura editoriale dei Niccolini", in: Cassanelli et al. 1997, 10–25

Ciarallo 2006
Annamaria Ciarallo, *Scienziati a Pompei tra settecento e ottocento*, Rome 2006

Ciarallo – De Carolis 1999
Annamaria Ciarallo – Ernesto De Carolis (eds.), *Homo Faber. Natura, scienza e tecnica nell'antica Pompei*, Venice 1999

Ciardiello 2012
Rosaria Ciardiello, "Die 'Antichità di Ercolano'. Rezeption in der europäischen Kunst und im Kunstgewerbe", in: Reinsberg – Meynersen 2012, 47–53

Cioffi – Grimaldi 2010
Rosanna Cioffi – Anna Grimaldi (eds.), *L'idea dell'antico nel decennio francese: atti del terzo seminario di studi "Decennio francese (1806–1815)"*, Naples 2010

Clay – Frederiksen 1976
Edith Clay – Martin Frederiksen, *Sir William Gell in Italy. Letters to the Society of Dilettanti*, London 1976

Coarelli 2002
Filippo Coarelli (ed.), *Pompeji*, Munich 2002 (It. original: *Pompei, la vita ritrovata*, Udine 2002)

Collezioni 1986/1989
Mariarosaria Borriello – Renata Cantilena et al., *Le collezioni del Museo Nazionale di Napoli*, vol. I, 1 and I, 2; Rome 1986/1989

D'Alconzo 2002
Paola D'Alconzo, P*icturae excisae. Conservazione e restauro dei dipinti ercolanesi e pompeiani tra XVIII e XIX secolo*, Rome 2002

D'Ambrosio – Guzzo – Mastroroberto 2003
Antonio D'Ambrosio – Pier Giovanni Guzzo – Marisa Mastroroberto (eds.), *Storie da un'eruzione*, exhibition cat. Milan 2003, Milan 2003

De Angelis 1993
Francesco De Angelis, "Giuseppe Fiorelli: la vecchia antiquaria di fronte allo scavo", in: *Ricerche di Storia dell'Arte*, 50, 1993, 1–16

De Caro 1994
Stefano De Caro (ed.), *Museo Archeologico Nazionale*, Naples 1994 (Eng. *The National Archaeological Museum of Naples*, 1996)

De Caro 1998
Stefano De Caro – Carolina Murat, "Michele Arditi e Pompei", in: *Il Vesuvio e le città vesuviane 1730–1860. In ricordo di Georges Vallet*, Naples 1998, 225–240

De Caro 2015
Stefano De Caro, "Visiting Pompeii. Progress in Excavations and Tourism in the Second Bourbon Age", in: Osanna – Caracciolo – Gallo 2015, 97–105

De Caro – Guzzo, 1999
Stefano De Caro – Pietro Giovanni Guzzo (eds.), *A Giuseppe Fiorelli nel centenario della Morte*, Naples 1999

De Carolis 2011
Ernesto De Carolis, "Alphonse Bernoud fotografo a Pompei", in: *Rivista di Studi Pompeiani*, 22, 2011, 49–60

De Carolis 2013
Ernesto De Carolis, *Robert Rive. Un Album fotografico di Pompei*, Pompeii 2013

De Carolis 2015
Ernesto De Carolis et al., "Pompeii Portrayed in Nineteenth-Century Photographs", in: Osanna – Caracciolo – Gallo 2015, 276–300

Desrochers 2003
Brigitte Desrochers, "Giorgio Sommer's Photographs of Pompeii", in: *History of Photography*, 27, no. 2, 2003, 111–129

Descamps-Lequime 2013
Sophie Descamps-Lequime, "The Ferdinand IV Donation to the first Consul and his Wife: Antiquities from

the Bay of Naples at Malmaison", in: Mattusch 2013, 141–176

Döhl – Zanker 1979
Harmut Döhl – Paul Zanker, "La scultura", in: Zevi 1979, 177–210

Dönike 2013
Martin Dönike, *Altertumskundliches Wissen in Weimar*, Berlin and Boston 2013

Dwyer 2010
Eugene J. Dwyer, *Pompeii's living statues*, Ann Arbor 2010

Echlin 2014
Alexander Echlin, "Dynasty, archaeology and conservation", in: *Journal of the History of Collections*, 26, no. 2, 145–159

Eschebach 1970
Hans Eschebach, *Die städtebauliche Entwicklung des antiken Pompeji*, Heidelberg 1970

Eschebach 1979
Hans Eschebach, *Die Stabianer Thermen in Pompeji*. With contributions by Harald Mielsch, Mariette and Arnold De Vos, Berlin 1979

Eschebach 1993
Liselotte Eschebach (ed.), *Gebäudeverzeichnis und Stadtplan der antiken Stadt Pompeji*, Cologne, Weimar and Vienna 1993

Ficacci 2000
Luigi Ficacci, *Piranesi. The complete etchings*, Cologne 2000

Fotografi a Pompei 1990
Fotografi a Pompei nell'800: dalle collezioni del Museo Alinari, Florence 1990

Franciosi 2006
Vincenzo Franciosi, *Il "Doriforo" di Policleto*, Naples [2]2006

Gardner Coates – Seydl 2007
Victoria C. Gardner Coates – Jon L. Seydl (eds.), *Antiquity Recovered. The Legacy of Pompei and Herculaneum*, Los Angeles 2007

Gardner Coates – Lapatin – Seydl 2012
Victoria C. Gardner Coates – Kenneth Lapatin – Jon L. Seydl (eds.), *Decadence, Apocalypse, Resurrection. The Last Days of Pompeii*, Los Angeles 2012

Germer 1990
Stefan Germer, "Stillgestellte Geschichte. Ingres und die Historienmalerei", in: Ekkehard Mai (ed.), *Historienmalerei in Europa. Paradigmen in Form, Funktion und Ideologie*, Mainz 1990, 193–208

Giannetti – Muzii 1997
Anna Giannetti – Rossana Muzii (eds.), *Antonio Niccolini architetto e scenografo alla Corte di Napoli*, Naples 1997

Gordon 2007
Alden R. Gordon, "Subverting the Secret of Herculaneum", in: Gardner Coates – Seydl 2007, 37–58

Guzzo 2006
Pietro Giovanni Guzzo (ed.), *Argenti a Pompei*, exhibition cat. Naples 2006, Milan 2006

Guzzo – Wieczorek 2004
Pietro Giovanni Guzzo – A. Wieczorek (eds.), *Pompeji. Die Stunde des Untergangs*, exhibition cat. Mannheim 2004/2005, Milan 2004

Hennemeyer 2014
Arnd Hennemeyer, "Wilhelm Zahns Pompeji-Publikation: eine Inkunabel der Farblithographie", in: U. Hassler (ed.), *Maltechnik & Farbgebung der Semperzeit*, Munich 2014, 98–123

Italienische Reise 1989
Italienische Reise: Pompejanische Bilder in deutschen archäologischen Sammlungen, Naples 1989

Jacobelli 2008
Lucia Jacobelli (ed.), *Pompei. La costruzione di un mito. Arte letteratura, aneddotica di un'icone turistica*, Rome 2008

Kockel 1998
Valentin Kockel, *Phelloplastica. Modell in sughero dell'architettura antica nel XVIII secolo nella collezione di Gustavo III di Svezia*, Stockholm 1998

Kockel 2000
Valentin Kockel, "Archäologie und Politik. Francesco Piranesi und seine drei Pompeji-Pläne", in: *Rivista di Studi Pompeiani*, 11, 2000, 33–46

Kockel 2002
Valentin Kockel, "Pompeji", in: *Der Neue Pauly. Rezeptions- und Wissenschaftsgeschichte*, vol. 15, 2, Stuttgart, Weimar 2002, 472–490

Kockel 2006
Valentin Kockel, "Gelehrsamkeit versus Anschauung. Vitruv, Piranesi, Mazois und die Entdeckung des römischen Hauses in Pompeji", in: Kathrin Schade – Detlef Rößler – Alfred Schäfer (eds.), *Zentren und Wirkungsräume der Antikenrezeption*, Münster 2006, 39–45, pl. 5–7

Kockel 2006b
Valentin Kockel, *Pompeji 360 Grad. Die beiden Panoramen Carl Georg Enslens aus dem Jahr 1826* (It. and Ger.), Milan 2006

Kockel 2012
Valentin Kockel, "Pompeji vermessen. Plan, Modell und andere Techniken zur Visualisierung der Ausgrabungen im 18. und frühen 19. Jahrhundert", in: Reinsberg – Meynersen 2012, 54–65
Kockel 2015
Valentin Kockel, "I modelli di Pompei dal Settecento al 'grande plastico'", in: Osanna – Caracciolo – Gallo 2015, 42–51
Koloski Ostrow 1990
Anne Koloski Ostrow, *The Sarno bath complex*, Rome 1990
Lamers 1995
Petra Lamers, *Il viaggio nel Sud dell'Abbé de Saint-Non*, Naples 1994
Langner 2001
Martin Langner, *Antike Graffitizeichnungen*, Wiesbaden 2001
La Regina 2001
Adriano La Regina (ed.), *Sangue e Arena*, exhibition cat. Rome 2001/2002, Milan 2001
Lichtenstern 2012
Christa Lichtenstern, "Lebensspuren und Körperzeichen – Pompejis Tote in der Skulptur der 2. Hälfte des 20. Jahrhunderts", in: Reinsberg – Meynersen 2012, 155–164
Lorenz 2008
Katharina Lorenz, "Bilder machen Räume. Mythenbilder in pompeianischen Häusern", Berlin et al. 2008
Mansi 1999
Maria Gabriella Mansi, "I primi tempi dell'impresa Cuciniello e Bianchi", in: Vladimiro Valerio – Gennaro Alifuoco (eds.), *Vedute, ritratti, scene popolari: Gli esordi della litografia a Napoli*, Naples 1999
Mansi 2008
Maria Gabriella Mansi, "Libri del re. Le antichità di Ercolano esposte", in: Cantilena – Porzio 2008, 115–145
Martorelli 1995
Lucia Martorelli, "L'organizzazione del lavoro dei disegnatori di Pompei", in: *PMM Immagine*, 24–28
Mattusch 2008
Carol C. Mattusch, *Pompeii and the Roman Villa*, exhibition cat. Washington 2008, Washington 2008
Mattusch 2013
Carol C. Mattusch (ed.), *Rediscovering the Ancient World on the Bay of Naples, 1710–1890*, New Haven and London 2013
Maupoix 1999
Michel Maupoix, "Désiré Raoul-Rochette, Choix des Peintures de Pompéi", in: Albore-Livadie 1999, 117–156 (text and colour reproductions of all the original plates)
Meller – Dickmann 2011
Harald Meller – Jens-Arne Dickmann (eds.), *Pompeji, Nola, Herculaneum. Katastrophen am Vesuv*, exhibition cat. Halle 2011, Munich 2011
Meller – Sampaolo – Melillo 2013
Harald Meller – Valeria Sampaolo – Luigia Melillo (eds.), *Gladiator. Täglich den Tod vor Augen – Looking on Death Every Day*, Darmstadt 2013
Migl 1998
Joachim Migl, "Die Bilder im Druck – Techniken und Bedeutung", in: Marion Mannsperger – Joachim Migl (eds.), *Bilder aus Pompeji. Antike aus zweiter Hand*, Stuttgart 1998, 27–40
Milanese 2007
Andrea Milanese, "Nostalgia dell'antico o nostalgia d'un contesto? Sale neopompeiane nel Museo Nazionale di Napoli tra1864 e 1870", in: Eugenia Querci – Stefano De Caro (eds.), *Alma Tadema e la nostalgia dell'antico*, exhibition cat. Naples 2006/2007, Milan 2007, 168-179
Miraglia – Piantanida 1992
Marina Miraglia – Paolo Piantanida (eds.), *Giorgio Sommer in Italien*, Heidelberg 1992
Moormann 2015
Eric Moormann, *Pompeii's Ashes. The reception of the cities buried by Vesuvius in literature, music and drama*, Berlin 2015
Mühlenbrock – Richter 2005
Josef Mühlenbrock – Dieter Richter (eds.), *Verschüttet vom Vesuv. Die letzten Stunden von Herculaneum*, exhibition cat. Haltern et al. 2005, Mainz 2005
Oettermann 1980
Stefan Oettermann, *Das Panorama. Geschichte eines Massenmediums*, Frankfurt 1980
Osanna – Caracciolo – Gallo 2015
Massimo Osanna – Maria Teresa Caracciolo – Luigi Gallo (eds.), *Pompei e l'Europa 1748–1943*, Milan 2015 (Eng.: *Pompeii and Europe 1748–1943*, Milan 2015)
Pagano 1991/1992
Mario Pagano, "Metodologia dei restauri borbonici a Pompei ed Ercolano", in: *Rivista di Studi Pompeiani*, 5, 1991–92, 169–191

Piggott 2004
Jan R. Piggott, *Palace of the people. The Crystal Palace at Sydenham 1854–1936*, London 2004
Pirson 1999
Felix Pirson, "Giuseppe Fiorelli e gli studiosi tedeschi", in: De Caro – Guzzo 1999, 25–41
Pinto 2012
John A. Pinto, *Speaking Ruins*, Ann Arbor 2012
Pisani 2009
Salvatore Pisani, "Herkulaneum und Pompeji", in: S. Pisani – K. Siebenmorgen (eds.), *Neapel. Sechs Jahrhunderte Kulturgeschichte*, Berlin 2009, 337–350
Pisani 2011
Salvatore Pisani, "'Luxusmarke' Pompeji", in: Stephanie-Gerrit Bruer – Detlef Rößler (eds.), "*... die Augen ein wenig zu öffnen". Der Blick auf die antike Kunst von der Renaissance bis heute*, Ruhpolding 2011, 129–139
Pisani 2012
Salvatore Pisani, "Die Entdeckung von Herculaneum und Pompeji. Ihre politische Bedeutung für das Königreich Beider Sizilien", in: Reinsberg – Meynersen 2012, 22–32
Pohlmann 2002
Ulrich Pohlmann, "Lawrence Alma Tadema und die Photographie", in: B. Klein (ed.), *Nobilis arte manus*, Dresden 2002, 441–464
Pompei, Tempi 1981
Pompei 1748–1980. I tempi della documentazione, exhibition cat. Rome 1981, Rome 1981
Pompéi, Travaux 1981
Pompéi. Travaux et envois des architectes français au XIXe *siècle*, exhibition cat. Paris and Pompeii 1981, Naples 1981
Pompeii AD 79, 1977/1978
Pompeii AD 79, exhibition cat. London 1977, London 1977; Boston et al. 1978, Boston 1978 (catalogue by John Brian Ward-Perkins and Amanda Claridge)
Querci – De Caro 2007
Eugenia Querci – Stefano De Caro (eds.), *Alma Tadema e la nostalgia dell'antico*, exhibition cat. Naples 2006/2007, Milan 2007
Reinsberg – Meynersen 2012
Carola Reinsberg – Felicia Meynersen (eds.), *Jenseits von Pompeji. Faszination und Rezeption*, Darmstadt and Mainz 2012
Ridely 1983
Ronald T. Ridley, "Dumas père, Director of excavations", in: *Pompei, Herculaneum, Stabiae*, vol. 1, 1983, 259–288
Roberts 2013
Paul Roberts, *Life and death in Pompeii and Herculaneum*, London 2013
Sampaolo – Hoffmann 2014
Valeria Sampaolo – Andreas Hoffmann (eds.), *Pompeji. Götter, Mythen, Menschen*, exhibition cat. Hamburg 2014/2015, Munich 2014
Sampaolo 2015
Valeria Sampaolo, "From the Herculanense Museum to the Museo Archeologico Nazionale di Napoli", in: Osanna – Caracciolo – Gallo 2015, 29–35
Staub Gierow 1994
Margareta Staub Gierow, *Casa del Granduca. Casa dei Capitelli figurati*, Munich 1994
Staub Gierow 2008
Margareta Staub Gierow, *Pompejanische Kopien aus Dänemark*, Rome 2008
Stefani 2015
Grete Stefani, *Pompeii, the State and Photography*, in: Osanna – Caracciolo – Gallo 2015, 331–335
Steiner 2005
Ulrike Steiner, *Die Anfänge der Archäologie in Folio und Oktav. Fremdsprachige Antikenpublikationen und Reiseberichte in deutschen Ausgaben*, Ruhpolding 2005
Strocka 1991
Volker Michael Strocka, *Casa del Labirinto (VI 11, 8–10)*, Munich 1991
Stroffolino 2012
Daniela Stroffolino, *L'Europa "a volo d'uccello": dal Cinquecento ad Alfred Guesdon*, Naples 2012
Van der Poel 1981
Halsted B. Van der Poel (ed.), *Corpus Topographicum Pompeianum*, vol. 5 (Cartography), Rome 1981
Wood 1996
Nicholas Wood, *La casa del poeta tragico. The House of the Tragic Poet. A Reconstruction*, London 1996
Zanker 1995
Paul Zanker, *Pompeji. Stadtbild und Wohngeschmack*, Mainz 1995
Zevi 1979
Fausto Zevi (ed.), *Pompei 79*, Naples 1979
Zevi 1988
Fausto Zevi, "Gi scavi di Ercolano e le Antichità", in: *Antichità di Ercolano*, Naples 1988, 11–38
Zevi 1996
Fausto Zevi, "La casa del Fauno", in: Borriello – D'Ambrosio – De Caro – Guzzo 1996, 37–57 and passim

GLOSSARY

Aedicula A small temple-like building, in archaeological terms not necessarily signifying a religious function.
Aedile One of two annually elected "officials" of a Roman town, subordinate to the → duumviri and responsible amongst other things for the provision of markets and the gladiatorial games.
Ala Literally "wing". A room at the back of the atrium, open on one side.
Apodyterium The changing-room in Roman baths.
Arca (plural: arcae) Solid wooden chests with ornate metal fittings and locks. They were kept in the → atrium and served as a conspicuously impressive safe for coins and valuables.
Archaistic A stylistic reference to the "stiff" forms of early Greek (Archaic) art. A manner particularly popular in the early Imperial age which was employed to lend artistic representations the appearance of being much older.
Askos A drinking vessel made of various materials in the stylised shape of a wineskin.
Atrium The central room of the traditional Roman house, partly open to the skies. The roof section may extend freely or be supported by columns (→ tetrastyle atrium). Beneath the opening was the → impluvium. Petitioners, freedmen and dependants of the → *patronus* were received in the atrium, which was where the → *arcae* were kept and the portraits of the householder's family.
Bisellium A double-width seat of honour which could be installed, for example, at the theatre. A symbolic means of honouring citizens noted for their charitable donations.
Caldarium A room with warm-water pool and heating in Roman baths.
Cavea A semi-circular theatre auditorium.
Cella A room in ancient temples that could be closed off, and which contained the image of the deity.
Colonia A town whose inhabitants have Roman citizenship and thus a close relationship with Rome. Pompeii was named *Colonia Veneria Cornelia Pompeianorum* around 80 BC, when it was settled by military veterans.
Corona civica A wreath of oak leaves, which was awarded as the highest honour. In the early Imperial age, a reference to Augustus and his successors.
Dilettanti Art lovers. The Society of Dilettanti in England was made up of members of the aristocracy who had completed the → Grand Tour. It also financed archaeological research projects in the Mediterranean region.
Duumvir (plural: duumviri) Elected annually, the duumviri were the two most senior officials of a Roman town, corresponding to the consul in Rome.
Emblema (plural: emblemata) Greek, literally the "inserted". An archaeological term for a particularly finely crafted mosaic design made in a workshop and then inserted as the central motif into a larger floor.
Eros (plural: erotes) In Latin, Amor or Cupid. Strictly speaking, the son of Aphrodite/Venus. In the plural used to denote small, naked boys whose presence evokes an "eroticised" atmosphere. They may be compared with Baroque putti in appearance (→ psyches).
Exedra A room adjoining a courtyard, open at the front and usually wider than it is deep. Its ground plan can be semi-circular or rectangular, and the entrance may be decoratively fronted with columns (e.g. the Alexander exedra in the Casa del Fauno).
Fauces The entrance vestibule of a Roman house, leading to the → atrium.
Frigidarium The cold room in Roman baths, featuring a large cold-water pool.
Grand Tour A term referring specifically to the extended tour of Continental Europe made by young English aristocrats as part of their education, with Italy as its main destination. Members of the upper classes from other European nations also undertook such tours, especially in the 18th century.
Impluvium The water tank in the → atrium of a Roman house, partly fed by rain falling through the opening in the roof. Marble tables for guests and small statuettes may be positioned around its edges.
Insula In Latin, meaning both a "tenement" and a "block of houses". The word is used in this latter sense in Pompeii (and elsewhere) to designate the different blocks of houses and in the modern identification system is part of a house's address, e.g. Casa del Fauno (VI 12, 2) = Regio VI, insula 12, entrance 2.
Kantharos (plural: kantharoi) A goblet-shaped drinking vessel with two high handles.
Kline A couch in a Roman house, used for sleeping and during meals with invited guests (→ triclinium).
Krater A large vessel in which wine was mixed with water.
Lanista The owner of a group of gladiators, also employed as a referee in combats.
Lararium A small shrine, mostly in the form of an → aedicule, found in every Roman house and in which the local gods (lares, snakes) and other divinities were worshipped.

Macellum A public market for the sale of foodstuffs, often in a richly decorated architectural complex.
Nymphaeum A fountain with a decorative façade, in Pompeii usually characterised by a wealth of mosaics and statues.
Oecus A Greek name for a large living room. In archaeological terminology also often used for smartly furnished rooms that were suitable for various kinds of entertaining.
Palaestra An open square, usually surrounded by colonnades, used for sports training.
Pantheon Greek, literally "shrine to all the gods". In Pompeii the now obsolete name used by the Niccolinis for the → Macellum.
Patronus Patronage signifies a relationship of protection on the one side and dependence on the other between a former slave-owner and a freedman. The *patronus* receives freedmen and other dependents/petitioners in the → atrium of his house. As an honorary title, *patronus* can also signify a duty of care towards a town.
Peristyle In general, a courtyard surrounded by a colonnade. In Pompeii, a regular feature of large houses from the 2nd century BC onwards. The most important reception rooms were situated around the peristyle.
Praedium (plural: praedia) A larger property inside or outside the town that could also be rented out or leased. In Pompeii, the *praedia* of Julia Felix (II 4, 1–12) are situated in one of the first areas to have been excavated (1754–1757).
Predella An Italian term used in art history and archaeology to denote a long, flat pictorial zone beneath a main scene. Common in the 3rd and 4th style in Pompeii.
Protome A decorative element projecting from a wall or cornice, often in the shape of an animal or human head.
Psyche (plural: psyches) The beloved of Amor/Cupid. In the plural the name is commonly used in archaeology for the female, usually winged pendants of the → erotes.
Sacellum A small shrine taking various shapes, e. g. that of an → aedicule.
Sistrum A metal rattle used in the Egyptian cult of Isis.
Situla A bucket-shaped container made of metal or clay.
Skyphos A cup with a flat base and two handles, in most cases projecting horizontally from the body.
Styles, four Pompeian The division of Pompeian wall painting into four chronologically successive styles, introduced in 1882 by August Mau, is still in use today. The terms are, however, not altogether precise, since they refer to different organisational systems within Pompeian wall decoration and not necessarily to different styles of painting or artistic signatures.
Strigil A metal scraper used to remove oil and sand from the skin after sport and before bathing.
Taberna A shop or workshop usually consisting of one room, in which the proprietors also lived.
Tablinum
The largest room attached to the → atrium, opposite the → fauces. Originally the bedroom of the house-owner and his wife, later a main reception-room or even a passage into the → peristyle.
Tepidarium A room maintained at a lukewarm temperature in Roman baths. Often smaller than the → frigidarium and the → caldarium.
Terra sigillata Fine-quality, shiny red tableware, initially manufactured in Arezzo/Central Italy in the 1st century AD but later chiefly produced in southern Gaul. It was used throughout the Roman Empire.
Tetrastyle atrium Ancient term for an → atrium with four columns forming roof supports and surrounding the → impluvium.
Theatrum tectum Literally "covered theatre". The name of the small theatre as recorded in an inscription only in Pompeii, which might also be called an odeum and probably provided the setting for cultural and political events.
Triclinium A room furnished with three couches (→ kline) and used for small social gatherings.
Tropaion A wooden post on which, as a sign of victory, the weapons of a defeated opponent were mounted.
Viridarium A courtyard for an ornamental garden. In Pompeii often painted with appropriate themes (landscapes, gardens, hunting scenes).

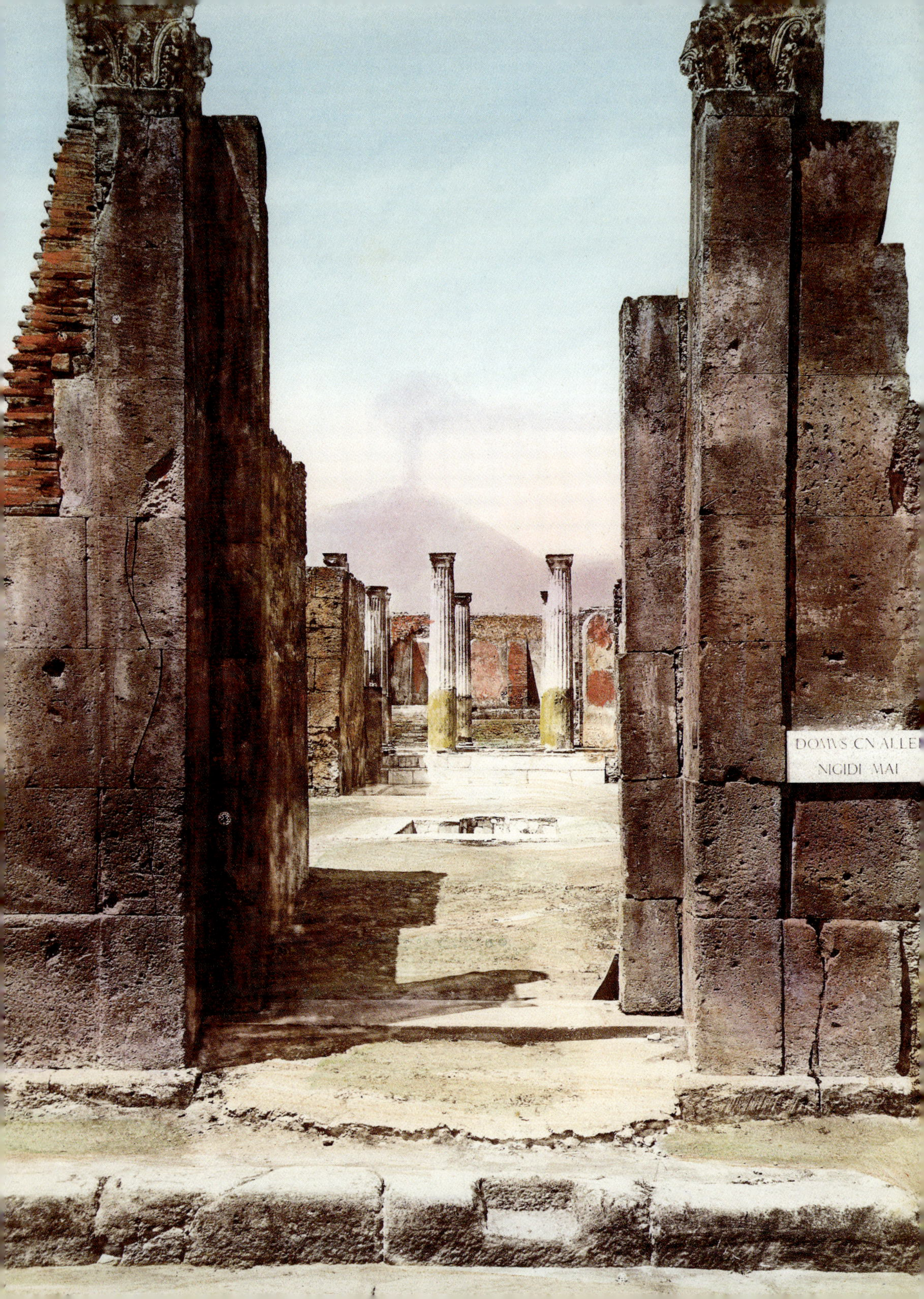
DOMVS CN ALLE
NIGIDI MAI

AUTHORS

Valentin Kockel studied classical archaeology in Marburg, Freiburg, Rome and Göttingen, where in 1978 he obtained his doctorate under Paul Zanker with a thesis on the necropolises of Pompeii. After five years as a research assistant at the German Archaeological Institute in Rome, he joined the architecture faculty in Darmstadt and qualified as a professor with a thesis on the Roman portrait. In 1995 he was appointed Professor of Classical Archaeology at Augsburg University, where he taught until 2014. Kockel headed excavations in Ostia Antica and at the Forum in Pompeii over a period of several years and published his findings in academic journals and books, most recently *Die Ehrenbögen in Pompeji* with Klaus Müller (2011). Another major area of his research is the history of the reception of Antiquity and in particular the techniques employed to visualise ancient cities and ancient art in the various imaging media of the 18th and 19th centuries, specifically: prints, drawings, panoramas, plaster casts and models. In this context he also conceived the exhibitions *Ansicht, Plan, Modell* (Augsburg 1998) and *Daktyliotheken. Götter & Caesaren aus der Schublade* (Augsburg, Göttingen from 2006). He was likewise prominently involved in the exhibitions *Rom über die Alpen tragen* (Munich 1993) and *Musées de papier* (Paris 2011).

After completing his studies in art history, classical archeology and ancient history in Berlin, Rome, Cologne, and Bonn, **Sebastian Schütze** joined the academic staff of the Bibliotheca Hertziana (Max-Planck-Institut für Kunstgeschichte) in Rome, where in 2001–2003 he headed the interdisciplinary research group "Strategies of Representation in the Early Modern Period". From 2003 to 2009 he held the Bader Chair in Southern Baroque Art at Queen's University in Kingston, Ontario. Since 2009 he has been Professor of the History of Early Modern Art at the University of Vienna. He is a member of the Academic Advisory Board of the Istituto Italiano per gli Studi Filosofici in Naples and a member of the Österreichische Akademie der Wissenschaften. In addition to a great many publications on Europe in the Early Modern Period, in particular, on art and patronage in Papal Rome and on painting in Naples, he has contributed significantly to a number of important international exhibitions, among them *Bernini Scultore* (Rome, Villa Borghese), *Melchior Lechters Gegen-Welten* (Münster, Westfälisches Landesmuseum für Kunst und Kulturgeschichte), *Barock im Vatikan* (Bonn, Bundeskunsthalle), *Caravaggio and his Followers in Rome* (Ottawa, National Gallery), *Bernini der Erfinder des barocken Rom* (Leipzig, Museum der bildenden Künste) and *Der Göttliche: Michelangelo als Inspiration* (Bonn, Bundeskunsthalle).

ACKNOWLEDGEMENTS

Author's acknowledgements
My thanks go to Johannes Bergerhausen, Stefano De Caro, Jens-Arne Dickmann, Domenico Esposito, Manuel Flecker, Carlo Gasparri, Rupprecht Goette, Andrea Milanese, Renate Miller-Gruber, Emmanuelle Rosso, Agnes Schwarzmaier, Grete Stefani, Mariette de Vos and most especially the indefatigable Irene Bragantini for all the information they have so kindly provided.

Publisher's acknowledgements
The present reprint of Fausto and Felice Niccolini's *Le case ed i monumenti di Pompei disegnati e descritti* is based on the copy from the Universitätsbibliothek Heidelberg (Naples 1854–1896; 6 vols.: C 3626 Gross RES::1, C 3626 Gross RES::2, C 3626 Gross RES::3,1 and 3,2, C 3626 Gross RES::4,1 and 4,2). We are grateful to Dr Karin Zimmermann for her unstinting support of this project from the outset. The digital reproduction of the original was carried out by the Göttingen Digitization Centre (GDZ) of the Niedersächsische Staats- und Universitätsbibliothek Göttingen, Germany. We would like to express our thanks to Martin Liebetruth of the GDZ for being so cooperative during all stages of the undertaking.

PHOTO CREDITS

Carlo Carrà © VG Bild-Kunst, Bonn 2026: p. 66
Pablo Picasso © Succession Picasso / VG Bild-Kunst, Bonn 2026: p. 65
Mario Sironi © VG Bild-Kunst, Bonn 2026: p. 63

Archives of the publisher, authors or collectors: pp. 32, 69, 72–3, 497–8, 499
Archivio dell'Arte, Luciano Pedicini, Naples: p. 16
© Les Arts décoratifs, Paris / Jean Tholance: p. 53
Bibliothèque nationale de France, Paris: pp. 7–8, 15, 34
bpk / Hamburger Kunsthalle / Elke Walford: pp. 58–59
bpk / Staatsgalerie Stuttgart: pp. 70–71
Getty Research Institute, Los Angeles: pp. 44, 47
© INHA, Dist. RMN-Grand-Palais / image INHA: p. 20
© Montauban, musée Ingres: p. 56
Luciano Romano, Naples: pp. 26–27
Musée des Augustins, Toulouse, photo: Daniel Martin: p. 49
National Trust Photographic Library / Bridgeman Images: p. 50
Niedersächsische Staats- und Universitätsbibliothek, Göttingen: endpapers, pp. 1, 2, 74–75, 110–111, 242–243, 238–239, 418–419, 430, 431, 434–435, 438–439, 443–443, 444, 448–449, 478–479
© Museo Nazionale Archeologico, photo: Giorgio Albano, Naples: pp. 25, 26–27
© RMN-Grand Palais (musée d'Orsay) / Hervé Lewandowski: p. 60
© RMN-Grand Palais (musée Picasso) / Jean-Gilles Berizzi: p. 65
© Scala, Florence / Mauro Ranzani, 2015: pp. 63, 66
© Scala, Florence – courtesy of the Ministero Beni e Att. Culturali, 2015: p. 55
Universitätsbibliothek Heidelberg: pp. 13, 19, 21, 29, 39, 40

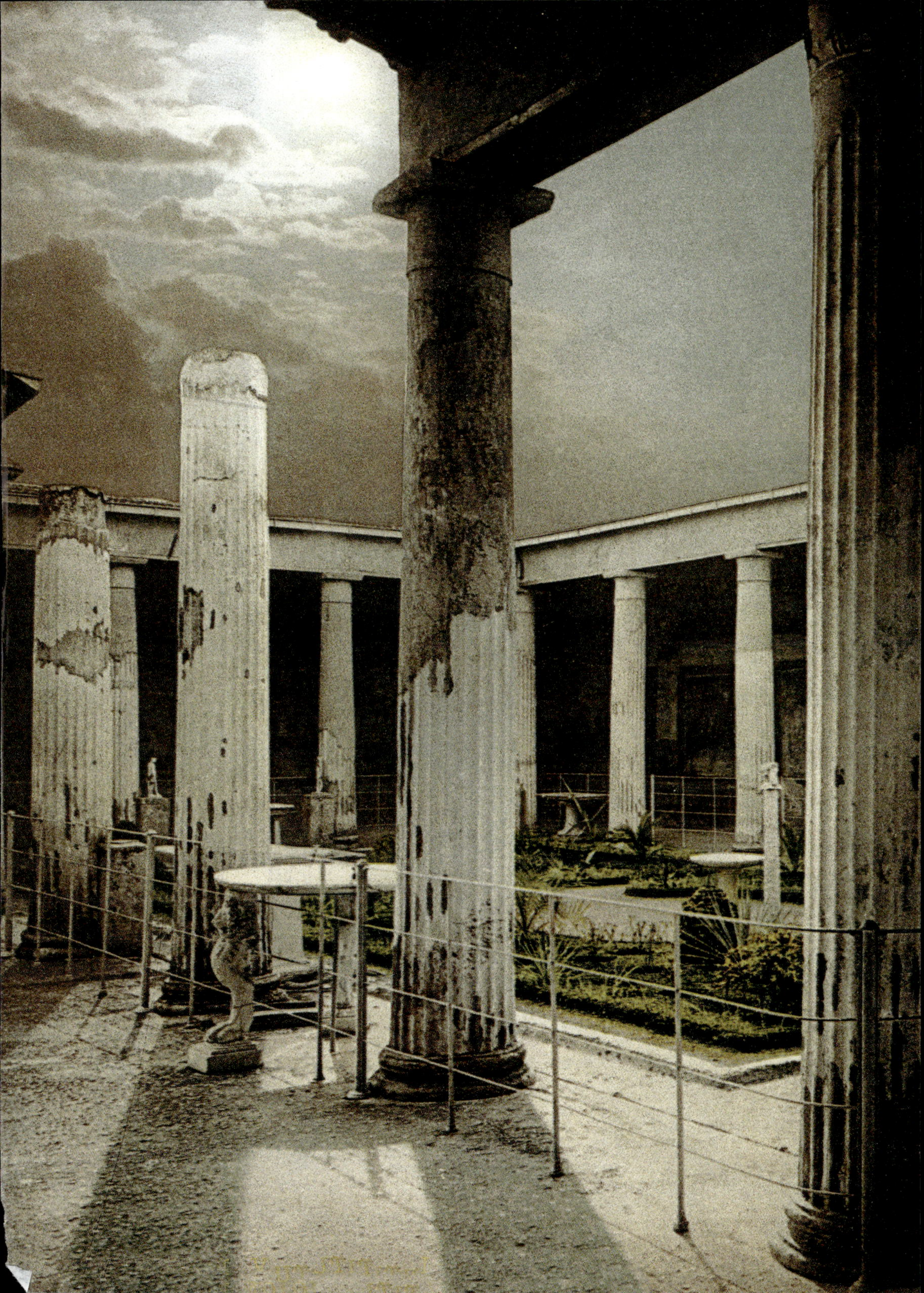

IMPRINT

PAGE 1
Title-page
From: *Le case ed i monumenti di Pompei*,
vol. I, Naples 1854

PAGE 2
Sarno, ground floor (detail)
See pp. 464–465, plate 2 (vol. IV)

PAGES 4–5
Mosaic floor from the tablinum (detail)
See p. 80, plate 3 (vol. I)

PAGE 6
Casa del Fauno, Impluvium (detail)
See pp. 236–237, plate 36 (vol. II)

PAGES 496–497
View across the Forum from the Southeast, ca. 1890 (?)
Photochrome. Private collection

PAGE 498
View across the Forum from the South; on the Left, the Porch of the Basilica, ca. 1890 (?)
Photochrome. Private collection

PAGE 508
Entrance to the Casa di Pansa, ca. 1875
Coloured photograph. Private collection

PAGE 511
View of the Peristyle at the Casa dei Vettii, Looking Southwest, ca. 1900
Photocrome. Private collection

Hohenzollernring 53, D–50672 Köln
www.taschen.com

English translation: Karen Williams,
Rennes-le-Château

Printed in Bosnia-Herzegovina
ISBN 978-3-7544-0019-7